West Africa
a travel survival kit

Alex Newton

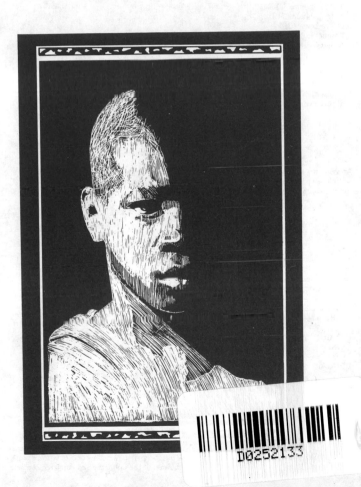

West Africa - a travel survival kit
  1st edition

Published by
  Lonely Planet Publications
  Head Office: PO Box 88, South Yarra, Victoria 3141, Australia
  US Office: PO Box 2001A, Berkeley, CA 94702, USA

Printed by
  Singapore National Printers Ltd, Singapore

Photographs by
  Chris Brown (CB)
  Eliot Elisofon (EE)
  Jerry Johnson (JJ)
  Jill T Johnson (JTJ)
  Claire Lewis (CL)
  Samuel Rubin (SR)
  Albert Votow (AV)

  Front cover: Niger River, Mopti, Mali (EE)
  Back cover: Kids on stilts, Seribougou, Mali (JJ)

Cartoons by
  Tony Jenkins

Published
  September 1988

Although the author and publisher have tried to make the information as
accurate as possible, they accept no responsibility for any loss, injury or
inconvenience sustained by any person using this book.

National Library of Australia Cataloguing in Publication Data

Newton, Alex.
  West Africa, a travel survival kit.

  Includes index.
  ISBN 0 86442 028 5.

  1. Africa, West - Description and travel -
  1981- - Guide-books. I. Title

  916.6'04

Alex Newton

Born in Atlanta, Georgia, Alex Newton was one of the many Americans affected in the 1960s by John Kennedy's challenge to join the Peace Corps. Following almost three years' service in Guatemala as an agricultural advisor and four years on Wall St as a lawyer, he studied French and development economics and ended up in West Africa, where he has spent seven of his last ten years working on development assistance programs. Travelling by plane, river boat, new trains and cockroach-infested ones, buses and pick-up trucks stuffed like sardines, and on top of lorries, he has visited all sixteen countries in West Africa and crossed the Sahara as well. Since there aren't many guidebooks on West Africa and since no class of traveller is spared the hassles of travelling in this area, Alex decided it was time someone wrote a book that addressed the needs of all levels of travellers. This is his first book. An avid kayaker and now living in Quito, Ecuador, he bids travellers look him up and says on weekends he can be found most likely at the nearest squash court, running with the Hash House Harriers or scouting the rapids.

Dedication

This book is dedicated to my mother and the Washington DC river rafting gang.

Lonely Planet Credits

Editor	Peter Turner
Design, Maps, Cover	Peter Flavelle
Design & Illustrations	Joanne Ryan
Typesetting	Ann Jeffree

Thanks also to Vicki Beale and Valerie Tellini for additional maps and Katie Cody for proof-reading.

Acknowledgements

My foremost thanks go to Olivier Leduc, who put together most of the maps and provided comic relief while I was slaving away on this book in Abidjan. Special thanks also to Robert McLean who tipped me off about the fabulous slide collection of Eliot Elisofon.

I should also like to particularly thank Phil Jones who spent endless hours reading and editing each chapter, Jerry Johnson who wrote a major part of the introduction and sent two volumes of slides, Sid Bliss who made invaluable contributions to the Togo chapter as did Kelly Morris, Buddy Roberts for sending me a computer and gathering facts in West Africa, Steve Nelson for his advice on computers and the use of his office, Jennifer Ellingston for daily comic relief and stimulating conversations during the last gruelling months, those who sent photographs – Jill Johnson, Claire Lewis, Belinda Barrington, Glenn Anders and Susan Lloyd, Diana Putman, the Warren Putmans, Chris and Betsy Brown, Bob Hellyard – and those who sent comments on particular chapters – Micky Lang and Chris Konarsky, Jill Hough, Barbara Fisher and Chuck Pill, Ann Lancaster (the introduction), among others.

And lastly, I'd like to thank the Lonely Planet team in Australia, particularly

Tony Wheeler and Jim Hart who followed me around Africa by letter during our initial 'scoping out' period, Peter Turner who undertook the arduous editing task, and Peter Flavelle and Joanne Ryan who did the artwork and maps.

A Warning & A Request

Things change – prices go up, schedules change, good places go bad and bad places go bankrupt – nothing stays the same. So if you find things better or worse, recently opened or long since closed, please write and tell us and help make the next edition better! All information is greatly appreciated and the best letters will receive a free copy of the next edition, or any other Lonely Planet book of your choice.

Extracts from the best letters are also included in the *Lonely Planet Update*. The *Update* helps us make useful information available to you as soon as possible – it's like reading an up-to-date noticeboard or postcards from a friend. Each edition contains hundreds of useful tips, and advice from the best possible source of information – other travellers. The *Lonely Planet Update* is published quarterly in paperback and is available from bookshops and by subscription. Turn to the back pages of this book for more details.

The Kingdom of Benin was at its most powerful from the 14th to 17th centuries, and it was during this period that the court artists produced the finest bronzes in Africa, such as this ram's head belt ornament.

Contents

Introduction

Call it mystique or adventure, whatever, West Africa has a power of attraction which, despite its sometimes primitive conditions, continues to entice westerners to spend time and even careers here. They certainly don't come because it's 'comfortable'. In the rural Sahel, people live in hamlets scattered about the hot and dusty landscape studded with huge baobab trees. Others live in tropical cities such as Freetown and Monrovia where every time it rains the electricity goes off and the sewers overflow.

Which isn't to say that the environment isn't interesting. You can experience sandy deserts and rain forests, and everything in between. But the physical environment and the wildlife are not West Africa's principal attractions as they are in East Africa. West Africa's draw card is

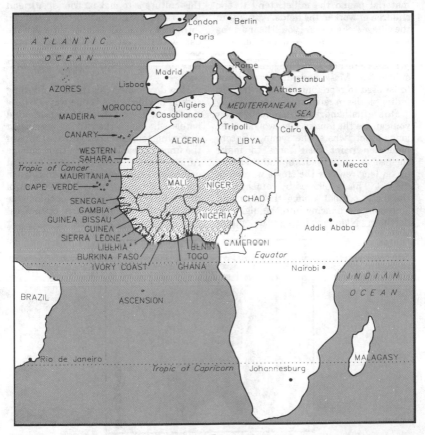

the people. If you're interested in art, music or traditional African culture, head for West Africa, not East Africa.

In Timbuktu and elsewhere in the Sahel, you'll see nomadic Tuaregs perched on their camels and covered with flowing embroidered material. Only their penetrating eyes appear from the white or indigo material wrapped around their heads. In the villages, you'll see men in traditional dress gathered around the chief discussing important village matters or shooting the breeze, while the women dressed in brightly coloured African material pound the millet, tend to the children or work in the fields. At night in the villages, chances are you'll hear drums and, in the Sahel, be offered the ritualistic three glasses of tea.

Masks are not something men carve only for sale. Masks and puppets continue to be used to represent spirits or help in telling stories in ceremonies that you may get to see firsthand. In September in Niger you can see the famous Gerewol, a week-long event where the young Bororo herdsmen paint their faces to make themselves more beautiful and then line up on long rows for the single women to inspect. This is followed by camel races, ritualistic combat among the men and long hours of dancing into the night. In northern Nigeria, during the major

Muslim celebrations, you'll see long processions of the most elegantly dressed men who gallop in mad fashion through town on their elaborately decorated horses.

What is just as interesting, however, is simply meeting people in the markets and villages. Africans are interested in people and one of the best ways to meet them is in the mud bars and local markets, talking with bread women, cigarette vendors, town crazies or millet beer drinkers.

Africans have a different world view to westerners, and the only way to penetrate this culture is to make a friend. A friend will take you to his or her village, introduce you to the family, show you the bars with the best music in town, and tell you when you're getting ripped off and how to accomplish tasks in the best way.

How do you meet this friend? Travelling second or third class is one way. Just be sure to get beyond those Africans around hotels who make their living serving or disserving tourists. Try the Peace Corps or the universities. If you're in francophone Africa, every student or former student will enjoy a conversation with an English speaker. Plus they usually have lots of time – little money and lots of time. One friend and you will see how open West Africans can be.

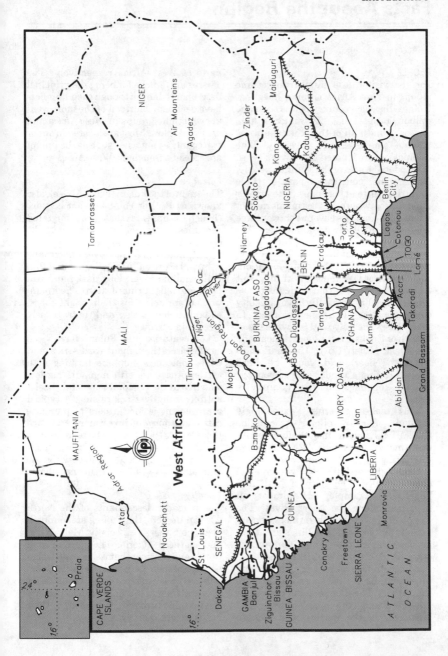

Facts About the Region

PEOPLE

For the visitor, the number of ethnic groups in West Africa is mind boggling. Guinea-Bissau, a country of less than one million people, has 23 major ethnic groups. Almost all of the other countries have a similar ethnic diversity. The colonial powers ignored this diversity, so that today the area of the Malinké people, for example, constitutes part of three countries instead of one. The major difference between countries in this respect is that some countries have one or two ethnic groups which clearly predominate; other countries do not. In Mali, for example, the largest ethnic group, the Bambara, represent only 23% of the total population.

This pattern is repeated throughout Africa. The result is that Africans of the same nationality frequently have difficulty communicating with one another. In many cases the only way is by means of French or English, but a lot of Africans do not speak either. Go to the market in Niamey (Niger) and you'll be hard pressed to find a vendor who speaks the official language of the country – French.

This makes governing exceedingly difficult. For travellers, it can be frustrating but it is this ethnic diversity that makes travel in West Africa so interesting.

Each group has its own special characteristics. The Bozo of Mali and Niger, for example, are almost all fishermen along the Niger River. The Dogon in Mali are mostly farmers who are famous for their cliff dwellings and their intensive agriculture. The Fulani on the other hand, are professional herdsmen.

Some ethnic groups are clearly more important, or at least more well known, than others. The Bambara and the Hausa have probably the most widely used languages in the western and eastern parts of West Africa respectively. The Tuareg are famous for being the principal desert nomads even though their numbers have declined. Thirteen of the more well-known ethnic groups in West Africa and are listed below. Most are located in one or two countries but a few such as the Fulani are spread throughout West Africa.

Fulani

The origin of the Fulani (Fou-LAN-ee), also known as Peul or Foulbe, is not certain, though it appears that they migrated centuries ago from Egypt and may even be of Jewish origin. Some are so fair-complexioned that they look Caucasian.

Fulani are usually tall, elegant and thin with aquiline noses, long dark hair, oval faces and a light complexion. The Fulani women are noted for their bright robes, elaborate hair-does, and outrageously large gold earrings.

For centuries the Fulani have been cattle raisers throughout West Africa, and while some now combine farming with cattle, others are still nomadic herders who live in the pastoral zone and subsist entirely from livestock raising. A typical arrangement is for farmers to purchase cattle as a form of investment and turn them over to the Fulani, who tend them in return for occasional sacks of rice. Fulani herdsman can recognise every single animal in herds of 300 cattle and more.

Tuareg

The nomadic descendants of the North African Berbers, the Tuareg are found all over the Sahara, especially Mali, Niger and southern Algeria. They are a proud people and consider themselves Caucasian because of their Berber heritage. They are relatively easy to recognise by their fairer skin and their nomadic outfits, especially the ink-blue turbans covering all of their heads except their eyes.

Historically, they were warriors and raiders and were known for their possession of slaves, the Bozo. Since the drought of the 1970s when their herds were devastated, many have had to abandon the nomadic existence for farming and village life and the transition has not always been successful.

Moors

The Moors are peppered throughout West Africa but are located primarily in Mauritania, as well as Senegal and the desert areas of Mali. The Moors have been, historically like the Tuaregs, nomads living from cattle and sheep raising. Located also in desert oases, they became involved in the date trade and other commerce and are now well known as merchants.

The racial conflict between the Moors, caucasians Muslims of Arab Berber origin, and the Negro Africans is fierce.

Until 1980 when slavery was finally abolished in Mauritania (in law if not entirely in fact), Moors had black African slaves who were permanently attached to the households.

Bambara

The Bambara (BAM-bah-rah) are the major ethnic group of Mali. They are mostly farmers, and control the government. Their language, Bambara, is not only the dominant language of Mali but almost identical to Djoula, the market language of the Ivory Coast, Guinea and Burkina Faso. The Bambara are famous for their art and their antelope-like masks called Chiwaras, are the most well-known masks of African art.

Malinké

The Malinke (Mah-LEEN-kay) are the major ethnic group in Guinea with a significant presence in southern Mali, the

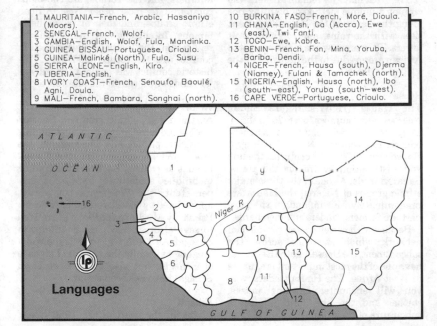

1 MAURITANIA—French, Arabic, Hassaniya (Moors).
2 SENEGAL—French, Wolof.
3 GAMBIA—English, Wolof, Fula, Mandinka.
4 GUINEA BISSAU—Portuguese, Crioulo.
5 GUINEA—Malinké (North), Fula, Susu.
6 SIERRA LEONE—English, Kiro.
7 LIBERIA—English.
8 IVORY COAST—French, Senoufo, Baoulé, Agni, Doula.
9 MALI—French, Bambara, Songhai (north).
10 BURKINA FASO—French, Moré, Dioula.
11 GHANA—English, Ga (Accra), Ewe (east), Twi Fanti.
12 TOGO—Ewe, Kabre.
13 BENIN—French, Fon, Mina, Yoruba, Bariba, Dendi.
14 NIGER—French, Hausa (south), Djerma (Niamey), Fulani & Tamachek (north).
15 NIGERIA—English, Hausa (north), Ibo (south—east), Yoruba (south—west).
16 CAPE VERDE—Portuguese, Crioulo.

ATLANTIC OCEAN

Niger R

Languages

GULF OF GUINEA

northern Ivory Coast and Guinea-Bissau. They are closely related to the Bambara and are famous for having had one of the great empires of West Africa. It was during the Malinké Empire of Mali in the 14th century, when Timbuktu, Djenné, Gao and Agadez began to blossom. These were not just the leading cities on the Sahara trade routes, they were centres of Islamic learning with major universities and palaces.

Songhai

Located primarily in northern Mali and Niger along the Niger River between Niamey and Timbuktu, the Songhai (SAUN-ghi) have traditionally been farmers and fishermen as well as herders. They are a very proud people famous for having the last and most expansive of the Sudanic empires of West Africa in the 16th century, extending from Senegal to Niger.

The great majority remain farmers who employ a unique method of planting rice along the banks of the Niger River as it rises with the rains, and sorghum as it lowers. They are now one of the poorest of African groups due to the droughts of the 1970s and 1980s.

Hausa

The Hausa (HOW-sah) are Sudan Negroes and number over 20 million. They are centred mainly in northern Nigeria and southern Niger. The largest Hausa city is Kano, for centuries the hub and distribution centre for the trans-Saharan trade. As one of the three major ethnic groups of Nigeria, the Hausa are predominately Muslim and for the most part are farmers, traders and merchants.

Because of their well-known commercial network which stretches across the subcontinent, the Hausa, like the Bambara, have one of the most important languages in West Africa. The Hausa traders, who you will encounter hawking masks, statues and the like, forms almost a subculture of their own.

Yoruba

The Yoruba (YOH-rou-bah) are one of the three major ethnic groups in Nigeria and are concentrated in southern Nigeria. They are pure Negroes and predominantly Christian, and generally rather robust in outlook. In their ceremonies they wear distinctive facial masks. They are a significant ethnic tribe in West Africa if only because of their large numbers and the fact that their principal city, Lagos, is the largest in Black Africa. In addition, however, the Yoruba are significant because of their early exposure to western education and their well-known art, which is found in museums around the world and is still practised today in the villages.

Ibo

The last of the three major ethnic groups in Nigeria, the Ibo (E-bow) are centred mainly in south-eastern Nigeria and are pure Negroes like the Yoruba. Their numbers, like the Yoruba, are enormous compared to most other West African ethnic groups, and their art is similarly famous. Intelligent and industrious by reputation, the Ibo have always been in conflict with the Yoruba and Hausa. This historic conflict was one of the catalysts for the Biafran war in the late 1960s.

Wolof

As the major ethnic group in Senegal (38%) and also present in surrounding countries, particularly The Gambia, the Wolof (WOH-loaf) are, like the Hausa, famous as traders. Because their trading technique sometimes appears overly persistent, the Wolof are not always appreciated by travellers or other Africans. Primarily Muslims, the Wolof are related to several other major ethnic groups in Senegal. As a result, not only is the Wolof language virtually the national language of Senegal, but also tribal rivalries in Senegal have not been strong.

Ashanti

Living in the heart of the 'Gold Coast'

African masks

(Ghana) and once wealthy from gold, the Ashanti (ah-SHAN-tee) developed one of West Africa's richest cultures. The largest tribe in Ghana, the Ashanti live in the cocoa and gold regions of central Ghana, with Kumasi as the capital. Their kings used to be weighed down with gold ornaments and their houses were some of the most elaborate in Africa. The Ashanti's traditional wealth is reflected in their art and fabrics, especially the colourful and expensive *kente* cloth made originally with finely woven silk, now more often with cotton.

Mossi

Occupying the central area of Burkina Faso and comprising about half the population of Burkina Faso as well as the bulk of the Ivory Coast's migrant labour force, the Mossi (MOH-see) are noted for never having been conquered by the Muslims. As a result, in great contrast to neighbouring Mali and Niger, Burkina Faso is no more than 20% Muslim. During their heyday, the Mossi had four kingdoms in Burkina Faso, each with its own courts and ministers maintaining a rigid social order. The Mossi have held on to their traditions very strongly, as can be witnessed today in Ouagadougou at the weekly Mora Naba ceremony.

Dogon

Numbering only about 300,000, the Dogon (DOH-ghon) are, nevertheless, quite famous for their art and their cliff dwellings. As a result, their villages are a hot tourist attraction today. Located in Mali east of Mopti, their houses are perched on cliffs and resemble those of the cliff-dwelling Indians in the USA. The Dogon are equally famous for their art – the doors and locks to their houses, for example, are some of the most artistically carved in Africa.

SOCIAL CUSTOMS

The saying is that people go to East Africa to see the animals and West Africa to see the people. To the extent this is true, knowing the social customs takes on added importance in West Africa, not only to avoid embarrassing situations but to enhance your possibilities of getting to know people.

Greetings *(les salutations)*

One of the basics is the great importance Africans place on greetings. For example, when the Senegalese Wolof greet one another they observe a ritual that lasts up to half a minute, starting with 'Peace be unto you', 'Do you have peace?', 'How are you doing?' to 'Where are the people of your compound?', 'Is your body in peace?', 'Thanks be to God'. The typical African greetings go into all kinds of inquiries about the family, one's health, work, the weather, etc. Even if one is at death's door, the answer is always that things are fine.

In the cities, the traditional greetings may give way to shorter greetings in French or English. In either case, it's a social blunder to get down to business immediately or to walk past an adult in a house without greeting them. Those who do are likely to meet with a hostile or negative attitude.

If you can learn the ritual in the local language, you will make an incredible hit. Even if you can't, all it takes is a few words and you will find many friends. In the chapters dealing with the various countries, five phrases are given in the most popular local language in the capital city. The unfortunate part is that many countries have four or five major languages and often another 20 or so minor ones. At least they'll know you're making the effort.

The emphasis on greetings makes the handshake important. It's a soft handshake, not the western knuckle cracker. In some coastal areas, particularly around Togo, you should try to learn the handshake between friends, which always ends up with a snap of the fingers. Even if you never succeed, Africans will find it amusing to teach you. Not to shake a man's hand when entering and leaving a social or business gathering is a real gaffe. In social settings you must go around the room, greet everyone and shake hands with the men. You do the same when you leave. In most areas men and women don't shake hands unless the woman extends her hand. This takes a little getting used to at first but eventually it becomes natural. In the French-speaking countries the thrice-kissed cheek greeting (starting with the left) is the norm for friends and even casual acquaintances of the opposite sex.

Women have traditionally been considered inferior to men and for this reason they tend to show deference to men in their greetings. As noted, they usually don't shake hands, but African men usually shake the hands of western women. In the Sahel women travellers may encounter an elder who, in strict compliance with the Koran, refuses to shake hands.

Another consideration is eye contact, which is usually avoided, especially between men and women and particularly in the Sahel. A boy does not look his father in the eye. If he does, his father will be suspicious. Don't think that because a woman avoids eye contact she's being cold. Some eye contact is perfectly OK as long as it doesn't develop into a gaze. So if you're accustomed to looking people in the eye and associate this with honesty, remember that this is not the case in Africa.

Begging

You've also got to look at beggars a little differently than you might elsewhere. In Africa, the only social security system for the great majority of people is the extended family. There is no government cheque to help the unemployed, sick or old. Most beggars are cripples, lepers, or those blinded by onchocerciasis (*oncho*). If you see an old man singing and being led around by a child, he is probably blind from oncho. Nevertheless, because of the effectiveness of the extended family in providing support, as well as the general respect that Africans give to their elders, there are remarkably few beggars considering that West Africa is the poorest area on earth.

For travellers, the point to remember is that Africans do not look down on beggars. Almsgiving is one of the pillars of Islam and to give to beggars is one of the means by which Muslims gain entrance into paradise. For those studying with a *marabout*, they are even expected to beg in order to feed themselves. For this reason, you will see even relatively poor Africans giving to beggars. Travellers with foresight will do everything possible to keep small change on them for this purpose. They're not asking for a lot, usually a coin equivalent to US 5c or 10c. If you don't have any just say 'next time' ('*la prochaine fois*'); they'll usually go on.

Gifts (le cadeau)

One thing foreigners tend to notice immediately is how many people come up to them asking for handouts. This is not begging in the traditional sense. You see kids all the time going up to foreigners with their hands out saying, 'cadeau, cadeau'. A guy will take you a block to point out the place you're looking for, and then ask for a cadeau. The girl at the bar may want a cadeau for just talking. Everybody's looking for a cadeau and the reaction of many foreigners is negative.

The point is, however, that the concept of giving gifts is very important in African society. It's also fairly structured. You are expected to give gifts to those above you in the social hierarchy, or to respected people. If your mother-in-law comes for the day, a gift to her is in order. It's not so much a case of reciprocity, rather, it's that if Allah has been good to you, you should be willing to spread some of it around. Since non-African foreigners are thought to be rich, they're expected to be generous. It's something you have to keep in mind everywhere you go.

If you're travelling near the desert, for example, take some tobacco with you for the men. Perfume makes an excellent gift for either sex, at least in the Sahel. You'll find yourself rewarded many times over. Even matches in places where they are scarce, such as upcountry Guinea-Bissau and Guinea, will be greatly appreciated. Similarly, the smart businessman will bring small items from the States or Europe to show his appreciation. One of the best gifts of all is a photograph, and it may even be worth bringing a cheap polaroid as a second camera.

Dress (les costumes)

In general, Africans place great importance on clothing, giving it a huge portion of the non-food budget. Western informality is definitely not the norm, although it is making a few inroads with the young in the bigger cities. Visitors are in for a real treat because Africans can dress with a regal quality.

In the traditional areas of West Africa both men and women wear long dress or outfits. The most common name for the most elaborate outfits is the *grand boubou*. For men, this is an embroidered robe-like garment reaching the ground with pants and shirt underneath. A kaftan is a less elaborate variation on the same theme. They are invariably worn at important occasions, and sometimes at work or on holidays.

The woman's *boubou* is similarly regal, long and embroidered. For more everyday wear, women wear a loose top and a length of cloth (*pagne*) around the waist for a skirt; this is made from the colourful cotton prints you see everywhere. The same wax or wax look-alike cloth is used in making men's casual clothes, which look like pyjamas. Because the designs are so distinctively African, it's initially surprising to learn that much of the better quality cloth actually comes from Holland. Yet the most unique are the handmade design fabrics, such as the tie-dye, indigo wood-block prints and batiks, which are produced in individual cottage-type establishments.

With clothing such as this, it is not surprising that in the more traditional areas, especially the Sahel, shorts worn by either sex and tight pants worn by women are considered offensive. This may seem like a double standard because African women often go bare breasted in the villages, yet they would be ridiculed for wearing tight pants. It's all a bit confusing, but women should keep in mind that clothes should not be revealing or suggestive. For men, standards are less strict.

Standards are different in the big cities such as Dakar. You'll see everything from the latest Parisian fashions to the most traditional outfits. Yet you will not see shorts being worn by either sex (unless jogging) or, in the Sahel, African women in pants. As for the villages, women would do well to purchase some colourful wrap-around pagnes or wear very loose fitting long pants with socks.

As with clothes, Africans are particular about cleanliness. You can be packed in a store in downtown Ouagadougou in terribly hot weather and, quite frequently, not smell other bodies. That's because a bucket bath is a morning ritual for the great majority of Africans. In this respect, it's interesting to note that many Africans think that most foreigners stink.

Eating Traditional Style

African food is eaten with the hands in the villages, as well as in African-style homes in the cities. Only the nomadic Tuaregs of the Sahara traditionally used utensils. Visitors will usually be offered a spoon, if there is one. A bowl of rice and a bowl of sauce will be placed on the ground and those eating will sit around on a mat and dig in, but never before washing their hands. It is usually polite to take off your shoes.

The head of the household will distribute meat and vegetables to the visitors. Take a handful of rice or other staple and part of the sauce or meat, then form a ball – this is the hard part – and eat. Don't shy away, it's usually a lot of laughs for everyone. It won't be pleasant the first time getting your hands all gooey but remember, a wash basin is always passed around afterwards. You may even grow to like this way of eating because of the increased 'family' feeling that it fosters.

As with the Arabs, only the right hand is used in forming the ball of food because of the ancient practice of using the left hand for personal toiletries. A violation of this rule will cause a silent turmoil. Just because you're a tourist won't make much difference. Eating with the left hand would be as offensive to Africans as a stranger drinking from your glass would be to you. Never wanting to create a scene, they'll continue eating while wondering just how 'developed' the western world really is.

Social Events

Much of African life centres around special events, such as weddings, baptisms, funerals, holidays and village celebrations (fêtes). If you get an invitation, by all means accept. Just be sure to bring your dancing shoes because, except at funerals, there will probably be dancing. At baptisms guests bring gifts for both the mother and the father; a small amount of money is perfectly acceptable. There will be a ceremony followed by a meal, typically a slaughtered sheep or goat.

At weddings there is likely to be an official ceremony at the mayor's office followed by eating and dancing at someone's home. The civil ceremony is not always boring. If the mayor is feeling his oats, he may go on for 10 to 15 minutes giving the wife, and then the husband, advice as to how each should act. The wedding is only the culmination of a week of activities involving visits to relatives, meals, and the exchange of gifts; only relatives and the closest friends are invited.

The offering of kola nuts plays a special role in all of this (as well as at other occasions). They are the extremely bitter nuts sold everywhere on the streets and known for their mildly hallucinogenic effects. Foreigners looking for a 'high' are usually disappointed and find them too bitter to stomach.

Marriage is such an expensive affair for the groom that many African men cannot afford to get married before their late 20s or 30s. Gifts to the bride's family can easily cost several hundred dollars in sheep, money and the like – not exactly peanuts in an area of the world where incomes of US$200 a year are typical. Still, in traditional society men who could afford more than one wife usually would marry more. (The Koran allows up to four.) Despite what you may hear to the contrary from African men, the first wives definitely don't like the custom of multiple wives. On the other hand, there's not much they can do except go to their families, where they're unlikely to be welcomed with open arms if the husband's only 'sin' was taking a second wife.

Other celebrations of particular interest to foreigners are the village fêtes. They may range from something fairly common, such as celebrating the end of the harvest, to something a little different, such as honouring the dead. There's usually traditional African dancing in a circle. Don't worry – you won't be asked to join in. If there's modern African music, however, you can expect to do some dancing.

Each fête is a little unique. In Niger, for example, they may include camel races or a wrestling match (la lutte). In other areas you may see African puppets used to tell stories, and elaborate dances with masks. The chapters on the various countries mention some of the more important celebrations. They are not easy to see, so if you get the chance by no means pass it up.

GEOGRAPHY

West Africa is mostly flat. The principal

hilly areas, rising to about 1000 metres and all good for hiking, are the Man area of western Ivory Coast and north-eastern Liberia, the Fouta Djallon area of north-western Guinea, the Jos area of central Nigeria, and the Kpalimé area of south-western Togo. The highest peak in West Africa, rising well over 2000 metres, is Mt Fogo in Cape Verde.

The coastal areas are close to the equator, however, all of West Africa is above the equator. Abidjan is only 5° north of the equator, Dakar 14°.

West Africa has far fewer rain forests than Central Africa. Nonetheless, Liberia is almost completely covered in rain forests, as are large parts of Sierra Leone and south-western Ivory Coast.

As you go north from the coast, the climate becomes drier and by the time you reach the southern areas of Mali, Burkina Faso and Niger, you'll be in the Sahel which extends northward to the edge of the desert. The landscape consists primarily of scrub trees and brush along with large baobab trees (the ones that look like they are turned upside down with the roots in the air) and lots of natural laterite. Northern Mali and Niger and virtually all of Mauritania are pure desert.

CLIMATE
Heat
You probably think Africa is very hot. Look at the average highs in Centigrade of the following cities in 1986:

	July	August
Washington	30	29
Rome	31	31
Tokyo	28	30
Singapore	31	30
Lagos (Nigeria)	28	28
Accra (Ghana)	28	28
Dakar (Senegal)	31	30
Cairo (Egypt)	35	35

In most of West Africa high humidity is the problem, not heat. The only area that gets really hot is the Sahel near the desert (Senegal, The Gambia, Mauritania, Mali, Burkina Faso and Niger), but not all year round. Only from March to May does it get noticeably hotter in most of West Africa. Put your face in front of a hair-drier and you'll know what it's like riding in a car with the windows down in the Sahel during this period. At least it's dry heat, however.

If heat (even dry heat) is really your bête noire, don't travel to West Africa from March to May. However, most people travelling around West Africa during this period don't lose their sanity because of the heat, especially if they're in air-conditioned environments now and then.

While the Sahel can easily get 20°C hotter from March to May, many people prefer this to the humidity. Moreover, in the shade, temperatures can be a good 10 to 15°C less. So if March to May is the only convenient time to travel, don't cancel or postpone your trip unless you are one of those who sit by the air-con all summer long.

Rain
The rainy season in West Africa is from June to September. In the wetter of these countries (Guinea, Sierra Leone and Liberia) May and October are also rainy months.

The wettest areas of West Africa are, from west to east, Guinea, Sierra Leone, Liberia and south-eastern Nigeria. If possible, you should definitely avoid visiting these areas during the heavy rainy period. The sun rarely shines and most dirt roads, except for the main arteries, become impassable.

In the rest of West Africa the skies are not cloudy all day during the rainy season. In the Sahel some people actually prefer this time of the year. The sun is not incessantly beating down on you and temperatures are a little lower.

The main problem during the rainy season is travelling upcountry off the

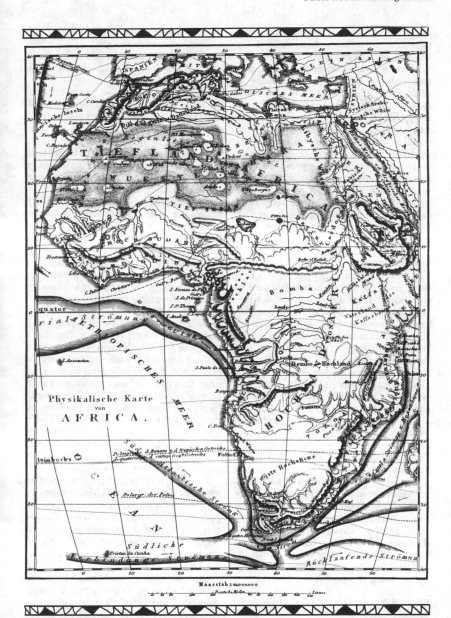

German map from the 19th Century

major roads. Many of the dirt roads are passable only with four-wheel-drive vehicles, and the driving times are double. Without a four-wheel-drive vehicle, you may have no hope of reaching some of those more remote spots you may have read about. This is true even in the Sahel. In late July on the edge of the Sahara, you can find yourself surrounded by lake-size puddles of water that refuse to be absorbed by the lifeless soils. People on tours shouldn't be concerned because four-wheel-drive vehicles are invariably used. Others who expect to do a lot of upcountry travel should have patience, a sense of humour and a good book – and be thankful that most major roads are either paved or all-weather.

The Harmattan

The November-February period may be a little cooler, but December-February is the time of the Harmattan winds when the skies of most West African countries are grey from the sands blown south from the Sahara. On bad days visibility can be reduced to a km, occasionally even less, resulting in plane delays or cancellations. Take a trip to the hilly areas of Guinea in December, for example, and you'll get none of the views that make it so popular, especially with hikers.

The Harmattan usually begins in late November or early December and lasts several months. In the Sahel, the skies will remain hazy until the first May rains. Fortunately, however, some days are fairly clear, which is probably why most travellers aren't too troubled by the Harmattan. People with contact lens should be prepared for problems regardless. Photography nuts are going to be disappointed with the hazy results and professional photographers in particular will end up shooting themselves if they come during this period.

ECONOMY
The Bad News

Overall, the economic situation in West Africa is bleak, with 10 of the world's 36 poorest countries located there. The poorest in West Africa are Burkina Faso, Mali and Guinea-Bissau, all with GNPs below US$225/person.

The Sahel tends to be poorer because the rainfall is so much more unreliable. A 50% drop in rainfall in Niger may mean a zero harvest – the same in rainy Liberia would not have nearly the same effect. The situation is so bad in the Sahel that many rural families cannot afford to have their only daily 'luxury' – a small glass of tea in the shade after a meal.

The problem is that the situation is not improving. To the contrary, despite considerable assistance from Western Europe and North America, many countries are worse off now than 25 years ago at independence. The classic example is Ghana, the most prosperous country in West Africa at independence. Now it's barely in the middle group. Other economic disasters are Guinea (which refused French assistance after independence) and Sierra Leone (only a few have benefited from its diamonds). Most West African countries were self-sufficient in food production in 1960. Now they are net importers of even basic grains except in years of adequate rainfall, which seems to have been about 50% of the time during the past 10 to 15 years. It's not just a question of rainfall; the population growth rate has not been matched by a concomitant growth in the agricultural sector even during years of good rainfall.

The situation has not been reversed by assistance from the west. Many observers believe that a major reason has been the governments' socialist policies. Almost everywhere that the governments of these young countries have interfered with the market mechanisms, the result has been disastrous.

No government in West Africa has received more outside assistance during the past 25 years than Senegal, yet its real growth rate per capita (markedly improved in 1985-86) has been zero over that period.

Instead of letting food prices be determined by market forces, the governments all over West Africa have set official prices for the farmers. The intentions may be noble, but invariably the set prices have been too low with the result that farmers have had little incentive to produce more than they can consume. In Mali, farmers used to go to jail for refusing to sell part of their harvests to the government at ridiculously low prices.

With policies like these, no matter how much money western governments put into projects they were probably doomed to failure. (Plus many were just poorly conceived.) There was always the hope that even if the projects failed, the governments would learn from their experiences. Foreign governments also hoped that by hanging in there, they might persuade the governments to change their policies during the course of the projects. Change was not to come that fast and many well-publicised failures were the result. The USA financed the most, so its failures got the most publicity.

The United States . . . spent $4.6 million for a cereal-production project in Senegal that did not increase grain output by a single bag. It spent another $13 million on a livestock scheme in Mali and later admitted that nothing whatsoever had been achieved.

The Africans by David Lamb.

With droughts occurring almost every second year, the pressure has been relentless to 'do something'. At the price of having some notorious failures, 'hanging in there' has had an effect. Gradually, governments all over West Africa are handing segments of the economies back to private enterprise, or ordering the state-run enterprises to make a profit or close down. Time will tell whether the situation will turn around.

The Good News

There are some real success stories in West Africa. That of the Ivory Coast is the

most well known. Togo is another, although in recent years the economy has become stagnant from over-investment in tourism. The wealthiest countries on a per capita basis are the Ivory Coast (US$1000) and Nigeria (US$750), while the rest have per capita incomes ranging from US$180 up. Here's how the top countries in West Africa, based on per capita incomes, stack up now compared to several years after independence:

1963	1985
Liberia	Ivory Coast
Ghana	Nigeria
Ivory Coast	Mauritania
Senegal	Liberia
Sierra Leone	Senegal
Mauritania	Togo
Guinea	Ghana

Oil is the reason Nigeria is near the top of the list. However, with the drop in oil prices, all of the oil-producing countries in Africa went into a significant slump during the first half of the 1980s and are only slowly recovering.

As the model economy in West Africa during the 1960s and 1970s, the Ivory Coast is the only net exporter of food in the area. Its success has come from cocoa (the world's largest producer), coffee (the world's third largest producer), cotton (highest in Francophone Africa), rubber (approaching the highest in Africa) and timber. Plus it has one of the region's most astute political leaders – Houphouet-Boigny.

Don't lose perspective – Nigeria is the economic goliath of West Africa. Nigeria's GNP is greater than that of all the rest of West and Central Africa combined. Why? People for starters – 100 million plus. One out of every five Africans is a Nigerian and there are as many Nigerians as there are Africans in the rest of West and Central Africa excluding Zaire. Oil is another reason. With high oil prices, Nigeria prospered even with corruption and poor planning. Today the Nigerian economy is in the doldrums, yet far better off than most.

MUSIC

Perhaps nothing is more interesting about African culture than the music and dancing. Because it takes some getting used to, few travellers get interested in this aspect of African life. It's too bad. After all, the origin of much of our pop music can be traced back to Africa. Moreover, this is another area where West and Central Africa stand out above the rest of the continent. Amongst Africans, the pop music from West and Central Africa dwarfs in popularity that from the rest of Africa. The music is so interesting that a tour of West Africa focusing solely on music would be entirely possible.

But travellers tend not to be interested because they don't know anything about it. Even if interesting, all the music over the radio may sound similar and without knowing who is singing or what country the music is from, most travellers find the whole music scene incomprehensible. One solution is to buy *The Music of Africa*, a brand new (1987), four-record anthology of modern African music by Hilton Fyle of BBC fame. This section may also help to demystify the music scene. It's followed by a reference section of the best-known recording artists. You still may not be able to identify these singers, however, unless you go out and buy a few of their cassettes. An amazingly simple way to do this is to walk into almost any music store (even those in market places), listen to some records, and then have them record one or more on a cassette on the spot. The price rarely exceeds US$4.

If you want records of African music, don't expect to be able to find them outside Africa without great difficulty. The best stores by far for African music in New York, Washington, London and Paris are as follows: African Record Centre Ltd (2343 7th Avenue, New York, New York; tel 212-2812717); The African Music Gallery (1722 Florida Avenue, NW, Washington, DC 20009; tel 202-4628200. Metro stop Dupont Circle); Stern's African Record Centre Ltd (116 Whitfield St, Covent Garden, London W1P 5RW; tel 01-3875550); Afric Music (3 Rue Plantes, 75014 Paris; tel 01-45424352. Metro stop Alesia).

Traditional Music

When people talk about African music, there are really two types – the traditional village music and the modern pop music. It shouldn't be surprising that the former is much harder for foreigners to appreciate than the latter. For one thing, very few of the instruments have scales. Rhythm has precedence over melody. To the uninitiated, it may sound monotonous when in fact there is a lot going on.

Several things set traditional music apart from pop music. Historically, music has been the prerogative of only one social group known as *griots*. They are the villages' entertainers as well as historians and genealogists. At a wedding, for instance, it's usually a griot who does the entertaining. Others usually of higher social status are content to leave music to them. A second unique feature of traditional music is that it serves a social purpose. Not only does each social occasion having its own type of music but, in addition, there are different kinds of music for women, young people, hunters, warriors, etc.

A third aspect of traditional music which sets it apart is the instruments. Unlike the pop groups with electric guitars and the like, the griots use only instruments that they themselves can make with local materials, such as gourds, animal skins, horns, etc. Included in this group are, foremost, drums and stringed instruments. A quick visit to almost any museum in Africa will give you a good idea of the variety. Nowhere is there a more imaginative assortment of drums than in Africa – cylindrical, kettle and frame drums as well as goblet and hourglass-

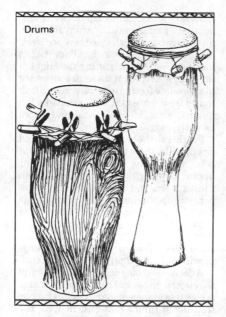

Drums

from half a large gourd and covered with a stretched goat skin. It looks and sounds something like a harp. You're especially likely to hear one in Senegal, Guinea, Mali or the Ivory Coast. In Guinea, all you have to do is wander down the streets of Conakry any evening and you're likely to see a street dance; the kora is an indispensable part of the scene (as is the balafon, a xylophone-like instrument with small gourds hanging on the underside that give it a hollow sound). In Senegal, you can go out any Sunday to the Benedictine monastery outside Dakar and hear the kora and other traditional instruments being used to play Bach and the like – truly unique.

A third general category of traditional instruments to look for are wind instruments. Included in this group are flutes made from millet stalks, bamboo and gourds, as well as animal tusk horns and trumpets made from gourds, metal, shells or wood. Again, they are found everywhere in West Africa and take a slightly different form in each area. If you're looking for something a little unique to collect but light and inexpensive, flutes are a good buy. One of the best new books on traditional African music is *The Music of Africa* by J H Kwabena Nketia (Victor Gollancz Ltd, 14 Henrietta St, London WC2E 8QJ).

shaped drums. There is a certain mystical aspect of musical instruments in Africa, as though they were alive with their own language of sounds. The fact that goats are the most talkative animals and their skins are used almost exclusively in making drums is no coincidence. One reason, perhaps, for the variety of drums is that they serve not only as musical instruments but for communication as well. The drums used for long distance messages are often made from the trunks of trees and can easily weigh several hundred kg.

Stringed instruments come in about as many varying forms as drums, ranging from a one-string lute to the 21-stringed *kora*. Because it's one of the few traditional instruments with a scale, the kora is probably the most interesting instrument to foreigners – and certainly one you should not miss hearing before leaving the continent. The kora is made

Pop Music

Turn on the radio and if the song is African, there's a 50% chance it is Congolese-Zairoise, a 25% chance it is Cameroonian, and a 25% chance it is a local group/singer. That's stretching things a bit because musical tastes vary a good deal throughout West and Central Africa. However, if there's any one music that is king just about everywhere, it's unquestionably the modern Congo-Zaire sound. Hearing it for the first time, you may think it's Latin. That's because there's a lot of Latin influence in African popular music. Indeed, African pop music is an incredible mishmash of traditional,

Latin and Black American music with elements of American jazz and rock.

It all started about 90 years ago with the coming of the colonial era. Africans for the first time were introduced to music with ballads. The influence came from three sources. First, there were the Africans who were forced to become members of regimental bands associated with the forts. The music they played was typically European – polkas, marches and the like. Second, there was the impact of the Christian religious groups with their songs. Finally, the increased trade with Europe brought sailors from all over the world and they brought not only their favourite ballads, but also instruments such as guitars, harmonicas and accordions. It may seem a little weird seeing a small accordion in some remote village, for instance, but you may.

Ghana was the richest country in the area and, not surprising, was where this influence was felt the most. What emerged was a westernised music called 'Highlife'. The western influence was greater in the dance bands which played to the black elite in the cities than those which played in the hinterland. The latter combined acoustic guitars with rattles, drums and the like and developed a type of Highlife that was substantially different from that of the dance bands. During WW II, Allied troops were stationed in West Africa resulting in the spread of more new

musical ideas, especially the then-popular 'swing' music. After the war, there were bands with sizeable repertoires, including calypso sounds. They began touring West Africa igniting the Highlife fire everywhere, but at the same continuing to assimilate foreign musical styles. Black music from across the Atlantic had a big impact, especially jazz, soul and, more recently, reggae.

Further to the south in Leopoldville and Brazzaville, there was another movement going on. During WW II, radio stations began popularising the early Cuban rumba stars, and new 'Congo-bars' were popping up offering not only refreshments but also dance music. The music was predominantly acoustic with solo guitars being accompanied by small brass ensembles. Bottles struck like gongs provided the rhythmic accompaniment.

A decisive turning point was the arrival of the electric guitar and amplification. Large orchestras emerged, many elaborating on traditional rumba patterns. In 1953, the popular band African Jazz featuring Dr Nico was established, followed three years later by the famous OK Jazz. In the late 1960s when President Mobutu of Zaire began his well-known 'Authenticité' movement, new orchestras began trying to remain more faithful to traditional sounds while at the same time experimenting with some of the North American rhythms. The result was enormously

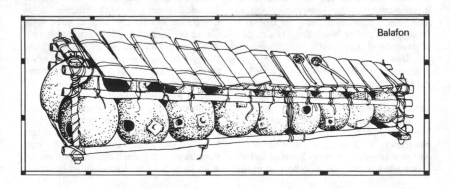

Balafon

successful, bringing a deluge of new orchestras that have dominated the African musical scene ever since.

As a result of all this assimilation, a variety of musical styles are heard throughout West Africa. African groups have incorporated African rhythms and developed their own unique sounds, with the result that African music is now having an impact on western music. The major styles that have developed are listed below. Most of the stars are male. There are a few big stars who are left out simply because they either do no fall within any major style (Aicha Kone) or because the music is not uniquely African, such as Alpha Blondy – the reggae superstar – and Nayanka Bell (all from the Ivory Coast).

Afro-Beat A fusion of African music, jazz and soul, Afro-Beat along with juju is the most popular music today in Nigeria. Unlike the other styles, there are so many variations that it's hard to classify. The undisputed king of Afro-Beat is Fela Anakulapo-Kuti. Fela went to the USA in the 1960s and was greatly influenced by James Brown. He took Brown's jazz and mixed it with the many cultural intricacies of his own African music and developed Afro-Beat. The instruments used by his orchestra are mainly non-African: guitars, trumpets, saxophones and electric pianos as well as drums. Yet the sounds are substantially African inspired. Because his lyrics are always controversial and frequently political, he has never been popular with the politicians. In 1984, he was detained on false currency smuggling charges and sentenced to 5 years in prison. The outcry was loud and in 1986 he was released. Other musicians whose music falls under the general title of Afro-Beat include Nigeria's Mono-Mono, Ghetto Blaster, and Sonny Okosun with his 'Jungle Rock' music, Benin's popular Polyrhythmic Orchestra and Ghana's African Brothers.

Juju Music Juju music had its origins in Nigerian Yoruba music. As far back as the 1930s, the Highlife bands began playing it. The Nigerian civil war gave rise to the popularity of juju music. Many members of the Highlife bands went east to Biafra, leaving a dearth of entertainers in Lagos. So the people turned to juju. Today, it's one of the most popular music styles in Nigeria; outside of Nigeria its popularity is rather limited. The leading singers are Ebenezer Obey and Sonny Ade, the latter being influenced by Afrobeat and particularly popular with the younger crowd.

Popular Sahelian Music This is sort of a catch-all category of non-traditional music played today by groups from Mali, Guinea and Senegal. What distinguishes this music perhaps is the greater use of traditional instruments, such as the kora and the balafon. Mory Kanté, a Guinean but now living in Abidjan, is the undisputed king of the kora but his jazzed up version bears little resemblance to what you hear in the villages. Touré Kunda is an internationally known musician from Senegal whose African jazz music falls under this category. Thionne Seck, Youssou N'Dour and the group *Xalam* are others from Senegal that are well known. In Mali, there are various dance bands, such as the *Super Rail Band* and *Les Ambassadeurs du Mali* and singers Boncana Maigo and Fanta Damba, which make substantial use of traditional instruments in producing their rich, complex rhythms, but their popularity outside Mali is limited.

Cape Verdian Music Only minimally popular in West Africa, Cape Verdian music is nevertheless worth mentioning because of its distinctive, fast-paced Latin style. The dominant role of the guitar and electric piano without traditional African instruments are part of what sets it apart from other Latin-inspired music, such as that from Zaire. The leading musicians can change quickly; those

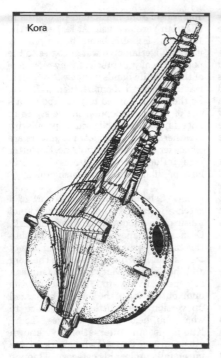

Kora

currently popular include Bana and Paulino Vieira.

Congo Music The Congo music from Zaire and neighbouring Congo is at the top of all the 'pop' charts. For one thing, it's some of the best dance music. If it sounds Latin, it's probably Zairois. If not, it's probably from neighbouring Congo or Gabon. Fifteen of the biggest stars/groups include the following. Male: Tabu Ley, *OK Jazz*, *Langa Langa*, Samaguana, *Bella Bella*, M'Bongo, Papa Wemba, Dr Nico (deceased), Pierre Moutouari and Pamelo Mounk'a (both from the Congo), and Akendengue (Gabon). Female: Pongo Love, M'Bilia Bel, Tshala Muana (all from Zaire) and Nayanka Bell (Ivory Coast).

Makossa Music Cameroon has a distinct style of music that may be second in popularity in West Africa excluding Nigeria. Makossa music is a fusion of Cameroonian Highlife and Soul. Like Congo music, the beat makes you want to dance which, of course, is part of the reason for its popularity. Recognising it, however, requires a little structured listening. The biggest stars are all male: Manu Dibango and Sam Fan Thomas along with Sammy Njondji, Moni Bile, Tamwo, Toto Guillaume and Ekambi Brillant.

One of the more interesting things to do while wandering downtown in any major city is to go into a record shop and ask to hear some of the local recording stars – under the impression that you might buy something, of course. There's no better way to learn the different styles, and maybe you will buy something. Records or cassettes typically sell for about US$10. You can get cassettes a lot cheaper at music stores in the business of making cassettes from their own records or from ones you give them. Bring your own good quality blank cassettes – the ones they use are invariably of low quality. Each country chapter lists the most popular local recording stars. Chances are they'll be the leading stars five years hence.

As for hearing live African music, the sad fact is that there are few groups which perform on a regular basis. In some countries, it's virtually impossible to hear an orchestra unless it's at a tourist hotel or there's a special occasion. The best cities in West Africa for hearing live performances are Lagos and Accra. In Accra and elsewhere in Ghana, on the weekends one can find live bands at many of the nightclubs. Other cities where there are groups playing on a regular basis are the capital cities of the Ivory Coast, Burkina Faso, Cape Verde and Guinea. If you're in West Africa in December 1988, head to Dakar for *FESPAC*, the Pan-African music festival that seems to crop every 10 years or so. The last one held in Lagos in 1977 was a great success.

WOALEY

If you like games of intellectual challenge, one of the first things you should do upon arriving in Africa is to learn woaley – a game similar to backgammon. The game goes by many different names, including *woaley* or *awalé* in the Ivory Coast, *aju* in Togo and Benin, *ouri* in Senegal. For starters, buy a woaley board. Most are rectangular, about a half-metre long with two rows of six cups each. Some boards also have a cup at one or both ends for storing captured peas (48 come with the game).

Even if games aren't your bag, you won't find a better way to meet Africans, especially if you're having trouble communicating. Woaley is a major pastime of Africans of all ages and has been since it originated in Egypt thousands of years ago. While it is designed for two people, teams are also possible. Finding an opponent is rarely difficult – opening the board amongst onlookers is usually all that's required.

The basics of play are not difficult, but mastering the game requires time. In Africa, one thing you will find is time, whether waiting for a bush taxi or simply cooling off in a bar or under a shade tree. There are several versions of the game played by different ethnic groups and varying in complexity. So don't be surprised if your opponent's rules are slightly different from those explained here.

Rules

1 Moves are always left to right, counterclockwise.
2 A move is made by picking up all of the pieces in a chosen cup and dropping them one by one (and only one) in each consecutive cup to the right, starting with the cup to the right of the cup from which the peas are taken.
3 You can initiate a move by picking up peas from a cup only on your side of the board.
4 A move may be made from any cup on your side that has peas. (In some versions, a move can be made from only cups containing at least two peas.)
5 You are entitled to only one move at a time. (In some versions, play continues until you 'capture' a cup.)
6 In some versions, if there are so many peas in the cup that you go completely around the board dropping peas back to the original cup, you skip the original cup.
7 Peas may be 'captured' from either side of the board. (In some versions, the initial captured cup – always the last cup in a move – must be on the opponent's side.)

Starting Play

All woaley boards have 12 cups and 48 peas. Four peas are placed in each cup. Either player may start. The first player picks up all the peas in a chosen cup (from the player's side only) and drops one at a time in each consecutive cup, counterclockwise. If you capture any peas, you put them to the side. Then the opponent does the same, and so on.

Capturing Peas

A player scores by capturing peas; the winner is the one with the most captured peas at the end of the game. A player captures peas only when the last pea dropped falls in a cup containing one or two peas (ie, two or three peas after the move).

In a well-executed move, a player may capture several cups of peas at a time, but only if they have three peas or less after the move and are in a row immediately preceding the last cup. For instance, if the last pea falls into a cup with two peas and, say, the three cups immediately preceding it each contain three peas or less after the move, the player would capture the peas in all four cups (including the peas he put into them). But if, after the move, the next to the last cup contained two peas and the second to the last cup contained more than three peas, he would capture the peas only in the last two cups.

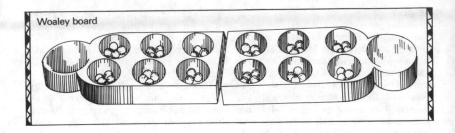

Woaley board

End of Game

The game ends when Player A has no peas left on his/her side and Player B must play at least twice consecutively in order to reach the opponent's side of the board. (In that instance, if Player B has various alternative moves but only one will allow him to get to A's side of the board, he has no option – he must make that move in order to keep the game going.) Ending up with no peas does not mean you win the game, although it is beneficial in the scoring.

Scoring

Each player counts the peas he/she has captured plus any peas remaining on the opponent's side of the board. Since there are 48 peas, any peas over 24 constitute a point. If, for example, your total is 30 peas (your opponent will have 18 peas), you will receive six points and your opponent zero. A match is whatever you decide – three games, 100 points, two hours, etc.

RELIGION

Before the Muslims began making inroads into Africa about 1000 years ago, the traditional religions in Africa were almost all animistic and involved ancestor worship. Now, roughly half of all West Africans are Muslim, particularly those living in the Sahel except in Burkina Faso, where the Mossi warriors successfully resisted the Islamic invaders. The country with the highest percentage of Muslims is Mauritania (95%), followed by The Gambia, Niger, Senegal, Mali, Guinea and Nigeria (primarily in the north) – all with more than 50%.

Christians, mainly Catholics, are concentrated along the coast with the highest numbers found in Ghana (40%), followed by Togo, Liberia, Benin and the Ivory Coast. The second longest cathedral in the world is the new cathedral in Abidjan, consecrated by the Pope in the mid-1980s.

Animism

Each ethnic group in Africa has its own religion, so there are literally hundreds of traditional religions in West Africa. However, there are some factors common to all of them.

Virtually all are animistic and accept the existence of a Supreme Being as well as reincarnation. The Creator is considered to be too exalted to be concerned with humans but there are numerous lesser deities with whom one can communicate, usually through sacrifices, as well as deified ancestors. There are no great temples or written scriptures, and beliefs and traditions are handed down by word of mouth.

The lesser deities, who act as intermediaries between the Creator and mortals, are frequently terrifying and correspond to natural phenomena or diseases. The Ewe of Togo and Ghana, for example, have over 600 deities including one representing smallpox. Africans pray to these deities in order to gain good health, bountiful harvests and numerous children. It would not be unusual to see an

African offering a few ritualistic words to one of the deities before taking libations. Many of the village celebrations are in honour of one or more deities. The Dogon of Mali, for instance, have celebrations before planting and after harvests to ensure good crops.

The ancestors play a particularly strong role in African religions. Their principal function is to protect the tribe. They are also the real owners of the land, and while you can enjoy it during your lifetime, you cannot sell it without incurring their wrath. Ethnic groups are usually broken down into clans, which include all individuals who can trace their origins to a particular ancestor. Each has its own taboos in relation to its protective genies. Certain ones cannot kill lions; others refrain from slaughtering pythons or caimans.

Magic is another element common to native African religions. Good magic keeps away evil spirits. The medicine men, or juju priests, are the ones who dispense charms, tell fortunes and give advice on how to avoid danger. They are frequently seen around the markets, usually with bags full of fetishes such as birds' skulls and shells. The charms worn around the neck are called *grigris* (gree-gree) and are found all over West Africa. In the Sahelian countries, it is not unusual to see a person with six or seven grigris around his or her neck, each warding off a particular evil. If it hasn't been blessed by the medicine man, it's worthless. I wouldn't be caught dead without mine.

Islam

In the early 7th century in Mecca, Mohammed recieved the word of Allah (God) and called on the people to turn away from pagan worship and submit to the one true God. His teachings appealed to the poorer levels of society and angered the wealthy merchant class. By 622 AD life had become sufficiently unpleasant for Mohammed and his followers that they were forced to flee to Medina. This migration, the Hejira, marks the beginning of the Islamic calendar, year 1 AH or 622 AD. By 630 AD they had gained a sufficient following to return and take Mecca. Mohammed died in 632 but within two decades most of Arabia was converted to Islam.

Muslims began infiltrating Africa about a thousand years ago. The Berbers from Morocco, for example, began raiding the Sahelian areas, bringing about the demise of West Africa's first major kingdom, the Empire of Ghana. By the 14th century many African rulers, particularly in the Sahel, had adopted Islam, at least in part. The second great West African kingdom, the Empire of Mali, was almost always ruled by Muslims and Timbuktu became a major centre of Islamic teaching.

Islamic penetration through the coastal forests was quite another matter. Even today there are not many adherents of Islam in the coastal areas except for the immigrants from there.

Islam is the Arabic word for submission and underlies the duty of all Muslims to submit themselves to Allah. The Five Pillars of Islam are the basic tenets which guide Muslims in their daily lives. These tenets are the *shahada, salah, zakat, ramadan* and the *hadj*.

The shahada – 'There is no God but Allah and Mohammed is his prophet' – is the basic profession of faith and the fundamental tenet of Islam. Salah is the call to prayer when Muslims must face Mecca and pray five times a day – at dawn, midday, mid-afternoon, sunset and nightfall. Zakat is the act of giving alms to the poor and needy. Ramadan is the ninth month of the Muslim calendar when all Muslims must fast from dawn to dusk. It commemorates the month when Mohammed had the Koran revealed to him. The hadj is the pilgrimage to Mecca and it is the duty of every Muslim who is fit and can afford it to make the pilgrimage at least once.

Islamic Customs It is worthwhile remembering a few basic points lest you commit some social error or miss out on some of the goings on. First, whenever you visit a mosque, take off your shoes. In some mosques, women are not allowed to enter; in others, there may be a separate entrance since men and women pray separately. Second, if you have a taxi driver or guide for the day, he may need to do his prayer ritual. Be on the lookout for signs he may express indicating he wants a few moments off, particularly around midday, late afternoon and sunset.

Third, despite the Islamic proscription against alcohol you may have heard that some Muslims drink like fish. Even so, it's impolite to drink alcohol in their presence unless they show approval. Fourth, if a Muslim man refuses to shake hands with a woman, remember he's only following the Koran so don't take offence. Fifth, there are some important Islamic holidays, during which time little gets done (see Festivals & Holidays.)

FESTIVALS & HOLIDAYS
A consideration in planning your itinerary are the special events throughout the year. The more important ones are listed below and discussed more fully in the country chapters.

January
1 New Year's Day is celebrated all over Africa.
1-22 Paris-Dakar Car Rally. This is Africa's biggest auto race. The route changes slightly every year. The drivers arrive in Niamey (Niger) around the 15th of January, Mali a few days later, and Dakar on the 22nd.
13 Togo Liberation Day. A vast parade makes its way through the streets of Lomé.

February
15-17* Argungu Fishing Festival, Sokoto State, Nigeria. This festival offers displays of barehand fishing, duck hunting,

swimming and diving competitions, and canoe racing. Drinking, drumming and dancing continue into the night.
20-30* FESPACO in Ouagadougou, Burkina Faso. This all-African film festival is held every odd year.

March
Mardi Gras in Cape Verde and Guinea-Bissau. This is Cape Verde's major celebration, with street parades every day leading up to Lent.
14-16* Tilsm Festival near Kanté (Togo). The Bassar people spend over three days in this dry month trying to predict the crop. Men perform *sintou*, a magical dance that can last as long as the festival.
15-21* Cultural Week in Burkina Faso. Held every even year about the third week in March in a different town, this event sponsors dancing, theatre, parades, etc.

April
4 Senegalese National Day. This is Senegal's biggest public celebration and coincides with the West African International Marathon and a 10-km race in Dakar.
8-9* Gomon Festival in central Ivory Coast. You'll see dancing, healing ceremonies and sacrifices.
15 Niger's National Festival. This is a major holiday in Niger involving one week of traditional dancing, wrestling and camel races.

May
17* Feast of Ramadan (estimated 1988 date, 6 May 1989 – moves back 11 days every year). This is the second major Islamic holiday, celebrated everywhere in West Africa following the annual 30-day Muslim fast. Especially interesting are the Sallah celebrations in Kano and Katsina (northern Nigeria).

July
6* Great Magal, Touba, Senegal. This is a special celebration in Touba that draws

huge crowds and occurs thirty days before Tabaski.

25* Tabaski (estimated 1988 date, 14 July 1989 – 11 days earlier every year). This is the major Muslim holiday and celebrated everywhere in West Africa. It's particularly interesting in Kano and Katsina (northern Nigeria), and Agadez (Niger).

August

3 Oshun Festival, Osogbo, Nigeria (near Ibadan). There's dancing, among other things.

4 Burkina Faso's Revolution Day.

September

1-30* Niger's Cure Salée. There is no event on the continent more interesting than the annual celebration of Niger's Bororos, nomadic Fulani cattle herders who get together once a year to celebrate.

The courtship rituals are particularly famous. The date is not fixed, but almost always occurs sometime in September, usually the latter half. The celebration lasts a week, but the major events only about two days. The location is also not fixed; the principal Cure Salée (there are several) usually takes place about 200 km west of Agadez, north of In-Gall.

2* Yams Festival, Bassar, Togo. At the beginning of September, this festival has folk dancing, fire dances and traditional costumes.

8-11* Guin Festival, Glidjo-Aného, Togo. This four-day festival starts on a Thursday before the second Sunday in September. Processions the first two days are followed by dancing and celebrations during the last two days.

28-15 October* New Yams Festival, Imo State, Nigeria.

Senufo dancer near Korhogo, Ivory Coast (EE)

December
10-12* Mali cattle crossing at Diafarabé. The exact date is not fixed until November. This is a very interesting event, when Fulani herders from the desert bring hundreds of thousands of cattle to an area about 200 km north-east of Ségou to cross the Niger River in search of greener pastures.
7-15* Igue Festival, Benin, Nigeria. In this colourful seven-day festival, Oba people perform traditional dances in full regalia, and their chiefs hold a mock battle and dance in procession to the palace to reaffirm their loyalty.
25 Christmas is celebrated everywhere.

* approximate date.

Islamic Holidays

There are some very important Islamic holidays, when almost all of West Africa's commercial life comes to a stop. Since the Islamic calendar is based on 12 lunar months, with 354 or 355 days, these holidays are always about 11 days earlier than the previous year. The exact dates depend on the moon and are only announced about one day in advance.

End of Ramadan (Id ul Fitr) Ramadan is the ninth month of the Islamic lunar-based calendar (the year is usually 354 days). During the entire 30-day month, Muslims are supposed to fast during the daylight hours. The fast is sometimes referred to as *le carême* (kah-REM). Muslims who do the carême (many do not, particularly those living in the cities) are usually weak during the afternoon because they are not allowed to eat or drink (except for athletes, pregnant women, and a few other exceptions) from sunrise to sunset. Work hours usually end around 1 or 2 pm.

You might think that people would lose weight during this period, but some actually gain weight because of the huge meals served after sunset and before sunrise. In general, it's a very festive time, something like the Christmas season, and people go more frequently to the mosque and visit friends at night. For 1988/89/90, the fast is expected to begin on 18 April, 7 April and 27 March.

The end of Ramadan is the second most important Muslim holiday – celebrated by a big feast, known as the Feast of Ramadan or the Small Feast, beginning on the evening of the 30th day. The centre of attraction is usually a roasted sheep, or possibly a goat. The estimated dates for 1988/89/90 are 17 May, 6 May and 25 April.

Tabaski (Id al Kabir) Also known as the Great Feast, Tabaski is the most important celebration throughout all of West Africa. This is the day that Muslims kill a sheep to commemorate the moment when Abraham was about to sacrifice his son in obedience to God's command, only to have God intercede at the last moment and substitute a ram instead. It also coincides with the end of the pilgrimage (hadj) to Mecca. In the preceding two weeks, sheep prices can jump 50% or more.

One-third of the sacrificed animal is supposed to be given to the poor, one-third to friends, and one-third for the family. Those who cannot afford a sheep are really embarrassed – most will do anything to scrape up the money. If you can manage to get an invitation, you'll be participating in what is for most West Africans the most important and festive day of the year. It's mainly lots of eating and visiting friends following several hours at the mosque. In most countries, it's a two-day public holiday, even in those not predominantly Muslim. The estimated dates for 1988/89/90 are 25 July, 14 July and 3 July – 69 days following the Feast of Ramadan.

The Hadj Ask a wheat farmer from near Timbuktu what he's going to do with any profits from a development assistance project and he's likely to tell you that he'll use it to finance a pilgrimage to Mecca.

Many other Muslims would say the same. All Muslims who are of good health and have the means are supposed to make the pilgrimage at least once in their life.

Those who do the pilgrimage receive the honorific title of Hadj for men, and Hadjia for women. For some, this can involve a lifetime of savings, typically several thousand dollars. It's not unusual for families to save up and send one member. Before the aeroplane, it used to involve a journey overland of a year or more, sometimes requiring stops on the way to earn money. So if you meet someone with the prefix Hadj or Hadjia, you may appreciate the honour this bestows on them in the community.

GAME PARKS

A saying you may hear is that people go to East Africa to see the animals and to West Africa to see the people. You may also hear that there are no game parks in West Africa worth your time visiting. If you like sitting on the porch of your hotel and having the animals led by, you won't like West African game parks. But if you like the idea of stalking the animals as much as simply observing them, then you may find the West African game parks quite interesting.

The people who are usually disappointed with the West African parks are those who have been to East Africa. It's fairly rare for a first-time visitor to Africa to return disappointed from a West African game park. You can see elephant, lion, buffalo, wart hog, birds galore, various species of antelope, and hippo.

The main problem with game parks in West Africa isn't the lack of animals – it's the remoteness of the parks. All except W National Park near Niamey (Niger) are at least a day's drive from the nearest capital city, or much longer. The parks are usually open from late November to the end of May or early June.

The major parks in West Africa are:

Comoé National Park in north-eastern Ivory Coast (a day's drive from Abidjan)
Arly National Park in eastern Burkina Faso (a day's drive from Ouagadougou)
W National Park in south-western Niger and northern Benin (a three-hour drive from Niamey and part of the same park network as Arly.)
Niokolo-Koba National Park in south-eastern Senegal (a long day's drive from Dakar)
Yankari Game Reserve in eastern Nigeria (several hours drive from Jos)

LANGUAGE

Of the 16 countries in West Africa, French is the official language in nine (Senegal, Guinea, Ivory Coast, Togo, Benin, Niger, Burkina Faso, Mali and Mauritania), English in five (Nigeria, Ghana, Liberia, Sierra Leone, The Gambia), Portuguese in two (Cape Verde, Guinea-Bissau), and Arabic (and French) in one (Mauritania).

Some say it's an awful legacy of the colonial period that the official languages are non-African. Far from it. To choose one of the many local languages for the official language would be politically disastrous. Moreover, few would be able to speak it.

Niger riverboat - MALI

Facts for the Visitor

VISAS

Exemptions

Travellers of the nationalities below are not required to have visas to the following countries:

Americans Togo.
Australians Gambia.
Belgians Burkina Faso, Niger, Togo.
British Algeria, Gambia, Ivory Coast, Niger.
Canadians Togo, Gambia.
Danes Algeria, Benin, Gambia, Ivory Coast, Niger, Sierra Leone, Togo.
Dutch Burkina Faso, Gambia, Niger, Senegal, Togo.
Finns Algeria, Gambia, Ivory Coast, Niger, Togo.
French Algeria plus all French-speaking countries in West Africa.
West Germans Benin, Burkina Faso, Gambia, Ivory Coast, Niger, Togo, Senegal. Visas to Ghana are required in principle but usually not in practice.
Italians Algeria, Benin, Burkina Faso, Gambia, Mauritania, Niger, Senegal, Togo.
Norwegians Algeria, Gambia, Ivory Coast, Niger, Togo.
Swedes Algeria, Benin, Gambia, Ivory Coast, Niger, Togo.
Swiss Algeria.

Visa Requirements

In addition to anywhere from one to four photographs, some embassies may require that you possess an airline ticket with a flight out of the country (to show proof of intention to leave the country). What they don't always tell you is that they will accept a photocopy of the airline ticket and that, sometimes, they'll accept a letter or guarantee from your travel agent instead of your bank. Otherwise, if the ticket is lost in the mail, you may not get reimbursed for quite a while.

If you buy a one-way airline ticket to Africa, you're asking for a headache – some countries won't issue you a visa unless you submit a bank statement or guarantee (*caution bancaire* in French) showing proof of adequate funds to return, ie at least the price of a return airline ticket.

African embassies in Europe and North America are, if anything, stricter in enforcing these requirements than those in neighbouring countries in Africa. If you're travelling on the cheap and cannot afford what they request, some people recommend getting the visa in Africa where enforcement is sometimes more lax. This won't help in the case of Niger, but it may with some countries.

One quirk is that some embassies will issue visas of only very short duration. Don't get upset. In every case, it's relatively easy to get an extension once you're in the country. Also, in Togo and Benin you may not be able to leave without an exit visa, which is required whenever the visitor has stayed over 10 days.

Another quirk is that every so often an embassy will not issue you a visa if, theoretically, you could have gotten one in the country of your residence. The Ghanaian embassy in Burkina Faso won't issue you a visa if you reside, say, in the USA or in the UK.

Most African countries refuse to issue visas in passports with South African visas. If yours has one, most countries including the USA will recognise this as justification for issuing you another passport. South African border officials used to insert removable visas if you asked them. They no longer do this.

Multiple-entry Visas

In addition to single-entry visas, some embassies issue multiple-entry visas, allowing you to re-enter many times. It's amazing how many visitors to Africa think that, for example, they can take the three-hour trip from Lomé (Togo) to Accra (Ghana) and re-enter Togo using the same visa. Sorry. Once you've left a country, you'll need another visa to re-enter. This may seem senseless, but ask an African about the ordeal of getting a visa to the USA and you may be a little more understanding.

Multiple-entry visas are almost always more expensive than single-entry visas. Most embassies won't tell you about the availability of a multiple-entry visa unless you ask. Once they are in Africa, many tourists regret that they didn't obtain such visas, even if their itinerary didn't include re-entry. Plans always change.

Obtaining Visas In Africa

Try to get all the visas you can before leaving. Still, there are some countries for which visas are easily and quickly obtainable in Africa, and others for which this is not the case. If you don't have time to get all the visas you need, be selective and get the ones that are more difficult to obtain in Africa. The list follows:

Easy Benin, Burkina Faso, Ivory Coast, Togo (obtainable from French embassies), Gambia and Sierra Leone (obtainable from British embassies), Guinea-Bissau and Senegal (both obtainable at the airport).

Difficult Ghana (one to four day service depending on the city), Mali and Niger (neither has more than three or four embassies in all of West and Central Africa), and Nigeria (takes three to four days in most African cities).

West African Diplomatic Missions Abroad

Diplomatic missions of the following West African countries plus Algeria can be found in:

Bonn All countries except Cape Verde, Guinea-Bissau and Gambia.
Brussels All countries.
Canberra Ghana, Nigeria.
Copenhagen Burkina Faso, Ghana, Ivory Coast, Nigeria.
The Hague Algeria, Cape Verde, Liberia, Nigeria.
London Algeria, Gambia, Ghana, Ivory Coast, Liberia, Nigeria, Sierra Leone, Togo.
Ottawa Algeria, Benin, Burkina Faso, Ghana, Guinea, Ivory Coast, Mali, Niger, Nigeria, Togo.
Paris All countries except Cape Verde, Guinea-Bissau and Gambia.
Rome Algeria, Ghana, Guinea, Ivory Coast, Liberia, Nigeria, Sierra Leone.
Stockholm Cape Verde, Guinea Bissau, Liberia, Nigeria.
Tokyo Algeria, Ghana, Ivory Coast, Liberia, Nigeria.
Washington All countries except Gambia (visas are obtainable in New York). Roughly half the countries also issues visas at their UN mission in New York.

Visas to Ex-Colonies

British embassies usually have authority to issue visas to Sierra Leone and The Gambia (and Kenya) wherever those countries don't have embassies. French embassies have the same authority for the Ivory Coast, Burkina Faso and Togo but, generally speaking, not the other francophone countries in West Africa. Portuguese embassies have authority to issues visas to some of their ex-colonies.

Visa Agencies

The following tip is easily worth the cost of this book. If you need visas to a number of African countries, it'll take a little time tripping around to all the embassies. In Britain and the USA, there are businesses that will do this for you. In the telephone directory, they're listed under the heading 'passport' or 'visa service'.

Some are apparently better than others. Five among many are Perry International

(4327 Harrison St, NW, Washington, DC, tel 202-9661760); Embassy Visa Service (2162 California St, NW, Washington, DC 20009, tel 202-3871171); Travel Agenda (119 West 57th St, Suite 1008, New York, NY 10019, tel 212-2657887); The Visa Service (411 Oxford St, London W1R 1FG, tel 01-6297276); and P & O Passport & Visa Service (77 Oxford St, London WC1, tel 01-8311258).

Travel Agenda, for example, charges US$10 to US$20 per visa, depending on the country, plus the embassy's fee. The Visa Service charges £7 per visa, plus the embassy's fee. They will mail you application forms and you must return them with your passport, photographs and, for some countries, your health card. Businesses rely heavily on these agencies, and many travellers who have used them wouldn't do it any other way. But if you only need one visa, it's quicker to do it yourself.

EMBASSIES & CONSULATES
The following non-communist countries have embassies and consulates in West Africa:

Australia Nigeria.
Belgium Ivory Coast, Niger, Nigeria, Senegal, Togo. Consulate: Mali.
Canada Burkina Faso, Ivory Coast, Nigeria, Senegal.
France All countries except Gambia.
West Germany All countries except Cape Verde, Guinea-Bissau.
Italy Ghana, Guinea, Ivory Coast, Liberia, Nigeria, Senegal, Sierra Leone.
Japan Ghana, Guinea, Ivory Coast, Liberia, Nigeria, Senegal.
Netherlands Burkina Faso, Ghana, Ivory Coast, Nigeria, Senegal. Consulate: Mali.
Sweden Guinea-Bissau, Ivory Coast, Liberia, Nigeria.
Switzerland Ghana, Guinea, Ivory Coast, Liberia, Nigeria, Senegal. Consulates: Mali, Togo.
UK Gambia, Ghana, Ivory Coast, Liberia, Senegal, Sierra Leone.
USA All countries.

MONEY
CFA
One French franc equals 50 CFA. This is a fixed rate. So if the French franc and the US dollar are trading, say, 6 to 1, you'll get 300 CFA for US$1. In late 1987, after the stock market crash, US$1 equalled about CFA 280. Almost half of the countries in West Africa (all the former French colonies except Mauritania and Guinea) use the CFA franc. By tying the CFA to the franc and exchanging it freely with the French franc, France has given West Africa perhaps its greatest gift – a hard currency. This means you can go from one CFA country to the next without exchanging money.

However, exchanging CFA in other countries isn't easy. In East Africa, the banks act like it's funny money. In the USA, even major banks won't accept them. In short, the CFA is hard currency only in West and Central Africa and France. So don't get caught with excess CFA. If you're returning home via France, no sweat. You can exchange them for French francs at de Gaulle airport.

One hitch is that there are actually two CFAs – the West African CFA (used in Senegal, Ivory Coast, Mali, Burkina Faso, Niger, Togo and Benin) and the Central African CFA (Cameroon, CAR, Chad, Congo, Equatorial Guinea and Gabon). While there's usually not too much difficulty exchanging one for the other at a bank or at a major hotel, don't expect the man on the street to do the same. So avoid getting caught on the weekend with the wrong kind of CFA.

Black Market
The black market scene in West Africa has changed dramatically since 1983. Then, there were nine countries with black markets and the differences in rates were enormous. In Ghana, the difference used to be 5000% – 50 to one! An orange on the

street used to cost the equivalent of US$1.50 – the real value being US 3c. Now, not a single country in West Africa has a substantially over-valued currency (though this could easily change). Guinea-Bissau was the last to join the boat, although a small parallel market (or black market) persists there, as well as in Nigeria, Ghana and Guinea. The official exchange rates in these four countries, however, are now almost as favourable as the black market rates. In Guinea, the franc is tied one to one to the CFA but a minor black market persists. In Sierra Leone, because of new floating exchange rates, the parallel market has virtually disappeared. However, inflation, which almost invariably follows a devaluation, has gotten out of control there.

Changing money on the black market is of course illegal, but even many conservative bankers consider the greater evil to be overvalued currencies which allow black markets to persist. Many travellers used to take the chance, risking stiff jail sentences. With the benefits having dropped dramatically, it's now hardly worth the risk. Those risks are considerable in a few places, especially Nigeria, but slight in most – at least for the experienced.

Sometimes there's no way to avoid exchanging money on the black market. If you're travelling overland by bush taxi, you're not likely to find a bank at the border. How do you pay for the onward taxi? You purchase currency at the last town before crossing the border.

As for the logistics of black markets, if a country has currency declaration forms at the airport or border and you declare all your money, you cannot use the black market – on departing the country, you won't be able to prove that you exchanged all your money at the official rate. You'll find money dealers in a number of places but almost invariably around the markets and at the borders.

In some places it operates openly. If you're walking towards the Lomé market,

for instance, and guys are hissing at you, you'll know what they want – hard currency for Ghanaian cedis. They even accept travellers' cheques! In other places, it's quieter. Taxi drivers frequently are in the business themselves or they act as agents and you may never see the money dealer.

Importing Currency

There is never a limit to the amount of foreign currency that you may import into a country unless, possibly, it's a huge amount. Bringing in local currency is another matter. Except in CFA countries and Liberia (which uses both the American dollar and Liberian dollar coins), it is either prohibited or severely restricted – typically limited to the equivalent of about US$10. You can get into serious trouble violating this rule, particularly in Ghana and Nigeria.

Exporting Currency

CFA Countries The rules for exporting CFA are unclear and unevenly enforced. In many CFA countries, tourists are theoretically supposed to be able to take out more than

local business people, and the limit is supposed to be higher if you're travelling to another CFA country. However, most border officials don't seem to know exactly what the rules are. In West Africa, taking CFA out of a CFA country is rarely a problem if you don't have more than about CFA 75,000. If you should run into problems, playing the ignorant tourist should help. Exporting other currencies from CFA countries is not a problem and currency forms aren't even used.

Non-CFA Countries The rules in non-CFA countries are quite different. You are never allowed to take out more than the equivalent of about US$5 to US$10 in local currency; in some countries you can't take any. Except in The Gambia, on leaving you won't be allowed to reconvert your local currency into foreign currency. So don't get caught with a lot of local currency on you. As for taking out other currencies, there's no limit anywhere in West Africa. On leaving, you will probably have to fill out a currency declaration form with bank receipts proving you exchanged the money that you brought with you at the official rate.

Exchanging Money at the Airport
Don't expect to be able to change your money at every airport. If you can, don't hesitate to do so – the exchange rate is invariably as good as the banks downtown. There are banks at most but not all of the airports serving major capital cities (Lagos, Abidjan, etc) and at about half of the smaller capital cities.

Even in the larger cities, you'll sometimes find the airport banks closed. Don't worry. There are always taxi drivers who'll accept dollars, French francs and frequently pounds, but don't expect the best exchange rate in town. In non-CFA countries, drivers may actually prefer to be paid in hard currency. If you're in a non-CFA country and you declared all of your currency, you cannot pay the driver in hard currency without incurring big

problems when you leave the country. You won't be able to show that all your money was exchanged at banks. No sweat – exchange money at the hotel and tip your driver well for the wait.

Credit Cards
The most widely accepted credit card is American Express (AE); Diners (D) is second. Although increasing in usage, Visa (V) and Carte Blanche (CB) are much less widely accepted, and Master Charge (MC) and Eurocard (EC) are all but worthless. As for restaurants, only the fairly expensive ones accept credit cards, and even then usually only American Express or Diners.

Travellers' Cheques
Take American Express – you'll find many more banks accept American Express cheques than other kinds, and you'll be reimbursed faster if you lose them. American Express travellers' cheques are accepted at almost all major banks in West Africa, but not always at banks upcountry. In Timbuktu, for example, don't expect to be able to exchange your money (cheques or bills) unless the cheques are in French francs because they won't have the foggiest idea what the day's exchange rate is. Anticipate this problem in any town or city outside the capital cities.

As for Thomas Cook, Citicorp, Barclays and Bank America travellers' cheques, you probably won't encounter any problems in the largest capital cities but elsewhere, you'll find that many banks do not accept them. In English-speaking countries, you shouldn't encounter many problems with Thomas Cook and Barclays checks; elsewhere you will.

If you lose your cheques, American Express have more representatives in Africa and generally seem to reimburse much faster. With others you may wait weeks, particularly if the issuing bank has no branch where you are. Just finding which bank, if any, is the correspondent bank is problem enough. If you lose your proof of purchase slip, getting reimbursed will take much longer – easily two weeks. So make photo copies of the purchase slip with numbers and put them in various bags and give one to your travelling companion. Also, bring a good amount of cash in small bills (preferably US dollars and/or French francs) for emergencies.

Wiring Money
Wiring money can take weeks, and problems are often encountered. The bank may deny receiving money which has actually arrived. So don't rely on money being wired to you. If money is wired, arrange for the forwarding bank to send a separate confirmation with full details. You can then go into the African bank with the much needed proof that your money has been sent

Foreign Banks
Citibank Abidjan, Dakar, Lagos, Monrovia, Niamey.
Barclays Abidjan, Accra, Freetown, Lagos
Chase Manhattan Abidjan, Lagos.
Chemical Abidjan.

COSTS
If you're travelling on the cheap, you can budget about US$10 a day in West Africa (double this amount in Liberia). This includes the cheapest lodging in town, eating on the street or in the cheapest African restaurants, and using the least expensive means of transportation – and nothing else.

As for hotels, travellers going first class should expect to pay US$70 to US$120 a night for a single. But don't think that anything less than the best will be intolerable. The best are usually deluxe, and a lot of travellers don't really need or want such luxury. For example, you can stay at a very decent two- or three-star hotel with pool, good restaurant and nice view for about half what the best hotels costs. In Niamey (Niger), this difference means paying US$23 versus US$55; in

Abidjan US$35 versus US$65. Those who find this attractive can budget for an average of only US$30 to US$40 a night except in Nigeria and Guinea.

As for restaurants, many countries in greater West Africa are so poor that there are few or no African restaurants. A restaurant is, after all, a luxury. So what you will find is that most restaurants serve continental cuisine, and it's not cheap, particularly if some of the ingredients are flown in from Europe. Eating relatively modestly can easily run you $US10 to US$20 a meal, and sometimes a lot more. On the other hand, it is possible to find inexpensive restaurants everywhere; it all depends on whether you're willing to take the risk of getting stomach problems. Even at these restaurants, however, if you stick to things like meat and rice and stay away from raw vegetables and fruits, the risk is actually minimal.

In relatively expensive places such as Abidjan, you can have an excellent meal of braised chicken and rice for US$5; foreigners go to these restaurants all the time. Those travelling on the cheap should expect to eat African food everywhere. The cost will frequently be less than US$1 a meal, especially if you eat on the street.

TIPPING
Tipping is a problem in Africa because there are few clear rules applicable to all people. Africans are not in the habit of tipping but a small amount of tipping is expected from wealthier Africans. Tipping to most Africans is related to the concept of a gift (*cadeau*); rich people are expected to give cadeaux. Almost all foreigners appear rich, therefore a cadeau is expected unless the person obviously looks like a hitchhiker. Anyone going to a fancy hotel would be expected to tip but there would not be the same expectation from a backpacker in a cheap hotel.

Everyone, even Africans, are expected to tip 10% at the better restaurants but check the bill closely to see if service is included. It frequently is at restaurants and hotels in French-speaking Africa. At the other end of the scale are the African restaurants with almost all African clientele – no tipping is expected from anyone. There's a grey area between these two classes of restaurants. Tipping at these restaurants is rarely expected from Africans and those who are obviously backpackers, but tipping is expected sometimes from local expatriates and almost always from wealthier tourists. Even the wealthier Africans will sometimes tip at all-African restaurants, not so much because it's expected but because it's a show of status.

As for taxis, tipping is generally not the rule but well-heeled travellers are expected to tip about 10%, except for rides in shared cabs where tipping is almost unheard of. In bigger cities with numerous foreigners such as Dakar, Abidjan and Lagos, the taxi drivers are becoming more like those in New York every day. A small tip may still be hoped for even from backpackers, though few do.

If you can afford it, you can spread a lot of good will by tipping, even for such things as brochettes purchased on the street – you're likely to make a few friends in the process. My favourite brochette man, for instance, gives me an extra one every time I order. Rather than tipping excessively at fine restaurants, you may spread wealth around and a lot of good will as well if you tip frequently and for things the locals would never tip.

CONCERNS OF BUSINESS PEOPLE
Business Cards

Bring lots of *cartes de visites* with you. Without them, you have no legitimacy at all. Be generous with the distribution of the cards as all Africans like to think they have a sugar daddy in the USA or Europe who's going to send them a plane ticket to deliver them from all this mess. And take them with you everywhere; it seems people never have them when they need them. They're even useful when the police

stop your cab for a routine check and your passport is back at the hotel.

Social Customs

Greetings are extremely important to Africans, more so than to Europeans and Americans. You never start a conversation until you say 'Good Morning' or the like. This means that when you go to the airline reservation office, for example, you do some small talk before getting down to reserving your flight. For getting appointments, this means being very friendly with the person's secretary. Those who fail to follow this custom are going to find it difficult to get things done.

Another thing to keep in mind is that the handshake is much more important in Africa than in the USA or Europe. The firm grip used by Americans is definitely not the style. In social settings, when entering and leaving you greet everybody no matter how many people are in the room. In many countries men and women do not customarily shake hands unless the man extends his hand first; if in doubt, shake hands because it's never in bad taste. The thrice-kissed greeting and leave taking (left cheek first) is practised between friends of the opposite sex, even casual acquaintances, in French speaking countries. It may seem awkward at first to go around the room and establish contact with each person individually, but it is very important to do so and gradually it becomes automatic.

Regarding dress, Africans are fairly formal. This means you dress no differently in Africa for business meetings than you would in western nations. For social gatherings, at homes of Americans and Europeans, informality usually governs. At Africans' homes, you can expect to dress more formally. For women, the long African dresses go well in either setting.

Law Firms

The only American law firm with offices in West Africa is Duncan, Allen & Mitchell, a Washington, DC based firm

(1575 Eye St, NW, Washington, DC 20005, tel 202-2898400, telex 440106) with offices in Abidjan (LMGL Building, 11 Avenue Joseph Anoma, 01 BP 3394, Abidjan 01, Ivory Coast, tel 225-326766, telex 2435) and Kinshasa (BP 12368, Kinshasa, Zaire, tel 243-30659, telex 21340). They are involved primarily in commercial law, helping companies setup operations and the like. Working with local lawyers, they will provide similar services in neighbouring countries on a case by case basis when required by the client.

GENERAL INFORMATION
Post
Mail service in Africa bears the brunt of many jokes, but the reality is that the service is quite reliable in most of West Africa – it just takes a while getting there. From the USA the typical delivery time is two to four weeks depending on the town's size/remoteness. From Europe, the delivery time is about one-third less. London-Abidjan, for example, takes about 10 days. However, delivery times considerably longer than this occur just frequently enough to make it impossible to rely on the mail for matters involving critical time-constraints.

Contrary to what you may hear, it's rare that governments open the mail. But then there's the Peace Corps volunteer who was thrown out of Togo for making unflattering remarks about the government on a postcard. Courier service is an alternative; DHL, for example, is located in almost every capital city in West Africa and in some of the other major cities as well.

Telephone
Telephone connections between Africa and Europe/USA are much better than one might think. First-time users are invariably surprised by the good quality of the reception. That's because international calls now usually go by satellite. Calls between African countries, however, are frequently relayed through Europe, in which case the reception is usually bad – if you can get a call through.

Calling from the USA or Europe to Africa is usually easier, and always less expensive, than vice versa. Direct dial is possible to a number of African cities. Between 5 pm and 6 am, the direct dial rate from the USA and Britain to most of Africa is about US$0.75 a minute. This is also the easiest time to get a line. If you call during business hours in the USA or Europe, you may find it very difficult to get through – after 5 pm your chances increase significantly.

Calling from Africa to Europe or the States is sometimes a problem. It's about seven times more expensive and there are no reduced rates at night. Secondly, the waiting time can be minutes or hours depending on the locality and time of day. Thirdly, in several countries calls to the USA must still be relayed through Europe and the reception is highly variable. Don't let this discourage you from trying. From major cities such as Dakar, the problems are minimal – you just pay a lot more.

Electricity
The electricity supply throughout West Africa is 220 volts, except for Liberia where it is 110 volts. Plugs are usually two round pins, ie like those in Europe.

HEALTH
Vaccinations
Everyone must carry an International Health Certificate with a record of vaccinations. Only two are sometimes required to enter West African countries – cholera and yellow fever, and even then usually only if you come from an infected area. These two are essential if you will be travelling extensively.

The average traveller also needs hepatitis and typhoid shots, and anti-malarial tablets starting two weeks prior to departure. In addition, vaccinations for TB, tetanus, meningitis and polio are recommended for those planning to live in Africa awhile and those travelling on the cheap who may encounter fairly unsanitary conditions.

Yellow Fever Required by all West African countries (about half of these waive the requirement if you're not coming from an infected area and staying less than two weeks – but how many airport officials know this?). The yellow fever shot is valid for 10 years, and you need to start the injections about three weeks prior to departure.

Cholera Required in Benin, Ivory Coast, Niger, Liberia and Sierra Leone. Also required in Gambia, Mali, Mauritania and Senegal if you come from an infected area. It must have been taken within the past six months.

It's a well-guarded secret that the vaccination against cholera is ineffective. Rather than waste the effort, a number of doctors will simply stamp your card as having received it. If you'll be travelling to

several countries, don't think you don't need one just because the country doesn't require it. There are periodic outbreaks and you may be refused entry without it. If you cannot get a doctor to stamp your health certificate without taking the vaccination, go ahead and take it rather than risk being stabbed with a dirty needle at an airport or border station.

Hepatitis The gamma globulin shot is given for hepatitis and should be taken just before departure because its effectiveness decreases rapidly. Moreover, it does not prevent hepatitis but only reduces the severity of the disease. Some doctors shrug off the efficacy of the gamma globulin shot, but some protection is better than none.

Typhoid This is the last of the four vaccinations that every traveller should have. If you've had a booster shot within the last three years, you won't need one.

Other Vaccinations There are four additional recommended vaccinations – polio, tetanus, meningitis and TB.

Polio is still common in developing countries but not a major problem. Most people will only require a booster shot. Tetanus is more likely to be a potential problem for those travelling on the cheap. Again, a booster shot is probably all that will be needed.

Type 'A' and 'C' vaccine for meningo-cocca meningitis is recommended for people planning more than a short visit, especially in The Gambia, Mali, Burkina Faso and Niger. As for TB, short-term visitors are very unlikely to get it. So forget about it unless you'll be staying awhile and/or likely to drink a lot of locally made yogurt that is not sold in containers. Finally, smallpox has now been completely eradicated (the last case was reported in 1977); vaccination is no longer required anywhere in the world.

AIDS

A virus very similar to one carried by green monkeys, AIDS (SIDA in French) has been traced back as far as 1959 to a case in Zaire. Still, it is only conjecture that it originated there. As of 1987, the following twelve African countries were the worst hit by the AIDS epidemic: Tanzania, Uganda, Zambia, Rwanda, Burundi, Kenya, Angola, Zimbabwe, Malawi, Central African Republic, Zaire and the Congo.

While none of these countries even border West Africa, the disease is spreading rapidly, the risk being many times greater in the cities than in the rural areas. Many prostitutes in Abidjan, for example, reportedly have it. In Africa, AIDS is primarily a disease not of homosexuals but of, as a Nigerian newspaper phrased it, 'women of loose virtue', though this applies equally to men. Avoiding sex with prostitutes is not enough, however, because Africans from all walks of life are known to carry the virus.

Another problem in West Africa is contracting the disease through blood transfusions and injections. Avoid needle happy doctors, but if this is not possible, make sure that a new syringe is used. Some travellers recommend bringing your own syringes for such instances, but be prepared for a lot of explanations if border officials find one in your bag.

Malaria

Malaria is probably the most serious disease in Africa, affecting about one in five Africans yearly (and yearly killing about one million people worldwide). Nevertheless, in general there is no need for short-term travellers who take their malaria suppressant tablets religiously to get worked up over this somewhat mysterious tropical disease. There is a rare type of malaria that is fatal and death can occur in a day or two. So anyone not taking their tablets regularly is playing with death except in the very dry northern-most areas of the Sahel where mosquitoes are almost nonexistent.

Malaria is usually not fatal and frequently only lasts a few days. Someone not taking preventive medicine may contract it many times during the year. When someone told me for the first time that their child had malaria 'last night', I responded: "What do you mean 'last night'." I thought the kid must be on death row. You learn that these things happen all the time, especially with the Africans who can't afford the daily or weekly treatment. It puts you on your back and a typical African farmer may have malaria 25% of the time.

Diagnosing malaria is not easy because it can mimic the symptoms of other diseases – high fever, lassitude, headache, pains in the joints, and chills. Be a little skeptical if some Joe Doe is 100% certain you've got it. The only sure way to diagnose malaria is by thorough examination of blood smears, and it's not everywhere that this can be done.

So to avoid contracting malaria take malaria suppressant tablets such as aralen or chloroquine once a week starting two weeks before you arrive and continuing four weeks after you leave. In Africa, aralen is not easily obtained. An equally effective substitute is nivaquine, which contains chloroquine, but must be taken every day. Chloroquine only acts to suppress malaria; it does not prevent it. If you get malaria, the treatment is the same for prevention, only in higher doses. Moreover, once you get malaria, traces remain in the blood so that you can never again donate blood. Also, if you've taken aralen, you shouldn't donate blood for three years.

There is a strain of malaria (plasmodium falciparum) with varying degrees of resistance to chloroquine. This is found, however, only in East Africa and the eastern regions of Zaire.

Drinking Water

Foreigners can easily get sick from drinking the local water, whether it is impure or not. For travellers on the cheap, the best solution is to take iodine or halazone tablets (not available in Africa), and avoid fresh vegetables and unpeeled fruits. In a pinch, you can use clorox/ammonia, but it's not as effective. Filtering water, by the way, clears the water but does not sterilise it.

For those with a little money, the solution is to buy bottled water, available in every capital city in West Africa and quite frequently even in the smaller cities and towns. The cost is not prohibitive, ranging between US$0.50 and US$1 per litre in most places (supermarket prices that is, because the hotels will sell it for three times that amount).

It's easy to avoid drinking bad water. The real problem is taking in bad water through others means, most commonly when eating raw vegetables or unpeeled fruit. The only solution is to avoid salads and the like altogether no matter how tempting they are or how fancy and modern the restaurant may be. It's an extremely rare restaurant that soaks its vegetables in an iodine solution. Hotels like the Hilton simply import their vegetables from Europe, but this doesn't avoid potential contamination through handling. So just bring along some vitamin tablets if you're a health nut.

Fortunately, most water in African cities and towns comes from potable sources. The problem is that the water can become contaminated in the pipes. African water systems operate under low pressure so that seepage of sewerage and the like into the pipes is quite possible. This is a much bigger problem during the rainy season, so consider this if you're faced with drinking untreated water.

Dysentery & Diarrhoea

You may think that diarrhoea is inevitable, but there are in fact many short term visitors to West Africa who never get it.

It's water - not meat, noodles, rice, African dishes such as *foutou* and the like - that has the greatest likelihood by far of giving you diarrhoea. But it's not just drinking water - your Coke and fries may be safe but not the glass or utensils.

In some respects, eating at restaurants may be more risky than eating on the street with your hands. (The opposite is true when street food is eaten with plates and utensils.) Street food is usually safe because the ingredients are purchased daily. (In restaurants, you never know how long that fish has been in the refrigerator, and how many blackouts have there been?)

If you are very careful about the water and still get diarrhoea, it doesn't mean you've got dysentery - it's probably caused by the change in food and a change of bacteria in the intestines. The treatment is simple - starve it out for at least 24 hours and drink plenty of unsugared liquids such as tea, bouillon soup and bottled water. A nourishing preparation containing salt, potassium and water is: the juice of one orange and a quarter teaspoon of salt together with 10 ounces of water. Adequate replacement of fluids is essential to avoid dehydration. Moreover, the flow of fluids will help wash out whatever is down there.

As improvement occurs, one or two days of soup and bread or soda biscuits or unsugared oatmeal (easy to find) should follow. In general, drugs are not recommended. Lomotil, however, will help to reduce the symptoms of diarrhoea if not the cause. If this doesn't work, a very effective French drug available locally that some people swear by is ercefuryl. If that's not available, try centercine.

If you have a very bad case of diarrhoea and nothing is working, there's always a chance you've got dysentery. For this you need to see a doctor but beware of needle happy doctors. Africans tend to have an overly high regard for medicines taken by needles and most doctors comply. In most cases, medicine taken through pills is just as effective as those taken by injection. If you're far from a doctor, your main worry is to avoid dehydration, which means drinking lots of fluids. Drinking also helps wash out the system. Finally, if the diarrhoea is accompanied by severe stomach cramps, drink tea or fruit juice with salt to help relieve the pain.

Venereal Diseases

To hear the doctors talk, there's no way to describe venereal disease in Africa other than rampant. Health officials estimate that 25% of the people in the Sahel, for example, have venereal disease. There are about 12 kinds, and many aren't so terrible. Many male expatriates in Africa take advantage of the Africans' disdain for sexual restraint without acquiring anything other than pleasant memories. Indeed, your chances of acquiring a venereal disease are probably less than if you partook of a hot number on Paris' famous Rue St Denis. While this may not be exactly comforting, the point is that the greatest risk by far is from prostitutes.

Weird African Maladies

You may have heard that you should never go swimming in a lake or river because you might come down with some weird African disease that over a period of time ages you about 20 years, or another that causes blindness. It's no joke. The first is called bilharzia or schisto, the latter oncho.

Bilharzia - Schistosomiasis Bilharzia or

'schisto' is a disease caused by tiny blood flukes (worms) which enter the veins and lay eggs. It is spread by snails which live just at the edge of lakes or slow moving rivers (there are few fast flowing rivers in West Africa). Anyone in the mud or shallow water along the edge is susceptible to having these microscopic worms penetrate the skin; labourers in irrigation ditches are particularly susceptible. A good case of the disease is mildly painful and can have a very debilitating effect over the years.

The symptoms are blood in the urine and intestinal pains. For a mild case, there may be no clear signs at all, which is why anyone living overseas for a few years must get checked for schisto upon return. Until recently, the only cure was a dangerous treatment with strong dosages of arsenic which killed the worms but, hopefully, not you. Now it's just a case of taking pills for a week.

Onchocerciasis 'Oncho' or river blindness,

is a disease that threatens the eyesight of 30 million people in the world. You'll know it's a big problem in the Sahel when you see your first blind person singing a song as they are led around by some eight year old. Then you see another and another and another. It's a very sad sight.

Entire villages along the Volta rivers in Burkina Faso have been vacated because of the severity of oncho in some areas. Oncho is transmitted by the bites of female black flies that like to lay their eggs in the foam found on the edges of turbulent rivers (just the opposite of schisto which requires slow moving rivers such as the Niger). After picking up the disease from an infected person they have bitten, the flies then bite uninfected people and lay eggs on the bitten areas. These become infected skin nodules under which the adult worms are found. It's pretty easy to treat in the early stages, but if left untreated, these worms produce thousands of microfilariae which after a few years will make their way to the retina where they die and cause blindness.

In a medical breakthrough, a new drug, Ivermectin, which kills these worms went on the market in France in 1987. Travellers to Africa do not really have to worry about getting oncho, but it's good to know, in case you happen to go into a river area infested with black flies.

Tumba Larva You may have heard that if

your clothes aren't ironed or dried in a clothes drier, you'll get worms. It's true. A wet piece of clothing hanging outside to dry is the tumba fly's favourite place to deposit her eggs. If they are not ironed, the eggs will become larvae and bore into your skin. Often a small white spot can be seen at the site of the lesion. Fortunately, the larva always stays just below the surface of the skin. Even many old African hands don't know how simple the treatment is – put vaseline over the wound to suffocate the worm. It will come out, although a little push may be necessary. Left untreated, these worms become the twice the size of rice from eating your juicy flesh and are quite painful.

Sleeping Sickness Another weird malady caused by biting insects in Africa is trypanosomiasis (sleeping sickness), which causes physical and mental lethargy. It is caused by the tsetse fly, which is about twice the size of the common fly. The main problem is that it kills horses and cattle, leaving large areas of central Africa with few or no such animals. Fortunately, the risk of infection to travellers is virtually nil, and the cure for the disease is effective.

Medical kit

Bring Lomotil (only for cases of severe diarrhoea), Pepto-Bismol (better for ordinary diarrhoea), prescription drugs (stored in two separate bags in case one is lost), malaria tablets, mosquito repellent and salt tablets (dehydration in rural areas of the Sahel is frequent). Travellers on the cheap should also include antiseptic ointment (Bacetracin is widely used), iodine or halazone tablets (for purifying water – they're not readily available in Africa), and petroleum jelly for cracked feet. If you'll be in the Sahel or desert, your feet can get very dry and hard and, as a result, begin cracking. The French call this 'le croco'. The cracks can go very deep and they can be amazingly painful and get infected.

THEFT & SECURITY

From what you continually read in the papers about the atrocities in Uganda, the rioting in South Africa and the civil wars in Angola and Sudan, you are probably prepared to hear that security is a problem in West Africa as well, and that roasted tourist in peanut sauce is considered a delicacy. The good news is that if you feared this, you're wrong. West Africa stands out as being one of the safest places in the Third World, and certainly safer than most large cities in the USA if not Europe as well. Which is not to say there aren't problems, only that they're less than in most other areas.

The Sahel is much safer than the coast. It may even be the safest major area in the world; that is no exaggeration. All the capital cities there are certainly among the lowest five percent in the world in terms of theft and muggings. A drunk can still go wandering around the streets of Bamako (Mali) with nothing to fear except maybe the police. Even in major cities along the coast, such as Abidjan and Dakar where safety precautions are a must, it has only been recently that some petty thieves have taken to carrying knives. The worst that usually happens is a loss of money and papers. It's still fairly rare to hear of thieves carrying guns, but when they do, the news spreads like wildfire. Expatriates, it seems, frequently distort the picture.

On a scale of one to 10, many South American cities would rate about an eight in terms of danger versus three or four for Abidjan, Dakar, Kano and Monrovia, two for the remaining coastal cities, and one for all the Sahelian cities.

Lagos (Nigeria) is a special case. On the same scale it might rate a 10, Ibadan (Nigeria) an eight. If you're the least bit worried about safety, avoid both cities. This includes changing airlines in Lagos because even taking a cab downtown at night is risky. Most visitors experience no problems, but even so, security can be a worry. Most business people simply do not go out at night. Travellers on the cheap are just as vulnerable.

Theft

Petty theft is the main concern. Women are more vulnerable and they have been robbed while jogging alone on seemingly safe beaches, and had their purses and jewellery snatched while leaving the grounds of hotels and restaurants.

Most thefts are due to the traveller's lack of foresight. The most common error is forgetting what you've got on. Avoid the temptation of wearing that new gold necklace or watch. Even seasoned veterans in Africa slip up, going to risky areas with jewellery and watches, even passports bulging out of their shirt pockets. Frequently, it's because at the beginning of the evening they didn't expect to end up in the hot district of town. Purse snatching in the market and near the entrance to restaurants and nightclubs is fairly common in the coastal cities. At nightclubs, you can't dance with your purse and leaving it at the table only invites theft.

My advice is to leave your purse or wallet behind. Either hide your money, take a small pouch bag which can be worn at all times, or wear clothing with lots of pockets – and leave most of your money, passports, IDs, credit cards, even watches at the hotel. It's surprising how few travellers use hotel safety boxes!

If the police hassle you for not carrying a passport, the worst that usually happens is you have to fetch it or pay a bribe. Better that than to risk having your passport stolen. It's a rare expatriate, for example, who carries around a passport except when going upcountry.

A final suggestion is to hire a guy to accompany you when walking around a risky area. It's usually not too difficult to find a kid hanging around who wouldn't mind picking up a few shillings warding off potential molesters.

Sexual Harassment

A frequent complaint of western women living in Africa, particularly single women, is sexual harassment. You may have an 'admirer' who won't go away, or a border official may abuse you verbally. Rape, on the other hand, is statistically insignificant, perhaps in part because Black African societies are not repressive sexually.

One reason for such harassment is that western women are frequently viewed as being 'loose'. Dress is sometimes a factor. Although you'll see African women in western clothes in the larger, more modern cities of West Africa, most still dress conservatively, typically with skirts to the ground. When a visitor wears something significantly different from the norm, she will draw attention. In the mind of the potential sexual assailant, she is dressing peculiarly. He may think she's asking for 'peculiar' and aggressive treatment.

In general, the problem of dress is easy to resolve; look at what other women are wearing and follow suit. Long pants are usually not a problem but long dresses are much better. If you want to wear shorts, bring along a wrap-around skirt to cover them when you're in public. Going braless is ill-advised; it's also more uncomfortable when you're in bouncing vehicles on bad roads.

If you're in an uneasy situation, my advice is to act prudish – stick your nose in a book. Or invent an imaginary husband who will be arriving shortly either in the country or at that particular spot. Or, if you are travelling with a male companion, introduce him as your husband.

PHOTOGRAPHY
Permits & Limitations

There are a few peculiarities about photography in Africa. The main one is that a photo permit is required in Burkina Faso, Guinea-Bissau, Liberia, Mali and Niger. In no place does this take more than 24 hours. If you take a photo in downtown Monrovia (Liberia) without a permit, the cops will pounce on you almost instantly.

As for video cameras, most countries

Niafounké, between Mopti and Timbuktu, Mali (JJ)

treat them like regular cameras. However, in a few countries you may run into problems. The governments' concern is that you may be a commercial film maker, in which case special permission is required virtually everywhere. If you wear a Hawaiian shirt and look like a tourist, you may be more convincing. Alternatively, contact the country's embassy and ask them to cable for clearance but don't expect the embassies to know the precise rules.

A second peculiarity is that in almost no country in this book may one photograph militarily sensitive installations. This includes most or all government buildings (even post offices!), airports, harbours, the presidential palace, the ministry of defence buildings, dams, radio and TV stations, bridges, railroad stations and factories. In short, any photos that might aid a potential coup d'etat – and more. Photographing policemen or military personnel is a major blunder. The problem for tourists is that prohibited areas are rarely put in writing or stated in specific terms. When in doubt, ask first.

In Liberia, even if you have a permit, what you can photograph will be greatly restricted – no dilapidated houses, for instance. Other countries prohibit photographing native religious services. The rules change from country to country. In Dakar, you can even take pictures of the Presidential Palace. In Togo, if you did the same, your camera would probably be confiscated and you would be put under intense interrogation for a day for two.

Photographing People

Every respect must be shown for others' customs and beliefs. In some places the camera's lens may be seen as taking away something personal. As for objects, some are sacred and should be treated as such. The golden rule is to ask permission – and take 'no' for an answer. In some instances, dress may be important. Wearing long pants and removing your shoes in mosques, for instance, may make it more likely that your guests won't object.

Usually Africans enjoy being the subject of photos, especially if you are friendly. There are very few things more valuable to Africans than photographs of the family, relatives and friends. Your promise to send them one will be taken seriously; moreover, it is one of the most appreciated, and yet inexpensive, ways to express your friendship. The great pity is that maybe only one in 10 travellers actually send that promised photo.

If you really want to make a hit in Africa, buy an inexpensive Polaroid camera and bring it along as a second camera. Despite the poverty everywhere, a nice photo is worth much more than money. In some instances, it may be the only photo that they have. More than once in the Sahel I have received a special request to take a private picture of the family patriarch. Imagine a household of 10 or 15 people without even a photo of the head of the household. Just be sure you let them know that there's only one shot remaining or everyone in the village will want their picture taken too.

Regarding paying for pictures, there's no simple answer. Some people recommend having some candy ready to give children who have been the camera's subject, while others believe is only encourages begging. If you're taking a series of shots of a craftsman, the answer is clearer – it's only fair that he should expect you to make a small purchase afterwards. Fortunately, it's pretty rare in West Africa for people to demand money for photos; the exceptions are the few touristy places, such as the 'Roots' village in The Gambia.

Special Concerns

Film in Africa is expensive – US$5 to US$20 a roll – and only the most widely used film is sold. Also, light conditions vary widely, so bring all the film you'll need and a variety of ASAs (100, 200, 400). In Africa, you'll find lots of 100 ASA film and some 200 ASA, but rarely 400 ASA. That's because the sunlight in Africa is frequently very intense. In the rainy season, you'll want more 200 ASA, even 400 ASA in the wetter coastal areas.

As for equipment, bring everything with you, especially extra batteries and cleaning equipment. Dust and dirt can get into your equipment, making it filthy in no time. A filter is also a good idea.

For two or three months starting in December, the Harmattan winds cover the sky with fine dust particles from the desert. Visibility even along the coast can be reduced on some days to a km or two; in the Sahel it's even worse. If photography is a primary reason for your visit, pick a time other than between December and mid-February.

All too often, pictures of Africans come out with the faces too dark, with little or no detail. You've got to compensate for black faces. If you use a light metre, the general rule is to open up one or 1½ stops from what the metre reads.

Finally, older model x-ray machines for checking baggage at airports can damage undeveloped film. With the newer models, this is not a problem. Since you can never be certain that a particular machine is safe, bring some protective lead bags – they're fairly inexpensive. While customs officials will usually let you carry film separately and avoid the x-ray, this isn't the case in all countries.

FOOD

African food is written off by many tourists as being too risky and seemingly unappetising. For people who cannot tolerate hot pepper, it's probably wise to avoid it. The rest will be missing an interesting experience.

Don't think that what you may sample in a restaurant or on the street is the best available. It often takes a few years in Africa to learn that good African food has many more ingredients than what you normally get in a local chop house. In cities, Africans are accustomed to eating street food, but they rarely eat at restaurants. When they do, they tend to prefer simple things such as braised chicken or fish. For this reason, there are few restaurants serving really good African food.

The best place to find good African food is at somebody's home. Africans eat very well if they have enough money to buy a lot of interesting ingredients. If you want to sample the best there is, make friends with an African woman and then give her some money (what you would have used for a restaurant) to make a meal. You won't be imposing because she can make a terrific meal and at the same time feed not only you but whomever else she normally feeds. If you're curious about African ingredients and spices, accompany her to the market. Most African food is quite hot, but as you get closer to the desert, you'll find fewer hot dishes.

If someone tells you they don't like African food, it's more likely due to the texture or excessive pepper than to the taste. The pepper is sometimes controllable; the hot sauce is frequently offered as a side dish. As for the texture, a number of African dishes are made with okra – the result is a slimy concoction. In the rural environment you may be eating native style (with your hands) in which case it's like dipping your hand into a bowl of raw eggs. There are any number of staples with which this can be eaten. One is banana *foutou*; another is *fufu*. The former is basically a glob of mashed plantains and cassava, the latter a glob of fermented cassava. Picture mashed potatoes mixed with gelatin and very sticky. You grab a portion (with your right hand, please!) and dip it in the sauce while forming a ball.

If you're turned off by slimy okra, you won't be the only one. Lots of people who love African food aren't particularly fond of it either. There is a much greater variety of African dishes than most

foreigners come across. Because okra dishes are plentiful on the streets, it's easy to get the false impression that there's not much else.

African food typically consists of a staple plus some kind of sauce. The preferred staple everywhere is rice; it is also more expensive because much of it has to be imported. In the Sahel, millet is the most common staple. It's a cousin of sorghum but produces a smaller grain, and has foliage resembling a corn plant. The grain is placed in a wooden receptacle and pounded, sometimes for several hours – not exactly one's idea of a fun way to spend the afternoon. African villages are too small to support the mills seen in most towns and cities, and even in the cities many people cannot afford the extra cost of the service. (It's close to slavery. Ask a group of women in a small village to make a wish list, and a mill will be at the top.) The resulting white mound is hardly what makes the juices run – but neither is plain white rice. Eaten with a tasty sauce, it can be surprisingly good.

Sauces-Recipes

Sauces are the heart of African cuisine and each country has its own specialities. The spices commonly found in Mali, for example, can differ widely from those in Nigeria. Because groundnuts (peanuts) are grown almost everywhere in West Africa, groundnut sauce is one of the most common. Peanut butter can be used as the main ingredient.

Senegalese *jollof rice* is a close cousin of Spanish paella and is one of the few African dishes that is well known throughout West Africa. Senegalese *poulet yassa* is a chicken dish which makes liberal use of onions and lemons. As for deserts, they are not a part of traditional African cuisine, however, fresh fruits are sometimes eaten afterwards.

Many of the African sauces are difficult to duplicate outside Africa for lack of the proper spices. The following three recipes require no special ingredients.

Groundnut Stew (Ghana)

l lb (450 grams) beef, cubed
½ lb (225 grams) peanut butter
3 dessertspoons tomato paste
1 large onion chopped
1 quart (litre) water
2 whole lemons squeezed
4 medium-size tart tomatoes
8 medium-size okra
½ lb (225 grams) pumpkin
1 teaspoon salt
2 hot chillies, crushed, or 1 teaspoon cayenne
   pepper
1-inch piece ginger, crushed

Cut the meat into cubes. In a heavy pan, cover the meat in hot fat, add water and seasonings, cover and boil for 20 minutes then reduce the heat. In another pan boil the tomatoes, okra and pumpkin. Then add this and the remaining ingredients to the stew and bring to a boil, stirring vigorously to avoid sticking. Reduce the heat and simmer for 45 minutes. Serve with rice. Serves four.

Poulet Yassa (Senegal)

1 large chicken
1 lb (450 grams) shredded onions
⅓ lb (180 grams) butter
4 big peppers (mildly hot)
1 lemon
2 heads garlic, crushed
2 bay leaves
1 dessertspoon black pepper
salt to taste
Chicken stock/water

Cut the chicken into four pieces, sprinkle with lemon juice and salt, and grill until brown. Melt the butter in a saucepan and sauté the chicken. Add the other ingredients and chicken stock/water (not too soupy), cover, and cook until tender. Garnish with tomato and lemon slices. Serve with rice. Serves four.

Jollof Rice (Nigerian style)

1 lb (450 grams) meat (chicken, ham, beef,
   lamb)
½ lb (225 grams) rice
1 lb (450 grams) tomatoes
1 5-oz (140 grams) tin tomato puree
2 onions, sliced
1 large green pepper, sliced
1 teaspoon cayenne pepper or paprika
½ teaspoon thyme
3 dessertspoons butter
½ teaspoon allspice
1 teaspoon black pepper
½ cup (1/8 litre) oil
salt to taste

Cut the meat into small pieces and brown in a large saucepan with heated oil. Then put to one side. Fry the tomatoes, green pepper and onions in the same oil until soft, and then add the meat with the tomato puree and spices. Add the water and bring to a boil. Then reduce the heat and simmer until tender. Add the rice to the pan and cook until all the water is absorbed and the grains are soft. Serves four.

DRINKS

While African cuisine is not everybody's cup of tea, everybody agrees that African beer is good by any standard. It is certainly better than the watery stuff in the USA and cheaper than that in Europe.

In all, there are about 45 beers

(including about 10 European beers) brewed in West Africa, with Nigeria alone producing about 30. In Togo, German tourists say that Beer Benin is as good or better than what they're accustomed to drinking at home. Part of the reason may be that the brewery in Togo was started by the Germans around the turn of the century and they still own an interest. While everyone has their own favourite beer, the following are some to be on the lookout for:

Best: Beer Benin (Togo)
Runners-up: Club (Liberia, Ghana, Nigeria), Flag (Ivory Coast, Senegal), Star, Harp and Gulder (Nigeria, Ghana).

Then there's the beer from Guinea-Bissau. Some say it's a little yeasty but if the brewery closes down for lack of bottles or caps, then these same people act like it was water from the fountain of youth.

Except for the coastal area between Sierra Leone and Nigeria, the great majority of Africans don't drink beer. (Probably fewer than one percent of the women drink alcohol.) That's because so many are Muslims.

Homemade brew, on the other hand, is popular everywhere, even in Muslim areas. In West Africa palm wine is a staple in villages along the coast. Yeast is added to the juice tapped from the palm oil tree, and this brew is allowed to ferment overnight. In Nigeria it's even bottled in factories. In the Sahel where it's too dry for palm oil trees, it's the cheap 'millet beer' that gets the men and Peace Corps volunteers wasted in the villages.

That's enough said about alcohol, because the great majority of Africans prefer soft drinks to beer. There's one non-alcoholic drink that is consumed so much throughout all of Africa that it could be entitled the continental drink of Africa – a drink made with so much ginger that it burns the throat. In remote villages, they may have nothing else to offer you. Most foreigners find the burning sensation too

strong. If you drink the local water (most travellers should definitely not), look for it on the streets; it is frequently sold in old soft drink bottles. The name changes from place to place.

artist, NIGER.

BOOKS & BOOKSTORES

The following books are all available in paperback and can be obtained through the mail. Only two are out of print. If you only have time to read one book and are looking for something informative and entertaining, it's hard to beat David Lamb's *The Africans*.

History - Africa in General

The Story of Africa by Basil Davidson (Mitchell Beazley London, 1984). This is a superbly illustrated and engaging book which was published to accompany Davidson's eight-part documentary series on the history of Africa for British TV.

A Short History of Africa by J D Fage & Roland Oliver (Cambridge University Press, Cambridge). This is also a very good, less expensive book.

Africa Since 1800 by Roland Oliver & Anthony Atmore (Cambridge University

Press, Cambridge, 1981). This is the last of a trilogy, the others being *Africa in the Iron Age* and *The African Middle Ages 1400-1800*. The book has three parts: the precolonial period up to 1875, followed by the partition and colonial rule, thematically rather than by region, and finally the roads to independence taken by different African territories, plus the post independence decades.

Modern Africa by Basil Davidson (Longman Ltd, Harlow Essex, England, or Longman Inc, White Plains, NY, 1983). This book focuses on African history since 1900.

History – West Africa

History of West Africa edited by J F Ade Ajayi and Michael Crowder (Cambridge University Press)

West Africa: An Introduction to Its History by Michael Crowder (Longman, 1977).

The Revolutionary Years: West Africa Since 1800 by J B Webster and A A Boahen (Longman, 1981). This book gives more of an in-depth treatment of later African history.

Social History

The African Genius: An Introduction to African Social & Cultural History by Basil Davidson (The Atlantic Monthly Press, Waltham, Maine, 1969).

Art

African Art in Cultural Perspective by William Bascom (W W Norton & Co, London or New York, 1985). This is an excellent paperback, but out of print, focusing solely on sculpture and covering West and Central Africa region by region.

African Art by Frank Willett (Oxford University Press New Jersey, 1971). Out of print. Almost 400 pages long, the book offers an in-depth discussion for those with a keen interest in the subject. Several other good paperbacks, such as *African Sculpture* by Fagg and Plass, are also out of print.

African Arts is a quarterly published by the African Studies Centre, UCLA. This is an excellent magazine with good photography and articles.

Novels

In 1986, Wole Soyinka of Nigeria won the Nobel Prize for Literature, only the fifth person from a Third World country to win the prize. He has written two books, including *The Interpreter*, but he is primarily a playwright. *A Dance of the Forests*, *The Man Died*, *Opera Wonyosi* and *A Play of Giants* are some of his more well-known plays. A man with a social vision who doesn't mind lambasting those in power, he uses a language which is far from simple, which is why relatively few Nigerians have read his works.

For an African novel, try one of the following classics:

The African Child by Camara Laye of Guinea (Fontana Books Douglas, Isle of Man, UK, 1954). Camara Laye was born in Guinea in 1924, studied in France, and returned to write this largely auto-biographical work of his childhood among the Malinké tribe, surrounded by ritual magic and superstition, and his emergence into manhood and independence. All the patience, curiosity, resolution and ferretings of the most accomplished anthropologist could not have elicited these facts. For additional books, ask Fontana Books for a list of their other 23 fiction books by African authors, including Wole Soyinka.

The Palm-Wine Drinkard by Amos Tutuola of Nigeria (Grove Press, New York, 1954). For those seeking humour, there is no book more amusing than this 1952 Nigerian classic about an insatiable drunkard who seeks his palm-wine tapster in the world of the dead.

Things Fall Apart by Chinua Achebe of Nigeria (Heinemann Educational Books, London, 1958). This is the most well-known African novel and has sold over a million copies. It is a classic that is still worth reading even though the theme is slightly dated. The tragic story takes place in the mid-1890s at the time of the colonial take-over. The main character, a powerful tribal figure, is divided between the past and the present during rapidly changing times. Achebe's historical imagination coupled with a mastery of the English language have led critics to compare him with Conrad and the like. Ask Heinemann for their free African Writers Series catalogue.

The Beautyful Ones Are Not Yet Born by Ayi Kwei Armah of Ghana (1969), and *God's Bits of Wood* by Sembene Ousmane of Senegal (1970) are also published by Heinemann and are especially recommended. The former got rave reviews from *The New York Times*. Sembene's novel tells of the struggles of strikers on the Dakar-Niger railway line in 1948. Heinemann has about 270 other titles in their African Writers Series.

A Bend in the River by V S Naipaul (Random House Inc, 1979). The story takes place in Zaire. It's a good selection for those wanting a novel on rural African life by a Pulitzer Prize winner.

Political & Economics

The Africans, by David Lamb, (Nomadic Books, Seattle, 1984). A portrait of modern-day Africa which is rich in political and social detail, this books gets rave reviews from travellers. Lamb, who has been twice nominated for the Pulitzer Prize, spent four years travelling to 46 countries, talking to both guerrilla leaders and presidents, and catching midnight flights to coups in little-known countries where desert people were supposedly doing unspeakable things to each other.

Africa: The People and Politics of an Emerging Continent by Sanford Ungar (Simon & Schuster, New York, 1986). This guide to the present-day political, economic and social realities of Africa, makes sense out of a complex continent, and is highly readable and entertaining. It pays particular attention to Liberia, Nigeria, Kenya and South Africa.

The Political Economy of Africa edited by D Cohen & J Daniel (Longman Ltd/Inc, 1981). This gives a leftist viewpoint.

West African States edited by John Dunn (Cambridge University Press, 1978). For a book focusing solely on West Africa, this is probably the best you'll find.

The best book for economic analyses is *The Economies of West Africa* by Douglas Rimmer (Hatchards, London, 1984). It's a new book with an analytical and systematic economic survey of West Africa by a senior academic at the University of Birmingham.

Ecology

Africa in Crisis by Lloyd Timberlake (Earthscan, Washington DC). This book focuses on the political and environmental factors contributing to drought and famine in Africa, particularly the roles international aid organisations and African leaders have played in recent environmental disasters.

Cookbook

The Africa News Cookbook by Africa News Service Inc (Viking Penguin Inc, New York, or Middlesex, UK, 1985). This appears to be the only African cookbook in print. It's quite good and covers the entire continent. Each recipe has been carefully chosen to ensure that all ingredients are obtainable in the west.

Magazines

West Africa by (West Africa Publishing Co, London). This weekly magazine has a high reputation for the accuracy of its news coverage.

Jeune Afrique (in French), (Le Groupe Jeune Afrique, Paris). This popular weekly magazine covers both Central and West African and world events, always with an African perspective.

New African, (IC Publications, London). This monthly has a reputation for accurate and balanced reporting, with a mix of political reporting, financial and economic analysis, features on social and cultural affairs, plus regular country and topic surveys.

Political Publications

The best in terms of giving the inside scoop is, unquestionably, the twice-monthly *Africa Confidential* (Miramoor Publications, London).

Commercial Publications

There are several annual publications. *Africa Review* (World of Information, Essex, UK) is an annual publication providing a concise and up-to-date digest of economic and commercial data on African countries, along with general information on the African business environment.

Africa South of the Sahara (Europa Publications, London) is a well-known annual publication containing similar but more detailed information.

Africa Contemporary Record (Holmes & Meier, London), published annually, is even more detailed.

You'll also find a number of monthly publications. *Africa Business* (IC Publications Ltd, London), is a monthly magazine providing a wide variety of news items, commentaries and feature articles.

Africa (Africa Journal Ltd, London), is a monthly magazine covering business, economics and politics.

The best weekly is *Economic Digest* (Middle East Economic Digest, London), a report providing business news, economic analyses and forecasts.

Bookstores

Bookstores in West Africa are listed under each country. Don't expect to be able to pick up any interesting reading in English outside Lagos, except with great difficulty. Books in French, however, are abundant. For specialist books on Africa, it is better to buy them at home.

London *Foyle's* (113 Charing Cross Rd, London WC2H OEB) is one block from Cambridge Circus and may be the world's largest bookshop. Ask for their Africana section. Their travel section is not good. *Waterstone's*, next door to Foyle's, is much better for maps and travel guides.

Even better for maps, with a fairly good selection of travel guides as well, is *Stanfords* (12 Long Acre St, Covent Garden, London WC2P, tel 01-8361321). They even have maps of individual countries in Africa. Several blocks away, the *Africa Book Centre* at the Africa Centre (38 King St, Covent Garden, London WC2 8JT, tel 01-8361973) has a small bookshop, and is a good place to get practical first-hand information on Africa. *Operation Headstart* (West Green Rd, London N15 5BX) has books exclusively on Africa, including a section on African cookery. *Knightsbridge Books* (32 Store St, London WC1E 7BS) specialises in African and Asian studies.

USA In New York City, the two stores with the best Africana sections appear to be *Liberation Book Store* (421 Lenox Avenue, corner of 131st St, Harlem, tel 212-2814615) and *Barnes & Noble* (5th Avenue at 17th St, tel 212-8070099). For maps and travel guides, your best bets are *Travellers Bookstore* (22 West 52nd Avenue, tel 212-6640995), *Complete Traveller Bookstore* (199 Madison Avenue at 35th St, tel 212-6859007), and *Scribner Book Store* (597 Fifth Avenue, between near 49th St, tel 212-7589797).

In Washington, DC, the best store for travel books and maps is *Travel Books Unlimited* (4931 Cordell Avenue, Bethesda, MD, tel 301-9518533). Downtown, *The Map Store* (1636 Eye St, NW, tel 202-6282608) carries Michelin maps of Africa.

Travel Centres of the World (Box 1788, Hollywood, CA 90078) specialises in very detailed maps and travel guides. Write for their catalogue.

Europe In France, try *L'Astrolabe* (46, Rue de Provence, 75009 Paris, tel 1-42854295, Metro stop Chaussee d'Antin). They specialise in books and maps for travellers and may be the best of that type. *Gilbert Joseph* (26, Boulevard St Michel, 75006 Paris, tel 01-43255716, Metro stop St Michel) has an excellent selection of maps and travel guides. *Hachette*, one block away, has some books not found at Gilbert Joseph. Several blocks from Gilbert Joseph is *Presence Africaine* (25 bis, Rue des Écoles, 75005 Paris, tel 01-4326588), which specialises in serious books on Africa, many by African authors, but has no travel guides.

In Holland, your best bet may be *Geografische Boekhandel* (Overtoom 136, 1054 HN Amsterdam, tel 020-121901). In West Germany, try *Daerr Expedition-service GmbH* (Hauptstrausse 26, D-8011 Kirchheim/Munich, Ortsteil Heimstetten, tel 089-9031519).

SPORTS

One of the secrets of meeting people in Africa is to look for activities in which they're involved. Sport is one way to meet Africans but you've got to be a little selective. You're not going to find many Africans sailing and deep sea fishing or on sail boards or on the golf links. Tennis, squash, football (soccer) and basketball, on the other hand, are favourite African sports. If you want to meet the entire spectrum of expatriates, run with the Hash House Harriers or head towards the nearest tennis club.

If you're a fairly good tennis player, there's hardly a private club in West Africa that will not invite you to play at least a game or two. If you can give one of the club's top players a battle for his life, you're in, win or lose. If you're not quite that good, you can still probably finagle a temporary membership if you're friendly and buy lots of drinks. One way to enter is to arrange a game when the courts are empty – the local African pro is the guy to approach because he wants your business hitting the ball even if non-members are not technically allowed. Become friendly with him, and he may come to be your 'in', in addition to becoming a friend.

So don't leave your sports equipment behind as it may prove to be your best 'in' to Africa. And don't leave behind balls, etc, because they're sometimes hard to find and invariably expensive. What follows is an overview of sporting opportunities in West Africa. The country chapters give the specifics.

Basketball & Soccer

These two win the sports popularity contest hands down. Bring along a deflated football (soccer) for a village family, a boy or group, and you'll be the hit of the day. Seeing a game of football is easy as there are games almost every Sunday in the major cities.

The biggest sports event in Africa is probably the Africa Cup football matches held every even year in the spring. People are glued to their radios and tubes. If you want to play, the universities and municipal stadiums are by far the best places to find a game.

Tennis & Swimming

You'll find tennis courts and swimming pools in almost every city over 100,000 and in many smaller cities as well. Many major hotels have these facilities and even if you're not a guest, you can usually use them – for a small price, of course.

Squash

There are more courts than one might expect – in Dakar, Banjul, Conakry, Freetown, Monrovia, Abidjan, Yamoussoukro (Ivory Coast), Grand Bassam (Ivory Coast), Ouagadougou, Accra, Lagos, Kaduna and Kano (Nigeria).

Hash House Harriers

In case you think this has something to do with hashish, you're a little off target. Picture a group of 25 to 60 young to middle-aged expatriates running once a week along a marked course through African villages, downtown boulevards, along the beach, through cassava patches and university grounds, and stopping perhaps for a beer along the way, shouting 'on on', and downing cases of beer afterwards while singing an occasional bawdy song – you'll be much closer to the mark. You won't find a better way to meet the expatriate community.

It all started in 1939 when a bunch of Aussies in Malaysia with nothing better to do than drink beer began meeting to run through rice paddies and anywhere else so as to build up a thirst for drinking still more. It's now an international organisation. In West Africa there are all-male groups in Nouakchott, Dakar, Banjul, Monrovia, Abidjan, Accra and Lagos.

The runs are weekly (usually Saturday or Monday) and generally not so tough as to prohibit non-joggers from participating. Since the starting point changes weekly, the only way to find the Hash is to call the British Embassy or, if there isn't one, the American Embassy Marine guards.

Foot Races
The West African International Marathon and 10 km race is held on 4 April in Dakar (Senegal) and attracts a few name runners. Other than this, there are a few short distance races in Abidjan, Monrovia, and possibly elsewhere.

Ife bronze, 1200 AD

Mountaineering-Hiking
West Africa is not exactly a climber's paradise. The weather is hot and the mountains are not particularly high. The possibilities for mountain climbing are better in Central Africa, though in Cape Verde there is the 2839-metre-high volcano, Mt Fogo.

The main attraction is the hilly areas where people sometimes go hiking. The most popular is the western area of the Ivory Coast around Man, the nearby Yekepa area of Liberia, the Kpalimé area of south-western Togo, the Fouta Djalon/Dalaba area of Guinea, and central Nigeria around Jos. Guinea, in particular, offers superb hiking possibilities in the hilly Fouta Djalon, a savannah area with magnificent views. Few people seem to know that the Fouta Djalon is also one of the best two or three places in West Africa for serious rock climbing – it's all limestone with a minimum of cracks, making it relatively safe.

The best places for technical rock climbing besides the Fouta Djalon is Hombori (Mali). Hombori is a village on the Mopti-Gao highway. There are some spectacular rock formations jutting out of the desert, reaching over 1000 metres in parts. A spectacular rock formation called Le Main de Fatma (or Aiguilles de Garmi), 12 km from Hombori, attracts experienced European rock climbers and some peaks or routes have apparently not yet been conquered. Africans in nearby villages will act as guides.

Golf
Abidjan and Yamoussoukro (both in the Ivory Coast) have the only two courses with grass greens and both are in very decent shape. The club house in Abidjan is so futuristic in design as to be suitable for a James Bond movie. The next best courses are in Monrovia (Liberia) and various cities in Nigeria.

The remaining cities, all with sand greens, are recommended only for addicts, or those wanting a good laugh and a few good photos showing golfing conditions those back home won't believe. From west to east, the courses are in Dakar, Banjul, Freetown, Monrovia, Ouagadougou (semi-desert conditions), Abidjan, Yamoussoukro, Accra, Lomé (bad), Lagos, Kano, Kaduna and Oguta (Imo State, Nigeria).

Sailboards

Sailboards are available for rent in (from west to east) Dakar, the Casamance beach area in Senegal, Banjul, Freetown, Monrovia, Abidjan, Sassandra (Ivory Coast), Lomé and Lake Togo. The sport is practised everywhere, even on rivers in the Sahel. On the river, however, you risk taking home one of those weird African diseases – bilharzia.

Sailing

There are sailing clubs in most major cities along the coast, but renting one is virtually impossible except for hobbycats in Dakar, Banjul and Monrovia. Day sails on 10- to 18-metre crewed yachts are available in Dakar, Banjul, Freetown and occasionally Abidjan.

Fishing

The countries where most deep sea sports fishermen head for are Senegal, Mauritania, Ivory Coast and The Gambia, but there's fishing everywhere along the coast. From The Gambia to Liberia, fishing for barracuda is very popular, while in Cape Verde tuna is the main catch. Only the deep sea fishing world is on to the fact that Dakar is one of the three or four best places in the world for sailfish; it's also excellent for blue marlin. Less well known is that other places along the coast, especially Abidjan, are right up there when it comes to blue marlin (also good for wahoo, barracuda and tuna). Mauritania is noted for surf casting and courbine is one of the main catches around Nouâdhibou. Air Afrique has a fishing centre there.

Charter boats are available only in (west to east) Dakar, Banjul, Conakry, Freetown and Abidjan. The season for

blue marlin and sailfish is generally from June to September. In Abidjan, there's a second season from November to mid-January.

The major agencies offering special fishing trips are located in Paris:

Jet Tours (Departement Chasse et Pêche, 19, Avenue de Tourville, 75007 Paris, tel 01-4602-7022 and 4705-0195). They offer one-week fishing trips to the Ivory Coast, Senegal and Mauritania. Prices range from about 10,000 to 20,000 FF depending on the numbers (one to four).
Au Coin de Pêche (50, Avenue de Wagram, 75017 Paris, tel 01-4227-2861/4168). Their prices are lower. *Orchape* (6, Rue d'Armaille, 75007 Paris, tel 01-4380-3067 and 4754-7857, telex 640771).
Dominique H Dhouailly (37, Rue la Fayette, 75009 Paris, tel 01-4874-3133). He concentrates on the Ivory Coast and Senegal.

Diving

The diving off N'Gor Island just outside Dakar is excellent for marine life, less so in terms of coral. The diving is good down to about 30 metres. There is also a diving club in Abidjan though conditions are pretty murky and there's not a whole lot to see. There are diving clubs/shops in both cities. Sierra Leone also offers fairly interesting diving south of Freetown.

Surfing

Surfing is rare in West Africa. However, there are excellent reefs just outside Dakar near the airport, discovered by the *Endless Summer* surfers. Reefs along the coast of Mauritania would undoubtedly make this one of the best places. Generally speaking, from Guinea eastward the waves are the one-big-crash type. Still, the *Endless Summer* surfers found some acceptable spots east of Accra and near Lagos.

Softball

There are laid-back games on weekends throughout West Africa. Americans are naturally the main participants but outsiders are always welcomed. The Marine guards at the US embassies invariably know the details. You'll find teams in Nouakchott, Praia, Dakar, Monrovia, Abidjan, Accra, Bamako, Ouagadougou, Niamey and Lagos.

Rugby

There are clubs in almost all the ex-British colonies. Visiting players are usually welcomed.

Cycling

Cycling expeditions are a very rare occurrence in West Africa. Most countries in West Africa are connected by paved roads, but certainly the only sane time to attempt such an expedition would be the 'winter' period from December to February. Be prepared for some long distances between major stops. As a competitive sport, cycling is popular in a lot of major cities, especially Abidjan and Dakar.

THINGS TO BUY

If you like art or textiles, there is a much greater selection of good art work in West Africa there than in the rest of Africa.

Masks are as imaginative, and frequently amusing or terrifying, as anything you've dreamed. There are textiles rarely seen in Europe or the USA with a variety of pleasing colours and patterns. You can buy silver and gold jewellery as well as beads at prices far below what you'd pay elsewhere, and there is a fascinating assortment of spears, musical instruments, agricultural tools, etc. These are just some of the reasons you might get hooked on African art. Yet African art is an acquired taste.

Two suggestions: before arriving, buy a book on African art (see Books & Bookstores herein) and, after arriving, go to a museum or good art shop. In Dakar, pass by the Museum of Dakar and *Bruno's* artshop at 2 Place de l'Indépendance in the dead centre of town. In Abidjan, try the *Rose d'Ivoire* in the basement of the Hôtel Ivoire. Then you'll have some standard of comparison. There's also a maturing process regarding taste – what you may find interesting at first may not

appeal to you later. You're likely to get tired of the cheaper, mass-produced items very quickly. So when travelling, it's almost always better to purchase things during the latter half of the trip.

Knowing the context in which an object is used is important in terms of both appreciation and in detecting artificially used or aged pieces. Unlike western art, almost all African art has a use. Masks, for instance, are for dances. Half the interest in a piece is sometimes knowing just how it is used. A knife may seem like any other knife until you learn, for example, that it's used only for circumcision. I know one couple who collects those small pieces of clothing which covers one's private parts – the use is at least half the interest!

No one likes to lug around souvenirs, so mail them back. Shipping is actually fairly reliable. Purchases not exceeding US$25 in value that are mailed to the States enter duty-free, and you may bring with you goods worth up to US$400 in value without paying duty; the US$400 includes all purchases mailed as well. The customs regulations in Europe and Canada are similar.

Keep in mind that many developed countries do not charge duty on goods from underdeveloped countries to help them improve their export trade. In the US, under the Generalized System of Preferences (GSP), goods from all countries of West Africa (except Nigeria) are exempt from duty. The major exceptions to this are textiles and shoes; and gold, silver and jade have certain restrictions in terms of duty-free treatment.

Textiles

If you like textiles, West Africa is the place to go. An obvious advantage of collecting textiles is that they're easy to carry. Some of the most expensive, well-known textiles include the bright *kente* cloth from Ghana, the elaborate Yoruba textiles from Nigeria, Tuareg wedding blankets found in Mali, and various textiles from the Sahel region (especially Mali, Burkina

Faso and Niger). But almost every country has interesting textiles. The blue indigo cloth of the Tuareg is popular all over West Africa, though some is not real indigo. The real stuff will rub off all over you. (Soaking in vinegar or very salty water will stop the running.) Some 'African' materials are actually made elsewhere, eg much of the colourful wax cloth comes from Holland.

You don't always have to go to the country where the textiles are made. The markets in Lomé and Abidjan, for example, probably have the widest selection of Ghanaian materials, as well as lots of textiles from Nigeria and the Sahel.

Wooden Carvings

Masks are sold all over West Africa and are not cheap unless mass produced. Other objects in wood include colourful puppets, African game boards, carved doors, latches, figurines and boxes. Each area has its own specialities.

Art which is authentic and valuable cannot be exported under the laws of most African countries. However, since very little art purchased by non-experts fits this description, it's more a matter of being hassled by the police than doing something illegal. In Nigeria, however, you won't be allowed to export even mediocre art work if it looks at all old.

Don't expect to travel upcountry and find something really valuable. Most of the museum quality stuff has already been purchased. Also, knowing the difference between the real thing (ie old and used) and a forgery requires seeing and handling thousands of pieces; no book or sixth sense will enable you to by-pass this process. Africans are extremely clever when it comes to artificially aging wooden objects and making them appear used. Even museum curators can be fooled by a mark made by sandpaper rather than normal wear.

What's old and used will invariably bring a much higher price than what's new. But that doesn't mean all pieces made today are aesthetically inferior (although most are). Prices of the better pieces, like all art, can be pretty subjective. As for mass produced items, the prices are a little more uniform and you can certainly be 'taken'. The only way to learn the price range is to ask knowledgeable locals or expatriates, or visit a fancy store and then bargain for one-third to one-half less at the local market (but beware – the quality may be inferior).

Two major concerns with all wooden objects from West Africa are cracking and beetles. Buy a new wooden carving and you may find it cracked by the time you get home. New wood must be dried slowly. Wrapping in plastic bags with a small water tray enclosed is one technique. If you see tiny bore marks with white powder everywhere, it means the powder post beetle (frequently confused with termites) is having a fiesta. There are two remedies – stick the piece in the freezer or cover it with lighter fluid.

Ivory

Elephants are an endangered species and are being slaughtered by the thousands in Africa, mostly by poachers. In early 1987, for example, police investigating a traffic accident in central Tanzania discovered 476 elephant tusks hidden in a secret compartment of a single trailer! Elephants have been entirely killed off in some countries such as Sierra Leone, and are rarely seen elsewhere except in game parks.

While many say that they believe African countries don't have the resources or determination to stop the killings, more often than not they seem to be simply groping for reasons to justify their purchases. Certainly such purchases only drive the price still higher, encouraging poachers to take even greater risks. Quite simply, those with a conscience do not purchase ivory. There's nothing illegal about it, however. In the USA, you can import small amounts of ivory in the form of jewellery and the like, but not for commercial reasons.

If you are toying with the idea of purchasing ivory, why not first check out the readily available substitutes? One is bone and another is wart hog tusk; both age very nicely. Unfortunately, the bone is often from an elephant, which makes it just as bad. Another substitute is plastic which is almost indistinguishable from ivory – even to experts! The only sure way to tell the difference is to put it under a flame or, better, touch it with a lighted cigarette. Plastic will melt and bone will be scorched. Ivory, on the other hand, will not scorch but can be discolored if the flame is left too long.

If it's so hard to tell the difference, one wonders why plastic wouldn't do just as well. In addition, there is the beautiful green malachite jewellery from Zaire sold throughout Africa. With all these alternatives, it takes a heartless creature to buy ivory.

Gold & Silver

Instead of ivory, why not buy gold? Almost all gold and silver is sold by the gram, the art work being included in the price. The art work is decent but not exceptional. Most people are more than pleased with the workmanship and the prices, which in the CFA zone are approximately US$15 to US$17 (CFA 4500 to CFA 5000) a gm for gold and US$1.70 to US$5.00 (CFA 500 to CFA1500) a gram for silver, depending on the quality. Despite what you may hear to the contrary, prices vary little from country to country. Within the CFA zone, for example, prices of gold and silver are only about 10% lower in the Sahel than in places such as Abidjan.

Quality is not a serious problem with gold. Getting cheated with the carats is fairly rare. The jewellers want you to return, and just because you don't speak French doesn't mean they won't believe you're a long-term resident. If you do get cheated, many countries have laws such as in Mali and you can return it.

With silver, quality is a major problem and this is why some people prefer to stick with the more expensive gold. The problem is that silver in most of West Africa is not sterling. It tends to tarnish quickly, so that it has to be cleaned fairly regularly. In Mauritania, the quality and workmanship are better, but far from what they were 10 years ago.

Beads

You'll find beads all over West Africa. In the markets, they are sold by the string, one type of bead per string, while in the shops you can sometimes find ready-made necklaces with a variety of beads. The Treichville market in Abidjan has a particularly wide selection and, surprisingly, prices are relatively low. Several hundred major bead styles are sold in Africa, including a variety of glass beads and shells. Prices vary considerably and some beads are quite expensive. Most travellers don't realise that you can go to the market and have a necklace made to order. The vendors will usually string them for you on the spot.

Brass

It is found all over West Africa, more so perhaps in the Sahel and in Benin. Finding a piece that's not mass produced isn't easy.

Baskets

Because of their bulkiness, baskets are not a hot item with travellers. Some of the best are found in Liberia and Nigeria.

Gourds

West Africa abounds in gourds carved with interesting designs. Nigeria and Niger seem to have some of the best.

MARKETS

The markets in West Africa are the most vibrant and interesting in Black Africa. The best are those in Bamako, Lomè, Abidjan, Dakar, Kano and Niamey. But don't think you'll be wasting your time at some of the lesser markets. Those in small towns frequently offer not only a surprisingly large variety of items but also some items not found in the bigger markets.

Hassling Most travellers love the markets, but a few find them extremely intimidating or annoying experiences – people grabbing you by the arm and not-so-gently pulling you over to the stall 'pour voir seulement' (just to see). There's a huge difference between markets, however. Traders in the markets in the Sahel (Bamako, Ouagadougou, etc) are not very pushy, while those in Dakar and Abidjan definitely are. (The latter are also known to have thieves.) If you're hesitant about the markets, don't start off with those two. Also, go early when the stalls are just opening and the vendors aren't in high gear; it's cooler then as well.

As for strategies in dealing with overly persistent traders, if you are really not looking for anything in that section, say no and move on. If they keep pulling you and you find it really offensive, let them know in no uncertain terms – if your actions are clear, they'll stop most of the time. The problem is that one tends to get mad and ends up not seeing as much, which isn't why you came there. My recommendation is to go with the flow. Head towards the stall, then they no longer have any reason to pull you. Give things a good look and go from there. Above all, try to view it as a game.

Bargaining Bargaining, of course, is the name of the game. Most travellers expect the initial price to be three times the 'real' price. This is usually true, but not always. With African cloth sold by the yard, for example, you can expect little or no lowering of the price. The same is true of gold and silver. If the lady tells you the price and you come back with an offer one-third that amount, don't be surprised if she becomes extremely ticked off, folds up the material and refuses to talk further. You'll feel like a real fool. So try to get a feel for prices beforehand. Ask knowledgeable locals or check out one of the hotel shops; prices in the market are typically half those in the stores.

Thieves As for the potential thieves, the solution is rather simple. Dress as if you were going horse riding – leave your watch, jewellery, passport, most of your money, etc at the hotel, locked in your suitcase or in the hotel's safety deposit box. Then hide your money and wallet on you or hold your bag firmly. (Pants with lots of button or zipper pockets are advantageous.)

WHAT TO TAKE
Clothes

Travel light. For one thing, the airplane baggage limit is 20 kg, not two pieces of luggage as in the US. Travelling light will give you space for souvenirs, while permitting you to buy the loose-fitting African clothes. Clothes which can serve a dual purpose (eg a blouse which can be worn with both jeans and fancier outfits in the evening) will help you pack lighter. Also, bring clothes you can leave behind.

As for dress codes, in East Africa you'll see travellers in safari outfits, pith helmets and all. In West Africa, you'll get laughed at if you show up like this. Keep things simple to avoid standing out like a sore thumb – it only makes you easy prey for hustlers. Buy things as you go. Women, for instance, can leave long dresses at home and buy the long, flowing African dresses sold everywhere and popular with foreigners. Business people on the other hand should expect to dress for meetings as in the west, ie a coat and tie for men.

Shorts are useful for the beaches and travelling upcountry, but women should not expect to wear them anywhere in public, even in modern cities such as Abidjan. One suggestion is to bring several wrap around skirts to put on over your shorts as needed. Men can wear shorts anywhere, but doing so will only accentuate the differences with the locals, especially in the Muslim-dominated Sahel.

Pants are acceptable everywhere. But in the Sahel, western women usually find it easier to develop a good rapport with African women if they wear similar clothes, ie long dresses. This is particularly true in the villages. The men's used-jean market throughout West Africa, by the way, is fabulous.

A sweater is advisable all year round but especially in the December-February period, particularly for countries bordering the desert, and Cape Verde. Those crossing the desert in the winter months should bring a heavy sweater.

Essentials
Medical kit See the health section.
Tampons, pads and contraceptives They're often impossible to find outside major cities.
Suntan lotion You'll use less than you think. It is frequently available but usually not the kind you want.

US$10 bills Hide about five US$10 bills (or pounds or French francs) where no one will ever find them. If you arrive on a weekend or a holiday, you may be forced to change money illegally. Small bills are easier to change.
Extra photos Bring lots. You'll need two or three for every visa and visa extension, and one or two for a photograph permit in countries where such is required. Visa-type photos are readily obtainable everywhere if you run out.

Recommended Items
Map Michelin's map of West Africa (No 153) is far superior to others. Finding one in West Africa is frequently difficult.
Film & photographic accessories Bring a variety of ASA film; lighting conditions vary considerably. Film and accessories are expensive in West Africa. Moreover, most shops offer only a limited range of film types and cameras/accessories.
Polaroid Camera Africans love photographs, but they typically have few of themselves. If you want to be a good will ambassador, buy a cheap Polaroid.
Alarm clock Hotels cannot always be relied upon for waking you up.
International Drivers Licence Sometimes required to rent cars.
Credit cards American Express is the most widely accepted, followed by Diners, with Visa a distant third. Others are almost worthless. Cards are required by most rental agencies and are useful for hotels and emergencies.
Pocket Purifier This is an ingenious device that purifies water on contact and works like a straw. Filters up to 190 litres. Available at better camping stores or send US$16 to Handsome Rewards, 19465 Brennan Avenue, Perris, CA 92379.
French phrase book Don't expect to find one easily in Africa.
Books Good books in English are hard to come by. Lagos is the best place.
Small calculator This can facilitate bargaining in the market immeasurably, especially if you don't speak French.

Small mirror & flashlight Women should realise that even in good hotels, room lighting is occasionally poor. Plastic bags and a washcloth are also useful.

Business cards Calling cards are very important in West Africa. Africans like to make friends; giving someone your card is an indication you want to keep in contact. They can even be useful in dealing with policemen.

Gifts Some businessmen pack things like solar-powered calculators and micro-recorders to give as presents to colleagues.

Especially for Budget Travellers

Cassettes Africans love music with a good beat from the west. Hard-core blues and complicated jazz go over like a bad joke. You can be sure bus and taxi drivers and many other Africans with cassette players will, for a change, want to hear your music. And cassettes make great gifts to leave along the way.

Plastic rain poncho This can double as a ground mat, and it's easier to carry than an umbrella.

Camping gear Camping gear is useful only if you'll be crossing the Sahara, travelling in your own vehicle, or hiking in the relatively few hilly areas. Except for those with vehicles, camping is not as popular as in East Africa and there are only a handful of camping spots in all of West Africa.

Student ID Unfortunately this is of little use but you may be able to wangle a discount somewhere with it.

WHEN TO TRAVEL

When to travel? 'Go in the cool, dry period from November to February,' you may hear. For many this is the best time but other important factors to consider are the Harmattan, rain, heat, tourist season congestion and, for some people, the game park season. My recommendations are:

1 Those who wilt in the heat – avoid visiting during the hot period, March to May.

2 Photography nuts – you'll get much better photographs in the rainy season from December to April. During the dry season, the skies get dusty from the Harmattan winds that blow from the Sahara.

3 Animal lovers – you'll miss seeing the animals if you visit during the period from June to mid-November when the game parks are closed.

4 Sun and beach vacationers – you won't get much sun if you visit during the rainy season, June to mid-October.

5 Travellers to Guinea, Sierra Leone and Liberia – for the same reason, pick a time to visit other than May through October.

Tourist Congestion

If you think this is a joke, you're not far off the mark. Still, you will find a good number of tourists in The Gambia, Sierra Leone, the Casamance area of Senegal, and the Dogon area of Mali. Hotels along the coast of Togo, Sierra Leone and The Gambia are literally packed with sunbathers on package tours from Europe from December to March (and to a lesser extent, in November and April). Also, the Casamance region of Senegal and the Dogon-Timbuktu area of Mali are a small Mecca for Europeans during the extended Christmas season – but that's only six to eight weeks out of the year. So if you don't have hotel reservations in these areas or just want to avoid other travellers, pick another spot in West Africa during these periods – unless you're travelling on the cheap, in which case you can usually find a mattress somewhere.

PLANNING AN ITINERARY

There are a number of factors to consider in selecting an itinerary, particularly if you have some choice as to countries. Basically, there are two environments – the dry savannah area called the Sahel (most of Senegal, Gambia, Mali, Burkina Faso and Niger) and the more tropical coastal areas. Nigeria has substantial areas of both types of environment.

Top left: Bororo man, Niger (EE)
Top right: Bororo married woman, Niger (EE)
Bottom left: Children selling fish along the Niger River, Mali (EE)
Bottom right: Bozo woman, Mali (EE)

Top: Family compound of the Samba people, Benin (AV)
Bottom left: Granaries and houses of a Dogon cliffside village,
Sanga region, Mali (EE)
Bottom right: Somba house near Atakora, Benin (AV)

Usually, it's more interesting to see some of both. A third environment is the desert, but most people don't see it because of the great distances involved in getting there. However, Nouakchott, the desert capital of Mauritania, is only a seven-hour drive from Dakar.

Major Sites of Interest

At great risk of creating controversy, I have given below my own assessment of the 16 places in West Africa that travellers seem to find the most fascinating. Just don't lose sight of the fact that in West Africa, people are more interesting than 'things' and places. Bamako, for example, is on the list, but the 'must' places won't take you more than half a day to see except for the market. You can have a memorable trip without seeing any of the places. Still, some environments are unique and particularly interesting, the villages of the Dogon cliff dwellers and the edge of the Sahara are examples. These places are all discussed in the country chapters. My list of the top places follows (random order):

Mopti-Djenne-Dogon area of central Mali
Casamance area of southern Senegal
Dakar (Senegal) and environs
Atâr-Chinguetti-Ouadâne desert-oasis area of Mauritania
Agadez (Niger) and Air Mountains
Northern Nigeria, especially Kano.
Coastal area of Ghana between Cape Coast and Dixcove.

Runners-up (random order):

Fouta-Djallon area of Guinea
Timbuktu and surrounding area of Mali
Bamako (Mali)
Korogho-Comoé Park area of northern Ivory Coast
Cape Verde, especially Mindelo
Niamey and 'W' Park area of Niger and northern Benin
Man area of western Ivory Coast
Banc d'Arguin coastal area of Mauritania
Lomé-Kpalimé-Ganvié area of southern Togo and Benin

Getting There

FROM NEW YORK

Only Air Afrique (tel 800-2372747) and Nigeria Airways (tel 212-9352700) now offer direct flights from New York to West Africa. Pan Am has discontinued its service. Air Afrique is more professionally run than Nigeria Airways. Air Afrique has twice weekly flights stopping in Dakar (Senegal) and Abidjan (Ivory Coast). Nigeria Airways has two flights a week to Lagos via Monrovia.

Iberia (tel 718-7933300) and Air Maroc (tel 212-9743790) both offer service to Africa and charge the same as the direct flights. You must transit in Madrid or Casablanca – an advantage if you want a few days or more in Spain or Morocco. For all other flights via Europe, you'll have to change planes and pay about US$300 more.

Regular economy fares to and within Africa are about the same as they are in the USA. New York-Abidjan is US$1780 for a roundtrip economy fare; New York-LA is half the distance and costs about half as much. (New York-Lagos is US$112 less roundtrip even though Lagos is further to the east.) The airlines also offer some special fares to Africa. If for whatever reason you fly to Africa on a full fare economy ticket, buy only a one-way ticket because you can buy the return fare in local currency for about one-third less than the fare in dollars!

Most travellers take advantage of one of the airlines' two special roundtrip fares – APEX and excursion fares. APEX is cheaper – about a third less than the normal economy fare (ie New York-Abidjan US$1216 versus US$1780). Excursion fares are set midway between the economy fare and APEX. With both fares, you must return within 45 days. You cannot change the return date without a 25% penalty and you must stay at least 13 days. With APEX, however, you must reserve at least 30 days in advance, and you are not allowed a stopover.

An excursion ticket, on the other hand, can be purchased up to the last minute and you are allowed one or more stopovers. For instance, you can fly Air Afrique to Abidjan and stop off in Dakar. Or take Iberia and stop over in Spain. If you want to stop over elsewhere in Europe, you'll have to pay about US$300 more for an excursion ticket (ie about the full economy fare direct to Africa).

Travellers from 12 to 23 years of age can take advantage of Air Afrique's youth fare. The fare is about the same as APEX (US$1174 roundtrip New York-Abidjan). The big advantage is that there are less restrictions – no advance purchase requirement and no 45-day return restriction. Nigeria Airways does not offer a student fare from the USA, but they do offer student discounts within Africa, eg they give up to 40% off from Lagos to Nairobi, which is a huge saving but the flight is still not cheap.

The cheapest way to get to Africa is to buy a ticket from one of the following travel agencies in New York: *Maharaja Travels* (518 5th Avenue at 44th St, New York, NY 10036, tel 212-3910122 and 800-2236862); *Travelow International* (136-75 37th Avenue, Flushing, New York 11354, tel 718-4458429 or 800-2315561); and *Lan-Si-Aire-Travel* (303 5th Avenue at 31st St, New York, NY 10016, tel 212-8895478). These are not fly-by-night companies and they have been in business for quite a few years.

All three companies offer a special roundtrip fare on Air Afrique to Dakar and Abidjan for about one-third less than the APEX fare (eg US$756 New York-Abidjan). The restrictions are identical to those of APEX, the big difference is that you must return within two weeks instead of 45 days. If you want to stay much longer than two weeks or pay less than 30 days in advance, call all three. You will find that they're not all sticklers for the rules.

You could also go with *Friends of Togo* (Box 666, Durham, NC 27702), an organisation of mainly ex-Peace Corps volunteers to Togo. Twice a year, they negotiate special roundtrip fares to Lomé (Togo) for two to three weeks duration, open to members and non-members alike. There is one flight around the third week in June and another a week before Christmas. The cost is about US$760.

Only if you must stay longer than 45 days does it pay to fly to London or Amsterdam and buy a ticket from a bucket shop or, alternatively, fly to Paris and buy a ticket from Le Point (if you can get a seat). The other advantage of buying your ticket in Europe is that you can combine a trip to Africa with a trip to Europe. Unfortunately, some bucket shops are too understaffed to respond to mail, but you can always call. The only way to make a reservation is to pay for the ticket, which can be done by mail. Except during the Christmas holiday season, you'll be taking little risk by waiting until you get to London or Amsterdam to buy your ticket; the chances of getting a flight within a day or two are usually good, however, the wise will call first.

FROM LONDON

Full fare economy tickets to Africa cost about what they do in Europe and the USA. Roundtrip London to Lagos (Nigeria) costs £834 (London-Boston, the same distance, costs £780). The only special fare offered by the airlines is the excursion fare, which limits your stay to a maximum of 30 days.

It's usually cheaper to go through a travel agent than buying from the airlines directly and the savings can be as much as 50%. In London (and Amsterdam), there are two distinct kinds of travel agencies. The first kind are the well-known ones like Thomas Cook which offer virtually no fare reductions (eg £800 London-Abidjan

roundtrip) unless you go on one of their all-inclusive tours. The second group, known colloquially as bucket shops, offer rock bottom prices on European and African airlines. These travel agencies are small operators (typically three to five people) and for the most part are quite reliable. They get their name from the fact that the airlines sell them a 'bucket' of tickets at a discount – you get the savings.

Typical roundtrip fares offered by bucket shops from London to coastal West African cities range from £360 to £540. There's no advance purchase requirement and return dates can be changed. Which airline you choose makes a difference. Aeroflot is the cheapest – £360 London-Abidjan roundtrip and £420 London-Brazzaville roundtrip – but you'll have to spend at least a night in Moscow, at the airline's expense. Sierra Leone Airlines is almost as cheap. If you insist on flying on a European airline, it'll cost you about £50 or so more than if you take an African airline.

The length of stay also effects the price of the ticket. Roundtrip tickets with a 30-day maximum return restriction (typically £400 to £440) are about £70 to £100 cheaper than those with the return portion valid up to one year (typically £470 to £540). Bucket shops also offer cheap one-way fares.

Some people think that because the tickets are so cheap, there must be something fishy going on. It's not true; the great majority of bucket shops are quite reliable. The problem is that every now and then one goes bust, giving their reputation a black eye.

It's important to see at least three or four agencies because they don't all deal with the same airlines. Some refuse to deal with Sierra Leone Airlines and Aeroflot, saying the former is too unreliable and the latter only marginally cheaper than other more direct flights. Consequently, you'll find a wide variation in prices and availability of flights to a particular destination. Warning: Tickets from bucket shops sell out much more quickly for flights in December and January than during the rest of the year. Also, reservations cannot be made without payment.

One other possibility is to try the tour companies who offer package deals to The Gambia from November to March. These are usually not very cheap, but occasionally they offer heavily discounted 'flight only' tickets on their unfilled charters. Roundtrip fares range from an astonishing £59, to £180. The maximum stay is usually two or three weeks but at this price if you want to stay longer you can discard the return ticket or try to sell it in Banjul. Most travel agents are unwilling to help you with these flights but the charter companies are listed under Package Tours. These tickets are subject to availability and can only be bought a few days in advance, so you have to be well organised and have your vaccinations, visas, etc, beforehand.

As for youth fares, STA Travel (74 Old Brompton Rd, London SW7, tel 01-5811022) offers special fares for those under 26 years of age, but the fares aren't any lower than those offered by the bucket shops.

The following bucket shops appear to be the most reliable; most of them will even respond by mail to inquiries:

Trailfinders Ltd (46 Earls Court Road, London W8 6EJ, tel 01-6031515. You cannot find a better agency than this one. They deal with most airlines except Aeroflot. Ask for a copy of their magazine Trailfinder.
Euro Asean Travel Ltd (Gucci House, 27 Old Bond St, London W1X 3AA, tel 01-4996615/4408). An agency that will respond immediately and informatively by letter to inquiries, they do not deal with Aeroflot or Sierra Leone Airlines.
The World Sports Supporters Club (40 James St, London W1M 5HS, tel 01-9359107). Equally well-known and reliable, this agency offers roundtrip fares that are about £100 more expensive than most of the others. They are unique in that they sell tickets on flights originating in Africa.

African World Travel Services (Radnor House, 93 Regent St, London W1R 7TG, tel 01-7347181/2/3). They are agents for almost all airlines serving West Africa from London. As an example of their fares. London-Accra roundtrip on Ghana Airways is £470, valid for one year. They also offer one-way fares.
Tourtrav Ltd (22 Old Quebec St, London W1, tel 01-4091868). They are well-established agents for almost all airlines serving West Africa.
Hogg Robinson Ltd (84 Bishops Bridge Rd, London WC2, tel 01-8714455). Not a bucket shop but a major travel agency, they offer equally cheap fares if you use this special telephone number.

Additional bucket shops which are well established and seem reliable are: Afro-Asian Travel Ltd (Linen Hall, 162 Regent St, London W1R JTB, tel 01-4378255/6/7); they are agents for most airlines serving West Africa. Allied Air Travel (90 Regent St, London W1R 5AP, tel 01-7346080); the entrance is at 29 Glasgow St. Economic Air Travel Bureau (93 Judd St, London WC1H 9NE, tel 01-3871211). Super Fare Travel (231 Oxford St, London W1, tel 01-7347927). Levitas Travel (147 Oxford St, London W1, tel 4390880). AZAT Travel (61 Charlotte St, London W1, tel 01-5804632/3); they are agents for most airlines serving West Africa. African Travel Systems (6 North End Parade, London W14, tel 01-6025091/2).

FROM PARIS

Most airlines offer excursion fares with a 30-day return restriction, plus UTA and Air Afrique offer a youth fare (ages 12 to 23) with a one-year return restriction for about 40% less than the regular economy roundtrip fare (ie about 4000 FF Paris-Abidjan). The special fares offered by travel agencies in France are, in general, slightly cheaper than those offered in London. However, most of them limit you to a maximum stay of 30 days. Some agencies offer special roundtrip fares valid for a year for about 25% higher than the 30-day flights.

One company, however, is unique – *Le Point Mulhouse* (2, Place Wagram, 75017 Paris or, on the Left Bank, 54, Rue des Écoles, 75005 Paris, tel 01-47632258). Le Point offers the cheapest flights from Europe to Africa – even cheaper than the bucket shops. They offer flights to Burkina Faso and the CAR with the return portion valid for up to a year. Examples of their roundtrip fares are: Paris-Burkina Faso for 2920 to 3220 FF (US$487 to US$537) and Paris-CAR for 3300 to 3820 FF (US$560 to US$637) (ie about half the excursion fare). They also have one-to four-week fares to Senegal, the Ivory Coast and Cameroon for about two-thirds the normal excursion fare.

Because of these incredibly cheap fares and the flexibility of their tickets, Le Point is the number one choice of travellers on the cheap. It is unique in offering tickets valid for up to a year, one-way fares and flights originating in Africa – Burkina Faso and the CAR only, however. For these two countries, departures are from Paris with a change over in Marseilles. If you leave from/go to Marseilles instead of Paris, the fare is about US$60 less. The fare is about US$60 more if you travel during the high season (summer and Christmas time). One-way only is about 65% of the roundtrip fares. As for flights to the Ivory Coast, Senegal and Cameroon, they offer much less flexibility and have the usual one to four weeks return restriction, with no one-way or Africa-origin options. There are about five to eight flights a month to/from Burkina Faso (more in the summer and Christmas time), about two flights per month to/from the CAR, and one per week to the rest.

The problem with Le Point is that reservations must be made well in advance and only upon full payment. You cannot make reservations by phone or pay by wire, which means that travellers from North America cannot make reservations until they arrive in Europe. Still, calling can be useful to find out what's available and also to find the names of travel agencies in

Europe which have special arrangements with Le Point for receiving payment.

The wise will give alternative departure dates. There's a fee for changing departure dates, and notification of the change must be made well in advance. Flights are frequently full a month or more in advance, especially during the summer. Reconfirmation is required in person; one day in advance of the flight is usually sufficient even though they say three days, the only problem is that Le Point sometimes cancels a flight that has numerous vacant seats and/or late reconfirmations.

Other French travel agencies offering special fares are:

Nouvelles Frontières (74, Rue de la Federation, 75015 Paris, tel 01-42732525) offers roundtrip fares to Senegal, Mali, Ivory Coast, Togo, Cameroon and the Congo for about two-thirds the excursion fare. Roundtrip Paris-Abidjan is 3400 FF. One of their flights (to Togo – for a little more) is valid for up to six months; otherwise the one– to four-week limitation holds. There are limited cancellation rights. Ask about their reduced hotel rates and excursions.

Jeunes Sans Frontières (31, Quai des Grands-Augustins, 75002 Paris, tel 001-43293550) offers similar fares with the usual four-week return restriction and limited cancellation rights.

Uniclam (63, Rue Monsieur-le-Prince, 75006 Paris, tel 01-4321236) has some unbeatable fares. Tickets can be purchased to eight countries, from Senegal to the Congo, most good for one year. Roundtrip Paris-Dakar is 3580 FF. Prices are about 600 FF less if the trip does not exceed four weeks.

GO Voyages (22, Rue de l'Arcade, 75008 Paris, tel 01-42661818) has fares that are not quite as attractive. They offer 20 to 25% reductions on the normal seven– to 30-day excursion rates, plus roundtrip tickets valid up to a year for 25 to 50% more. Departures are from Paris and Brussels, some from London. Destinations include about half of the countries covered herein.

OTU (137, Boulevard St-Michel, 75005 Paris, tel 01-43291288) is a university tourist organisation offering special fares to students and young people.

FUAJ (Federation of Youth Hostels, 10, Rue Notre Dame-de-Lorette, 75009 Paris, tel 01-42855540) offers special fares to young people as well as organised tours.

FROM MUNICH & BRUSSELS

ARD (Konigwieserstrabe 89, 8 Munich 71, tel 089-7592609/45) specialises in African travel. Munich-Abidjan return, for example, costs 1550 DM (US$2800) with a 35-day return restriction, and 50% more with a one-year return restriction.

Uniclam (1, Rue de la Sablonnière, 1000 Brussels, tel 02-2185562) offers the same fares as Uniclam in Paris.

Nouvelles Frontières (21, Rue de La Violette, 1000 Brussels. tel 02-5118013) offers the same fares as Nouvelles Frontières in Paris.

Acotra (Rue de la Montagne, 38, B-1000 Brussels, tel 02-5125540/8607) offers special prices to teachers, students and recent students under 31 years of age. Destinations include Bamako, Brazzaville, Kinshasa, Lagos and Monrovia. Roundtrip prices range from 23.550 FB (US$615) to Bamako and 44.750 FB (US$1210) to Kinshasa. The return portion is valid for up to a year. All flights have a one-way option which costs 55 to 65% of the roundtrip fare.

CJB (6, Rue Mercelis, 1050 Brussels, tel 02-5116407) also has special fares for students and young people.

FROM AUSTRALIA

There are no direct flights from Australia to West Africa. The three basic options are to fly via East Africa, North Africa or Europe.

The only direct flight to continental Africa is with Qantas to Harare but at around A$2300 return from Sydney or Melbourne this is one of the most expensive options. From Perth you can fly direct to Harare for A$1850 return, but there are no cheap flights to West Africa from Zimbabwe.

A better option is to fly to Nairobi and then pick up a return ticket to West Africa

from there. This usually involves flying to Singapore and connecting with another flight to Nairobi. PIA (Pakistan Airlines) seems to have the cheapest flights and you can pick up a return Sydney-Singapore-Karachi-Nairobi ticket for around A$1690. A slightly cheaper alternative is to fly via Manila and connect with a PIA flight there.

If flying with PIA doesn't attract you, other carriers fly from Singapore to Nairobi but they are usually more expensive. One interesting alternative is to fly Air Mauritius from Singapore to Nairobi with a stopover in Mauritius for about A$1800 return from Melbourne or Sydney.

Internal flights in Africa are not cheap and the published price for a Nairobi-Lagos ticket is A$490 one way or A$680 for a return ticket valid for only one month. Other destinations in West Africa are slightly more expensive. However, Nairobi is the one of the best places in Africa for airline tickets. Whilst Nairobi travel agents don't compare with London bucket shops, they should be able to undercut the scheduled fare and sell you a more flexible ticket.

To go via North Africa, one of the best deals is with British Airways and Royal Jordanian Airlines to Casablanca or Tunis for around A$1500 return. From North Africa you can then travel overland across the Sahara or pick up an air ticket to West Africa, but don't expect to find any bargains.

The high cost of flying to Africa makes flying via Europe a viable alternative. A low-season ticket to Europe costs around A$1450 return and you can then buy a bucket-shop ticket to West Africa in London or Paris. There are also reasonably priced tickets that can be bought in Australia, eg a ticket with Swiss Air to Zurich and then a connection with one of their flights to Abidjan or Accra, costs around A$2400 return.

The most important thing is to shop around. Travel agents offer different flights and prices, airlines occasionally have special deals, and it is best to get as many quotes as possible before deciding. A good place to start looking is STA (Student Travel Australia) which has offices in all Australian capital cities.

PACKAGE TOURS

For those who have significant fears of Africa even after reading this book (or because of it), package tours are probably the best solution. Moreover, some of their more exotic offerings, especially with the French companies, allow you to do things that you could not possibly do otherwise. Nouvelles Frontières, for example, offers a one-week chartered sailing trip in the Casamance area of Senegal for US$425 plus airfare.

Le Point has two-week, fairly rustic expeditions in Mali, Togo, Ghana, Comoé Game Reserve, and Burkina Faso all for about US$390 to US$460 depending on the season plus airfare (2920 FF/US$485). The tours depart from Burkina Faso and are coordinated with Le Point's Paris-Ouagadougou flights. You can also take trips through the desert in Mauritania or you can live in an African village in Burkina Faso for a week for only about 1200FF (US$200).

Of the American companies, Travoa is typical of the more deluxe outfits. They offer two tours of West Africa, one covering seven countries in 22 days for US$5440 and another covering 11 countries in 40 days for US$10,992. Others are not so expensive. Henderson Tours out of Atlanta has tours covering 11 countries from Senegal to Gabon. A 14-day tour of Senegal, The Gambia, Liberia and the Ivory Coast, for example, costs US$1490 plus airfare (US$1069 from New York).

African American Heritage Studies Program offers study/travel programs intended to increase your awareness of the many cultures in Africa. Examples include 'Traditional Healers and Religion Program' to Senegal, Nigeria, Togo and Benin, 15 days for US$2500; 'Senegal, Gambia Special', eight days for US$995;

'West African Kingdoms' to Senegal, Nigeria, Benin, Togo, Cameroon, 15 days for US$2685 including airfare.

In Britain, there are few package tours of the adventurous nature and they are mainly beach vacations in The Gambia and Sierra Leone coupled with a few side trips into the interior. These two countries, and Senegal, offer miles of beautiful sand beaches and, unlike most of West Africa, safe swimming, plus hotels located far enough away from the capital cities to allow people to forget they're in Africa if that is their choosing. The high season (no rain) is from November to April. The Gambia and Senegal are unique in that even during the rainy off-season (June to October), there is still more than enough sunshine for an enjoyable vacation.

Two weeks in The Gambia during the high season costs £400 to £680 (depending solely on the date) including roundtrip airfare from London and half board. During the Christmas period, prices are £100 to £150 more. Package tours to Sierra Leone often cost about a third more, with no obvious advantages.

From the USA

The leading deluxe tour operators specialising in West Africa are *Travcoa* (875 Michigan Avenue, Chicago, Ill 60611, tel 800-9922005); *African Step Tours Inc* (118 East 59th St, New York, NY 10022, tel 212-3083816); *African Travel Advisors* (8949 South Stony Island, Chicago, Ill 60617, tel 800-6216165); *Hemphill Harris Travel Corp* (16000 Ventura Boulevard, Suite 200, Encino, CA 91436, tel 800-4210454); *Olson-Travel World* (Box 92734, Los Angeles, CA 90009, tel 800-4212255).

For more moderately priced tours, try *African American Heritage Studies Program* (120 South LaSalle St, Suite 1144, Chicago, Ill 60603, tel 312-4430929); *African Holidays* (Box 36959, Tuscon, AZ 85740, tel 800-5280168); *Scantravel Africa* (Box 13248, Tuscon, AZ 85732, tel

800-5285151); *East/West Holidays, Inc* (80 Fifth Avenue, New York, NY 10011, tel 800-2231784); *Henderson Tours* (931 Martin Luther King St, Atlanta, GA 30314, tel 800-2414644).

Beach Holidays – from Britain

Thomas Cook represents most of the following: *Horizon Holidays Ltd* (41 Old Bond St, London W1X 3AF, tel 01-4937446); *Blue Sky Holidays Ltd* (London Road, East Grinstead, West Sussex RH19 1HU, London tel 01-8368499); *Thomson Holidays Ltd* (Greater London House, Hampstead House, Hampstead Road, London NW1 7SD, tel 01-4392211/4358431); *Enterprise Holidays* (c/o Thomas Cook); *Kuoni Travel Ltd* (Kuoni House, Dorking, Surrey RH5 4AZ, London tel 01-4998636); *Wingspan Travel*, 6 Great Queen St, London WC2B 5DG, tel 01-2423652).

From France

Nouvelles Frontières (previously listed); *Le Point Mulhouse* (previously listed); *Airtour Afrique* (36, Avenue de l'Opera, 75083 Paris, tel 01-42669089); *Africatour* (9/11, Avenue Franklin Roosevelt, 75008 Paris, tel 01-47237859); *Rêve-Vacances* (9, Rue Kepler, 75016 Paris, tel 01-

47206333/6478); *BVJ* (Bureau des Voyages de la Jeunesse, 20, Rue Jean-Jacques-Rousseau, 75001 Paris, tel 01-42368818), *FRAM* (79, Avenue Champs Elysées, 75008 Paris, tel 01-47235445); *Jet Tours* by Air France (19, Avenue de Tourville, 75007 Paris, tel 47050195); *Uniclam* (previously listed).

From Belgium & Germany

Uniclam (Brussels; previously listed); *CJB* (Brussels; previously listed), *Afrika Tours Individuell* (Schwanthalerstrabe 22, 800 Munich 2, tel 089-596081); *Air Conti Flugreisen GmbH* (Neurhauserstrabe 34, 8000 Munich 2). *ARD* (Konigswieserstrabe 89, 8 Munich 71, tel 089-7592609/45) is an agent specialising in African tours and cheap airline fares.

ADVENTURE TRIPS

Some organisations and travel agencies specialise in adventure travel, from canoe trips down the Niger River to camel trips across the desert. People on these trips experience Africa in ways that even most people living in Africa never have. Wilderness Travel, for example, offers a 23-day Mali adventure including a boat trip on the Niger River to Timbuktu for US$1890 to US$1990 plus airfare, as well as a two-week desert safari in southern Algeria.

International Bicycle Fund offers a 15-day and a 30-day bicycle trip of West Africa, typically one trip in November and another in December, covering Liberia east to Benin. The emphasis is not on testing people's stamina but on meeting local people and learning the history and culture of the region. The cost excluding airfare is US$700 for the 15-day trip and US$1050 for the 30-day trip. Forum Travel sponsors approximately 15 different Sahara expeditions, some involving camel and canoe rides.

Operation Crossroads Africa sponsors, every summer, seven-week Peace Corps-type experiences in rural Africa including, usually, Sierra Leone, Ghana, Ivory

Coast, Liberia. 'Volunteers' participate in projects (construction, museums, etc) for five weeks followed by two weeks of in-country travel. The cost is approximately US$3000. Many participants get churches and other organisations to sponsor them, reducing part of their costs.

Terres d'Aventure, in Paris, offers two weeks trekking in Guinea's Fouta Djalon area plus a 16-day adventure in Mali's Dogon area for 10,500 FF and 11,200 FF, respectively. Another Paris based outfit, Explorator, is involved in a wide assortment of adventure tours, including two and three week trips in Mali's Dogon area, the Agadez-Air Mountains, and southern Algeria. The 16-day Mali trip, for example, costs 11,000 FF including airfare.

The following comprehensive list includes agencies with tours of the Sahara desert in southern Algeria.

From the USA

Wilderness Travel (1760-AT Solano Avenue, Berkeley, CA 94707, tel 800-2476700); *Operation Crossroads Africa* (150 Fifth Avenue, New York, NY 10011, tel 800-4223742); *Bicycle Africa* (International Bicycle Fund, 4247 135th Place SE, Bellevue, WA 98006, tel 206-7461028); *Turtle Tours* (251 51st St, New York, NY 10022, tel 212-3551404); *Mountain Travel* (1398 Solano Avenue, Albany, CA 94706, tel 800-2272384); *Forum Travel International* (91 Gregory Lane, No 21, Pleasant Hill, CA 94523, tel 415-6712900).

From France

Visages du Monde (26, Rue Poliveau, 75005 Paris, France, tel 01-45870404); *Nouvelles Frontières* (previously listed); *Terres d'Aventure* (16, Rue Saint-Victor, 75005 Paris, tel 01-43299450); *Explorator* (16, Place de la Madeleine, 75008 Paris, tel 01-42666624); *Hommes et Montagnes* (Chateau Revel, 38500 Voiron, France, tel 76-051028); *Le Point Mulhouse* (previously listed).

From Elsewhere in Europe

Jerrycan Expedition (Rue Sautter 23, 1205 Geneva, Switzerland, tel 022-469282); *Explorado* (61, Avenue Legrand, 1050 Brussels, tel 02-6482269); *Nomadis* (Obere Bachgasse 20, 8400 Regensburg, Germany, c/o BERS Touristik, Germany, tel 0941-59136); *Sliva Expeditionen* (Postfach 548, 8000 Munich 33, Germany, tel 089-294336); *Explorer* (Huttuttenstrabe 17, 4 Dusseldorf, Germany, tel 0211-379064).

OVERLAND EXPEDITIONS BY TRUCK

There are numerous companies in Britain and some on the Continent which take travellers across the Sahara Desert to West Africa or to East Africa via West Africa. The latter typically go through Niger, Nigeria, Chad, Cameroon, CAR and Zaire en route to Kenya. These trips take one to five months and are not for everybody by a long shot. Breakdowns of the truck and border closings requiring drastic changes in itinerary are warnings that shouldn't be taken lightly. The overland vehicles are almost invariably huge trucks with seating down the sides and take 10 to 15 people. Clients are usually in their 20s, rarely over 40.

The price is very reasonable considering the distance covered and the time involved. Guerba Expeditions, for example, charges about £1335/US$2000 for a two-month trip overland from Tunisia to Togo and back via Timbuktu. The price includes food and the London-Tunis-London flight. *Exodus Expeditions* has trips ending in Burkina Faso and Cameroon, as well as trips between these points and Nairobi. Ten weeks Ouagadougou to London, for example, costs £850/US$1270 including food plus airfare.

The price of a five-month overland trip from London to Kenya including the food kitty and one-way airfare runs about £1400 to £2650, depending on the company. *Hobo Trans-Africa* is a little different from the others in that they cross the Sahara via the Reggane-Gao route into Mali and Burkina Faso, passing through Timbuktu and the Dogon area, thus including more of West Africa.

These trips offer the opportunity at a very reasonable price to see just about every kind of environment that Africa has to offer. The disadvantage is that they involve a lot of time in a fairly slow truck.

A group that I saw passing through Cameroon had just passed near Rumsiki, an area with spectacular almost knife-like mountains jutting out of the ground. André Gide considered this spot to be one the most beautiful in the world and there's hardly a tourist brochure on Cameroon without at least one picture of the area. Yet neither the trip leader nor anyone in the group had ever even heard of it. Since the quality of the guides varies greatly, be sure that you meet your trip leader before signing up; a bad one can ruin the whole trip. These trips do offer an unforgettable adventure at a cheap price for those with a little time to blow.

Most of the British companies offering such trips advertise in *Time Out*, *LAM*, *TNT* and the Saturday edition of *The Guardian* personnel section, all published in London. There are about 10 or 20 small travel companies in England offering such trips. In Germany, they advertise in *Abenteuer & Reisen* and *Tours*. The following are the most established and well known:

British Companies

Guerba Expeditions Ltd (101 Eden Vale Rd, Westbury, Wiltshire BA13 3QG, UK, tel 0373-826611); *Encounter Overland* (267 Old Brompton Rd, London SW5, UK, tel 01-3706845; or c/o Adventure Centre, 5540 College Avenue, Oakland, CA 94618, tel 415-6541897); *Exodus Expeditions* (All Saint's Passage, Department LM, 100 Wandsworth High St, London SW18 4LE, UK, tel 01-8700150; or c/o WestCan Treks, 17 Hayden St, Toronto, Ontario M4Y 2P2, tel 403-4390024); *Trans Sahara* (Continental Pullman Holding BV, 83 Upland Rd, London SE 22, tel 01-6937468);

Hobo Trans-Africa (Wissett Place, Halesworth, Suffolk IP19 8HY, UK, tel 09867-3124); *Long Haul Expeditions* (56 Bohun Grove, East Barnet, Herts, UK, tel 01-4401582); *Tracks* (12 Abingdon Rd, London W8 6AF, tel 01-9373028).

American Companies

Himalayan Travel Inc (Box 481, Greenwich, CT 06836, tel 203-6220055); *Overseas Adventure Travel* (6 Bigelow St, Cambridge, Mass 02139, tel 800-2210814); *Adventure Centre* (5540 College Avenue, Oakland, CA 94618, tel 800-2278747; 800-2288747 for CA only).

European Companies

Caravanes de Jeunesse Belge (6, Rue, Mercelis, Brussels 1050, tel 02-5116406); *Jerrycan* (previously listed); *Travel Overland* (Barerstrabe 73, Munich 78, Germany, tel 089-272760); *West African Travel* (Wilhelm Leuscher Strabe 228, 6103 Griesheim, Germany, tel 06155-63336); *Lama Expedition* (Roderbergweg 106, 6000 Frankfurt, Main 60, Germany, tel 069-447897).

BY FREIGHTER

From North America, there is no longer any company that offers regularly scheduled passenger-carrying freighters from anywhere in the USA to West Africa. There are only vessels chartered for a particular shipment. While they might accept a passenger or two, you'd have to go down to the docks to find out about them. In other words – forget it. From Europe, there are still a few romantics who occasionally hop a freighter. It is only for those with a few extra shekels. A typical trip from Europe, say Antwerp, takes about nine days to Dakar, 13 days to Abidjan, and 17 days to Zaire.

Of the lines serving West Africa, you cannot do better than the Swiss *Nautilus Line* (c/o Keller Shipping AG, Holbeinstrasse 68, 4002 Basle, tel 061-237940; Douala c/o Socopao, Quai de la Marine, 5; Abidjan c/o Transcap). Their freighters which are reportedly quite clean, leave from Genoa and Marseilles to the Congo, stopping at Dakar, Tema (Ghana), Lagos (Nigeria) and Douala (Cameroon). Nautilus charges about 2200 Swiss francs (US$ 1475) one-way to the Congo (about 875 SF to Dakar); the price includes meals. If you're shipping a vehicle, count on paying about 50 to 75% extra for the vehicle, depending on its length and weight.

From Britain, you can take a *Nigerian Shipping Lines* freighter once a month from Liverpool to Lagos (Nigeria), stopping in Dakar, Banjul (The Gambia), Freetown (Sierra Leone), and Takoradi (Ghana) on the way. The one-way cost for the owner's suite/first class is £428/397 to Dakar and £594/504 to Lagos, including meals. The trip takes about one week to Dakar and another week to Lagos. Contact Nigerian Shipping Lines' agent, Brown Jenkins & Co Ltd (Dunster House, Mark Lane, London EC3, tel 01-5911700).

From France, *SITRAM* (Tour Atlantic, 92080 Paris Cedex 6, France, tel 01-49000201; or 01 BP 1546, Abidjan 01, Ivory Coast, tel 225-369200) has freighters twice a month Bordeaux-Abidjan (Ivory Coast). The trip costs 7540 FF (about US$1255, ie about twice the one-way economy airfare). When there's not a full load, the ship stops in Dakar, otherwise, there are no intermediate stops. *Compagnie des Croisières Paquet* no longer offers service from France to Dakar.

From Antwerp, you can take *Compagnie Maritime Zairoise* or *Compagnie Maritime Belge*, both of which offer service to Zaire, stopping in Dakar and Abidjan. From Hamburg or Rotterdam, there's *Polish Ocean Lines* (c/o Gydnia America Shipping lines Ltd, 238 City Rd, London EC1, tel 01-2539561; or c/o Pakhold-Rotterdam BV, Box 544, Van Weerden Poelmanweg 25-31, Rotterdam, tel 302911), which has service twice a month to the Congo, with 10 stops.

For more information, consult the monthly *ABC Shipping Guide*, available in some libraries and from World Travel Centre (tel 0582-600111) in Dunstable, UK LU5 4HB. Or, better, contact *Carolyn's Cruises* (32 Garner Drive, Novato, CA 94947, tel 415-8974039) or *Freighter Cruise Service* (5925 Monkland Avenue, Montreal, Quebec H4A, tel 514-4810447). Both specialise in passenger-carrying freighter service. Freighter Cruise publishes a free newsletter thrice yearly with freighter schedules. They can tell you all about *Compagnie Maritime Belge*, for instance, which costs US$3890 to US$4980 for a 38-day roundtrip to Zaire. You can also get leads from the *Freighter Travel Club of America* (Box 12693, Salem, Oregon 97309). The US$16 membership dues include a question & answer service as well as a monthly magazine.

CROSSING THE SAHARA

The first crossing by automobile was in 1922 when a group of Frenchmen in five Citroen trucks made the north-south crossing in 20 days. Now the trip is done all the time but it's still high adventure. From November to early March, temperatures are fairly tolerable.

The desert offers lots of surprises. One you've probably heard about is how cold it can get at night. Another is that it's not all sand dunes like you saw in Lawrence of Arabia. On the contrary, huge sand dunes are seen only occasionally on the most popular routes. You'll see spectacular mountains in some areas, hard flat sand in other areas, and lots of rocks in still other areas, with an oasis now and then to clean your dirty body and perk up your spirits.

Each environment offers its own special memories. Don't be surprised if you see a camel caravan or two, with a princess perched on a fancy saddle with flowing white material draped over four posts to shield her from the sun. When you see this, you'll know you're really there. If you meet a few Tuaregs in the middle of nowhere, there's nothing to worry about even though they used to be famous fighters and to this day would no more be seen without their swords than cowboys used to be without their guns.

Why do people get a charge out of crossing the desert? For a motorcyclist it's the challenge and thrill of crossing 1500 km of flat sand at cruising speeds of 120 km/hour or more, with side trips off the beaten path to areas few, if any, non-nomads have ever seen. To others, flat sand offers only boredom.

It's the side trips, such as into the rocky Air mountains, that create the most lasting memories. Or maybe it's just the incredible vastness, the stillness, the wind, being in the middle of nowhere and the surprise of seeing anything resembling life, whether another vehicle, a bush, or a nomad appearing from the middle of nowhere and seemingly going to nowhere. I have never met anyone who regrets having taken the trip, despite temperatures of up to 50°C, inevitable problems with the vehicle, canned food and no place to take a crap without everyone seeing you.

Despite what you may have heard and read, the trip is not particularly dangerous if the minimum precautions are observed. It's done all the time, even by motorcyclists, who frequently go off the main routes and chart their own course. One warning, however, concerns crossing the Sahara during the hottest period, June to August. Only a few vehicles cross then and if you're hitchhiking, be prepared for some long waiting periods. Those driving will have their equipment and provisions inspected by the Algerian police. If you don't seem prepared, they may not allow you to cross.

The best book from a logistical standpoint is the *Sahara Handbook* by Simon and Jan Glen. You can get a copy of the 1987 edition by sending £17.95/US$30 to Roger Lascelles Publishers (tel 01-8470935) at 47 York Rd, Brentford, Middlesex, UK TW8 0QP. For a guide to the sights and the best deals in Algeria and Morocco, as well as Tunisia, see Lonely Planet's forthcoming *North Africa – a travel survival kit*.

Route through Niger

The Algiers-Tamanrasset-Agadez route, called the Route du Hoggar, is by far the most popular route – and, consequently, the safest. For better or worse, it's paved except for about 500 km. If your vehicle breaks down in the unpaved section, you are fairly assured of being able to hitch a ride if necessary. It's 1975 km between Algiers and Tamanrasset (Tam), another 835 km to Agadez, and 1020 km more to Niamey, for a total of 2830 km.

The straight driving time is only 12 days (six days from Algiers to Tam, three days more to Arlit, and another three to Niamey). However, most people who rush the trip regret it afterwards. Allowing three to four weeks would be far more desirable. Nonetheless, people do it in two weeks all the time and thoroughly enjoy it. Agadez is one of the most interesting desert towns in West Africa, plus there are fabulous mountains along the way, making this one of the most interesting areas in all of West Africa. However, getting to and from the mountains requires a detour of at least a few days. The Hoggar mountains are north-east of Tam; the Air Mountains are accessible from Agadez.

Between Algiers and Agadez the route is paved except for about 500 km between Tam and Arlit. The In Salah-Tam portion, however, is in terrible condition. You must drive the entire way off the main road, and it's quite rocky. It's actually more difficult than the unpaved Tam-Agadez section! What was once a one-day trip now takes up to three days; this will all change once the repaving is finished. South of Tam the pavement ends after about 100 km. Try to time your departure so that you spend the night in Gara Eckar, an area about 260 km south of where the pavement ends and 60 km north of In Guezzam. You'll know you're there when you see the magnificent outcrops of wind-eroded sandstone rocks – ideal for photography in the later afternoon or early morning.

From the Niger border control post at Assamakka, you have the choice of going via Arlit or Tegguidam Tessoumi. The latter route is less travelled but allows you to see the salt evaporation ponds at Tegguidam Tessoumi, where camels are loaded with salt for transport to northern Nigeria and elsewhere.

Don't worry about getting lost. The unpaved section has clearly visible stakes every few km, so it's fairly difficult to lose your way. Count on three to four days from Tam to Agadez. In Tam, you must pass by the police and through customs. As for petrol, there are stations in Tam and in Arlit and you must have enough jerrycans to make the 592 km between the two, but bear in mind that you will use more petrol than normal. There is a petrol station (and water) at the border post, In Guezzam, but you cannot rely on the petrol supply as it is often limited and army gets priority.

Hitchhiking Hitchhiking is not difficult except during the hottest part of the year, June to August. If you refuse to pay, however, anticipate long waits. You can try to get away with not paying between Algiers and In Salah; further south, forget it. And don't expect to get away cheaply. Count on a minimum of 25,000 CFA/US$83 (dinars are usually not accepted) for the Tam-Agadez crossing.

The waiting point for southbound travellers is Tam. For northbound travellers it is usually Agadez, sometimes Arlit. Anticipate waiting anywhere from a day or two in Tam in winter to a week in the summer. In Tam, the best places to catch a truck going south are the customs post and the gas station; you can also try restaurants, such as the Restaurant de la Paix.

Women travelling alone will have fewer hassles if there are other travellers in the vehicle. There's safety in numbers against, for example, border officials who sometimes have nothing better to do than to get drunk and try to seduce women.

Others should make a point of giving the police cigarettes, food, or whatever to humour them. They have been known to give some travellers a hard time.

Between Agadez and Niamey and between Tam and Algiers, you can hitch or take a bus. There are daily buses Algiers-Ghardaia, Ghardaia-In Salah, and In Salah-Tam. You could also fly Algiers-Tam; the cost is only about 50% more than the bus ticket.

Route through Mali

The 1503-km Adrar-Gao route through Mali, known as the Route du Tanezrouft, is far less travelled, making hitchhiking extremely difficult. There are some misconceptions about this route, eg that it takes longer and is more rugged. Neither is true. For motorists and motorcyclists, there are even certain advantages. The route is technically easier than the Tam-Agadez route even though the unpaved section is over 2½ times longer (1317 km as opposed to about 500 km). This is because there are fewer sections of soft sand along the way (plus the 600-km asphalt stretch between In Salah and Tam on the other route is in terrible condition).

The paved section ends in Reggane, 185 km south of Adrar. From there it's a two to three-day drive to the Malian border (Bordj-Moktar). It is hard flat sand all the way and a little monotonous. High markers are placed every 10 km and you can usually see them from a long distance. The only place the going gets a little rough is about half-way between the border and Gao. Count on another two to three days for that section. After Gao it's another long day on dirt road to Niamey (or two days on asphalted road to Bamako). So time-wise, the routes through Niger and Mali are about the same.

Many who take the Mali route find that the desert's vastness gives a heightened sense of adventure and exhilaration. A very isolated week in the desert simply leaves a greater impression than the more travelled Tam route involving only three or four days off asphalted road. Some may consider the near absence of other travellers an advantage. This consideration is more than outweighed by the significantly increased risk factor. Travelling alone is simply out of the question unless you really don't mind risking your life. Police in Adrar may insist that you travel with at least one other vehicle.

You'll find petrol stations and water in Adrar, Reggane, Bordj-Moktar and Gao. The pump at the border is sometimes empty, in which case you may have to wait a few days. You can find out at Adrar or Gao whether there's petrol in Bordj-Moktar or when it should arrive. In any event, this is not a good route for petrol-guzzling vehicles. Bordj-Moktar is also the only place for water between Reggane and Gao.

In Adrar, you must pass through customs (le douane), while in Reggane, you must pass by the police for an inspection of your equipment and documents. You'll also have to pass by the police in Bourem and Gao. If you're heading south, you'll have to pay CFA 1000 per vehicle at the border, so be sure to carry some CFA or French francs.

If you are hitchhiking, expect a good week's wait because there are only about five or six trucks a week that make this run. The best places to catch rides are Gao and Adrar, not Bourem or Reggane. There are regular buses between Adrar and Ghardaia as well as between Gao and Niamey. Between Gao and Mopti (now paved), there are now daily bush taxis but between Gao and Timbuktu, you may have to wait a few days. The turn-off point for Timbuktu is three km north of Bourem but this section is worse than any part of the Reggane-Gao stretch.

Finally, getting petrol in Algeria is no problem, but in Gao and Timbuktu it is sometimes rationed. Don't worry. There's almost always black market gas available; ask the filling station attendant.

What to Take

A complete medical kit is indispensable for motorcyclists and highly recommended for everybody else. Make sure it includes salt tablets to avoid dehydration, ointment for the eyes (for sand irritation), plus skin cream, sun screen and chap stick. Because you won't be able to get quickly to a doctor in an emergency, bring an antibiotic as well. Flagyl (metronidazole) is good for amoebic dysentery but difficult to obtain; tetracycline is another.

From December to February, you'll need warm clothing at night as near freezing temperatures are not unusual. During the rest of the year, except from May to August, it can still get chilly at night, so bring a sweater. You'll need a sleeping bag/pad for the same reason, also sun glasses and a hat. Pick up a cheche, the cotton cloth that Tuaregs wrap around their heads. It can be useful to help prevent dehydration and it keeps the sand out of your eyes. Plastic bags come in very handy since sand gets into everything. If you'll be crossing by motorcycle, consider bringing some facial mist spray. Some motorcyclists swear by it, saying they wouldn't think of crossing again without this short-lived luxury.

If you're driving, don't wait until arriving in Algeria to get 20-litre jerrycans. They cost about 10 times as much in Algeria as they do in Britain. Count on using at least twice as much petrol per km as usual.

Sand ladders (plaques de desensablement) are indispensable. You can buy them along the way, but they become much more expensive south of Ghardaia. You'll also need a compass and a mirror, two good spare tires, a three-tonne hydraulic jack with wide supporting board, and a fire extinguisher – overheated engines have been known to catch on fire.

As for water, count on using at least seven litres per person per day. Obviously, it's best to have an extra supply.

You are permitted to bring in duty-free one bottle of scotch or two bottles of wine per person, plus a carton of cigarettes. Hold firm if customs officials say you cannot bring in liquor. They want it desperately. Alcohol, even Algerian wine, is not sold anywhere in Algeria except at major hotels, and then only to tourists at exorbitant prices. Naturally, the Algerians want this forbidden fruit. So don't be surprised if a border official asks if you have any to sell. The selling price of whiskey (not less then 200 dinar) is the equivalent of a night at the best hotel in town plus a meal or two. Wine, on the other hand, is much less valuable. Cigarettes make such good presents that you should consider bringing some even if you don't smoke.

In London you can get everything you need (sand ladders, jerrycans, shovels with a large blade, tow rope, tyre pumps, puncture repair kits, etc) at *Brownchurch Components* (tel 01-7293606), 308 Hare Row off Cambridge Heath Rd. In Nice, try *Nice Off-Road Centre* (tel 93-821977) at 107 Avenue Cyrille Besset.

Type of Vehicle

What one usually reads and hears is that a four-wheel-drive vehicle is required for crossing the Sahara. This is baloney. I crossed it a 10-year-old Volkswagon van without problem; others have crossed in more inappropriate vehicles. You are likely to see more Peugeot 504s than Land Rovers and you'll undoubtedly see a few Deux Chevaux as well.

This is not to say that a Land-Rover or the equivalent isn't preferable; of course it is, but the advantage is not the four-wheel drive. Four-wheel drive can be worthless in the sand and it's speed, not traction, that will keep you from getting stuck. Once you're stuck, it's the sand ladders that'll get you out. The main advantage of a Land-Rover is its high clearance. Then you won't have to do what we did, which was to straddle the track with the wheels on the centre ridge and one side so as to elevate the car as much as possible.

The point is that just about every

vehicle under the sun has been used at one time or another to cross the desert, and yours will make it too if it's in good condition and you're prepared to do some painstaking driving in the soft spots.

Vehicle Documents

International Drivers Licence Despite what you may have heard, such licences are not required in West Africa except in Nigeria – but get one anyway. While your regular licence is legally sufficient, don't expect the local African policeman to know this. He probably will have never seen a licence the likes of yours and may doubt its validity. Secondly, for those who get into trouble with the law, having two licences will allow you a certain amount of liberty, shall we say, if the police take your international licence and tell you to report somewhere.

In the USA, they are obtainable from any office of the Automobile Association of America (AAA). All you need is two photographs, a drivers licence and US$5; they're issued on the spot. It can all be done by mail if you send them a photocopy of your licence. Write or call the AAA (8111 Gate House Rd, Falls Church, VA 22047, tel 703-3313000). In the UK, both the AA (Automobile Association, Overseas Operations Department, Leicester Square, London WC1) and the RAC (Royal Automobile Club, Box 92, Croydon CR9 6HN, UK, tel 01-6862314) issue them; the cost is negligible.

Insurance Almost no country in Africa will allow you to drive without third-party automobile insurance – a green card (*la carte verte*). Getting insurance in Europe is next to worthless because coverage does not extend below about 20° latitude north (ie only Algeria, Morocco, Tunisia, Libya, Egypt).

Whether or not you have a carte verte, many countries in West Africa (Niger, Mali and Algeria among others) require you to buy insurance locally. You can usually buy it at the border or in the closest major town. In Mali, the minimum 15-days insurance costs CFA 18,000 (US$60). In Algeria, it's cheaper – about 65 dinar for 10 days. Many Europeans travelling on the cheap simply take their regular insurance card along and count on the fact that the border guards won't look in the back to see in which countries the insurance is valid. In Nigeria and some other countries, this assumption usually proves correct.

The following companies/organisations issue insurance: Campbell Irvine Ltd (46 Earls Court Road, London W8 6EJ, tel 01-9379407), Automobile Club de France (6, Place de la Concorde, Paris 8e, tel 01-42653470), and ADAC (11 Konigstrasse, Munich; or Bundersalle 9-30, Berlin 31).

Carnet de Passage A *carnet de passage en douane* allows you to bring a car into a country without paying the normal customs duty or lodging a deposit with customs. It is intended to ensure that you don't sell your vehicle en route without paying duty. If the vehicle is not exported when you leave, the country can obtain payment of the duty from the issuing organisation – and eventually you.

Carnets are issued by automobile associations in most countries (RAC and AA in Britain, AAA in the USA, ADAC in Germany). All of them demand a guarantee. There are two types – bank guarantees and insurance company guarantees. For a bank guarantee, you must put up collateral equal to the estimated amount of the duty. The cost is frequently prohibitive. In Australia, for example, the AAA requires a bank guarantee equal to 300% of the value of the vehicle!

Insurance companies, on the other hand, demand much less up-front money. They will issue a bond upon payment of a refundable premium equal to a small percentage of the estimated amount of the duty. If the company must pay on a claim, it has the right to collect the same from you. In Britain, the AA uses Alexander Howden Ltd (22 Billiter St, London EC3M 2SA); their premium is only 3%. A bond takes about a week to get.

There was a time when a carnet posed a major problem for travellers in West Africa. Those days have passed. While Nigeria and many other countries in Africa require a carnet, Algeria, Morocco, Tunisia, Niger, Mali and the Ivory Coast do not. In Benin and Togo, they can be purchased at the border. In Senegal, they are no longer required for stays of up to 30 days. (The customs office will issue you a free *passavant de douane* valid for 30 days.) This means that you can drive from Europe to the coast of West Africa (but not Nigeria) without getting one beforehand, regardless of which route across the Sahara you choose. It's hard to find a motorcyclist these days who obtained such a carnet before leaving Europe.

Selling Vehicles
Most new or used automobiles can be sold in Africa for about the same price or a little more than in Europe. Previously, they could be sold for a nice profit; those days have long since passed. If you'll be staying awhile in West Africa, it makes sense to bring your own vehicle. The paperwork is less in Togo and Benin, making them the most attractive places to sell automobiles, followed by the Ivory Coast and Senegal. In Niger, temporarily imported vehicles cannot be sold unless the owner has resided there at least two months. Left-hand drive Peugeot 504s and non-diesel Mercedes 280S are the easiest to sell. As for large motorcycles, Abidjan and Dakar are the best markets.

You could also ship your vehicle to/from Europe. Dakar and Abidjan are the best ports. Travellers shipping vehicles on the Swiss *Nautilus line* have reported satisfaction with the service.

Mediterranean Ferries
From France From Marseilles, *Société Nationale Maritime Corse-Méditerranée* (SNCM) and *Compagnie Tunisienne de Navigation* (CTN) (Marseilles only) offer

ferry connections to Tunis, Algiers and Oran. From Sete, SNCM and *Compagnie Nationale Algerienne de Navigation* (CNAN) have ferries to Algiers, Oran and Tangiers.

Since Marseilles and Sete are the two most popular points of departure, getting a reservation for an automobile during the summer is difficult. You can reserve by calling SNCM (Paris tel 01-42666019/6798; Brussels tel 02-2194788; Marseilles tel 91-919220; Sete tel 67-747055). Their agent in Britain is P & O Ferries (Arundel Towers, Portland Terrace, Southampton SO9 4AE). If you use an agent, book at least several weeks in advance. Otherwise, on arrival you may find that they have no knowledge of your reservation.

The journey takes 1½ days. The cost for a vehicle one-way is expensive (there are reductions for roundtrip fares), averaging about 1500 FF regardless of which route you take. The exact cost depends on the length of the vehicle and the season (about 20% more expensive during the summer). These boats are not like the average ferry but are one-class tourist ships with comfortable accommodation, superb meals and nightly entertainment. For travellers, the price is about 700 to 1200 FF. There are reduced rates for students and young people.

From Italy CTN offers service from Genoa to Tunis for about half the price of Marseilles to Tunis. It is represented in Europe by SNCM. The Italian company *Tirrenia* offers service to Tunis from Genoa, Naples, and Sicily (Palermo and Trapani). You can take a slow train from Naples to Sicily. There are no reductions for roundtrip fares, but they do offer reduced rates for students in the off season. Tirrenia is represented by CIT (Paris tel 01-45009950; Brussels tel 02-5138599; Geneva tel 315750; Amsterdam tel 020-241677). Their tourist ships are similar in quality to those of SNCM.

From Spain In Spain, you can cross the Mediterranean from one of three ports: Algerciras (southern tip of Spain), Alicante and Malaga. Ferries from Algerciras go to Morocco (Tangiers and Ceuta), while those from Alicante and Malaga go to Melilla (northern Morocco). Algerciras-Ceuta is the cheapest route (about 60/250 FF per person/vehicle) and serviced six days a week, several times daily. The trip takes only 90 minutes, but during the summer you have have to queue for many hours. Algerciras-Tangiers costs about 50% more, and there are half as many crossings a week. Alicante-Melilla (or Malaga-Melilla) is over twice as expensive as Algerciras-Ceuta and takes eight hours. But you can cross every day except Sunday, and you'll save petrol and about 1000 km of driving to Algeria.

There are also connections between Alicante and Oran/Algiers, but they are less frequent (several times a week to Algiers; once a week to Oran in the summer). For more information, call Melia in Paris (tel 01-47427059). Both Melilla and Ceuta are free ports. If you will have significant purchases to make (petrol, alcohol, cigarettes, etc), it may be worth your while to go via one or the other.

TRAVELLING THROUGH ALGERIA
Visas
Algerian visas are not required for citizens

of Denmark, Finland, Ireland, Italy, Norway, Spain, Sweden, Switzerland and the UK. If you travel from south to north through Algeria, you can get a visa at the Algerian Embassy in Bamako (Mali) or Niamey (Niger). Going north-south, you can get one at the airport in Algiers or at the Algerian consulate in Tunis or the UAE embassy in Rabat (Morocco). In Algiers, you can get visas to Niger and Mali within 24 hours, frequently the same day if you go early. They are also available in Tam. When going south to Niger, you no longer need to get an exit visa from the police in Tam; they'll give it to you at the border.

Money
US$1 = 5.43 dinar
£1 = 10.15 dinar

The official currency is the dinar. You must buy 1000 dinar (US$220) at the border regardless of how long you stay. This can make a short trip through Algeria very expensive. Don't expect to be able to reconvert dinar into hard currency at the border. Students used to be exempt, but there are no longer any exceptions. Some travellers coming from Morocco have avoided this requirement by crossing the border at Figuig. There's no place to change money, so the police will give you a currency form and tell you to change money at the nearest bank.

You are allowed to bring only 50 dinar into Algeria. There is a substantial black market that brings as much as three times the official rate (four times in Morocco). Most travellers are only passing through and therefore the compulsory 1000 dinars is usually enough. Bank hours are Saturday to Wednesday 9 am to 3 pm and Thursday 9 am to 12 noon. Be sure to keep every bank receipt, otherwise you'll have serious problems at the border when leaving. If you must change money on Friday, go to the most deluxe hotel in town; those run by the government are supposed to change money even for non-guests.

Hassles
Algeria sometimes gets a bad press. The problem is not with the ordinary citizens but the police and border officials. How you dress and act may make a difference with both police and ordinary citizens. Women, in particular, face difficulties. From the age of 12, women are virtually locked up, never to appear in public again without a veil. Thus western women are considered to be 'loose'. Just because a woman is with her husband doesn't mean she won't be approached. Conservative dress will help. Also, unmarried couples are sometimes not allowed to take the same room at hotels.

Algiers (El Djezair)
The place to head for in Algiers is the Kasbah, an old section of town with narrow winding streets. The sights to see are the old fortress (good view of the city), the Grand Mosque, the Mosque des Ketchaoua, the palace Dar Hassan Pacha, and the Musée des Arts et Traditions Populaires.

As for other areas of the city, the Musée des Beaux-Arts in the Quartier d'el Anasser section of town has one of the finest collection of paintings and sculptures in Africa. Also not to be missed in the town centre is the Musée du Bardo, a 17th century villa with an extensive collection of musical instruments, clothing and jewellery.

Places to Stay Getting a hotel room in Algiers is frequently quite difficult. Those on the cheap frequently stay at the lowest grade hotels (*dortoirs*) or at the Turkish bath houses (*hammams*) which are found in almost every town in Algeria. Your bed at a bath house will be a mattress on the floor and the cost is usually no more than D7 a night. Women are frequently not allowed. There are quite a few in the centre of town, especially around the train station, but finding one that's not full is no easy task.

You can find more decent hotels in the

D60 to D75 range. *Rose*, 3 Rue Debbih Cherif, is downtown and costs about D75 for a double. *Hôtel Regina*, near the main post office on the same street as the Hôtel de l'Angleterre, costs about the same. It's comfortable and fairly clean, with breakfast included in the price. *Hôtel de Geneve* (20, Rue Abane Ramdane) is similar and also recommended. *Grand des Étrangers* (1, Rue Ali Boumenjel, Place Port Said) has large rooms with sink and toilet and offers breakfast. Cheaper still are the *Hôtel des Bains de Chatres*, up the hill from Place Port Said, and *Hôtel Central Tourist* (9, Rue Abane Ramdane), near Hôtel de Geneve. The latter is tolerably clean but has no showers.

Among the medium priced hotels, the *Angleterre*, 11 Boulevard Ben Boulaid, is a good buy; consequently, getting a room can be difficult. Three others are the *Djemila Palace* (tel 633413) Rue Bettignies; *Hôtel Terminus* (tel 636177) Rue Ksentini; and *Hôtel Michelet* (tel 633413) Rue Bounaffa.

Hôtel Aurassi (tel 64855), with rooms for about D200, is the city's best. It's a 10-minute drive from downtown overlooking the Bay of Algiers. Two other hotels in the same price range are the four-star *St George* (tel 665300), 10 minutes from downtown, and *Hôtel Aletti* (tel 635040/6) on the promenade near the commercial centre.

Ghardaia

The most interesting oasis town on the entire route if not all of Algeria, Ghardaia deserves exploration. It is really five separate hill towns, the largest being Ghardaia, and is inhabited primarily by a somewhat pious Muslim sect known as the Mozabites.

As for things to see, several of the mosques are open to visitors except on Friday, and include the mosques in El Atteuf and Melika (two of the five towns) but not in Beni Isguen. One of the more interesting things to do is to walk down the clean streets of Ghardaia, especially in the market area and commercial centre. You might also check out the artisanat, a fairly expensive place to buy artisan goods but worth a look. Finally, there's an interesting auction at 5 pm in Beni Isguen, the holy town, but get there on time because it doesn't last long.

Places to Stay & Eat *Camping Souleila* at the southern entrance of town is popular and convenient, although expensive at D20 per person, D15 for a site and D10 for a car. It is pleasant, shaded and privately operated.

For cheap hotels, about D50 a double, try the *Hôtel 'Les Mille et Une Nuits'*, facing Cinema l'Étoile. It has clean rooms and a good restaurant. Others in the same price range are the *Hôtel du Carrefour*, which is fairly quiet, and the *Le Napht*, in the centre of town. The latter is clean, friendly and has a decent restaurant. The cheapest of all may be *Maison de Jeunesse*, on the main street below the Transatlantique. It costs D15, but apparently you can only stay there one night. An alternative is the *Hammam*, for men only, near the SNTV bus station.

The city's top hotel may now be the new 600-room *Hôtel du M'Zab* on the northern edge of town. Near the centre of town, *Les Rostemides* costs about D200 and has a pool. The *Transatlantique*, also near the centre, is a more interesting and pleasant hotel even though less deluxe. It has a pool and a garden, and the suite for four is reasonably priced.

Two inexpensive restaurants are the *L'Étoile* opposite the Mille et Une Nuits and *Restaurant des Voyageurs*. The latter offers a moderate selection.

El Golea

Surrounded by vast palm groves and gardens which spread out at the base of the Grand Erg Occidental sand sea, El Golea is one of the most beautiful oasis towns in Algeria. The gardens contain not just palm trees but also fruit trees, vegetables and even flowers. If you're there at the right time, you'll even see roses. A few km out of town two km off the paved road to In Salah there's a salt lake where you might see some birds if you're there at the right time of year. If you'd like to pick up a rug, bedspread, or items made from camel skin, the Artisanat in El Golea is not a bad place to shop. Prices are fairly steep. If you'll be going to Tunisia or Morocco, its better to wait, but of course the items for sale won't be the same.

Places to Stay & Eat There are two camping spots. The *Camping* at the northern entrance to town opposite the SNTL parking lot is much more popular than the government-run campsite south of town. The management is very hospitable and there are showers and drinkable water. It's also a good place for hitchhikers to look for rides.

The air-con Saharan-style *El Boustan*, is expensive but worth a visit even if you don't stay there. On occasion, they will change your money if you are not a guest. The location in the palm groves with a pool and a view of the old Ksar is perfect.

As for restaurants, the *Restaurant de l'Oasis* is inexpensive and recommended. *Le Restaurant des Amis* is even less expensive but also good. *Café du Peuple*, two blocks from the Tademait, is the best breakfast spot in town.

In Salah

A less interesting oasis town than the others, In Salah is distinguished by its houses of red mud and is one of the hottest towns in the Sahara. One of the more interesting things to see is the Palmerie d'El Barka, a pleasant palm grove with petrified wood.

Places to Stay & Eat *Camping Tidkelt* is close to town, and is clean with very basic facilities. *Hôtel Tidikelt*, near the oasis, is new and the only hotel in town, with air-con and a pool. As for restaurants, the best is the *Restaurant du Carrefour*, near the market with four-course meals. *L'An 2000* facing the commissariat prepares good inexpensive meals.

Tamanrasset (Tamenghest)

Tam is geographically the centre of the Sahara and the starting point for the major desert crossing to Niger and trips to the Hoggar Mountains – perhaps Algeria's major tourist attraction. If you're lucky enough to be there between December 25 and January 10, you can witness the region's biggest festival which includes camel races and dancing. The open air market is where you'll find the Tuareg nomads who dominate this area of the desert.

The main attraction near Tam is the lunar-like Hoggar Massif. It averages about 2500 metres in altitude, with Mt Le Tahat reaching 2918 metres. Ancient volcanic upheavals created this unearthly lunar maze of metallic-coloured mountains, jagged and curved, pointed and arched, the most bizarre of all being the Atakor. It has here that the science fiction movie 'Dune' was filmed.

The third highest summit of the Atakor is the 'Assekrem', reaching over 2700 metres. Father Charles de Foucauld, the French monk and mystic, chose this site in 1906 for his Hermitage, where he devoted the remaining five years of his life to studying the Tuaregs. A 10- to 30-minute walk up the mountain from the parking lot, the Hermitage is a fantastic place for hiking, with one of the most unforgettable sunrises and sunsets in the entire Sahara. Don't miss it. You'll find a 30-bed refuge there for sleeping. Since it's 2700 metres above sea level, be prepared for sub-freezing temperatures. The 6.15 am mass alone is worth the trip.

The Hermitage is only 84 km from Tam, but a trip there takes three hours due to boulders in the road. Because of the boulders, don't attempt it without a high clearance vehicle. A guide is not necessary, but some may prefer one. Guides and Land-Rovers are available from *Agence*

Akar Akar on the main drag, *Agence Mero-N'Man* (tel 734032) next door, and at the camping ground. Ask them about renting camels. The hard part is usually finding enough people to keep the price down. Count on paying about US$200 a day for a Land-Rover. The man to talk to is Mokhtar, the owner of Akar Akar and Tam's most renowned citizen; he also manages Camping Les Zeribas.

If you're having car trouble, try Rikab Mohammed Rabah, downtown across from the bookshop on the road leading south towards Hôtel Tahat. If you want to fly to Algiers, you'll have to change the price of the flight on the currency declaration form, in addition to the 1000 dinars you changed at the border!

Places to Stay & Eat The best camping facilities are at *Camping Les Zeribas*, on the southern end of town, 300 metres south of Hôtel Tahat. You can stay in a rustic bungalow (D40 per person) or camp for D20 per person plus D10 for a car. The facilities are very good, including showers (running water 8 to 10 am, 4 to 7 pm only) and a washing area. Some people prefer

La Source, a camping spot 15 km northeast of town, or camping on their own in the desert, which is prohibited within 10 km of town.

Another possibility is to stay overnight at the waterfalls in Tameskret, 48 km east of Tam off the *piste* to Tarhaouhaout. You'll need a guide to find them.

Hôtel Tahat (tel 734474, telex 53646) is expensive at D170 for a double. It's on the southern end of town on the road towards Adriane and usually full by mid-afternoon. *Hôtel Tin Hinane*, downtown on the main drag (Avenue Emir Abdel Kader), is a quaint, run-down hotel with an acceptable restaurant. There's a cheap *Hammam* as well.

Tam now has 10 or more restaurants that are quite cheap even at official exchange rates. For local cuisine and cheap prices, you could try the well-known *Café-Restaurant de la Paix*. *Tassili*, on the main drag, and *Restaurant Tropique* are two more. Around the corner from Tropique you'll find a small café popular with hitchhikers and Tam's younger set.

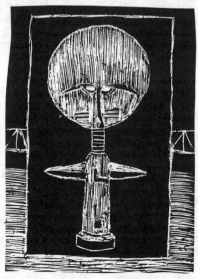

Getting Around

AIR
Confirming Reservations
You must reconfirm your reservation in person before the flight, otherwise you won't have a reserved seat even if the ticket says 'OK'. Telephone reconfirmations are never accepted because your ticket must be stamped. The regulations say to reconfirm within 72 hours of the flight – that means not later than 72 hours. You can usually reconfirm up to a week in advance, sometimes more. If you reconfirm within less than 72 hours, you will more than likely find that your reservation is still valid. Even the day of the flight is usually not too late unless the flight is full, in which case your reservation may be cancelled. If someone will reconfirm for you, don't forget that they'll need your ticket. Flight schedules change frequently so maybe it's just as well that tickets must be reconfirmed.

If you're put on the waiting list, don't panic. African airlines usually don't overbook, so your chances of getting on are frequently good. It's usually not how far up the waiting list you are that counts, but who gets to the check-in counter first. The standard check-in time is two hours before flight departure; get there even earlier if you're on the waiting list. The check-in line will probably resemble a rugby scrum, so look immediately for a young man (a 'friend') who'll assist you – it's worth every cent.

African Airlines
African airlines have been described by readers of the *African Economic Digest* as frightening, unreliable, dangerous, unpleasant, unpredictable, uncaring, overbooked, impertinent and dirty. Service varies greatly even with the same airline. Sometimes it is excellent. Take Ghana Airways from Abidjan westward and it'll be half full with very good service; take the same airline from Abidjan to Accra and you may think you're on a cattle car. There's some correlation between service and safety, but not always. The real concern is the quality of the maintenance operations. Foreign pilots operating in Africa say it varies greatly. Most of the airlines are serviced routinely in Europe and many have contracts with foreign airlines which provide the pilots and maintenance personnel. There is, then, an element of control.

So despite the horror stories you may hear, in general you need not worry about flying on African airlines. There's no reason, however, not to try taking one of the better airlines, but in many instances there is no choice. If the American ambassador wants to get from Bissau to Dakar, he or she will take the local airline – and so will you. Don't be terribly surprised if, on occasion, you have to wait at the airport a half day or so (never go to the airport without a good book and several magazines), or during the flight they're doing things to keep the door from coming off, or the luggage is stuffed in the back prohibiting an emergency exit. These things happen every now and then. If it's any comfort, many of the pilots are experienced European or well-trained African pilots. When you do have a choice, the list of airlines below in descending order of quality (safety and service) is intended to give you some basis for choosing:

1 *Ethiopian Airlines, Air Afrique, Air Gabon* and *Cameroon Airlines* – the order in which the readers of *Africa Economic Digest* in 1985 rated the African airlines serving West Africa.
2 *Air Mauritanie, TACV* (Cape Verde) and *Air Ivoire* seem to have the best reputation of the airlines offering primarily in-country service.
3 *Ghana Airways* and *Nigeria Airways*. Between these two, Ghana Airways (seemingly improving every day) wins hands down in

terms of service. Nigeria Airways' service is good only within Nigeria. On its inter-Africa routes, Nigeria Airways has one of the worst reputations of any airline in West Africa. It's the type of airline you board without knowing whether there's really a seat for you. In terms of safety, however, Ghana Airways and Nigeria Airways seem to be on an equal footing and superior to those in category four. There have been, apparently, few or no accidents on either airline – no proof, however, that their maintenance operations are adequate.

4 All other African airlines operating in West Africa are included here except for the three in category five below. Foreigners take these airlines all the time, especially when there's no alternative. If it's any comfort, most are flown by European pilots.

5 *Air Mali* (always on the verge of bankruptcy) and *Air Liberia* have the worst reputations. An Air Mali plane crashed outside Timbuktu in 1985, confirming many people's suspicion that it is one of the worst airlines in Africa. Air Liberia has just returned from bankruptcy. Both should be avoided.

Changing Tickets

Tickets written by Nigeria Airways and Ghana Airways are not accepted by other airlines unless written outside Africa, ie paid for in hard currency. If you buy a ticket on Nigeria Airways in Dakar, for example, and want it endorsed to another airlines, keep dreaming.

Hassles at the Airport

For all too many travellers, the most harrowing experiences are at the airport. Lagos airport has the worst reputation by far. Checking in can be a nightmare. You don't have to have been in Saigon the day it fell to know what it was like getting on the last plane out. In Africa it's like that on every flight. It's rare that the good guy who respects the queue doesn't get on the plane, but it's just frequent enough to cause many people, Africans and foreigners alike, to lose their civility.

There is a way out of this, however. Find one of the enterprising young men who makes a living by getting people checked in. They rarely rip you off. If they take your baggage, they're not going to run away because they know they'll be nabbed by the police the next time they show up for 'work'. Which doesn't mean you should go have a *pastis* (a popular drink in West Africa) while they perform their magic. The point is that they are there to earn an honest living – even if they give you the line that they're only being your friend. It will only cost you a dollar or two, more when you don't have a confirmed seat, and don't be surprised if the guy behind the counter insists you show your appreciation to him as well. So don't worry about these guys; it's the taxi drivers who are much more likely to rip you off.

All of the above is usually worse in the case of big airports such as Lagos or Accra, but it can happen in the smaller ones as well. Sometimes you have no choice but to get in there and fight your way to the counter; just remember that if you choose not to, you'll still probably get on. One of the advantages of being on a tour is that you avoid this hassle. You lose some of what makes a trip to West Africa truly an adventure, but a lot of people would just as soon not make it too much of an adventure.

Airport Tax

In about half the countries in West Africa, the airport tax is included in the ticket price. In the others, the tax is levied at the airport when you're leaving. If you're not prepared, you may have to cash a US$50 bill to pay a US$10 tax.

Costs of Flying

Flying in Africa is not cheap because distances are fairly long (Dakar to Abidjan, for example, is half way across the USA), and you can't get anything cheaper than the roundtrip excursion fare (two-thirds the standard economy fare). To get this special roundtrip fare, you must stay at least seven days. But take a four-day trip from, say, Lomé to Niamey or Abidjan to Bamako (about 1000 km) and you'll pay the full economy fare both ways (about US$300 roundtrip). Occasionally, you can get a cheaper fare with smaller airlines such as Air Ivoire and Air Burkina.

BUSH TAXIS *(taxis de brousse)*

You may think that bush taxis are those beat-up old vehicles that take three hours to fill up and are packed like sardines, with an accident rate you'd just as soon not know about. The answer is yes, but not for all bush taxis. There are three classes of overland transport that could come under the title 'bush taxi':

Peugeot 504 Station Wagons These cars, all of them assembled in Nigeria, are quite comfortable when relatively new and not packed like sardines (more than eight including driver). Usually, all it takes to change a nightmare to a pleasant ride is to buy an extra seat. Even then, the price is reasonable. The average cost of a seat in a bush taxi throughout the CFA zone is only US$3 to US$4 per 100 km. The 1200-km trip from Bamako (Mali) to Abidjan (Ivory Coast), for instance, is CFA 14,000 (US$46).

There's usually some correlation between the quality of the vehicles and the wealth of the country. Comparing bush taxis servicing Lagos-Kano (Nigeria) and Bamako-Mopti (Mali), for example, is like equating diamonds and glass. The latter are generally in terrible condition; the former may be relatively new. So just because it's a bush taxi doesn't mean the trip will be unbearable.

It's also not true that the waiting time is always long. For well-travelled routes such as Dakar-Banjul, Abidjan-Bouake, Lomé-Accra and Lomé-Cotonou, the waiting time is typically no more than 15 to 45 minutes. In Nigeria, the average waiting time is more like five minutes. On the other hand, going from Bamako to Ouagadougou could involve a half day's wait or more, especially if you arrive at the wrong time. In most cases, 6.30 to 8.30 am is the best time to catch bush taxis.

Bush taxis are almost always located at a bush taxi station *(gare routière)*. Just remember that most major cities have several, one for each major road leading out of town.

Bush taxis, however, can be quite dangerous. The better the roads, the more the danger. That's because it allows the drivers to drive like maniacs, which they all do. Don't sit there like most people with your eyes shut; pay him extra to go more slowly or say you have a heart problem. For the adventurous and those on-the-cheap, bush taxis are the only way to travel. Travellers on higher budgets should not write them off. If a well-driven route is chosen, such as Dakar-Banjul, chances are that the experience will produce a few good stories to tell back home and some cherished memories.

If you want to charter a Peugeot all to yourself, the price is easy to calculate if all you're doing is going from A to B and back. Take the price of one seat and multiply it by the number of available seats and then do the same for the return portion. Don't expect to pay a cent less just because you're saving him the time and hassle of looking for other passengers – time is not money in Africa.

Small buses At many bush taxi parks, you may find no Peugeot 504s, but only small buses (or both). Slightly less expensive, they are not necessarily less comfortable, particularly if the Peugeots are packed with four people on the second seat. The big disadvantage is that they are always a little slower and have longer waits at the numerous police checks because of the larger number of passengers to search.

Pick-ups *(bâches)* With wooden seats down the sides, covered pick-ups are definitely second-class, but sometimes the only kind of bush taxi available. These trucks are invariably stuffed with, not only people, but probably a few chickens as well, and your feet may be higher than your waist from resting on a sack of millet. The ride is guaranteed to be unpleasant unless you and your companions adopt the African attitude, in which case each time your head hits the roof as the truck descends into yet another big pothole, a roar of laughter will ring forth instead of a cry of sympathy. There's nothing like African humour to change an otherwise miserable trip into a tolerable, even enjoyable experience.

Trucks While not falling under the general title of bush taxi, in a few instances the only thing available is a truck stuffed with what at first glance you may think is cattle. Even unflappable, old African hands are taken back by the fact that until 1986, this was the only mode of overland transportation offered on a regular basis between two neighbouring Sahelian capitals, Niamey and Ouagadougou. Fortunately, a recent World Bank project has improved not only the condition of the road but, as a side effect, the sub-human transportation system as well. The chapters on the individual countries give the details.

BUS

Buses are generally not as popular as bush taxis because they are usually slower. Many don't have fixed schedules, in which case the waiting time is longer as well. There are some exceptions, however, the most notable being Ghana, where the state transportation system is top notch, has a set schedule, connects all the major towns and is dirt cheap. The problem is that it is so popular that getting a bus is frequently difficult. Niger is another country with a good bus system. Buses there are as fast as bush taxis and more comfortable. Consequently, to get a seat you must invariably reserve a day or two in advance, sometimes more.

In Nigeria, where everyone seems to be in a rush, buses are slower than bush taxis but much faster than the trains and, hence, are an excellent way of travelling

long distances at night. The Ivory Coast also has some modern comfortable buses with fixed schedules but, unlike Ghana, serve only the major cities. In Burkina Faso, the buses are far from luxurious but they are the cheapest in West Africa, part of the government's socialist policies, and serve all the major towns. You don't have to reserve in advance but you do have to get to the station several hours before departure.

The only other countries you might take buses are Sierra Leone, where they are in bad shape but frequently the only alternative, and Cape Verde, where bush taxis don't exist. Otherwise, count on using one type or another of bush taxi.

As for city buses, the only cities where you'll find well-developed systems are Abidjan and Dakar. In Freetown and Banjul, there are frequent buses connecting downtown with the suburbs. In most other cities, the shared taxi system takes the place of buses.

TRAINS

Over half the countries in West Africa have trains and many are fairly decent. The train cars in Senegal and Mali are all European-made and new (since 1980) with sleeping cars. Some of the cars on the Ivory Coast-Burkina Faso line are just as new, and those in Nigeria and Ghana are of the same quality but older. All but the last have air-con, but whether it's working is something else. My experience is that the air con on most of these trains is more likely to be working than not, although sometimes it's not very noticeable.

On the Gazelle connecting Abidjan and Ouagadougou, you'll be served a decent steak & frites with wine on a white tablecloth, and may even be offered a choice of aperitifs and after-dinner drinks. Just be prepared for a bumpy ride in the Bobo-Ouagadougou section; if you doze off, you may dream you're on a horse.

On both the Dakar-Bamako and Abidjan-Ouagadougou runs, the air-con sleeping cars are limited to two people, giving you a bit of privacy. On the others, the chances are that the 1st class sleeping cars won't be filled, so that you'll have privacy anyway. In Nigeria the trains are a little older but still offer air-con, meals and sleepers. Just be prepared for a later arrival than the schedule indicates.

The real adventure seekers could consider taking a train in one of the four countries where the trains are surely among the world's worst. Take the 2nd-class Conakry-Kankan (Guinea) train, and you may be the first non-African to board since independence. Or take some wine cooler along on the seven-hour train ride in Togo – arriving on time only spoils the party.

Below is a summary of the possibilities;

Best Trains
1 Ivory Coast-Burkina Faso (Abidjan-Ouagadougou) 23 hours
2 Senegal-Mali (Dakar-Bamako) 30 hours
3 Nigeria (Lagos-Kano and Port Harcourt-Maiduguri) both 34 hours

Other Trains
1 Ghana (Accra-Kumasi and Kumasi-Takoradi)
2 Togo (Lomé-K'Palimé and Lomé-Blitta) seven and eight hours
3 Benin (Cotonou-Parakou) nine hours
4 Guinea (Conakry-Kankan) 24 hours

DRIVING

If you'll be travelling a lot by road, the location of the principal routes is a major consideration. Some dirt roads are all-weather while others are not and you can't necessarily tell this from the Michelin road map.

As for travelling times, the major routes/times are given below. A 'day' means seven to 10 hours driving time in a private vehicle, eight to 14 hours in a bush taxi.

Dakar to: Nouakchott (one day), Banjul (one short day), Casamance (one day), Bamako (four to five days, or 30 hours on the train – you can take a vehicle), Conakry (three to four days, four to five by bush taxi), Bissau (two days, three by bush taxi).

Abidjan to: Monrovia (two days), Freetown (four days), Bamako (two days), Ouagadougou (two days, 24 hours by train), Accra (one long day), Cotonou (two days).

Ouagadougou to: Bamako (one long day, two by taxi), Mopti (two days), Lomé (two days), Niamey (one day, two by taxi), Accra (two days, two to three by taxi/bus)

Niamey to: Agadez (one to 1½ days), Gao (one to 1½ days, same by bus), Ndjamena (one week), Kano (one to 1½ days)

Lagos to: Kano (two days, 16 hours by taxi), Enugu (one day).

TAXIS

Taxis at the Airport

Only in Dakar and Abidjan do taxis have meters (*compteurs*). For all others, either bargaining is required (especially the bigger cities), or you'll be given the legally fixed rate which is not negotiable. Typical fares are given in the country chapters. Fares do not go up annually, so be a little suspicious if the quoted price is much higher. If you can't speak French, be content if you pay no more than a 25% premium. The price always includes the luggage unless you have a particularly bulky item. Also, fares invariably go up sometime between 9 pm and midnight; the country chapters specify the time. Don't be surprised if the driver tells you an earlier hour.

Do not expect that bargaining is always required with taxis. The fare at most airports into town is fixed by law. Not all the drivers received their training in New York – many are honest and will quote you the correct fare. The problem is how to tell whether the quoted fare is the correct one. The wise will ask an airport official before throwing themselves to the wolves.

Warning: Drivers tend to be sleepy from 18-hour workdays and may race along at hair-raising speeds, particularly in the big cities. The sheep will say nothing, while the rest will raise their voices to intolerable levels – which language makes no difference.

Taxis Downtown

Except for metered taxis in Dakar and Abidjan, prices are usually fixed by law but in reality are sometimes negotiable. The zone system operates, only it's never clear where they begin and end. The locals always know. Frequently, the quoted price will be the correct one. Keep in mind that there are two bases for calculating taxi fares – one when you hop in a cab with other people going in the same direction, and another when you 'charter' (as they frequently say in English-speaking Africa) one to yourself. (In French-speaking countries, the word *déplacement* is sometimes used.)

From the hotels, the rate is always the charter rate, plus there's usually a 50 to 100% premium on top of that to cover their waiting time. When you hail a cab on the streets downtown, it's not always easy to know which rate you're being offered. In Monrovia (Liberia), unless you're being picked up at a hotel or wearing a Hawaiian shirt, they almost never quote the more expensive charter fare. In Banjul (The Gambia), on the other hand, the taxi drivers assume that if you can afford a plane from London and two weeks on the beach, you can surely afford the charter rate. That's because there are hordes of tourists in Banjul and hardly any in Monrovia. In most cities, it's not so cut and dried and you'll have to discuss the rate before getting in.

As for the ease of finding taxis, in Abidjan, Dakar and Monrovia they're thicker than flies. In other cities it's more like looking for shooting stars. In the latter, there will usually be locations (*taxi gares*) where taxis wait for people wanting a charter, and/or there will be certain streets which are heavily travelled by taxis. Stand a block away and you may find yourself losing your cool.

The major hotel in town is invariably a place to pick up a taxi, sometimes by phoning. The problem is that it may take an exhaustive walk to get there. So maybe you should consider looking for a young kid who'd like to earn some pocket money finding you one. All too many visitors to Africa are so intimidated by Africans or the language barrier that they don't make use of people willing at every step of the way to make your stay much more pleasant – at a cost of less than the price of a doughnut. And you don't have to speak French to say 'taxi' to a young kid – he'll usually get the message.

CAR RENTAL

There are car rental agencies in almost every capital city. In all but four or five countries, all you have to do is go to the city's major hotel to find one. There is little difference in price between car rental agencies except in large cities where there may be a number of small operators.

If the small operators charge less, it's usually because the vehicles are older and sometimes not well maintained. While you can sometimes get a good deal, the problem is that you can never be sure about the car's condition. If you can't afford to be stuck in the middle of nowhere with a broken down vehicle, stick with Hertz, Avis and Eurocar. As in the USA and Europe, you will usually need to have a credit card to guarantee payment, or put down a sizeable deposit. Nowhere in West Africa may you take a rental car across a border or leave it in another city.

Hertz, Eurocar and Avis are all well represented in West Africa, but they are not the only ones. Avis, Hertz and Eurocar brochures sometimes fail to include some of their more obscure representatives. Their locations are listed under each country.

Before you rent a car consider whether you might not be better off hiring a taxi by the day. If your rental car breaks down, it's your problem instead of the taxi driver's and if you don't speak French and you're in a French-speaking country, the headache will be greater. You may, for instance, find yourself stuck on the road after getting the wrong type of gas. Also the chances of finding some remote spot or the African nightclub that you're looking for may be slim – especially if you don't speak French. More importantly, if you get a friendly driver, chances are he'll show you some things you'd never otherwise see – maybe his home, for example.

For those on a limited budget, the major consideration will be the cost. The following table compares rental cars (fairly uniform throughout West Africa) with all-day taxis (highly negotiable, anywhere from CFA 8000 to CFA 15,000 plus gas – if you bargain well):

	Renault 12 Berline	Taxi
100 km	CFA 29,300	CFA 16,500
200 km	CFA 42,450	CFA 19,750
300 km	CFA 55,600	CFA 23,000

These prices in Niger include all costs, such as estimated gas usage, insurance, driver (required in Niger and other countries outside the capital city), etc.

The major problem with hiring taxis by the day is that many taxi drivers have never done it before and may not understand your terms, ie you will pay for the petrol separately. If you negotiate a price including petrol, you'll be asking for trouble. He'll reduce his speed to a slow trot and complain incessantly every time you take even the most minor detour. His attitude will ruin your trip, no joke. Getting him to agree to a fixed rate plus petrol is conceptually easy for him to understand and requires no estimate of petrol consumption. If you change your itinerary, it won't matter to him because you're the one paying for the petrol. Still, it's not always easy to negotiate because he may not speak English or French very well. The solution is to go to the nearest major hotel and explain to the doorman what you want and then have him explain it to the driver. Once this is settled, your only other problem is calculating the petrol usage. If his petrol meter is not working, you're asking for an argument at the end of the day. Get another driver!

The second major problem with hiring a taxi is that it is more likely to break down than a rental car. More than one weekend trip has been ruined when the taxi broke down miles out of the capital city and couldn't be quickly repaired – and no refund. The lesson is to inspect the car beforehand; if you hear a lot of rattling, choose another.

Benin

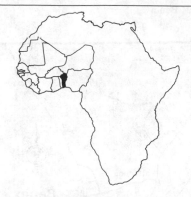

Benin has one of the hottest tourist attractions in all of West Africa – Ganvié – a fishing village built on stilts in the middle of a lagoon. It's only a 25-minute drive from downtown Cotonou to the launching point where you'll find canoeists ready to take you around the lake, and over to this town of 12,000 inhabitants. Half the tourists to Togo make a side trip to Benin just to visit Ganvié. There is a great contrast between Ganvié and Cotonou – Ganvié is remarkable, Cotonou is not. Indeed, Cotonou's lethargy may be more noticeable than Ganvié's uniqueness, because many leave Benin unimpressed.

Many travellers, however, don't make it into the countryside, which is a big mistake. The changes under the leftist government are hardly as pervasive as, say, those in Cuba. In the rural areas, life in some respects goes on unchanged. Voodoo, which has its origins in Benin and eastern Togo, still plays a prominent role, as it does in Haiti. Even today, fetishism is prevalent. You'll get a sense of this in Ouidah, the old slave trading centre along the coast, and Abomey, the centre of the Kingdom of Dahomey, one of the greatest empires in West Africa. The history of the king's palace, once the largest in West Africa and now a museum, is unique in that only women were used to protect the king. Up north, you can visit one of the better game parks in West Africa and, nearby, the fascinating castle-like settlements of the Somba, some of whom still don't find much use for clothes. In short, except for the capital city, Benin has more to offer in some ways than its ever-popular neighbour, Togo.

HISTORY

Benin is a small obscure country, but when it does something, it does it in a big way. The people in this area established one of the largest slave trading operations in West Africa and became one of the most powerful kingdoms. Since independence, they have had the second highest number of coups in Africa (Nigeria is number one) and adopted Marxism, the only country in West Africa to do so wholeheartedly.

Over 350 years ago, there were numerous small principalities. One of the chiefs had a quarrel with his brother and around 1625, moved to Abomey. He then conquered the neighbouring kingdom of Dan, which became known as Dahomey, meaning 'in Dan's belly' in Fon. Each successive king of the dynasty pledged to leave more land than he inherited, a pledge they all kept by waging war with their neighbours, particularly the powerful Yorubas of Nigeria. At the same time, Portuguese and then other European powers established trading posts along the coast, notably at Porto-Novo and Ouidah. The Dahomey kingdom soon became rich by selling slaves, usually prisoners of war, to these traders and received luxury items and guns in return, thus increasing the internal strife. Thousands of slaves, averaging about 10,000 a year for well over a century, were shipped to the Americas, primarily Brazil and the Caribbean and particularly Haiti, taking their knowledge and practice of voodoo with them. As a result, southern Benin became known as the Slave Coast.

What was a city in Benin like in the 17th century? Not what you imagine. A Dutch visitor described Edo city thus:

Benin

was made in education. Dubbed the 'Latin Quarter of West Africa' by the French, Dahomey become famous for its educated elite. This elite were employed by the French and the Senegalese as principal advisers to government officials throughout West Africa. This eventually backfired as the educated elite became extremely vocal and began agitating for assimilation and equality, even forming their own newspaper that attacked the French.

No progress whatsoever was made, however, in developing the palm industry. Incredibly, Dahomey was exporting the same amount of palm products on the eve of independence in 1960 as it was in the mid-1800s.

Independence

After WW II, the people of Dahomey formed trade unions and political parties, with Hubert Maga becoming a famous politician during this period. When Benin became independent in 1960, along with France's other African colonies, he became the country's first president.

Almost immediately, the former French colonies started deporting the Dahomeyans who had been running the administration. Back in Dahomey without work, they were the root of a highly unstable political situation. Three years later, after seeing how easily some disgruntled army soldiers in Togo staged a coup, the military did the same in Benin. During the next nine years, Benin became the Bolivia of Africa. There were four more successful military coups, nine more changes of government and five changes of constitution – what the Dahomeyans called in jest *le folklore*. At the same time, reflecting the civil manner of the Fon, not a single president was ever killed! When the army deposed General Soglo in 1967, they politely knocked on his door and told him: 'You're through'.

Finally, in 1972, Lt Col Mathieu Kerekou, a Catholic from the north, representing a group of middle and junior-grade officers, seized control and

As you enter it, the town appears very great. You go into a great broad street, not paved, which seems to be seven or eight times broader than the Warmoes Street in Amsterdam ... The houses in this town stand in good order, one close and even with the other, as the houses in Holland stand ...

In the late 1800s, the French gained control of the coast and defeated the kingdom of Dahomey, making it a colony and part of French West Africa. During the 70-year colonial period, great progress formed a revolutionary government, renaming the radio station 'the voice of the revolution'. Anti-white sentiment erupted a few months later, with crowds attacking the foreign-owned stores and the French Cultural Centre. Initially portraying themselves as a group of officers outraged with the tribalism and political chaos, Kerekou's government soon attracted more radical elements.

The Revolution

Two years after the coup, Kerekou announced that Marxism would be the country's official ideology. To emphasise the change, he renamed the country Benin. The transition was rough. A Presidential guard assassinated the Minister of Interior over a moral scandal implicating Kerekou's wife; the USA withdrew its ambassador; and workers held strikes in Cotonou for higher salaries. In 1977, in a coup attempt presumably instigated by Beninese exile groups, a force of Europeans and Africans headed by a French mercenary landed at Cotonou airport, only to fly away after several hours of unsuccessful fighting. A commission of inquiry later revealed that Gabon and Morocco had helped organise the operation and the French were also implicated. Outraged by the accusations, Gabon broke off diplomatic relations and expelled all 9000 Beninois living there, and the French reduced their aid by a third.

As part of the revolution, the government required schools to teach Marxism, set up collective farms and ordered students to work part-time on them. It assigned areas of cultivation and production goals to every district and village, formed state enterprises, created a single central trade union, inculcated a more militant spirit in the army, and warned churches to support them or get out – à la the Soviets.

Today

Even though the country appears self-sufficient in staple food crops, except in years of drought, the economic picture remains unpromising. Structural changes in the economy have at best been modest. The revolution has always existed more in rhetoric than reality, and even some of those changes have been undone by the decision in 1982 to reduce the number of parastatals. Most farming remains in private hands and state and collective farms represent no more than 10% of the cultivated land. In the commercial sector, private businesses continue to handle about two-thirds of the trading.

There are also some signs of political liberalisation. The government now holds elections to the national assembly and even though the party must approve all candidates, the party clearly considers whether the candidates are acceptable to the local communities. Benin has also set out to improve relations with the west as well as with its neighbours, renewing friendly relations with the Ivory Coast and Togo in the process. The USA, in turn, sent back its ambassador. After having seen many of its citizens expelled from Benin and their land expropriated after the 1977 coup attempt, France is back on good terms with Benin. Once again, the French are helping to finance the recurrent budget deficit. Foreign aid from many sources continues to pour in, but only at half the rate of the 1970s. Despite student unrest stemming from the government's decision in 1985 to stop the practice of automatically hiring all new secondary school graduates, Kerekou remains firmly in power. Benin is now one of the most stable countries in Africa – quite a contrast to the first 12 years following independence.

PEOPLE

Despite the government's strident Marxist rhetoric, the people are friendly even to those travellers from stridently free-enterprise countries. Curious about the west and anxious to make contact with travellers, they are apt to be quite open-minded on political issues.

Over half of Benin's four million people

are members of one of three ethnic groups – the Fon (and the related Adja), the Yoruba and the northern group composed of Bariba and Somba. Only a third of the people are Christian or Muslim; the rest are animists, and many practise voodoo.

Voodoo does not involve morality. The practice of worshipping voodoo spirits (or fetishes) stems from the belief that God created hundreds of them, each with unique supernatural powers to affect human lives. Below the voodoo are the spirits of the dead and the priests. The priests are imbued with a part of the fetish and are the only humans who can communicate with the voodoo and the dead spirits. Below the priests are the fetishers, who help them in their rites. Each tribe or clan worships a particular voodoo, typically in a fetish temple. You'll see man-made fetishes for sale. If you buy one, make sure you learn which voodoo spirit it represents. By making offerings to them, people hope to gain special favors, such as the birth of twins. In addition, if they don't appease the evil force, Legba, represented by a phallus, bad things can happen.

Fifteen percent of the land, all in the south, has half the country's population. This is Fon and Yoruba country. They were involved in the slave trade prior to the arrival of the French. During the colonial period they enjoyed educational privileges and became prominent in administration throughout French West Africa.

You'll find the Somba and the Bariba in the north. Because this is a barren and undeveloped area, they have always been poorer and less westernised, producing a significant regional and ethnic split between northerners and southerners – a major factor contributing to the political instability following independence. The Somba are concentrated in the north-west around Natitingou, and the Bariba, a Muslim tribe, around Kandi, Nikki and Kouandé. If you happen to attend a Bariba festival, you're in for a treat. The horsemen are famous for their displays, racing their horses through terrified crowds, only to stop them at the last minute.

The Fon are well known for their art. As was generally the case throughout Africa, men produced the sculpture. The Fon kings used both appliqué artists and brass and silver artisans to enhance their status as rulers, and until the 19th century forbade them to work outside the palace walls. At the royal palace at Abomey, you can still see some of the polychrome bas reliefs in clay that were used to decorate the palace, temples and chiefs' houses. Their brass and iron sculpture was some of the most remarkable in Africa and depicted scenes of men hoeing, chiefs with their retinues, and dances of the religious cults. The huge royal tapestries in Abomey that depict, for example, hunting scenes and events from the lives of rulers, are the best examples of the ancient appliqué work. You won't have any problem finding modern-day examples – black material with figures cut out of imported coloured cloths and sewn thereon, illustrating, for example, animals, hunting scenes, and the panther god, Agassou. It's sold everywhere in Cotonou as well as up and down the coast of West Africa, making it one of the most popular – and portable – souvenirs in West Africa.

GEOGRAPHY
Roughly 650 km long and 120 km wide in the south expanding to over 200 km wide in the north, Benin is a small country, about two-thirds the size of Portugal. Most of the 120-km coastal plain is a sandbar which obstructs the seaward flow of several rivers. As a result, you'll see lagoons a few km inland all along the coast. The biggest lagoon is Lake Nokoué which forms the northern city limits of Cotonou, and the southern limits of Porto-Novo, the country's nominal capital. It's easy to visit Cotonou without ever seeing the lagoon, consequently, most travellers don't realise how close it is. Lake Nokoué's outlet to the sea passes through

Niger River, Niamey, Niger (EE)

Top left: Indigo dye pits in Kano, Nigeria (EE)
Top right: Ashanti cloth weaver, Ghana (EE)
Bottom left: Bambara wood carver, Mali (EE)
Bottom right: Fon applique cloth from Abomey, Benin (EE)

Cotonou, dividing the city almost in half. The famous fishing town of Ganvié is constructed on stilts in this lagoon. The country's major river, the Ouémé, flows southward into Lake Nokoué and has a wide marshy delta with considerable agricultural potential.

As you travel inland, the land remains flat but the coastal plains are replaced by a forested plateau with dense vegetation. The country's third and fourth largest towns, Parakou and Abomey, are in this area. In the far north-west, the site of Benin's two major game parks, Pendjari and 'W', is the Atakora Mountains, which reach a maximum height of 457 metres.

CLIMATE
In the south, there are two rainy seasons, April to mid-July and mid-September through October, while the north has one rainy season from June to early October. In the hottest part of the year, March and April, temperatures in the north sometimes reach 44°C – about 10°C higher than in the south.

VISAS
Visas are not required by Danes, French, West Germans, Italians and Swedes. South Africans are not admitted. There are Benin embassies in both neighbouring Nigeria and Niger but not in Togo or Burkina Faso. If you're travelling from Togo, you can get them at the border on the coastal road. The border is open 24 hours, but visas are issued only on weekdays, 8 am to 12.30 pm and 3 to 6.30 pm, and Saturday 8 am to 12.30 pm. No other Benin border station issues visas.

Visa extensions of up to one month are issued without problems in 24 hours by the Immigration office near the French embassy. You'll need two photos.

Upon arrival in Cotonou, you're supposed to get a CFA 100 white tourist card (*carte blanche*) from ONATHO (tel 312687), a block or two inland from the Hôtel du Port. Like all government offices, the hours are weekdays 8 am to 12.30 pm and 3 to 6.30 pm, closed Saturday and Sunday. Don't fail to do this unless you want to be harassed by police throughout your trip. They have been known to send travellers in Parakou and elsewhere back to Cotonou to get one.

In addition, when travelling upcountry, you're theoretically supposed to get a *permit de circulation* in each town where you stay overnight. In large towns, most travellers don't do this and experience no problems. In small towns, however, if you don't get one, the police may get suspicious.

Exit visas are required unless you're leaving by road. But check this – the rule changes every so often. They're issued while you wait from the immigration office, but not on Saturday or Sunday.

Diplomatic Missions Abroad
Abidjan, Accra, Algiers, Bonn, Brussels, Kinshasa, Lagos, Niamey, Ottawa, Paris, Washington.

MONEY
US$1 = 287 CFA
£1 = 537 CFA

The unit of currency is the West African CFA. There's a thriving black market for the Nigerian naira. If you're at the airport and the bank is closed, you can always take a 20-minute walk to the Sheraton and cash it there. You don't have to be a guest at the hotel and they don't charge a commission on travellers' cheques. The only bank downtown that changes money is the Commerce Extérieur branch of the BCB. Banking hours: weekdays 8 to 11 am and 3 to 4 pm; closed Saturday and Sunday. Banks: BCB (Banque Commercial du Bénin), Banque Beninoise de Developpement.

LANGUAGE
French is the official language. Over half the people speak Fon; Mina, Yoruba, Bariba and Dendi are others. Greetings in Fon:

Good morning	*AH-fon GHAN-jee-ah*
Good evening	*KOU-doh BAH-dah*
How are you?	*AH-doh GHAN-jee-ah*
Thank you	*AH-wah-nou*
Goodbye	*OH-dah-boh*

GENERAL INFORMATION
Health
Yellow fever and cholera vaccinations are both required. The Polyclinic *Les Cocotiers* (tel 301431/20) is a private clinic in Cotonou and likely to be better than the National Hospital (tel 300155/300656). For general practitioners, try Dr Daouda Soule (reads English) at the Polyclinic and Dr B Lam (tel 321171/314766) at *Clinic les Grâces* (speaks English).

The most well-stocked pharmacies in Cotonou are *Pharmacie l'Éternité* (tel 321232) on Wologuede road off l'Étoile Rouge, *Pharmacie de la Radio* (tel 314951) around the corner from the US embassy, and *Pharmacie Jonquet* (tel 312080). The name of the all-night pharmacy (Pharmacie de Garde) is posted in pharmacy windows.

Security
Despite the poor lighting in downtown Cotonou, it's one of the safer West African cities. Thefts from parked vehicles used to occur frequently, but army crackdowns have reduced this significantly. Nevertheless, there are occasional pickpocketing incidents, and armed muggings have occurred along the beach and in the Jonquet section of town. A popular beach called La Crique, next to the PLM hotel in Cotonou, is particularly prone to robbery. Beaches are closed at night, and you can be arrested if found there after dark. In addition, the beach road behind the Presidential Palace beginning at the Hôtel du Port is off limits from 7 pm to 7 am. The area around the Presidential Palace is off limits at all times.

Business Hours
Business: Weekdays 8 am to 12.30 pm and 3.30 pm to 7 pm; Saturday 8 am to 12.30 pm.

Government: weekdays 8 am to 12.30 pm and 3 pm to 6.30 am.

Public Holidays
1 January, 16 January, Easter Monday, 1 May, End of Ramadan (17 May 1988, 6 May 1989), Tabaski (25 July 1988, 14 July 1989), 1 August (Independence), 26 October, Mohammed's Birthday, 30 November, 25 December, 31 December.

Photography
Taking photos in cities and major towns is a problem. The rule is that you don't need a permit to take photos of the countryside, monuments, non-religious folklore dances and scenes of local life. On the other hand, taking snapshots of the harbour, bridges, airport, TV and radio stations, dams, all government buildings and military installations (ie anything potentially useful to a group trying to stage a coup) plus museums, convents, fetish temples and cultural and religious ceremonies can land you in the clink. These rules may seem clear cut but they aren't. The only way to avoid risking a major hassle with the police is to ask permission from the nearest policeman before taking photos in Cotonou and major towns. For more information, ask at ONATHO when you get your white tourist card.

Time, Post, Phone & Telex
When it's noon in Benin, it's 11 am in London and 6 am in New York (7 am during daylight savings time). The post office and poste restante are good in Cotonou. You can make overseas calls from the Sheraton, but the cost is almost double that at the post office (CFA 7000 for three minutes to the USA). Service is interrupted frequently during the rainy season. Otherwise, the service is good except to Nigeria and Ghana. Telexes can be sent from the Sheraton and from the post office.

GETTING THERE
Air

From Europe, the direct flights are from Paris. From London, the cheapest route is via Moscow on Aeroflot with a ticket purchased from a bucket shop; this involves a stop-over in Moscow. From New York, you could take Air Afrique, transferring in Abidjan, or Nigeria Airways to nearby Lagos. You could also fly to Togo – a taxi from Lomé to Cotonou takes only three hours. Returning to Europe, some travellers reportedly buy tickets on Aeroflot from Cobenham's Travel Agency in Cotonou using black-market naira; the price comes out to about US$250. Air Benin has frequent flights to Parakou (CFA 15,000) and Natitingou (CFA 18,500) at least once a week, and to Niamey and Lomé.

Car

The border with Nigeria is open again. Driving time from both Lagos and Lomé to Cotonou is only three hours. Avoid arriving in Lagos at rush hour – it's a mess. The coastal route to Lomé is open 24 hours. The Cotonou-Parakou road is now paved; so you can travel the entire 1062 km from Niamey (Niger) on tarred road – an easy two-day drive. The northern border of Benin is open 7 am to 7.30 pm. The 200-km dirt road from Parakou to Lama-Kara (Togo) is in good condition; this increases your options. Black cars are not allowed into Benin, because that is the colour of government vehicles.

Bush Taxi

Bush taxis leave all day and into the early evening from Jonquet square in Cotonou to Lomé and Lagos; the trip takes about three hours. Getting a taxi to Parakou is no problem; from there to the Niger border takes about six hours.

GETTING AROUND
Air

Air Benin has regular flights from Cotonou to Parakou and Natitingou.

Bush Taxi/Bus

You can usually get a bush taxi in Cotonou to Lomé or Lagos within five to 20 minutes. There are also buses for Abomey and Parakou, though the waiting time is considerably longer. Most people travelling from Cotonou to Parakou prefer the train.

Train

The Cotonou-Parakou train takes about 10 hours and you'll see some beautiful countryside on the way. To see Abomey, get off in Bohicon, only eight km away. First class is as comfortable as that on any train in West Africa – working air-con, cold drinks, uncrowded, tolerable bathrooms – but there are no compartments, sleeping cars or restaurant. You can, however, pick up food on the way. The seats in 2nd class are hard, and the cost, about CFA 3200, is not cheap compared to that of a bush taxi. On the other hand, it's seldom crowded. The train leaves once a day in both directions, and they change the schedule every now and then. Most recently, trains departed Parakou at 1.45 pm. If all you want is to ride on a train, you could also take the much shorter Cotonou-Porto Novo line.

Cotonou

Cotonou has the lethargy of a Sunday morning. Shifting your life style into low gear won't make you like Cotonou, but it helps. Have a drink, lie in the sun, and be thankful this place isn't as crowded as many African cities. In addition to some fairly good beaches only a few km from the centre of town, Cotonou offers several good nightclubs, a four-star hotel, a few decent restaurants (but nothing compared to those in Lomé) and one of the best craft markets on the coast of West Africa. Only a 25-minute drive from downtown brings you to the launching point for a trip to Ganvié, one of the hottest attractions in West Africa for foreigners and Africans alike. Most important, the Beninois are quite friendly, and because there aren't so many foreigners in Benin you're likely to get special attention. So while Cotonou may seem a little boring at first glance, making an effort is worth it.

The heart of town is the intersection of Avenue Clozel and Boulevard Sekou Touré. Going eastward on Avenue Clozel, one of the city's two main drags, you'll pass over the old bridge (the one closest to the ocean) into the Akpakpa section; the road eventually turns into the highway to Porto-Novo and Lagos. The new bridge, financed by the USA, is the one further inland and the wide Boulevard St Michel (or Avenue du Nouveau Pont), the other main drag, passes over it into Akpakpa, eventually connecting with Clozel. The nicest residences are in the opposite direction, out near the US embassy and the Sheraton – the Patte d'Oie, Haie Vive and Cocotiers sections.

Information
Tourist Office ONATHO (tel 312687, telex 5032) is the government-run tourist office. This is where you get your tourist card. It is down the street across from the Hôtel du Port.

Embassies Algeria, Egypt, France (Rue de Cocotiers, BP 766), West Germany, Ghana, Niger, Nigeria, USA (Rue Caporal Anani, BP 2021, tel 300650/301792), Zaire.

Bookstores & Supermarkets *Librairie Notre Dame* is the best bookstore but nothing special. It is near the intersection of Clozel and Sekou Touré, behind Notre Dame Cathedral. It's open 8 am to 12.30 pm and 4 to 6.30 pm except Monday morning and Sunday. Others are *La Plume d'Or* near the US embassy and *Sapec* on Avenue Clozel near the post office; the latter sells a colourful book on Benin. For postcards, try the Sheraton.

The best supermarkets, both in the heart of town, are *CFAO* and *Somico* on

the so-called 'Rue des Libanais'. You'll find, for instance, Possotome, locally bottled mineral water, for CFA 170 a bottle. For specialty items, *Amelco* in Cocotiers is the best.

Travel Agencies Benin-Tours (at the Sheraton, tel 300702/300546, telex 5111); Cobenham Voyages (air fares). ONATHO organises guided tours to places near and along the coast as well as to the far north.

Grand Marché de Dan Tokpa
The only must see in town is the Grand Marché de Dan Tokpa, which is held every four days and borders the lagoon. As opposed to the Marché Central which has only foodstuffs, the lively Dan Tokpa market has everything from dungarees, wax cloth, baskets, religious paraphernalia and pottery, to bats' wings and monkeys' testicles.

Places to Stay – bottom end
Camping anywhere in Benin is illegal, even in a car, and if they find you, you'll spend a day in jail. The worst possible place is the beach – the thieves are notorious, and you'll get arrested.

A good place for the money is *Hôtel Pacific* (tel 331760), with 12 rooms for CFA 2500 to CFA 4000 (CFA 4000 with separate beds) and a sidewalk terrace for drinks and three meals a day. A fan costs CFA 500 extra. The rooms not facing the street are fairly quiet. It's a 10-minute walk from the heart of town on the main drag, Avenue Clozel, just across the old bridge in Akpakpa. About four km further out on the same road is *Hôtel Miva* (tel 321206/18); look for the large bright green building on you right. The rooms are much better, and only a 15-minute walk from a good beach, but you won't find many clients there, probably because of the remote location. A room with fan costs only CFA 3500 (CFA 4500 for two people of the same sex) and CFA 4000 to CFA 6500 with air-con (CFA 3500 to CFA 4500 extra for two people of the same sex).

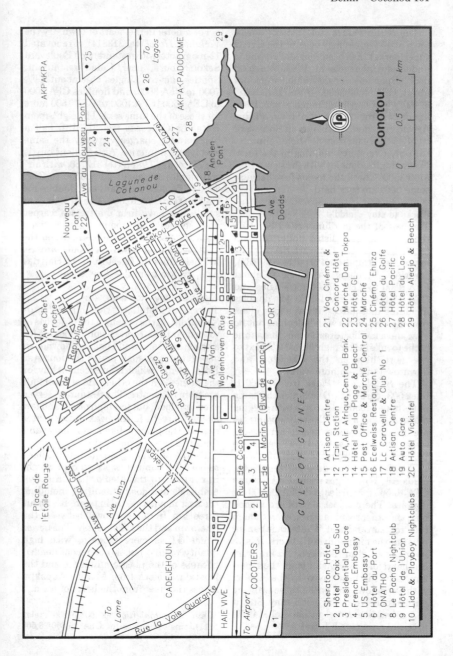

Conotou

0   0.5   1 km

1   Sheraton Hôtel
2   Hôtel Croix du Sud
3   Presidential Palace
4   French Embassy
5   US Embassy
6   Hôtel du Port
7   ONATHO
8   Le Pacha Nightclub
9   Hôtel de l'Union
10 Lido & Playboy Nightclubs
11 Artisan Centre
12 Train Station
13 UTA, Air Afrique, Central Bank
14 Hôtel de la Plage & Beach
15 Post Office & Marché Central
16 Ecelweiss Restaurant
17 Lc Caravelle & Club No 1
18 Artisan Centre
19 Auto Gare
2C Hôtel Vickinfel
21 Vog Cinéma & Concord Hôtel
22 Marché Dan Tokpa
23 Hôtel GL
24 Marché
25 Cinéma Ehuza
26 Hôtel du Golfe
27 Hôtel Pacific
28 Hôtel du Lac
29 Hôtel Aledjo & Beach

The *Bénin Palace* (tel 312596), downtown at 15 Guinkomey back of the CFAO supermarket, has been remodelled and is under new management. It's now a good deal. Spacious singles/doubles go for about CFA 4500/5500. *Hôtel Babo* (tel 314607) is cheaper but much worse. It's a km or two from the heart of town on Rue Agbeto-Amadore, two blocks off Boulevard St Michel, not far from St Michel church – the only five-storey building in the area. Noisy singles/doubles with fans cost CFA 3100/3500. Check the rooms first because some beds are rock hard.

Places to stay – middle
The best of the medium priced hotels is the *Croix du Sud*, listed under top end hotels because it's first-rate despite the lower cost. *Hôtel du Port* (tel 314443/4, cards AE, D), charges a little less – about CFA 9500 to CFA 12,000 for singles and CFA 11,500 to CFA 14,000 for doubles including mosquitoes. It has a long clean pool, decent rooms with balconies but no view and a mediocre restaurant. It has one of the town's better nightclubs. It's next to the port between the Sheraton and downtown (a 25-minute walk).

The *Hôtel de la Plage* (tel 312560/1, telex 503, cards AE, D) charges the same but is not as good – old rooms with sagging mattresses and a pool. The only advantages are the not-so-clean beach across the street, the restaurant and the location – a 10-minute walk from the heart of town.

The 30-room *Hôtel du Golfe* (tel 330955, cards AE, D) charges about CFA 7500 to CFA 10,500 for singles and CFA 12,500 for doubles. The cheaper singles are a good buy; the other rooms are not, even though they're clean and neat. The terrace bar is a plus but the nightclub is mediocre. It is on Avenue Clozel in Akpakpa, 1½ km from the heart of town. Ask about their new annex on the beach next to the Aledjo, with bungalows and pool – those wanting an inexpensive beach hotel may find it very attractive. *Hôtel du Lac* (tel 314970) is terribly managed; forget it.

For a hotel in the heart of town, try the *Vickinfel Hôtel* (tel 313814), a renovated 12-room hotel with restaurant off Boulevard Sekou Touré, near Calao restaurant. Spotless air-con singles cost about CFA 7000 to CFA 8000, and doubles CFA 8000 to CFA 9500 (CFA 1000 to CFA 1500 more for those of the same sex). The eight-room *Hôtel Le Concorde* (tel 313313), half a block away, charges virtually the same and is much inferior. An excellent buy is the *Hôtel de l'Union* (tel 312766, with air-con singles for about CFA 6500 to CFA 8000 (CFA 4000 with fan) and doubles for CFA 8000 to CFA 10,000. The 10 rooms are small, but have firm mattresses, carpet and spotless bathrooms, plus a bar-restaurant and TV room. It is in the north-west section of town on Boulevard St Michel across the street from the Hall des Arts, 1½ km from the heart of town.

Places to Stay – top end
The best hotel is the huge *Benin Sheraton*, on the beach on the outskirts of town near the airport. If you're looking for a beach hotel and won't be going downtown very often, you may prefer the four-star *Hôtel Aledjo*, which is an excellent buy for the money, on the other side of town four km from the centre. The restaurant serves excellent food, but has high prices and few clients. Except in the peak of the winter season, the place is like a mortuary, and finding a cab can be a pain.

For the price and good quality, it's hard to beat the popular *Croix du Sud* which, in contrast to the Aledjo, has an active ambience and good amenities, including the best movie theatre in town. It's about three km from downtown between the Sheraton and the US embassy. The newer *Hôtel GL* is more modern, with high quality rooms, but is not recommended because of the plastic ambience and the location, a block from Marché Akpakpa across the river from the heart of town.

Benin Sheraton (tel 300100/301256, telex 5111), singles/doubles for CFA 25,500/28,500

(CFA 3000 more for an ocean-view room) and bungalows for CFA 34,000/36,000, round pool, tennis courts, sauna, disco, casino, shops, Hertz, cards AE, D, V, EC, MC.

PLM Hôtel Aledjo (tel 330561, telex 5180), 55 large singles/doubles for CFA 17,000/19,000 (CFA 3000 more for an ocean-view room), tennis, pool, casino, cards AE, D, EC.

Croix du Sud (tel 300954/5, telex 5032), single/double bungalows for about CFA 11,500/13,500, long pool, bar, nightclub, movie theatre, cards AE, D.

Hôtel GL (tel 331617, telex 5311), singles for about CFA 12,000 to CFA 13,000 and doubles for CFA 13,500 to CFA 14,500, pool, cards AE, D.

Places to Eat

Cheap Eats In the dead centre of town at the intersection of Clozel and Sekou Touré is the ever-popular *La Caravelle*, open every day from 7 am to midnight. They serve beer, food and pastries on the upstairs terrace, where there is a panoramic view of downtown. Between La Caravelle and the post office on Avenue Clozel is the highly popular *La Gerbe d'Or*, a long-standing pastry shop beyond the common man's means. It has fruit tarts, pizza, hamburgers, ice cream flown in from France, famous croissants, and air-con you can really feel.

For much cheaper meals, head for Boulevard St Michel; there are a number of small restaurants all along the way. If you're in the lively section of town around the Lido Club nightclub, across the street you'll find *Restaurant Seneglaise*.

Lebanese One of the best restaurants in town is the *L'Oriental*, which serves an excellent Lebanese meze in a pleasant outdoor setting. Open every evening, it's located in Quartier Haie Vive not far from the Sheraton. Prices are moderate.

French The *La Fourchette*, closed Thursday, has the reputation of being Cotonou's best, but it's over-price and not so great. It is downtown one block west of Boulevard Sekou Touré, several blocks from Cinema Vog. *Hibiscus* is slightly less expensive

and fairly good. Closed Sunday and Monday, it's in Cotonou II near the Golfe Hôtel, which is two km from the heart of town on Avenue Clozel.

For moderate prices, you can't beat *Le Calao* (tel 312426), a good small restaurant in the heart of town on Boulevard Sekou Touré four or five blocks from the intersection with Avenue Clozel. Closed on Wednesday, they serve a variety of dishes, including couscous and various fish and seafood dishes. Also moderately priced and attractively decorated is *Edelweiss* (tel 313138), closed Thursday and in the heart of town, several blocks from the intersection of Clozel and Sekou Touré. They offer a huge selection, including Continental, African and Asian cuisine. Another restaurant which reportedly serves very good cuisine is the French-run *Chez Dede la Choucroute* (tel 320751), which has an orchestra and dancing on Saturday. You'll have to take a taxi to get there; it's next to Club Onu. The cheapest French restaurant is *La Verdure* (tel 312132), downtown behind the CFAO and popular with sailors, among others.

Of the hotels, the *Sheraton* offers no surprises. The popular restaurant at the *Hôtel Croix du Sud* is more moderately priced and serves a CFA 3000 fixed price Continental meal and a CFA 2000 special African plate. Or there is a large à la carte menu. The quality of the restaurant at the *Hôtel de la Plage* is far superior to that of its rooms. They offer a CFA 3200 special plus many à la carte selections.

Chinese *China House* serves the best Chinese food, but it suffers in comparison to Chinese restaurants in Lomé. Prices are moderate, and it's open every day. It is a few km from downtown on the road to Lomé, next to the Soviet Cultural Centre – fairly convenient to the Sheraton and Croix du Sud. Downtown on a dirt road next to the Cosmos Club, two blocks from the Cinema Vog on Boulevard Sekou Touré, is *La Pagoda*, which also serves decent Chinese food at moderate prices.

Italian *Sorrento* is the only place to get decent Italian food. About two km from the heart of town behind the Hall des Arts, they serve good pizza and other Italian and French dishes.

Entertainment & Sports

Bars The most popular watering hole is *La Caravelle* in the heart of town, with big beers for CFA 425. *Le Memphis* is a late night American-style bar, popular with expatriates. It is one km from the Sheraton in Quartier Cadjehoun, a block from La Voie Quarante road.

Nightclubs The top nightclub by far is *Number One*, which is new and plush and popular every night, and packed on weekends. It's in the heart of town half a block from La Caravelle; taxis are parked outside late at night to take you back to your hotel. The cover, which includes a drink, is CFA 2000 weekdays and CFA 2500 weekends. *King's Club*, at the Hôtel du Port and open Friday, Saturday and Sunday only, is sometimes lively and has a CFA 1500 cover. *Le Teke*, at the Sheraton and closed Monday, has a CFA 2000 cover but is usually pretty dead. *Le Safari*, at the Croix du Sud and open every night, is usually no livelier.

For live music, be on the lookout for announcements about orchestras playing at *Le Pacha* near the huge Hall des Arts on Boulevard St Michel.

For a decadent dancing place, try the ever-popular *Lido Club* on Rue des Cheminots, half way between the heart of town and the Hôtel de l'Union as the crow flies. Drinks are CFA 1000, but higher on weekends. Next door is *Playboy*, Cotonou's most disreputable nightclub. Men pay nothing to enter if they come without a female companion. You'll find lots of women inside and rooms by the hour upstairs. Taxis are parked outside all night long.

Movie Theatre *Les Cocotiers* (tel 301605) at the Hôtel Croix du Sud has air-con and shows first rate films nightly at 6 and 9 pm. *Cinema Vog* downtown on Boulevard Sekou Touré is less expensive and shows karate flicks among others at 5.30 and 9 pm. The *Centre Culturel Français* shows excellent films several times a week; the mosquitoes are a problem.

Sports In addition to the private beach at the Sheraton, there's a small beach in front of the Hôtel de la Plage, and 'La Crique' just beyond the Aledjo. La Crique is very crowded on Sunday with expatriates and Africans because of the weak undertow, but watch out for your valuables. It's a good three km from downtown, so most people take a taxi. If you're looking for an uncrowded beach, one that has been recommended is near the airport. Take the road to Lomé and just after passing the railroad tracks near the airport, turn left down a very long sandy road. You'll find African villages nearby.

If you're not staying at one of the top hotels with pools, you can swim in the long pool at the Hôtel du Port for only CFA 500. The pool at the Aledjo is short; the Sheraton's is round and costs CFA 2000.

You can play tennis for free at the Aledjo if you buy a drink, or pay about CFA 2000 to play at one of the Sheraton's. You might also be able to pick up a game at the Club du Tennis in Cotonou II, 100 metres beyond the Hôtel du Lac. They have three courts in fair condition.

Things to Buy

Artisan Goods For crafts, head for *L'Artisanat* downtown next to the river. Go down Avenue Clozel and it's on your right as you approach the old bridge to Cotonou II. It's a series of 20 or so shacks. Benin is famous for its appliqué black cloth with bright quilted birds and other animals. L'Artisanat also has a wide variety of other artisan goods, including wooden carvings, batik, tie-dye materials, bronze statues, sandals, ivory, malachite, leather work and tablecloths. The government agency, ONATHO, also sells artisan goods but at higher prices. Their largest outlet is at the ONATHO headquarters, one block inland from the Hôtel du Port. The Sheraton has another outlet.

Music For records or cassettes of Beninois music, you'll have to search for one of the small African shops that records music. Polyrhymic Orchestra is well known throughout West Africa for its Afro-beat music; Yonass Pedro is also popular.

Getting There & Away
Air Air Benin has frequent flights to Parakou and flies to Natitingou at least once a week.

Bush Taxi/Bus Bush taxis and minibuses for Porto-Novo and points along the coast leave from the Auto Gare near the vieux pont (old bridge).

For buses north (Abomey-Calavi for Ganvié, Abomey, Parakou) the station is off Avenue Sekou Touré near the Vog cinema.

Train There are trains to Parakou and towns on the way, as well as the line to Porto-Novo. The train is reasonably comfortable and not crowded. There is one train per day in either direction travelling on the Cotonou-Parakou line, and stopping in Bohicon near Abomey.

Getting Around
Airport Transport There's a departure tax of CFA 2500. You'll find a bank, bar, Hertz, Avis and Eurocar. A taxi into town (5 km) is supposed to cost only CFA 1000 (CFA 500 to the Sheraton), but most drivers will refuse to take you for less than CFA 2000 because of the long wait between planes. Returning to the airport, you should be able to get the official price.

Taxi Fares are CFA 100 for a shared taxi (double for fairly long trips) and CFA 500 for a taxi to yourself. By the hour, taxis cost only CFA 1000, CFA 500 more if you

include the Sheraton in the trip. Rates double at 9 pm. You'll find it difficult to negotiate a fare for the entire day – CFA 10,000 to CFA 12,000 plus petrol would be a fair price.

Car Rental Hertz (tel 301915, cards AE, D), Avis (tel 315138, telex 5130, cards AE, D), and Eurocar all have booths at the airport; Hertz and Avis also have offices at the Sheraton. Others, some of which might be cheaper, include Locar Benin (tel 313837), Socar Locar (tel 313157), Sonatrac (tel 312357), and the government tourist office ONATHO (tel 312687). A Renault 4 without driver will cost you about CFA 20,000 plus petrol for the day, assuming you travel 150 km.

AROUND COTONOU
Ganvié
The number one attraction near Cotonou is Ganvié (ghan-vee-AY), a frequently photographed village whose 12,000 inhabitants live in bamboo huts on stilts several km out on Lake Nokoué, just north of Cotonou. Even if you normally avoid touristy things, don't write off Ganvié. Africans themselves are fascinated by Ganvié; you'll see as many African tourists as westerners. The Tofinu moved here in the 18th century from the north where the land was no longer sufficient to feed everyone. The swampy area around Lake Nokoué was excellent protection against the Fon and Dahomey kingdoms because a religious ban prevented any warrior from Abomey from venturing into the water or areas liable to flooding.

The people live exclusively from fishing. As much breeders of fish as fishermen, the men plant branches on the muddy lagoon bottom. When the leaves begin to decompose, the fish congregate there to feed. After many days, the men return to catch them in a net. Most of the canoes (*pirogues*) are operated by women, who do the selling. Loaded with spices, fruits and fish, these pirogues are a colourful sight. Inside, there's invariably a woman wearing a straw hat with a huge rim. Everything takes place on the water where peace and quiet contrasts with the bustle of the mainland.

The best time to see Ganvié is in the early morning when the mist is lifting and there are no tourists, or late afternoon when the sun has lost its force.

Places to Stay & Eat When you return to the launching point, you can eat at *La Pirogue*, a pleasant restaurant which offers a four-course meal for CFA 3000 plus á la carte. Next door is *Ganvié Bungalow Hôtel* (tel 360039), which has four very decent air-con rooms for CFA 5500. More interesting, but less comfortable would be to sleep in Ganvié itself; the locals are well accustomed to renting rooms. Expect to pay about CFA 1700.

Getting There & Away To get to Ganvié you must go 18 km around the lake to Abomey-Calavi, a 25-minute ride. A taxi to yourself from Cotonou will cost CFA 6000 – high because of the large number of well-heeled tourists headed there. The locals usually take a bus, leaving near CFAO supermarket in Cotonou, or a shared taxi for about CFA 500.

You can catch a motorised boat or pirogue to Ganvié across the lake. By motorised boat, the trip over and back will take two hours. You'll feel much less like a tourist by taking the non-motorised pirogue, which takes only about an hour longer. The cost varies according to the number of passengers. The cost per person of a pirogue is CFA 6000 for one, CFA 2500 for three or four, and CFA 2000 for five or more. The price of a motorised boat varies from CFA 8000 to CFA 2500. Don't expect to bargain much, if any.

It's possible to get a cheaper ride with some of the independent pirogue men, but finding them is no easy task. One traveller reports that if you go five km north of Abomey-Calavi to the village of Akassato, it is possible to rent pirogues for CFA 2000 to CFA 2500 per boat.

The South

PORTO-NOVO
Not many people living in Africa would guess that the capital of Benin is not Cotonou. Even though the President lives in Cotonou and everything transpires there, Porto-Novo, 32 km to the east, remains the nominal capital. Dating back to the 16th century, Porto-Novo has seen better days. It's now a ramshackle city of 150,000 people with massive buildings, most dating from early colonial times. The wealthy families of Benin once lived here. Walking down the narrow streets, you'll see high red earth walls surrounding the old homes of Yoruba traders.

Musée Ethnographique
One of the benefits of President Mitterand's visit in 1983 was his agreement to renovate this museum in the centre of town. It is open 8 am to 12 noon and 4 to 7 pm and well worth a visit. The museum retraces the history of the kings of Porto-Novo, offering a fine collection of Yoruba masks, arms, musical instruments – including some interesting carved drums, implements and costumes.

Grand Marché d'Adjara
This market is held every fourth day, eight km east of Porto-Novo on the road to Nigeria and is one of the most interesting markets in Benin. You'll find drums and other musical instruments, unique blue and white tie-dye cloth, some of the best pottery in Benin, locally made baskets, and bicycles as well as the usual fare. Pirogues are used to transport goods from nearby Nigeria. Watch it all as you're sipping some of the excellent palm wine sold in the market.

Other
Next to the market is an interesting old Brazilian-style **church** that has been converted into a mosque and coloured pink. The **Palace of King Toffa** (Palais du

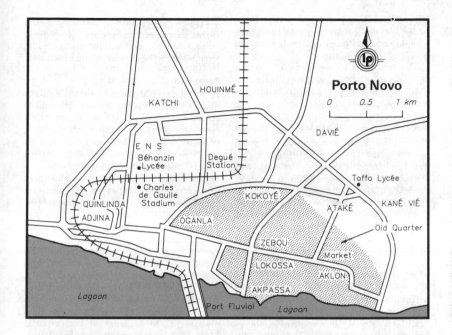

Porto Novo

0   0.5   1 km

Roi Toffa), who signed the first treaty with the French, is in the eastern part of town in Quartier Gbecon; they'll let you inside for a small donation.

If you make friends with some of the local fishermen, they may let you ride along as they work on the lagoon. You'll see some interesting lagoon villages with not a single tourist.

Places to Stay & Eat

For cheap accommodation, try *Hôtel Detente* near the ocean or, possibly, the *Mission Catholique*. If you're looking for a good place to eat, try *Le Souvenir* or the *Dona*.

Downtown and operated by ONATHO, *Hôtel Dona* (tel 213052) is the best hotel and has a restaurant, bar, nightclub and 22 rooms, some with air-con and others with fans. *Hôtel Beau-Rivage* (tel 213038), which is not as nice, has 19 air-con rooms.

OUIDAH

Another potential excursion from Cotonou is Ouidah, the voodoo centre of Benin and only 42 km west of Cotonou. Until the wharf was built at Cotonou in 1908, Ouidah (population 30,000) had the only port in the country. Its heyday was from 1800 to 1850, when Ouidah was the port where slaves were shipped from Benin and eastern Togo to the USA, Brazil and Haiti, where the practice of voodoo remains strong.

Things to See

The three major attractions are the old **Portuguese Fort** built in 1721 and the **Musée d'Histoire** (or the Voodoo Museum) therein, the cathedral, and the **Sacred Python Temple** (le Temple des Serpents) Forget about the snake temple – you'll be led to a grumpy old man who will demand CFA 500 for the experience of seeing the pythons. He will then lead you into a very small room, lift up some boards, and *voilà* – four harmless, sleeping snakes. In any case, this guy has a good business going.

Musée d'Histoire (Voodoo Museum)

The museum, on the other hand, is definitely worth a visit even though it's not as good as the one in Porto-Novo. It's in the mansion of a Portuguese family that was ousted in the early 1960s – the old 'governor' used to raise a Portuguese flag every morning, claiming the fort was Portugal's! The exhibits focus on the slave trade and Benin's consequent links with Brazil and the Caribbean. There are all sorts of strange artefacts of the voodoo culture and pictures of people in trances in Benin, Cuba, Brazil and Haiti. You'll be shown skulls, ghost clothes, centuries old Portugese gifts to the kings of Dahomey, mural-size blow ups of old maps and engravings, photographs showing the influence of Dahomeyan slaves on Brazilian culture, and traces of Brazilian architecture that the repatriated slaves brought back with them to Africa.

Places to Stay

You can sleep at the government-owned *Hôtel Gbena*, with rooms for about CFA 8000, or a small hotel with rooms for about CFA 2200 and a pleasant terrace bar – the military like to stop by the latter and rap with travellers.

LOKOSSA

If you come from Togo and head straight for the north, you will pass through Lokossa. *Hôtel Étoile Rouge* has a bar-restaurant and 20 rooms, four with air-con.

ABOMEY

If you have time to visit only one town outside Cotonou, Abomey is a good choice. It's only 144 km north of Cotonou on asphalt road and it is an extremely interesting town. Abomey is Fon country and was the capital of the great Dahomean

kingdom. The main attraction is the Royal Palace of the Fon, which is slowly being restored, and the Museum inside, which covers the history of the kingdoms.

Royal Palace

Before the arrival of the French, the palace must have been the most incredible structure in West Africa. It was first constructed in the 17th century; each successive fon king enlarged it so that by the 19th century the palace was huge, with a four-km-long perimeter and a 10-metre-high wall enclosing an area of 40 hectares and a court of 10,000 people. The museum consists of only the palaces of the last two kings to build there. Fleeing from the French in 1892, their successor ordered the palace to be burned. So only a small part of the original palace is standing – the courtyards and ceremonial rooms, and the houses where the king's wives lived.

King Glele was said to have had about 800 wives, 1000 women slaves to attend to them, an army of 10,000 soldiers and, most unusual, 6000 Amazonian bodyguards. He and the other kings apparently believed that women were less treacherous than men. There was also a colony of artists who worked exclusively for the king.

A large part of the palace was devoted to altars for dead kings, who were buried there. The people thought it befitting that their deceased kings have an entourage of people in the afterlife, so they held an annual human sacrifice – mainly convicts and prisoners of war.

Museum

Inside the rundown museum, you'll see the great thrones behind which hang the famous Abomey royal tapestries, depicting the country's history. One of them shows a scene of Glele using a dismembered leg to pound his enemy's head in a mortar. You'll also see lots of voodoo, skulls, Portuguese artefacts ranging from pistols to sets of china, and the royal huts of the king's 800 wives. You may not take photos of any of this!

Centre des Artisans

The museum tour takes half an hour, at the end of which your guide will take you to the Centre des Artisans next door where you'll see artisans working on all kinds of modern-day crafts (wooden carvings, bronze statues, etc) for sale at prices about as low as anywhere. The quality is nothing to write home about, but the items at least make good souvenirs.

Other

Besides the temple, you could visit the very good market, which takes place every four days and is not too touristy. Then look for some of the fetish temples in the countryside. Each is dedicated to a different divinity (death, smallpox, etc) – the practice of voodoo is still very active here. Cycling is a good way to see the rural areas; you might get lucky and find a local who'll rent you a bicycle for the day.

Places to Stay & Eat

For a dirt cheap hotel, your only real choice is *Foyer des Militants* because *Hôtel Routière* is closed. The quiet Foyer is two km out of town and costs about CFA 2200 to CFA 3300 for rooms with mosquito nets but no fans. Nearby, 300 metres up a small track, you'll find *Chez Monique*. She has rooms for CFA 1000, but they're not always available. Regardless, Monique serves good chicken and fries.

The best hotel in town, which isn't saying much, is *Motel d'Abomey* (tel 500068), with six simple rooms, a bar and a restaurant. Most 1st-class travellers now stay at the new *Hôtel Dako* in Bohicon, eight km away. It has decent singles/doubles with breakfast for CFA 8500/14,000 and a pool.

Getting There & Away

Getting there is no problem. Take a train from Cotonou to Bohicon, then a taxi eight km to Abomey, or one of the many buses which leave daily for Abomey from Boulevard Sekou Touré in Cotonou.

DASSA ZOUMÉ

Dassa Zoumé lies roughly half way between Cotonou and Parakou. If you stop over here, you'll find a motel with 11 rooms and a restaurant.

The North

PARAKOU

Parakou (population 70,000) is a bustling town at the end of the railroad with wide avenues and nothing of great interest to see. It is, however, a handy stopover point for the north and the game parks.

Places to Stay & Eat

As for cheaper accommodation, *Hôtel les Canaris* (tel 612294) has ventilated rooms for about CFA 3300 to CFA 5500, and serves fairly decent food. *Hôtel-Restaurant Bon Gout* near the train station is not bad for the price. The friendly people there serve decent food and charge about CFA 2200/3300 for singles/doubles free of bed bugs and roaches. Really low on cash? Try the *Gare Routière*, where you should be able to find a dormitory bed for about CFA 700.

You'll find a decent hotel, *Hôtel les Routiers* (tel 612127), with pool, tennis courts, a good restaurant and 20 air-con rooms for about CFA 5500 to 8500. Two other hotels with decent rooms, but not cheap, are *Hôtel Benin*, at about CFA 7500 for a double with air-con, and *Buffet-Hôtel OCDN*, with two air-con singles/doubles for about CFA 5500/7500.

DJOUGOU

One of the more interesting things to do in Djougou is to take an excursion to see the nearby Taneka villages; their picturesque round houses have banco walls and grass roofs topped with jars. You can stay at *Motel de Djougou*, which has 12 rooms and a bar-restaurant, or *Hôtel Nantho*, which reportedly isn't bad for the low price.

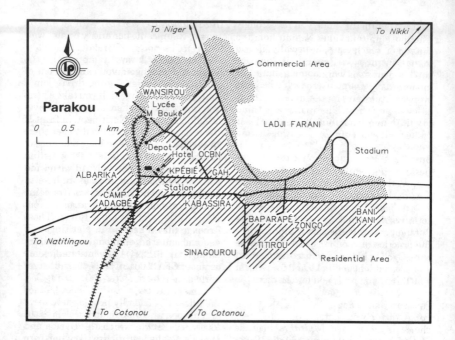

GAME PARKS & SOMBA COUNTRY

Benin has two national parks in the far north – Pendjari Park and, about twice as large, 'W' Park. Pendjari is adjacent to Arly Park in Burkina Faso, while 'W' Park is adjacent to the park of the same name in Niger. All three in effect form one big park. For those interested in hunting, these parks are surrounded by buffer zones managed for hunting: Pendjari, Alfakoara and Djona. All are open from the end of November through May, the best viewing time being January through March.

The types of animals you might see are elephant, hippo, lion, cheetah, crocodile, various species of antelope, baboon, buffalo, hippo, wart hog, and various species of birds. Half the fun is stalking the animals; don't expect to see large numbers of them.

The Somba

What's most fascinating about the Somba is their houses. The Somba dwellings, called *tatas*, consist of small, round, tiered huts that look like miniature fortified castles. The ground floor is reserved for the animals. The kitchen is on the intermediate level. From there, you ascend to the roof where there are rooms for sleeping and a roof terrace for daytime living. The somba are more concentrated to the south-west of Natitingou in the plain of Boukoumbe, and south-east around Perma. They live in the middle of their cultivated fields, and none of the compounds are close to one another.

The Somba, who have avoided Islamic and Christian influences, practise hunting with bows and arrows, which make great souvenirs. It's not unusual to see them going about their daily business completely naked. They don't like people taking photos of them, and you're strongly advised not to get out of your car and approach the houses, especially if you have a camera. Of course, if someone invites you to their home, that's an entirely different matter. Don't hesitate to accept.

Places to Stay & Eat

Many visitors stay in Natitingou and make excursions from there, but there is also good accommodation closer to the park.

In Porga at the entrance to the park is the *Hôtel Porga*, a tourist-class hotel which has 21 unadorned rooms and a restaurant which reportedly serves good food, including tasty wart hog during the hunting season. *Hôtel Pendjari*, inside the park, consists of five large bungalows with 25 rooms but it has been closed for years. It is reportedly going to reopen as an inexpensive campement.

NATITINGOU

Pleasantly located at 440 metres altitude in the Atakora Mountains and 110 km south-east of Porga, the entrance to the park, Natitingou is the centre of excursions to both Pendjari Park, sometimes called Porga Park, and Somba country.

Places to Stay & Eat

For rock bottom prices, try the *Campement de Natitingou*, which is clean, peaceful and serves food, or *Hôtel Soda-Tourisme*. The best in Natitingou is the PLM *Hôtel*

Tata Somba (tel 821124) with 26 air-con rooms, restaurant, bar and a pool.

Getting There & Away

To get to Natitingou, you can take one of Air Benin's regular flights, drive, join a tour, or take a bush taxi. If you take a bush taxi from Parakou, there's a car that leaves around 9.15 am for Natitingou in front of the post office, but you need to get there two hours in advance to have a chance of getting a seat. Otherwise, take a taxi to Djougou, then another to Natitingou. You can't hike in the park, so go to the hotel in Natitingou and make friends with travellers who have vehicles. Or arrange to rent Hôtel Tata Somba's Land-Rover. Those driving will find petrol in Natitingou. If you encounter mechanical problems, try Garage St Joseph – the mechanics are reportedly competent and their charges are fair.

KANDI

Kandi is worth a stop for two reasons – the lovely market, to which the Bariba and the Peul give a distinctive northern character, and the *Campement*, well placed behind two voluptuous mango trees. You may find they have no water, however. For food, there's the *Gargoterie de Kandi* behind the market.

MALANVILLE

This town is on the Niger border. You'll find a dirty campement at the entrance to town.

Burkina Faso

If you ask someone what there is to see in Burkina Faso, 'nothing' may be the response. Yet its popularity among travellers is tops in the Sahel – proof again that in West Africa, people count more than places. Ouagadougou (WAH-gah-DOU-gou) is smaller than most Sahelian capitals – you can walk everywhere downtown – and you might think life in one of the five poorest countries on earth would be fairly tranquil. Far from it. You'll find bustling streets crammed with mopeds and the market is one of West Africa's most active. One reason travellers like 'Ouaga' is that it is so easy to meet the locals in the morning at one of the many street-side tables serving coffee and bread, or in the evening at one of the many bars for which the city is famous. Only one in four Burkinabé is Muslim. So don't be surprised that it has more places for light drinking (drunks are rare) than Bamako and Niamey combined. In Ouaga, the night-time is the right time.

In the rest of Burkina, village life is fascinating. Finding a way to experience it is the problem, but *Le Point Mulhouse* has the answer. In Gorom-Gorom, a dry northern area near the desert, you can live in Le Point's African-style huts and participate in village life, and even weed and pound millet if you like.

In the far south, sugarcane fields, verdant plateaux, waterfalls and lakes provide an entirely different typography. Many travellers' favourite spot is Bobo-Dioulasso, the country's former capital and second major city. It has wide shaded streets, a vibrant market and an interesting array of possible excursions. Despite the present leader's militant style and the profusion of arms-toting militia, the country retains its good 'vibes' – a major reason travellers continue to give it high marks.

HISTORY

Before the colonial era, the largest political unit in much of Africa was the village. Burkina Faso was one of the exceptions. Various Mossi kingdoms ruled over many villages with an iron hand and developed a rigid social structure. In destroying this, the French perhaps laid the foundation for the country's post-independence turmoil. There have been six coups, a number equalled in Africa only by Nigeria.

The first kingdom of the Mossi people was founded over 500 years ago in Ouagadougou. Three additional Mossi states arose thereafter, each paying homage to Ouagadougou, the strongest of the four. The governments were highly organised, with ministers and courts, and a cavalry known for its devastating blitz attacks against the Muslim empires in Mali. They also fostered a rigid social order, with the other ethnic groups within their domains at the bottom. Only a few groups in the south-west, including the Bobo, Lobi and Senufo, escaped subjugation by these centrally organised states.

In the late 19th century, the French in West Africa became so accustomed to fighting for their territories that they were less willing than the British to negotiate. Rather than trying to reach a reconciliation with the Mossi, they chose to break them up. Exploiting the states' internal rivalries, the French accomplished their mission before 1900. The Ouagadougou

112

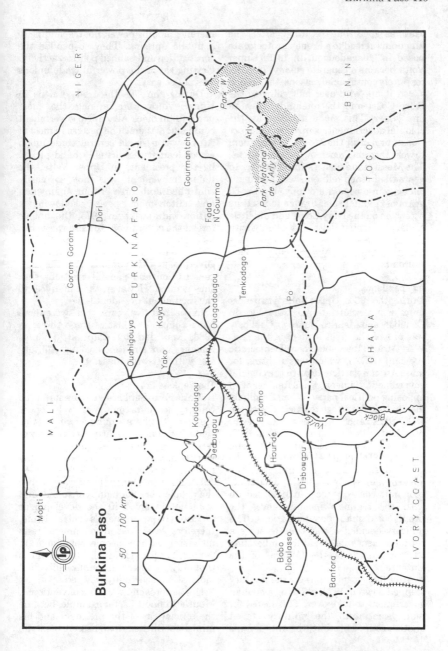

Burkina Faso

king escaped but returned after the kingdoms agreed to a French protectorate based in Ouagadougou. In 1919, Upper Volta became a separate colony. In 1932, for purely commercial reasons, the French sliced it up, with over half going to the Ivory Coast and the remainder to Mali and Niger. This made it easier for the colonial government, centred in the Ivory Coast, to recruit the Mossi, forcing them to work there on French-owned plantations. The Mossi made such a stink that after 15 years the French relinquished, making it once again a separate colony. During 60 years of colonial rule, France focused its attention on the Ivory Coast and did little to develop Upper Volta. It was only with the forced labour of the Mossi and others that they built the Abidjan-Ougadougou railroad.

Independence

During the 1950s, Upper Volta's two most prominent African statesmen were Ouezzin Coulibaly and Maurice Yameogo. Coulibaly was one of the great leaders of the pan-West African Rassemblement Democratic Africain (RDA), which was fighting for more African participation in the colonial government. Yameogo was a founder of an opposing political party. When Coulibaly died in 1958, Yameogo reconciled with the UDC-RDA and became a shoe-in for president following independence in 1960.

Yameogo became increasingly autocratic and banned all political parties except the UDC-RDA, and he administered the government poorly, with disastrous economic consequences. In 1966, fed up with the regime's incompetence, the people held mass demonstrations. The military decided it was time to stage a coup and sent him to jail for embezzling £1.2 million from the Council of the Entente.

After four years in power, the military stepped down in 1970, allowing a civilian government to take over. This lasted for four years, until the military staged another coup. This time, the military was

merely grabbing power, not responding to a public uprising. They suspended the constitution and banned political activity. Getting rid of the powerful trade unions was not so easy.

During the '70s the trade unions in Upper Volta were among the most powerful in black Africa. No government could ignore them. The pattern in most of Africa was a single central trade union whose leader was virtually hand-picked by the president. In Upper Volta, the union movement was not so easily controlled and three or four unions had real autonomous power. Following a nation-wide strike in 1975, the unions forced the government to raise wages but labour leaders were still not satisfied. In 1978, after several years of pressuring the government, the unions got the new constitution and general elections that they wanted. However, their man lost to the incumbent president.

In the next five years, there were three more coups. The last of these three, in 1983, was led by Captain Thomas Sankara, an ambitious young military star with left-wing ideas.

The Sankara Era

Burkina Faso, Sankara's new name for the country, became a country of revolutionary idealism. Sankara wondered why it was that after almost a quarter of a century of receiving more foreign aid per capita than just about any country in Africa, Burkina remained one of the world's five poorest nations. He concluded that it was because the people were not being consulted, and were not involved in the development process. His government's central theme, therefore, was that development rests ultimately with the people, not foreign aid donors. The flip side of this Maoist coin, is that only group action counts; individual motivation is virtually frowned upon.

His approach was unconventional. Modest Renault-5s, for example, became the official car of the president and his ministers. Blitz campaigns were his style.

In one 15-day marathon, the government vaccinated 60% of the children against measles, meningitis and yellow fever. UNICEF called it 'one of the major successes of the year in Africa'. Adopting the Chinese barefoot doctor model, Sankara called on every village to build a medical dispensary. The government sent several people from each village for training, making them frontline medical advisors. Between 1983 and 1986, over 350 communities built schools with their own labour, and the education of children increased a third to 22%.

Ouagadougou looked a bit shabby, so he ordered all houses on the principal streets to be painted white, then levelled the central market, thinking that some foreign government would surely help finance a new one. None have. In 1985, he dismissed all but three of the cabinet members, sending them to work on agricultural cooperatives. It was mainly show. A month later, they were back at their old jobs. Then Sankara ordered an across-the-board 25% cut in government salaries and ordered all rents for 1985 to be handed to the government instead of the landlords.

His pet project was the Sahel railway, a 375-km railroad project connecting Ouagadougou and Tambao at the Niger border, the site of rich manganese and limestone deposits. The project so far has no western backing because economists say it won't be profitable. Undaunted, Sankara moved ahead. In early 1987, they inaugurated the first leg, the 33-km stretch to Dousin, all done with 'voluntary' village labour.

The bluntly honest Sankara was immensely popular with the masses. In early 1986, he brought the country to war with Mali over an ancient border dispute involving Agacher, an area supposedly rich in manganese (but too costly to mine). His popularity soared still further. It ended five days later, but not before both sides had dropped a few bombs, causing an estimated 60 deaths.

Today

While Sankara was popular with most Burkinabé, he antagonised trade unions, landlords and many western countries. By his constant attacks on western imperialism and his back-slapping antics with Libya's Gaddafi, Sankara also alienated the French and the Americans. Sankara was one of the most interesting political figures in West Africa and his motives seemed irreproachable, but he did not live to see if his socialist policies would work. In late 1987, a group of junior offices seized power. Sankara was taken outside Ougadougou and shot.

PEOPLE

With about seven million people, Burkina Faso is one of the more densely populated countries in the Sahel. It's also over-populated, which is why the country's major export is people – over half a million Burkinabé work in neighbouring countries, primarily the Ivory Coast. While the remittances they send home assist the economy, the emigration of so many young men is a catastrophe for agriculture. It all helps intensify the famines that occur during the periodic droughts.

Concentrated in the central plateau area, including Ouagadougou, the Mossi are only one of about 60 ethnic groups in Burkina, each with its own language. You'll encounter the Bobo in the west around Bobo-Dioulasso, the Fulani or Peul (Sankara is Fulani-Peul) primarily in the north, the Gourmantché in the east, and the Lobi in the far south.

The Mossi are famous for having the longest continuous royal dynasty in West Africa, dating back about 500 years, when the war-mongering Mossi founded an empire in Ouagadougou. There were four Mossi kingdoms, each with its own king, or Naba. Strongly individualistic, they were one of the few people in the Sahel to successfully resist the Muslims. They even sacked Timbuktu, a Muslim stronghold, at the height of its power in 1333. As a result, today not more than 25% of the people are Muslim. The dynasty continues because the chief of the Ouagadougou kingdom escaped the French. You can see the Mossi emperor Friday mornings at the weekly Moro Naba ceremony (Moro is singular for Mossi).

Burkina would be a good place to look for masks if they weren't so large. The Mossi are best known for their tall antelope masks, usually painted red and white and well over two metres long. Used in funeral rites, they are also recognised by their oval faces and the vertical strip down the centre of the face. The Bobo, too, are famous for their masks, especially the butterfly mask which is over a metre wide with a small round mouth and a triangular face, and is painted red, white and black. Since butterflies tend to swarm after the first rains, they are associated with the planting season and the masks are used by dancers in agricultural rituals.

GEOGRAPHY
Landlocked in the Sahel, Burkina Faso is a flat arid country of bush, scrub and reddish laterite soil. As you move north, the vegetation thins out and the land becomes sandy and desert-like. In the far south around Banfora, below Bobo-Dioulasso, the rainfall is heavier and there are forests and irrigated sugar cane fields. The area from Banfora eastward to Ghana has beautiful rolling plateaux and green woodlands.

The French named the country Upper Volta after its three major rivers – the Black Volta, the White Volta and the Red Volta. All of them flow into the world's largest man-made lake – Volta lake in Ghana. You might think these rivers are the saviour of this arid country, but the waters attract black flies which transmit river blindness disease. As a result, Burkina has the world's highest incidence of this dreaded disease. Entire villages along the rivers have been evacuated because of it and the victims are the beggars in Ouaga and elsewhere, who are led around by small boys, chanting for money.

CLIMATE
The weather pattern is similar to the rest of the Sahel. Rain falls June to September. December to February the weather is cooler and the harmattan winds produce hazy skies. The hot season is March to May.

VISAS
Visas are required of everyone except nationals of Belgium, France, West Germany, Italy, Luxembourg and the Netherlands. Visas are easily obtainable because French embassies can issue them in countries where Burkina is not represented. Exit permits are no longer required.

You can get visas in Ouagadougou for Togo, the Ivory Coast and Chad (all at the French embassy) but not to Mali, Niger or Benin. Before the war, if you could convince the Malian border officials that you were residing in Burkina and couldn't get a visa, they would often allow you through provided you applied for a visa upon arriving in Bamako. This didn't work, however, for those arriving in Bamako by air. Chances are this may be resumed. Visas to Ghana are obtainable in Ouagadougou within two or three days but only if you indicate on your application form that you reside in a country without a Ghanaian embassy.

Diplomatic Missions Abroad
Abidjan, Accra, Bonn, Brussels, Cairo, Copenhagen, Lagos, Ottawa, Paris, Washington.

MONEY
US$1 = 287 CFA
£1 = 537 CFA

The unit of currency is the West African CFA. There's no restriction on the import or export of currencies. Banking hours: weekdays 7 to 11.30 am and 3.30 to 5 pm; closed Saturday and Sunday. Banks: BIAO, BICIA (Banque Internationale pour le Commerce, l'Industrie et l'Agriculture); Banque Nationale de Paris.

LANGUAGE

The official language is French. There are a number of African languages. Over half the people speak Moré (MOR-ay), the language of the Mossi. Dioula (JOU-lah) is the major language spoken in the market. Greetings in Moré:

Good morning	*YEE-bay-goh*
Good evening	*NAY-zah-bee-ree*
How are you?	*lah-fee-bay-may*
Thank you	*un-POS-dah BAR-ee-kah*

GENERAL INFORMATION

Health

A yellow fever vaccination is required. Cholera is required only if you've been in a country with a recent outbreak. The *Hôpital Yaldago Ouedraogo* (tel 334641/3/6) should be used only in emergencies. One of the better pharmacies in Ouagadougou is *Pharmacie Nouvelle* downtown near Ciné-Burkina.

Security

Burkina is one of the safest countries in Africa.

Business Hours

Business: weekdays 8 am to 12.30 pm and 3 to 6 pm; Saturday 8 am to 12.30 pm. Government: weekdays 7 am to 12.30 pm and 3 to 5.30 pm; closed Saturday and Sunday.

Public Holidays

1 January, 3 January, Easter Monday, 1 May, End of Ramadan (17 May 1988, 6 May 1989), Ascension Thursday, Whit Monday, Tabaski (25 July 1988, 14 July 1989), 4 August (Revolution Day), 15 August, 1 November, Mohammed's Birthday (22 October 1988, 11 October 1989), 25 December. The major holiday is Revolution Day. Independence (1 December) is no longer celebrated.

Photography

A photo permit is now required. They are issued by the Ministry of Tourism, which is open normal government hours. You will need to buy a fiscal stamp. Even with a permit, you cannot photograph any government buildings, military installations or personnel, airports, reservoirs, TV/radio stations, or religious ceremonies.

Time, Phone & Telex

When it's noon in Burkina, it's noon in London and 7 am in New York (8 am during daylight savings time). Calling Europe or the USA is usually not difficult. You can call from the main post office downtown every day until 8 pm; thereafter, you'll have to use the more expensive hotel phones. As for telexes, you can use the post office in Ouagadougou or the Silmandé and Indépendance hotels.

GETTING THERE

Air

From Europe, there are direct flights from Paris and Marseilles. From the USA, you'll have to transfer in Paris, Dakar or Abidjan. There are numerous flights from Abidjan to Ouagadougou but only two a week from Dakar to Ouagadougou. Air Burkina has flights to Bouaké and Abidjan (Ivory Coast), and Bamako (Mali). The cost on Air Burkina is about 25% less than on Air Afrique.

The cheapest connections between Europe and Africa are with *Le Point Mulhouse*, which has about eight flights a month from Marseilles to Ouagadougou. The cost is only about US$375 return and US$250 one-way. Flights are usually booked up at least a month in advance, sometimes two or more months during the summer months and around Christmas. Le Point makes reservations only upon receipt of full payment, so reservations by phone are impossible. French francs or CFA sent by cable with alternative departure dates are accepted. It may be possible to reserve in the UK; Le point apparently has an agent there for receiving money. For more details, see the introductory Getting There chapter. In Ouagadougou, Le Point is now on the Po road, several blocks from the main drag (Avenue Binger).

From London, the next cheapest way to get to Burkina Faso is on Aeroflot via Moscow with a ticket purchased from a bucket shop; the return fare is about £400.

Car

The straight driving time from Ouagadougou to Lomé (Togo) or Abidjan is about 20 hours. The route to Accra (Ghana) is paved the entire distance but is in bad repair between Kumasi and Tamale. Driving will take considerably longer until the repair work is completed, probably in 1988. You can also drive all the way from Ouagadougou to Niamey (Niger) and Bamako (Mali) in about nine and 12 hours, respectively; both routes are paved all the way. Borders with Togo, Ghana and Mali close at 6 pm; the Niger border closes at midnight. The Ivory Coast border never closes, but foreign cars need a *laisser passer*, which is issued only from 6 am to 6 pm.

Bush Taxi

From Ouagadougou there are bush taxis for Niger, Togo and Ghana. Service to Niamey is quicker now that the new asphalt road has been completed. The cost of a taxi direct to Lomé is about CFA 13,000. The price comes out about 50% cheaper if you buy a ticket to Dapaong (northern Togo) and take another from there to Lomé.

Bus

If you're headed for Ghana, one advantage of taking the bus is that you'll probably make it to the border before 1 pm, when the Ghana state bus leaves from the border to Tamale. But there are only two buses a week to Po and the border – Tuesday and Thursday.

Train

The Ouagadougou-Abidjan train leaves twice daily. The *Gazelle* has air-con,

which works temperamentally, sleeping cars (*couchettes*) with two people to a room, clean linen and wash basins, plus a decent dining car. The *Express* is cheaper, has a sleeping car with four people to a couchette, a decent dining car, and takes several hours longer. One leaves invariably in the morning, the other in the late afternoon. The schedule changes almost yearly, with the Gazelle leaving in the morning one year and the Express leaving in the morning the next year. The cost of the Gazelle is approximately: CFA 20,600 for 1st class (CFA 4500 extra for a couchette) and CFA 14,400 for 2nd class. The cost of the Express is approximately CFA 16,500 for 1st class (CFA 3500 extra for a couchette) and CFA 13,800 for 2nd class. The Gazelle takes about 22 hours and the Express about four hours longer – if there are no derailments. Ouaga to Bobo-Dioulasso is a 6 to 7 hour trip. There is a third series of trains, the *Rapides*, which cost about a third less than the Express and take longer still, but you'll have to change trains if you're going all the way to/from Abidjan.

GETTING AROUND

Air

From Ouagadougou, Air Burkina has flights five times a week to Bobo-Dioulasso, and twice weekly to Gorom-Gorom.

Bush Taxi/Bus

Bush taxis connect Ouagadougou with all the major towns. The buses are significantly cheaper, consequently, it isn't easy to get a seat unless you arrive an hour or two before departure. Most buses leave around 8 am. Throughout Burkina there are long waits for the bush taxis to fill up.

Train

There are three trains a day in both directions between Ouaga and Bobo. Between Bobo and Banfora there are two.

Ouagadougou

In spite of the arms-toting police everywhere, Ouaga retains its relaxed atmosphere and continues to be a favourite among travellers. You can cover most of the central area by foot. Meeting Africans and other travellers is relatively easy and the pastry shops downtown facilitate this by attracting both Africans and many overland travellers. One of the first things you'll see is the city's outstanding eyesore – a flattened area in the centre of town where the market used to be. Sankara had it levelled in 1985 and that's how it'll remain until the necessary finance is found. To find interesting crafts and materials, you'll have to go to the outskirts of town to the temporary market. Spread thinly over a vast area, it lacks the vitality of the former market.

Unlike most other major Sahelian cities, Ouaga is not dominated by Muslims, hence the night life is better than just about anywhere else in the Sahel except Dakar. Several places have live music almost every night of the week; some of it is in the open-air, some inside. Sankara wanted the common man to be able to enjoy the fruits of life, so all of them except the Silmandé's are dirt cheap due to government regulation of prices.

The best time by far to be in Ouagadougou is during FESPACO, the Pan African Film Festival held every odd year for about 9 days, usually starting the third or fourth Saturday in February. Typically, about 60 films are shown during the festival, about eight every evening starting around 6 pm in various theatres around town. The city's atmosphere is festive, plus the films, almost all produced by African, are fascinating and an excellent way to learn about Africa.

Information
Tourist Office *Direction de Tourisme* is 100 metres from the Hôtel de l'Indépendance.

If you want to stay at Arly Game Park, make your booking here.

Bank The *Bank International du Burkina* on Rue Brunnel gives good rates and efficient service.

Embassies Algeria, Canada (BP 548, tel 332093, telex 5264), Egypt, France (BP 504, tel 332270, telex 5211), West Germany (BP 600, tel 336094), Ghana, Netherlands, Nigeria, Senegal, USA (BP 36, tel 335442/4/6, telex 5290). Belgium, Spain, Sweden and Switzerland are represented by diplomatic missions.

A Bobo helmet mask from Burkina Faso

Bookstores & Supermarkets Three of the best supermarkets are *Mini-Prix* downtown next to the defunct Hôtel Michael and *Casino* on the main drag across from the Maison du Peuple. English newspapers and magazines arrive Tuesday afternoons at *Librairie Attie*, located at the Indépendance and also downtown near Ciné-Burkina.

Travel Agency Le Point Mulhouse (BP 4580, telex 5460), near downtown on the Po road and open Monday to Saturday 8 am to 1 pm, offers a number of excursions, including trips to Mali's Dogon area, the Ivory Coast, and a one-week trip to Gorom-Gorom about 300 km north-east of Ouaga, where you live in a typical African village for a week.

Moro-Naba Ceremony

The only 'must see' is the Moro-Naba ceremony (*la cérémonie de Nabayius Gou*) which takes place every Friday around 7.15 am. Take the Po road a block or two beyond the cathedral, then about two blocks to your right until you reach the far side of the Moro-Naba palace. Some travellers will undoubtedly find it boring. It's a very simple ceremony accompanied by drums that lasts only 15 minutes. It recounts an old story of when the preferred wife of the Moro-Naba, king of the Mossi, asked that she be permitted to go see her parents. He consented on condition that she return in three days. Infuriated when she did not return on time, the emperor mounted his horse the next morning, a Friday, to fetch her. As he was to depart, his ministers and the people begged him not to go. Showing his generosity, he agreed, dismounted and returned to the palace. The horse and people are all dressed in traditional costumes. Photographs are not allowed.

Musée National

This interesting museum faces the hospital. In addition to some good masks from various ethnic groups, you'll find a good collection of pottery with geometric designs that all serve different purposes – to store jewellery, clothes or grain. There are also magic pots for storing medicines. This ethnology museum also has a good collection of traditional materials, including an entire Mossi chief's outfit. Hours are 9 am to 12.30 pm and 3.30 to 5.30 pm, Tuesday to Saturday.

Other Sights

Besides the various places where artisan goods are sold there is the unique **Maison du Peuple**, a public auditorium on Avenue du Binger.

Places to Stay – bottom end

For the price, you can't do better than the popular *Hôtel Pavillon Vert* (tel 323551), which costs about CFA 5000/5500 for singles/doubles with air-con. The clientele is a mixture of Africans and foreigners, and the restaurant, with grass-covered *paillotes* in the central courtyard, is a favourite of many. It is a good km behind the train station next to the Marché de Sankariare, about two km from the town centre. If you don't go early in the morning, the chances of their having an empty room are slim. Five blocks away, you'll find *Hôtel l'Entente*, which is an excellent buy at about CFA 2300 to CFA 2800 for a clean single with fan and CFA 2800 to CFA 3300 for a double (about CFA 4000/4500 for air-con singles/doubles).

If you prefer to be in the heart of town, you will get less value for the money. *Hôtel Delwende* (tel 336314), half a block from the old central market near the defunct Hôtel Michael, charges about CFA 4500/5500 for a room with fan/air-con and a pleasant balcony for drinks and eats. The nightclub is on the same level as the rooms. *Hôtel Royale* is opposite the market and apparently charges about half as much for its rooms.

Along Avenue Yennenga, you'll find five or six places to stay; not all of them have signs. About five blocks from the old central market on Avenue Yennenga is the well-known *Hôtel Idéal* (tel 335765), which costs about CFA 4500 to CFA 5500 for a room with air-con. Don't let the hotel's respectable-looking exterior fool you; the rooms are poorly maintained. A little further down the street you'll find the slightly cheaper *Hôtel de l'Amitié* (tel 333023). On the same street, 100 metres from the mosque, is *Hôtel Yennenga* (tel 335824), which has poorly maintained singles/doubles for about CFA 3500/4500 with fan and CFA 5000/5500 with air-con. *Restaurant Rialle*, nearby, has somewhat cheaper rooms. Further out near the square Yennenga and the airport, you'll find *Hôtel Oubry* (tel 332936), with clean rooms, a tranquil terrace, African music and decent food – highly recommended.

For the cheapest, most basic accommodation, *Chez André* behind the Le Point office, and *Pierre Dufour* next to the cemetery have been recommended. A bed costs around CFA 1000.

Camping The best place is *Ouaga Camping* (or Chez Bouda Abel), which is one km behind the new Gare Routière on the south-eastern outskirts of town. Follow the signs behind the gare; it's down a dirt road in a village. They charge about CFA 500 per bungalow with good beds, clean toilets and showers. *Les Volta Fleuries* (tel 333717), 12 km on the road to Bobo, welcomes campers plus it has a good restaurant.

Places to Stay – middle
The colonial-era *RAN Hôtel* (tel 334255, telex 5273) on Avenue Binger near the train station, gets high marks from foreigners and Africans for its pleasant ambience, long pool and central location. The restaurant is mediocre. The 34 air-con rooms cost about CFA 11,000 and CFA 13,000. During the high season, November through February, a number of tour groups specialising in inexpensive overland adventures stay at *Hôtel Ricardo* (tel 333042). It is well managed by a friendly Italian and has relatively low prices (CFA 9000/11,000 for (singles/doubles), a long and usable pool, and one of the best hotel restaurants, with good pizza among other things. However, it is inconveniently on the outskirts of town behind Reservoir No 2, and finding a taxi is not easy.

Hôtel Tropical (tel 333418, telex 5418) is less expensive than the RAN and more conveniently located than the Ricardo. Air-con singles/doubles cost about CFA 9500/10,500 and the hotel is on a major street (Avenue Dimdolobsom), a 20-minute walk to the centre of town. The rooms are about as good as those at the Ricardo and the RAN.

If you want to be closer to the town centre, try *Hôtel Central* (tel 333417) in the dead centre of town, next to the defunct central market. It has the best restaurant of any hotel in town and singles/doubles for only about CFA 8000/9000 including tax, but the quality of the rooms is much inferior – the air-con barely cools the rooms, and the water pressure is low. If you have a ticket with Le Point, they'll reportedly knock off about CFA 3000 from the price.

Places to Stay – top end
The best hotel in town is Frantel's *Hôtel Silmandé*, but the restaurant is nothing to rave about and it's inconveniently located on the outskirts of town next to the reservoir. The liveliest hotel is the newly renovated 135-room *Hôtel l'Independance*, which is one km from the heart of town and doing a thriving business because of the reasonable prices and pleasant ambience, and it has a long pool. Next door is the city's major tennis club, to which guests have limited access.

The best deal in town for the money and good quality rooms is the *Ok Inn*, which has a pool and very decent restaurant. Prices are lower because of the poor location – next to the Gare Routière on the southern outskirts of town, about seven km the town centre. They do offer, however, free mini-bus service into town six times a day.

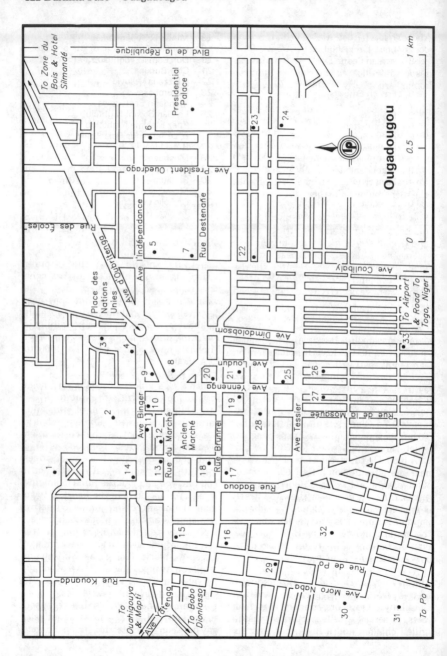

Ougadougou

1	Train station	18	Mini Prix Supermarket
2	Maison du Peuple	19	Librairie Attie
3	Artisan Centre	20	Don Camillo Nightclub
4	Post Office	21	Ciné Burkina
5	Hôtel de l'Indépendance	22	Il Pizzeria Vesuvio
6	French Embassy	23	US Embassy
7	Tennis Club	24	Mandarin Restaurant
8	Palais de Justice	25	Le Flamboyant Nightclub
9	L'Harmattan	26	Chez Maxime Nightclub
10	Bonbonniere		& Le Terminus Restaurant
11	La Chaumiere Restaurant	27	Hôtel Idéal
12	L'Eau Vive Restaurant	28	Mosquée
13	Hôtel Central	29	Ghanaian Embassy
14	RAN Hôtel	30	Stadium
15	Air Afrique	31	Moro Naba's Palace
16	Le Point	32	Catholic Church
17	Hôtel Delwende & King Snack	33	Tropical Hôtel

Hôtel Silmandé (tel 333635, telex 5345), singles/doubles for CFA 22,000/26,000, pool, tennis, nightclub.

Hôtel de l'Indépendance (tel 334186/7/8, telex 5201), singles/doubles for about 14,300/16,500, long pool, bar with billiard table, TV/video, bookstore and shops.

Ok Inn (tel 336766, telex 5418), 20 singles/doubles for about CFA 10,500/11,500, five bungalows for CFA 15,000, short pool, shuttle bus.

Places to Eat
Cheap Eats Downtown on Avenue Yennenga, next to Maxime's disco and three blocks from Ciné-Burkina, you'll find *Le Terminus*, a popular Peace Corps hangout which serves edible food for CFA 500 to CFA 1000. On the street a few blocks away near the mosque you'll find *Un Soir au Village*, which has good food and low prices. *L'Escale* nearby on the same street is another possibility. Equally good and popular is *Café de la Paix*, a block east of the market and near Ciné-Burkina. The upstairs balcony of the *Hôtel Delwende* is a nice setting for a meal.

African *Le Maquis* is about two hundred metres from the airport on Avenue Coulibaly. Outdoors under thatched roofs, it serves excellent chicken yassa, grilled chicken and a few other African dishes. Downtown, try the popular *L'Harmattan* one block across from the post office and open every day. The cuisine is mostly French, but they also have well-prepared daily African specials for about CFA 2000. Another possibility is *The King Snack*, half a block from Hôtel Michael; most dishes are CFA 1000 to CFA 1500.

French *L'Eau Vive* (tel 333512) is a Ouaga institution known throughout West Africa. It is run by an order of nuns and, naturally, it is closed Sunday. It has a garden terrace that is the city's most pleasant dining area. The food is very good, service comes with a smile, prices are quite reasonable, and if you stay until 9.30 pm, you can join the nuns in singing 'Aves'. You'll find it in the heart of town facing the vacant central market, 50 metres from Hôtel Central. The best food, however, is probably served at *La Chaumiere* (tel 334423), which is on the opposite side of the same block, facing the Maison du Peuple on Avenue Binger. Closed Monday, it's also more expensive, and serves Alsatian and Belgian specialities.

The air-con *Le Safari* also has very good service and food. It's downtown about halfway between the Hôtel de l'Indépendance and the airport, near *La Toque*, a new French-run restaurant with a pleasant ambience. Closed Monday, it charges about CFA 3000 for most main courses except the braised chicken, which is CFA 1800. If charcoaled meat dishes are what you're looking for, head for the *Ok Inn* on the outskirts of town. The restaurant is quite good and open every day. You can dine outside along the pool or inside with air-con. For excellent crepes try *Le Relais-Creperie* several blocks from Hôtel de l'Indépendance in the direction of the airport. Closed Tuesday, the French owners offer a wide selection of crepes, soft music, and inside or outside dining.

Italian Ouaga's best restaurant may actually be at the *Hôtel Central*, which is a little surprising in view of the hotel's run-down appearance and rooms. The cuisine is Italian and French, and includes seafood and the house speciality, spaghetti flambé. You also have the choice of indoor or outdoor dining. Open every day, it's downtown next to the market area. Another crowd pleaser is *Il Pizzeria Vesuvio*, where prices are very reasonable; a large pizza costs CFA 3000. They also serve numerous other Italian dishes. Open evenings only and closed Monday, it's on the same street as the Hôtel de l'Indépendance, three blocks away in the direction of the airport.

Others prefer *Hôtel Ricardo* behind reservoir No 2, about three km from the heart of town. Open every day, Ricardo offers his customers excellent pizza cooked in a wood burning oven as well as numerous Franco-Italian dishes.

Asian For good Chinese and Vietnamese food, you have only one choice, *Le Mandarin* (tel 332375), closed Monday and a block south of the US embassy. However, the service is slow and prices are moderately high by Ouaga standards.

Lebanese The *Oriental* (tel 332009) serves Lebanese and French food plus pizza

under straw huts for about half what you'd pay at the 'name' restaurants. It's downtown across from Ciné Burkina and open every day.

Pastry Shops Ouaga is noted for its pastry shops, most of which serve as social meeting places; the hours are usually 6 am to 12 noon and 3 to 7 pm. The most well known is *La Bonbonniere*, on Avenue Binger across from the Maison du Peuple. Others include *La Patisserie Nouvelle* across from Ciné-Burkina and *Patisserie de Koulouba*, about five blocks south of the Indépendance on the same street.

Entertainment & Sports

Bars The most popular place for a drink among well-heeled travellers is *Hôtel de l'Indépendance*; you have a choice between a drink around the pool or inside with air-con and a billiard table. The *RAN Hôtel* is fairly popular and has a more mixed African and non-African clientele. Those on the cheap prefer the bars along Avenue Yennenga, particularly *Don Camillo*, which doesn't get lively until the evening, and the balcony of *Hôtel Delwende*.

Nightclubs *Don Camillo* is a Ouaga institution, something no traveller should miss. No other nightclub in West Africa outside of Ouaga can claim these ingredients – a big dance floor, no cover, big reasonably priced beers, virtually packed every day of the week and, most important, live entertainment nightly. And if you need a dancing partner, that's no problem either. It's in the heart of Ouaga, on Avenue Yennenga, one block east of the vacant central market. Another advantage is that it gets lively around 9 pm, not 11 pm like many nightclubs.

La Palladium is similar in most respects and three blocks down on the same street, next to *Le Flamboyant*, which is a popular disco with strobe lights and a cover charge of CFA 300 on weekends. Packed weekends, it has cheap drinks and women available. *Maxime's* is similar in all respects, two blocks away on Avenue Loudun, and preferred by many. *L'Harmattan*, one block in front of the post office, is similar and open every day. The only classy disco is at *Hôtel Silmandé*, which has a cover of CFA 2500 and expensive drinks. Nearby, is *La Galaxie*, which is similar to Maxime and Le Flamboyant. At the opposite end of town, about two km beyond the airport, is *L'An 2*, a new nightclub which has paillotes outdoors. If you're looking for a bar where you can both dance and meet friendly Africans, try *Chez Alex*, a Ghanaian hangout for the common man. It's about four km from downtown near the Zone du Bois.

Movie Theatre *Ciné-Burkina* was built for FESPACO in the late '60s. With a wide screen and good seats, it's still one of the better movie theatres in West Africa. Shows are usually at 6.15, 8.15 and 10.15 pm. It's downtown across from the mosque, two blocks from the central market area.

Sports There are pools at the top five hotels. The longest are at the Indépendance and the RAN. The latter charges CFA 700 weekdays, CFA 1000 weekends. For tennis, try the Silmandé or the *Club de Tennis* next to the Indépendance. You have to be invited to play at the latter, but if you want to hit with the club pro (CFA 2000 an hour), he'll find a way to get you on the court.

The Americans have an open-air squash court behind their International School. They play volleyball there as well on Sunday at 4 pm. Golfers may get a chuckle playing the 18-hole, laterite course at the *Ouagadougou Golf Club*, about 12 km from downtown on the Po road. The greens are rolled sand and slightly oiled.

Things to Buy
Artisan Goods Temporarily located on the outskirts of town, the *Grand Marché* is one of the best in West Africa. Materials are a particularly good buy as are baskets, leatherwork, bronze and pottery. Downtown, behind the post office is the *Centre Artisanal* (tel 333221), which has a mediocre selection of batiks and other materials, pottery and bronze. It's open weekdays 8 am to 12 noon and 4 to 6 pm, Saturday 4 to 6 pm.

Embroidered tablecloths and napkins are the speciality of *Le Centre de Formation Feminine Artisanale*, a women's cooperative sponsored by the Austrian Catholic Mission. It is off the road to Bobo-Dioulasso, several km west from the city centre. Further out of town you'll find the tannery, *Le Centre de Tannage* (tel 334457), which makes purses, small boxes and wall hangings among other things. Or pass by one of the tannery's outlets downtown – at Hôtel de l'Indépendance and on Avenue Loudun between the mosque and the Petit Marché. The quality is not exceptional, but you may find a good souvenir.

Music For cassettes of African music, look outside the Bonbonniere pastry shop. Burkina is not noted for its music. Some of the better known singers are George Ouedrago, Opportune and Cissé Abdoulaye (traditional).

Getting There & Away
Bush Taxi Bush taxis for Niger, Togo and Ghana leave from the Gare Routière on the southern outskirts of town, about eight km from the centre. The cost of a taxi direct to Lomé is about CFA 13,000. The price comes out about 50% cheaper if you buy a ticket to Dapaong (northern Togo) and take another from there to Lomé.

Bush taxis make the trip to Bobo-Dioulasso quicker than the train. They cost from CFA 2500 (Peugeot 404 pick-ups) to CFA 3500 (Peugeot 504s), but they're less comfortable.

Bus There are connections from Ouagadougou to all the major towns. Buses leave from Gare 'X9' on the north-west side of Ouaga. The departure time for most destinations is 8 am. If you get there later than 7 am, you're unlikely to get a seat. If you're headed for Ghana, one advantage of taking the bus is that you'll probably make it to the border before 1 pm, when the Ghana state bus leaves from the border to Tamale. But there are only two buses a week to Po and the border – Tuesday and Thursday. If you're headed just to Bobo-Dioulasso, you could also take a bus. They are cheaper and slightly faster, and are near the train station, to your left.

Train There are rail connections for Koudougou, Bobo-Dioulasso and Banfora, though the buses and bush-taxis are quicker. For the Ivory Coast, the Gazelle leaves Ouagadougou at 4.10 pm and the Express at 7 am, but these may change so check at the RAN station in Ouaga (tel 333751).

Getting Around

Airport Transport At Ouagadougou airport, there's no departure tax. You'll find a bar-restaurant, shops and car rental (Avis). The cost of taxis to downtown (four km) is posted outside the airport where the taxis are stationed – CFA 1000 (50 to 100% more to the Hôtel Silmandé). You could also catch one of the cheap public buses, but you may have to walk a number of blocks to one of the major routes.

Taxi Fares are CFA 200 for a shared taxi, about CFA 500 for a taxi to yourself (more for long journeys), about CFA 1750 by the hour, and about CFA 10,000 plus petrol by the day. Bargaining is required. Taxis are not always easy to find during the day, even on the main road, Avenue Binger-Avenue de l'Indépendance. The Hôtel de l'Indépendance is the only sure place to find one. At night about the only place you may find one is on Avenue Binger in front of the RAN hotel, in front of the Hôtel Central, and at the Hôtel de l'Indépendance.

Car Rental There are numerous car rental agencies in Ouagadougou. Rent a Car/Avis (tel 333229) is at the airport, Hôtel Silmandé and on Rue de la Chance. Avis will reportedly sometimes allow you to drop the car off in Abidjan. Burkina Auto Location (tel 335552/332621) is at the Hôtel de l'Indépendance and accepts AE and D cards. A Renault 4 will cost you about CFA 13,500 a day plus CFA 80 per km, 22% tax and CFA 3500 for a chauffeur (required). Other agencies include TT Car Transit c/o Marie-Pierre Diallo (tel 333106) and Express Auto Location (tel 334255/70) at the Ran hotel.

The West

BOBO-DIOULASSO

'Bobo' is the No 1 favourite West African city of many travellers. It's easy to understand why. It has wide shaded streets, a thriving market, a sidewalk café for drinks, one of the best value hotels in West Africa, a relaxed pace of life in a city with about 150,000 inhabitants, and a number of possibilities for out-of-town excursions.

Things to See

The **Grande Marché**, which is closed on Friday, is one of the best in West Africa for a city of its size. To the east of the market is the old **mosque** built in 1880 and a good example of Sudanese architecture. The main points of interest are just out of Bobo – see the Around Bobo-Dioulasso section.

Places to Stay – bottom end

Near the Gare Routière, you'll find three places. The *Mission Protestante Americaine* (tel 990467) is friendly to travellers and has cooking facilities and neat rooms for about CFA 2800 a person. It is near *Hôtel de la Paix* (tel 990100), which borders the Gare Routière. For about CFA 2300 to CFA 2800 a room, the Paix is reasonable and they serve decent cheap food. About a block or two away is *Hôtel Hamdallaye*, which charges about CFA 3300/3800 for singles/doubles with showers and a fan.

In the centre of town, there are several more cheap hotels. *Hôtel du Commerce* (tel 990311), which borders the market, is not a good buy – about CFA 4500/5500 for singles/doubles with fans and CFA 6500/7000 for singles/doubles with air-con. A better buy is *Soba Hôtel* (tel 991048), which is near the Auberge and has singles/doubles for about CFA 2200/2800 (bungalow), CFA 4000/4500 (fan), and CFA 6500/7500 (air-con). It also has a pool.

If these are all full, which is often the case, try *Hôtel de l'Unité* (tel 991401), a good km from downtown but not far from the train station. Ventilated singles/doubles cost about CFA 3300/3800 (CFA 2000 more for air-con). Near the outskirts of town you'll find *Hôtel de l'Amité* (tel 990746), which has clean decent rooms for about CFA 3300 and private shower (CFA 500 more with fan and CFA 2000 more with air-con).

Places to Stay – top end
The well-managed *L'Auberge* (tel 990184) is simply fantastic for the price. For about CFA 7700/8300 (singles/doubles), you get a decent air-con room, a clean pool, a bar with billiard table, a terrace for drinks and watching the crowds, and one of the three best restaurants in town. It's in the dead centre of town. Even if you don't stay here, you can use the pool for CFA 1000. You'll find newer, more modern facilities and a pool at the 40-room *RAN Hôtel* (tel 990649/999684) which is across from the train station, a km from the heart of town. Singles/doubles cost about CFA 13,300/15,500. You can make reservations at the train station in Ouaga, Abidjan or Bouaké.

Two other decent but inferior hotels are *Relax Hôtel* (tel 990442, telex 8218), with singles for about CFA 7700 to CFA 10,500 and doubles for CFA 8300 to CFA 11,000), and *Watinorna Hôtel* (tel 991079), with

rooms for about CFA 7000 to CFA 8200 (CFA 1000 more with air-con) and a pleasant patio. Both are several blocks from the Auberge. If these are full, try *Hôtel le 421* (tel 990652), also downtown but closer to the train station, with clean air-con rooms for about CFA 7700 and a nightclub.

Places to Eat
L'Eau Vive (meaning living water), closed Sunday, is the sister restaurant of the one in Ouaga and equally good. It's downtown across from *Cafeteria du Relax*, which is a very popular inexpensive restaurant and a meeting place for the locals. The restaurant at the *L'Auberge* is open every day and a great buy – a three-course meal with wine for about CFA 2500. They also have a big à la carte menu which includes pizza. Across from the Auberge you'll find another good restaurant, *La Boule Vete*, which is run by a pleasant French woman who charges only CFA 1600 to CFA 2000 for all her main courses.

Two blocks from the Auberge, facing the post office, is a great outdoor bar-restaurant, *Le Mankno*. Run by two French men who serve both European and African meals and play good music (Rolling Stones, reggae, hard rock), this place has very cheap beers. Back of the post office is another popular place, *Le Renaissance*. The music is a major attraction here as well, but it's more traditional.

For much cheaper fare, you have many choices. At the Gare Routière is *Le Metropole*, which serves excellent steak among other things, *Restaurant de la Paix* nearby and, on Avenue de l'Unité between the Gare Routière and the market, *Yan-Kady*, which serves traditional African cuisine.

Nightlife
The nightclubs are all in the heart of town. Three of the best are *Black & White* near the Hôtel du Commerce, *Horphée* 150 metres from Relax hotel, and *Le 421*

several blocks away. On weekends, there's frequently dancing at *Le Mankno*; the music is sometimes live.

AROUND BOBO-DIOULASSO

The following places of interest can easily be done as day trips from Bobo.

La Mare aux Poissons Sacres de Dufora

This unusual fish pond, 10 km from Bobo, is not to be missed. The setting in a crevice below a cliff is memorable. You'll find Africans there virtually every day of the week. They come with chickens, which they kill and feed to the huge fish. A taxi there and back will cost you about CFA 5000 if you bargain well; the excursion shouldn't take you more than two hours. You'll have to walk 10 minutes or so from the taxi. Around the pond you'll see chicken feathers everywhere. The people say the fish are more active Monday and Friday and that photographs make them hide. Also, wearing red is prohibited.

La Guinguette

Another possibility is an excursion to La Guinguette, a bathing area about 18 km west of Bobo in a verdant forest, le Forêt de Kou. In colonial times, it was reserved exclusively for the colonialists. Now, it's a popular place for Africans on weekends. The water is crystal clear and during the week you'll have the place to yourself. Camping and swimming are apparently both possible.

Koumi

For an interesting village, head for Koumi, 16 km south-west of Bobo on the road to Orodara and Sikasso. You'll see two-storey houses that are reminiscent of those of Indian tribes in south-western USA. Consult the chief before taking photos.

BANFORA

The town of Banfora is nothing special, but the surrounding area is certainly one of the most beautiful in Burkina – perfect for a tour on a motorcycle or bicycle. The major attractions around Banfora are Les Cascades and Lake Tengrela.

Places to Stay & Eat

The best hotel is the two-star *Hôtel La Canne à Sucre* (tel 880107), on the road to Abidjan, about one km from the train station. Air-con rooms range from about CFA 6500 to CFA 9000, and you can dine inside or outside. The next best is *Hôtel Fara* (tel 880117), 300 metres from the train station (take a left as you leave the station). Decent rooms cost about CFA 3300 to CFA 3800 (fan) and CFA 5500 (air-con), all with private showers. The meals, however, are not as cheap as at *Hôtel le Comoé* (tel 880151), which is near the stadium, about two km from the train station. The rooms, which cost about CFA 2250 (CFA 3800 with fan and CFA 5500 with air-con), open on to a garden full of plants, giving the place a pleasant feeling.

AROUND BANFORA

Les Cascades

These are 12 km west of Banfora off the road to Tengrela. The waterfalls are interesting all year round, but more so during the rainy season. Camping is possible but the water might be infested with bilharzia. Those without vehicles will either have to hike or rent someone's motorcycle or moped. In the dry season, a bicycle will suffice. On the way, you'll pass through irrigated sugarcane fields – quite a contrast to the dry land in most of Burkina.

Lake Tengrela

This lake is about 10 km due west of Banfora. You'll see fishermen in their boats bringing in the nets and hippo heads bobbing up and down. Give a few coins to one of the men and he'll take you for a boat trip. Camping is also possible along the lake.

BOROMO

Boromo is half way between Ougadougou and Bobo-Dioulasso. *Le Campement* is one of the better places to stay. It costs about CFA 1700 for a room with shower.

KOUDOUGOU

Koudougou is Burkina's third largest city. There's nothing to see in particular, so take a break from sightseeing and enjoy yourself.

Places to Stay & Eat

Koudougou has a surprisingly decent hotel, the six-room *Hôtel Toulourou* (tel 440170) owned by Burkina's first president, Maurice Yameogo. It is two blocks east of the train station. Air-con rooms cost about CFA 4500 with outside bath and CFA 6500 with private bath. The air-con restaurant offers a big selection; most dishes are CFA 900 to CFA 2000. Four flocks away is *Hôtel Yéléba*, with ventilated singles for about CFA 2800, and air-con doubles with shower for about CFA 4500. At the shaded patio restaurant, you can get braised chicken and steak & fries, among other things. *Hôtel de la Post*, near the post office, is similar in quality and has a decent restaurant.

A block from the Toulourou is the *Hôtel Oasis*, which charges about CFA 1200 a night for one of its 10 rooms and serves food as well. A block from Oasis, is *Chez Tanti*, where you can get African chop. Facing Tanti is *Snack bar Gazelle*, which serves drinks outside under paillotes. Another major watering hole is *Snack bar Sport*, a 10-minute walk north-east from the train station and lively even in the morning.

The East

KOUPÉLA

Koupéla is 127 km east of Ouaga on the way to the game parks, at the intersection of the main road to Togo. You'll find *Hôtel Bao Fougou* at the intersection and *Hôtel le Bon Sejour* 200 metres away. The latter has a bar and restaurant.

GAME PARKS

Forêt de Mazinga

A three or four hour drive south from Ouaga via Po is the Forêt de Mazinga. It's not a park but a game reserve managed by Canadians who are working on a project to determine how much wildlife a given area of land can support and what can be done to increase the land's carrying capacity. The numerous elephants are the main attraction. There are also various species of antelope, monkey, baboon, wart hog and birds, but no lion. Unlike traditional game parks, you can walk amongst the animals without restrictions. An empty shed without beds is available for those staying overnight, but the 'ranch' managers prefer advance warning of your arrival. (Call the Canadian embassy.)

Parc National d'Arly

You'll find all the animals here that you do in the neighbouring Pendjari park in Benin – elephant, wart hog, baboon, monkey, lion, hippo, leopard, crocodile and various species of antelope and birds – but their numbers are few so spotting them won't be easy. The park is 520 km south-east of Ougadougou, a six to seven-hour drive on mostly paved road. It is open early December through May.

Places to Stay & Eat

For CFA 13,300/15,500 (singles/doubles), you can stay in an air-con bungalow at the PLM *Hôtel Campement d'Arly*, which has a bar, restaurant and pool. To make reservations, see the Direction du Tourisme in Ouga. To get there, you must travel east on asphalt road to Kantchari, then south on dirt road to Arly on the eastern side of the park. For much less money, you can stay on the western edge of the park in Pama at *Chez Madame Bonanza*, who has 20 or so bungalows and serves excellent food. Her husband was apparently eaten by one of the lions.

Parc 'W'

This park is about 70 km east of Arly and

an extension of the same park in Benin and Niger. The animal life is virtually the same. You can stay at Arly or at the park entrance in Diapaga, where there's a *Campement* with five bungalows and a restaurant.

The North

OUAHIGOUYA

This is 181 km north-west of Ouagadougou and is the largest town in the north. During the dry season, it is quite feasible to drive to Dogon country in Mali. The best hotel is the family-run *Dunia*. The *L'Amitié* is another.

KAYA

Kaya is 98 km north-east of Ouaga and can be used as a stop-over on the way to Gorom-Gorom. *Hôtel de l'Oasis* has large rooms and a shower but no restaurant.

DORI

Dori is in the north-east, about 50 km south of Gorom-Gorom, The *piste* (track) between the two towns is bad There's a big market on Sunday and you can get petrol and cold beer here. If you're lucky you'll find a bed at *Chez Jean* at the market facing the bank.

GOROM-GOROM

Gorom-Gorom is a very pleasant town where the mud architecture blends in perfectly with the environment. The market, which takes place Thursday, is one of the most interesting in Burkina. You'll see various ethnic groups (Bella, Peul, Songhai, Tuareg), a variety of animals and a wide selection of artisan goods (cloth, leather, goods, jewellery).

Places to Stay

Le Point has constructed a *Campement* in the style of traditional African houses where tourists live for a week or so, experiencing life in an African village as it really is. By the mid-1990s the campement will be turned over to the villagers. It is closed July and August. Air Burkina has flights to/from Ouagadougou on Tuesday and Friday.

MARKOYE

Markoye is about 45 km north-east of Gorom-Gorom and can be visited as a day trip if you're staying in Gorom-Gorom. The attraction here is the Monday camel and cattle market, which is the equal of, or better than, that in Gorom-Gorom.

Cape Verde

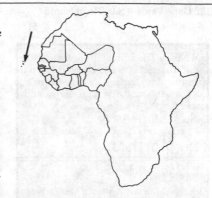

The Galapagos Islands are not the only place that provided Charles Darwin with the inspiration for his theory of evolution. Cabo Verde (VER-dee) played a role too. Only the fit survive here. By some measures it's the driest country in Africa; most of these islands receive rainfall only once or twice a year and on one island it hasn't rained in over 10 years. Years ago, if you were living on one of these islands some 620 km out in the Atlantic, what did you do when a drought came along? You either died with thousands of others, fled the country on the next boat out, or stuck it out and went about building terraces and dykes and planting trees so that the next time it rained, the water didn't end up in the sea along with your topsoil.

If you have any interest in how people have adapted to a seemingly life-defying environment with limited resources, you'll find visiting the interior fascinating. Certainly that's the effect it had on Darwin when he visited here over a hundred years ago. As he said in the *Voyage of the Beagle*:

The island would generally be considered as very uninteresting; but to anyone accustomed only to an English landscape, the novel aspect of an utterly sterile land possesses a grandeur which more vegetation might spoil.

But there's more to Cape Verde than the environment. The people, for instance, are like none on the continent because they look and act more Portuguese than African. So don't be surprised by the absence of African tribal life and umpteen local languages. There are Portuguese-style houses with verandas upstairs, plazas with an orchestra in the middle, cobblestone-like streets, *vino verde* with your Portuguese meals, distinctive fast-paced music with Latin rhythm and African inspiration, and a relatively well-educated mestizo people – almost all with relatives in the USA. If the idea of an island with a Portuguese ambience and a lunar setting seems intriguing, chances are you'll be delighted by the Cape Verde islands, especially during Mardi Gras time. It may not be action packed, but it is picturesque.

HISTORY

The history of Cape Verde is dominated by three overriding facts: there were no people of any sort on the islands when the Portuguese first arrived; the environment has become increasing fragile over the centuries, largely due to man and over-grazing; and it's further from the African continent and closer to the Americas than any other African country. It's hardly surprising, therefore, that Cape Verde developed along lines somewhat different from the rest of Africa. As a result, of the 52 countries in Africa, Cape Verde probably deserves the title of being the most unique.

Early History

When Portuguese seamen first landed on the Cape Verde islands in 1456, the islands were barren of people but not of vegetation. Seeing the islands today, you may find it hard to image that they were sufficiently *verde* (green) in those years to entice the Portuguese to return six years later to the island of São Tiago to found Ribiera Grande, the first European city in the tropics.

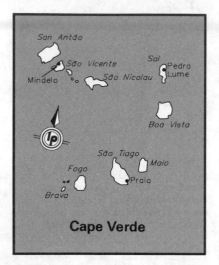

Cape Verde

Working on the plantations was no easy task, so almost immediately the Portuguese began bringing slaves from the West African coast to do the hard labour. Because of their location on the sailing route to points further south on the African continent, the islands were also a convenient base for ships transporting slaves to Europe. With the addition of the Americas in the 16th century as a destination for the slaves, Cape Verde was sitting pretty – the slaving ships could hardly avoid the islands.

Vineyards added to the prosperity and the wine exported to Portugal was of excellent quality. But all wasn't rosy. The prosperity of the islands attracted pirates, who occasionally attacked the towns, and England's Sir Francis Drake sacked Ribiera Grande in 1585.

Droughts

Cape Verde continued to prosper – until the first drought. In 1747, the islands were hit with the first of a series of droughts that have plagued the islands ever since. Why? Too many people and goats. People chopped down trees and goats destroyed

the ground vegetation which provides moisture. The Portuguese government sent almost no relief during any of the droughts (except the most recent one starting in 1969). Three major droughts in the late 18th and 19th centuries resulted in well over 100,000 people starving to death. The total population killed in each was incredible: 44% in 1773-76, 42% in 1830-33 and 40% in 1863-66. The decline of the lucrative slave trade in the mid-19th century was a second blow. Cape Verde's heyday was over.

It was then, in 1832, that Charles Darwin passed by. The country's landscape had become the antithesis of the Galapagos. His description in *The Voyage of the Beagle* still holds true:

A single green leaf can scarcely be discovered over wide tracts of the lava plains; yet flocks of goats, together with a few cows, contrive to exist. It rains very seldom, but during a short portion of the year heavy torrents fall, and immediately afterwards a light vegetation springs out of every crevice. This soon withers; and upon such naturally formed hay the animals live. It had not now rained for an entire year. When the island was discovered, the immediate neighbourhood of Porto Praya was clothed with trees, the reckless destruction of which has caused here, as at St Helena, and at some of the Canary islands, almost entire sterility. The broad, flat-bottomed valleys, many of which serve during a few days only in the season as water-courses, are clothed with thickets of leafless bushes. Few living creatures inhabit these valleys.

Cape Verdeans started emigrating to New England in droves. Why New England? Because whales abounded in the waters near Cape Verde, and as early as 1810 whaling ships from Massachusetts and Rhode Island began recruiting crewmen from the islands of Brava and Fogo. Many of them used this as a means to escape to the US and leave behind their precarious existence. Within just six years, the Americans had established a consulate on the islands. But the islands were not finished. With the advent of the ocean liner, their position astride Atlantic shipping lanes made Cape Verde an ideal location for resupplying ships with fuel (imported coal), water and livestock. The deep protected harbour at Mindelo on São Vicente became an important commercial centre.

The droughts continued. During the first half of the 20th century, the following percentages of the population didn't make it through: 15% in 1900-03, 16% in 1920-22, 15% in 1940-43, and 15% in 1946-48. Starvation was becoming a way of life, but the Portuguese did nothing, neither helping to build water retention dams nor taking other measures to cope with the droughts. The Portuguese needed workers, however, for their cocoa plantations in São Tome, so between 1900 and independence, over 80,000 Cape Verdeans signed up for four year contracts at a time. The only problem was that they were treated like slaves, and transported in ships where they were packed like animals. An international boycott of São Tomé cocoa in the early 1900s did nothing to change their living conditions.

Independence

Despite this bad treatment, the Cape Verdeans at least fared a little better than Africans in the other Portuguese colonies because of their lighter skin. A small minority received an education; Cape Verde even had the first school for higher education in a Portuguese colony. By the time of independence, a quarter of the population was literate, compared to 5% in Portuguese Guinea (now Guinea-Bissau).

This ultimately backfired when the literate Cape Verdeans became aware of the pressures building up on the mainland for independence and started their own joint movement for independence with the natives of Guinea-Bissau. It was the Cape Verdean intellectual, Amilcar Cabral, who got the movement going when he founded the political party PAIGC in 1956. Because the Cape Verdeans were so much better educated

than the Guineans, they naturally took over the leadership.

The Portuguese dictator Salazar wasn't about to give in like the British and French. So there was no escape from fighting, but it all took place in the jungles of Guinea-Bissau because the liberation movement simply wasn't as strong in Cape Verde. Middle-class Cape Verdeans were not so keen to disassociate themselves from Portugal, and the islands were more isolated. It took 14 years of war using guerrilla tactics (discussed in the Guinea-Bissau chapter) to gain independence in 1975. For five years after, Cape Verde and Guinea-Bissau talked about a union of the two countries, but a 1980 coup in Guinea-Bissau that deposed the president (of Cape Verdean origin) put an end to that.

Today

In 1986, Cape Verde had its heaviest rains in almost 20 years, possibly ending its longest and harshest drought ever – 17 years from 1969 – except that people didn't die this time. The USA and Portugal made up most of the 85% food deficit and are continuing to do so. However, the islands' livestock was almost wiped out. The number of cattle, for instance, is about one-third of what it was in 1968. Only Santo Antão island remains green enough to warrant the islands' original name. More than ever, survival is the name of the game, and coping with the elements is the only strategy. But there's a gamble in everything they do. If a farmer plants before the rains and the rains are minimal, he could lose everything.

Whether the latest rains were merely a freak incident or a return to the norm, nobody knows. The drought has continued for so long that some people are beginning to wonder if it is now the normal weather pattern. After all, 1985 was drought year number 31 in the 20th century. The norm these days is four to eight inches of rain in September or October, followed by another 11-month drought. In two days of rain in September 1984, the rains caused intense flash flooding and two major bridges were swept away near Tarrafal and Porto Formoso. Precious water and top soil went right into the sea.

When you take a trip into the countryside you'll see some of the 15,000 dykes and 2500 km of water-retaining walls that have been built in the last few years to keep this from happening. It's working and they're building more. You may think they're for irrigation too, but they're not. Pumping water would require resources way beyond Cape Verde's means.

You'll also see new trees being planted. Local experts and research by international organisations have produced a variety of acacia which is well adapted to the conditions of the islands. Some 23,000 hectares have been planted since independence, and by 1990 the government expects to be self-sufficient in wood fuel for the first time in over 300 years.

So Cape Verde is not without hope. Indeed, based on what is known as the Quality of Life Index, Cape Verde comes in near the top in West Africa. That's because the education level and health standards are the highest in West Africa; almost 60% of the state budget is spent on health and education. From 1975 to 1983, life expectancy increased an astounding 39%, from 46 years to 64, possibly the highest in Africa. Cape Verde has the most successful food-for-work program in Africa, maybe the world, and people can find employment if they want to work. Everywhere on the islands, you'll see roads being built in much the same way the Romans did – rocks chiselled by hand and then placed by hand into the ground, without mortar. Over 35% of the economically active rural population, mainly unemployed farmers, are employed this way!

How can this be? The gross domestic product (GDP) only comes to about US$150 a person, about the same as Guinea-Bissau. Simple. For every US$1 earned at home, Cape Verdeans get another US$1 from relatives abroad, and another US$1 in the form of foreign aid and – explained further on – receipts from South African Airways. People have been emigrating for years, over half a million in the last 100 years. There are as many Cape Verdeans living overseas (roughly 350,000) as there are in Cape Verde. Most are living in Massachusetts (particularly the greater Boston area) and Rhode Island. They haven't forgotten their homeland. The remittances they send back to Cape Verde are estimated to be slightly higher than the GDP itself. In 1981, it was US$25 million in remittances as against a GDP of US$20 million. Forty percent of the government's budget comes from these remittances.

Cape Verde also receives assistance from many countries. Eighty percent of its investment budget comes from foreign aid. The US alone provides most of its grain and Cape Verde is the highest per capita recipient of US grain in Africa, if not the world. Third, South African Airways (SAA) cannot make its long-haul flights to Europe and New York (now banned) without refuelling. Denied landing rights at almost every other airport in Africa, the planes stop at Sal Island. Although the US ban on SAA costs Cape Verde an estimated US$3 million annually in lost revenues, the landing fees and refuelling charges reportedly still equal 15 to 20% of Cape Verde's foreign earnings.

Politically, the country is stable. The party maintains a certain Marxist orientation, but the country's ties are all with the west. Certainly that's where the aid comes from. The Soviet fleet isn't even allowed to use the ports.

One of the things you'll remember most about your trip to Cape Verde is the strength of the people's attachment to their homeland. Even if the weather never returns to 'normal', Cape Verdeans aren't about to desert these islands. True, there's still a trickle of people leaving the islands every year, but talk to some of the older people and you'll find some who have spent most of their lives abroad, yet returned here to retire.

PEOPLE

Cape Verde probably has the lowest population growth in Africa. It is also the only country in West Africa with a primarily mestizo population. The arrival of white people in significant numbers dates back five centuries, long before colonial settlement on the continent. The miscegenation between the Portuguese settlers and their African slaves began early and forged a distinct Cape Verdean nationality with its own highly individual culture.

The vestiges of the Portuguese culture are much more evident than those of the African, although this is less true on São Tiago Island, which has a significant number of people of pure African stock. There's little trace of the African in their dress, their houses or their religion (Catholic). The food is basically Portuguese, but the music is distinctive – Latin in rhythm but with a different pace, usually much faster. The guitar and the electric piano dominate, but the usually ubiquitous African drum is difficult to find.

GEOGRAPHY

There are 10 major islands, nine inhabited and all of volcanic origin. The most important is São Tiago, which contains the capital city of Praia and almost half of the population. São Vicente has the country's major harbour and second largest city, Mindelo. These two islands along with Santo Antão, which has the highest rainfall and the second highest population, and Fogo with the islands' highest peak, Mt Fogo (2839 metres), are where most of the islands' 310,000 inhabitants live.

The island of Sal, as its name suggests, produces salt, enough for export. It has an international airport, but only 6000 residents. The island of Brava, still famous for its 19th century importance as a whaling centre, has few inhabitants

today but is picturesque and fairly accessible by boat.

CLIMATE

Because of the numerous micro climates, rainfall is not evenly distributed. On the western slopes of Fogo, for example, there is sufficient rainfall to grow coffee. In most areas, however, it is limited typically to one or two downpours between late August and October. The rest of the year is marked by gusty winds and, particularly between December and February, low visibility from dust originating in the Sahara Desert.

Cape Verde is one of the cooler West African countries. The hottest period is September when it reaches 27°C. Due to ocean currents, the sea is also considerably chillier than along the West African coast. From December to February, you'll need a heavy sweater; during the rest of the year, a windcheater is advisable because of the winds.

VISAS

Only nationals of Guinea-Bissau do not need visas. Almost everyone on the African continent gets them in Dakar (Senegal). The embassy in Dakar is downtown in an office building on Rue de Relais, off Avenue Ponty. Visas are issued in one day for most nationalities if you apply in the morning. You should bring a letter of recommendation from your embassy, otherwise the process will take about a month and even then you may not get one. If there's no Cape Verdean embassy where you are, try the nearest Portuguese embassy. They will usually process your application.

Diplomatic Missions Abroad

Algiers, Bissau, Conakry, Dakar, The Hague, Lisbon, Luanda, Washington.

MONEY

US$1 = 72 CVE
£1 = 140 CVE

The unit of currency is the escudo (CVE). It's not a hard currency, but there's no black market. Inflation is fairly low. You may have to fill out a currency declaration form when you arrive.

Banking hours: weekdays 8 am to 12 noon (cash transactions only). If you arrive in Praia on the weekend, the Hotel Praia Mar will exchange your dollars or CFA for escuodo. The hotel will also accept American Express travellers' cheques. Banks: Banco de Cabo Verde, Banco Nacional Ultramarino.

LANGUAGE
Portuguese is the official language, but the everyday language of most people is Crioulo, an Africanised creole Portuguese.

GENERAL INFORMATION
Health
A yellow fever vaccination is required if you're travelling within six days from an infected area. The hospital (tel 442) in downtown Praia on Rua Martines Pidjiguita has Cuban doctors and is not too bad, but the one in Mindelo (Avenida 5 de Julho, tel 2030) is definitely better. Ask for the German doctor in Mindelo, Andreas Kalk. Two of the better pharmacies are Farmácia Higiene (tel 288) at Prace 12 de Setembro in Praia and Farmácia Higiene (tel 2007) on Rua Liberatadores d'Africa in Mindelo.

Security
Praia is one of the three or four safest capital cities in Africa. Mindelo is equally safe.

Business Hours
Business: weekdays 8 am to 12 noon and 2.30 to 6 pm; Saturday 8 am to 12 noon. Government: weekdays 8 am to 12 noon.

Public Holidays
1 January, 20 January, 8 March, Good Friday, 1 May, 19 May, 1 June, 5 July (Independence), 12 September, 25 December.

Photography
No permit is required. You should not encounter any problems, nevertheless, avoid photographing military installations.

Time, Post, Phone & Telex
When it's noon in Cape Verde, it's 1 pm in London and 8 am in New York (9 am during daylight savings time). Postal service is very reliable. Calling Europe and the USA is no problem. The cost to the USA is 300 CVE a minute, less than half of what it is elsewhere in West Africa. None of the hotels have telex facilities; try the post office.

GETTING THERE
Air
The flights from New York to Sal Island with South Africa Airways have stopped because of the sanctions against South Africa. From Europe, South African Airways has direct flights to Sal from Amsterdam, Frankfurt, Lisbon and Paris. You can also fly Lisbon-Sal on TAP, and Dakar-Praia on both Air Senegal (Saturday) and the Cape Verdean airlines TACV (Wednesday).

Getting a flight from Dakar to Praia is not easy. Even if the ticket reads 'OK' and your travel agent swears that it has been confirmed 'OK', it isn't. Why? Because Air Senegal and TACV only take reservations by someone walking in the office and putting your name on 'The List'. Maybe your travel agent can try contacting a Dakar travel agency to do this for you. The problem presents itself not once but twice since, as with all flights in Africa, you must reconfirm your reservation. If you're arriving in Dakar several days in advance of the flight, no problem. Otherwise, the same person who made your reservation should reconfirm it 72 hours before the flight.

Returning from Praia to Dakar, you'll have the same problem. Someone must walk into the TACV or Air Senegal office in Praia to make your reservation. Otherwise, when you arrive in Praia and (immediately!) go to the TACV or Air Senegal office to make a reservation, they may tell you that there are no seats for the next two weeks. This is not unusual because the flights are almost always full. So your one-week trip could easily turn into a two-week trip or more. During Mardi Gras time, count on staying a month unless someone has previously reserved and paid for you.

Still, if TACV tells you the plane is full, it's only a half-truth. Five of the 45 or so seats on most flights are reserved for the government. TACV can't sell any of the five until it has received word from the government of how many will be used, usually a day or two before the flight leaves. So it's not unusual for several spaces to become available in that time. If you're desperate and know someone with pull, get them to plead with the government to let TACV sell you a seat. The chances of this working are fairly good if all five aren't needed. But ask TACV first; they may have already received word that all of them will be used.

Boat

As for connections to the outside world, there is reportedly a ship that connects Dakar and Mindelo about once a month, but few travellers have taken it. This might be a possibility for leaving the islands; at least it would be much easier getting information there than in Dakar.

In Mindelo you might even find a freighter headed for Portugal or the USA (Delta Lines carries the food shipments). There's nothing on a fixed schedule basis, but you might get lucky. Just don't expect it to be free. It'll probably cost you as much as the plane. If you are very lucky, you might even find a yacht headed towards the USA or the Caribbean. Those leaving from the coast of West Africa almost all stop here.

GETTING AROUND
Air

Between Praia and Mindelo there are one or two flights daily, and between Sal and either Praia or Mindelo, there are several flights a day. Between Praia or Mindelo and the other islands, however, once or twice a week is typical. The price of tickets is not expensive, about 2000 CVE (US$23) for Praia-Mindelo, for example.

Reserving seats on the roundtrip portion of inter-island flights is a problem. TACV in Praia and Mindelo (tel 2804) may tell you that if you want to go to a particular island, you must wait until you arrive to reserve your flight back. Don't believe them. It's a matter of radioing the TACV office on the island and making a reservation. If they say there are problems with the radio, be skeptical. The problem is that the TACV office is usually deluged with people, especially in Praia, and they don't want to take the time to do this. Catch them when the office isn't so swamped, usually first thing in the morning or late in the afternoon, and let them know very clearly, and nicely, that you simply can't risk taking the flight without some certainty of getting back by a given day.

A final problem is the harmattan, the winds from the Sahara desert that bring dust and reduce visibility, sometimes to less than one km. This happens from December through February. One day it may be relatively clear, the next may be much worse. Sometimes it won't let up for a week or more. Your return flight to Dakar may be postponed, even cancelled, or you can be left stranded on an island for days. Many people would never risk it. If you're going to be travelling a lot around the islands, this problem alone is a good enough reason to plan your trip during another part of the year.

Boat

There are ferry connections to all nine inhabited islands. Some follow a regular schedule, others do not. The ferry that ploughs between Praia and Mindelo has an irregular schedule, averaging about two trips a week. The trip takes 16 hours and costs about 600 CVE. The *Furna* connects Praia with Fogo and Brava. She leaves Praia on Tuesday and Thursday at 9.30 pm, and arrives at Fogo in 12 or 16 hours depending on whether she stops at Brava en route (longer) or afterwards. Returning to Praia, she leaves Fogo on Monday at 6 pm and Wednesday at 5 pm; the trip takes 12 or 16 hours depending, similarly, on whether she stops at Brava en route.

The cost is only about 350 CVE. You cannot buy a ticket on board. In Praia, tickets for all ferries must be purchased at the Agência Nacional de Viagens (tel 307) downtown around the corner from the US embassy. In Mindelo, this same company (tel 2420/1) is downtown on Avenida de la Republica.

The major problem with these ferries is that they have no cabins. There are only a few benches, and they aren't comfortable. So you must resort to looking for a corner, and it'll probably have to be outside where it gets very cold and windy. Be prepared for a miserable night.

São Tiago Island

São Tiago was the first island to be settled and the major island of Cape Verde. For the visitor there is the relaxed capital Praia, the first settlement, Cidade Velha, or the deserted beaches around Tarrafal.

PRAIA

The centre of Praia is on a fortress-like plateau overlooking the ocean. The principal residential sections are on surrounding plateaus and in the valleys between. The streets are very clean, cars rare and the people pleasant. Tranquility rules in this small city of 40,000 inhabitants. The central market is small by West African standards, but still interesting.

There are several places on the plateau where you can get something to eat, all fairly proletarian. The hole-in-the-wall bars are full of unemployed men, drinking Portuguese wine or *grogo*, the local sugar cane mash. At night things liven up wherever there's electricity (blackouts are common). In the heart of town you'll find the Esplanada, the central plaza with a covered bandstand. From 6 to 9 pm or so in the evening, the young people congregate here, walking around the circle, eyeing the opposite sex and waiting for the next show at the cinema. If there are areas of town where the electricity hasn't been cut off, chances are you can find an animated place to get a drink and maybe even listen to some of the local music, one of the best treats that Cape Verde has to offer. The beaches are another. There are two near Hotel Praia Mar on the edge of town.

Information
Embassies Brazil, France (tel 220), Portugal (tel 408/710), Senegal, USA (tel 761). Honorary consuls: Belgium, Netherlands, Norway.

Bookstores & Supermarkets For books on Cape Verde, good records and cassettes of superb Cape Verdean music, and not-so-good postcards, your best bet is *Galerias Praia*, the town's major department store on Avenida Amilcar Cabral, and *Serbam* next door. Popular male singers include Bana, Paulino Vieira (guitar), Masa Abrantes, Chico Serra (piano) and Luis Morais. The Praia Mar also has postcards.

The *Instituto Caboverdiano do Livro* next to Restaurante Avis also sells some books and maps. For food, there's the central market and *Galerias Praia*, which has the best supermarket in town.

Travel Agency There's an agency at the Hotel Praia Mar. You'll probably have to deal directly with either TACV (tel 612/3/4) on Rua Guerra Mendes or Air Senegal (tel 717) nearby.

Places to Stay – bottom end
There are frequent blackouts, and only

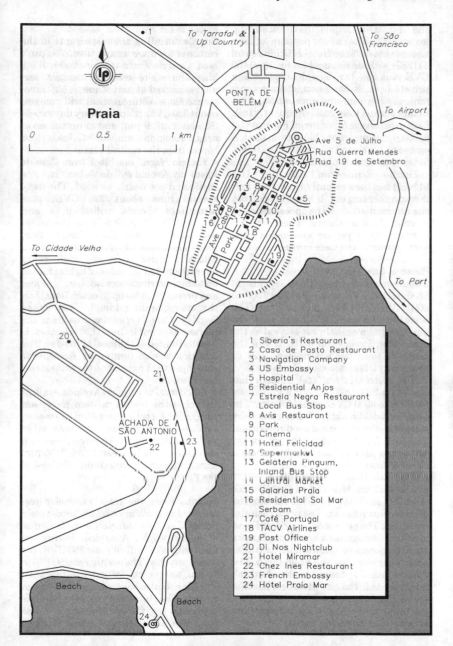

Praia

0   0.5   1 km

To Tarrafal &
Up Country

To São
Francisco

PONTA DE
BELÉM

To Airport

Ave 5 de Julho
Rua Guerra Mendes
Rua 19 de Setembro

To Cidade Velha

Ave Cobral

Park

To Port

ACHADA DE
SÃO ANTONIO

Beach

Beach

1   Siberia's Restaurant
2   Casa de Pasto Restaurant
3   Navigation Company
4   US Embassy
5   Hospital
6   Residential Anjos
7   Estrela Negra Restaurant
    Local Bus Stop
8   Avis Restaurant
9   Park
10 Cinema
11 Hotel Felicidad
12 Supermarket
13 Gelateria Pinguim,
    Inland Bus Stop
14 Central Market
15 Galarias Praia
16 Residential Sol Mar
    Serbam
17 Café Portugal
18 TACV Airlines
19 Post Office
20 Di Nos Nightclub
21 Hotel Miramar
22 Chez Ines Restaurant
23 French Embassy
24 Hotel Praia Mar

the top two hotels have stand-by generators. The most popular of the cheaper hotels is the *Hotel Felicidade* (tel 611289) with singles/doubles for 700/1400 CVE plus 10% tax. The doubles have a private bath. It has plain, clean rooms, fans, good lighting and a restaurant. It is in the centre of town and is frequently full. Less expensive is *Residencial Paraiso* (tel 613539), downtown one block from the US embassy. It's clean and costs 600/850 CVE for singles/doubles plus 10% tax.

Pensão Residencial Sol Mar (tel 613455) has been recently renovated and is worth checking out. It is one block from the central market on the opposite side of Avenida Amilcar Cabral. There's also a cheap unnamed pensão downtown on the same corner as the Café Portugal.

Places to Stay – top end

The *Residencial Anjos* (tel 613892) costs 1200 to 1500 CVE for singles and 1600 to 2000 CVE for doubles, plus 10% tax. The price includes breakfast. It's an excellent buy, and has rooms almost as good as the Praia Mar, Praia's top hotel. It's in the centre of town but has no generator or restaurant (there are several nearby).

The *Hotel Marisol* (tel 613460) has singles for 2500 to 3000 CVE and doubles for 3000 to 3500 CVE, plus 10% tax. The price includes breakfast. It has a stand-by generator, decent rooms, good restaurant and fans. It is overlooking the sea on the same road as the Praia Mar but one km closer to town.

The best hotel by reputation is the *Pousada Praia Mar* (tel 614363/614253, telex 79) at 3000/3500 CVE for singles/doubles plus 10% tax. The price includes breakfast. The price is 500 CVE less for an identical room without hot water. It has a stand-by generator, tennis court, saltwater pool, ocean-view bar and a nightclub. The air-con usually doesn't work, but it's rarely needed. The city's two best beaches are nearby, but the hotel is three km from the town centre. Travellers' cheques are accepted but not credit cards.

Places to Eat

City Centre All of the restaurants in the centre of town are inexpensive. You can't beat *Casa de Pasto* (or *Amélia's*). It's a blue and white collar restaurant and always packed at lunchtime. A big three-course Cape Verdean meal will run you about 300 CVE. It's open every day except Sunday until 9 pm, and is on the main drag, Avenida Amilcar Cabral, four blocks from the central plaza.

Estrela Negra, one block from Casa de Pasto on Avenida 5 de Julho, is more rustic and not nearly as good. The daily special runs about 225 CVE, plus sometimes there's grilled pork and chicken. The *Hotel Felicidade* also serves very good but basic Cape Verdean fare, including lobster when in season. *Cachito Snackbar* across from the main plaza offers the widest selection of lighter meals, including various sandwiches, croques and pregos. It's also open much later than the others, until midnight, but closed Sunday. *Café Portugal* across from the market is similar but the selection is usually limited to the meal of the day. The selection is also limited at *Restaurant Avis*, open to 11 pm and on the same street one block away.

Geladeria Pinguim on Avenida Amilcar Cabral is the town's modern ice cream parlour, with a good selection of ice creams, sundaes and other fancy concoctions, as well as sandwiches. However, you can order these only between 4 and 10.30 pm; only drinks are served during the rest of the day.

Suburbs Even the most expensive restaurants in town are all very moderately priced. The *Hotel Marisol* is the favourite of many people. A typical Portuguese meal with wine will run you 550 CVE. It's open every day. The evening hours, 7.30 to 10 pm, are typical for most restaurants. The Marisol also has a very good ice cream parlour. The *Pousada Praia Mar* is a close runner-up but the atmosphere is not as good. The *Mira Mar* in Cidade Velha 15 km away offers the nicest setting. Watch the sunset from the old fort, then order dinner on the terrace overlooking the ocean. The speciality is lobster.

Casa Inês is more like a family restaurant, basic, but extremely popular, in part because it has a generator. The grilled meats are particularly good. Most of the nine selections are 150 to 300 CVE. Between the Marisol and the Praia Mar there's a road leading up the bluff. Go to the first main intersection at the top, veer to your right, and stop at the first houses on your right for directions. It's to your right about 150 metres down an alley at the edge of the bluff.

Ponte has an entirely different ambience – like a nightclub with low lights, a bar and few tables. The menu is very limited but the Portuguese fare is good, and most dishes cost 250 to 550 CVE. It's in a residential section, two km from the downtown plateau on the main road inland.

Casa de Pasto Churrascaria with an outside terrace is on the same road but 200 metres toward town. The speciality is grilled meat with most plates costing around 400 CVE. It's open every day. *Churrascaria Siberia* is better known and noted for its grilled chicken, about 500 CVE a plate. It's also about two km from the downtown plateau but in a different location.

Entertainment & Sports

Bars Downtown, the best places for a drink are *Café Portugal*, *Avis* with its wood-panelled surroundings, and the Esplanada, Praia's central plaza where throngs of people mingle around from the late afternoon on. For local colour and a sip of the local brew, grogo, try *Casa de Poto's* bar. The local expatriates tend to head more toward the terrace bars at the *Marisol*, the roof-top terrace of *Hotel Felicidades* and, for the best ocean view, the *Praia Mar*.

Nightclubs *Di Nos* is the best in town, inexpensive, with open-air dancing, usually to the very lively sounds of a Cape Verdean orchestra. The crowd is fairly young and sometimes rowdy. It's usually open Friday to Sunday starting around 10.30 pm, but not if there's a blackout in that area of town. It's a 20-minute walk up the bluff from the Marisol.

Pilon on the Praia Mar has taped music, mostly American but some Cape Verdean. It's very popular weekends, but otherwise dead. There's a cover charge except for guests at the hotel. *5 de Julho* is a park in the new part of town that apparently has music on weekends starting around 10.30 pm. You might also try *A/Teia* ('The Spider's Web') in the Fazenda section of town.

Movie Theatre Cine-Teatro on the same block as the Felicidade shows American films now and then, all dubbed in Portuguese. Shows are at 6.30 and 9.30 pm.

Sports For tennis, your only choice is the court at the Praia Mar. The fee for people not at the hotel is 150 CVE (200 CVE at night). The Praia Mar also has the only pool; it's saltwater and crowded on weekends. The coast is rocky, so there aren't many beaches. The most popular is a tiny beach right next to the Praia Mar. It too is packed on weekends.

Less crowded and great for body surfing is a beach about a 10-minute walk in the opposite direction of the Praia Mar. For no crowds at all, you'll have to drive 30 minutes to São Franciso Beach. Or go to Tarrafal, the prettiest beach at the opposite end of the island. There is a rocky cove with caves for snorkelling and diving about one km east of Tarrafal Bay. The water is never very warm, and from December to March it's downright cold.

Getting There & Away

Air There are daily flights from Praia to Mindelo and Sal Island.

Bus There are buses to towns in the interior. There is no bus station as such, only designated places on the streets depending on the destination. The bus to Tarrafal via São Domingos leaves one block from Geladeria Pinguim on the main drag, Avenida Amilcar Cabral. The departure hour is 3 pm from Praia and 6 pm from Tarrafal. The bus to Santa Catarina leaves Praia every day at 3.30 pm, and Santa Catarina every day at 6.30 am.

Getting Around

Air Transport There's no airport departure tax. You'll find a snack bar but nothing else at the airport in Praia. A taxi into Praia (4 km) is 200 CVE including baggage. There are no buses.

Bus You can catch buses on the plateau to every section of the city, but a lot of people walk because of the infrequent service.

Taxi Fares are 80 CVE for a short trip in town. They are not accustomed to hourly rates so bargaining is required. Expect to pay not less than 700 CVE. Taxis are black and not too difficult to find on the plateau. There are no taxis at the hotels, but the hotel receptionist will gladly call the taxi company for you. The pick-up charge is 80 CVE. After 8 pm, taxis disappear, but you can call the taxi beforehand and arrange to be picked up at just about any hour. Rates are negotiable. There are no car rentals.

TARRAFAL

A trip to the interior of São Tiago Island is a must. One suggestion is to head for Tarrafal, a small fishing village at the opposite end of the island with perhaps the best beaches on the island.

SÃO DOMINGOS

On the way to Tarrafal, you could stop in São Domingos at a bar-restaurant called *Pedra Badejo* overlooking the ocean. Tarrafal can be reached by bus, and you can stay overnight at the *Aldeia Turística*, an inexpensive pension next to the beach which serves very decent food, as does *Tata* downtown.

CIDADE VELHA

For a half-day trip, go to the old city, Cidade Velha, 10 km from Praia and the first town built by the Portuguese on the islands. The ruins of the old fortress and the first cathedral are of particular interest. It's a good place to head for in the late afternoon to look at the ruins followed by a drink and meal at sunset.

ISLAND TOUR

A taxi is about the only way to get there other than hitchhiking, which usually isn't too difficult. Those with bucks can rent a taxi by the hour and head towards São Jorge (lovely gardens and picnic spot), Monte Chota (high in the hills), São Domingos (on the coast with a restaurant) and, for the most scenic drive but several hours from Praia, Santa Catarina (also with bus service and a restaurant). You could hitchhike to these villages; Cape Verdeans are great about picking people up. Just don't expect many vehicles with extra seats to pass by.

São Vicente Island

MINDELO

Mardi Gras is the best time by far to be in Cape Verde but also the most crowded. While celebrations and parades are held all over the islands, those at Mindelo are the best. Preparations begin several months in advance and on Sundays you can see the various groups practising and marching up and down the streets.

With 35,000 inhabitants and the country's deepest port, Mindelo hardly plays second fiddle to Praia. It's a somewhat more lively town, perhaps because of the ships passing through. Certainly the bars and nightclubs are more numerous and the restaurants a cut above. The Amilcar Cabral park is the liveliest place in town from 6 to 11 pm; don't miss it. These places are not hard to find. Half of what there is to see and do is

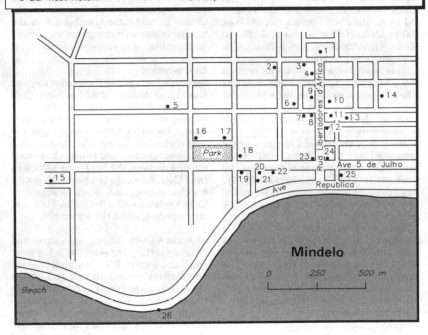

1 Palácio du Gobierno
2 Casa Miranda
3 O Cordel Restaurant
4 Pastelaria Algarve
5 Disco Pimm's
6 Pensão Casa Rialto
7 Discoteca do Bana record shop
8 Café Portugal
9 Bar Rest Ratem
10 Defunct Mercado
11 Xe Nu Bar
12 Café Royal
13 Taxi Stand
14 Cathedral
15 Hotel 5 de Julho
16 Cine Edin Park
17 Hotel Porto Grande
18 Hospital
19 Geladeria
20 Aparthotel Avenida
21 La Terrasse Restaurant
22 TACV
23 Pensão Chave d'Ouro
24 Banco do Cabo Verde
25 Navigation Company
26 Port

located on just two intersecting streets, Rua Liberatadores d'Africa and Avenida 5 de Julho.

The colonial houses are particularly picturesque. Most are two-storey houses with balconies and shuttered windows, and the architecture is very Portuguese. Filling out the picture are streets in stone, palm trees and a variety of other trees, small bars with their own special character on every other corner, all surrounded by the sea on one side and tall barren hills on the other. In the USA, this town probably would have been restored and become a tourist trap. Left as is, the town has a lot of charm.

Places to Stay – bottom end

Pensão Casa Rialto has singles/doubles for 400/550 CVE plus 10% tax. There are only three or four rooms with a common bathroom, but the rooms are clean and the beds are fairly comfortable. It's one block back of Café Portugal.

Pensão Chave d'Ouro (tel 2402) costs 550/650 CVE for singles/doubles plus 10%

tax and is highly recommended. It's in the heart of town across from the main bank and one floor up. It is like a big old Portuguese house, with high ceilings, shared baths, and a darn good restaurant with filling meals.

Places to Stay – top end
Many people still prefer Mindelo's grand old hotel, the *Porto Grande* (tel 2446) at 900 to 1100 CVE for singles and 1200 to 1550 CVE for doubles, plus 10% tax. The price includes breakfast.

This hotel has a lot of character even though it's a bit rundown. Each room has a balcony overlooking the city's beautiful park; the scene of a lot of activity in the evening. Or see it all from the hotel's popular terrace bar.

Hotel 5 de Julho (tel 2704) is a newly renovated and fairly large hotel in the same price range, but the atmosphere is a little sterile. There's a fair view of the city, but it's a 10-to 15-minute walk to the centre of town and getting a cab could be very difficult.

The hotel with the best rooms is *Aparthotel Avenida* (tel 2689, telex 44) at 1300 to 1600 CVE for singles and 1600 to 2000 CVE for doubles, plus 10% tax. The price includes breakfast. It's a small new hotel downtown near the ocean with wood-panelled rooms. There's no life to the hotel, however.

Places to Eat
Even the most expensive restaurants in town are at best moderately priced. *O Cordel* is quiet with a small restaurant, air-con and impeccable service, and is a good three notches above any restaurant in Praia. The main dishes are 250 to 350 CVE. It's downtown across the street from the pink Palacio du Gobierno. *Ratem*, with soft music, air-con and some interesting selections, seems about as good. Most main dishes are about 350 CVE. It's in the heart of town on Rua Liberatadores d'Africa across from the defunct Mercado Municipal.

La Terrasse (tel 2527) is downtown overlooking the ocean and on a hill behind the Aparthotel Avenida. It is owned by a French/Cape Verdean couple, is a good place for lobster and it's one of Mindelo's three best restaurants. *Pensão Chave d'Ouro* is unquestionably the best place for traditional Cape Verdean food. A full meal will cost about 225 CVE. For snacks, the *Geladeria*, next to the Aparthotel Avenida, has six choices of ice cream, crepes, banana splits, milkshakes and sandwiches.

Entertainment
Bars *Café Portugal*, in the heart of town on Rua Liberatadores d'Africa, and *Café Royal* across the street, are two of the most popular with Cape Verdeans and travellers alike. They serve coffee, beer, pregos and sandwiches. *Pastelaria Algarve* is another on the same street and two blocks toward the pink Palacio. *Xe Nu Bar*, a half block from Café Royal, is a fancy small bar with a quiet setting, and seems to appeal to Cape Verdeans with a few bucks. For grogo, try some bars along the waterfront.

Nightclubs *Disco Pimm's* has a small and intimate setting and seems to be the most popular in town. It's open almost every day starting around 10 pm, and on the street behind the Porto Grande, about two blocks away. *Katem* is a nightclub downtown next to Ratem that seems worth checking out. *Je t'aime* and *Bar Calipso*, nightspots in the fringe area of town, may also be worth inquiring about.

Other For movie theatres, Cine Edin-Park next to the Porto Grand has a lot of American films. Shows are at 6 and 9 pm. The most popular beach on weekends is just outside of town. Alternatively, you could walk or take a taxi up Monte Verde just outside Mindelo for a fine view of the city and harbour. If you're looking for a supermarket, try Casa Miranda. For records of Cape Verdean music, the best place is *Discoteca do Bana* back of Café Portugal.

Getting Around
Taxi A taxi from the airport into town (10 km) costs about 300 CVE. There are no buses. Hitchhiking shouldn't be too difficult. The taxis are found one block behind the old Municipio Mercado building just off Rua Liberatadores d'Africa.

Fogo Island

The major attraction of Fogo is Mt Fogo (2839 metres), which had the islands' last volcanic eruption, in 1951. The major town is São Felipe.

SÃO FELIPE
São Felipe has brightly painted houses with balconies as in Praia and Mindelo. It looks like a sleepy town in Portugal.

Places to Stay
For only about 100 CVE, there is an unnamed pensao half a block from the market with big rooms and decent beds but no restaurant.

The surprisingly good *Hotel Xaguate* (or *Hotel São Felipe*) has singles for 800 to 1200 CVE and doubles 1000 to 1400 CVE, plus 10% tax including breakfast. The more expensive rooms have balconies. It has a tennis court and a good restaurant. Reservations can be made in Praia at the Praia Mar hotel.

MT FOGO
It's an hour's drive from São Felipe to Cha das Caldeiras, a village at the base of the Mt Fogo. There, it's easy to get a guide to take you to the top for a magnificent view of the volcano's eight-km-diameter crater and a good idea of how this entire archipelago was born. The climb takes four or five hours. The cinder makes the climbing tough; you slide with every step, making progress slow. Coming down is almost like skiing.

Getting There & Away
The problem is getting to Cha das Caldeiras. There are taxis in São Felipe, but they could easily charge you 10,000 CVE, and that wouldn't include waiting for your return. Hitchhiking is possible, but you may have to wait a few hours because there aren't many vehicles and they probably won't be going that far, although most drivers will pick you up.

Climbing the Crater
An alternative to climbing the volcano is climbing the tremendous crater that circles the volcano. The advantage is the savings in time and money. Take the same road as though you were going to Cha das Caldeiras and get off at the base of the crater where the road splits in opposite directions around it, about 12 km from São Felipe. You can get a taxi one-way for about 5000 CVE, otherwise, hitchhike. Ask the locals to point out the path leading up. The trip to the top can be done in three hours if you're in good shape, and the view is about as good as from the volcano. When you get back down, even if no cars pass by, São Felipe is within walking distance.

THE CALDERA
You could also drive or hitchhike up into the Caldera area. The villages there are inhabited by the ancestors of French royalists who escaped from Napoleon. They make their own wine – full-bodied reds.

Other
Instead of returning to São Felipe, you could head to the delightfully secluded black sand beaches on the west coast of Fogo and to the south of São Felipe. Or take a ferry to Brava island. The trip only takes three hours and there are ferries every day except Sunday. It's mountainous, with good hiking possibilities. As on Fogo, seemingly everyone has relatives in the USA.

Sal Island

The only reason to go to Sal Island is to catch a flight to Europe. *Novotel Belorizonte* is brand new and the best hotel on the island, with single/double bungalow rooms for 3800/4200 CVE, pool, tennis and windsurfing. It's in Santa Maria village 18 km from the airport and on the beach, and it offers a free shuttle bus from the airport. The *Morabeza* is in the same village and is where the flight crews stay. The *Pensão Dona Angela*, in the village nearest the airport and within walking distance, is cheap and has good food.

The Gambia

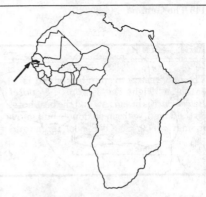

Tourism is to The Gambia in West Africa what it is to Kenya in East Africa. Its vast stretches of relatively undeveloped beaches with little undertow, guaranteed sunshine nine months of the year, and a peaceful, safe environment make The Gambia a Mecca in the wintertime for Europeans. Another reason is the abundance of all-inclusive package tours from London, starting at £270 a person for a week's stay – cheaper than a roundtrip ticket from a cut-rate bucket shop!

Travellers on the cheap are attracted by the country's cost of living, the lowest in West Africa. Bird watchers are in for a real treat – over 400 species have been recorded. Others come more for the cultural experience, particularly to visit Juffure, the site of Alex Haley's world famous novel *Roots*. You can also visit several nature preserves, take a cruise up the Gambia river and fish in the ocean. People are friendly everywhere, plus they speak English. By African standards, the adventure is with a small 'a' but for those wanting to see a bit of Africa with little hassle and affordable accommodation, The Gambia may be the perfect choice.

HISTORY

The history of this tiny country seems inevitably linked to outside influences. First, it was a battleground between the French and English for control of the slave trade. More recently Senegal, its much larger neighbour, has caused the most problems. Yet union with Senegal may offer the only real hope for economic prosperity. So don't be surprised by all the attention given in the local newspapers to the new Senegambia confederation.

The Gambia has been populated for a long time, at least since 750 AD. In the 13th century, the area became part of the empire of Mali, with Muslim Mandinka traders from present-day Mali spreading into the area. So Islam was dominant in Gambia from early on.

The first white men were the Portuguese who arrived in 1455. It was they who introduced peanuts – now the mainstay of the economy – and cotton. Never very numerous, the Portuguese sold their trading rights in 1581 to the British, who took Fort James, 24 km up river in 1661. This was their first garrison in West Africa and one of the most infamous slaving posts. The French had a trading post just across the river. For almost a century and a half they rivalled each other for slaves, ivory and gold which they exchanged primarily for tobacco and gunpowder. Fort James changed hands several times during the periodic clashes. With the Treaty of Versailles in 1783, Britain gained all rights to the Gambia. But the rivalry for slaves continued.

When the British had a change of heart and abolished slavery in 1807, they were not content with letting others continue on the wicked path. So with almost equal vigour, they began capturing slave vessels of other nations headed for the New World, converting Fort James from a dungeon for slaves to a haven for those who escaped. They soon concluded that the mouth of the Gambia river was a better place from which to patrol the slave trade. So in 1816, the British leased Banjul Island from a local chief and founded Banjul, then called Bathurst. They laid streets and planned MacCarthy

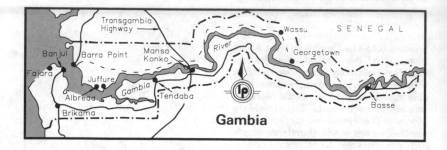

Square, but the town was never prosperous. As an economy measure, the British sometimes administered the colony from Sierra Leone until 1888 when they made the Gambia a crown colony and fixed the colony's snake-like boundaries, completely surrounded by French Senegal except for the small coast.

For the next 75-odd years of colonial rule, the British did virtually nothing to develop the area. In the 1950s, there was one hospital, one school and no paved roads outside Bathurst.

Independence
In 1960, when the rest of West Africa was gaining independence, the Gambia was still uncertain of its future. That was the year Dawda Jawara, a veterinary surgeon and Mandinka from upcountry, founded the People's Progressive Party (PPP). Britain doubted that complete independence was possible. The UN sent a team of specialists to study the feasibility of a union with Senegal. They concluded that a complete political merger was impossible at the time and recommended a federation.

So in 1965, Gambia became independent, with Jawara as its first president. Without any official explanation, Gambia was renamed The Gambia. Some say it was to avoid confusion between the country and the river; others say it was to avoid confusion with Zambia. Bathurst became Banjul. Few thought the country had a viable economic future but during the next

10 years, the world price for groundnuts (peanuts) increased significantly, raising the country's GNP almost three-fold. The number of tourists grew even more dramatically, from 300 in 1966 to 25,000 10 years later – equal to Banjul's population.

Politically, there were two viable parties and no political prisoners. Everything seemed relatively calm until 1981 when Jawara was in London at the royal wedding of Prince Charles and some disaffected soldiers staged a coup. Pursuant to the mutual defence pact between Senegal and The Gambia, Jawara asked the Senegalese government to oust them, which it did, and the Senegalese troops have remained there ever since.

Acknowledging his debt to Senegal, Jawara announced that the Gambian and Senegalese armed forces were being fully integrated and that full confederation was needed. A year later, the Senegambia confederation came into effect, with the president of Senegal as its president and the president of The Gambia as its vice president. Each country maintains its independence and sovereignty, however.

Today
The country's financial picture is gloomy. Recent government policies – such as devaluing the currency, reducing payrolls and selling off unprofitable parastatals – may produce a turnaround. Still, the

balance of trade has been negative for every year since 1975 and is growing. Saddled with a huge debt incurred during several droughts, the government can barely repay its IMF loans. Also The Gambia has a one-crop economy – more so than any other country in West Africa. The government's attempt at diversification has failed. Groundnuts still account for 85% of all export earnings, and world prices have not been favourable.

The number of tourists, mostly Scandinavians, is now about 50,000 a year. Tourism contributes more in percentage terms to export earnings than in any country in West Africa, yet this figure is only 15% and there are few spin-off effects. Virtually all tourists are on package tours; most rarely sample a restaurant outside the hotel. Only about 2100 jobs have been created from tourism, mostly in low paying positions over the six-month tourist season. Yet the government continues to spend a significant portion of its capital development budget on tourist-related projects, diverting funds from those sectors directly benefitting Gambians, such as agriculture.

Politically, the Senegambia confederation is, to say the least, not working as envisioned. Cultural differences are an impediment. People in Senegal, a former French colony, simply don't think the same way as the Gambians, even though the ethnic composition of the two countries is similar. Smuggling is another major problem. Duties tend to be higher in Senegal, making some imported goods there more expensive, and prices for groundnuts in the two countries are never the same. So the Gambians have been active for years in smuggling goods and peanuts into and out of Senegal, periodically provoking minor border incidents.

The Gambians are sensitive to Senegalese troops on their soil and afraid of being engulfed by their much larger neighbour. So they are moving cautiously. Their adoption of the CFA as official currency, for instance, is unlikely. Senegal, on the other hand, wants unification badly. Thus, tensions occasionally flare. At a football match in Banjul, rioting provoked the Senegalese High Commissioner in Banjul to call in Senegalese troops to protect the players. The Gambia responded by asking Senegal to recall him.

Despite its problems the country is a political paragon in Africa. It has stability without one-party statism, no standing army of its own, no political prisoners and it is probably the leading advocate of human rights on the continent. With all these virtues, The Gambia probably feels entitled to even more support from the west.

PEOPLE

With about 700,000 people in an area smaller than Connecticut, The Gambia is the continent's fourth most densely populated country. About 40% are Mandinka who are particularly numerous inland. They are the descendants of the rulers of the empire of Mali, which flourished in the 14th and 15th centuries. About half of the Africans in Banjul are Wolof, the tall, pitch black traders who predominate in Senegal. One out of five persons is a Fulani. Traditionally they are herders and live throughout West Africa; they have lighter skin and relatively straight hair. There are another 10 major ethnic groups and the intermarriage between the groups has made The Gambia a melting pot. The common denominator is religion – over 90% follow Islam. In West Africa, only Mauritania has a higher percentage of Muslims.

GEOGRAPHY

Looking like a worm in the side of Senegal, The Gambia best epitomises the absurdity of the national boundaries carved by the European colonial powers. Averaging only 35 km wide, the country follows Africa's most navigable river, the Gambia River, as it snakes through dense mangrove swamps bordered by cotton trees, bamboo forests and salt flats. As the crow flies, it's

322 km long, but by the river, The Gambia is 487 km long. Except for the 48-km coast, it is entirely surrounded by French-speaking Senegal. Along the river banks and the marshes, you'll find a truly amazing abundance of birds.

At the mouth of this remarkably blue river are Banjul and Barra, with a ferry connecting the two. Twenty-four km upstream you'll come to Fort James Island, Albreda and Juffure, then Tendaba after 130 km and, much further up river, Georgetown and Basse. There, the river is only 200 metres across, compared to several km in width at Banjul. A good asphalt road runs along the southern banks east to Basse.

The Gambia teeters on the southern edge of the Sahel. So you won't find rain forests but, rather, savannah and open woodland with tall grasses and shrubs – perfect for growing groundnuts. A fifth of this perfectly flat country is saline marsh. This marsh makes improvements in the country's agricultural situation difficult, as does deforestation and over-grazing due to over-population.

CLIMATE

The rainy season is short – July to September. The dry season is so pleasant that many people find air conditioners unnecessary. Temperatures reach their peak between February and May.

VISAS

Visas are not needed by nationals of Australia, Belgium, Canada, Denmark, Finland, West Germany, Iceland, Ireland, Italy, Luxembourg, Netherlands, New Zealand, Norway, Spain, Sweden and the UK. British embassies issue visas to The Gambia in countries without Gambian representation. Visas in Dakar are issued the same day. You're supposed to have an onward airline ticket if you arrive by air (not necessary if you arrive by land); in practice, the requirement is usually ignored. Visas are not obtainable at the border. Visa extensions are easily obtained

from the Ministry of Interior, Anglesea and Dobson St, Banjul.

Diplomatic Missions Abroad

Brussels, Dakar, Frankfurt, Freetown, Lagos, London, New York, Zurich.

MONEY

US$1 = 7.5D
£1 = 11D

The unit of currency is the dalasi (dah-lah-see). Travellers' cheques frequently have a higher exchange rate than cash. The dalasi has been devalued, virtually wiping out the black market but causing prices to almost double. At the airport, you may still have to fill out a currency declaration form. The restriction on exporting foreign currencies – the equivalent of 250D – may still be in effect as well.

Outside greater Banjul, you won't find any banks except in Basse. Banking hours: Monday to Thursday 8 am to 1 pm; Friday to Saturday 8 to 11 am. Banks in Bakau are also open from 4.30 to 6.30 pm. Banks: Standard Bank, BICIS (Banque International pour le Commerce et l'Industrie du Senegal).

LANGUAGE

English is the official language. A number of African languages are spoken, the principal ones being Wolof, Mandinka and Fula. Greetings in Mandinka:

Good morning	ee-SAM-ah
Good evening	ee-wou-RAH-rah
How are you?	EE-bee-dee
Thank you	ah-bah-RAH-kah
Goodbye	AH-lah-mah, nee-ah-JAH-mah-lah

GENERAL INFORMATION
Health

A vaccination against yellow fever is required, as is one against cholera if you're coming from an infected area. There are three hospitals and clinics in Banjul: the private Westfield Clinic (tel 92213), a German clinic on Pipeline Rd, and the government hospital, Royal Victoria Hospital in Banjul. For emergencies, try Dr Peters or Dr Palmer at Westfield Clinic.

Security
Banjul is very dark at night, but it and the beaches are fairly safe considering the huge number of potential pickpocketing victims. However, there are occasional thefts; so you must definitely be on your guard. Women should not walk alone on deserted beaches.

Business Hours
Business: Monday to Thursday 8.30 am to 12.30 pm and 2.30 to 5.30 pm; Friday to Saturday 8 am to 12 noon. Government: Monday to Thursday 8 am to 3 pm; Friday to Saturday 8 am to 12.45 pm.

Public Holidays
1 January, 1 February, 18 February (Independence), Good Friday, Easter Monday, 1 May, End of Ramadan (17 May 1988, 6 May 1989), Tabaski (25 July 1988, 14 July 1989), 15 August, Muslim New Year, Mohammed's Birthday, 25 December.

Photography
No permit is required, but taking photos of military installations, airports, Banjul harbour and major government buildings could get you into trouble.

Time, Phone & Telex
When it's noon in The Gambia, it's noon in London and 7 am in New York (8 am during daylight savings time). The telephone service is reasonably good. Calls from Banjul to the UK and USA cost only about US$3 a minute from the telecommunications office near the Atlantic hotel. There are telex facilities at the major hotels, the post office on Marina Rd in Banjul, and Gamtel Co (24-hour service).

GETTING THERE

Air
The only direct flights from Europe and from London are on British Caledonian. But there are many direct flights from all over Europe to nearby Dakar. From the USA, you'll have to transfer in Dakar or London. No airlines serve the interior. Service is much more reliable Dakar-Banjul than vice versa. Occasionally, airlines do not stop in Banjul as scheduled, and Air Senegal apparently refuses to give confirmed reservations.

Car
Travelling from Dakar to Banjul, you can take the Trans-Gambia highway from Dakar to Soma, then west to Banjul (480 km). Most people take the more direct route via Barra (320 km), and then the 25-minute Banjul-Barra ferry. The entire trip takes five hours if the ferry departs shortly after you arrive and doesn't break down, as occasionally happens. Otherwise, it can take six or seven hours. The ferry should leave Banjul every two hours between 8 am and 6 pm and Barra every two hours 9 am to 7 pm. But it cannot pass at low tide, so the schedule is never fixed. In Banjul, call the ferry (tel 28205) for the estimated departure time.

The 135-km road south from Banjul to Ziguinchor (Senegal) and the road inland to Basse are both paved. Driving time is about four hours to Basse via the south side of the river and two hours to Ziguinchor. The Gambia-Senegal borders are open 24 hours. If you're headed for one of the towns on the northern side of the Gambia river, such as Juffure, you can take a car/passenger ferry at Banjul, Soma, Georgetown and Basse (or a pirogue all along the river if you're without a car).

Bush Taxi/Bus
Bush taxis go in three major directions from Banjul – north to Dakar, east to Basse, and south to Ziguinchor. If you're

headed north to Dakar, take the ferry across the river to the Senegalese side. There, you'll find numerous Peugeot 504s and minibuses headed for Dakar. If you're headed south from Dakar, you'll find them at La Gare Pompiere. The cost for a seat in a Peugeot is about CFA 4000. By minibus, the fare is CFA 2500 to CFA 3000. They take about five hours, not including the ferry crossing, so plan on the trip taking six to eight hours depending on your luck with the ferry. If the ferry won't be leaving for several hours, you could try one of the pirogues (canoes). In Banjul, you'll find them along Wellington St.

Bush taxis headed south for Ziguinchor leave from Brikama. To get from Banjul to Brikama, take a public bus or shared taxi. The entire trip takes four hours or so and costs about CFA 1600.

You can also get to Basse by travelling in the opposite direction from Senegal. If you're coming from Tambacounda (eastern Senegal), you can enter The Gambia via Velingara (Senegal). There are good taxi connections between Tambacounda and Velingara. From Velingara to Basse, there's a good dirt road and a constant flow of trucks and bush taxis. The trip is over dirt road and takes about an hour. You may not find a border control, so check with police in Basse to avoid problems later on.

From Dakar and Ziguinchor, the easiest way to get to eastern Gambia (Basse, etc) is via the Trans-Gambia highway. Get off in Soma, which is two km south of the Mansa Konko river crossing. It's a major point for picking up transport.

GETTING AROUND
Bush Taxi/Bus
If you're travelling east from Banjul along the river, you can take bush taxis and trucks direct to Basse. There are two routes – the paved road along the southern edge of the river and the dirt road along the northern edge. If you take the northern route, you'll have to take a ferry to Barra and catch a taxi there, or cross

the river upstream at Mansa Koma-Soma, Georgetown or Basse. Naturally, most people take the southern route. Bush taxis and buses leave from Thomas St next to the Box Bar stadium off Independence Drive, and from the taxi park in Serrekunda. Most leave fairly early in the morning.

Those in the know, however, take the comfortable and highly recommended GPTC bus. The express leaves Banjul at 8 am and takes four hours. The non-express buses leave at 6.45, 9, 11.30 am, and 3.30 pm and, in principle, take an hour or two longer. You can catch them at the intersection of MacCarthy Square and Independence Drive.

Boat
The *Lady Chilel Jawara* used to plow the Gambia river, but in 1984, she went the way of the Titanic. Her replacement, if there ever is one, is likely to have similar facilities and schedule. The accommodation was fairly decent, with air-con, private baths, and two or four berths to a cabin, plus three meals a day. Those sleeping on the deck (only about US$6 one-way before she sank) used to buy food along the way. Even if service is resumed, the locals will undoubtedly prefer the faster bush taxis.

Banjul

Banjul is the country's major metropolis – with all of 50,000 inhabitants. Geographically, Banjul forms the tip of a peninsula at the mouth of the Gambia river, but technically, it's on an island. There's only one tourist hotel downtown – the Atlantic. At night, the streets are pitch black. The main street leading into town is Independence Drive, which ends at MacCarthy Square, the city's one public park. The two main streets run south from there – Wellington and Buckle – along which you'll find most of the shops. Albert Market is at the MacCarthy Square end of

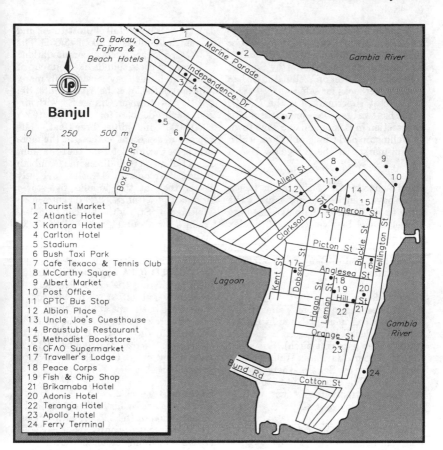

Banjul

0   250   500 m

1 Tourist Market
2 Atlantic Hotel
3 Kantora Hotel
4 Carlton Hotel
5 Stadium
6 Bush Taxi Park
7 Cafe Texaco & Tennis Club
8 McCarthy Square
9 Albert Market
10 Post Office
11 GPTC Bus Stop
12 Albion Place
13 Uncle Joe's Guesthouse
14 Braustuble Restaurant
15 Methodist Bookstore
16 CFAO Supermarket
17 Traveller's Lodge
18 Peace Corps
19 Fish & Chip Shop
21 Brikamaba Hotel
20 Adonis Hotel
22 Teranga Hotel
23 Apollo Hotel
24 Ferry Terminal

Wellington St; the ferry dock is near the far end of Wellington.

Bakau, Fajara and Serrekunda are the major suburbs. Fajara has five beach hotels, Bakau two. Most major restaurants and expatriate residences are in these two suburbs. Nearby Serrekunda is a major hub of activity for Gambians.

Information

Tourist Office This is next door to the Apollo hotel on Orange St. It is open Monday to Thursday 8 am to 2.45 pm and Friday and Saturday 8 am to 12.45 pm.

Embassies Addresses of some of the embassies are:

Guinea-Bissau (Wellington St next to the African Heritage Gallery café, tel 28134); Senegal (Buckle and Cameron Sts, tel 28469); Sierra Leone (Leman St, tel 28206); UK (48 Atlantic Rd in Fajara, Box 507, telex 2133/4); USA (Pipeline Rd in Fajara, Box 596, tel 92856/8).

Other embassies include: Liberia, Mali, Mauritania, Nigeria. Consulates: Belgium, Denmark, France, West Germany.

Bookstores & Supermarkets The two best bookstores are the *Methodist Bookstore* at Buckle and Cameron St and *Chaaku's* on Clarkson St near MacCarthy Square. *NTC* one block over on Wellington St has lots of paperbacks for sale.

The best supermarket is the *CFAO*, which has two branches – one at the major intersection in Bakau and one downtown at Wellington and Cameron. There's also a mini-market at the Bungalow Beach hotel.

Travel Agencies All of the major beach hotels have agencies offering virtually the same tours. Three of the major ones are Damel Travel Services (tel 28601, telex 2212) at the Atlantic hotel, Wing Afric (tel 92505/2259, telex 2215), and Gambia Tours (tel 28963 in Banjul and 92717 in Serrekunda).

Things to See

Anglophiles coming from Francophone Africa will feel more at home in Banjul where the English influence is notable (there's even a cricket pitch). But apart from the Albert Market on Wellington St near MacCarthy Square, there are no 'must sees'. The beaches out of town are the main attractions, so just wander around and enjoy yourself.

Places to Stay – bottom end

For the price, about 45/60D singles/doubles (20D more for a large room), you can't do better than *Uncle Joe's Guesthouse*. It is behind the Tropical Nightclub at the intersection of Cameron and Clarkson St. Breakfast costs about 12D. It's the small home of a portly old man who is hospitable and once lived in England.

Nearby, at 18 Dobson St, is the atrocious *Traveller's Lodge* (tel 28175), which has rooms for about 45D and prostitutes galore. If Joe's is full, try the *Teranga Hotel* (tel 28387) at 13 Hill St, which has rooms with fans for about 45D. *Brikamaba Hotel* around the corner at 24

Buckle St is noisy, full of prostitutes, and has singles/doubles for about 45/65D. The *YMCA* no longer offers accommodation.

If none of these sounds like your cup of tea, you'll have to pay considerably more. The best of the lot is the *Apollo Hotel* (tel 28184) downtown on Orange St, with air-con singles/doubles for 120/180D (CFA 6000/8000) including breakfast. The rooms are as decent as those at the more expensive Carlton hotel and the restaurant has a full menu including some Gambian dishes. The rooms at the Apollo are slightly better than at the popular five-storey *Adonis Hotel* (tel 28262/4) downtown on Wellington St, with air-con singles/doubles for about 115/160D (CFA 5400/7000) including breakfast, and the *Kantora Hotel* (tel 28715) one block from the Carlton, with small air-con singles/doubles for 110/145D (CFA 5000/6500) including breakfast. Since the city's electricity is frequently cut off at night, air-con is sometimes irrelevant at all of these.

If you prefer to stay near the beach in Bakau (15 km), ask the owner of In Revelation V across from Sambou's Bar in Bakau; he may be able to arrange something.

Places to Stay – middle

The best place by far for the price is the modern *Bakotu* (tel 92555), with singles/doubles without air-con for about 165/240D (£16/24) including breakfast. It's beyond Fajara across the street from the Novotel; hence, you can take advantage of its many facilities as well as the nearby Fajara Club. If it's full or closed (June to October), you could try the *African Village* (tel 92384, telex 2287) in Bakau, which has singles for 165D to 190D (£16 to £19) and doubles for 240D to 290D (£24 to £29) including breakfast (about 45D to 65D more for a sea view) and is open year-round. The pool is tiny and dirty, and the beach is rocky, but the nightclub is hot.

The only advantages of the *Wadner Beach Hotel* (tel 28119, telex 2219, cards AE) are that it's only three km from

Banjul and has a pool and tennis court. At about 285/335D (£28/33) for air-con singles/doubles with breakfast, it's not a particularly good buy compared to the similarly priced Bungalow Beach hotel, nor is it open from mid-May through September.

If you want to stay downtown, your best bet is the *Carlton Hotel* (tel 28258) on Independence Drive, which is a good two notches down and frequently full. It has singles/doubles for about 150/200D (£15/20) with breakfast, decent lighting and air-con. The electricity is frequently cut off in the city, however, so buy candles.

Places to Stay - top end

The Gambia is the only country in West Africa which has high and low season rates. High season dates vary from hotel to hotel – approximately 1 November through 30 April. Some hotels close down during the low season. Since the high season is also the cool season, some hotels offer rooms without air-con at lower prices. All of the six major hotels are of excellent quality and are outside Banjul except the *Atlantic Hotel*, which appeals to business people as much as to tourists, primarily the British. Although the Atlantic has a pool, tennis, squash, etc, it has two drawbacks – the beach is not as clean there, and the major restaurants and nightclubs are 15 km or so away.

The *Kombo Beach Novotel*, the *Senegambia* and the *Sunwing*, are all 15 to 25 km from downtown. If you're looking for the hotel with the best rooms or the most active night life, stay at the Novotel. The Senegambia, which caters to Scandinavians and the Swiss, has a more relaxed atmosphere. Rooms there are not fancy and cost significantly less if you don't insist on air-con. Attracting primarily Scandinavians, the Sunwing has the advantage of being near Bakau, a village with lively African bars and crafts.

A small notch down in quality and price are the *Fajara* and the *Bungalow Beach Hotel*. Many people prefer the Bungalow Beach because its prices are lower, all rooms have kitchenettes, the restaurant is one of the best, and you can take advantage of all the facilities of the Novotel next door. Guests at the huge Fajara hotel can use the golf, tennis and squash facilities at the Fajara Club next door; consequently, it offers as much as any hotel in terms of sports and entertainment.

Hotel prices are fairly stable in foreign currency but not in dalasi; therefore, the prices below are in British pounds.

Kombo Beach Novotel (tel 92465/6/7, telex 2216), air-con singles/doubles for £44/52 (440/520D), tennis, pool, active nightclub, windsurfers, surfboards, cards AE, D, V.

Atlantic Hotel (tel 28214/28601, telex 2250), air-con singles/doubles for about £44/52 (440/520D), no low season rates, pool, tennis, squash, windsurfers, sail boats, water skiing, cards AE, D, MC.

Senegambia (tel 92717/8/9, telex 2269), singles/doubles for about £32/44 (320/440D) including breakfast, about 25% less during low season, about £5 extra with air-con, showers only, pool, tennis, squash, mini-golf, volleyball, nightclub, cards AE only.

Sunwing (tel 92435, telex 2220), air-con singles/doubles for about £42/50 (420/500D) including breakfast, pool, tennis, windsurfers, catamarans, closed mid-April through October, cards AE only.

Fajara (tel 92351), singles/doubles with breakfast but without air-con for £29/42 (290/420D), about 25% less during low season, pool, tennis, squash, golf, lively nightclub, cards AE only.

Bungalow Beach (tel 92288), singles/doubles including breakfast for about £29/33 (290/330D), 33% low season discount, about £5 extra for air-con, pool, kitchenettes, supermarket, tennis, windsurfers available next door at the Novotel, cards AE only.

Places to Eat

Cheap Eats In addition to the restaurants downtown, try *Sambou's Bar-Restaurant* in Bakau; look for the sign about half a km before the Sunwing hotel. The menu is quite varied and includes a few Gambian dishes. Main courses are about 23D to

45D, and the selection is fairly large. The unpretentious *Cape Point Restaurant* next to the Sunwing is in the same price range and serves Gambian specialities as well as Continental fare. For rock bottom prices, try the *Seabreeze Bar & Restaurant* near Sambou's, the *Rising Sun* at the main intersection in Bakau, and *Kotu Bendula* at the Craft Centre next to the Novotel.

Downtown *Braustuble* (tel 8371) on Leman St near MacCarthy Square is Banjul's closest thing to a pub and highly recommended. A cold draft beer and a sandwich at the biergarten behind will cost you 18D. Inside, there's a full menu; the German sausages are recommended. You could also eat at the *Atlantic Hotel*, but prices are higher and the quality is variable. The *Apollo Hotel* on Orange St serves a businessman's luncheon for about 19D. They also have an extensive à la carte menu including sandwiches and African dishes.

Nearby on Leman St is *Fish & Chips Shop*, a Peace Corps hangout which serves inexpensive fish and sandwiches. Near the Carlton Hotel is the popular *Café Texaco*, which serves good, inexpensive Gambian dishes such as jollof rice (*benechin*) and peanut stew (*domoda*), as well as other fare including good brochettes in pita bread.

Asian All the Asian restaurants are in Fajara or Bakau. The Chinese proprietor of the *Bamboo Restaurant* (tel 92764) first came to the country as part of a team of rice-growing technicians and decided to stay on. Closed Monday, it is in Fajara near the junction of Pipeline and Atlantic Rd and serves good Chinese food at moderate prices, but the portions are small. You can eat inside or on the lawn beside the bamboo and flower beds. Or try *The Rice Bowl* (tel 92104) in Bakau on the old road to Banjul, about one km from the Sunwing. The menu is quite extensive, with most main dishes costing about 35D

to 45D. A special complete dinner is about 55D. The Chinese and Malaysian food at *Yellow Gate* (tel 92728) in Fajara, 300 metres off Pipeline Rd, about one km north of the US Embassy, seems to lack some critical Asian seasonings and ingredients.

Various Cuisines The area's best non-African restaurant is probably *Lamar Restaurant* (tel 92638) in Fajara on Pipeline Rd across from the US embassy. The cuisine is Lebanese and continental, the quality excellent, the portions large and the prices moderate. Their Lebanese peanut and fish dish is famous. On Saturday evenings from 8.30 to 10.30 pm, they serve a Lebanese buffet for only about 45D.

Bakadaji Restaurant, about 5 km from Fajara off the road to Serekunda, is highly recommended as the best place for Gambian food. Especially recommended are the Thursday and Sunday buffets for only about 27D. Local dishes include, for example, benechin, *plasas* (meat and fish cooked with vegetable leaves in palm oil and served with mashed cassava *foufou*). You can get continental dishes as well.

The garden ambience and soothing music are the principal attractions of the popular *Francisco's Grill House*, half a km from the Fajara Hotel. You can also dine inside with air-con. The menu is quite varied and includes sandwiches. Most main courses are about 35D to 45D, and it's open every day until midnight. For Italian food, your only choice is at the *Casino*; the restaurant is reportedly fairly decent.

Entertainment & Sports

Bars The terrace at the *Braustuble* on Leman St is unquestionably the most popular watering hole downtown. For a more derelict ambience, try the *Adonis Hotel*, a Peace Corps favourite for years.

In Bakau, the unpretentious *Sambou's Bar-Restaurant* is very popular. The Hash House Harriers guzzle beer there every Monday evening after their run. To meet Gambians, walk across the street to *In Revelation V*, a popular shanty-like bar with all Gambian clientele and reggae music. It's open late.

In Fajara, *Francisco's Grill House* near the Fajara Hotel has a popular terrace bar with a garden setting and music, and is open until midnight. Or have a drink at the nearby *Fajara Club* – non-members can use the bar. Among the hotels, one of the best places for a drink is the *Bungalow Beach Hotel*; the poolside terrace is packed every evening in the high season. For really cheap brew, try the *Kotu Bendula Bar* at the Craft Centre next door.

Nightclubs If you're downtown, try *Tropical Nightclub* on Clarkson St near MacCarthy Square. Virtually all the good nightclubs, however, are in Fajara, Bakau and Serrekunda.

In Bakau, the hottest place is *Club 98* at the Village Hotel near the CFAO supermarket. Open every day with a 20D cover on Saturday, it's very active, with some Gambians but mostly tourists. Almost equally good is *Casaurina* next to the Fajara hotel. Open every night with a 10D cover, it appeals to both Gambians and tourists. If you're looking for a place that is sometimes mobbed with tourists, head for the popular *Bellingo* at the Novotel. For roulette, black jack and slot machines, go to the *Casino* between the Novotel and the Senegambia, open every evening from 7 pm. If you're looking for a place with more local colour, try *City Disco* in Serrekunda, a nightclub that Gambians rave about.

Movie Theatres There are excellent videos open to the public at the Novotel every Sunday at 3, 7 and 9 pm for about 12D. The monthly schedule is posted outside the Novotel. Downtown, the best movie theatre is Banjul Cinema on Buckle St; Indian flicks are the main attraction.

Sports Unlike the beaches in most of West Africa, those in The Gambia are safe, with little undertow. All the major beach hotels have pools, but only those at the Senegambia and the Bungalow Beach are appropriate for doing laps.

Most of the beach hotels have wind-surfers; the typical charge is about 25D. At the Novotel, even guests must pay; at the Senegambia, hotel guests don't pay. You can get an incredibly good deal on lessons at the Senegambia – about 240D for 10 lessons. Learning in the surf, however, is difficult. Try the early morning when conditions are calmer.

Joggers can join the all-male Hash House Harriers group on Monday at 5.45 pm. The meeting pont is usually announced on the bulletin board at the Fajara Club. For squash, try the Senegambia, which has an African pro, the Atlantic Hotel, or the Fajara Club, which charges non-members 12D for 40-minutes.

You do not have to stay at the Fajara hotel or be a member of the Fajara Club (tel 92456) to play golf there. The green fee for the 18 holes is about 45D; club rental is about 25D. Those people interested in cycling can rent bicycles at many of the Beach hotels for about 23D a half day and 35D a full day. For half-day fishing trips, see the tour agencies at the beach hotels; barracuda, groper and snapper are the main catches.

Yacht Cruise Oyster Creek is a mangrove swamp about five km from Banjul on the main road inland towards the beach hotels. There, you'll find the *Spirit of Galacia*, a 14-metre yacht available for all-day outings on Saturday or Sunday, and weekdays according to demand. The creek is full of wildlife, especially birds. The most numerous are herons, hawks, grasswarblers, doves, swallows and king-fishers. After about six km, she stops for a picnic lunch and a swim just beyond Mandinari, and returns around 4 pm. The cost is about 210D. There's also the 23-metre *Wild Knight*, which takes two-day trips upriver to Tendaba Camp and back for about 925D.

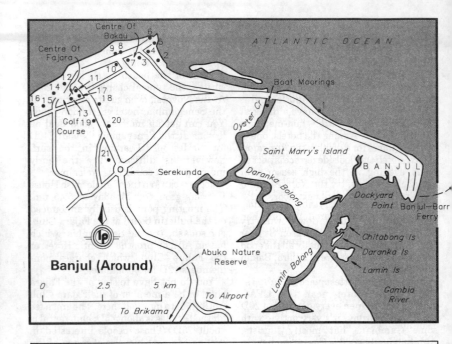

Banjul (Around)

1	Wadner Beach Hotel
2	The Rice Bowl Restaurant
3	In Revelation V Bar
4	Sambou's Bar/Restaurant
5	Cape Point Restaurant
6	Sunwing Hotel
7	CFAO Supermarket
8	Stalls where African material is sold
9	African Village Hotel
10	Rising Sun snackbar
11	Francisco's Grill House
12	Fajara Hotel
13	Fajara Club
14	Novotel, Bakotu Hotel, Bungalow Beach Hotel, Arts Centre Kotu Bendula, snackbar
15	Casino
16	Senegambia Hotel
17	Bamboo Restaurant
18	US Embassy
19	Lamar Restaurant
20	Yellow Gate Restaurant
21	Bakadaji Restaurantj

Wrestling Wrestling is the national sport and a major tourist attraction. He-men in loin cloths with charms (*grigis*) strut around, performing with an eye to the audience, while between matches there's a cacophony of sounds – drums, flutes, whistles, and girls chanting like cheerleaders. Anything goes – biting, kicking, punching – and no fancy hand-locks, technical throws, points, etc. Just get him down. You can see matches in the late afternoon 5 to 7 pm on most Saturdays and Sundays in Lamin, Serrekunda and Brikama. All the major hotels have buses leaving around 4 pm or so; the cost is about 60D.

Things to Buy

Artisan Goods The best place for art is *The Gambia Black African Arts Club Art Gallery* in Bakau just beyond Sambou's. Open Monday to Saturday 9.30 am to 12.30 pm and 2.30 to 6.30 pm, it offers batiks, pottery, paintings, sculpture, and graphics. The most popular souvenir items are the batik prints, tie-dye cloths, colourful 'gambishirts', gold and silver filigree jewellery, wooden carvings and leather goods. Downtown, the best place is the *Tourist Market* on Marine Parade out beyond the Atlantic hotel. *Albert Market*, on Wellington St near MacCarthy Square, has a bit of everything, including some crafts. It closes around 3 pm. For silver filigree, try the Mauritanian shop next to Braustuble. You'll find various stalls in Bakau at the main intersection and even more at the *Craft Centre* next to the Novotel.

Music For records of African music, ask the locals to lead you to one of the small recording places downtown. There are only a few Gambian recording artists. Two of the most popular are Famboling and Magadan.

Getting There & Away

Bush Taxi Bush taxis and minibuses for Dakar leave from Barra, a 25-minute ferry ride from Banjul. The ferry leaves Banjul roughly every two hours between 8 am and 6 pm. If you can't wait for the ferry, take one of the pirogues from Wellington St. Barra is also the place for transport along the northern route in The Gambia.

For Ziguinchor, bush taxis leave from Brikama. Bush taxis to the interior (that ply the more popular southern route along the river) leave from Thomas St next to the Box Bar stadium off Independence Avenue, and from Serrekunda.

Bus The comfortable and recommended GPTC buses run from Banjul to Basse five times per day. There is an express at 8 am and regular buses at 6.45, 9 and 11.30 am

and 3.30 pm. They leave from the intersection of MacCarthy Square and Independence Drive.

Getting Around

Air Transport At the airport, there's a departure tax of about 50D. You'll find a bar and a place to change money. Taxi prices are posted; the cost to Banjul (27 km) or to the major beach hotels is about 80D. Most drivers will quote you the official rate, so bargaining is usually not required. There are no buses from the airport. To cut costs, you could take the Brikama-Banjul bus, but the closest stop is at least 5 km away. Or take a cab to Serrekunda (about 45D) and catch a cab from there.

Bus Buses to Bakau, Fajara and Serrekunda leave about every 15 minutes between 6 am and 8 pm; the cost is a pittance. You can catch them along Independence Drive. If you're going to the Fajara Beach hotels, you'll still have to walk several km or more. You'll find minibuses to Serrekunda on Grant St opposite MacCarthy Square and those to Brikama at Albion Place and Grant St.

Taxi A short trip in town costs about 5D. Bargaining is definitely required. A seat in a shared taxi is about one quarter of this, but drivers do not like giving foreigners these rates. Taxis are plentiful during the day but difficult to find at night except at the major beach hotels. The rate is about 60D for Banjul-Fajara and about 40D for Banjul-Bakau.

Car Rental There are no regular car rental agencies, but you can rent one of the popular open-air Suzuki jeeps from Spot (tel 92657/8) at Serrekunda junction. Also ask the tour operators, particularly Damel Travel Services (tel 28601) at the Atlantic hotel.

The Interior

ABUKO NATURE RESERVE

Abuko is unique among West African parks in that it's fenced and accessible – only 20 km from Banjul, beyond the airport. What's also unusual is the amazing diversity of vegetation for a park of only 102 hectares. That's because a stream runs through the centre, allowing riverine forest to flourish surrounded by the more typical savannah vegetation in the drier areas. You can see up to 50 tree varieties, all numbered along the 2½ km trail, giving you a good idea of the diversity and variety of trees found in this part of West Africa.

The wildlife is pretty meagre by African standards – baboon, chimps, antelope, hippo and birds. Pythons and three poisonous species of snakes – puff adders, green mambas and cobras – also crawl about. Don't worry; the large number of park visitors tend to scare them away from the well-beaten paths.

The reserve is open every day from 8 am to 6.30 pm. To avoid the heat, go in the early morning or late afternoon; allow two hours for the walk.

JUFFURE, ALBREDA & FT JAMES ISLAND

Juffure is the small village that Alex Haley, the black American, put on the map with his famous novel *Roots*. Haley believes his great great grandfather, Kunta Kinte, was carried away from Juffure as a slave some 200 years ago. About 25 km inland, opposite James Island, Juffure is now an over commercialised tourist trap. Still, it's very much like the more obscure villages elsewhere in The Gambia and Senegal – a cluster of thatched-roof mud huts connected by dirt paths. Juffure's aging chief (*alkalo*) will give you a brief lecture on the history of the village followed by a request for a small donation. Many others will also ask for hand-outs. Binta Kinte, an old lady who purports to be a direct descendant of

Kunta Kinte, will ask for about 15D to let you come inside her compound and talk. You'll also see Kunta Kinte's compound, and the ruins of the slave trading station.

Several hundred metres away you'll find Albreda and its old trading house established by the French in 1681 – 20 years after the British had captured the nearby James Island fort, built by a German Baron in 1651. These two forts were the scene of the periodic battles between the French and British for control of the slave trade. While the British were occupied with the war for independence in America, the French sacked Ft James. It has been eroding ever since. Abandoned in 1829, Ft James now lays in ruins. All that remains are some walls, arches and muted cannons.

Getting There & Away

To get to Juffure, Albreda and Ft James Island, take the ferry from Banjul to Barra and catch a taxi from there to Juffure. You can reach James Island by dugout canoe. To make it to Juffure and back in one day, you'll have to catch the first ferry at 8 am. Or take a tour from one of the beach hotels.

TENDABA

About 130 km upstream, Tendaba is the site of the country's only inland tourist hotel. The major attractions here are trips to a nearby game reserve and African villages, and pirogue trips up the river. The camp has Land-Rovers and motorised pirogues for these trips.

Places to Stay & Eat

Developed by a Swedish sea-captain in 1972 and constructed to look like an African village, *Tendaba Camp* has eight singles, 26 doubles, and 10 triple mock-traditional huts plus a bar, restaurant, dirty swimming pool, generator, and camp-fire dances at night by the natives. Singles/doubles cost 80/160D; a good breakfast costs 20D more. The tour groups charge about 185D for an overnight stay.

GEORGETOWN

Georgetown has a surprisingly good *Government Rest House*, with clean rooms, hot water and even a lounge, all for about 80D. Inquire at the police station. For such cheaper but inferior accommodation, try the *Educational Centre* on the eastern edge of town.

WASSU

You'll undoubtedly hear about the famous, enigmatic Stone Circles – burial sites constructed about 1200 years ago with clusters of massive, reddish-brown laterite columns, numbering from 10 to 24, and weighing several tons, one to three metres high. Similar structures are found in Guinea and the Sahara, but the largest concentration is in eastern Gambia, particularly in Wassu.

Getting There & Away

You can reach Wassu by taking a bush taxi to Kuntaur and walking 3½ km from there.

BASSE

This is the largest upcountry town, 362 km from Banjul by paved road. You'll find the Dunia Cinema, a bank, the *Sahel Disco Night Club*, *Restaurant Jobot*, and a car ferry. The riverside market, however, is the main hub of activity. You can stay at the *GRMB Rest House* which is preferable to, and more expensive than, the *Apollo Hotel*.

Ghana

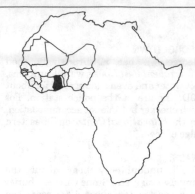

Everybody likes the Ghanaians. If an award were given for the country with the friendliest people in West Africa, Ghana would probably win. One of the best educated peoples in black Africa at the time of independence, Ghanaians understand western culture. So it's easy to make contact and you're likely to get into some pretty serious discussions. Ghanaians are a proud, open people and they like to do things their way.

Accra may not be the most beautiful city in Africa, but it's their city – not a city catering to tourists or western expatriates. And they like to have fun. Accra and Kumasi on Saturday night are jumping. If you like live bands, you can usually take your pick of at least four or five. Ghana is, after all, the place where the somewhat passé 'highlife' music got its start. Ghana also has some of the most beautiful fabrics in West Africa, the most well known is the expensive and colourful *kente* cloth made by the Ashanti.

Ghana is the old 'Gold Coast', where Europeans came 500 years ago searching for gold – and found it. Along the coast, you'll see a string of forts and castles that the Europeans left behind. Inside, your spirits will sink when you see how slaves were branded with hot irons, then crammed into wet dungeons and chained, waiting to be shipped to the New World.

Ghana also has one of the real 'in' spots in West Africa – Dixcove – where you can sleep on one of the most beautiful beaches in West Africa, or in one of the old forts for 50c a night, and eat giant crayfish and shrimp for the price of a cheap beer. Those on the cheap come away raving about Ghana and the chances are you will too.

HISTORY

For centuries, the Gold Coast was black Africa's richest area. Gold and slaves made the Ashanti one of the richest civilisations in Africa. During the colonial period, the old Gold Coast was a model colony for the rest of West Africa; it had the best education system, the most developed infrastructure and the wealthiest economy. After independence, Ghana became a different kind of model – that of how to destroy an economy. Ghana gets the award for the worst economic record since independence, a distinction it is now overcoming.

There is evidence of settlements along the Ghanaian coast dating back 30,000 to 40,000 years, but the ancestors of today's Ghanaians migrated primarily from the north, starting around the 12th century. What may have caused this migration was the fall of the Empire of Ghana, a kingdom to the north-west which incorporated parts of Mali, Mauritania and Senegal and is in no way related to present-day Ghana, except through this migration.

The Portuguese arrived in the late 15th century looking for gold. They found enough to justify building several forts along the coast, starting in 1482, but the real wealth turned out to be slaves. The fortunes earned in the slave trade attracted the Dutch, British and Danes in the late 16th century. During the next 250 years, Britain, Portugal, Holland and Denmark competed fiercely for this trade, building forts, capturing those of their rivals, then losing them. The average yearly 'take' in slaves was 10,000. When it all ended in the 19th century, they left 76 forts and castles of various sizes along the Gold Coast, an average of one every six km – certainly an African record.

Having outlawed slavery in the early 19th century, the British took over the forts to effectively impose customs duties along the coast, and they signed treaties with many of the coastal chiefs. They also stayed around to make sure that no one revived the slave trade, like the Ashanti had who profited handsomely from it. The Ashanti capital city, Kumasi, had many of the trappings of a European city, even employing Europeans in the late 19th century as military trainers and economic advisors. The Ashanti weren't about to give in, so the British attacked Kumasi in 1873. It took the British well over a year to sack the city, and immediately after they declared the area a crown colony.

Ashanti resistance continued until 1900, when the British governor demanded the Ashanti's golden stool – the equivalent of asking for the golden ark! Three days later, the Ashanti attacked the British fort there, but they eventually lost, and Kumasi was almost totally destroyed in the process. You can see many photographs of this famous war in the Military Museum in Kumasi.

Colonial Period

The British set out to make the Gold Coast a showcase. It was to be an African country, not a colony dominated by outsiders. So they allowed few Europeans to settle or even be employed there. The British administrators never numbered over 4000.

Cocoa soon became the backbone of the economy, overtaking Equatorial Guinea as the world's leading producer in the 1920s, the colony's most prosperous decade ever. In 1900, gold was the only ore exported – only about £20,000 worth. So to increase production, the British built railroads in all directions from Sekondi, the sole commercial port. Kumasi, the cocoa and timber centre, got its link in 1903. By WW I, cocoa, gold and timber made the Gold Coast the most prosperous colony in Africa. By independence, the Gold Coast was the world's leading producer of manganese and also exported diamonds and bauxite. It also had the best schools in Africa, the best civil service, a cadre of enlightened lawyers, and a thriving press.

Until 1948 when the British established a university at Cape Coast, they sent Africans abroad for advanced study. One of these students was Kwame Nkrumah, who spent 10 years in the USA, 1935 to 1945, studying and teaching at Lincoln University in Pennsylvania and reading the literature of pan-Negro aspirations, which fired him up, and Marxist writings, which influenced his revolutionary ideas.

In 1947, Nkrumah broke away from the country's leading political party, which advocated independence within 'the shortest possible time', and formed the Convention People's Party (CPP) aimed at the common man, with the slogan 'Self Government Now'. Two years later he called a general strike. The British responded by putting him in prison. While he was there, the CPP won the general elections in 1951. The British were so impressed by how efficiently the CPP had operated in gathering votes, despite Nkrumah's absence, that they released him and asked him to form a government.

Independence

Nkrumah agreed to abandon the party's slogan in favour of working with the colonial administrators, thereby gaining their confidence and enabling him to learn the ins and outs of government. In 1957, the strategy paid off when Britain granted independence. Nkrumah cast aside the name Gold Coast in favour of that of the first great empire in West Africa – Ghana – even though the country had only a romantic, tenuous connection with that kingdom. For Africa, it was a momentous occasion. Ghana was the first black African country to gain independence. For Ghana, it was the beginning of an

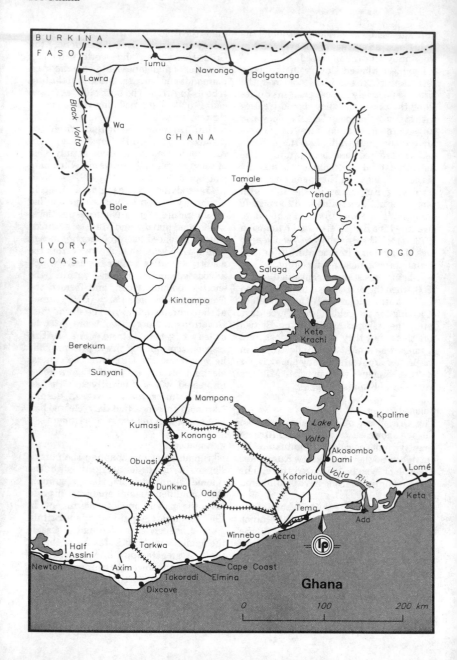

Ghana

economic nightmare, and 25 years of almost continuous decline followed.

Nkrumah borrowed heavily to finance his grandiose schemes. Many of the projects were wasteful – US$16 million was spent on a conference centre to host a single meeting of the Organisation of African Unity, US$2 million on Black Star Square, US$9 million for a showcase super-highway that extended only 23 km and is under used, US$17 million for a drydock and US$8 million for a state house. At independence, Ghana had almost half a billion US dollars in foreign exchange reserves; by 1966, the country was a billion in debt. World prices for cocoa didn't help matters any. They went tumbling from £247 a ton at independence to below £100 a ton by 1965-66.

Nkrumah's most grandiose project, though, was Akosombo dam. Valco, an American company controlled by Kaiser Aluminum, wanted it built to fuel its plants for smelting bauxite into aluminium. Ghana was to lose about a million hectares of land to be covered by Volta lake, but Nkrumah wanted the project desperately. He accepted Valco's offer to build the costly dam in return for the right to all the electricity it needed, virtually at cost – a sweet deal for Valco. Revenue from the projected sale of electricity was to permit Ghana to electrify the rural areas and finance the irrigation of the Accra plains, Ghana's potential bread-basket. With a steadily deteriorating economy, however, the projected private sector demand never materialised, and the electrification and irrigation programs were shelved.

To a continent of new nations desperate for political unity, Nkrumah was a hero. Handsome, charismatic and articulate, he espoused the cause of African unity on every occasion. He even sent soldiers off to the Congo to help keep the peace, though he could hardly afford it. When Nkrumah talked, people and nations listened. At home, however, he became ruthless. Within a year following independence,

Ghana had become virtually a one-party state. In 1958, he approved a law providing for up to five years detention without trial or appeal. Four years later, an estimated 2000 to 3000 people were held in jail without trial. In 1962, a coup attempt led to a wide-scale purge.

He alienated the business community by turning over a large portion of the economy to state-run enterprises, very few of which became profitable. He alienated the west by his never-ending denunciation of imperialism and neo-colonialism, the heavy accumulation of debts, and the rapid growth of commercial ties with the Soviet bloc. Perhaps worst of all, he alienated his own army by setting up a private army answerable to him alone. The public, which appreciated the significant improvements in infrastructure and social services, became disillusioned by the conspicuous corruption among the party's leaders. In 1964, there were food shortages for the first time ever.

It was all too much. In 1966, while Nkrumah was on a mission to Hanoi, the army staged a coup. There was general rejoicing in Ghana, though not by all. Exiled to Guinea, where Sekou Touré had given him the title of 'co-president', he died of cancer six years later.

The Great Decline

Between 1966 and 1981, Ghana suffered through six governments, all corrupt or incompetent except for one which lasted three months. Probably no ruler was worse than Col Acheampong, who 'redeemed' the country in 1972, and thereafter dissolved Parliament. He considered a previous devaluation of the cedi an affront to the country's honour, and did the unheard of – he revalued the currency upward by 44%, even though the currency was already way overvalued. Acheampong had a simple solution to all of Ghana's problems – print money. In 1976 alone, he increased the cedis in circulation by 80%. Inflation was wild and reached 12% a month! Prices went up every week. When he left office, the cedis was overvalued by 20 times the market value. Travellers who changed money at the bank had to pay the equivalent of US$1.50 for an orange. Little wonder they began to avoid Ghana or change money on the blackmarket.

As the cedi became increasingly worthless, more and more cocoa – up to 50,000 tonnes a year – was smuggled across the borders to Togo and the Ivory Coast. Meanwhile, production was falling, from 430,000 tons in 1965 to 265,000 tons in 1978, the year the army politely told Acheampong to step town. The military stayed in power, however, continuing its pilferage while promising new elections. Everybody in those days periodically hopped a bus to Lomé (Togo) to buy essentials like detergent, oil and milk. If you had been at the airport in Accra, you would have seen custom officials inspecting the suitcases of passengers coming from London only to find them 100% filled with detergent.

Two weeks before the promised elections in 1979, a group of young military officers led by Flight Lt Jerry Rawlings, not content on seeing their corrupt military bosses retire in a state of luxury, staged a coup. The elections proceeded, but before turning over the government, they relented to pressure from the lower ranks and publicly executed three former heads of state! Acheampong, who was accused of having stashed away US$100 million in foreign accounts, was among the three. In addition, hundreds of other officers and businessmen were tried and convicted by impromptu 'peoples' courts and given long sentences. Then, after only three months in power, Rawlings bowed out as promised – to everyone's amazement.

Adopting very conservative economic policies and austerity measures, the new president was unable to arrest the economy's downward spiral. Meanwhile, Rawlings remained enormously popular with the people and continued speaking out about the need for vigilance against corruption. At the end of 1981, after the new leadership had demonstrated its inability to halt the economic decline, Rawlings staged another coup. He became the only modern-day African ruler to gain power a second time after having previously given it up. This time he stayed.

Today

Rawlings has done the seemingly impossible. By 1986, articles in western newspapers were appearing with titles such as 'Ghana: Black Africa's Economic Showcase'. Since 1983, the economy has grown by more than 5% a year in real terms, while inflation has gone down from 122% in 1983 to just over 10% in 1985. Between mid-1983 and mid-1986, export earnings skyrocketed 44%, cocoa production alone increasing by 28% in just two years. What did Rawlings do? He did exactly what the IMF and the World Bank said to do. Between late 1983 and mid-1986, he devalued the currency 33-fold, raised prices to cocoa farmers four-fold, laid off 28,000 civil servants in one year alone, removed price controls on all but 23 essential commodities, and started getting rid of some of the unprofitable state enterprises. The government also renegotiated the agreement with Valco, raising its electricity rates by 200%. In return, the World Bank and the IMF have given Ghana some hefty loans.

The changes are visible. Owners are painting buildings in Accra, the government is rebuilding its roads from one end of the country to the other, farmers are busy replanting trees and reclaiming abandoned farms, Ghanaians from abroad are returning, ports are being rebuilt and, most noticeably, consumer goods are back in the stores.

Rawlings is not only a man with guts – he is a maverick. Instead of fostering the cult of personality, he ordered all pictures of him removed from public places. He rides around in a jeep, not a limousine.

In others ways, he's not so different. He

tolerates little dissent – when newspapers are even mildly critical, he closes them down. Those caught for corruption, like two Ghanaians and a Lebanese caught in 1985 for embezzling US$1.3 million, get the firing squad.

One might think that with Ghana's free-market revolution, Rawlings must be the darling of the west. He isn't. The problem is his leftist politics. When Libya's Gaddafi speaks, Rawlings applauds. When the USA votes one way in the UN, Rawlings votes the other. When the west talks about human rights, Rawlings talks about anti-imperialism. More importantly, he has lots of Ghanaian political enemies. There's been a major coup attempt just about every year he has been in office. It'll be interesting to see how he – and Ghana – fares.

PEOPLE
One of the more densely populated countries in West Africa, Ghana has 14 million people. About 40% are Akan, which includes the Ashanti whose heartland is around Kumasi, followed by the Ewe in the east, the Ga in the south around Accra, and various tribes in the north, including the Gonja and the Dagomba. Because of fairly enlightened government policies over the decades, the divisive tendencies which might be expected in a country with 75 different languages have not occurred. Rather, most Ghanaians have a strong national consciousness, which was fostered by Nkrumah. Christians outnumber Muslims about two to one, with the Muslims concentrated more in the north. The rest of the people – about one-third – practise the traditional ancestral religions.

GEOGRAPHY
Looking like a shoebox and about the size of the UK, Ghana is a flat, relatively homogeneous country. The dry coastal region consists mostly of low-lying scrubland and plains. Starting 20 to 30 km inland, thick rain forests take over and continue to the northern third of the country, a plateau area of about 500 metres elevation which is predominantly savannah and open woodland – ideal for cotton. Most of the cocoa comes from the central and southern area, the Ashanti being one of the principal cultivators of this historically lucrative crop.

Instead of mountains to break up the landscape, Ghana has Lake Volta – the world's largest man-made lake, about twice the size of Luxembourg. It's fed from Burkina Faso by the Black Volta and White Volta rivers; the latter formed the western boundary of German Togoland until 1922.

CLIMATE
Ghana has three rainfall zones. Along the coast including Accra, the rainfall is light and the wet seasons are from April to June, and October. Once the heavy forests take over starting 20 to 30 km inland, the rains become heavier and last longer. In the north, the weather becomes drier again, with one rainy season, May through September.

VISAS
Visas, or entry permits in the case of nationals of British Commonwealth countries, are required of all travellers. Visas are easily obtained in all neighbouring countries. The process typically takes three days in the Ivory Coast and Burkina Faso, but only one day in Togo. The Ghanaian embassy in Burkina Faso will not issue visas to travellers who put down as their place of residence a country with a Ghanaian embassy – unless they take a liking to you. Visas are not issued at the borders, all of which close promptly at 6 pm. Exit permits, as with extensive power shortages and curfews, are a thing of the past – for now anyway.

Visas are usually valid for 14 days. Extensions can be obtained in Accra from the Ministry of Interior near the stadium, as well as in Kumasi, Sekondi and Tamale. You will need two photos and a letter of invitation from a Ghanaian resident, so make a friend or ask a local expatriate for advice – they have to go through the same process. With such a letter, you shouldn't have any problem. Don't indicate tourism as the only reason for your extended stay.

Diplomatic Missions Abroad

Abidjan, Addis Ababa, Algiers, Berlin, Berne, Bonn, Brasilia, Brussels, Cairo, Canberra, Conakry, Copenhagen, Cotonou, The Hague, Lagos, Lomé, London, Monrovia, Ouagadougou, Ottawa, Paris, Rome, Tokyo, Tunis, Washington.

MONEY

US$1 = 188 cedis
£1 = 352 cedis

The unit of currency is the cedi (cee-dee). Inflation is in double digits, so expect prices to be somewhat higher than shown herein. In the early 1980s, Ghana was one of the most expensive countries in Africa. A single orange at the official rate could cost US$1.50. Because of a near 60-fold devaluation between 1983 and 1987, it's now fairly inexpensive. The currency is floated on a weekly basis. Each time there's a devaluation, prices rise somewhat, but because the medium priced and expensive hotels demand payment in hard currency, the devaluations have had no effect on their prices. (Only one hotel, the Ambassador in Accra, accepts credit cards.)

The devaluations are slowly killing off the black market. In early 1987, the rate was only 200 cedis to the dollar – hardly worth the risk. In Accra, you may still find black marketeers around Opera Square, the Arts Centre and Makola market. Even though it's illegal to import more than 20 cedis into Ghana, before the devaluations many travellers used to buy cedis in Lomé; you still can at the market there. Customs officials sometimes conduct thorough searches, sometimes not at all. When you leave, they are frequently lax at the borders, typically asking no more than to see your currency declaration form. Don't lose that form; you'll have serious problems if you do. At Accra airport, on the other hand, they may frisk you. All of this varies according to the border station, who's on duty, the time of day, and fate.

Banking hours: weekdays 8.30 am to 2 pm (open one hour longer on Friday). Banks: Bank of Ghana, Barclays, Ghana Commercial Bank, Standard Bank of Ghana.

LANGUAGE

English is the official language. You'll hear Ga in the south-east including Accra, Twi-Fanti around Cape Coast and Kumasi, Ewe in the east, and various languages in the north. Greetings in Ga are:

Good morning/ good evening   *ming-gah-bou*
How are you?   *tay-yoh-tain*
Thank you   *oh-gee-wah-dong*

Greetings in Ewe:

Good morning   *mou-DOH-boh-no, nee-fon*
Good evening   *mee-LIE-nee-ah*
How are you?   *nee-FOH-ah*
Thank you   *mou-DOH, ack-pay-noh*
Goodbye   *mee-AH-gah-DOH-goh*

GENERAL INFORMATION

Health

Vaccinations are required for yellow fever and cholera. The best hospitals in Accra are not the public ones. Foreigners generally prefer the Northridge clinic. The Police Hospital not far from the US embassy is another, but you may not be allowed to use it. Two of the best pharmacies in Accra are Kingsway Chemist (tel 662440) on Knutsford Avenue near TCU Motors, and Ghana Drug House (tel 663235) on Asafoatsee Nettey Rd opposite the ice company.

Security

For a city with over a million people, Accra has had relatively few pickpocketing incidents, perhaps because very few foreigners walk around downtown.

Business Hours

Business: weekdays 8 am to 12 noon and 2 to 5.30 pm; Saturday 8 am to 1 pm. Government: weekdays 8 am to 12.30 pm and 1.30 to 5 pm.

Public Holidays

1 January, 6 March (Independence), Good Friday, Easter Monday, 4 June, 1 July, 25-26 December.

Photography

No permit is required, but you should be particularly cautious in Accra - the numerous coup attempts against Rawlings keep soldiers suspicious. Important government installations are in the area around the old castle in Accra. Taking photos in this area will land you in jail, as will taking photos of any government buildings, dams, ports, airport, TV-radio stations, etc.

Time, Post, Phone & Telex

When it's noon in Ghana, it's noon in London and 7 am in New York (8 am during daylight savings time). The post office in Accra is on Nkrumah Avenue. Telephone communications from foreign countries to Accra are poor, sometimes taking days to get a call through. Calling to/from elsewhere in Africa is even more difficult. Cables can be sent from the post office. Telex facilities are available, and there is a public call office at Extelcom House, High St, Accra (open Monday to Saturday, 7 am to 9 pm).

THINGS TO BUY

Because they had so much gold and profited from the slave trade, the Ashanti developed one of the richest and most famous civilisations in Africa. Today, they are still well known for, among other things, their *kente* cloth - metre for metre, probably the most expensive material in Africa - their stools, which are among the finest in Africa, and their fertility dolls. Made only by men and originally with silk, kente cloth is an immense piece of brightly coloured cotton fabric with intricate patterns and a wealth of hues. Men in the south wear it draped like a toga. US$150 is not an unreasonable price.

Stools play a greater role in Akan culture than they do elsewhere in Africa. The first gift that a father gives to his son, and the first gift bestowed by a fiance on his future bride, is a stool. Everyone has his or her favourite; it would be heresy for someone to sell it or give it away. When a person dies, the relatives use the stool to sit the corpse on and bathe it, after which they place it in the room for ancestor worship. Chiefs consider stools to be their supreme insignia. The insignia of King Osei Tutu, the founder of the Ashanti kingdom, is a gold stool, which supposedly descended from the heavens, and the only gold one ever to exist. Not even the supreme Ashanti king may sit on this stool, which is brought out only on rare occasions and is itself placed on a special stool. You'll undoubtedly see these stools for sale as you travel around Ghana. If they weren't so bulky, they'd make great souvenirs.

Ashanti fertility dolls (*akua-ba*), on the other hand, are small and easily transported. These are the flat, circular-headed statues with long ringed necks sold everywhere. About a third of a metre high and carved in wood, they're treated like magic. Women who want children, and pregnant women who want their children to have beautiful heads and long necks, carry them on their backs like children.

If you buy wooden artefacts or paintings, you'll have to present a certificate from the museum in Accra to show that they aren't of historic value. No problem - they'll issue you one in five minutes.

GETTING THERE
Air
From Europe, there are direct flights from Amsterdam, Geneva, London, Marseilles and Rome. The cheapest way to get to Ghana is to buy a ticket from a bucket shop in London or Amsterdam. Rates on Aeroflot and Ghana Airways are the lowest, approximately £400 to £440 roundtrip. From the USA, you can take Air Afrique from New York, transferring in Dakar or Abidjan.

Once highly ridiculed, Ghana Airways is clearly improving. Planes are serviced in Britain. Fares must be paid for in hard currency unless you're travelling only inside Ghana. From Accra to Cotonou in Benin costs US$52.

Car
The roads in Ghana were the best in West Africa in 1960. By the early 1980s, they had become some of the worst. The country is now in the midst of a major road building program. All the major arteries in the country, including Accra-Kumasi-Berekum, Kumasi-Tamali and the entire coastal road stretching from the Togolese border to the Ivorian border, have been or are being paved or re-paved. The 580-km Abidjan-Accra coastal road is now a 12-hour drive, Accra-Lomé a three-hour drive, and Accra-Kumasi a four-hour drive. The 1010-km Ouagadougou-Accra road is tarred all the way except for 15 km. However, the 393-km Kumasi-Tamale portion will continue to take a full day until the road work is completed.

Bush Taxi/Bus
To/from Burkina Faso If you're going to Burkina Faso you can get a bus direct to the border from Accra. Buses start early. Those for Kumasi leave from 6 am to 4 pm and take four hours, the cost is about 250 cedis.

To/from Abidjan The best way to get from Abidjan to Accra is on the Ghana State Transport bus which leaves from near Treichville hospital in Abidjan at 6 am, costs CFA 7000, and takes a long day because of the tedious customs check at the border.

To/from Lomé Most people do not take the STC buses towards Lomé because it's quicker to take a taxi or minibus. You won't make it to Lomé unless you hit the road by 2 pm because the border closes at 6 pm sharp.

In 1987 this border was closed for a few months, but is now open again. After an attempted coup in Togo, the Togolese

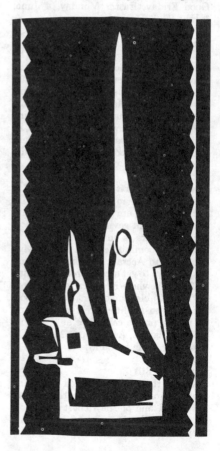

closed the border, believing that the culprits had come from Ghana. When they decided to reopen the border, Ghana, having been insulted, kept it closed for a few months more to get even!

GETTING AROUND

Air
The only interior flight destinations are Kumasi, Tamali and Sunyani. It's at least as quick to travel to Kumasi overland as it is by air.

Bush Taxi/Bus
You have the choice between a car-taxi, a 'mammy truck' and a State Transport Corp (STC) bus. Ghana is famous for the high quality of the STC buses – big comfortable, fast, punctual and inexpensive. They don't take on any more passengers than there are seats, and offer a total of 57 itineraries, including some very remote towns. Getting a ticket is the only problem.

The lowest class vehicles are the 'mammy trucks', so named because of their predominantly female clientele, travelling with cassava, yams and all manner of goods. The unpadded board, elbow in your side, and olfactory surprises come free with the ticket.

Train
There are three railway lines – Accra-Kumasi, Kumasi-Sekondi, and Accra-Huni Valley. The government purchased some used European trains in 1986, so the quality is now much improved. Because there are far more practical ways to travel, foreigners rarely take trains in Ghana and then only for a lark. The train station is downtown on the lower part of liberty Avenue opposite Kinbu Rd.

Boat
The *Makosombo Queen* is an adventurous trip if it is still operating. For years, it has been plowing Volta Lake from Akosombo in the south to Yapei in the north, starting Mondays and taking three days. The boat has 12 staterooms plus dormitories, but no restaurant.

Accra

Accra (ah-KRAH) is a lively town that used to attract travellers until the economic situation in Ghana got so bad in the late 1970s and early 1980s that life there simply became too difficult to enjoy. One could walk into a government-run store and find four or five people behind counters, all smiling and ready to serve you, the only problem being that the shelves were 99% empty. At nighttime, the streets were completely dark from electricity blackouts, forcing people to stay at home or in their hotels.

Change is in the air. Buildings are being painted and, unheard of until recently, Ghanaians abroad are even returning. Accra is big, with 1.2 million people and spread out in the English tradition. It's a logistical hassle. Finding an empty cab or one going your way is no easy task. The major roads are Ring Rd, a broad four-lane highway, and the two parallel downtown streets of Nkrumah Avenue (ex-Liberty Avenue) and Kojo Thompson Rd. Once you're downtown, plan on doing a lot of walking because of the taxi problem. It's possible to spend the entire day downtown without seeing a white face. That's because Ghana is the antithesis of Gabon and the Ivory Coast – Ghanaians run the show.

Information
Tourist Office This is on Kojo Thompson Rd and the staff are helpful. The KLM office, in Republic House on Nkrumah Avenue, has good city maps for free.

Embassies Benin (tel 225701), Burkina Faso (tel 224962), Canada (Box 1639, tel 228555), Denmark (tel 227715), France (Box 187, tel 228571), West Germany (Box 1757, tel 221311), Ivory Coast (tel 774611), Japan (Box 1637, tel 775616), Liberia (tel 225701), Niger (tel 224962), Nigeria (tel 776158), Switzerland (Box 359, tel 228125/85), Togo (tel 777950), UK (Box 296, tel

664651/776728), USA (Box 194, tel 774315/775347).

Other embassies include: Algeria, Austria, Brazil, Egypt, Ethiopia, Guinea, Italy, Mali, Netherlands, Spain, Togo, UK.

Bookstores The tiny *Omari* is Accra's best and has maps of Ghana plus a decent selection of novels. It's on Ring Road, about half a km east of Danquah Circle on your left. The bookstore at the University of Legon is another possibility, but it's a long way out of town.

Travel Agencies The major travel agencies are Jet Age Travel & Tours Ltd at the Ambassador hotel, Black Beauty Tours (tel 776542/776896) at the Continental Hotel, Universal Travel & Tourist Services (tel 222813/228049) at Republic House on Nkrumah Avenue, and Scantravel (tel 663134/666761) on High St. Making air travel arrangements is their major business. They offer no tours of the country, only a rental car with chauffeur in the case of Black Beauty and Jet Age. Universal represents Thomas Cook and Scantravel represents American Express.

Black Star Square
Black Star Square and Independence Arch, a huge area backed by the sea with a capacity for over 25,000 people, is to Accra what Red Square is to Moscow. Nkrumah built it in 1961 along with the huge stadium across the street, behind which is the State House built in 1965 for the OAU conference – all examples of his extravagant spending habits. From the square you can see Osu Castle off in the distance near the ocean. It was built by the Danes around 1659 and is now the seat of government. It is off limits to the public.

National Museum
Three blocks east of where Nkrumah Avenue intersects with Castle Rd, is the National Museum, which is open every day 8 am to 6 pm except Monday and well worth a visit. It houses an assortment of drums, chiefs' chairs, Ashanti cloth, stools, swords, implements, old photographs, masks, including numerous items not of Ghanaian origin.

Art Centre
If you follow High St from Black Star Square towards the centre of town, you'll

1	Tip Toe Gardens Nightclub	22	Art Centre
2	Kwame Nkrumah Circle	23	Riviera Beach Hotel
3	Terra Nova & La Reve Restaurants	24	Independence Arch
4	Blow Up Restaurant	25	Marriot International Hotel
5	Ringway Hotel		& Holiday Makers Hotel
6	Bus Stop Bar & Restaurant	26	Pearl of the East Restaurant
7	Adeshi Hotel		& All That Jazz Nightclub
8	North Ridge Hotel	27	Penta Hotel
9	Lemon Lodge & Korkdam Hotel	28	Tropicana Restaurant
10	YMCA	29	Mandarin Restaurant
11	Maharani Restaurant	30	Black Caesar's Restaurant
12	Crown Prince Hotel		& Nightclub
	& Hotel de California	31	Omari Bookstore
13	Restaurant 400	32	US Embassy
14	National Museum & YWCA	33	Danquah Circle
15	Avenida Hotel	34	Redemption Circle
16	Ambassador Hotel	35	Afrikoko Restaurant
17	Cocoa House	36	Star Hotel
18	Taxi & Bus Park	37	Peace Corps
19	Makola Market	38	No 37 Roundabout
20	Post Office	39	Continental Hotel
21	James Fort		

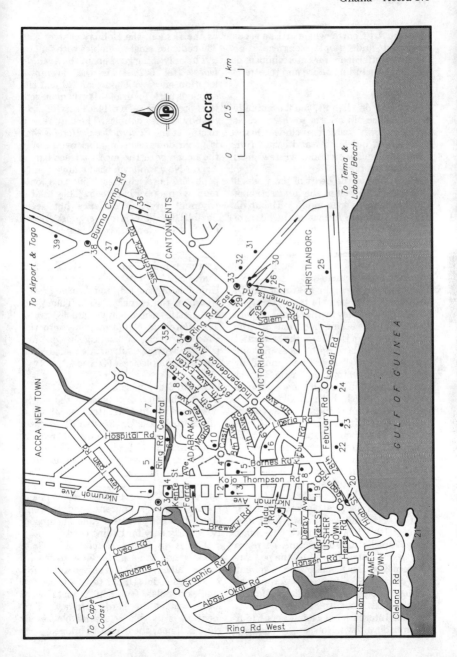

pass the Art Centre, where artisan goods are sold and people congregate on Saturday afternoons for entertainment of all kinds, including dance and theatre.

Other Sights

Continuing on High St, you'll eventually arrive in the old area of town known as James Town, which includes many dilapidated old houses and James Fort, now an inconspicuous whitewashed prison at the port.

Returning to the heart of town, you'll find Makola Market at the intersection of Independence Avenue and Kojo Thompson Rd. Up Nkrumah Avenue is the heart of Accra's commercial district - Cocoa House, the big GNTC department store, Kingsway and most of the banks.

Places to Stay - bottom end

It's worth staying at the YWCA or YMCA in Accra just to be able to say that you stayed at what may be the cheapest open-to-the-public accommodation in the world - less than US 25c (at the bank rate) for a dormitory bed! Both places are going strong and travellers are welcome. They are close to downtown on Castle Rd near the National Museum. If there's a course in progress and the beds are all taken, try the Presbyterian Guest House on Salem Rd in Kuku Hill (between Danquah Circle and Black Star Square) and the Methodist Church Headquarters across from Mobil House - the cost is only 100 cedis or so.

As for regular hotels, you'll be hard pressed to find better accommodation for the price than the spotlessly clean Lemon Lodge, which is several blocks off Ring Rd, next door to the well-known Korkdam Hotel (tel 226797). A room with breakfast costs 770 cedis, payable in cedis. There are only seven rooms. If it's full, the popular 19-room Korkdam has a Chinese restaurant and charges 960/1870 cedis for decent singles/doubles. Or try Holiday Makers Hotel, next door to the well-known Marriot International Hotel, about four km from downtown. Nowhere near as good

as the Lemon, the Holiday charges 550/730 cedis for singles/doubles with fan.

The only thing good about the Avenida Hotel (tel 662864) is the downtown location on Kojo Thompson Rd and the spacious patio for drinks. Poorly managed, the hotel charges 1108/1430 cedis for dirty shabby singles/doubles. The only reason to stay at the Riviera Beach Hotel is that it's near downtown on a rock overlooking the ocean with the nicest terrace bar in Accra. Now rundown with a huge empty pool, the hotel charges 1650 cedis for a room with a poor bathroom. They ask for payment in hard currency but seem flexible. The hotel is in a very dark area at night; walking around could be dangerous.

If you want to be in the heart of town and don't care about quality, three places to try are the 20-room Tropicana (tel 666292) on Tudor St, Hotel Memorial Nkrumah on Kojo Thompson Rd, and Crown Prince Hotel on the corner of Kojo Thompson and Castle, where doubles are 660 cedis. The Hotel de California, opposite the Crown Prince, is slightly better and popular with travellers. All rooms have fans and doubles cost 880 cedis.

Places to Stay - middle

One of the big advantages of the newly renovated Penta Hotel (tel 774529), with singles/doubles for US$27/40 with breakfast, is the location - near Danquah Circle on Cantonments Rd leading into downtown Accra and near many restaurants, nightclubs and available taxis. The Chinese-run Ringway Hotel (tel 228306) charges US$32 for a decent room, has a good Chinese restaurant, and is well-located on Ring Rd near Kojo Thompson Rd - fairly easy for hailing cabs.

The King David Hotel (tel 225280/229832) has some of the best rooms in Accra - all have TVs and refrigerators - for 2420/3300 cedis (US$27 to US$36.50) for singles/doubles. They don't seem to insist for payment in hard currency. The location is not bad - several blocks off Ring Rd, near the overhead bridge.

For the price, US$19.50 a room, the state-run *Star Hotel* (tel 777728/777326) is a good buy. The rooms are fairly large and the nightclub is one of the most popular in Accra on Saturday nights, but the bathrooms are in poor condition, the air-con doesn't work in many rooms, and it's about seven km from downtown and several km beyond Ring Rd. Finding taxis is a big problem. A better choice is *Adeshi Hotel* (tel 221307), which charges only US$13.50/22 for singles/doubles that are better maintained than those at the Star. Hailing taxis is not a major problem because it's on Ring Rd half-way between Kuame Nkrumah Circle and Redemption Circle.

Places to Stay - top end

The four top hotels are all quite different. The big state-run *Ambassador Hotel* was completely renovated in 1985 and is the only hotel rating three stars, primarily because of all its amenities, including a long pool. It is the closest major hotel to downtown, usually has taxis waiting outside and, unlike the others, accepts credits cards (American Express). Frequent travellers to Ghana who care only about the quality of the rooms, restaurant and hotel management prefer the *North Ridge Hotel*, a well-managed, privately owned hotel that has big rooms, a pleasant ambience and a good restaurant. It is just off Ring Rd, about four km from downtown. To hail a cab, however, you have to walk several blocks.

The brand new, seemingly well-managed *Marriot International Hotel* (not part of the Marriot chain) has the best rooms and is one block from a major road leading into downtown Accra, easy for hailing taxis. It's small, however, and you are unlikely to meet other travellers. The large state-run *Continental Hotel* near the airport is quite active and has a popular terrace bar, nightclub and taxis waiting outside, but it is not well managed. Pay extra for a renovated room, otherwise you'll get a shabby room, possibly with no running water at night.

If you like the idea of a small tranquil hotel that is pleasant, well managed and has a good restaurant, the *Granada Hotel* is 10 km from downtown and several hundred metres beyond the airport, but you need wheels.

By 1988, you may have some additional choices just outside Accra along the beach. In 1987, a 200-room bungalow-style beach resort at Labadi beach just east of Accra, a 50-room beach hotel at Charles Village, and a 20-room beach hotel at Oyster Bay were nearing completion - all part of the government's plan to push tourism in a big way.

Ambassador Hotel (tel 664646, telex 2113 Ambassador), US$27.50/49.50 for singles/doubles, tennis, long pool, casino, travel agency, car hire, shops, cards AE only, reservations by cable are not assured.

North Ridge Hotel (tel 225809, telex 3025 Northridge), US$49/60 for singles/doubles, accepts reservations by cable.

Marriot International Hotel (tel 774542, telex 2340 MNJGH), US$50 a room with breakfast, video/music in rooms, accepts reservations by cable.

Continental Hotel (tel 775361, telex 2113 Continental), US$27.50/39.50 for singles/doubles (US$49 for a renovated double), casino, nightclub, travel agency-car hire, reservations by cable are not assured.

Granada Hotel (tel 775343), US$40 a room.

Places to Eat

Cheap Eats The popular *Bus Stop* is not particularly cheap, but serves simple fare – sandwiches, khebabs, fish, chicken, beer, good orange juice, plus a few cheap Ghanaian dishes on Sunday. Open every day 9 am to 10 pm, it's on Ring Rd about one km east of Nkrumah Circle. *Terra Nova*, a stone's throw south of Nkrumah Circle, has a limited menu but the *al fresco* dining under thatched roofs is pleasant. Afterwards, you can visit some lively nightclubs next door. It closes at 10 pm and all day Sunday. This area, and the section further downtown around the Lorry Park, is where you'll find street food day and night.

Chinese Accra has the best Chinese restaurants in all of West Africa. The food is excellent at all the top five restaurants. Three of them are near Danquah Circle on Ring Rd, all are open every day. The newest 'in' Chinese restaurants are *Rickshaw* at the Ambassador hotel, which is particularly liked by Ghanaians, and *Hinlone* one long block north of Ring Road. Taxi drivers may not know the Hinlone but as you drive east on Ring Rd, take your first left (Labone Rd) after passing Danquah Circle (about half a km), then the next left.

Mandarin (tel 776378), which has a pleasant decor and big menu, is just off Ring Rd, about 300 metres on the opposite side (west) of Danquah Circle. The advantage of *Pearl of the East* (tel 774902), which has authentic Chinese vegetables and an interesting decor, is that you can have a drink next door at the popular pub-like *All That Jazz*. Go south from Danquah Circle for one block and take a left immediately after passing the Penta Hotel; it's on your right 100 metres down. The other two, *Boajin* (tel 775847) and *Lam's Restaurant* at the Grenada Hotel, are too remote.

Indian Not as good as the Chinese restaurants, *Maharani* (tel 226418) has the best Indian food, an Indian ambience and moderate prices. It's on Farrar Avenue between Nkrumah Avenue and Kojo Thompson Rd.

Continental One of the best is *Blow Up*, on Kojo Thompson Rd just south of Ring Rd. Open every day from 8 pm, they serve eight pasta dishes, pizzas with various toppings, plus beef, chicken and seafood dishes. Prices are fairly high for Accra. You'll find more moderate prices at *Restaurant 400* (tel 225108), which is one of Accra's better restaurants. Closed Sunday, it's in the heart of town on Nkrumah Avenue, one block from the Standard Bank. Near the Cocoa House on the same street is *Los Amigos*, which has a

small menu and a pleasant ambience except for the jukebox, and is open every day until midnight.

Lebanese *Phoenica* serves decent Lebanese fare and is downtown on Kojo Thompson across from NICR. On the same street is *Uncle Sam's* (tel 226558), with moderate prices and open every day except Sunday until 11 pm. The newly renovated *Tropicana*, several km from downtown and one block off Cantonments Rd near the Russian Cultural Centre, is expensive and not particularly good.

Ghanaian Pepper soup, groundnut stew, gari foto (eggs, onions, dried shrimp, tomatoes, gari) and kelewele (fried plantains with pepper and ginger) are some common Ghanaian specialties. The *Ambassador Hotel* has a well-prepared Ghanaian specialty every day. *After 8*, downtown on Kojo Thompson across from Avenida Hotel, serves Ghanaian and continental specialities. Further from downtown, there's *Afrikiko* on Independence Avenue leading towards the airport; fufu and jallof rice are on the menu. Another which has been recommended is *Pub la Rita* on Cantonments Rd in Markoffie.

Entertainment & Sports

Bars *All That Jazz* is highly recommended; this pub-like bar is popular with both Ghanaians and expatriates. Open every day, they charge a 200-cedi cover on weekends. It is just south of Danquah Circle, one block behind the Penta Hotel. The terrace of the *Continental Hotel* is still fairly popular. On Independence Avenue between the Continental Hotel and Ring Rd at Redemption Circle is a Peace Corps favourite – *Afrikiko*, a pleasant outdoor bar-restaurant. Going north, look for the big straw-covered structure on your left. You can get a big beer for 100 cedis as well as fufu, jallof rice and snacks. *Bus Stop* is closer to the downtown area and one of the more popular bars, also serving food.

Nightclubs Accra is one of the best places in West Africa for live music, especially on Saturday night. One of the most popular places is the *Star Hotel*, which has a live band Saturday 7 pm to 3 am and a 150 cedis cover, with lots of beer and a huge outdoor dance floor. The *Bukom Nightclub* at the Continental Hotel usually has a band on Saturdays from 8 pm to 1 am. It is air conditioned and very popular. On Saturday afternoons, you can hear a live band at the *Ambassador Hotel* for only 30 cedis.

The nightclub scene in Accra is fairly unstable, with clubs opening and closing frequently. One of the more popular nightclubs these days is *Apollo Club*; ask your taxi driver to find it. *Black Caesar's*, a long-standing favourite with Ghanaians and expatriates, has come back to life after being closed. It is on Ring Rd a stone's throw from Danquah Circle, and may still be open weekends only. Two blocks away is the new *Stage Coach Discoteque*, 100 metres behind the Penta hotel and next to the well-known All That Jazz bar. It's closed Monday and Tuesday. If you have wheels and a driver who knows his way, you might try *Stereo Spot*, a popular dancing spot with Ghanaians at Teshie Nungua Estates on the coastal road leading east towards Tema.

Nightclubs for the common man seem to have more staying power and are also around Ring Rd at Nkrumah Circle. A block to the north, is *Tip Toe Gardens*, one of Accra's most popular dancing spots. For only about 70 cedis, you can dance outdoors to a live band Wednesday to Saturday.

Just south of Nkrumah Circle are two of Accra's most disreputable nightclubs, *Le Reve* and *Premier Lodge* next door; neither has a cover charge. These hot spots are where both expatriate and Ghanaian men look for women – or vice versa. They're open every day from 8 pm and start getting lively from about 10 pm on.

Movie Theatres Two of the best are the Orion and the Globe.

Sports Ghana boasts beautiful sandy beaches and lagoons. The closest major beach, Labadi Beach, is a 10-minute taxi ride east of Danquah Circle on the coastal road to Tema. The undertow is strong and thieves are prevalent, so be careful. You will find other uncluttered beaches west of the city, especially 'mile 13', 'mile 14' and 'mile 16'.

For tennis or swimming, go to the Ambassador hotel where the charge is a mere 60 cedis. Golfers can try the course at the Achimota Golf Club (tel 776551). Expatriate Americans play softball on Saturday at 2 pm. Inquire at the American embassy; visitors are usually welcome. There are four unceremonious horse races downtown at the race track, next to the football stadium, every Saturday between 3 and 5 pm.

Barclays Bank has an unlit squash court in fair condition at its training centre. Going south from Redemption Circle on Independence Avenue, you'll see a Barclays sign on your right. Ask the guards to show you. As long as you are respectful, no one seems to mind. The luckier squash players get invited to play at the Tesano Club or Achimota School.

Joggers should call the British embassy (tel 664651) to find out where the Hash House Harriers meet for their weekly Monday run at 5 pm. This is an international group of runners who amuse themselves running through corn fields and back alleys, and then swallow lots of beer. Whatever you do, don't jog near the old castle, a high security area – you may get a rifle poked in your belly.

Things to Buy

Artisan Goods The first place to head for is the *Art Centre*. It is downtown on the ocean road (High St) near Black Star Square and is open every day. You'll see a wide assortment of crafts and carvings – not all Ghanaian. Next door, you'll find a wide assortment of materials, including the famous Kente cloth. On the outskirts of town several hundred metres beyond the Continental hotel is *The Ark*, open weekdays 8.30 am to 4 pm and Saturday 8.30 am to 1 pm, with a wide selection of wooden carvings and other crafts, many non-Ghanaian. For jewellery, try the *Nugget* on Farrar Rd two blocks south of Nkrumah Circle.

Music For records or cassettes of Ghanaian music, you'll have to search for an African shop that makes cassettes, or wander through the giant department stores downtown on High St. Ghana is not the leader in African music that it once was – highlife music is now passé. African Brothers is the most well-known group; others include Big Beats, Boombaya and Headzoleh.

Getting There & Away
Air There are regular flights to Kumasi, Tamale and Sunyani.

Bus There are two STC bus stations in Accra. One is downtown near the national museum, the other is on the western side of Ring Road beyond Kwame Nkrumah Circle. Seats fill up quickly, so most people buy their tickets well in advance. If you're going to Burkina Faso, you can get a bus direct to the border. Buses start early. Those for Kumasi leave from 6 am to 4 pm and take four hours and the cost is about 250 cedis. There are regular buses to Cape Coast for 190 cedis plus 60 cedis for luggage.

Bush Taxi Bush taxis and minibuses to Lomé and virtually all other destinations leave from the lorry Park in downtown Accra at the corner of Kojo Thompson and Kinbu. You won't make it to Lomé unless you hit the road by 2 pm because the border closes at 6 pm sharp. A bush taxi to Akosombo costs 140 cedis.

Train There are trains to Kumasi, Sekondi and Huni Valley. The station is downtown on Liberty Avenue opposite Kinbu Rd.

Getting Around
Airport Transport At Accra airport, there is a 200 cedis airport tax. You'll find a restaurant, a bar and a bank. A taxi to downtown (10 km) costs about 500 cedis; bargaining is definitely required. Many drivers demand foreign currency. There's no bus service into town, however, you could walk to the highway several hundred metres from the airport. It leads directly into town, so catching a shared taxi isn't difficult. You probably won't find one going exactly where you're headed, so count on changing taxis en route. It would be less hassle looking for other travellers to share a cab.

Only one major hotel, the Ambassador, is near the heart of town. Most of the others are somewhere between downtown and the airport. The Continental Hotel is only a km and a half away from the airport; the Granada is less.

Taxi There are no set rates when you 'charter' a taxi for yourself. A typical trip will run 150 to 250 cedis depending on the distance. Taxis by the hour are 500 cedis. The only places where you can be sure of finding taxis for charter are the Ambassador, Continental and Penta hotels. If you won't be staying at one of these, make arrangements with the taxi driver bringing you in from the airport to pick you up. Do not expect your hotel clerk to find you a taxi the next day. He couldn't even if he wanted to.

A shared taxi costs only about 40 cedis, but finding one going in your direction may be tricky. Don't try to learn by trial and error – you'll go nuts. Ask people what road you should be standing on. It may require a lot of asking because people tend to know only the routes they take. The problem is that it may take a little walking to get to that street because, again, Accra is spread out. Also, do not expect a cab to go exactly where you're going as they usually only go from circle to circle. You may have to go to one circle, then hail another – this is usually much quicker than waiting for a taxi going closer to your final destination.

Car Rental

There are only a few car rental agencies in Accra and none elsewhere. Black Beauty Tours (tel 776542/776896) at the Continental Hotel and Jet Age Travel & Tours Ltd at the Ambassador Hotel both rent cars. You may be required to hire one of their chauffeurs. Hertz is represented by Allways Travel Agency (tel 224590), and Avis by Speedway Rent-a-Car (5 Tackie Tawia St, tel 228799/228760, telex 2134). Antrak Car Ltd at Danquah Circle is another.

AROUND ACCRA

If all you have time for is a half-day excursion, there are several options. The **University of Legon** is about 12 km out of Accra beyond the airport and worth a visit if done in conjunction with a visit to the **Aburi Botanical Gardens**, which are even further away. Some of the sites at the gardens include the Bush House, which is a typical Ghanaian building, the tricky 'monkey pot tree' which traps monkeys, and a model cocoa farm.

Tema

If you find port areas interesting, head 30 km east via the more interesting coastal route to Tema, Ghana's major port – a sterile pre-fab looking city. Around 10 am, the fishing vessels drift back from their night at sea, and fish are sold on the spot.

Places to Stay & Eat You could eat at the *Dragon Restaurant* or at Tema's major hotel, the 12-storey *Hotel Meridien* (tel 2878), which has a great terrace on top for viewing the port. Singles/doubles for about US$14/22.

Akosombo Dam

Others are more interested in taking the 100-km trip north-east to Akosombo Dam, which dams the world's largest man-made lake, the 400-km-long Volta Lake. Nkrumah inaugurated it in 1966, a month before the army ousted him. Over two-thirds of the electricity goes to the American company, Valco, which built the dam and uses it for its aluminium foundry in Tema. Except when there are back-to-back droughts, as in 1983-84, there's enough left over to power all of Ghana and even a good portion of neighbouring Togo and Benin.

From Akosombo you can take the *Makosombo Queen* for the three-day trip along the lake.

Places to Stay & Eat You can eat and sleep at the rundown 40-room *Volta Hotel*, which dates from the early '60s and has a sweeping view of the lake, dam and surrounding hills.

The Coast

Travellers rave about the coastal area west of Accra, particularly Cape Coast, Elmina, Busua and Dixcove, which was described by one traveller as 'the best beach in Africa'. The major city, Takoradi, and its twin city, Sekondi, hold little interest besides the port. What makes the area special are the old slave-trading forts, the beautiful beaches and the incredibly low prices. Where else can you see 14 forts and castles along a 250-km stretch of beach, actually sleep in two for less than US$1, and feast on amazingly cheap seafood caught and prepared for you by the villagers? Before economic conditions became so pitifully bad in Ghana, the beach at Dixcove was one of the most 'in' places on the West African coast; Elmina and Cape Coast were not far behind. With the change in Ghana's economic fortunes, they are again becoming popular. Elmina's first-class tourist hotel is again full on weekends.

COASTAL FORTS

The major forts and castles, east to west

from Accra are: Fort Good Hope at Senya Beraku (61 km west of Accra), Fort Leydsaamheid at Apam (10 km west of Winneba), a fort a few km east of Cape Coast, Fort Williams and a castle at Cape Coast, Fort Saint Jago and Saint George's castle at Elmina, Fort Vredenburg and Komenda English Fort at Komenda (10 km beyond Elmina), a fort a few km east of Sekondi-Takoradi, Fort Metal Cross at Dixcove, Fort Prince's Town (between Dixcove and Axim), Fort Saint Anthony in Axim and Fort Beyin (between Axim and Half Assini). The major ones, all open to the public, are the ones in Cape Coast, Elmina, Dixcove and Axim.

Most of the forts were built during the 17th century; the Danes, Brits, Portuguese and Dutch all played a role, with the forts and castles constantly changing hands – some as many as three times in five years. The most famous castle, Saint George's castle at Elmina, was unusual in that it changed hands only twice – from Portuguese to Dutch to British. It is also the oldest, dating from 1482 when the Portuguese brought an expedition of 600 men, including 100 masons and 100 carpenters, to begin construction.

Elmina castle was not originally used for slave trading. The Portuguese came looking for gold and ivory, found both, and began building forts where they could store it until trading ships arrived. The forts were also useful in helping them defend their spheres of influence. By 1600, however, slave trading was solidly established. Portugal was forced to share its control of the coastal trade with Holland, Denmark and Britain, which began building some of their own forts as well as stealing some of the Portuguese forts. The castle at Elmina fell to the Dutch in 1637. As they did with the gold and ivory, the Europeans used the castles to literally brand and store the slaves until ships arrived. They packed up to two thousand into four or five rooms and chained them down.

The castle at Cape Coast, built by the British, captured a year later by the Dutch and recaptured by the British, has an interesting little museum that's open every day except Monday from 8 am to 6 pm. The castle in Elmina is even better. You'll leave with a deep impression of just how badly the slaves were treated. It's amazing any of them survived. The guide there is the most enthusiastic and knowledgeable on the west coast of Africa; tip him well. During his one-hour tour, you'll see the slave quarters, the quarters of the condemned people, the slave auctioning rooms and the governor's quarters.

Places to Stay & Eat

Cape Coast The town's best is the 16-room *Savoy Hotel* (tel 2868), on the eastern side of town. Singles/doubles with springy beds and shared bathrooms run about 550/990 cedis (1650 cedis for a suite). The restaurant offers five or six selections for about 350 to 500 cedis. On the western outskirts of town is the *Palace Hotel*, which has a bar and charges about the same as the Savoy for a clean room with a basin, but shared bathrooms. Ask for one of the second-floor rooms because they catch the breeze.

Dans Paradise has also been recommended as good value. It has air-con doubles with attached baths and king-size beds for 1100 cedis.

Elmina Only 13 km from Cape Coast, Elmina has rooms for all budgets. For a mere 50 cedis a person, you can stay at *San Iago Fort*, which is perched on a hill overlooking the castle and the fishing village below. The toilet is filthy, in part because there's no running water, but there are women who will bring you a bucket of water and may fix you a meal. There are only four rooms – usually no problem getting one during the week but very difficult on weekends. At the time of writing it was closed for renovation but should be open again soon. The *Hollywood Hotel* is a good cheapie. It is run by a

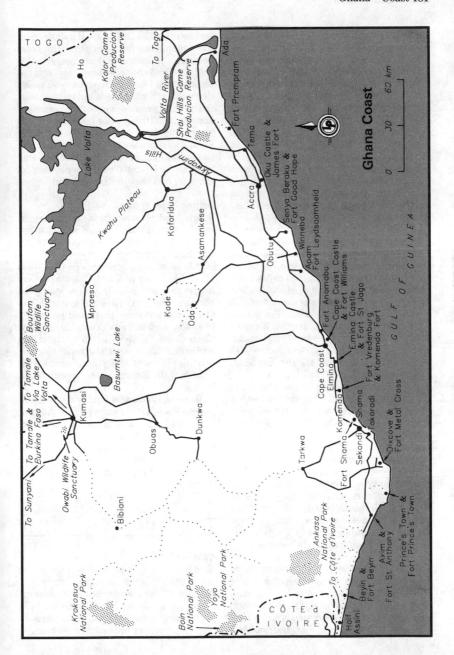

friendly family and the rooms are spotless. Doubles cost 650 cedis.

Elmina used to have the best-value hotel on the coast – *Elmina Hotel* (Box 100, Tel 2499), but it now costs about 2400 cedis for one of its cabins. All rooms have twin beds and porches that face the ocean, so the lack of air-con or fan is of no great concern. Meals are not cheap – one full meal with drinks can cost up to 1000 cedis. On Friday and Saturday nights during the dry season, it is frequently full with expatriates from Accra, so try to make a reservation. There are usually rooms available in Cape Coast if it's booked.

Takoradi In town near the Texaco station is an excellent hotel for the money – the new *Hotel Africana* (tel 2966). It has clean ventilated rooms and private baths for about 650 and 850 cedis (250 cedis more for air-con). The hotel's *Ahenfie Club Disco* is lively and the beers are cheap. It is open Saturday and Sunday. For rooms less than half this price, try the *Western Palace Hotel*, which has a restaurant, clean bathrooms, and big clean rooms with fans. Others cheapies are the *Embassy Hotel* and the dirtier *Hotel Arvo*.

The best hotel is the 70-room *Atlantic Hotel* (tel 3301/9), which is almost two km from the heart of town and has rooms with air-con for about 1900 cedis. The pool is in working condition and the nightclub opens on Saturday nights. There usually aren't many guests for a variety of reasons – the air-con frequently doesn't work, they may even have to bring water in buckets up to your room, and there are no screens on the windows, making the place a mosquito heaven. Nearby, along the sea, is the well-known *Mikado Restaurant*, the best in town and English-owned.

Dixcove-Busua You have the choice of sleeping in *Dixcove Castle*, which has four filthy bedrooms for 170 cedis a person including breakfast, or right on the beach at the *Busua Pleasure Beach* hotel, which charges 300/440 cedis (singles/doubles) for one of its 23 bungalows. If you sleep on the beach, stay far away from the hotel because the owner will charge you 200 cedis – and be prepared for lots of mosquitoes. During the week, you won't find many other travellers, but on weekends the place becomes a resort for western expatriates. Bring water because there is no potable water here. Food, on the other hand, is no problem – the local kids will immediately approach you offering large crayfish for 50 to 100 cedis, depending on the size, and they do the cooking!

Getting There & Away

Roads leading west from Accra are in excellent condition. The easiest way to get to Cape Coast and Takoradi is to take one of the comfortable STC buses. Getting a seat is usually fairly easy. The trip takes about 2½ hours to Cape Coast and four hours to Takoradi. If you're going to Elmina, which is 13 km beyond Cape Coast, the bus stops there and you don't have to get off in Cape Coast. To get from Cape Coast to Elmina, it's fairly cheap and easy to hire a cab. Returning to Accra, you might be able to hitch a ride back with a guest at the Elmina Hotel, especially on Sundays.

To get to Busua and Dixcove, which are several km apart, 32 km west of Takoradi, you could hire a taxi in Takoradi or, cheaper, take one of the regular buses. If you're coming by bush taxi from the Ivory Coast, ask them to let you off at the entrance to Busua and try to hitch from there.

The North

KUMASI

Kumasi is a sprawling city of 400,000 people, the heart of Ashanti country and the site of the country's major cultural centre and one of the country's three major universities. It is not an esthetically pleasing city, but at least it is vibrant.

National Cultural Centre

The city's major attraction is the National Cultural Centre, a 10-minute walk from the market. You'll find a museum of Ashanti art and culture, a theatre, library, craft shop, exhibition hall and restaurant. The museum, which contains a collection of clothing, jewellery, furniture and royal insignia, is constructed to look like an Ashanti chief's house, with four separate buildings opening onto a courtyard, and walls adorned with traditional carved symbols. It's open every day 9 am to 5 pm except Monday, when it's open 2 to 5 pm. The craft shop, which is open weekdays 8 am to 5.30 pm and weekends 8 am to 1.30 pm, has an assortment of inexpensive crafts which make good gifts and souvenirs. There is also a kente cloth centre, with some of the material for sale. Next to the cultural centre is the zoo, open every day 8 am to 5 pm (5.45 pm weekends).

Central Market

This market is one of the largest in Africa, with roughly 10,000 traders. The vultures perched on top of the market stalls add an ominous touch. If you're looking for kente cloth, Kumasi and the surrounding area have the lowest prices. To find some in the central market, you'll need someone to lead the way. It's usually sold only in huge pieces sufficient to make an elaborate toga; 8500 cedis is a very good price.

Military Museum

The Military Museum at Kumasi Fort, open weekdays 9 am to 2 pm and Saturday 9 am to 12 noon, is another attraction. Downtown one block from Kingsway, it focuses primarily on the British-Ashanti war of 1900, with lots of interesting old photographs and military regalia. A guided tour takes about an hour.

University of Science & Technology

This is on the outskirts of town in a pleasant setting. The sports facilities were at one time noted for being among the best in Black Africa.

Places to Stay – bottom end

You're going to have a hard time finding a cheaper place than the *Menka Memorial Hotel*, which has decent rooms for 450 cedis (550 cedis with fan, and 650 cedis with fan and private bath). It's on a major road between the heart of town and the stadium, less than two km from downtown. For quality accommodation, you can't beat the two-storey colonial *Presbyterian Guesthouse*, which costs 500 cedis a person and is downtown two blocks behind Barclays bank. You can use the kitchen to make your meals, but they charge about 200 cedis each time.

If you want to be in the heart of town in a hotel with lots of action, you may prefer the noisy 21-room *Hotel de Kingsway*, which has rooms for 550 to 880 cedis and rooms with air-con for 990 to 1200 cedis, plus tolerable bathrooms. In the centre of the hotel there's a big area for drinking that becomes a nightclub in the evening, occasionally featuring live music. Nearby, half a block from Prentice Agencies, is the quieter *Montana Hotel*, with singles/doubles without private baths for 550/660 cedis.

Other hotels, all about three km from downtown, include *Stadium Hotel* (tel 3647), with decent singles/doubles for 550/770 cedis (880 cedis with inside bathroom), *Hotel de Texas*, with ventilated rooms for 880 cedis and 1320 cedis with air-con, and *Kings Hotel*, with ventilated rooms for 550 cedis (1100 cedis with air-con).

Places to Stay – middle

Of the medium-priced hotels, the 47-room *Ashford Court Hotel* (tel 2917), which is several km from downtown and has a restaurant, is good for the price. Rooms with private bath go for 750 cedis without fan, 950 cedis with fan, and 1450 cedis with air-con. Sometimes, there's music and dancing in the restaurant.

Places to Stay – top end

For years, the city's major hotel has been the slightly run-down *City Hotel* (tel

3293), which is on a hill on the outskirts of town and has 75 rooms with air-con for 1980 cedis. The amenities include a nightclub, casino, tiny supermarket, shops, bookstore, and video lounge. However, two new privately owned hotels have sprung up – *Hotel Amissah* (tel 3046) and *Noks Hotel* (tel 4438/4162). While they are smaller and offer no amenities, the rooms are superior. Both are in residential areas near the stadium several km from the centre of town, charge 1800/2400 cedis for rooms/suites, and have a decent bar and restaurant. The only problem could be finding taxis. By comparison, the old state-run *Catering Resthouse* (tel 3656) seems overpriced at 1760 cedis for a bungalow with two beds and air-con; its only advantage is that it is closer to the centre of town.

Places to Eat
Ghanaian food is easy to find around the market. The YMCA, downtown half a block from Kingsway store, has a restaurant but no accommodation. The *Family Restaurant* is a good cheapie, as is the slightly more expensive *Lord's Restaurant*.

The best restaurant in town is probably *Chop Sticks*, which serves Chinese food and is about a km from the City Hotel. If you come by taxi, tell the driver to wait or you may have to walk back. After that, you might try *The Cabin Restaurant*, on Accra Rd near the university on the outskirts of town, which serves Chinese and European dishes. Otherwise, for continental cuisine, you'll have to stick to the hotels.

Nightlife
For live music, the *Hotel de Kingsway*, *City Hotel*, the *Cultural Centre* and *Star Nite Club* are all places where musical groups perform. For nightclubs, some of the favourites are *New Orleans*, *City Hotel*, *The Cameo* downtown, and *Pink Panther* near the stadium.

Getting There & Away
Bus/Bush Taxi Getting to Kumasi is no problem; STC buses leave Accra daily from 6 am to 4 pm. BMW bush taxis also go to Accra for 600 cedis. If you're headed to Abidjan by private bus, you should get to the bush taxi station next to the market by 7 am, otherwise you may not get a seat. They'll drop you in Agnibilekrou, 35 km within the Ivory Coast, where you'll find other taxis to Abidjan. The trip takes about 12 hours. If you're headed for Tamale, try to get a seat on the STC bus, otherwise you'll have to take a dilapidated private bus which leaves very early in the morning and takes all day.

Train For Takoradi, the train is recommended. The new German carriages are comfortable and the trip takes 7 hours. It costs 600 cedis in 1st class, 325 cedis in 2nd class.

AROUND KUMASI
Bonwire
If you're interested in seeing kente cloth being made, or buying large quantities, head for Bonwire, a village which exists almost entirely from weaving. Take the highway heading north-east towards Mampong and Tamale, and turn right on the Asonommaso road – a total distance of about 35 km. The town itself is interesting because most of the buildings are of the Ashanti style, with enclosed inner courts.

SUNYANI
Sunyani is a major town 127 km from Kumasi on the way to Abidjan. If you stop there, the eight-room *Catering Rest House* is apparently the best there is.

TAMALE
Tamale is a city of about 100,000 people and the capital of the northern region, an area that produces most of the country's rice and cotton. The city has many shade trees and is pleasantly spread out, but not particularly noteworthy. You'll find a Barclays bank and a Kingsway store

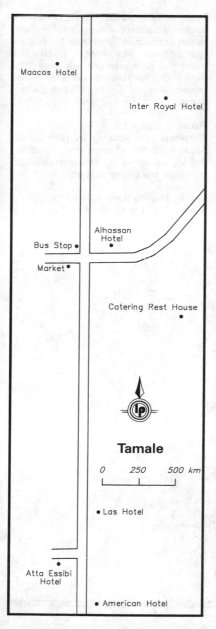

Maacos Hotel

Inter Royal Hotel

Bus Stop

Alhassan Hotel

Market

Catering Rest House

Tamale

0   250   500 km

Las Hotel

Atta Essibi Hotel

American Hotel

there. The 232-km road between Tamale and Kumasi is in nightmarish condition, but it is being completely paved – a project that will take at least several years to complete. If you can get your hands on some 'pito', the local brew made with millet, the ride may not seem so bad.

Places to Stay & Eat

For the price and the convenient downtown location, it's hard to beat the *Alhassan Hotel* (tel 2834), with rooms for 300 to 440 cedis. You have to use water from buckets to take a shower in the outside bathroom, but that's no different from all the other hotels. The big advantage is that it has a restaurant and is in the heart of town, about a block from the bus station and market. The *Cowrie Restaurant* charges about the same for meals and chilled beer. For cheaper accommodation, try *Maacos Hotel* on the northern end of town, which charges 220 cedis for a dirty tiny room.

In terms of quality, the *Catering Rest House* (tel 2978) has no competitors. You can pay either 880 cedis for a small ventilated room with fan, or 1650 cedis for a traditional-style bungalow, with air-con and a colourfully painted fresco on the outer wall. Don't be surprised if there's no running water. One km from downtown, it also has a bar with video and the best restaurant in town, with meals for 220 to 550 cedis. *Inter Royal Hotel* (tel 2247) is a good notch down. The rooms cost 495, 660 and 880 cedis; the most expensive includes air-con and a private bath without running water! The major problem is that it's two km from downtown in an area where taxis are rare.

On the southern end of town, about two km from the centre, are three hotels. The best is *Las Hotel* (tel 2217), which has a bar but no restaurant. The 550 cedis rooms, which are only marginally better than those at Alhassan, have a fan and private bath, but no running water. *America Hotel* and *Atta Essibi* charge the same or more and are not recommended.

Getting There & Away

The STC buses are far preferable to the trucks, but tickets are hard to get. If you can't get the bus it's a 12-hour bone rattler to Kumasi by truck for 650 cedis plus 100 for a backpack; to Bolgatanga it costs 200 cedis for the six-hour journey. Burkina Faso can be reached in one day via Bolgatanga and Navrongo, and then on to Paga at the border.

BOLGATANGA

Bolgatanga is the major town between Tamale and the Burkina Faso border. The best hotel is the *Black Star*; others include *Oasis*, *Central* and *Bolga*.

NAVRONGO

Navrongo is the last town before the Burkina Faso border. You'll see several large half-built structures here. They were begun in the mid-70s during the reign of Acheampong, who wanted to give this small village a nice gift – a huge hotel complex! Construction on this insane project stopped for good when he was deposed.

Places to Stay

There are no hotels, so try the *Catholic Mission* or the mission-run *Secondary School* nearby – a 15-minute walk south-east from the centre of town.

Getting There & Away

The STC bus heads south from Navrongo to Tamale and Kumasi every day at 1 pm.

Guinea

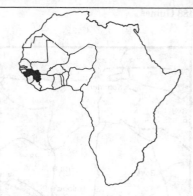

The vibrancy of the African culture and the spectacular beauty of the countryside are Guinea's major attractions. If you like to hike or motorbike, head for Guinea. The mountainous Fouta Djallon plateau offers some of the most striking scenery in West Africa and a relatively cool climate. Don't expect major hassles from the police either. Since Sekou Touré's death in 1984, the country has changed radically. You can almost feel the new liberty and economic vitality. Every month there seems to be another new restaurant in Conakry. Other things have not changed – such as the good music. Conakry has more major nightclubs than you can count, and you can also just walk around town any evening and frequently find a celebration in the streets accompanied by a several men playing traditional music. In Guinea, live music still reigns.

Guinea is not prepared for tourism, however. Outside Conakry, with one exception, all you'll find is 4th-class accommodation. Travellers on the cheap usually love it, with a double room costing US$2 to US$3, double that in Conakry. Those who insist on creature comforts are often disappointed. In Conakry, the only truly decent hotel costs US$100 a night for a double. In short, you may not like Guinea unless you're willing to rough it. Fortunately, it's one of the safest countries in West Africa, so travelling cheaply poses virtually no risk.

HISTORY

Guinea (Guinée in French) was a fairly obscure part of Africa until independence when Sekou Touré led Guinea in rejecting de Gaulle's proposal of a French 'community'. Touré became an all-African hero but he was a disaster as president. The country will take many years to recover.

Guinea was part of the great empire of Mali, which dominated most of the western Sudan and much of the Sahara from the 11th to the 15th centuries. The Malinké of Guinea are the descendants of those famous rulers. Fulani herders started migrating into the area around the 15th century and as a result of the Holy Islamic War of 1725, gained hegemony over the mountainous Fouta Djallon area.

The Guinean hero, Samori Touré, led the resistance against the French. It wasn't until 1898 that the superior-armed French captured him. Once the railroad to Kankan was completed, they began serious exploitation of the area, then part of French West Africa.

The most famous Guinean of all was Sekou Touré, a Malinké and a descendant of the legendary Samori Touré. From a poor family, he became the leading trade unionist in all of French West Africa and led the fight for independence. In 1956, while still holding communist views, he led a breakaway movement from the French parent union and formed a federation of African trade unions.

Independence

Shortly after coming to power in 1958, Charles de Gaulle offered the French colonies a choice between autonomy as separate countries in a Franco-African community or immediate independence. Led by Sekou Touré who declared that Guinea preferred 'freedom in poverty to prosperity in chains', Guinea was the only

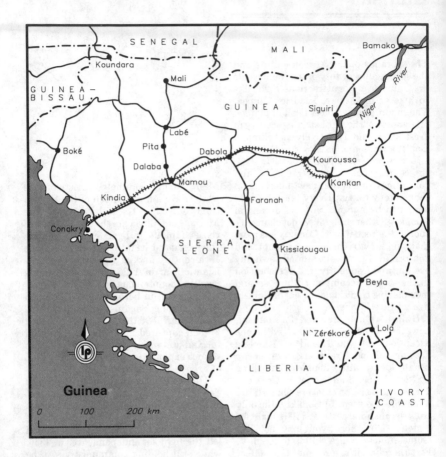

Guinea

0   100   200 km

French colony to reject De Gaulle's community proposal. Thus, Guinea became the first French colony to gain independence, and Sekou Touré became an African legend in his own time. Since Guinea had only one viable political party, that led by Sekou Touré, he became the country's first president.

The world soon learned how vindictive De Gaulle could be. Infuriated, he pulled the French out immediately, but not before they had ripped out the telephones and destroyed all military equipment and civilian archives, leaving nothing behind. French private citizens fled, withdrawing massive amounts of capital, thus assuring Guinea's economic collapse. Two years later, Sekou Touré made a decision that the present government is now strongly trying to reverse. Guinea withdrew from the franc zone and established its own currency, the syli.

With French economic assistance gone, the new country badly needed foreign aid. They turned to the Russians, but the honeymoon with the USSR was short-lived. In 1961, the Soviet ambassador was thrown out for 'interfering in the internal affairs of the country'.

The government continued on a socialist road, however, and in 1967 commenced a campaign of cultural revolution on the Chinese model, with state-run farms and weekly meetings of each revolutionary unit. It was an unmitigated disaster. As many as one million Guineans fled into neighbouring countries looking for work. Greatly depleted in numbers, the remaining farmers could work only one-quarter of the country's cultivable area. The USA had to give tonnes of food aid every year to keep people from starving.

The Reign of Terror
Sekou Touré appointed Malinké to virtually every major political position and treated his political opponents cruelly. Following an unsuccessful Portuguese led invasion of the country in 1970, he became paranoid, never once leaving Guinea for the next five years, and spoke of a 'permanent plot' against his regime. Waves of arrests followed. In 1971, 91 prisoners were sentenced to death. Torture became commonplace. Every year, Guinea was near the top of Amnesty International's list of the worst human rights offenders. In 1976, with the Fulani plot, he implicitly charged the entire Fulani population with collusion in an attempt to overthrow the government. The alleged Fulani leader of the plot was starved to death in prison. A quarter of the country's population, mostly Fulani, went into exile.

The revolt of the market women in 1977 was historic. As part of its programme to discourage private trade, the government decreed that all agricultural produce had to be delivered to the state-run cooperatives. For the market women, many of whom had been among Sekou Touré's most ardent supporters, this was too much. Riots started in Conakry, where the women destroyed various police offices

around Conakry, then spread to most of Guinea's towns, where they killed the governors of Kindia, Faranah and Boké. On hearing their complaints directly, he was deeply moved and again legalised petty trade. The day the revolt began, 27 August, is now a national holiday.

The riots seemed to turn him to more orthodox thinking in other ways as well. Soon after, he stepped up his *rapprochement* with France, with whom diplomatic relations had been resumed the year before. In 1978, Giscard d'Éstaing became the first French president since independence to set foot in Guinea. Touré then went on a 16-country tour of Africa, making amends with Senegal and the Ivory Coast.

Attempts against his life continued, however, until he died of heart failure in 1984, only months before a scheduled conference of the Organisation of African Unity (OAU) that he was to chair in Conakry. His death was followed by one of the most spectacular funerals in modern-day Africa, attended by numerous heads of state from Africa and elsewhere who had come to pay their respects to the old hero. Three days later, however, the people's real feelings came to light.

Military leaders toppled the government and quickly denounced Touré. They released a thousand political prisoners and promised an open society and the restoration of free enterprise. There was dancing in the streets of Conakry. The military government is still in power, with Colonel Lansana Conté, a Susu, in charge.

Today
Guinea is a remarkably different country today than it was just a few years ago. Free enterprise is on the march. People can once again talk freely and exiles are returning. The Susu and Lebanese communities are doing particularly well, evidenced by an estimated five-fold increase in the number of expensive automobiles and the construction of a number of new villas. There's even a new currency pegged to the franc as part of a

process of re-entering the franc zone. However, blackmarket operations continue to be highly profitable and diamonds are by far the most lucrative smuggling commodity, followed by gold.

Guinea is still a long way from losing its place on the list of the world's 25 poorest countries. It has some of the worst roads in West Africa that need vast sums to repair them. Reversing the disastrous decline in agricultural production won't be easy.

With the world's largest bauxite reserves, plus diamonds, iron, copper, manganese and possibly uranium, Guinea could be a rich country. Multinational corporations continue to exploit them, but these revenues alone will not restore the country's economy. Hard decisions lie ahead, like reducing the numbers on the government payroll and eliminating many unprofitable state enterprises.

PEOPLE

The Malinké, Fulani and Susu constitute about three-quarters of the country's 6.3 million people; 15 other ethnic groups make up the rest. You'll find more Susu along the coast and more Malinké and Fulani in the north and centre. Guinea is predominately Muslim and only about a quarter of the people are non-Muslim. Christians don't even constitute one percent.

The Malinké are the descendants of the empire of Mali. Despite their large numbers in Guinea, Mali, Senegal and elsewhere, Malinké art is extremely rare – quite the opposite of the Bambara in Mali, to whom they are closely related. If you find any wooden carvings, it's likely to be in the form of an antelope, a favourite subject. Sculptured human figures are almost nonexistent.

GEOGRAPHY

The Fouta Djallon hills are Guinea's most well-known geographical feature and the source of most of the Niger river. It is a beautiful plateau rising in the central west of the country to over 1500 metres, with the town of Labé in the centre. The hills were popular with the colonial administrators before independence because of the cooler climate and spectacular scenery.

Closer to the coast this plateau gives way to the Guinea highlands and, eventually, to a 65-km-wide coastal plain with areas of tropical swampland. Conakry is on a long narrow peninsula, and just south are some small islands which are popular spots on the weekends. In the south-east corner along the Liberian border, you'll find dense tropical forests.

Guinea has huge deposits of bauxite (which, when smelted, becomes aluminum) – an estimated 30% of the world's known reserves. Most of this is around Mt Nimba in the remote south-east. A quarter of the mountain is in Liberia; that alone justified foreign companies in Liberia building a railroad to the coast. Guinea, however, has done nothing with Mt Nimba. For starters, they'd have to build a 400-km railroad linking Mt Nimba with Kankan. So an American mining company exploits smaller deposits near the western coast at Boké and a French company operates closer to Conakry.

CLIMATE

Guinea is one of the wettest countries in West Africa. Rainfall along the coast is particularly high. Conakry, for example, receives about 4300 mm in a normal year, about half of that in July and August. While the central mountainous region receives less than half this amount, the rains are more evenly distributed throughout the rainy season, from May to October.

VISAS

Everyone must get a visa. If you don't have a visa, you can get one easily in all neighbouring countries except Mali. Entering and exiting overland is no longer a problem, nor is putting 'tourism' on your visa application. Visas are usually valid for only one month following the date of issue, su don't get a visa far in advance. Since Sekou Touré's death, you can travel anywhere in the country and there are far fewer police checks. Exit visas are no longer required except, possibly, for long stays. Visas to the Ivory Coast are available from the French embassy.

Diplomatic Missions Abroad
Abidjan, Accra, Addis Ababa, Bamako, Banjul, Berlin, Bissau, Bonn, Brazzaville, Brussels, Cairo, Dakar, Dar es Salaam, Freetown, Kinshasa, Lagos, Maputo, Monrovia, Nairobi, Ottawa, Rabat, Paris, Rome, Tokyo, Washington.

MONEY
US$1 = GF 280
£1 = GF 550

The unit of currency is the new Guinean franc (GF). Guinean importers get about a 13% better rate. The GF exchanges one to one with the CFA and many establishments will accept payment in CFA. In a few more years, Guinea will probably be allowed to convert to the CFA. Upcountry, a slight black market has developed, with CFA 1000 trading for GF 1200. At the top three or four hotels, you must pay your bill in hard currency (including the CFA) or credit cards. You may not export any Guinean francs whatsoever, and customs officials do check.

Banking hours: 8 am to 12 noon; closed Sunday. Banks: Banque Centrale de la République de Guinée, Banque Guinéene du Commerce Extérieur.

LANGUAGE
French is the official language. Many African languages are spoken – Malinké by 40% of the people, especially in the north around Kankan and Faranah; Fula by 30%; Susu by 23%, particularly in the south around Conakry. Greetings in Susu:

Good morning	*tay-nah-mah-ree*
Good evening	*tay-nah-mah-fay-yen*
How are you?	*oh-REE toh-nah-moh*

Thank you	*een-wah-lee*
Goodbye	*une-GAY-say-gay*

GENERAL INFORMATION
Health
Vaccinations against yellow fewer and cholera are required. Hôpital Ignace Dean, which is recommended only for dire emergencies, is downtown at the northern end of Avenue de la République. The pharmacies are all government operated and poorly stocked. One of the best is Pharmaguinée near the Madina market, about seven km from downtown.

Security
Guinea is one of the safest countries in West Africa. Pickpocketing is about as serious as things get. Be careful around the Conakry market where thieves abound.

Business Hours
Business: Some businesses work government hours. Others are open Monday to Saturday 8 am to 12.30 pm and 3 to 6 pm except Friday, when shops close at 12.30 pm. Government: Monday to Saturday 7.30 am to 3 pm except Friday, when offices close at noon.

Public Holidays
1 January, 3 April, Easter Monday, 1 May, End of Ramadan (17 May 1988, 6 May 1989), Tabaski (25 July 1988, 14 July 1989), 15 August, 27 August, 2 October (Independence), 1 November, Mohammed's Birthday, 22 November, 25 December. The biggest holidays are 3 April, the day the present regime came to power, and Independence Day.

Photography
Whether or not a permit is still required from the Ministry of Information, you risk having your camera confiscated by the police if you take photos without their permission, even if you're photographing something seemingly unobjectionable, such as a football match.

Time, Phone & Telex

When it's noon in Conakry, it's noon in London and 7 am in New York. To make an international call, you must go to the post office. The waiting time is typically three hours or so. Don't be surprised if you're cut off. You can apparently send telexes there as well.

GETTING THERE
Air

From Europe and North Africa, there are direct flights from Amsterdam, Brussels, Paris and Casablanca. The cheapest way to get there from London is on Aeroflot with a ticket purchased from a bucket shop, but the route through Moscow is also the longest. From the USA, you'll have to transit in Europe or Dakar. Air Guinée, which is flown by Air Lingus (Ireland) pilots, is fairly reliable and has flights to neighbouring African countries.

Car

The drive to/from Freetown (Sierra Leone) takes six hours, a little longer in the rainy season. About two-thirds of the 335-km road is paved. If you're headed to Senegal (Conakry-Dakar is 1393 km), the drive from Conakry to the border takes two long days in the dry season, with a stopover in Labé. The Conakry-Labé road is paved, but full of potholes. The unpaved 300-km section between Labé and the border is poor, the worst stretch being the last 150 km. This is a major truck route, however, and quite passable during the dry season. During the rainy season, trucks continue to pass, but motorists are advised to be prepared for the worst. The Senegal section is asphalt for all but 100 km, and even this is now being paved. If you're heading for Guinea-Bissau, take the route via Labé and Koundara, not Boké to the south.

Conakry to Kankan via Faranah takes about 16 hours; the entire route is paved but full of potholes. You can make it from Kankan to Bamako (Mali) in about 12 hours during the dry season; none of the 344-km road is paved. Between Kankan and the border, there are two ferries and four wooden bridges to cross. The dirt road is in fairly good condition, except for the washboard roads on the Malian side.

During the dry season, it is quite feasible to drive from Man (Ivory Coast) to Conakry via eastern Guinea. The more scenic, mountainous route is via Nzérékoré and Kankan; the shorter route (three days) is via Gbarnga (Liberia), Guéckédou and Kissidougou.

Customs officials at the Guéckédou border are notorious for swindling travellers. Their trick, reportedly, is to demand that travellers show them all their money, then they carry it into the woods and return it US$20 short. You can avoid this hassle by crossing at Macenta instead.

Bush Taxi
To/from Sierra Leone Conakry to Freetown by bush taxi takes a full day; buses from the border to Freetown take five or six hours.

To/from Senegal Bush taxis to Labé take about 10 hours. If you're headed to Senegal, expect the journey on the pitiful road between Labé and the border to be moderately slow during the dry season (typically 14 hours Labé-Koundara), and extremely slow during the rainy season – up to three days sometimes. The Conakry-Sambailo plane flies only twice weekly and are unreliable and often full. A truck from Koundara to Tambacounda (Senegal) shouldn't take you more than 10 hours or so in the dry season.

To/from Guinea-Bissau Almost everyone going to Guinea-Bissau takes the northern route via Labé and Koundara but be prepared to walk the last 20 km from Saidhoboron (the last small village in Guinea) to the border if there are no vehicles to take you. Otherwise, connections are not too bad. If you're crazy enough to want to go to Bissau via Boké, try to get to Boké before Saturday because a vehicle reportedly leaves on that day to Bissau,

Top: Abuko Nature Reserve, outside Banjul, Gambia (SR)
Bottom left: Abuko Nature Reserve, outside Banjul, Gambia (JTJ)
Bottom right: Woman returning from market, Banjul (CL)

Top: Barber shop in Bobo Dioulasso, Burkina Faso (AV)
Bottom: Barber shop signs, Benin City, Nigeria (EE)

otherwise the journey could easily take a week.

GETTING AROUND

Air

Air Guinéc has interior flights to about five towns including Kankan and, twice weekly, to Labé and Sambailo/Koundara. Air Liberia, which is back in operation but has a bad reputation, has unlisted flights from Conakry to Freetown and Monrovia.

Bush Taxi

Bush taxis are slow during the dry season and even worse during the wet. Bush taxis to Labé take about 10 hours.

Train

The 2nd-class train between Conakry and Kankan may be Africa's worst; the trip takes 20 to 24 hours. In theory, the train leaves twice weekly on fixed days. In fact, it leaves when it darn well pleases. Be prepared for some hard seats.

Conakry

After being left to run down by Sekou Touré for a quarter of a century, Conakry (KON-ah-kree) is definitely on the upswing. New shops, restaurants and nightclubs are constantly popping up. Once a city of tight-lipped people, Conakry is now open and vibrant. The city still looks shabby, but the streets have been recently repaved and cars are everywhere.

The city has a lot of African flavour too. If you walk in the African sections of town on a Sunday, chances are you'll see a celebration or two that usually blocks off a street. Onlookers form a circular area, and on one side three or four men play koras and the balafon. Moved by the music, a woman enters the area and dances frenetically for several minutes until she is totally exhausted, after which she retires and another enters spontaneously

to dance just as madly, only with different movements.

The city's location on a narrow peninsula is a mixed blessing. The good part is that the ocean is so visible. The bad part is that the city has nowhere to expand except northward, making the city longer and longer and increasingly difficult to travel from one end to the other – sometimes up to an hour in heavy traffic, which is every day until 11 pm. The main north-south drag is the Autoroute which, as you move south and closer to the heart of the city, becomes the Route du Niger and, in the heart of town, the Avenue de la République.

Information

Embassies Algeria, Benin (Corniche Sud next to Socomer), Cape Verde, Congo, Egypt, France (BP 373, tel 441655/81), Ghana (Corniche Sud), Guinea-Bissau, Italy, Japan (BP 895, 461438), Liberia, Mali, Morocco, Nigeria, Senegal (cnr Avenue de la République and 4th Boulevard), Sierra Leone, Switzerland (BP 720, tel 461387), USA (BP 603, tel 441520/1), Tanzania, West Germany (BP 540), Zaire.

Consulate: Britain (c/o Magus Ltd, BP 158, tel 443705/8).

Travel Agencies There are none; you'll have to deal directly with the airlines.

OAU Centre

Near the Hôtel de l'Indépendance you'll see how the African presidents are treated each time there's a week-long meeting of the Organisation of African Unity. There are 50-odd Moorish-style chalets, all identical and resembling miniature castles that seem amazingly out of place. In Guinea's case, the conference scheduled to take place here in 1984 was cancelled when Sekou Touré died, after all the preparations had been completed. They now house the offices of the World Bank, the IMF, various businesses, ministers and the like.

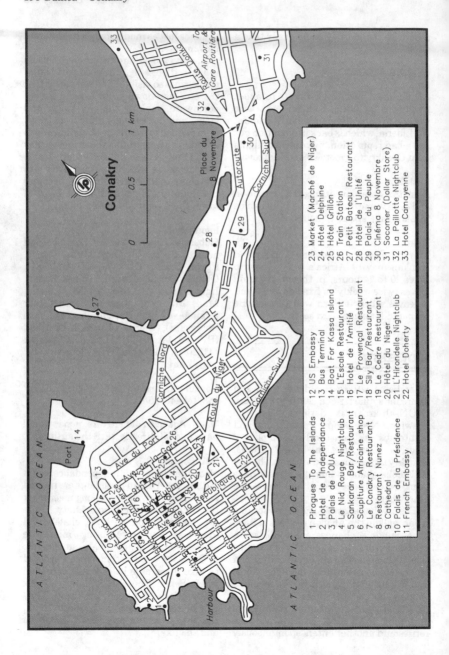

Conakry

1 Piragues To The Islands
2 Hotel de l'Independance
3 Palais de l'OUA
4 Le Nid Rouge Nightclub
5 Sankaran Bar/Restaurant
6 Sculpture Africaine shop
7 Le Conakry Restaurant
8 Restaurant Nunez
9 Cathedral
10 Palais de la Présidence
11 French Embassy
12 US Embassy
13 Bus Terminal
14 Boat For Kassa Island
15 L'Escale Restaurant
16 Hotel de l'Amitié
17 Le Provençal Restaurant
18 Sily Bar/Restaurant
19 Le Cedre Restaurant
20 Hôtel du Niger
21 L'Hirondelle Nightclub
22 Hotel Doherty
23 Market (Marché de Niger)
24 Hôtel Delphine
25 Hôtel Grillón
26 Train Station
27 Petit Bateau Restaurant
28 Hôtel de l'Unité
29 Palais du Peuple
30 Cinéma 8 Novembre
31 Socomer (Dollar Store)
32 La Paillotte Nightclub
33 Hotel Camayenne

Nearby is the OAU Conference Hall that was never used. Also nearby is the president's residence, the Palais de la Présidence.

Palais du Peuple

This is the huge Chinese-built auditorium on the Autoroute near the Hôtel de l'Unité. Occasionally, dancing groups perform there.

Îles de Los

From the southern end of Conakry you'll see the Îles de Los, a series of small islands five to 10 km south-west of Conakry, that are popular on Sunday.

The expatriates prefer the Île de Roume, which has a tranquil side good for youngsters and a rougher side with waves. To get there, you'll have to hire a motorised pirogue from the rocky beach near the Indépendance. A roundtrip *déplacement* costs at least GF 10,000.

The Guineans prefer Kassa Island Beach, which is crowded and a real scene every Sunday. There's a boat which leaves Sunday at 9 am from the port and returns at 5.30 pm. The roundtrip cost is only GF 200. Another possibility is to take one of the regular inexpensive pirogues over to the small village of Soro; they leave from the beach near the Indépendance and return the next day in the early morning.

Places to Stay – bottom end

For the price, it's hard to beat *Hôtel Delphine* (tel 443621) on 5th Boulevard which charges GF 2000 for a clean room without air-con. Downtown one block from the well-known L'Escale de Guinée restaurant, it's a notch above others in the same price range. There's a bar-restaurant too.

The *Hôtel de l'Amitié* (tel 443137) is two blocks away on Avenue Tubman and has rooms for about GF 2000. It has a reputation for thieves and prostitutes. You can get a room just as cheaply at *Hôtel le Grillon* (tel 444202) which is two blocks from the Delphine in the opposite direction and one block from the train station. The rooms go for about GF 2000 to GF 6000; the more expensive ones have air-con. It has a restaurant that serves filling meals for about GF 1000.

Another possibility is the *Hôtel du Niger* (tel 442454), which has large rooms for GF 5000 with overhead fans and high ceilings but no windows, dirty communal bathrooms, and an unpleasant manager. It's on Route du Niger, one block from the Marché du Niger.

Places to Stay – middle

If you're looking for a medium-priced hotel with air-con rooms, there's only one – the highly recommended *Hôtel Doherty* (tel 443137), with air-con singles/doubles for GF 10,500/12,500 including a good breakfast, hot plates in the rooms, lanterns in case of a blackout, clean bathrooms, firm mattresses and a TV/video room. The cheaper rooms have shared baths. The friendly lady who runs this place is a definite plus. It it half a block from Hôpital Ignace Dean on 5th Avenue, which runs parallel to Avenue de la République one block away.

Places to Stay – top end

The best hotel is unquestionably the *Hôtel de l'Indépendance* downtown overlooking the ocean, but it's not one of the better Novotels. Ask for one of the older rooms with balconies – the newer ones are small and much inferior. The restaurant is expensive and dinner will cost at least US$25.

The *Hôtel de l'Unité*, three km from the heart of town, used to be almost as good but it's poorly managed and going downhill. The rooms are fairly large and the pool is long, but the ambience is dreadful and the meals are poor for the price.

A better buy may be the newly renovated 120-room *Hôtel Camayenne*, which overlooks the ocean and is five km from the centre. One km from the airport, 13 km from the heart of town, you can stay at the 60-room *Hôtel Gbessia*, which has a pool and tennis court but small rooms and paper-thin walls. All of these hotels must be paid for in hard currency or credit cards.

Hôtel de l'Indépendance (tel 444681, telex 2112), US$91/114 for singles/doubles including tax and breakfast, round pool, tennis, TV/video, tennis, dinner dance every Saturday night, cards AE, D, V, CB.

Hôtel de l'Unité (tel 443137, telex 2139), US$55/68 for singles/doubles including tax and breakfast, long pool, lively disco weekends, cards AE, D.

Hôtel Camayenne, pool, scheduled for opening in 1987.

Hôtel Gbessia (tel 464747/464041, telex 775), US$53/69 for singles/doubles including tax, short pool, tennis, video lounge, nightclub, cards AE, D.

Places to Eat

Cheap Eats For large serves and cheap food but a limited selection, there's the popular *Sankaran*, on Avenue de la République across from the Sabena offices, and *Hôtel le Grillon*. *Au Fin Gourmet*, next to the US embassy, has numerous selections on the menu but few in reality. The service is quick, however, and it's one of the few restaurants open on Sunday. The cheapest food of all, and generally well prepared, is the street food around the markets.

Cedre is the best inexpensive downtown restaurant. A meal will run you GF 1500 to GF 2000. There are many Continental selections plus a few Lebanese ones. It's two blocks from Avenue de la République, three blocks down from Boulevard du Commerce. Another possibility is *Le Provençal*, about a block from the post office and closed Sunday. The upstairs terrace dining is a plus; the extremely limited selection and slow service are definite minuses.

French Conakry's best restaurant may be the new *Le Rustique* (tel 465241), which is about 10 km from downtown and closed Monday. The French menu is quite interesting, plus there are three African

specialities. Most main courses cost GF 2000 to GF 3500. The decor is pleasant to elegant, and there's air-con. To get there, take Route Donka for about six km. About one km before Cinéma Rogbane, you'll see a sign or two pointing to your left. It's several blocks off Donka.

The best restaurant downtown is the new *Le Conakry* (tel 444579, which is closed Sunday and is two blocks behind the Sabena offices, six blocks from the Novotel. This place was a hit from the day it opened. You'll find about 10 selections on the menu, a pleasant atmosphere, a popular bar and good service. A typical meal without wine will run you GF 5000.

Before Le Conakry opened, the most popular French restaurant downtown was the old *L'Escale de Guinée* (tel 442362), which is two blocks behind the US embassy and closed Sunday. Run by an elderly French woman who is something of a character, it is a little less expensive and you can eat on the terrace outside. Jumbo shrimp are one of the specialities.

The relatively inexpensive *Le Petit Auberge*, on Avenue Tubman and closed Sunday, offers a fairly standard menu, air-con and good prices. The restaurant with the nicest setting in Conakry is *Le Petit Bateau*, 300 metres out in the water on a tiny stretch of land with a great view of downtown Conakry. The food is nothing special – two French entrées and three main courses (grilled fish, grilled chicken and brochettes). The only problem other than the slow service is that the bugs like it here too.

For an excursion out of town, head north on the weekend to Coyah, where there's an unlikely but decent French restaurant, *Chez Claude*. Claude is a Frenchman who has been in Guinea for 20 years or so and married to a Guinean. The six or seven selections on the menu include wart hog and couscous. In Coyah, look for the sign on your right saying, strangely, Chez Julie; it's on your left a ways.

Vietnamese *Le Riz Perle* is one of Conakry's best restaurants and good by any standard. Open every day for dinner only, they offer about 25 selections, although about a third are usually not available. The big problem is the location – about 20 km or a 30 minute drive from downtown Conakry on the northern outskirts of town. One km beyond the Coca Cola plant on the Autoroute, look for a small sign on your right pointing to your left. It's several blocks away.

Italian For great pizza and a good variety of well-prepared pasta, seafood, chicken and beef dishes, head for the popular *Pizza Coco*, which charges GF 1800 to GF 2500 for most main courses. Closed Tuesday, it's about 11 km from downtown. Take Route Donka for about seven km. Half a km beyond Cinéma Rogbane, look for a sign pointing to the right. *Le Nunez* (tel 444893) is not as good but is more conveniently located downtown. Closed Sunday, they serve five kinds of pizza and spaghetti, plus fish and meat dishes and numerous entrées. You can eat on the sidewalk terrace or inside. Prices are moderate, and the service is good. You'll find it one block off Avenue de la République, one block from the Sabena offices on the other side of République.

African *Sily Restaurant* (or Madame Diop's) (tel 442547) is a Conakry institution not without reason. She serves excellent African cuisine including chicken in peanut sauce, chicken yassa, riz-gras, fonio, couscous and others. A three-course meal costs GF 3500 to GF 4000; you can bring your own beer or wine. For dinner, you must telephone or go by in the morning to order; for lunch, you must order the day before. It is closed Sunday.

Entertainment & Sports

Bars There are no bars where people head after work to drink and watch the crowds. Some French expatriates like the bar at *Le Conakry*. Among the seedier bars, the

Sankaran and the street-level bar of *Le Provençal* are fairly popular. Those looking for trouble prefer the *Hôtel de l'Amitié*.

Nightclubs Conakry has lots of good nightclubs, but the best are in the suburbs, not downtown. None of them get lively before 11 pm. Thursday, Saturday and Sunday are the biggest nights. The cover charges are relatively low.

There are four nightclubs in the airport area; the most popular is *Le Balafon*. It attracts a big Lebanese crowd and African women, and plays a wide variety of western, African and Cuban music. The cover is GF 1000. Not far away is *Zambezi* owned by the South African singing star, Mariam Makeba, who makes rare appearances. Modern, small and crowded, with a plush air-con interior, it's usually open from Thursday to Sunday. *Privilege*, just before Hôtel Gbessia, is new and currently popular with Conakry's middle class. You'll find a good variety of music, an interesting decor resembling an African bungalow, comfortable seating, and plenty of space except on Thursday and Saturday nights when it gets crowded. There's a GF 1000 cover on those two nights only. *Pili-Pili*, at Hôtel Gbessia, has a small dance floor and cramped seating and attracts mainly people staying at the hotel.

Out on Route Donka you'll find three more, all about three km from the centre. *La Miniere* is similar in terms of popularity, music and prices to Le Balafon. It offers a view of the sea as well as chicken and brochettes. About one km further out along Route Donka is *Le Village*, which offers similar music, prices and food and is open only during the dry season because the dancing is outside. Nearby, about one km beyond Cinéma Rogbane, a block off Route Donka, you'll find *Sabar*, which may be the best place in town for African music. Very popular with Guineans, it's open every night except Monday, and the cover is GF 1000.

The only respectable nightclub near downtown is *La Paillote*, an open air place with dancing where you may get to hear an orchestra. The well-known group Tambourins usually plays Thursday, Saturday and Sunday nights; there's a small cover charge.

One of the most popular places in the heart of town is *Le Bakoro*, across from Le Conakry restaurant. It is small and smoky, and open every night with a GF 500 cover. The dimly lit *Le Nid Rouge* nearby may be worth a try. The nightclub at the *Hôtel de l'Unité* is sometimes lively on weekends. The buffet-dancing Saturday night special at the *Hôtel de l'Indépendance* is popular with expatriates but must be reserved in advance if you want to be sure of a table.

If you're looking for a place for the working man with plenty of potential dancing partners try the ever-popular and always lively *Bembeya Club*, which is downtown opposite Le Provençal restaurant. Be very careful – the area is known for thugs and thieves. *L'Hirondelle*, on Route du Niger across from the Marché du Niger, is similar but safer and fairly popular on weekends, especially Saturday when there's a cover charge.

Movie Theatres The air-con *Cinéma Rogbane* is the best in town, with shows at 6 and 9 pm, but it's 10 km from downtown out on Route Donka. *Cinéma 8 Novembre*, on the Autoroute near the Palais du Peuple, is the next best. It has the same hours but no air-con.

Sports The Indépendance and Unité hotels have tennis courts and pools. The only squash court is at the US embassy warehouse – you need an invitation but they're always desperate for players. If you're interested in bridge, try the Indépendance on Tuesday around 7.30 pm when a French-speaking group meets. The best place to jog is along the Corniche Sud road because of the ocean view and the small amount of traffic.

Things to Buy

Artisan Goods You'll find artisan goods of mediocre quality sold on Avenue de la République across from the Sabena offices. For higher quality crafts, try *Sculpture Africaine* a block away across from Sankaran restaurant, about 30 metres off Avenue de la République. Guinea is the best place in West Africa to buy the harp-like kora. The regular ones are very bulky, but some smaller versions are available. For material, such as tie-dye cloth, tablecloths and napkins, look around for one of the women's cooperatives, *Les Centres de Promotion du Pouvoir Feminin*, in Conakry.

Gold & Silver Try the jewellers near the Marché du Niger. There's *Bijouterie Le Gerbe* next to Sily restaurant, *Bijouterie de la Nation* (tel 442223) two blocks from the market, and another near the Hôtel du Niger, among others. The general level of workmanship is not as good as that in Mali, Senegal and the Ivory Coast. Prices, however, are about 10% lower, ie GF 4000 to GF 4500 a gram for gold.

Music If you want records of Guinean music, go to *ENIMA*, inside the Palais du Peuple and open Monday to Saturday 8 am to 2 pm. Prices are low and the selection is good, including the popular Sory Kandia (dead but a national hero) and Fodé Kouyaté and the following orchestras: Bembeya Jazz National, Kaloum Star, Super Boiro Band, Les Tambourins, Horoya Band National, among others.

Various For foodstuffs, there's the *Marché du Niger*, about one km from the heart of town on Route du Niger, and the government-run grocery store, *Socomer*, which accepts US dollars only. Bottled water sells for about US$1 a litre. Four km from downtown, it's on the old airport road about one km beyond Cinema 8 Novembre, and open Monday to Saturday 9 am to 12.30 pm and, except Friday, 4 to 6.30 pm. There are no cash registers. They just drop the bills in a cardboard box and give you change in gum and candy.

Getting There & Away

Air Conakry is connected to virtually all the capital cities along the West African coast by various airlines. You can also fly to Conakry from Labé, Kankan and Sambailo/Koundara.

Bush Taxi You can get bush taxis from Conakry at the Gare Routière at the Madina market, on the Autoroute between downtown and the airport. Bush taxis to Labé take about 10 hours.

Train The train to Kankan is supposed to leave on Tuesday and Friday mornings but don't bet on it. It is slow, extremely uncomfortable and not recommended.

Getting Around

Airport Transport At Conakry's new airport, there's no longer a departure tax. You'll find a restaurant and a bank, which may not always be open, as well as Hertz, Avis and Eurocar. A taxi to downtown (13 km) costs GF (or CFA) 1500 to CFA 2000; bargaining is definitely required. There are no airport buses. For about a fifth the cost of a chartered taxi, you can walk over to the main highway about 100 metres from the airport and hail a shared taxi headed into town.

Taxi A seat in a shared taxi costs only GF 50 for a short ride (up to about six km), double for longer trips. When you hire a taxi to yourself, the minimum *déplacement* is GF 250. A trip to the airport will cost about GF 1000. Taxis waiting at the Hôtel de l'Indépendance charge about double this amount. Finding an empty cab is not easy. The only sure place is the Indépendance. Taxis are plentiful along the main drag. They usually have other people inside, so you only pay for the seat. A taxi by the hour should run you GF 1200 to GF 1500 if you bargain hard – more if you get one from the hotel.

Car Rental Hertz, Avis and Eurocar all have booths at Conakry airport and downtown at Novotel's Hôtel de l'Indépendance in Conakry (tel 444681, telex 2112). Another is Guinéenne de Location de Voiture (Avenue de la République near Route du Niger, tel 443926).

AROUND CONAKRY

Kindia

The best one-day excursion from Conakry is Kindia, a 2½-hour scenic drive north of Conakry in the foothills. The Institut Pasteur de Kindia, which is open every day except Sunday, is a research centre which has an interesting collection of snakes and monkeys.

Places to Stay If you stay in town, the uninspiring choices include the *Hôtel de Guinea* on the southern end of town and, on the northern end next to the train station, the rustic *Hôtel le Buffet de la Gare*, which has rooms for about GF 1000 a night.

Bridal Falls

The main attraction of Kindia is the Bridal Falls about 12 km beyond Kindia, a km or two off the road. You'll see a sign announcing *Le Voile de la Mariée* on your right. The falls are interesting only during the rainy season when the flowing water resembles a bridal veil. There are some open huts for picnic lunches and camping is also allowed.

Mamou

Mamou is 224 km from Conakry at the junction of the roads to Kankan and Labé. You can stay at *Hôtel Luna* for GF 800 a room or at the *Buffet de la Gare*, three blocks from the Gare Routière. *Hidalgo* near the petrol station serves food.

The Fouta Djallon

The single most interesting area of Guinea is that of the Fouta Djallon plateau, which includes the towns of Labé, Dalaba and Mali, among others. It is one of the best hiking places in West Africa and is also great for techinical rock climbing because it's all limestone with no cracks and therefore, relatively safe.

If you're without wheels, one possible itinerary that is not so back-breaking is to take one of the twice-weekly flights to Labé and hire a taxi from there to Dalaba, with a stop in Pita to see the Kinkon waterfalls. You can stay several days or longer at the pleasant bungalows in Dalaba, and then hire another taxi back to Conakry, stopping in Kindia to see the town and the Bridal Falls.

DALABA
Dalaba was chosen during the colonial period as a therapeutic centre because of its 1000-metre altitude and spectacular scenery. The centre is now in ruins, however, the Centre d'Acceuil (or Les Cases) on the southern outskirts of town is still intact, and is perched on a cliff overlooking the mountains. The president and Mariam Makeba have vacation homes nearby. The best time to visit is from November to January when it's cool. Between January and May, the dusty skies tarnish the view.

Places to Stay & Eat
The four large bungalows at the Centre d'Acceuil have four or five rooms off a central living area with sofa, chairs, refrigerator, and bathrooms with running water and showers. The cost is only GF 1000 a room.

Since Dalaba is a good six-hour drive from Conakry (an hour or two more by bush taxi) and there are about 18 rooms in all, and the place is almost never full. To get a room, go to l'Étoile du Fouta and ask for directions to the nearby home of the

Chef du Protocol. You need his permission, but it is virtually automatic.

Nearby is L'Étoile du Fouta, a huge pleasant old restaurant where you can have all your meals, but you must order in advance for each. At night, it's a nightclub.

PITA
As you travel north from Dalaba you'll pass through some fantastically beautiful mountains. An hour's drive north of Dalaba is Pita, where the major attraction is the Chutes du Kinkon waterfalls. You need permission from the Commissariat to see the falls, which you get to by passing through town and taking a left about a km or so beyond Pita. They're 10 km down a bad dirt road. The falls are below a lake and power station. Camping is definitely prohibited but picnicking is not. You'll see where a number of African presidents have etched their names into the rock.

Place to Stay & Eat
You can stay at Hôtel Kinkon for GF 500 a room, and eat there or in town at Momeal facing the old post office.

LABÉ
Labé is an hour's drive further north of Pita. It is a major transit point for those coming from Senegal and Guinea-Bissau. Between the Hôtel de l'Indépendance and the heart of town, you'll pass by a small shop where an artist draws interesting scenes on gourds; they make great souvenirs.

Places to Stay & Eat
There are two hotels – the Hôtel du Tourisme at the southern entrance to town, with a restaurant and rooms for GF 800, and the Hôtel de l'Indépendance at the Gare Routière towards the centre of town, with a restaurant and slightly inferior rooms for GF 500 to GF 1000. Neither place has running water. If they are both full, which is not unusual, make friends with one of the professors at the

Institut Poli-Scientifique or ask the Tourisme to let you sleep in one of their lounge chairs. On weekends, however, the lounge is noisy because the most popular nightclub in town, the *Tinkisso Club*, is directly below.

MALI
Not many travellers make it to Mali, 120 km north of Labé via a primitive dirt road. It's the highest town in the Fouta Djallon, with spectacular views of Senegal and the legendary rock, *La Dame de Mali* (1538 metres), which is seven km north-east of town and may not be photographed because it's sacred. You can stay at *La Dame de Mali* for about GF 400.

KOUNDARA
If you're on your way to or from Senegal or Guinea-Bissau, Koundara is a junction town near the border.

Places to Stay
Hôtel Mamadou Boiro charges GF 3000 for a decent room.

The East

KANKAN
This is Guinea's second city. There is a presidential palace and an extensive market here. If you stay at the *Hôtel Buffet de la Gare*, they may demand that you pay in hard currency, US$10 a room, and keep your passports overnight.

FARANAH
Faranah is the major overnight stop between Conakry and Kankan and the site of the country's major agricultural school.

Places to Stay & Eat
Hôtel Cite Niger charges GF 1500 to GF 2000 for a room. You can eat there or at *Le Regal*, a Senegalese restaurant on the western edge of town on the road leading to Mamou.

KISSIDOUGOU
Kissidougou is on the major artery from Conakry to both Liberia and Kankan.

Places to Stay
The *Hôtel du Kissi* has fairly decent rooms for about GF 1000, and serves steak and salad for about the same price.

MACENTA
Macenta is in the south-east between Kissidougou and Nzérékoré.

Places to Stay & Eat
Hôtel Vieux Libanais has rooms for GF 500 to GF 000 and serves food.

NZÉRÉKORÉ
In the far south-eastern corner of Guinea near bauxite-rich Mt Nimba and the Liberian border, Nzérékoré is on the less used, hilly scenic route between Liberia (or the Ivory Coast) and Kankan. This route is advisable only during the dry season.

Places to Stay & Eat
Hôtel Forêt Sacrée charges GF 750 for a room. You'll find a small restaurant in the dead centre of town.

Guinea-Bissau

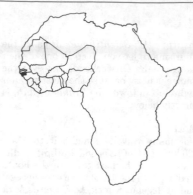

Guinea-Bissau (and Cape Verde) gained independence in 1974 after 14 years of guerrilla war waged by a classic revolutionary movement. All other West African countries gained independence with virtually no bloodshed – and many years before – but the Portuguese just wouldn't give up. It's hard not to admire a people who have gone through such a struggle and who were saddled with a colonial power that did nothing for the country except use it as a cheap source of agricultural produce. Yet today Guinea-Bissau is on very good terms with Portugal, its leading trading partner.

If this doesn't interest you, other things about Guinea-Bissau might. It has some of the friendliest Africans on the continent, small clean towns, and wide streets with flowering trees where pickpocketing is unheard of and not a tourist is in sight. Bissau, the capital, has pastel-coloured two-storey buildings with wooden verandas 'à la Portugal', a bar or two where you can meet people and quench your thirst, and it is one of the safest cities in Africa.

In the interior you can meet friendly Africans (and escape the unfriendly police of other countries), see authentic African dancing with a jungle touch, and find authentic African masks. Or visit the virtually deserted off-shore islands which would be a Mecca for tourists if there were an easy way to get to them.

But Guinea-Bissau is not for everybody, not by a long shot. If you insist on having your creature comforts and are looking for vibrant markets, interesting things to buy, unusual sights and historic edifices, pass on. You won't find them here.

HISTORY

The great Empire in Mali of the 14th century included part of present-day Guinea-Bissau. Before then, Africans had migrated into the area, seeking refuge from the earlier Empire of Ghana, also in Mali. Later, over 50 years before Columbus discovered America, the Portuguese sent ships to Guinea-Bissau and other areas along the coast to seek slaves, gold, ivory and pepper. In the 1500s, wars with the Mande people from upper Guinea provided an even greater supply of slaves.

The Portuguese built forts along the coast of present-day Guinea-Bissau and elsewhere in West Africa and had a monopoly of the trade until the early 1600s when the English, Spanish, French and Dutch captured most of their forts. The effects of the slave trade, particularly the social disintegration, were devastating. African was pitted against African, tribe against tribe, and the loser was sold as a slave. No area was hit worse than Guinea-Bissau because it was on the coast and closer to Europe and the Americas than most other areas of Africa.

Content to exploit the coast, Portugal didn't even lay claim to the interior until 1879 when European powers carved up the continent. Even after being 'given' what became known as Portuguese Guinea, Portugal was unable to gain full control of the entire area until 1915, after a long series of wars with the Guineans. In the process, Portuguese Guinea ended up with arguably the most repressive and exploitative of the colonial powers.

The Portuguese government, once it had 'pacified' the country, was more brutal than the other European colonial

202

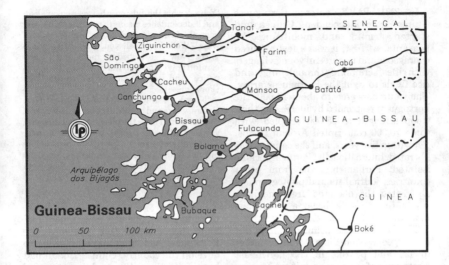

powers. Also, Portugal itself was hardly a rich country and had few resources, hence it did not develop its colonies.

Colonial Period

By the late 19th century, with the abolition of slavery enforced by British navy patrols, the export of agricultural products to Europe became the colonial powers' main interest in West Africa. But the republican government in Portugal was so weak that it found it convenient to allow non-Portuguese European companies to control and export the crops, mainly peanuts and palm oil. This didn't change until the 1926 coup in Portugal when the dictator Salazar came to power and imposed restrictive customs duties and laws against foreign companies, forcing them to sell out to Portuguese interests. It was only then that Portuguese colonial rule began in any complete or systematic sense. If you were a peasant, it meant you planted peanuts, like it or not.

When Britain and France gave up most of their African colonies between 1957 and 1962, because of their economic might they merely changed from being colonials to neo-

colonials, and still profited considerably from trade with their former colonies. But Portugal was so weak that if her colonies were freed, she could not impose neo-colonialism – other more powerful countries would assume the dominant trade position. So Portugal refused to follow suit.

War of Liberation

The result was the longest war of liberation in the history of Africa, a guerrilla war waged by the PAIGC (the African Party for Independence in Guinea and Cape Verde) with significant help from the Soviet Union and Cuba. From its inception in 1956, the PAIGC was committed to joint liberation of both the Portuguese colonies. The better educated Cape Verdians provided many of the leaders, including the head leader and co-founder of the party, Amilcar Cabral, one of Africa's modern day heroes. But it was in Portuguese Guinea that the mass movement was strongest. Guerrilla warfare became the adopted tactic, Marxism the ideology, and Portuguese Guinea the scene of action.

In 1961, PAIGC entered Portuguese Guinea from independent Guinea and started arming and mobilising the peasants. At first, it was a few hundred courageous and resourceful young villagers with rifles, scrambling through jungle and rice fields to fight the Portuguese army. Their numbers grew to about 10,000; the Portuguese responded by increasing their troop strength to 25,000 coupled with some 10,000 conscripted African troops. Yet within five years, half the country was liberated. Internationally, Portugal became isolated. Parliamentarians from other countries, journalists and photographers all visited the liberated area and as a result the struggle became front-page news during the early '70s.

The Portuguese continued to hold out in refugee-swollen Bissau, a few smaller towns, and pockets in the north-east where some of the more prominent Muslim Fula collaborated with the Portuguese in an attempt to preserve their social privileges. Their agents in Conakry were held responsible for the assassination of Amilcar Cabral. But the movement was too strong. By 1973, the PAIGC organised nationwide elections in the liberated areas and proclaimed its independence. Eighty countries quickly recognised it as the legitimate government. Still, it took Salazar's overthrow the following year for Portugal to call it quits.

Now viewed as a model, the movement was successful largely because of the PAIGC's political strategy during the war. They cleared 'liberated zones' and built schools, provided medical services and encouraged widespread political participation to help people realise the promise of a better life. Cabral said this was to be a war of revolution, not of revolt. Society had to be completely reorganised if the people were ever to be genuinely free.

What independence meant to Guineans is eloquently summed up by the military officer's comments in David Lamb's *The Africans*:

'You ask what the difference between colonialism and independence means to me,' the thirty-six-year-old Miranda said, filling my glass with wine. 'Well, I will tell you. The difference is great. Now I go to bed at night and I sleep comfortably. I do not worry about the secret police. And I do not tip my hat to the *Tuga* (Portuguese).

'Now I speak to a white man without fear. Before, white and black did not talk. But now at this moment I have the pleasure of sitting with you, a white, and I speak to you like a man. That is all we fought for, the right to respect. We did not hate the Portuguese people, only the Portuguese government. Even if you were Portuguese, I would still be happy to sit with you, because now we are equals.'

Once in power, the new government had more than a handful of problems. The Portuguese had done almost nothing to develop the country. Guinea-Bissau had been little more than a cheap source of peanuts and palm oil. They left behind a grand total of one brewery built for the Portuguese troops, a few small factories for peeling rice and peanuts, 14 university graduates, and not a single doctor. Only one in 20 people could read, life expectancy at birth was 35 years, and 45% of the children died before the age of five. During the war rice production had fallen 71% and many of the rice polders were ruined and would take years to rebuild. Rice had to be imported for the first time ever.

Politically, the PAIGC, led mainly by Cape Verdians, wanted a unified Guinea-Bissau and Cape Verde, but abruptly dropped the idea in 1980 when the President, Cabral's half-brother (also a Cape Verdian), was overthrown in a coup while he was visiting Cape Verde to negotiate the union. João ('Nino') Vieira, a native, took over and replaced the *mestiços* with Africans. He remains President.

Bissau under Marxism

The socialist state took over large parts of the modern sector, including some major enterprises. Marxist literature was everywhere and political dissent was banned. Hordes of Russian advisors came, but were rarely seen – socialising with the natives was and continues to be taboo.

Despite the Marxist dogma, pragmatism and political neutrality ruled. Private citizens continued owning most of the small shops. The Soviets provided military aid, just as they provided all of the PAIGC's military equipment during the liberation war. The west provided the non-military aid. Trade-wise, the west now completely dominates. It's the source of most of the country's imports and the purchaser of most of its exports.

In the government-run supermarkets, you'd see empty shelves except for four hundred or so tins of baking powder and a bushel or two of plantains. Whenever potatoes and wine from Portugal arrived, they remained on the shelves all of 30 minutes. Bars were full, in part because whenever the brewery ran out of caps only draft beer was available. The shops were almost empty except for uninteresting items from eastern bloc countries. Conditions were so bad that finding food was almost a clandestine activity – housewives spent four or five hours a day searching for food, relying on friends and relatives to give them a good tip, sometimes paying by barter. In the interior, foreign products were so scarce that matches made a welcomed gift.

Today

Change is on the way. After making no progress at all under Marxism and receiving precious little economic aid from the USSR despite the presence of numerous Russian advisors, the government in 1986 began selling off almost all of its enterprises. Now local produce abounds in the open markets. In the four new hard-currency stores you can purchase a wide assortment of imported items at fairly stiff prices – but at least you can buy them. On the outskirts of town there's a new market that specialises in expensive smuggled goods from Senegal and The Gambia – as

the government looks the other way. In 1986, Bissau got a pastry shop – the city's first since the Portuguese left – and Bissau's nightlife took a decisive upturn when two new nightclubs opened. The electricity supply is more regular and blackouts are becoming less and less frequent.

Still, the economy drags. Government revenues don't even equal the wage bill. Farmers are producing enough for themselves but little more. Why should they when all they receive is overvalued Guinean pesos with, until recently, little of interest to spend them on. If you're lucky and don't live far from the Senegalese border, you can at least smuggle your excess produce across the border in exchange for hard currency, the CFA.

Oil is one possible answer to the country's economic woes; there may be off-shore deposits. If not, the country has little hope of escaping the economic doldrums.

Perhaps a result of the country's continued economic plight is the alleged coup attempt in 1986. The conspiracy involved top officials including Vice President Correia, a hero of the independence war. All involved were executed after the attempt failed.

PEOPLE

Guinea-Bissau has 23 ethnic groups and a population of only 875,000, 95% of whom are farmers. About 30% of the people are Balante and 20% Fulani (Fula); the Manjaco and Mandinka follow them in numbers. There are also quite a few *mestiços* of mixed European and African descent. All but several hundred of the Syrian and Lebanese traders and Portuguese left in the 1970s following independence.

About a third of the people are Muslims, mainly Fula and Mandinga; both groups are concentrated more upcountry than along the coast. Except for a few Christians in the towns, the rest are ancestral worshippers and follow traditional animist beliefs.

Folk dancing is as strongly preserved

here as anywhere in Africa. So if you go upcountry, be on the lookout for a celebration. The harp-like kora and the xylophone-like balafon are used extensively, and women dance frantically in a circle of onlookers. In Bubaque, a typical men's group might be wearing masks picturing animals with horns, along with a variety of arm and leg bands, frequently with green leaves stuck into them. Some costumes make use of dry grass, giving a much more jungle-like appearance than those in, say, the Sahelian countries. But costumes change from area to area and dance to dance. In Bafatá, for example, dancers paint their faces white and wear simple costumes made primarily of thick pieces of rope with bells dangling from them.

If possible, try to hit Bissau at carnival time in February or March; the assortment of masks is incredible. Regardless, spirits are high then and it's a good time to meet people.

GEOGRAPHY

Guinea-Bissau is one of Africa's five poorest countries. But it differs from the others in that nobody seems to be starving in the rural areas. Rainfall is more dependable than in many African countries, and scarcity of land isn't yet a major constraint.

It's about the size of Switzerland and on the far west coast of Africa, nestled between Senegal and Guinea and just at the point where the coast begins its very gradual ninety degree turn eastward. The country is mostly flat lowlands, rising to no more than about 300 metres near the Guinea border. The rainy season is from June to October and the rainfall is almost twice as heavy along the coast as it is inland.

In the wet coastal plains, you'll find meandering rivers, tangled trees, rain forests and deep estuaries; it isn't easy to distinguish mud, mangrove and water from solid land. The relatively high tides periodically submerge the lowest areas,

and inlets indent the coast. Consequently, there are only a few rudimentary, zig-zagging roads. To get to many villages, you'll have to take a canoe.

Everything changes radically inland, where lightly wooded savannah takes over. You'll see rain fed rice grown everywhere, most of it in polders, as well as peanuts, manioc, maize and other subsistence crops. What you won't find are towns that can support more than one petrol station. Gabú, Bafatá and, on the coast, Cacheu are as large as towns come. Between Cacheu and the Senegalese border are the best beaches in Guinea Bissau.

Then there are the Bijagos islands, an offshore archipelago consisting of 18 main islands. The most important, with a cow paddock airstrip and a hotel, is Bubaque. The others are paradise and there is hardly anyone to disturb your tranquillity. Getting to them, however, is no easy task.

VISAS

Only Cape Verdians and Nigerians don't need visas. Visas are usually valid for two weeks. Exit visas (and visa extensions) are issued at the central police station but not required unless you stay longer than a month. Visas can be obtained at the airport and are payable in hard currency (CFA 2700).

The embassy in Dakar (Senegal) offers same day service if you get there not later than mid-morning. You may be asked for a letter of recommendation from your embassy. Service is about equally fast in Banjul (Gambia); visas are sometimes issued while you wait. On the other hand, in Bissau you cannot get a visa to The Gambia. The French embassy in Bissau issues visas to Burkina Faso, Ivory Coast, Mauritania and Togo.

Diplomatic Missions Abroad

Abidjan, Algiers, Banjul, Brussels, Conakry, Dakar, Lisbon, Stockholm, Washington.

MONEY

US$1 = 655 pesos
£1 = 1075 pesos

The unit of currency is the Guinea-Bissau peso. Over the past few years, the black market rate has been two to four times more favourable – usually around twice as favourable just after one of the periodic devaluations. In early 1987 the black market rate was four times the official rate, however, in mid-1987 there was a massive devaluation which all but wiped out the black market though it seems to have reemerged since but the rates are much lower than those of a few years ago. You'll find money changers around the market in Bissau, upcountry and in Ziguinchor (Senegal).

Inflation is running at about 20% a year, so expect prices somewhat higher than indicated here. You do not have to fill out a currency declaration form, but you may be asked to change money at the airport (about CFA 20,000) and at the border (about CFA 5000). Because of periodic devaluations, the country is no longer expensive at the official rate. You are not allowed to export pesos and they will be confiscated at the border if found on you.

Credit cards are not accepted anywhere except, perhaps, at the new Sheraton. You cannot use pesos to pay your bill at the two top hotels in Bissau. The commission on travellers cheques is low. Banks: Banco Nacional da Guiné-Bissau, Banco Nacional Ultramarino. Banking hours: weekdays 7.30 to 11.30 am (for cash transactions), closed weekends.

LANGUAGE

Portuguese is the official language, but at best a third of the people in town speak it. The principal African language is Crioulo.

GENERAL INFORMATION
Health

A yellow fever vaccination is mandatory if you come within six days from an infected area and you're staying for more than two weeks. Simão Mendes Hospital (tel 212816) is the best of the two hospitals in Bissau. Don't be surprised if your doctor is Cuban or Russian. You'll also find hospitals in Gabú and Bafatá. Two of the better pharmacies in Bissau are Farmácia Moderna (tel 212702), one block from Hotel Ta-Mar and not far from the port, and Luso-Farmaco two blocks from the Ta-Mar.

Security

Walking around downtown Bissau at night is safer than in just about any African capital city except, perhaps, Praia (Cape Verde).

Business Hours

Business & government: weekdays 8 am to 12 noon and 3 to 6 pm, Saturday 8 am to 12 noon.

Public Holidays

1 January, 20 January, 8 March, 1 May, 3 August, 12 September (National Day), 24 September (Republic Day), 14 November, 25 December.

Photography

A photo permit is reportedly required, but because it's so unusual for someone to ask for one, you may get the run-around. Inquire at the Ministry of Information.

Time, Post, Phone & Telex

When it's noon in Guinea-Bissau, it's noon in London and 7 am in New York (8 am during daylight savings time). The postal service is reliable. Phone calls to Dakar (Senegal) are not a problem, but to anywhere else it's next to impossible. It can easily take several days to get a call through to the US or Europe, and the operator will usually cut you off after three minutes. For a telex, try the new Sheraton hotel or the post office.

GETTING THERE
Air

There is no way to fly to Guinea-Bissau on a first-rate airline unless you take the twice weekly TAP flight from Portugal. Aeroflot flies to Bissau via Casablanca and Nouadhibou every other Thursday, returning by the same route on the Friday. Almost everyone else, including ambassadors, take one of the thrice weekly flights to/from Dakar. Beware: Even if your Dakar-Bissau ticket says 'OK', it never is. The same is true of your return flight from Bissau. Air Senegal and LIA (Linhas Aéreas du Guinea Bissau) make reservations only for those who walk in the door and sign up. Your travel agent might have a contact in Dakar who could do this.

There are also connections once a week with Conakry and Casablanca. There are no longer any direct flights to Cape Verde. The LIA ticket to Conakry is pretty cheap if purchased in Bissau. They don't ask where you changed your money. Even at the official exchange rate, the ticket costs only about US$40.

Car

From Senegal, there are three routes into Guinea-Bissau – via Farim, Cacheu and Bula but most people go via Farim. It is fairly simple to drive from Ziguinchor (Senegal) to Bissau via Tanaf (Senegal) and the border town of Farim. (You'll find a ferry at the Cacheu and Bula crossings.) All but 35 km of the 270 km total are paved. Count on six or seven hours. Most of the road blocks have been eliminated. The border closes at 6 pm, but the police on the Bissau side will let you through at any time of the day or night if you bring a small gift. There are no petrol stations on the way. Bissau to Conakry (Guinea) is another matter. The border has reopened. The 1000-km drive takes three days (or two long ones) – one to Koundara (Guinea), another to Labé (during the dry season), and another to Conakry.

Petrol is sometimes not available in Bissau. The chances of finding some in Gabú or Bafatá are even less, but there's no problem making it to Koundara on one tank. In Guinea, blackmarket petrol is easy to come by even if the petrol stations

have none. There's a good asphalt road from Bissau to within a few km of the Guinea border. The 300-km dirt road from there to Labé is pretty bad, possibly impassable at times during the rainy season, while the Labé-Conakry portion may hold the world's record for potholes.

Bush Taxi

To/from Senegal There are three ways to get from Ziguinchor to Bissau. The easiest, but longer and more expensive, is the route that most vehicles take via Tanaf (Senegal) and Farim. Finding a bush taxi to Tanaf is usually not a problem; the same is not true of finding a vehicle from there to Farim, a distance of 35 km. Though muddy during the rainy season, this section is the most well travelled; so your chances aren't bad. A lift should cost about CFA 750.

Coming from Bissau, there are daily buses to Farim leaving from the Mercado Bandim; just get there early. The total cost isn't much since buses in Guinea-Bissau are quite cheap. The border crossing at Farim is friendly and informal. Several km separate the Senegalese and Bissau border posts. You'll probably have to take a canoe across the river and wait for a vehicle. Take whatever comes because fuel is always in short supply and, consequently, vehicles too.

The second route is via Cacheu near the coast. From Ziguinchor to São Domingo (Senegal) is an easy 25-km bush taxi ride. There is one ferry crossing a day each way, leaving early in the morning from Cacheu and at noon from São Domingo; the trip takes two hours. From Cacheu it's 100 km to Bissau on paved road. Since Cacheu is one of the country's bigger towns, finding a ride shouldn't be too difficult, at least by Guinea-Bissau standards. You'll have to take another ferry on the way, and it frequently isn't operating because of the lack of fuel. In that case, you just hop a canoe across, and from there it shouldn't be too difficult to get a ride for the remaining 20 km.

You should be able to make the trip in one day from Ziguinchor, but coming from Bissau you'll undoubtedly miss the ferry, making the trip longer. So from Bissau, the route via Farim is definitely faster. The third route via Ingore (Senegal) isn't recommended because it's less travelled and connections are poorer, involving at least an hour's walk and possibly much more.

To/from Guinea The Conakry-Bissau route is for hearty souls with time to spare. Do not take the southern route via Cacine and Boké (Guinea) unless you want to spend a week or more making the trip. The 1000-km northerly route via Labé and Koundara (both in Guinea) is the one everybody takes. It's simple enough getting a bush taxi from Conakry to Labé (10 hours) or a bus from Bissau to Gabú (four hours). Labé to Koundara is a poor but well-travelled road and not too difficult except in the rainy season, in which case your truck may end up making it a two or three-day trip instead of one. From Koundara to the border and Gabú is 110 km – expect delays. Vehicles pass by so rarely that you may have to walk the 20 km from Saidhoboron (the last village in Guinea) to the border. There is, however, one scheduled lorry a week between Gabú and Koundara.

GETTING AROUND
Air
LIA has two flights a week to Bubaque Island.

Bush Taxi/Bus
In Bissau, buses and taxis go to all the smaller towns. Mercado Bandim one km from the centre is where you'll find them. Usually, only one bus a day runs to a given town, and you must get to the market no later than 7 am to be assured of a seat. You can also get bush taxis to most towns; the cost is low but the wait tends to be much longer than in other African countries. So bring a book. Road blocks are now rare.

Boat
There is a regular steamer service to the Ilha de Bubaque, as well as ferries to Bolama.

Bissau

When you arrive in Bissau (pop 125,000), you'll know you're in a socialist country because the streets are spotlessly clean, the cars few, the noise level low, and the commercial area lifeless – quite the opposite of most African capitals. But that's part of what makes Bissau refreshingly different.

You won't see any beggars or be molested by hawkers trying to sell you what you don't need; there's no danger of being robbed or falling into an open sewer or getting hit by a motorbike as you cross the street; and for once in an African city the word 'beauty' applies.

Those who stay a while will see that there's a lot more happening than meets the eye. Just following around a housewife to see how and where she collects the family's daily sustenance can be fascinating. Or stalking the Russian military advisors to see where they drink. Or walking down to the port area to catch a glimpse of the action there. But it all requires a little nosing around.

Information
Tourist Office The Centro de Informação e Turismo is on Avenida da Unidade Africana, near the Ministry of Education.

Embassies Algeria, Brazil, Cape Verde, France (tel 212633/4, Rua Eduardo Mondlane), Guinea (Rua 12), Nigeria, Portugal (tel 212741/9, Rua 16, No 6), Senegal, Sweden, US (tel 212816/7, 19A Avenida Domingo Ramos). Consulates: Belgium, Netherlands.

Bookstores & Supermarkets For postcards, your only hope is the Sheraton and the Hotel 24 de Setembro. For books and maps of Guinea-Bissau, the *Casa de Cultura* carries mostly communist text books in Portuguese but also has several colourful books on Guinea-Bissau, maps and records.

The government supermarket *Socomin*, one block from the cathedral on Avenida Amilcar Cabral, is virtually empty but interesting to see for that reason.

For imported goods, there are now four hard currency stores which accept payment only in hard currency, usually US dollars and CFA only. Prices are fairly high. The oldest is *Entreloja* near the port, also called the Dollar Store. They only accept US dollars. Wine, cheese, coffee, canned goods, chocolate, soups and juice are all available. It's at 14 Rua Guerra Mendes one block off the port going towards the Ta-Mar, and closes at 7 pm.

Travel Agencies There are none – only the airline offices, including TAP (tel 213933/91).

Things to See
There's no 'must see', but you might take a look at the port, the two markets, the **Presidential Palace** and, across the street in the PAIGC headquarters, the **Museum of African Artefacts**, which has a collection of early African carvings and artefacts.

Places to Stay – bottom end
For the price, about 1400 pesos a room (650 pesos more for the larger room no 5), *Hotel Ta-Mar* is not a bad place. Clean rooms with balconies, surprisingly good beds, passable lighting, a popular bar and a restaurant with full meals. At night you may have to use candles, and the hallway bathrooms are filthy. It's downtown at the corner of Avenida 12 de Setembro and Rua 3, four blocks from the port. The rooms at the *Hôtel de Portugal* on Praça Che Guevara may be a little cheaper, but they're usually full.

There is reportedly an unmarked pensão at 23A Avenida Amilcar Cabral which is cheaper than the Ta-Mar. However, if you're staying at least a week and want the cheapest lodgings possible, go to the tourist information centre (*Centro de Informaćão e Turismo*), which has a list of private houses where you can

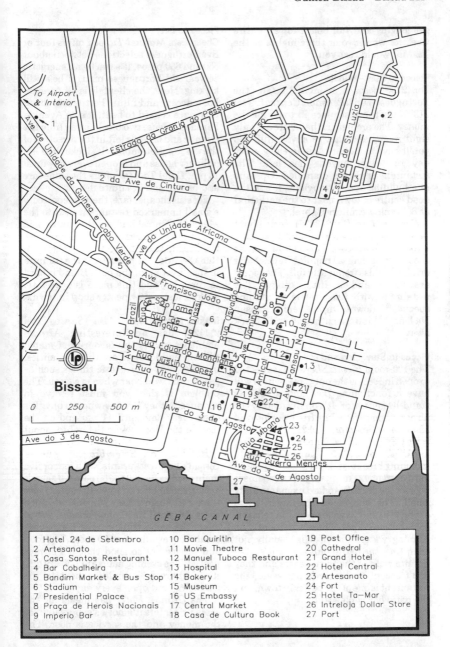

Bissau

0   250   500 m

GÊBA CANAL

1 Hotel 24 de Setembro	10 Bar Quiritin	19 Post Office
2 Artesanato	11 Movie Theatre	20 Cathedral
3 Casa Santos Restaurant	12 Manuel Tuboca Restaurant	21 Grand Hotel
4 Bar Cobalheira	13 Hospital	22 Hotel Central
5 Bandim Market & Bus Stop	14 Bakery	23 Artesanato
6 Stadium	15 Museum	24 Fort
7 Presidential Palace	16 US Embassy	25 Hotel Ta–Mar
8 Praça de Herois Nacionais	17 Central Market	26 Intreloja Dollar Store
9 Imperio Bar	18 Casa de Cultura Book	27 Port

get lodging and full board for an entire week for what two or three nights at the Ta-Mar would cost you.

Places to Stay – middle

For 2750 pesos a room with fan, the Portuguese-run *Pensão Central* (tel 213270) is the best place in town for the money. The problem is that there are only eight rooms and they're always full. So you'll have to call or come in early every day to see if anyone has left. The restaurant is always crammed. Upstairs in a building and not obvious, it's in the dead centre of town next to the cathedral at 8 Avenida Amilcar Cabral.

Grande Hotel (tel 213437), costs about 2400 pesos a room with fan, and 3200 pesos a room with air-con. This hotel is not as good but it has a popular terrace for drinks. It's also frequently full. The rooms are small and a little dingy. The restaurant with fixed menu is nothing special. It's downtown on Avenida Pansau Na Isna, behind the cathedral and a block away.

Places to Stay – top end

The 180-room *Bissau Sheraton*, expected to open in 1988, is the only hotel which will have a functioning pool and a reliable stand-by generator. It's on the road to the airport, about four km from downtown. *Hotel 24 de Setembro* (tel 215222/213766) costs US$25 to US$30 for rooms with a fan, and US$35 to US$60 for rooms with air-con, including breakfast. Bills must be paid in hard currency. The quality of the rooms is poor for the price. Standard rooms are fairly small. The bungalows are larger, more expensive, and have air-con and refrigerators but no carpet. There's frequently no running water, the pool is usually not operating, the bathrooms smell, it's a 25-minute walk to the town centre and they don't accept credit cards. However, the restaurant is one of the better in town, and the patio bar is pleasant.

Places to Eat

Cheap Eats *Manuel Tuboca* offers four or five Portuguese selections between about 550 and 650 pesos. It's run by an energetic 84-year-old Portuguese man, if he's still kicking. Here, the clientele is all African. For a decent and filling Portuguese meal, this place is hard to beat. It's on Avenida Pansau Na Isna, two blocks away from the Grande and on your left in the direction of the 24 de Setembro. It looks like an ordinary house and is open every day until 10 pm. *Hotel Ta-Mar* offers the same fare and prices, and it's quite decent.

For still cheaper fare, there is reportedly a small unmarked restaurant next to the Mercado Central and another unmarked one in the port area near the LIA offices. For bread, there's *Padaria Africana* on Rua Osvaldo, one block from the stadium in the direction of the port. Bread is hard to come by, and this place is open late. There's also a new pastry shop in town.

Major Restaurants *Casa Santos* (tel 211124) has an interesting African ambience and is the favourite of many. Shrimp and lobsters are the specialities, but they also offer exotic things such as gazelle and wild boar when in season. The problem is that you must reserve in advance so they'll know what to buy. It's open every day until 11 pm and on the road to the Hotel 24 de Setembro, about 400 metres before on your right.

Hotel 24 de Setembro has one of Bissau's best restaurants, with four or five main courses for 350 to 750 pesos. If there's a shortage of beer in town (frequent), get there early before they run out. It's open every day until 10.30 pm. *Pensão Central* offers the same three-course Portuguese meal every evening for 700 pesos. The food and service are so good that it's always packed. The evening hours are 7.30 to 9 pm. It's upstairs in a building next to the Cathedral and open every day.

The *Grande Hotel* has meals for the same price, but it's not as good value for the money and the service is poor. The fare at two of Bissau's nightclubs – *Ponta Neto*, eight km from downtown, and if it has reopened, the *Kora Club*, downtown – is also fairly decent.

Entertainment & Sports

Bars The *Hotel 24 de Setembro* offers the nicest outdoor setting for an alcoholic drink (there are no bottled soft drinks in Bissau), but *Confeitaria Império* and *Bar Quiritin* in the centre of town are much more popular with Africans and many local expatriates. They are both at the end of the main drag (Avenida Amilcar Cabral) where it turns into a big circle, with the Presidential Palace at the far end. They offer cheap draft beer on a street-side terrace and are open every day until 11 pm. The Quiritin also serves small plates of shrimps, clams and sandwiches.

The street-side terrace of the *Grande Hotel* is almost as popular. Another terrace bar, with umbrellas, African clientele and a few things to eat, is *Bar Cobalheira* near Casa Santos, on the road to the 24 de Setembro. It's closed Mondays. *Casa Santos* two blocks away has a bar inside, as does *Hotel Ta-Mar* downtown several blocks from the port. The latter is frequently crowded.

Nightclubs Two nightclubs opened in Bissau in 1986; one is near the port area. The *Kora Club*, one block behind the Cathedral, used to be the most popular in town until it was closed after the owner apparently went around town sporting a new Mercedes and the government began wondering where he got all the money. In Bissau, you never see a Mercedes! If it hasn't reopened, your only other choice for music, dancing and drinks is *Ponta Neto*. You'll need wheels to get there, however, because it's eight km from the centre of town. There's usually dancing after dinner starting around 11 pm. Bring bug repellent if you have any because the mosquitoes like to dance too.

Movie Theatre There's one downtown on Avenida Amilcar Cabral one block before the big circle. Screenings are at 9 pm.

Sports For tennis, the new Sheraton may have a court when it opens. Otherwise, your only choice is a court near the brewery, about 2 km from the centre of town. For swimming, the new Sheraton will have a pool. The one at the 24 de Setembro is usually either empty or half full. For basketball, the Africans get some pretty good games going near dusk on a court downtown about one block from the US Embassy. For jogging, Bissau is hard to beat. It's streets are not crowded, to say the least.

Things to Buy

Artisan Goods There are one and maybe two *Artesanatos* which sell art from Guinea-Bissau. One is downtown on Rua Mbana several blocks from the Ta-Mar; the other, which may be closed, is on the road leading to the airport, about one km on your right after passing Mercado Bandim. They offer a very limited selection of wood carvings and painted masks at reasonable prices. Dollars, CFA and pesos are all accepted.

Markets For local produce, try the *Mercado Central*, a block in front of the Cathedral. Fresh produce is becoming increasingly plentiful, especially in season, January through May. On the outskirts of town you'll find *Feira Popular*, an enclosed open-air market with expensive goods from neighbouring countries, especially Senegal.

Music You can also find records at the 24 de Setembro. The group *Super Mama Djombo* is popular locally, as are singers Dulce Maria Neves, Mario Cooperante and N'Kassa Cobra. Dulce Maria has been known to sing at the Kora Club.

Getting There & Away

Air Air Senegal has flights to Ziguinchor

and Dakar on Mondays and Fridays. In mid-1987 LIA (Air Guinea-Bissau) was temporarily out of action. When operating they fly to Dakar, Conakry and Bubaque Island.

Bush Taxi/Bus Bush taxis and buses leave from the Mercado Bandim. It's best to get there early. A bus to Gabú costs around 1800 pesos. For detailed information on travel to Senegal and Guinea, see the Getting There section earlier in this chapter.

Boat The boat to Bubaque leaves on Saturdays at 1 pm, and sometimes during the week. Contact Agência Guiné Mar (tel 212675/212836) at Rua 4 Guerra Mendes for tickets and information. The trip takes five hours and costs around 600 pesos. There are also smaller boats that do the trip, so if you can't wait for the regular boat ask around the port.

There are also daily ferries to Bolama; contact Agência Guiné Mar for details.

Getting Around
Airport Transport There is a departure tax of CFA 2500 or the equivalent. There are no facilities at the Bissau airport other than a currency exchange where you'll be required to exchange the equivalent of about US$50 upon arrival. A taxi into town (eight km) is 300 pesos. Since taxis are so few, people are pretty good about giving lifts.

Taxi Fares are about 35 pesos for a short trip in town of one or two km, 50 to 60 pesos for longer trips. They are very difficult to find on the streets; look for a blue Faf N'Haye (a small box-like Citroen assembled in Bissau). There are also several old buses running about.

Car Rental There are no car rental agencies. You'll have to negotiate with a taxi driver. The best place to find them is at the Sheraton or the Hotel 24 de Setembro. It's easier for him to calculate if the car and petrol are treated separately, and you pay for the petrol used. Otherwise, expect him to complain if you deviate the slightest from your original plan.

BUBAQUE ISLAND
The Ilha de Bubaque is one of the most beautiful of the offshore islands and a delightful place to stay. It's the type of island where, in the remoter areas, what you wear or don't wear on the beach doesn't phase the natives. If you have the time, this place should definitely be checked out. Food and water are scarce and a problem, but there is a hotel. There is electricity (5 to 10 pm) because the President has a villa there.

Places to Stay Eat
You may be able to stay at the *Swedish Mission*; they reportedly take travellers in. Otherwise, it'll have to be the *Estancia Boldeana du Bubaque*, the only hotel on the island. Payment must be in hard currency. Quite surprisingly, it's of the same general quality and price range as the 24 de Setembro. Built by the Swiss, it has a restaurant and 10 or so attractive bungalows with attached bathrooms. The only problem is that there is no cross ventilation in the bungalows and they can get very hot. There are fans but the electricity goes off at 10 pm. Water is a greater problem because it is on only two times a day. The hotel is a good place to eat and the meals are reasonably cheap. If you show that you are going to tip well, you may be able to arrange with the waiter to pay in pesos. Reservations can be made in Bissau at the 24 de Setembro.

The beach near the hotel is not particularly good. The best beach, Punta Anino, is at the far southern end of the island, about 14 km away. You can reach it by shuttle bus (45 minutes) and you may be able to rent African bungalows there.

Getting There & Away
LIA have resumed their flights on a 12-

seater Russian bi-plane, operating twice weekly. The price is only 1250 pesos. LIA's office in Bissau is about a block from the port. You can also take a steamer which leaves twice a week, stopping at Galinha Island en route. On Saturdays, it leaves at 1 pm and takes five hours. The cost is about 600 pesos one-way. You can get tickets and information at Agência Guiné Mar (tel 212675/212836) at 4 Rua Guerra Mendes, one block from both the port and Entreloja. It returns the following day, departing in the early afternoon.

OTHER ISLANDS

If you could get to some of the other islands of the Bijagós Archipelago, you would undoubtedly find them completely untouched by civilisation. There is little food or water and even tin cans and plastic containers are a rarity. Some sailing boat operators who cater to tourists have caught on to these islands and head towards them from The Gambia. There's definitely something very pristine about these islands. Ask around, you might find a way to get to them.

These islands are not only beautiful but the people's customs are also very interesting. On one island they are very superstitious about the dead and the cadaver is put into a canoe and sent to be buried on another island, so that no dead are buried on the island and the spirits do not stay around. On another island as soon as a young girl reaches puberty the young men line up and she chooses one. If she's not pregnant within a year, she throws him out and chooses another. When she does get pregnant the man stays around only until she gives birth and then he returns to the group and becomes eligible again for other liaisons.

BAFATÁ

One of Bissau's largest towns, it numbers only about 10,000 inhabitants. There are buses every morning from the market in Bissau and the trip takes about three hours. The only place to stay may be the Apartamentos next to the *Pensão Transmontana* for 550 or so pesos. It also serves inexpensive fare.

BOLAMA

The original capital of Guinea-Bissau during colonial days, it now lies in ruins but may be interesting for its old colonial architecture. Ferries run daily between Bissau and Bolama; you must buy tickets in advance from Agência Guiné Mar. There's no place to stay, but you can reportedly sleep on the beach on the other side of the island, with little worry of theft.

GABÚ

The only accommodation are some rather mouldy log cabin Apartamentos near the market for 600 pesos.

FARIM

You can eat and sleep at the *Pensão de Seripe* which has one mosquito infested room. Otherwise, make a friend.

Ivory Coast

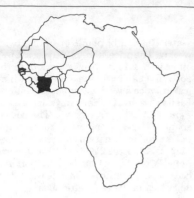

The economic showcase of Africa during the '60s and '70s, the Côte d'Ivoire is West Africa's wealthiest country. In Abidjan, you'll find skyscrapers, a beautiful lagoon setting without rival in West Africa, the Ivoire (black Africa's most famous hotel), a futuristic golf club which could serve as the setting for a James Bond movie, a bowling alley and an ice skating rink. The most recent addition is the new cathedral, the most stunning piece of modern architecture in West Africa, which dominates the landscape like the opera house in Sydney.

Known as the 'Paris of West Africa', Abidjan attracts Africans from all over the region, making it West Africa's most cosmopolitan city. Seemingly, one out of two Africans here is a foreigner. Talk to your taxi driver; chances are he is an immigrant to the Ivory Coast. You can find out as much in Abidjan about what's really going on politically in Burkina Faso as you can in Ouagadougou. Partially as a result of this migration, Abidjan has one of the most vibrant African quarters – Treichville – of any African capital; the nightlife is as lively as West Africa has to offer.

Elsewhere, you'll find the picturesque former capital of Grand-Bassam and Assini beach nearby, the mountainous region around Man, the capital Yamoussoukro, the fascinating Senufo area around Korhogo, Comoé game park (West Africa's largest), Grand-Béréby beach and the remote fishing village of Sassandra. All are easily reached by one of the best road systems in Africa. So even if Abidjan doesn't interest you, the rest of the country probably will.

HISTORY

The Ivory Coast never had any great kingdoms as in Mali, Ghana and Burkina Faso, and not much is known about the country prior to the arrival of European ships in the 1460s. The major ethnic groups in the Ivory Coast all came rather recently from neighbouring areas. The Krou people migrated eastward from Liberia around 400 years ago; the Senoufo and Lubi moved southward from Burkina and Mali. It wasn't until the 18th and 19th centuries that the Akan people from Ghana, including the Baoulé (BAH-ou-lay), migrated from Ghana into the eastern area and the Malinké from Guinea into the north-west.

The Portuguese were the first Europeans to arrive. Compared to neighbouring Ghana, the Ivory Coast suffered little from the slave trade. European slaving and merchant ships preferred other areas along the coast with better harbours. The French didn't take any interest until the 1840s when, under Louis-Phillipe, they enticed local chiefs to grant French commercial traders a monopoly along the coast. Thereafter, the French built naval bases to keep out other traders. The French began a systematic conquest of the interior after a long war in the 1890s against Mandinka forces, headed by the illustrious Samory Touré. Even then, guerrilla war by the Baoulé and other eastern groups continued until 1917.

Colonial Period

Once the French had complete control and established their capital, initially at Grand-Bassam then Bingerville, they had

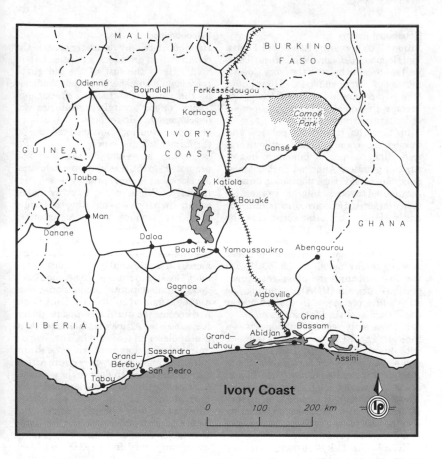

one over-riding goal – to stimulate the production of exports. Coffee, cocoa and palm oil were soon introduced along the coast, but the opening of the interior had to await the building of the railway. Because of its rocky plateau, Abidjan, not the capital Bingerville, was chosen as the railway hub. To build the railroad north to Ouagadougou and work the cocoa plantations, the French conscripted African workers from as far away as Upper Volta (now Burkina Faso). In 1932, to facilitate this, they even made Upper Volta part of the Ivory Coast. By then, cocoa was the country's major export. It wasn't until the late 1930s that coffee began to challenge cocoa as the main export earner.

The Ivory Coast stood out in West Africa as the only country with a sizable population of 'settlers'. Elsewhere in West and Central Africa, the French and English were largely bureaucrats. As a result, a good third of the cocoa, coffee and banana plantations were in the hands of French citizens. The hated forced-labour system was the backbone of the economy.

Houphouet-Boigny

Around 1905, a wealthy Baoulé chief had a son, Houphouet-Boigny (WHO-fuet BUIN-yee), who was to become the Ivory Coast's father of independence. Houphouet studied medicine in Dakar and thereafter became a medical assistant, prosperous cocoa farmer and local chief.

In 1944, he turned to politics and formed the country's first agricultural trade union – not of labourers but of African planters. Annoyed that colonial policy favoured French plantation owners, they united to recruit migrant workers for their own farms. He soon rose to prominence and within a year, after converting the trade union into the Parti Democratique de Côte d'Ivoire (PDCI), he was elected a deputy to the French parliament in Paris. A year later, he had allied the PDCI with the West African Rassemblement Democratique Africain (RDA), becoming the RDA's first president. In the same year the French abolished forced labour.

In those early years, Houphouet was a radical. The RDA was closely aligned with international Marxist organisations and staged numerous demonstrations in Abidjan that resulted in many deaths and arrests. It wasn't long, however, before Houphouet adopted a more conciliatory position. France reciprocated, making him the first African to become a minister in a European government.

Even before independence, the Ivory Coast was easily French West Africa's most prosperous area, contributing over 40% of its total exports. Houphouet feared that when independence came, the Ivory Coast and Senegal would end up subsidising the poorer colonies if they were all united in a single republic. His preference for independence for each of the colonies coincided with French interests. At independence in 1960, most of the former French colonies were lightly populated, weak and dependent on their former ruler.

Independence

Houphouet-Boigny naturally became the country's first president, a position he still holds. He is the last of the old guard presidents who ushered in independence in the early '60s. Leaders throughout Africa offered varying strategies for development. Houphouet was at one extreme, favouring continued reliance on the former colonial power.

He was also one of the few who promoted agriculture and gave industrial development a low priority – at least initially. While almost every other country in Africa was cheating the farmer with low produce prices to subsidise industrial development, Houphouet's government gave farmers good prices and stimulated production. Coffee production increased significantly, catapulting the Ivory Coast into third place behind Brazil and Columbia in total production. Cocoa did the same and by 1979, the Ivory Coast had become the world's leading producer. It also became Africa's leading exporter of pineapples and palm oil. The Ivorian 'miracle' was, foremost, an agricultural miracle. Almost everywhere else in Africa, agriculture failed to deliver the goods.

French technicians masterminded the programme. In the rest of Africa, Europeans were largely driven out following independence. In the Ivory Coast, they poured in. The French community grew from 10,000 to 50,000, mostly teachers and advisors. Critics complained that Houphouet had sold out to foreign interests. In 1975, two out of three top managerial personnel were foreigners, mostly French. However, Houphouet was clearly calling all the major shots and with a strong economy, few Ivorians complained. For 20 years, the economy maintained an annual growth rate of nearly 10% – the highest of Africa's non-oil exporting countries. Abidjan has grown from 60,000 people in 1945 to over two million today.

The fruits of growth were widespread. One reason was that the focus of development was on farming, the livelihood of most of the people. Another reason was the absence of huge estates. Most of the cocoa and coffee production, for instance, was in the hands of hundreds of thousands of small producers. Literacy rose from 28% to 60% – twice the African average. Electricity reached virtually every town and the road system became the best in Africa outside South Africa and Nigeria. Still, the numerous Mercedes and the posh African residences in Abidjan's Cocody section were testimony to the growing inequality of incomes and the beginnings of a class society.

Politically, Houphouet ruled with an iron hand. The press was far from free. Tolerating only one political party, he eliminated opposition by largesse – giving his opponents jobs instead of jail sentences. Several half-hearted coup attempts in the early '60s were easily suppressed. All those arrested were eventually released. Later, he even made one of them a minister.

Not all the investments were wise by a long shot. Houphouet was Africa's number one producer of 'show' projects. So many millions of dollars were poured into his village, Yamoussoukro, that it became the butt of jokes. The four-star hotel there still has an occupancy rate of less than 5%; the losses are staggering. Many of the state enterprises were terribly managed; graft was rampant. But the economy did so well that the government could afford to err.

The Big Slump

The world recession of the early '80s sent shock waves into the Ivorian economy. The drought of 1983-84 was a second wallop. For four years, from 1981 to 1984, real GNP stagnated or declined. In 1984, the rest of Africa was gleeful as the glittering giant, Abidjan, was brought to its knees for the first time with constant blackouts. Over-cutting of timber finally had an impact and revenue slumped. Sugar had been the hope of the north, but

world prices collapsed, making a fiasco out of the huge new sugar complexes there. The country's external debt increased three-fold and the Ivory Coast had to ask the IMF for debt rescheduling. Rising crime in Abidjan made the news in Europe. The miracle was over.

Houphouet did what was required. He slashed government spending and the bureaucracy, revamped some of the poorly managed state enterprises, and sent home a third of the expensive French advisors and teachers. Hard times had finally forced the government to keep its promise of increasing the number of Ivorians in management positions.

Today

The economy is back on track. Whether the country is doing well or poorly depends largely on the world prices for coffee and cocoa, both of which were down in 1987. Continuing to diversify, the Côte d'Ivoire is adding cotton and rubber to its trophies – number one in Francophone Africa in cotton, projected number one in Africa in rubber by 1990.

The main question is political – who will succeed Houphouet. *Le Vieux* (the old man) holds his cards tightly, keeping his closest advisors constantly guessing. Lots of names are mentioned, but no one has a clue. Clearly slowing down, Houphouet now hints that 1988 (the end of his present term) will be the year he steps down, but many people are skeptical.

A master politician, Houphouet plays no favourites. Tribal politics have torn other African countries apart, but not in the Ivory Coast. You'd never know he was Baoulé, certainly not from his three-piece suits. You won't hear about political prisoners either. When politicians cause major scandals, he holds no grudges. The biggest scandal of the '80s occurred in 1985 when the mayor of Abidjan couldn't account for US$58 million from the cocoa and coffee exporting company he headed. Houphouet let him escape in disgrace, then welcomed him back a year later.

Even democracy is making some headway. There's still only one political party, but voters now decide who will fill the deputy positions in the legislature and many posts are hotly contested.

PEOPLE

The country's 10 million people are divided into four ethnic groupings: the Akan (Baoulé and Agni primarily) in the east and central areas, the Krou (Bété and Yacouba primarily) in the west near Liberia, and the Senoufo and the Mande in the north. The Akan constitute about 35% of the population, with the largest single group being the Baoulé (15% of the population). The Akan are far from politically united however, which greatly reduces their importance as a coalition and obliges the powerful Baoulé lobby in the government to carefully court the country's other ethnic groups.

GEOGRAPHY

Except for the western area around Man, the Ivory Coast is fairly flat. In the south is Yamoussoukro, the country's new capital à la Brasilia, and all the cocoa and coffee farms. You'll see remnants of the rain forests that once covered the entire area. As you move north, the land becomes savannah. This is where you'll find Bouaké, the country's number two city and, further north, Korhogo and Comoé game park.

The coastal area is unusual in that a lagoon, several km inland, starts at the Ghanian border and stretches for 300 km along the entire eastern half of the coast. From Abidjan you can sail westward on this lagoon for a week and never see the sea. To get to the sea you must go through Vridi canal, built in the early 1950s to give Abidjan a harbour. Half of Abidjan is on the northern side of the lagoon, including the downtown and posh residential sections, and half on the southern side, with some of the major African quarters and industry.

CLIMATE

In the south, the rains fall heaviest from May through October, usually letting up in August. In the drier northern half, the rainy season is late May through early October, with no August dry spell. The south is humid, but temperatures rarely rise above 32°C (90°F). From early December through February, the *harmattan* blows down from the Sahara and greatly reduces visibility, especially in the northern mountain regions.

FESTIVALS

One of the best ways of learning about the people is to attend some of the many festivals in the Côte d'Ivoire. Most do not start on the same day every year, so finding the exact dates is no easy task. Some of the more well-known festivals are the Fêtes des Masques in Man (November or February), Fête de l'Abissa in Grand-Bassam (early November, lasting a week), the Fête des Haristes in Gbregbo near Bingerville (1 November), and the carnival in Bouaké (March).

If you're here in late April, don't miss the Fête du Dipri (yam festival) in Gomon, 100 km north-west of Abidjan. You'll see the turn-off sign near km 75 on the road to Yamoussoukro. For the exact date and information, contact the Bureau of Tourism (tel 320733) downtown in Immeuble de la Corniche, at the corner of Boulevard du General de Gaulle. In the local US embassy rag, Christina Robinson vividly describes the events leading up to the confrontation between the two secret societies, the Sékékponé and the Angrékponé:

The festival commences around midnight. The entire village lies awake within the security of their huts. Evil lurks about. The Angrékponé society chants in the distance calling for the Diori to be a failure. Slowly and quietly only the women and children sneak out of their huts and naked they carry out nocturnal rites to exorcise the village to be rid of the spells of the Angrékponé. Before sunrise, the chief appears and calls out to his people: 'O Loh Loh Ao! Chase out the evil.' Then the entire village emerges screaming out these words. The drums begin to pound, mass hysteria permeates the air, and the villagers covered in kaolin enter into trances. Bodies squirming in the dust, eyes roll up into their sockets, an adolescent beats himself, women cook eggs and bananas in their hands, and in the main street children beat the red dust with sticks. Pandemonium reigns. This frenzied behavior continues till noon, then the magic exercises begin. The Sékékponé plunge knives deep into their bellies. Onlookers gaze as the healing process begins immediately. Finally by late afternoon, the Sékékponé and Angrékponé confront each other. In a silent battle, the loser hands an egg to the victor and departs. The Abidji, as the sun sets, perform their final purifying ablutions and the festival comes to an end.

LANGUAGE

French is the official language. The principal African languages are Yacouba (Man), Senoufo (Korhogo), Baoulé (Yamoussoukro), Agni (Abengourou) and Dioula, the market language everywhere. Expressions in Dioula (JOU-lah):

Good morning	e-nee-SOH-goh-mah
Good evening	e-nee-WON-lah
How are you?	e-koh-kay-nay-WAH
Thank you	e-nee-chay
Goodbye	khan-bee-ah-FOH

VISAS

Nationals of Denmark, Finland, France, West Germany, Ireland, Italy, Norway, Sweden and the UK don't need visas. For a visa, you must provide the embassy with a copy of a return or onward airline ticket. Visas are valid for 90 days. French embassies issue visas to the Ivory Coast in those countries without Ivorian embassies.

In Abidjan, you can get visas for other African countries in one to two days, except for Ghana and Nigeria which take up to four days. The British embassy issues visas to Sierra Leone, Gambia and Kenya; the French consulate does the same for Togo and Chad. For the embassies represented in the Ivory Coast, see the Abidjan section.

Diplomatic Missions Abroad

Accra, Addis Ababa, Algiers, Amsterdam, Bangui, Berne, Bonn, Brasilia, Brussels, Cairo, Conakry, Copenhagen, Dakar, Geneva, Kinshasa, Lagos, Libreville, London, Madrid, Monrovia, New York, Ottawa, Paris, Rabat, Rome, Tokyo, Tunis, Vienna, Washington, Yaoundé.

MONEY

US$1 = 287 CFA
£1 = 537 CFA

The unit of currency is the West African CFA. As for CFA export restrictions, the rules are irrelevant because each airport official has a different interpretation. The best strategy is to be very respectful, wear a colourful African shirt with several cameras around your neck, follow the oldest lady in line and act like she's your mother. Don't crack jokes. With CFA 100,000 or less, you shouldn't have any problems. If you're going to another CFA country, you're supposed to be able to export more. Exchange rates at the hotels are poor, and changing money at the local banks is painfully slow. So if you arrive by plane, use the airport bank. It's open every day from the first arrival to the last. Barclays, however, offers better rates.

Banking hours: weekdays 8 to 11.30 am and 2.30 to 4.30 pm; Saturday 8 am to 12.30 pm.

GENERAL INFORMATION
Health

A vaccination is required for yellow fever but not for cholera. The best hospital by far is the new Polyclinique Internationale Sainte Anne-Marie (tel 445132) in Deux Plateaux, probably the best hospital in West Africa. The second page of the newspaper, Fraternité Matin, specifies which pharmacies are open at night.

Security

Thieves are a problem in Abidjan. Some carry knives; most don't. Treichville and, above all, around Vridi canal are the most dangerous areas, but no part of town is safe for walking alone after dark. Anybody who looks wealthy is at a greater risk than travellers on the cheap, but not even the latter are safe. Most thievery is not planned. Someone sees a bulging back pocket and goes for it. The trick is not to provide the temptation. Leave all jewellery, watches, purses and wallets at the hotel; most have safeboxes. The real value of what you're wearing makes no difference. My cheap watch was lifted while I was in a car at a stop light, with my arm at the window. If you've bought gold, don't wear it. You could get robbed going from a car to the restaurant. Fortunately, most major nightclubs now have doormen who escort people to and from their cars.

Business Hours
Business: weekdays 8 to 12 am and 2.30 to 6 pm; Saturday 8 to 12 noon. Government: 7.30 to 12 noon and 2.30 to 5.30 pm; Saturday 7.30 to 12 noon.

Public Holidays
1 January, Easter Monday, 1 May, End of Ramadan (17 May 1988), Ascension Thursday, Whit Monday, Tabaski (25 July 1988), 15 August, 1 November, 7 December (National Day), 25 December.

Photography
A photo permit is not required. The Côte d'Ivoire is not uptight about people taking snapshots but, as in virtually all African countries, taking photos of military installations and airports is prohibited.

Time, Phone & Telex
When it's noon in the Côte d'Ivoire, it's noon in London and 7 am in New York (8 am during daylight saving time). International phone connections are good. The Hotel Ivoire has booths open to the public for making international calls. The cost to the USA is CFA 2000 a minute. The PTT may charge slightly less. The major hotels have telex machines.

FOOD
Ivorian specialties include *kedjenou* (KED-jeh-nou) made with chicken, vegetables and a mild sauce, and *foutou*, boiled yams or plantains pounded into a paste. Foutou, rice and other staples are invariably served with a sauce, two of the more common ones being *sauce arachide* made with groundnuts, or a hot *sauce graine* made with palm oil nuts. Because of its sticky mashed potato-like consistency, foutou may not be to your liking.

Attiéké (AT-chay-kay), however, is universally liked. You may think it's couscous but in fact it is grated manioc. You'll find attiéké at all the *maquis* – the Ivory Coast's claim to fame in the African culinary world.

Visiting Abidjan without going to a maquis is like visiting Britain and not having fish & chips. A typical maquis is a cheap open-air restaurant with chairs and tables in the sand and some amusing African paintings on the wall, perhaps of a woman with her spider-like hairdo and a bottle of Flag, the country's most popular beer. All they normally serve is beef brochettes and braised chicken or fish smothered in onions and tomatoes, served with attiéké. Some also serve chicken kedjenou. I've never seen anyone get sick from eating at a maquis. If you're worried about the raw tomatoes or hot peppers, push them aside.

GETTING THERE
Air
From Europe and northern Africa, there are direct flights from Brussels, Cairo, Casablanca, Geneva, London, Madrid, Marseilles, Paris and Rome. From the USA, there are direct flights from New York to Abidjan with Air Afrique, with a stop in Dakar. Air Ethiopia offers direct flights from Addis Ababa, with connecting flights to/from Nairobi and Bombay. You can get direct flights from Abidjan to all capital cities in continental West and Central Africa except Guinea-Bissau, Chad and the Central African Republic.

Car

The road system is excellent. From Abidjan, the straight driving time north to Ouagadougou and Bamako is 20 and 24 hours, respectively. The route is paved all the way to both cities except the stretch from Ferkéssédougou to the border, a washboard road passable year round. Burkina Faso and the Côte d'Ivoire keep their borders open 24 hours, but the official who needs to see your vehicle papers reportedly leaves around 6 pm.

The coastal road connecting Abidjan and Accra (Ghana) is now paved almost the entire distance. The driving time is 12 hours. Until the bridge at the border is completed, you will still have to go via Frambo, where there's a ferry over to Jewi-Wharf (Ghana). The ferry takes 30 minutes and carries one vehicle (about CFA 10,000). The border closes at 6 pm.

Almost everyone heading west to Monrovia, a two-day trip, takes the route through Man, stopping there for the night. The unpaved section between Man and Ganta (Liberia) is in excellent condition, so you can pass year round. You can also go along the Ivorian coast via Tabou, Zwedru (Liberia) and Gbarnga; this route takes three to four days and is paved only about half the distance. Only expert drivers with four-wheel-drive vehicles should attempt it from May through November, when the Liberian section becomes very muddy.

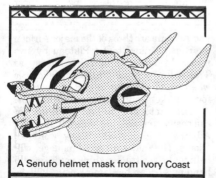

A Senufo helmet mask from Ivory Coast

Bush Taxi/Bus

The frequent bush taxis are a good way of entering the country, though most travellers headed to/from Burkina Faso take the train.

To/from Mali If you're heading to/from Mali, take the train on the Abidjan-Ferkéssédougou stretch and catch a taxi from Ferké to Sikasso (Mali), an 11-hour trip, and another to Bamako, seven hours more. If you go via Odienne, you'll probably be sorry as The traffic is very light between there and Bougouni (Mali). Travellers going west from Abidjan to Liberia can make it to Man in one easy day and from there to Monrovia in one long day. You'll find taxis all along the way; no walking is required.

To/from Ghana If you are travelling to/from Ghana, you can make it from Kumasi to Abidjan in one long day without problem. Abidjan-Accra takes longer, about 1½ days. From Abidjan you'll have to take a taxi to Aboisso and another on to Frambo, where there's a ferry about every 1½ hours over to Jewi Wharf. The last one leaves around 4 pm or so. Then, you'll have to take several more taxis to Accra.

You can make the Abidjan-Accra trip in one day if you take the Ghana State Transport bus, which leaves from near the Treicheville hospital at 6 am and costs CFA 7000. Anticipate a long wait at the border for everyone to clear customs.

Train

To/from Burkina Faso The Ouagadougou choo-choo is not just for laughs; it's the cheapest way to travel north as far as Ouagadougou and highly recommended – one of the best trains in West Africa. The *Gazelle* leaves Abidjan daily at 8.30 am sharp and the *Express* at 4 pm. From Ouagadougou, the Gazelle leaves daily at 4.10 pm and the Express at 7 am. The Gazelle takes about 23 hours and the Express about four hours longer, if there are no derailments. The schedule changes almost yearly, but there's always one train leaving in the morning and one in the afternoon. Call the RAN station in Abidjan (tel 320245).

The Gazelle has temperamental aircon, sleeping cars (*couchettes*) with two people to a room, clean linen and wash basins in the couchettes, plus a decent dining car. The Express is cheaper, has a sleeping car with four people to a couchette with no air-con, and a decent dining car. The couchettes on the Gazelle are frequently fully booked but rarely more than a day in advance.

The Gazelle costs approximately CFA 20,600 for 1st class (CFA 4500 extra for a couchette) and CFA 14,400 for 2nd class. The Express costs around CFA 16,600 for 1st class (CFA 3500 extra for a couchette) and CFA 13,800 for 2nd class. There is another series of trains, the *Rapides*, which cost about a third less than the Express and take longer, but you have to change trains to get to Ouaga.

GETTING AROUND
Air
Air Ivoire flies to all major inland cities, including Bouaké, Korhogo, Man and San Pedro. To charter a plane, contact Air Transivoire (tel 368415).

Bush Taxis
The Côte d'Ivoire has a good system of bush taxis running throughout the country. Some are Peugeot 504s; others are minibuses. If the Peugeots are too crowded for your liking, buy an extra seat.

Bus
The big luxury buses are much more comfortable than the bush taxis and cost about the same. There are connections daily from Abidjan to Yamoussoukro, Man, Bouaké and Korhogo.

Train
The only train line in the country is the one to Ouagadougou. This is a good way of

getting to the major towns of the interior. There are train connections to: Anyama, Yapo, Agboville, Dimbokro, Bouaké, Katiola, Tafire and Ferkéssédougou.

Taxi
City taxi drivers are notorious for rigging their metres. Also, rates double at midnight when the red No 2 meter is used. Africans and the local French don't tip, but taxi drivers often expect tips from foreigners and those going to hotels.

Abidjan

Abidjan was an unimportant town until 1951 when the French finished Vridi canal connecting the lagoon with the ocean, giving the city an excellent harbour. Since then, the city's population has skyrocketed, from less than 100,000 people to two million, spread over four peninsulas around the lagoon. Abidjan has two faces. Visitors travelling 1st-class tend to see only the wealthy side, especially Le Plateau, the downtown section with the skyscrapers, and Cocody, the posh residential section where you'll find the Hotel Ivoire. Les Deux Plateaux, another posh residential section, is nearby. At least half the residents of the nicest residential sections are Ivorians.

The sections where the ordinary people live are far more interesting. For sheer vibrancy, day and night, no city in Africa can top Abidjan. Treichville, Marcory and Adjamé are three of the major African quarters. Linked to Le Plateau by two major bridges, Treichville, known as Trashville by some English speakers, is where you'll find the largest of the city's four markets and the most nightclubs. A thorough tour of the Treichville market can easily consume half a day. The one in Adjamé is also good. A few words of Djoula, the major market language, will help make the traders think you're an old hand at African bargaining.

Top: Man region of western Ivory Coast (EE)
Left: Dan acrobatic dancers, Man region, Ivory Coast (EE)
Right: Masked stilt dancer, Ivory Coast (EE)

Top: Wambele dance, Ivory Coast (EE)
Bottom: Casamance region, Senegal (JTJ)

At night, you'll find street food everywhere in Abidjan's famous *maquis*, which sell better chicken and fish than you'll find in any fancy European restaurant. Eating at one is a must. Sailors and the more adventurous then head for Treichville's most famous nightlife street – Rue Douze. You may even find some of the local fire water – *koutoukou*. There are also many more respectable nightclubs.

Information
Tourist Office The Bureau of Tourism (tel 320733) is downtown in Immeuble de la Corniche, at the corner of Boulevard du General de Gaulle.

Banks Barclays (tel 322804) in Immeuble Alpha 2000, Citibank (tel 324610) across from the famous Pyramid building, Chase Manhattan (tel 331041), BIAO (Banque International pour l'Afrique Occidentale), BICICI (Banque Internationale pour le Commerce et l'Industrie de la Côte d'Ivoire), SIB (Société Ivoirienne de Banque).

Embassies Virtually all of the following embassies are on the Plateau:

Benin (tel 414484)
  Cocody
Burkina Faso (tel 321313)
  2 Avenue Terrasson de Fougeres
Canada (tel 322009)
  Trade Center, BP 4104
France (tel 326749)
  BP 1393
West Germany (tel 324727)
  Immeuble SMGL, BP 1900
Ghana (tel 331124)
  Residence la Corniche, Boulevard du General de Gaulle
Guinea (tel 328600)
  Immeuble Diana, Rue Crosson Duplessis
Japan (tel 323043)
  Immeuble Alpha 2000, BP 1329
Liberia (tel 222359)
  Immeuble Le General
Mali (tel 323147)
  Boulevard Pelieu

Netherlands (tel 222712)
  Immeuble Les Harmonies, BP 1086
Niger (tel 355098)
  Boulevard Achalme, Marcory
Switzerland (tel 321721)
  Immeuble Les Arcades, BP 1914
UK (tel 226850)
  Boulevard Carde, Immeuble Les Harmonies, BP 2581
USA (tel 320979) BP 1712

Other embassies include: Algeria, Argentina, Austria, Belgium, Brazil, Cameroon, CAR, Egypt, Ethiopia, Gabon, Guinea-Bissau, Italy, Mauritania, Morocco, Nigeria, Norway, Spain, Tunisia, Zaire.

Bookstores & Supermarkets The best bookstores downtown are *Librairie de France*, in the tall Alpha 2000 building on Avenue Chardy, and *Pociello*, two blocks away on the same street. For books on the Ivory Coast, magazines and newspapers, the bookstore at the Hotel Ivoire is the best.

Nour-al-Hayat, one of the best supermarkets, is a block down from the Alpha 2000 building. Another is *Score*, across from the Marché du Plateau.

Travel Agencies CATH Voyages (tel 327073) in Immeuble Alpha 2000, Avenue Chardy, is the number one travel agency for inland tours. They offer package tours to Man, Korhogo, Comoé Park, Yamoussoukro, Abengourou, etc. Another major one is Socopao (tel 227505/228381) in the same building; they represent American Express. Others include Express Voyages (tel 324462) on Avenue Delafosse, Akwaba Travel (tel 324045) on the same street and Ata-Toubia (tel 327523) on 5 Avenue Nogues. Akwaba has more unusual offerings – a trip down the Niango river and all-day trips to an Ebrié village, including a pirogue ride.

Hotel Ivoire
The city's number one attraction is the Hotel Ivoire, which has everything from an ice skating rink, bowling alley, cinema

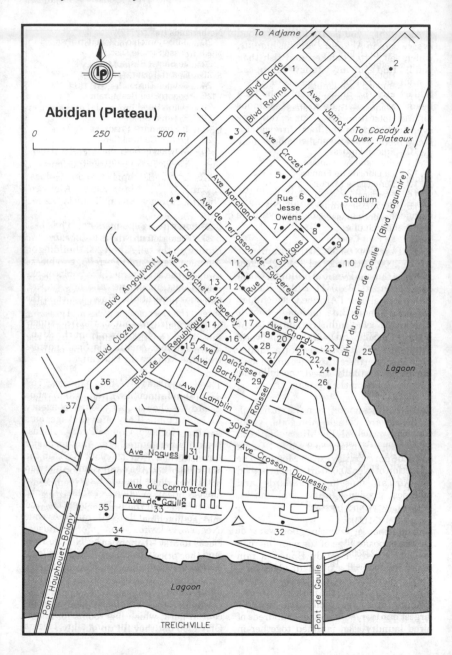

Abidjan (Plateau)

0   250   500 m

To Adjame

Blvd Carde

Blvd Roume

Ave Jamot

To Cocody &
Duex Plateaux

Ave Crozet

Ave Marchand

Ave de Terrasson de Fougeres

Rue Jesse Owens

Gourgas

Stadium

Blvd Angoulvant

Ave Franchet d'Esperey

Rue

Ave de la Republique

Ave Chardy

Blvd Clozel

Ave

Ave Delafosse

Ave Barthe

Rue Roussel

Blvd du General de Gaulle (Blvd Lagunaire)

Lagoon

Ave Lamblin

Ave Crosson Duplessis

Ave Noques

Ave du Commerce

Ave de Gaulle

Pont Houphouet–Boigny

Pont de Gaulle

Lagoon

TREICHVILLE

1	La Baguette d'Or Restaurant & British Embassy	20	Il Don Antonio's Restaurant
2	Cathedral	21	Passé Simple Disco
3	Hôtel Ibis	22	Le Santal Restaurant
4	Burkina Faso Embassy	23	Chalet Suisse Restaurant
5	Eloka Restaurant	24	Oxygèn Disco
6	Maquis du Stade Restaurant	25	Lagon Bleu Restaurant
7	Hotel Tiama	26	Hilton Hotel
8	US Embassy	27	Pyramid Building & Shawarma Snack-bar
9	Maison des Combattants Bar	28	French Cultural Centre
10	French Embassy	29	Mayflower Bar
11	Brasserie Abidjanaise	30	Open-air Restaurant (serves bats)
12	La Librairie de France	31	Le Son des Guitares
13	Senegalese Market	32	Grand Hôtel
14	Marche du Plateau	33	Novotel
15	SCORE Supermarket	34	Ferry Stop
16	Regency Brasserie	35	Bus Station
17	Scotch Club	36	PTT (Post Office)
18	Le Paris Cinéma	37	Plateau Train Stop & Restaurant
19	Les Deux As Bar		

and casino to a grocery store and a major art shop.

Cathedral

The city's spectacular cathedral is the largest Catholic cathedral in the world after St Peter's. It is best seen on a Sunday (9.30 am, when there's a chorus, and 11 am); during the week it's closed.

Museum

Several blocks inland from the cathedral, on Boulevard Nangui Abrogoua, you'll find the museum, Le Musée National d'Abidjan, which is open 9 am to 12 noon and 3 to 6 pm every day except Monday. The collection of over 20,000 art objects is good by African museum standards and includes wooden statues and masks, pottery, ivory and bronze.

Parc du Banco

On the opposite edge of town on the road to Dabou is the Parc du Banco, a rain forest reserve and a pleasant place for a walk. Several hundred metres beyond the dirt road entrance to the park you'll see an unforgettable spectacle, the world's largest outdoor launderette – hundreds of hired laundry men jammed together in the middle of a small stream frantically rubbing clothes on huge stones held in place by old car tyres. Afterwards, they spread the clothes over rocks and grass for at least half a km, never getting them mixed up. Get there before noon; in the afternoon all you'll see is drying clothes.

Zoo

The zoo, on the north-east edge of town, is one of the best in West Africa, but nothing special by western standards.

Golf Club

If you have wheels, you could take in the futuristic new Golf Club on the eastern outskirts of town beyond the Forum Golf hotel. You don't have to be a member to have a meal or drink. The setting is spectacular. All the pool lacks is a wave-making machine!

Places to Stay – bottom end

For the price, you can't beat *Centre Bethanie* which charges about CFA 1600 per person in a four-bed room and CFA 600 for a generous breakfast. Another possibility is the *Mission Catholique*, near a small central park, which has rooms for about CFA 2200 but they fill up quickly.

Many travellers want to stay in Treichville because it's the centre of activity. It's also slightly more dangerous. You're unlikely to find lodgings cheaper than at *Hôtel Fraternité* on Avenue 21 and Rue 44. Filthy rooms there cost CFA 1300. *Hôtel aux Tourbouroux* (tel 326448), on Avenue 13 at Rue 8, is only slightly better with rooms for CFA 1500, CFA 2000 (fan) and CFA 3000 (air-con) – still no bargain for what you get.

For a half-way decent hotel, the following three are roughly comparable: *Hôtel le Prince* (tel 327127) on Avenue 20 and Rue 19 Barre near the mosque, with air-con singles/doubles for CFA 4400/4900; *Hôtel California* (tel 355566) on Avenue 23 and Rue 44 near Cinéma l'Entente, with air-con rooms without hot water for CFA 5250; and *Hôtel Atlanta* (tel 332469) on Avenue 15 and Rue 14 Barre, with air-con singles/doubles for CFA 4300/5800.

In Marcory (bordering Treichville), you'll get more for your money. There are a number of inexpensive but decent hotels around Avenue de la TSF, the main drag leading off the autoroute.

Hôtel Konankro (tel 350578) charges CFA 5500 for a tiny room with double bed and air-con and a decent bathroom. It's on Rue TSF, about four blocks off the auto-route. Two blocks beyond and one block to your left, you'll find *Le Souvenir* (tel 351256), which has rooms just as good for the same price. One block away and one block off Rue TSF, you'll find *Hôtel Le Repos* where rooms cost CFA 6500 (also hourly rates) with TV and fancy wood carving on the walls. This is where the married African big shots bring their girl friends.

For a decent inexpensive hotel in Adjamé, try *Hôtel Liberté* (tel 371564) on Avenue 13 just north of the Gare Routière, three or four km from downtown. Rooms cost CFA 4000 to CFA 4500 with fan and CFA 6000 with air-con. Two blocks away near the big roundabout where traffic heads into Abidjan, you'll find the incredibly cheap *Hôtel La Rocade* which has small rooms with shower for CFA 1000 and a balcony with a great view of the street life below. Nearby at the Gare Routière, *Hôtel de la Gare* (tel 371856) has rooms for CFA 3000 (CFA 4000 with air-con and CFA 4500 with two beds).

If you'll be sleeping in your vehicle in Abidjan, try the parking lot of the Hôtel Akwaba (tip for the *gardien*) or the Parc National du Banco in the north-west corner of town, on the road to Dabou.

Places to Stay – middle

One of the best buys in Abidjan is the *Grand Hôtel* (tel 321200, telex 23807), a very respectable hotel on the Plateau that charges about CFA 9000/12,300 for singles/doubles. For a decent hotel with African ambience, try *Hôtel du Nord* (tel 370463) – popular with Africans on per diem who want to save money. They charge about CFA 6000 for their small ground floor rooms with air-con and CFA 7000/7500 for singles/doubles upstairs. It's in a safe but active area in Plateau Nord, two blocks from the well-known Lodgments 2000 and three km from downtown.

If you want to be in the most active African section of town, *Hôtel Ekoumatan* (tel 359036) on Avenue 16 in Treichville or even better, *Treichotel* (tel 328965) on the same street are both highly recommended. They charge CFA 6500/8500 and CFA 8000/9000 respectively for singles/doubles with air-con and private bath.

If you'd like to be on the beach try *Le Baron*, a fairly new African-run hotel that has decent rooms with air-con for about CFA 8000 (CFA 4000 for several hours). Occasionally there's live music on weekends. It is a CFA 1750 taxi ride from the Plateau past the airport on the road to Grand-Bassam. Just down the road is *La Vigie* (tel 367128), which has a fairly decent restaurant with a CFA 4300 menu. Singles/doubles cost about CFA 6600/7700.

Places to Stay – top end

The most famous hotel in all of West and

Central Africa is the 750-room *Hôtel Ivoire*. It has a movie theatre, casino, supermarket, ice skating rink and seven tennis courts. Nevertheless, the *Hilton* has a higher occupancy rate and is preferred by business people because of the superb management, cosier atmosphere, newer rooms and downtown location. The less expensive *Novotel*, also downtown, is quite decent but nothing special.

Bordering the lagoon, the *Forum Golf Hôtel* is almost as nice as the Ivoire and the Hilton and is much better value. The only problem is the location – about five km beyond the Ivoire, a good 15-minute taxi ride to downtown. *Le Wafou*, also a 15-minute drive from the Plateau, is Abidjan's most unusual hotel. It has 50 bungalows with sundecks on stilts in the lagoon, with one of the hottest nightclubs and best restaurants in town. The inconveniently located *Sebroko* has about a 15% occupancy rate and is not recommended. The older *Palm Beach*, a 20-minute drive from downtown, is recommended only if you want to be on the beach or near the port area.

For the price and downtown location, the *Ibis Plateau* and the *Tiama* are both recommended. The Ibis has better rooms and the Tiama a better location. The *Ibis Marcory* is better if you want an overnight hotel near the airport.

Hôtel Ivoire (tel 441045, telex 23555), CFA 33,500/38,500 for singles/doubles (CFA 3000 extra for the tower), pool, tennis, bowling, ice skating, sauna, movie theatre, casino, nightclub, supermarket, Eurocar, cards AE, D, V, CB.

Hilton (tel 328322, telex 22636) CFA 31,000/37,000 for singles/doubles (CFA 34,000/40,000 with lagoon view), pool, tennis club nearby, Eurocar, cards AE, D, V, CB.

Forum Golf (tel 431044, telex 26112), CFA 24,000/28,000 for singles/doubles (CFA 28,500/33,000 with lagoon view), pool, tennis, windsurfing, cards AE, D, V, CB.

Novotel (tel 320457, telex 23264), CFA 25,000/28,000 for singles/doubles (CFA 27,500/31,500 with lagoon view), pool, Eurocar, cards AE, D, V, CB.

Le Wafou (tel 359893, telex 42199), CFA 21,000/24,000 for singles/doubles, pool, tennis, rooms with sundecks, cards AE, D, V, CB.

Sebroko (tel 320933, telex 23828), CFA 22,500/23,000 for singles/doubles, pool, cards AE, D, V, CB.

Tiama (tel 320822, telex 23494), CFA 20,000/22,000 for singles/doubles, Eurocar, cards AE, D, V, CB.

Ibis (Plateau tel 320157, telex 22608; Marcory tel 369255, telex 42130), CFA 18,500/20,500 for singles/doubles, pool (Marcory only), cards AE, D, V, CB.

Le Palm Beach (tel 354216, telex 42236), CFA 16,000/18,500 for singles/doubles (CFA 2000-4000 less for bungalow rooms), saltwater pool, cards AE, D.

Places to Eat

Cheap Eats For rice and sauce and the cheapest food in town, look around any of the markets. There are several places on the Plateau near the Pyramid building and in Treichville that sell Lebanese shawarma sandwiches for CFA 450. Abidjan's equivalent to McDonalds is *Super Chicken*, downtown one block from the Pyramid building, and in Treichville on Rue 13 near Avenue 20. Everything except the food comes directly from the USA, even the silver hamburger wrappings. The hamburgers at the Ivoire's bowling alley are 10 times better, but also more expensive at CFA 1500 for a huge burger with fries.

African A visit to Abidjan is not complete without a meal at a *maquis*. They serve braised chicken, braised fish and *attiéké* and some have local specialties such as *kedjenou* and *foutou*. Everyone swears they know the best maquis in town. They all serve the same food for about CFA 2000 to CFA 2500 a person plus drinks. What changes is the ambience – those in Marcory and Treichville tend to be friendly and lively. Unfortunately, maquis have become so popular that some normal restaurants have taken the name. If a place has tablecloths and more than four selections, you're at a fancy imitation. Ask a taxi driver if he knows 'un vrai

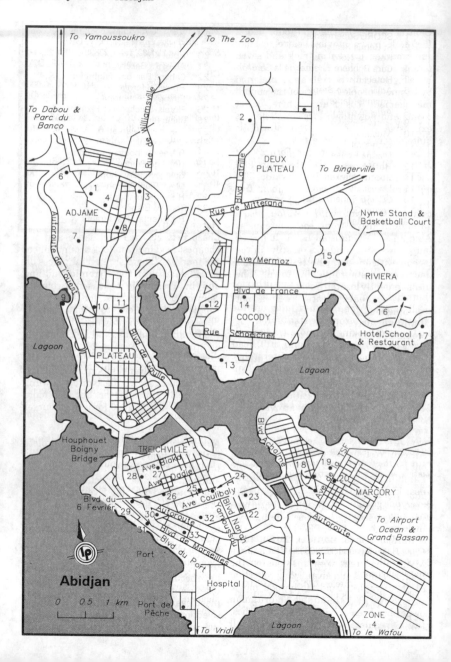

To Yamoussoukro

To The Zoo

To Dabou & Parc du Banco

Rue de Williansville

DEUX PLATEAU

Blvd Latrille

To Bingerville

Rue de Mitterand

Nyme Stand & Basketball Court

6

1

4

3

ADJAME

8

7

Ave Mermoz

15

RIVIERA

Blvd de France

Autoroute de l'Ouest

9

10   11

12   14

COCODY

16

Rue Schoelcher

Hotel, School & Restaurant

17

Lagoon

Blvd de Gaulle

PLATEAU

13

Lagoon

Houphouet Boigny Bridge

TREICHVILLE

Ave Biaka

Blvd Achalme

28   27 Ave Dadie

18

19   TSF

Blvd du 6 Fevrier

26   25

24

20

MARCORY

29   30

Ave Coulibaly

23

Blvd Nangui Abrogoua

22

Autoroute

To Airport Ocean & Grand Bassam

31

32

Blvd Valery Giscard d'Estaing

33

Blvd de Marseilles

21

Port

Blvd du Port

Abidjan

0   0.5   1 km

Port de Pêche

Hospital

ZONE 4

To Vridi

Lagoon

To le Wafou

1	SCORE Supermarket	19	Hôtel Le Souvenir
2	St Remis Restaurant		& Hôtel Le Repos
3	Hôtel de Nord	20	Hôtel Konankro
4	Gare Routière & Hôtel de la Gare	21	All-night Bakery
5	Hôtel Liberté	22	Cabane Bambou Nightclub
6	Adjamé Train Stop	23	Hôtel California
7	Adjamé Market	24	Ethiopia Restaurant
8	Adjamé gare routière	25	Hôtels Treichotel & Ekoumatan
9	Hôtel Sebroko	26	Janic Bar
10	Museum	27	Treichville Market
11	Cathedral	28	Canne à Sucre Disco
12	Marine House		& Chez Babouya Restaurant
13	Hôtel Ivoire	29	Hôtel de France
14	Cocody Market	30	Gold jewellery shops
15	University	31	Main Train Station
16	SCORE Supermarket	32	Hôtel International
17	Forum Golf Hotel	33	Tout Va Bien
18	Good Maquis		& l'Oriental Restaurants

maquis' or just head for Marcory and ask there. You'll find a number near the main drag, Avenue de la TSF. For an authentic but slightly higher-class maquis, try the well-known *Maquis du Stade* on the Plateau, across from the stadium.

If you're looking for more traditional, every day African food (foutou, etc), head for *Éloka*, a modern, clean cafeteria that serves a number of authentic African dishes. Open 7.30 am to 10.30 pm, it's one block from the Maquis du Stade at the Ministry of Finance building. For Ethiopian food, try the popular *Ethiopia* (tel 323920) on Rue 38 in Treichville. For really cheap food at lunch, try the most popular African 'restaurant' on the Plateau, an outdoor eating area between Avenue Lamblin and Avenue Crosson Duplessis, near Hollando. Get there by noon, before everyone gobbles up the house specialty – bat (*chauve-souris*). It's not bad, but a little boney.

Abidjan's most unusual restaurant is *Chez Babouya* (tel 323928). It resembles a Mauritanian tent with cushions on the floor, low tables and an amazing collection of photographs of old Hollywood movie stars. Since 1965, the affable Mauritanian owner has been serving only four dishes, two Senegalese and two Moroccan, all

well prepared. The cost including wine comes to only CFA 3000 to CFA 3500 a person; order one of everything. You'll find it on Avenue 7 in Treichville, a block behind the well-known Canne à Sucre nightclub. It's open every evening but is closed during August and September.

Seafood *Chez Cakpot* (tel 352978) gets rave reviews and is highly recommended. The selection is limited, primarily lobster and prawns, but the location is special. You're seated only 30 metres from the ocean, with waves breaking right before you and ships passing nearby. It's a 20-minute drive from downtown and is open every day from noon to 10 pm. Your taxi may have to wait for you. The cost is about CFA 6500 a plate.

The best seafood restaurant is probably the *Restaurant des Pêcheurs* (tel 354235) near Treichville in Zone 4, opposite the fish market, Le Port de Pêche. It is rarely crowded but suffers from a subdued ambience and moderately high prices. If you stay on the Plateau, try *Lagon Bleu* (tel 328468), a good but moderately expensive restaurant on a boat in the lagoon, 200 metres from the Hilton. It is closed Sunday.

Italian Abidjan's most popular restaurant may be *St Remis* (tel 415140). It has the best pizzas in town for CFA 2000 to CFA 3000, various French dishes and the most affable restaurateur in Abidjan, Remi. It is on the wide Boulevard Latrille in Deux Plateau, a five-minute drive from the Ivoire and a 10-minute drive from the Plateau. Downtown, the best pizza and Italian food is served at *Il Don Antonio's* (tel 327086), half a block from the landmark Pyramid building. In Treichville, try the informal, ever-popular *Tout Va Bien* on Boulevard Marseilles, open every day until 11 pm.

Asian Abidjan has some excellent Vietnamese restaurants. The three best, all on the Plateau, are moderately priced. *La Baguette d'Or* (tel 325724) is on Boulevard Carde in the same building as the British embassy and *La Rose d'Asie* (tel 324192) is down the hill from the famous Pyramid building. *Le Dalat* (tel 327950) at 12 Rue Paris, is a small restaurant and has been reviewed in the *New York Times* no less.

Abidjan's Chinese restaurants, on the other hand, are fairly expensive and nothing special. *La Grande Muraille* (tel 322506), on Avenue Terrasson de Fougeres facing the Alpha 2000 building, is as good as any and less expensive than some.

Lebanese The two best Lebanese restaurants are *Istanbul* (tel 322762) in Treichville on Avenue 16 and *L'Oriental* (tel 323685) a good km away on the well-known Boulevard de Marseilles. Both are medium priced. The latter has music, the former has slightly better food.

French Abidjan's most spectacular restaurant is at the *Golf Club*; you don't have to be a member to eat there. The silky fabrics and fancy interior panelling, the space-age building overlooking the lagoon with Abidjan in the distance, and the fabulous food and service all make this place memorable. A typical meal runs about CFA 20,000; reservations are not required because it's never full. Your taxi will have to wait.

If awards were given to the city's two best restaurants, the winners would likely be the expensive 'institutions' *La Brasserie Abidjanaise* (tel 329235) on Boulevard de la République and *Le Grenier* (tel 323494 on Avenue Crosson Duplessis, both on the Plateau. Reservations are necessary. The restaurant at the *Hilton* is in the same league. *Le Chalet Suisse* (tel 325480) is more moderately priced and always full. It's on Avenue Chardy, near the lagoon and the Hilton.

Entertainment & Sports

Bars Abidjan is not noted for its bars. During the day, *La Maison des Combattants* on the Plateau 150 metres from the US embassy is popular and has a breezy, colonial atmosphere. You can also get a decent three-course meal for about CFA 2800. At night, the French barmaids are the attraction of the tiny but ever-popular *Scotch Bar*, downtown on Avenue Chardy.

After work, one of the most popular places is the *Hilton*. What's special is the opportunity to hear the *kora*, the African version of a harp. The music is entirely different from the Indian sitar, but the emotional impact is similar. Mory Kanté, a Guinean who now lives in Abidjan, is the undisputed king though hearing him or any kora player is actually fairly difficult. Besides the lobby of the Hilton in the late afternoon, try the Golf hotel on Fridays between 7 and 11 pm.

Nightclubs Abidjan's two best-known nightclubs are *La Canne à Sucre* and *La Cabane Bambou*, both in Treichville. These are the only places in town where you can dance to an African band. Finding a dancing partner or a cab when you leave is never a problem. Both have doormen-bouncers. As at most major nightclubs, the cover (CFA 3500, higher on weekends) includes a drink. People don't begin showing up until 11 pm.

All the other 'name' nightclubs are fancy, undistinguished discos with recorded music and are well-attended by the French, the Lebanese, the African jet-set and the university crowd. On the Plateau, you'll find the four liveliest discos all within two blocks of each other: *Oxygén* facing the lagoon and half a block from the Hilton, *Lagoon Bleu* in a boat 100 metres away, *Passé Simple* on Avenue Chardy around the corner from the Oxygen, and the *Scotch Bar* (upstairs) nearby on the same street. In the port area, try *Cobra Bleu* at Le Wafou, the only hotel with a decent nightclub. The place is huge and typically mobbed.

Treichville is where the action is and where the sailors head. Women are everywhere; so are rogues. On Rue 12 you'll find about six lively but disreputable bars with dance floors. Unlike the fancy discos, they get going early, around 9 pm. The most famous is *Janic Bar*, where beers and cokes are CFA 600. Many of the women are salaried and their job is to coax the men into buying them mixed drinks. All it takes is two drinks for you to be CFA 5000 out of pocket. Couples can have fun too, but don't be surprised if the women make passes at the man. On Rue 11 in an unmarked, dilapidated two-storey apartment 1½ blocks from Janic Bar, Tanti will serve you some delicious firewater, *koutoukou*, for CFA 100 a shot – a terrific way to start the evening. If you can't find her, ask around; someone else will surely oblige.

Movie Theatres All movies from English-speaking countries are dubbed in French. The best theatres, all good by western standards, are at the *Hôtel Ivoire* (showings at 6 and 9 pm) and on the Plateau – *Cinéma Paris* on Chardy Avenue, *Le Sphinx* on Rue du Commerce, and *Les Studios* on Boulevard de la République near the market. The *French Cultural Centre* (tel 225628) downtown next to the landmark Pyramid building has all kinds of cultural events, usually announced in *Fraternité Matin*.

Sports Abidjan has some of the best blue marlin fishing in all of West and Central Africa. Tuna, wahoo, ray, coryphee and sailfish are the other principal deep sea fish found off Abidjan. For ocean fishing, the season is late April to the end of June and, better, November to December. The Marlin Club (Zone 4, tel 368927) rents boats for about CFA 130,000 for a maximum of three people. Jet Tours offers nine-day, all-inclusive fishing trips from Paris starting from 13,000 French francs.

The Hôtel Ivoire has seven tennis courts and the Forum Golf has two. The Ivoire is also a good place to go swimming; the fee for non-guests is CFA 1000. At the Forum Golf, the CFA 2200 lunch ticket includes free use of the imaginatively curved pool with an island. There are also windsurfers for rent. A km beyond the Forum Golf is the huge clubhouse (tel 430845), with the best 18-hole golf course in West and Central Africa. The second best is in Yamoussoukro. Both are tournament quality. The green fee is CFA 10,000 for non-members (CFA 15,000 on weekends) plus CFA 1500 for rental clubs. Right across from the Forum Golf hotel, is the old nine-hole course (tel 431295), which also has grass greens and clubs for rent. For CFA 4000 (CFA 6000 weekends), you can go around as many times as you like.

For a squash court with air-con, try the golf club or the *Sporting Club* in Deux Plateux; the latter charges non-members CFA 2500. From about June to late-September, the ice skating rink at the Ivoire turns into an indoor tennis court. During the rest of the year, you can skate there every day until 10 pm for about CFA 1500 including skates. You can bowl there as well, every day until midnight.

Joggers can join the Hash House Harriers on their weekly jaunt on Saturdays at 5 pm. The location changes weekly. Even though about 80 people show up, finding someone who knows the location isn't easy. Try the British embassy (tel 226850), DHL (tel 331553) or Deloite Haskins & Sells.

Things to Buy

Markets About a km from the Hôtel Ivoire is the *Marché de Cocody*, which is a good place to find art work and fabrics. Prices, however, are slightly higher than at the other markets.

In the heart of town amongst the skyscrapers and shops, you'll find the *Marché du Plateau* and, a block away, the *Marché Senegalais*, good for crafts. Both the *Marché de Treichville* and the *Marché de Adjamé* are better but require a taxi or bus from the Plateau.

Artisan Goods The best place to find good quality masks and other wood carvings is *La Rose d'Ivoire* (tel 349255) in the basement of the Hôtel Ivoire; it's open every day. For fabrics, beads, ivory, bronze, cheap wood carvings and malachite, head for the markets. The *Marché de Treichville* (top floor) is the best, especially for beads and cotton materials. It's safe, but beware of pickpockets. Prices for the wax cotton prints vary widely, from about CFA 1000 to CFA 4000 a metre, depending on where they're made (those from Holland are the most expensive), the number of colours and the popularity of a given print. The top floor of the *Marché de Cocody* is more compact and less confusing but slightly more expensive. On the Plateau, try the *Marché Senegalese* along the wide Boulevard de la République and the *Marché au Plateau* one block away.

Gold & Silver The best selection is at the Ivoire where they also accept credit cards but Treichville is cheaper. You'll find several small jewellery shops with significantly lower prices across from the brewery, La Brasserie de Bracody, one block from the wide autoroute. Everything is sold by the gram – about CFA 5000 for gold and CFA 600 for silver.

Music Abidjan is one of the better places in West Africa to buy recordings of African music. The record shop at the Hôtel Ivoire is the best. On the Plateau, try *Studio 33*

on Avenue Chardy next to the Librairie de France and *Disc Discount* nearby, on the top floor of Nour Al Hayat. Cassettes sold on the street are a third the price but of poor quality. If you don't want records or can't afford those at the Ivoire, look on Avenue 16 in Treichville for an African-run record shop; occasionally, they will agree to record your selections of their music on your blank cassettes. Go to the Ivoire or elsewhere for high quality blank cassettes. Three Ivorian *vedettes* known Africa-wide and in Europe are the reggae superstar Alpha Blondy, and female vocalists Aicha Koné and Nayanka Bell. Three other well-known singers are Jimmy Hyacinte, Francois Lungar and Mariatou.

Alpha Blondy, who wears the shades and charisma of a pop idol, became enamoured with Bob Marley while studying at Columbia University. Outspoken in defence of Africa and the poor, he feels reggae 'is a kind of newspaper for the Third World. Reggae helps us communicate.' Two of his biggest hits were *Apartheid is Nazism* and *Cocody Rock*. He once told a reporter: 'In Africa man, if you're head of state, you don't move too long from your chair. You go pee, and find somebody's taken over.'

Getting There & Away

Air Air Ivoire flies to all major inland cities including Bouaké, Korhogo, Man and San Pedro.

Bush Taxi In Abidjan, you'll find the north-bound taxis at the Gare Routière in Adjamé and those headed east to Grand Bassam and Aboisso at the Gare Routière in Treichville.

Bus There are connections daily from Abidjan to Yamoussoukro, Man, Bouaké and Korhogo. In Abidjan, you'll find them at the Gare Routière in Adjamé.

Train There are train connections to: Anyama, Yapo, Agboville, Dimbokro, Bouaké, Katiola, Tafiré and Ferkéssédougou. For more information see the Getting There section at the start of this chapter.

Getting Around

Airport Transport At Abidjan airport, there's no airport tax. You'll find a bank open until the last flight each evening, a restaurant, shops and free shuttle service to the major hotels. If you reserve ahead, Hertz, Avis and Eurocar will meet you there with a car. A taxi costs about CFA 800 to Marcory, CFA 1100 to Treichville, CFA 1400 to downtown (16 km) and CFA 1900 to Cocody (Hôtel Ivoire area). If the rate is higher, suspect fraud. You won't find any buses at the airport, but you will on the autoroute a good two km away; taxi drivers are likely to refuse such a short trip.

Bus SOTRA buses cover every corner of the city. The main station on the Plateau, the Gare du Sud, is at the foot of the Houphouet-Boigny bridge. From the Plateau (the Gare du Sud and along Boulevard de la République), buses No 5 and 25 head for Treichville while buses 16, 20, 27, 30 and 37 head north towards Adjamé and beyond. If you're heading for the Gare Routière in Adjamé, get off at the mosque, several blocks away.

Taxi Taxis have meters and are reasonably priced. If you're travelling at night, the taxi should not be using tariff 2, which is double the rate, unless it's after midnight. Scream, holler, do anything to keep them from racing on the freeways at death-defying speeds. The number of fatal accidents is surely Africa's highest. If the cops catch you without a seatbelt on, you can be fined.

Car Rental You'll find Eurocar (tel 351135/358806, telex 3494) at the Hilton, Golf, Tiama and Ibis hotels; Hertz (tel 357163/357356, telex 43167) on Boulevard Giscard d'Éstaing; Avis (tel 328007/320457, telex 32542) at the Novotel; Budget (tel 356354, telex 42258) at Hôtel

Palm Beach and in Zone 4 at 81 Ruc Blanchard; Locauto (tel 355495) in Immeuble Francisco on Rue Pierre et Marie Curie; Civcars (tel 358951) at 165 Boulevard de Marseilles in Zone 4; Mattei (tel 323034) downtown on Boulevard de la République. At the airport, you'll find Hertz (tel 368943), Avis (tel 711687) and Eurocar (tel 368943).

Ferry Downtown, across the street from the Gare du Sud, you'll find the Plateau stop for the cheap (CFA 100) *bateau-bus* (*la gare lagunaire du Plateau*) – a great way to see Abidjan. It's a ferry with connections to various points around the lagoon. If you get off in Yopougon, you'll find one of the famous Harris churches (a Christian-animist mixture), which has a Christ figure on a cross outside – unusual for Africa. The CVA, a private sailing club, is 400 metres away as the crow flies.

You can also take a special sight-seeing tour, a 1½ hour ferry ride, that takes you around the lagoon and costs CFA 1300. To catch it, go to the Plateau stop for the bateau-bus on Wednesday at 3 pm, Thursdays at 9 am and 3 pm, Saturday at 11 pm and Sunday at 2 pm. At least 10 people must show up, and the boat does not operate from June to September. If you wish, you can reserve a seat (tel 321737); the cost is about CFA 1300 a person.

AROUND ABIDJAN

There are two nearby excursions that can be done as day trips or weekend excursions. They are easily reached by public transport.

Île du Boulay

If you want to spend a lazy day on the beach, instead of going to Grand-Bassam, you could take a ferry to this island several km from the Plateau. It has a beach, inexpensive cabins (CFA 6000) for an overnight stay, and a seafood restaurant with authentic Ivorian recipes and tables on the sand. On Sundays at 10 am you can catch the ferry at the bateau-bus stop on the Plateau. It returns around 5 pm. The CFA 8500 price includes the meal which is quite a sumptuous spread. Reservations (tel 443574) are unnecessary.

Bingerville

Another possibility, only 15 km away, is Bingerville. A charming town on a plateau overlooking the lagoon, it was the capital until the 1930s. A walk through the old botanical gardens near the centre of town is a must. The governor's palace, now an orphanage, is a particularly good example of colonial architecture. The Atelier d'Art, a school of art for young Africans, has a number of rooms displaying their work. It is open 8 am to 6 pm.

The Coast – East

GRAND BASSAM

The best one-day excursion from Abidjan is Grand-Bassam, 40 km east of Abidjan. What you'll find are the remnants of a bygone era. The narrow strip of land between the ocean and the lagoon is where the first French colonists set up their capital, separating themselves from the natives whose own town across the lagoon began as servants' quarters.

A yellow fever epidemic in 1899 prompted the French into changing the capital to Bingerville. Grand-Bassam, it seemed, was headed for oblivion. Construction of a jetty two years later, however, brought new life. Buildings went up everywhere; spacious balconies, shuttered windows and pretentious archways were 'in'. In 1931, this 30-year golden age came to an end when the French built another jetty in Abidjan. Customs houses, the governor's palace, a tax office, an elegant post office, huge ornate storehouses and numerous two-storey homes with elegant verandas were all left to decay. The 'coup de grâce' was the opening of the Vridi canal in Abidjan in 1951.

Today, expatriates from Abidjan head here on Sundays during the dry season to soak up the sun and have lunch at one of several hotels along the beach. At the entrance to town, you'll find a long series of stalls filled with local crafts – a good place to pick up souvenirs.

Places to Stay – bottom end

Finding a cheap hotel isn't easy. If *Chez Antoinette* is still open, it should cost about CFA 4000/5000 for singles/doubles. You'll do better going to one of the nearby villages and act like you own one of the paillotes which line the beach. They're full on Sundays and vacant the rest of the week. Or ask them to rent you a vacant one.

Places to Stay – top end

Grand-Bassam has four first-rate hotels all on the ocean: *La Taverne Bassamoise* (tel 301062), *La Paillote* (tel 301076), *Assoyam Beach Hôtel* (tel 301557) and *Le Wharf* (tel 301533). With a pool, tennis and singles/doubles for about CFA 17,500/

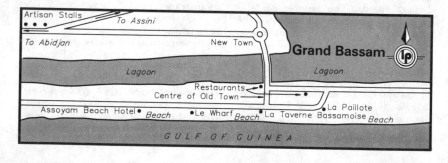

25,000 including half board, the Bassamoise is a notch above the rest. Nevertheless, many people prefer the Paillote because it has a friendly, more informal atmosphere, excellent food and the lowest prices, about CFA 11,000/16,000 for singles/doubles with half board. Both of them are the clear favourites for Sunday lunch.

The Assoyam has a pool, tennis and squash courts, and singles/doubles for about CFA 12,300/13,500 including breakfast, while the Wharf offers only the beach and rooms for about CFA 10,000 or CFA 15,000/20,000 with half board.

ASSINIE
Assinie has the best beaches near Abidjan. The only problem is that they're almost a two-hour drive east of Abidjan, and you must leave your car on one side of the lagoon and hire a canoe to take you across. Many foreigners own bungalows there, but usually stay only on Sundays. During the rest of the week, you'll find very few people except for the Africans guarding the huts.

Places to Stay
The two resort hotels are the *Club Med* (reservations tel 323580) catering to the French, and *Les Palétuviers* (reservations tel 300712), catering to the Italians. Sporting activities include swimming, water skiing, tennis and archery. Open only October-April, both give priority to people on package tours from Europe and accept reservations in Abidjan only a few days in advance. The charge per person is about CFA 32,000 including meals (CFA 16,000 for the day including lunch).

In Assouindé nearby, there's a more reasonably priced place several hundred metres from the sea – *SITOUR* (tel 353685), which has 45 bungalows for CFA 20,000/36,000 (singles/doubles) with half board. Without a reservation, you can't get in.

The Coast – West

JACQUEVILLE
Only about 50 km west of Abidjan, Jacqueville is a two-hour drive from Abidjan via a ferry crossing. If you're hitching, the best time to go is Sunday when expatriates escaping the Grand-Bassam crowds head that way. The beach there is actually a little nicer than at Bassam; the one in front of *Hôtel Le M'Koa* (tel 327980) is for guests only, unless you eat at their over-priced restaurant.

DABOU
Dabou is 49 km east of Abidjan near the turn off to Grand Lahou. If you get stuck there, the principal hotel in town is *Le Fromager*, which has rooms for CFA 7000 with air-con and CFA 3500 without and meals for CFA 2000 to CFA 2500.

TIEGBA
About 60 km west of Abidjan, half-way between Abidjan and Grand Lahou, Tiegba is a fascinating village. The houses there are built on stilts. To get there, you'll have to pass over some dirt roads through rubber plantations. There's someone in the village who has several rooms for rent.

SASSANDRA
A five or six hour ride in a minibus over some bad roads from Abidjan, Sassandra is an interesting fishing village with plenty of palm wine (*bangui*) and beautiful beaches. Most travellers adore it. The town was once a slave port, so you can still see the slave building and old colonial buildings such as the governor's house.

Places to Stay & Eat
For a younger crowd, friendly managers and a less touristy, more laid-back atmosphere, head for the highly recommended *Hôtel Ouest* (tel 720464). It's at the opposite end of town, on the road to San Pedro, a km from the centre. Singles/

doubles cost CFA 5500/6000. If it's full, try *Hôtel Grau* (tel 720174), near the Campement. It's a pleasant little hotel that has a restaurant with superb service and clean singles/doubles with overhead fans for CFA 5500/6500.

The only upmarket hotel is the *Campement* (tel 720515), a comfortable tourist hotel on the eastern outskirts of town overlooking a small fishing harbour, with a patio on the beach. Unfortunately, the beach is too cluttered to use. Singles with air-con cost about CFA 7200 to CFA 8000, doubles CFA 1500 more. They offer French cooking and all kinds of activities – tennis, windsurfing, ping pong, and trips up the river in a pirogue (canoe) to see the monkeys and wildlife. The guide service offered by the hotel is quite expensive; you'll do better finding your own. They'll take you up the river, show you to the bars in town with reggae music, buy a lobster on the beach and cook it for you, and get you anything, including all the bangui you can drink.

Nightlife

The most famous bar in town, if not in the Ivory Coast, is *Chez Masters*. Inside, you'll find blue lights, music and women. What's unusual is the sheer number of women who live there, each in one of the scores of tiny cubbyholes – a sad sight.

SAN PEDRO

A seven-hour, bush-taxi ride from Abidjan (or one hour by plane), San Pedro is a bustling industrial city, the country's second major port. Much of the country's timber and palm oil is exported from here. Most travellers head on to Sassandra, 60 km to the east, or Grand-Béréby, 52 km to the west.

Places to Stay & Eat

For a less expensive downtown hotel patronised by both Africans and travellers, try the 15-room *Hôtel Bahia* (tel 212733), a good buy at about CFA 6500/7500 for a single/double with air-con. Alternatively,

Le Napolean (tel 711357), near the post office on the main drag leading from the bus station, has 10 singles/doubles with air-con (possibly not working) for CFA 7000/8000 and a super restaurant serving African and European food. The big concrete *Hôtel Atlantic* (tel 711825) on the main drag (Boulevard de la République), with 82 singles/doubles for CFA 7500/8500, is boring and not recommended.

In the residential Quartier du Lac, two km from downtown and near the bus station, you'll find two small African hotels – *Hôtel Olympic* (tel 711010) with clean air-con rooms for CFA 6000, and *Hôtel Mondial* (tel 712294) with air-con singles/doubles for about CFA 5000/6000.

The two best hotels are *Motel Arso* (tel 712474/712557) and *Le Balmer Plage* (tel 711275). The Arso, which has 27 rooms, 30 bungalows, pool and cars for hire, is the favourite of tour groups. My favourite is Le Balmer, three km west of town past the port – a CFA 1000 taxi ride and fairly isolated. Overlooking the sea, it has bungalows with thatched roofs and air-con, a great view, bartenders with white jackets, and an excellent but expensive restaurant. Singles/doubles at both cost about CFA 10,000/11,000. For an apartment with three bedrooms in a tall building on the beach, try the *Residence Mohikrako* (Abidjan tel 361482, telex 43145).

Nightlife

For nightclubs with lots of dancing partners, try the *Pussy Cat* or *Play Boy*, about five blocks from Le Napoleon. *La Baraka*, downtown on the main drag, and *La Cloche* are classier.

GRAND-BÉRÉBY

The best beaches in the Ivory Coast are in Grand-Béréby, a seven-hour drive from Abidjan. You can also fly there; the hotel will meet you at the airport. The *Beau-Rivage* (Abidjan tel 326012, ask for Madame Daguero) is a very popular hotel, with clean bungalows right on the ocean. The cost is CFA 16,000 half board and CFA

21,500 full board. Getting a room is next to impossible around Christmas time and on any three-day weekend. Langouste is on the menu every night. If you make arrangements in advance, they'll take you on an early morning guided tour of the nearby game reserve. You'll see as many animals as at Comoé.

TAI NATIONAL PARK

If you'll be in Grand-Béréby or San Pedro, consider a side trip to Tai National Park, directly north of Tabou only a few km from the Liberian border. This is not an easy park to get around and you'll need a guide. The owner of Beau Rivage arranges trips, but only if you call ahead. In a very rainy humid area, Tai is one of the last remaining areas of primal rainforest in West Africa.

The best time to visit is December to February, when there's a marked dry season. You'll see trees up to 46 metres in height, with massive trunks and huge supporting roots. Some of the wildlife you might see include elephants, leopards, golden cats, pygmy hippos, buffalos, wart hogs, forest duikers and other antelopes, monkeys and chimpanzees.

BOUBÈLE

Boubèle is recommended if you're travelling to/from Liberia overland via the coastal route or you're looking for an out-of-the-way place on the beach. About 19 km east of Tabou (near the Liberian border) you'll see an arrow pointing south towards Boubèle and the beach. You'll probably have to walk four km through a superb palm tree forest to Boubèle. There, you'll find the 10-room Village Hôtel de Boubèle (BP 60, Tabou) in a superb location along a river and near the ocean. It costs about CFA 19,000 with full board. An hour's walk down the beach will bring you to Toulou where, for CFA 1000 a person, you can rent one of the six palm leaf huts on the beach. Fresh water is available and the people are very friendly. This place is fantastic.

The North

KORHOGO

An all-day drive north from Abidjan, Korhogo is famous for its cloth – coarse raw cotton, like burlap, with painted, mud-coloured designs. The weavers use a natural vegetable dye mixed with black mud and a knife with a thick curved blade to paint the geometrical figures. It's used solely as a wall hanging and found in all the markets in Abidjan. It makes a good inexpensive souvenir and costs CFA 3000 to CFA 4500 for a metre-long design. In theory it's washable, but some will fade after the first wash. In Korhogo, you'll find it at the market and outside the major hotels. For wood carvings and other crafts, head for the new Grande Mosquée. In the quartier artisanal nearby, you'll find lots to buy.

Places to Stay – bottom end

For a place with rock bottom prices, try the Mission Catholique, which charges CFA 1500 per person and is one block from the Hôtel du Nord. If it's full, try Hôtel le Pelèrin (tel 860588) at the market. They have decent small singles/doubles with clean bathrooms and fans for CFA 3000/4000 – excellent for the price. It's much better than the similarly priced Hôtel Syndicat a block away.

Places to Stay – middle

The best buy is unquestionably the Motel Agip (tel 860113) in the heart of town – highly recommended. French run with a decent sidewalk restaurant, it has eight clean, high-quality singles/doubles for CFA 5500/6800. Hôtel du Nord (tel 860858), three blocks from the Mt Korhogo hotel, costs about CFA 5500 a room and is not a good buy in comparison to the Agip. Next door is La Voute, reputedly the most popular nightclub in town.

For a decent hotel with a real African ambience, try Hôtel des Avocats (tel 860569), one km from the centre of town and not far from Hôtel Kadjona. The CFA 7000 to CFA 8000 rooms have air-con and modern bathrooms. The CFA 11,000 apartments have TVs, music, air-con, refrigerators, lots of lounge chairs and a separate bedroom.

Places to Stay – top end
Le Mont Korhogo (tel 860400, telex 63108), where tour groups stay, is the best hotel in town. Within walking distance of the market, it has a pool and small singles/doubles with air-con for about CFA 13,000/14,500. The next best hotel is probably *Hôtel Kadjona* (tel 860289), on the main road leading into town. It has 50 decent singles/doubles for CFA 7500/9500 with air-con, TVs, a pool that doesn't work, and the Club Kadjona Kassoum nightclub.

Places to Eat
The *Hôtel du Nord* has a good Lebanese restaurant with full meals for CFA 1300 and Lebanese shawarma sandwiches for much less. Next to the Mt Korhogo Hôtel is *Ayakaly*, a good African restaurant with a wide variety of authentic African specialties (foufou, sauce graine, etc) for CFA 550.

AROUND KORHOGO
What's particularly interesting about Korhogo are the villages surrounding the area. You may want to stop by ONT (Office National du Tourisme) for some advice and maps to the major sites – Waraniéné for weavers (*tisserands*), Fakaha for the famous Korhogo cloth (*les tapis*), Koni for blacksmiths (*forgerons*), and Sinématiali for potters (*potieres*).

Waraniéné
The most touristy village is Waraniéné. It has a weavers' cooperative with set prices that are half those in Abidjan. They see more tourists because there's lots for sale and it's only five km north from Korhogo on the road to Sikasso (Mali).

Koni
Koni is not quite so touristy and is 17 km north of Korhogo on the road to M'Bengue. The blacksmiths there mine iron ore and use it for making agricultural implements. If you're lucky, you'll see the entire process from ore to iron in one visit. They are closed on Sunday. Blacksmiths hold a special position with the Senoufo. Their relationship with the earth invests them with power, and their caste presides over funerals. When someone dies, the corpse is carried through the village in a long procession, while men in enormous grotesque masks chase away the soul. Immune to evil spirits, the blacksmiths dig the grave and carefully position the corpse inside, after which they present a last meal to the dead, then feast and celebrate.

Fakaha
The sleepy town of Fakaha is 36 km southwest on the road to Kanaroba. Most of the wall hangings you'll see everywhere in Korhogo come from there. As in Waraniéné, there's a cooperative, but bargaining is possible. **Katia**, 11 km further on, produces the same weavings.

Sinématiali
This pottery centre is 30 km due east on the paved road to Ferkéssédougou. Once a village of traditional round huts, it now has ugly modern structures with metallic roofs.

Places to Stay The only inexpensive hotel you'll find in the towns near Korhogo is *Hôtel Le Womadeli* in Sinématiali. It has 10 air-con rooms and a restaurant.

Kouto
This village, 129 km north-west of Korhogo, is a recently 'modernised' village like Sinematiali. You'll find blacksmiths, carvers and weavers, plus a 17th century mosque falling into ruin.

Kasoumbarga

On the way to Kouto stop in Kasoumbarga for a look at a highly unusual mosque dating from the 17th century. It is round with a thatched roof and there is a barely recognisable monastery next door. It's 14 km west of Korhogo down a small dirt road leading north off the paved highway.

Getting There & Away

To get to these villages, travellers with vehicles usually take a guide (they're everywhere), in part to keep from getting lost. If you're without a vehicle, the easiest way is to rent a taxi. CFA 12,000 to 15,000 for the day (or CFA 2000 to CFA 2500 by the hour) plus petrol is a fair price. If you negotiate a price that includes petrol, the driver will balk every time you make the slightest detour.

BOUNDIALA

The main attraction of this town, 152 km west of Korhogo, is the *Hôtel de Dala* (tel 820054). Quite a few travellers stay a night at this tourist-oriented hotel. Built and managed by the local village association, the Dala has 24 round, traditional-style huts with air-con. On Saturday nights, you can witness Senoufo dancing around a bonfire and baobab tree.

ODIENNE

If you're headed to Mali via this route, good luck. You'll find very few vehicles heading north. The daily bus south for Man leaves from the truck park in the morning whenever it fills up.

Places to Stay & Eat

Not far from the post office, *Le Campement* is quite clean, in good condition and costs about CFA 4000 with fan and CFA 5000 with air-con. For very cheap eats, try *La Bon Auberge* facing the Grand Marché. Odienne also has a two-star hotel with pool – the 30-room *Les Frontières* (tel 800405).

FERKÉSSÉDOUGOU

Ferkéssédougou is on the major road north from Abidjan to Mali and Burkina Faso. The bitumen road ends there and the road is fairly bad from Ferké to the border. The train for Abidjan and Ouagadougou passes by twice daily. You'll find nothing of interest; it is just a transit point to Korhogo and Comoé National Park.

Places to Stay & Eat

Ferké does have a surprisingly good hotel, the *l'Auberge de la Reserve* (tel 85) at the south end of town along the highway. It has a long pool, 35 air-con singles/doubles for CFA 7000/9000, and a good restaurant with a CFA 3800 full-course meal.

About four blocks behind the l'Auberge, you'll find *La Muraille*, with spotlessly clean rooms for CFA 4500 with air-con, CFA 3000 with fan, and CFA 2500 without private bath – a good buy but about three km from downtown. For a cheap hotel in the centre of town, try *Hôtel Koffikro*, two blocks behind the BICICI bank, about a km from the train station. Their rooms are decent and cost about CFA 3000 with fan and CFA 3500 with air-con.

For a dirt cheap hotel, try *La Gazelle*, 150 metres from the train station, or the similar *Hôtel Campement* next door. At CFA 1000 a room, it's hard to complain about the filthy conditions.

COMOÉ NATIONAL PARK

In the north-east corner of the country, 600 km from Abidjan, Comoé is one of the largest game parks in West Africa. Those who haven't been spoiled by the parks in East Africa usually find it interesting. There's an excellent chance of seeing both lions and elephants as well as wart hogs, green monkeys, hippos, waterbucks, kobs, roan and other species of antelope, and perhaps even a baboon. Leopards exist, but are rarely seen. Birds are not particularly abundant either. The park is open from late November to mid-May; the best viewing time is at the crack of dawn and late afternoon.

Places to Stay & Eat

The park has two equally good tourist hotels with pools. The *PLM Comoé* (Savana Tours, Abidjan tel 323842, telex 23328) is at the southern entrance in Gansé and *Comoé Safari Lodge* (Soaem, Abidjan tel 327525) is at the northern entrance. The cost for a small but clean room is about CFA 28,000 for two people with half board. The *Campement* in Kakpin, 15 km beyond the PLM, is much cheaper. It has 17 traditional huts with private bathrooms but no air-con for CFA 6000, and a thatched-roof bar/restaurant with plain food such as spaghetti and canned tomato sauce. At all three places you'll find guides, who will greatly increase your chances of seeing animals.

Getting There & Away

Getting to the park is time-consuming – about 10 and 12 hours driving time from Abidjan to the southern and northern entrances, respectively, the last three hours being over washboard road whichever entrance you take. The turn-off point is Katiola for the southern entrance and Ferkéssédougou for the northern entrance.

The alternative is to fly to Korhogo, where the tour operator will arrange for you to be driven to the Comoé Safari Lodge – roughly CFA 110,000 per person from Abidjan for a two-day package deal. Alternatively, you could take the train from Abidjan, and get a taxi from Ferké (about CFA 20,000) or hitchhike (fairly difficult).

KONG

For an interesting village on the way to Comoé, stop in Kong between Ferké and the park, 34 km south of the main road connecting the two. The Sudanese architecture, with flat-roofed buildings and 12th to 13th century mud-covered mosques with protruding wooden beams, is reminiscent of Mali.

The West

MAN

Nestled in lush green hills, an eight-hour drive north-west of Abidjan, Man has the most beautiful location of any inland city. Man itself is not particularly attractive, but the market is first-rate. You'll find a wide assortment of fabrics and wooden carvings on the top floor, some of high quality.

Another good place to pick up carvings is the artisan shop outside the Hôtel les Cascades. The blackened masks with big lips and slit or hollow eyeholes, are Dan; they're used to keep women from seeing the uncircumcised boys during their initiation into adulthood. The dark spoons which stand on two feet are also Dan. If you see some less naturalistic, fairly grotesque masks, they may be Guere.

The best time to be in Man is for La Fête des Masques, in November, during which you'll see more than 100 masks from neighbouring communities. The masks vary in importance; each village has several great masks which represent the memory of that village. Masks in this area play a particularly important role. They are not made simply to disguise the face during celebrations or to be looked upon as works of art. The mask is for ritual. It's a divinity, a depository of knowledge. It dictates the community values that protect society and guard its customs. No man ever undertakes any important actions without first addressing the mask to ask for its assistance. Whether the crops will be good or bad depends upon the mask, whether you will have a son or daughter depends on the mask. So the Africans here glorify it during times of happiness and abundance.

La Cascade

The number one attraction in Man is *La Cascade*, a waterfall in a superb bamboo forest five km west of town. You'll find a

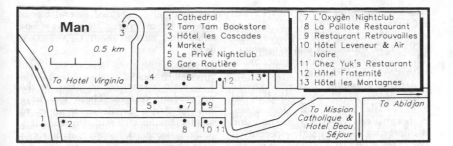

Man

0   0.5 km

To Hotel Virginia

1 Cathedral
2 Tam Tam Bookstore
3 Hôtel les Cascades
4 Market
5 Le Privé Nightclub
6 Gare Routière

7 L'Oxygèn Nightclub
8 La Paillote Restaurant
9 Restaurant Retrouvailles
10 Hôtel Leveneur & Air
   Ivoire
11 Chez Yuk's Restaurant
12 Hôtel Fraternité
13 Hôtel les Montagnes

To Mission
Catholique &
Hotel Beau
Séjour

To Abidjan

swinging bridge made of vines (*pont de lianes*) and a restaurant in the gorge. It's a touristy site even the locals frequent. At first glance, the bridge looks authentic but look again. It's French engineered with cables for support. You'll find the real thing in Gueoule, a village outside of Danane, an hour's drive south-west towards the Liberian border.

Hiking
For hikers, a major attraction is *La Dente de Man*, a steep tooth-shaped mountain 14 km north-east of town, considered to be the guardian angel of Man. Find a kid in Glongouin, the village below, to act as your guide. Without one, you're sure to lose the jungle path. I did even with a guide. The climb takes about an hour and gets fairly steep in places. A panoramic view on top awaits you if it's not the harmattan season. For a bigger challenge, try *Mt Tonkoui* (1225 metres) 20 km north-west of town, on the road leading to the waterfalls, or *Mt Nimba* (1752 metres) on the Liberian border via Danane.

Places to Stay – bottom end
For the price, you can't beat the *Mission Catholique*, which has a seminary on the western side of town. They frequently have rooms available even during the school season (October-June). The cost is only CFA 1300. The major drawback is the location – a 30-minute walk from the centre of town. For a hotel in town, try *Hôtel Fraternité* (tel 790689), which has a

restaurant with African dishes and rooms for about CFA 3000 (CFA 3500 with fan). On the same side of town (eastern entrance), a 10-minute walk from downtown, you'll find *Hôtel les Montagnes* (tel 790086). It has a restaurant with African specialities, a bar, a nightclub and a more active ambience but slightly inferior rooms. Rooms cost about CFA 2500 (CFA 3500 with fan and CFA 4500 with air-con). *Hôtel Virginia* is on the outskirts of town in the opposite direction and is not recommended.

Places to Stay – middle
For a good medium-priced hotel, head for *Hôtel Leveneur* (tel 790039), in the heart of town. It's highly recommended for the atmosphere and the price – clean rooms with air-con and private bathrooms for CFA 6000 to CFA 7000 and a pleasant restaurant with full course meals for CFA 3000. The street-side terrace is a good place to have a drink and meet people, and you're within easy walking distance of everything in town.

Places to Stay – top end
The two best hotels in town are the *Hôtel les Cascades* (tel 790251) on a hill overlooking the city, a 15-minute walk from downtown, and *Hôtel Beau-Séjour* (tel 790991) on the eastern outskirts of town, about three km from downtown. The only advantage of the Cascades is the location and the pool. Many travellers with vehicles prefer the Beau-Séjour,

which has bungalow rooms with TV and refrigerators for CFA 11,000 a room compared to CFA 14,000 at the Cascades (CFA 11,500 without TV and refrigerator). The Beau-Séjour also has ordinary rooms with air-con for CFA 5500.

Another possibility is the village-like PLM *Motel Les Lianes* (Abidjan tel 327503, telex 23328) in Gouessesso. Although it's not very lively, you may find it interesting for one night, especially if you're travelling 1st class and are not the adventurous sort. They charge CFA 18,000/26,500 for single/double bungalows with half board (obligatory). You'll find a hammock in front of each room and there's a pool, tennis court and Africans making crafts. However, it is closed from June to October.

You could also stay in Touba, 71 km north of Gouessesso. *Le Mehou* (tel 58) has 20-air-con rooms and a pool and is comparable to the best hotels in Man.

Places to Eat

The cheapest places are around the market. For superior African home cooking, head for *Tanty J'ai Faim* near the gare routière, where you can eat under a thatched-roof paillote. It's in Quartier Avocatier; you may need a guide to find it. Other places serving inexpensive African food are hotels Fraternité and les Montagnes and *Restaurant Retrouvailles*, a half block from the gare routière. For about CFA 900, you can get a full meal at all of them.

For European food, try the *Hôtel Leveneur* in the centre of town, *Chez Yuk's* next door, or *La Paillote* half a block away. All are quite good. At the Paillote, you eat outside under huts with straw roofs. Yuk's is a sidewalk café with a pleasant indoor dining room. The plat du jour at all of them is about CFA 1400; the full menu is double that.

Nightlife

The two most active nightclubs downtown are *L'Oxygén*, half a block from the Leveneur, and *Le Privé* several blocks away on the main drag. Both have strobe lights and charge about CFA 1200 a drink.

AROUND MAN

The main attraction of Man is the surrounding villages. Those who have been in Africa awhile often prefer to wander around on their own without a guide. Newcomers, however, are likely to meet fewer people and commit a serious faux pas without a guide. You'll find them around the hotels. Village elders and kids may expect small tips, so bring cigarettes and candy.

Some 13 km east of Man on the road to Fakobly, you'll come to **Tieni** and **Siabli**, on a cliff overlooking two verdant valleys. The chief has seen tourists before and knows what they want – a photo of him in his full regalia with his wives. The CFA 1000 tip must come first. Ask for his permission to hike through the area. Nine km further east you'll come to **Facobly**, where you should have no problem finding a pirogue for a trip on the water.

Travelling north of Man on the paved road to Touba, at km 44 you'll come to **Biankouma**, a village full of fetishes. Twelve houses may not be photographed, so ask before taking pictures. Look for the sage who makes the hats; he's quite a character. **Gouessesso** is five km to the west. There, in a cocoa farm, you'll find the PLM *Les Lianes*, an unusual tourist hotel constructed to look like an African village – unique in the Ivory Coast. It's well worth a look, perhaps even a swim in the pool. Four km away there's a bridge made of vines; you'll need a guide.

Further north on the road to Touba, you'll come to **Gouana**. Don't miss the enormous tree, its girth is larger than most African huts. **Niena** is up the road and famous for its mask dancers.

Zala, the last village before Touba, is the centre for the famous Yacouba stilt dancers, well publicised in tourist brochures. During the three to five years of training,

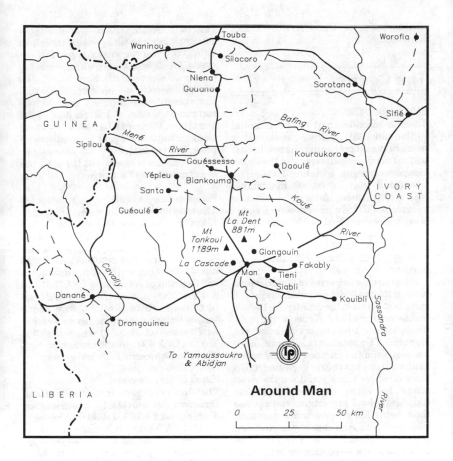

Around Man

0   25   50 km

To Yamoussoukro & Abidjan

the men must tell no one, not even their wives, what they're doing. Once initiated, they become empowered to communicate with the spirits who, in turn, direct their elaborate, acrobatic stunts, all to the sounds of chanting and drums – and the crowds' delight.

Many people say the dry season is the best time to visit. What they usually fail to mention, however, is the harmattan which greatly reduces visibility from early December through February or later, and completely spoils the magnificent moun-

tainous landscape. Unless you have no choice, don't come during the harmattan. November and March-April is the ideal time.

Gagnoa

Gagnoa lies halfway between Abidjan and Man. There's nothing of interest, but it is a convenient place to break the journey to Man. Gagnoa has a first-rate hotel, *Le Fromager* (tel 772036), with singles/doubles for CFA 9000/11,500 and a pool. For about CFA 2500, you can get a grubby double room at the *Hôtel Syndicate d'Initiative*.

The Centre

YAMOUSSOUKRO

Yamoussoukro became the official capital in the mid-1980s, but it's the capital in name only and probably will remain that way for many years. Starting in the 1960s, Houphouet began spending lavishly on this small town of 50,000 inhabitants which is (surprise, surprise) his native village. You'll find almost deserted, eight-lane highways lined with lights, and avenues that end right in the jungle. There's no city like it in Africa. This small version of Brasilia is definitely not bustling.

It has an amazing array of facilities for a town of its small size including one of the three best hotels in the country, an 18-hole tournament-quality golf course, the party headquarters, two modern colleges, the Houphouet Foundation (á la Rockefeller), a mosque and the president's huge home, with walls one km square enclosing it. On one side of his home you'll see the moat where he keeps the crocodiles that supposedly lend protection. You can see them being fed every afternoon around 4.30 to 5 pm. And don't miss the two colleges, INSET and INSTP. The government spared no expense in building them. If you ask at the gate, the student guards will give you a guided tour. Even compared to schools in the west, the architecture is outstanding.

Because the city is so spread out, the easiest way to see it is to rent a taxi, about CFA 2500 an hour. Otherwise, you'll be doing a lot of walking.

Places to Stay – bottom end

For a dirt cheap hotel, try *Hôtel Waka Waka* on the street behind the Houphouet-Boigny Foundation. Their bare minimum rooms go for CFA 2000. Still, it's better than

Hôtel de la Paix on the main drag near the Shell station; the filthy rooms there cost CFA 1300. You get what you pay for.

At CFA 4500 for a room with air-con, big beds and showers, it's hard to beat *Le Cameo* opposite the mosque. You'll find the woman owner friendly and the bar-restaurant under a big paillote quite attractive. Rooms at *Le Bélier*, two long blocks away, are equal in quality and price, but the location is less convenient, the restaurant is closed and the hotel has the atmosphere of a morgue.

Places to Stay – middle

The nicest of the medium-priced hotels is *Hôtel la Residence* (tel 640004). They charge about CFA 9000/11,000 for rooms with TV. On the main drag, you'll find three less expensive hotels. The French-run *Motel Agip* (tel 640040) downtown has decent rooms for about CFA 7500 and a CFA 3800 menu. *Motel Shell* (tel 640024) has rooms for CFA 6500 and a simple French restaurant. Even better is *Le Paysan* (tel 64 0031) where the CFA 7500 to CFA 9500 rooms are a good buy. The hotel's pizzeria isn't bad either.

Places to Stay – top end

The town's finest is Sofitel's *Hôtel President* (tel 640158/81), where singles/doubles cost CFA 27,000/30,000, but only about CFA 19,000/21,500 if you ask in advance for their golfers weekend special. Technically, you're supposed to be a member of the golf club in Abidjan, but they don't enforce this. You'll only get this special rate if you reserve in advance and ask for it. If you play golf, you'll have to pay a green fee of CFA 10,000. The President also has a pool, movie theatre, tennis and squash courts, sauna, a disco (lively on Saturday nights only), and a spectacular restaurant on the 11th floor overlooking the city – a great place to have a drink if it is too expensive to dine.

Places to Eat

One of the more popular restaurants is

Tout Va Bien, a French-run open-air restaurant with friendly service. Another is *Restaurant Ty Breiz*, a creperie that also uses paillotes for dining outside. The menu is small but the cost is moderate and the ambience is pleasant. It is opposite the Tropicana hotel and behind the SIB bank; look for the sign on the main drag.

Nightlife

One of the best nightclubs in town is *Klin Kpli*, a fancy nightclub with almost all African clientele. The cover is CFA 2000 and it's active weekends only. The young French all go to *La Paillote*, which has a similar cover and almost no African clientele. The *Kokou* at the Hôtel President is crowded on Saturday night; the other nights it's usually fairly dead. The common man's nightclub is *Marco Polo Club* one block behind the Texaco station.

BOUAKÉ

In the heart of Baoulé country, Bouaké is big, with about half a million inhabitants, but it's not a particularly interesting city and there's nothing of interest other than the market.

Places to Stay - bottom end

For rock bottom prices, try *Hôtel Bakary* 200 metres behind the RAN station. Rooms there cost about CFA 2600 and are pretty basic but quite acceptable. If it's full, try the inferior *Hôtel de la Gare* 300 metres away. They charge about CFA 2200 for a room (CFA 500 more with fan).

Places to Stay - middle

The *Hôtel de l'Air* (tel 632815) is excellent and highly recommended. It has a French restaurant and is a superb buy for the money – about CFA 8000 for an excellent room. The only drawback is the location, about five km from the heart of town. The French-run *Hôtel le Provincal* has one of the best restaurants and most popular terrace bars in town. It is directly opposite the RAN station. Singles/doubles there cost about CFA 7000/9500 and are

frequently full. For another no-frills hotel near the centre of town, try *Hôtel du Centre* (tel 633278), which has singles/doubles for CFA 8000/9500, a bar, nightclub and a medium priced restaurant. *Hôtel Ville Nord*, several long blocks from the RAN station, is a better buy at CFA 7000 for a decent room with TV.

Places to Stay - top end

The two best hotels are *Hôtel Harmattan* (tel 633195, telex 2493) a km from the centre of town and the *RAN Hôtel* (tel 632016) next to the train station. The Harmattan has a pool, tennis court, nightclub, shops, a French restaurant and rooms for about CFA 15,000. Singles/doubles at the newer RAN Hôtel cost about CFA 15,200/17,500. It has a long pool and a very popular bar with orchestra, the *Nivagueen*.

Places to Eat

Restaurant du Sahel, three blocks from the Hôtel du Centre, is very popular and a cut above the other maquis. It has about 10 selections but costs no more than an ordinary maquis. Several blocks from Hôtel du Centre is another maquis, *Walé*, and *Les 3S*, a popular Lebanese restaurant with shawarma sandwiches, chicken and other Lebanese fare. Both are across the street from *Savannah*, probably the most popular nightclub in town. The cover charge there is about CFA 2000. *Club 6* is also lively and not far away.

For foreign cuisine, in addition to the Provincal, try *Tien-Long* (tel 633722), a Chinese restaurant that's highly recommended for its reasonable prices. Most selections are in the CFA 1300 to CFA 2200 range. It's two long blocks from the RAN station and open every day. Another is the small *Le Calao*, an expensive French restaurant two blocks from the RAN station and closed Sunday.

Getting There & Away

The train passes by about three times a day in both directions. The fastest and most comfortable way to travel to Abidjan, however, is by one of the big luxury buses, which you'll find at the huge market. The last one for Abidjan leaves at 10 pm.

KATIOLA

An hour's drive north of Bouaké, Katiola's main attraction is the huge pottery shop on the eastern outskirts of town. The main hotel is the modern 50-room *Hôtel Hambol* (tel 654432/357331), with 50 modern rooms for about CFA 9500, a pool and a nightclub. For a cheaper hotel, try *Hôtel de l'Amitié* (tel 654363).

Liberia

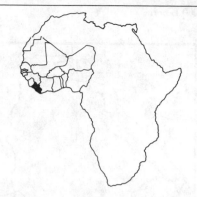

Liberia gets bad press these days. You may hear that there is nothing of interest to see or do in Liberia, that it rains all the time, and that there are blackouts almost daily in Monrovia. Only the last point is entirely true.

Liberia has some beautiful old houses built during the first part of the 19th century which resemble the old mansions in the southern USA. In the north, the hills reach up to 1000 metres and more, providing a refreshing climate for hiking and weekend excursions. Liberia also has its fair share of prized masks and other wooden carvings as well as some of the best basket weavers in West Africa. If it's adventure in the tropical forests you're seeking, there's nothing to beat travel in upcountry Liberia. You may have your first taste of bush rat, see an adolescent's initiation rite, or wander upon a pygmy hippo, which is about the size of a pig and unique to Liberia and western Ivory Coast.

Still, Liberia is relatively small and suffers in comparison to many other African countries in terms of markets, traditions, music, clothing and facilities for travellers, especially those going upcountry. It is very wet from May through October and gets about 4650 mm of rainfall a year. What makes Liberia special is the people. Many foreigners find Liberians easier to meet than other Africans, which may be a reflection of their historical ties with the States. Liberians are known for their zest for living and sense of humour, plus the food and the Club beer are unsurpassed in West Africa. So maybe it's not surprising that Liberia produces a wide spectrum of opinions, from 'It's a screwed up country with no traditions and nothing of interest to see' to 'I never had a better time in Africa'.

HISTORY

Liberia is unique. It is one of only two African countries (the other being Ethiopia) that did not suffer from the yolk of colonialism. It has the freest press in West Africa, opposition political parties, the largest commercial fleet of ships in the world (almost all foreign-owned), and the wettest capital city in Africa. Since 1980, it has achieved another distinction – the worst economic nose dive in Africa.

Before 1822, when the first group of black American settlers arrived, only a few Africans lived in the area because the tropical forests covering almost the entire country were simply too inhospitable. Consequently, no great civilisations developed. The settlement of Liberia was sponsored by the American Colonization Society (ACS), which was supported by James Madison and Thomas Jefferson. The project made strange bedfellows – white supporters wishing to correct the injustices done to blacks joined with whites who just wanted to get rid of the blacks. The Congress enacted legislation designating the ACS as the custodian of Africans who had been rescued by slave-patrolling ships. President Monroe couldn't give direct financial aid because of the controversy surrounding the society, so instead, he interpreted this legislation rather imaginatively to justify funding a 'transit camp' in Africa for these recaptives.

In 1820, two ships with free American

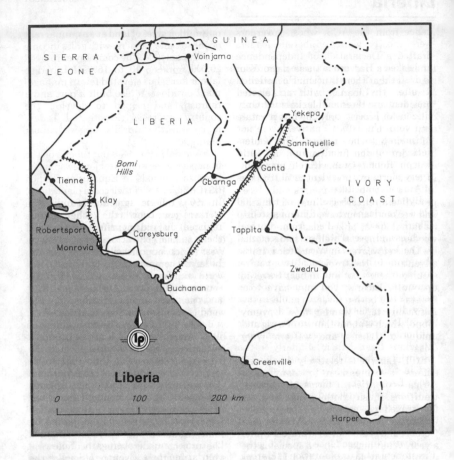

Liberia

0   100   200 km

blacks arrived in Sierra Leone but disease killed so many that the expedition failed. A year later, another ship arrived. The expedition leaders negotiated with the Bassa chiefs for a strip of land stretching 100 km along the coast in present day Liberia. The price tag came to about US$300 in beads, tobacco, cloth, rum and gunpowder. In early 1822, they proceeded down the coast and took possession of Providence Island, a tiny island between what is now downtown Monrovia and the port. Fever and attacks by hostile Africans

decimated the original group and many others returned to the USA. Nonetheless, they managed, in part with the assistance of the US Navy, and within two years had enacted a constitution.

Independence

The success of the venture prompted several colonisation societies in several states to sponsor similar settlements at Harper and Greenville. They quarrelled amongst themselves but eventually merged. By 1846, they wanted independence from the ACS, whose governors were mostly whites. Liberian leaders drafted a Declaration of Independence and asked a Harvard law school professor to draft them a constitution. He modelled it after the USA's, with an elected president and bicameral legislature. Only citizens of Liberia could own real estate and vote. Until 1904, 'natives' were not considered to be citizens. The leaders declared independence in 1847 and Joseph Roberts was elected president. Every successive president until 1980 was of American ancestry.

By the mid-19th century, of the 5000 black Americans who had immigrated to Liberia, 2000 had died from tropical diseases and several hundred had returned to the USA. The Americo-Liberians, as they came to be known, constituted only a tiny fraction of the total population. The colonising societies had intended for the settlers to 'civilise' the natives but in fact they did very little except to dominate them. It's ironic that in imposing their authority over the natives, the Americo-Liberians treated them similarly to the way whites treated blacks worldwide.

The Masonic Order, established in 1851, became the symbol of Americo-Liberian solidarity and many political issues were discussed and decided upon in the lodges. Five presidents, starting with Roberts, were grand masters.

Between independence and 1926 when Firestone started its plantation at Harbel, Liberia floundered politically and economically, losing 40% of its territory to the British and French during the scramble for colonies in the late 1800s. Economically, Liberia was in sad shape. Her primary exports, coffee and palm oil, were no longer attractive on the world market. Nearly everything, including food, was imported.

Firestone Era
Looking around the globe for a cheaper source of rubber, Firestone ended up with a real coup in Liberia in 1926. It secured one million acres of land at an annual rent of only 6 cents per acre, with gross income taxed at only 1%. The company employed 20,000 workers, 10 to 15% of Liberia's labour force, but elevated few to management positions. It also built a port and a railroad, and helped to develop the country's hydroelectric potential. Today, it is still the world's largest rubber plantation.

A scandal in the 1930s put Liberia on the front page of the world's major newspapers. Spanish colonials in Equatorial Guinea needed labourers for their cocoa plantations. In 1905, Liberia agreed to supply the workers on contract. Village chiefs rounded up young men and supplied them to the contractors; the labourers received no salary until they returned to Liberia. The League of Nations published a scathing report equating the system to slavery and implicating both the president and vice-president of Liberia as part of the syndicate of Americo-Liberians receiving a cut in the lucrative venture. Liberia's 'Watergate' ended with both the president and vice-president resigning.

WW II solidified Liberian-American relations. The USA built air bases and black Africa's first truly international airport at Robertsfield, next to Firestone. About 5000 black American troops were stationed in Liberia during the war and anti-submarine patrols were flown by sea planes based at Lake Piso, near Robertsport. Roosevelt even landed there. Even the US dollar was made official currency. Today, a Voice of America transmitter near Monrovia, a satellite tracking station, as well as military and private investment, motivate the US to maintain good relations.

The Era of Prosperity & the Coup
For 20 years following the war Liberia sustained the highest growth rate in black Africa, raising per capita incomes to the highest in West Africa by the early 1960s. Twenty-four American companies joined Firestone in making major investments in Liberia and the total amount rose to

US$800 million. Much of the credit went to Liberia's most famous president, William Tubman, president for 27 years and the 'Maker of Modern Liberia'. Nonetheless, the road network was primitive and until 1945 it was not possible to travel from Monravia to Liberia's three neighbouring countries. Only in 1967-68 were Robertsport, Greenville and Harper, all major towns on the coast, connected by road to Monrovia.

The big news of the 1960s was the establishment of iron ore mining operations in the north near Yekepa by Lamco (the Liberian American Swedish Minerals Company). Yekepa grew from next to nothing to over 20,000 people. The company became the largest private enterprise in Black Africa, and built a railroad from Yekepa to Buchanan as well as a port in Buchanan. Today, Lamco accounts for about half of Liberia's annual iron ore output; Bong Mining Company, 70 km north of Monrovia, is number two. By the early 1980s, the Lamco ore deposit under exploitation was nearing depletion. Production fell and employees were fired. Still, Liberia remained the largest iron ore producer in Africa.

Liberia's economic boom came to an end in the mid-1970s after Tolbert took over from Tubman. While he initiated a series of reforms, the upper levels of government continued to be controlled by about a dozen, related Americo-Liberians. Tolbert's brother, brother-in-law and son-in-law were all senators as well as prominent businessmen. Corruption continued unabated. Official vehicles became, in essence, private vehicles and contractors had to pay kickbacks to various levels of government not only to win contracts but just to get paid. The governing Americo-Liberians used the money to enrich themselves and buy loyalty. Extravagant public works projects increased the budget deficit enormously.

The rice riots in early 1979 were an ominous event. For decades, the government had subsidised rice prices to appease city dwellers. This policy made rice growing unprofitable and brought thousands of people into Monrovia looking for work. Monrovia had grown from a sleepy town of 12,000 in 1940 to around 250,000 by 1980. Strapped for money, the government decided to raise rice prices by about 20%. The Tolbert family, with large-scale rice farms, stood to profit handsomely. The people rioted and the government closed the university and suspended due process.

In April 1980, a small group of non-commissioned offers led by Samuel Doe staged a successful coup and killed Tolbert. For the first time Liberia had a chief-of-state who wasn't an Americo-Liberian, giving the indigenous population their first taste of political power, and their first opportunity for vengeance. Doe shocked the world by ordering 13 people, including ex-ministers, to be executed by firing squad on a public beach before TV cameras.

Today

Liberia is going down the tube, and Doe seems to be doing little to halt it. Having lost roughly 25% of its per capita income between 1980 and early 1987, Liberia recorded the worst economic performance in Africa in the 1980s (although incomes remained significantly above those in most Sahelian countries). Unemployment in Monrovia exceeds 50%. Blackouts are now so frequent that only hotels with their own generators usually have electricity. Bankrupt and no longer able to repay its debts, the government reduced salaries by a full 25%. By the mid-1980s, the World Bank and the IMF had halted their lending programs. The only significant donor remaining was the US, which gave more aid per capita to Liberia from 1980 to 1986 than to any other African country – over US$432 million since Doe came to power. Corruption continues at the same level as during the Tubman-Tolbert years, only now the government can't afford it.

If the economy collapses, no one will be

surprised. Doe's government is bankrupt and doing little to initiate reform. In desperation, Doe agreed in 1987 to accept 17 Americans to work at the highest levels in various ministries in an effort to curb corruption. The US dollar remains official currency, but you won't see US dollars anywhere. They are immediately hoarded whenever tourists hand them over. They have become so scarce that since 1985, Liberian dollar coins and US greenbacks no longer exchange at par on the local market. Merchants offer discounts to those paying with US dollars. Hotel owners' eyes light up when they see travellers paying with 'real' dollars.

Food production is mysteriously on the increase, suggesting that people may be heading back to the farms. Even though Bethlehem Steel threw in the towel and sold its 25% interest in LAMCO, most American companies are sticking it out. Their investments in Liberia (approximately US$500 million) still represent about half of the total foreign investment. Firestone, with about 10,000 workers, remains the largest employer.

As promised, Doe held elections in late 1985. The political parties of Doe's two major opponents were declared ineligible. One party put up Jackson Doe, a political unknown, and political spectators surmised that it was a silly attempt to confuse the voters. Still, according to BBC reporters, Jackson won. The government, however, declared Samuel Doe the winner. An unsuccessful coup attempt followed. Doe jailed key opposition political leaders, then released them after tremendous pressure from the US Congress. With US backing, he remains in power.

PEOPLE
Ethnic groups in Liberia have not put a stamp on the country as they have in other African countries. None of them clearly dominates numerically. The Kpelle and the Bassa are the most numerous, with 19% and 15% of the population, respectively; the seafaring Kru and the Vai are also well known. There's been too much inter-marriage for any of these tribes to be culturally homogeneous or united into a single political unit. The Americo-Liberians have received the most attention because of their political and economic dominance, but they account for less than 3% of the population. Some 5000 or so Lebanese traders seem to own half the shops in Monrovia, but Indians now vie with them for control of the retail trade, very little of which is run by Liberians. The disproportionate share of economic power in the hands of the Lebanese and Indians causes considerable resentment.

Adherents of non-indigenous religions constitute roughly half the population and are split fairly evenly between Christians and Muslims. The settlers were primarily Baptists and Methodists but they did little missionary work among the indigenous peoples, leaving that to foreigners. Even within a given denomination, the Americo-Liberian and indigenous congregations did not mix and had separate churches. Membership in a recognised church was relevant to social position. Before the coup, some church leaders charged that the typical Americo-Liberian tended to regard the church as if it was a club. Politics and religion were closely inter-meshed and if a person lost political office, he was likely to lose his church office as well. The 1980 coup broke, perhaps forever, this tie between the church and politics.

Secret Societies
The Poro and the Sande secret societies, centred primarily in the north-west, are fascinating. The Poro are for men, the Sande for women. Non-members cannot attend their meetings and rituals, and decisions are often executed in secrecy. Each has rites and ceremonies whose purpose is to educate young people in the customs of the tribe, preserve the group's folklore, skills and crafts, and instil discipline. Their contribution in preserving traditional ways has been significant.

Membership is not restricted to a

particular ethnic group and, in principal, everyone in the community should be initiated. Traditionally, the uninitiated couldn't engage in all the political and ritual activities of their particular tribe. The initiations, which used to involve as much as four years of training, now usually less, take place when the children approach puberty. The initiates are easily recognised by their white painted faces and bodies and their shaved heads but what they actually do is anybody's guess. These societies are very hierarchical. The most extreme example are the Poro among the Vai, which traditionally had 99 levels. Lower ranking members cannot acquire the esoteric knowledge of higher ranking members or attend their secret meetings. Ascending in the ranks depends on birth (the leadership is frequently restricted to certain families), seniority, and the ability to learn the societies' beliefs and rituals.

The role of these societies has traditionally gone beyond religion and the education of the young. They control the activities of indigenous medical practitioners, and they often judge disputes between members of high-ranking families. A village chief who doesn't have the support of the Poro on important decisions can expect trouble enforcing them. They may even punish people for such things as theft, incest and murder, sometimes by execution. Today, while secret societies are still fairly important among some tribes, modern customs and institutions are undermining them.

GEOGRAPHY
Rain forests are everywhere and cover about three-quarters of the country. With only 2.3 million inhabitants in an area the size of New York state, Liberia hasn't had to worry so far about the forests being wiped out. In the far north around Yekepa, you'll find the huge Lamco iron ore operations and the Nimba mountains, reaching up to 1752 metres. Rivers are also everywhere. Eleven major ones empty into the Atlantic Ocean, the biggest being the St Paul which passes through Monrovia. The water flow on the St Paul can be tremendous, on occasion exceeding 1,000,000 litres per second in August – more than twice the normal flow of the Colorado River in the Grand Canyon.

Marshes, creeks and tidal lagoons intersect the narrow coastal plain, with five major towns dotting the coast: Harper, Greenville, Buchanan, Monrovia and Robertsport. Only the last three are connected by a coastal road. To get to the others, you must fly or travel several hundred km inland. Sarpo National Park, which is also in eastern Liberia and incorporates some of the best primal rain forests in Africa, presents the same logistical problem.

CLIMATE
Liberia is in the heart of the tropics and Monrovia, on the coast, is one of the two wettest capital cities in Africa (Freetown, Sierra Leone is the other). Monrovia averages 2.5 mm (one inch) of rain a day during the six-month rainy season, May to October. Inland, the average rainfall drops to about half this. The best time to visit is obviously in the dry season. The temperature never gets over 33°C in Monrovia; inland it gets a little hotter, but not much.

VISAS
Only Nigerians are not required to get visas to Liberia. If you transit within 48 hours and have an onward ticket, no visa is required and you'll be given a transit visa at the airport. If you stay more than 15 days, you must report to the immigration office, downtown on Broad Street. You'll need two photos. In Monrovia, you can get visas to all neighbouring countries except Mali. Visas for the Ivory Coast cost US$20 and Ghanaian visas cost US$12.50 and take one day to issue. The French Embassy issues visas to Togo and Burkina Faso.

Diplomatic Missions Abroad

Abidjan, Accra, Addis Ababa, Berlin, Berne, Bonn, Brussels, Conakry, Freetown, The Hague, Kinshasa, Lagos, London, Nairobi, Paris, Rome, Stockholm, Tokyo, Washington, Yaounde'.

MONEY

The US dollar and the Liberian dollar (all in coins) are both legal currency. Their official value is identical, but not on the street where you'll get $1.50 in Liberian coins for US$1. You can exchange the two at whatever rate you can get since they're both legal tender. In stores, you can sometimes negotiate a lower price if you agree to pay in US currency. The money situation is deteriorating constantly. It is difficult to find small coins and the new five dollar coin isn't helping matters any. Don't be surprised if the government takes the country off the US dollar standard; in practice, it has long since happened.

Banking hours: Monday through Thursday 8 am to 12 noon, Friday 8 am to 2 pm. Banks: Citibank (Ashmun St, tel 221329), Bank of Liberia, International Trust Co of Liberia. Citibank charges about US$5 per transaction for cashing travellers' cheques other than its own, so don't change small amounts.

LANGUAGE

English is the official language, and everybody speaks it. Speaking Liberian English is a blast and the following will help you get started:

Dash	Bribe
Hard to spend	Stingy
Sweet	Delicious (sweet soup)
Weak	Lazy
His speed is cold	Not popular with the girls
To run speed on a girl	Ask for a date (We got high speed on that girl)
Waste	Discard (waste the milk)
Eat money	Embezzle

GENERAL INFORMATION

Health

A cholera vaccination is required as is yellow fever if you're travelling within six days from an infected area. The best hospital in Monrovia for emergencies is Elwa Hospital (tel 271512) in Paynesville. As for doctors, Dr Befus and Dr Frank Young, both at Elwa Hospital, are recommended by some people. Two of the best pharmacies in Monrovia are the American Drug Store on Benson St, and Sitaram Pharmacy on Randall St.

Security

Downtown Monrovia is full of pickpockets, especially at night. So it is important to avoid wearing jewellery and watches and carrying important documents. It is rare to see a foreigner walking along the streets at night and those who don't have cars invariably use taxis. Even when there's electricity street lighting is practically non-existent except on Broad Street which, along with the appropriately named Gurley Street, at least seems safer because they are the most popular areas at night. Elsewhere in Liberia, security is not a significant problem.

The major problem travelling in Liberia these days is the police. They love to hassle travellers and try to extract bribes. One traveller was told by border officials that because he didn't have a photo permit for his camera, he would have to pay US$1500 in fines or return to Monrovia to face trial. When the distraught traveller broke down and cried, they screamed that it was a trick. In the end, he got away with giving them a packet of chewing gum, a flourescent marker pen and US$1.

Business Hours

Business: weekdays 8 am to 12 noon and 2 to 4 pm; Saturday 8 am to 12 noon. Government: weekdays 8 am to 12 noon and 1 to 4 pm.

Public Holidays
1 January, 11 February, Decoration Day
(2nd Wednesday in March), 15 March,
Easter Friday, 11-12 April, 14 May, 26
July, 24 August, Liberian Thanksgiving
Day (first Thursday in November), 29
November, 25 December.

Photography
A photo permit is required. In Monrovia,
the police will definitely question you if
you are seen taking photographs. If you
don't have a permit, expect to be escorted
immediately to headquarters. Permits are
issued by the Ministry of Culture and
Tourism on 14th St in the Sinkor district
of Monrovia. The permit takes one day,
and you can only photograph what you
specify in the request.

Time, Post, Phone & Telex
When it's noon in Liberia, it's noon in
London and 7 am in New York (8 am
during daylight savings time). The post is
fairly reliable. Calls to other African
capitals are a problem because the lines
are often down. Calling Europe and the
States is easier. For telexes, try the post
office or the Ducor Palace Hotel.

GETTING THERE
Air
Pam Am no longer offers service from New
York. You'll have to take Nigeria Airways,
Air Afrique (transferring in Dakar or
Abidjan) or go via Europe. There are
direct flights from London, Brussels,
Geneva and Amsterdam. The cheapest
flight is with Aeroflot on a ticket
purchased from a London bucket shop.

Car
The road north from Monrovia to Ganta is
paved and in excellent condition, as is the
road east from Monrovia to Buchanan.
But there is no road east of Buchanan to
the border, so the best route from the Ivory
Coast is the road via Man (Ivory Coast),
Sanniquellie and Ganta. Monrovia-
Abidjan is asphalted for all but the 250-km

stretch between Man and Ganta, which is
a well-maintained, all-weather dirt
road.

Your other option is to travel along the
coast of the Ivory Coast until Harper, and
then north from Harper to Ganta via
Zwedru. This route is much more
difficult. You will almost certainly get
stuck on the Harper-Zwedru section in
the heavy rainy season from June to
October. The coastal road from Monrovia
to the Sierra Leone border is being paved
but the onward section in Sierra Leone is
nearly impassable from July to October.

To get to Guinea, you can travel on the
coastal route via Sierra Leone, or westward from Gbarnga to the Guinea border.
This latter stretch can be passed during
the wet season, but the driving is slow.
Driving times: Monrovia-Man (10 hours),
Monrovia-Ganta-Harper (15 hours, much
longer during the wet season), Monrovia-
Gueckedou (11 hours), Monrovia-Yekepa
(six hours), Monrovia-Sierra Leone
border (three hours).

Bush Taxi
Bush Taxis are the principal means for
getting to Liberia from the Ivory Coast,
Sierra Leone and Liberia. The routes are
outlined in the preceding Car section.
From the Ivory Coast border you'll have to
change in Sanniquellie and Ganta.

GETTING AROUND
Air
For flights to the interior towns, Air
Liberia is back in business but is not
recommended unless you hear that it has
improved significantly. On the other
hand, Weasua Airlines, a charter company,
is reliable.

Bush Taxi
Cars are by far the most common kind of
bush taxi but there are also pickup trucks
converted into cabs and a few buses. They
can be found near the centre of town next
to the bridge. Bush taxis going north and
towards Buchanan are plentiful and there

Top: Kolon Sorgho harvest, Mali (JJ)
Bottom left: Fixing hair, Mali (JJ)

Top: The famous mosque at Djenné, Mali (AV)
Bottom: *Togu Na* with altar, Dogon village, Mali (EE)

are also several every day from Monrovia to Robertsport and the Sierra Leone border. Heading towards Man, you'll find no taxis going to the border; you'll have to change in Ganta.

The frequent road blocks are annoying and the soldiers are often looking for a bribe. Travellers have been charged US$2 for having their bags searched.

Train
The Yekepa-Buchanan train no longer takes passengers.

Bus
Buses are almost non-existent except for minibuses.

Monrovia

Chances are you'll hear some uncomplimentary things about Monrovia. It is bad enough that it is one of the rainiest capital cities in the world but as well there are the frequent blackouts which can make nighttime a drag, the shabby condition of most buildings, the lack of any interesting stores, and the dearth of artisan goods for sale. No wonder many travellers are inclined to strike Monrovia off their list of places to visit.

But if you've come to see and experience the real Africa, Monrovia with 350,000 inhabitants is certainly that. If you like places with a seedy character don't cross Monrovia off your list. Throughout the older part of town, especially between Broad Street and the water, there are three-storey mansions like those in Gone With The Wind and all seem to be inhabited by four or five families. The houses have broken window panes, shutters falling off, rusty tin rooves, paint (what little there is) peeling off and clothes strung out everywhere, but if you look carefully you'll see that many of them have doorways and columns as fine as those in the southern USA.

Then walk into several stores downtown. Even if you don't find anything interesting, you'll at least appreciate why there's friction between the Liberians and the Lebanese/Indians – the latter practically run the city.

Information
Embassies France (Box 279, telex 4360); West Germany (Box 34, tel 226460, telex 4230); Italy (Box 255, telex 4438); Japan (Box 2053, tel 221227, telex 4209); Sweden (Box 335, telex 4255); Switzerland (Box 283, tel 261065, telex 4559); UK (Box 120, tel 221055); USA (Box 98, tel 222991/2/3).

Other embassies include: Algeria, Cameroon, Egypt, Ethiopia, Ghana, Guinea, Israel, Ivory Coast, Nigeria, Sierra Leone, Spain, Zaire. Consulates: Netherlands, Norway.

Bookstores & Supermarkets *Captan's* at Broad and Randall, and *National Bookstore* nearby at Carey and Mechlin, are unquestionably the best. They offer English novels, books on Liberia, magazines of all sorts, maps of Liberia, etc, including one of the most entertaining novels by a Liberian on Liberia, *Red Dust on the Green Leaves*. *Saranna's News Stand* downtown on Randall St stocks *Time*, *Newsweek* and the *International Herald Tribune*, as does the Pan-African Plaza on Tubman Boulevard. The Ducor Palace Hotel bookstore has a fair selection of English novels.

For supermarkets, the best are *Choitram's* supermarkets. There are several, including two downtown (one at the corner of Carey and Gurley, and one on Randall St) as well as one on Tubman Boulevard in Sinkor.

Travel Agencies Morgan Travel Agency (tel 223586) 70 Ashmun St, is the American Express representative, and Brasilia Travel Agency (tel 222378) Broad St.

Waterside Market

This downtown market is not to be missed. It's a hub of activity if not a storehouse of interesting artisan goods. At night the adventurous will take a stroll on the appropriately named Gurley Street, lined with 10 or 12 dives that offer Club beer, women and song every night until the sun comes up.

Masonic Temple

Now in ruins and inhabited by squatters, the Masonic Temple was Monrovia's major landmark until the 1980 coup. Since most of the Masons were Americo-Liberian descendants of the original settlers, the Temple was the most prominent symbol of the previous regimes. It was vandalised after the coup, when the Masonic Order was banned. Photographs are not allowed.

Museum

A new museum downtown was under construction and is scheduled to open soon.

Zoo

Somewhat unique is the privately owned zoo, the only one in Africa where you can see a dwarf pygmy hippo. It's about a 15-minute drive from downtown near the old airport; all the cabbies know where it is.

Providence Island

This is where the first expedition of freed American slaves landed. It is between the centre of town and the port. It's now a cultural park where you can see traditional dancing, concerts and special programs. Even if there's no performance, it's worth a trip as there may be groups practising.

Places to Stay – bottom end

Prices qouted here do not include the 10% government tax.

The YMCA (Box 147, tel 221520), downtown at 12 Broad St, is the cheapest place in town at US$6 a bed, but you have to go through bureaucratic hassles to one. Rooms are not available at the YWCA. A better buy for the money is the United Methodist Church in Sinkor at 12th St, next to the beach. They charge US$7.50 a bed, in a single or double room. You can wash your clothes there too. For US$15 a room, you can stay at the Lutheran Mission two blocks down at 14th St, next to the beach. The staff are friendly and the baths have hot water.

The hotels charge a lot more for a lot less. The Nevada, in the heart of town on Gurley St, and Maxim Hotel (tel 222252) nearby both have singles/doubles with aircon for US$15/22. Florida Motel (tel 221690), downtown on Front St, has aircon rooms for US$14.

Places to Stay – middle

For the price, US$22/33 for singles/doubles, the Ambassador (tel 223147) is the best buy. It has completely renovated wood-panelled rooms, a salt water pool and a fairly good restaurant. However, the hotel is dead, and at night the area is too dark and unsafe for walking anywhere. It's next to the ocean on UN Drive near the British embassy, a 10 to 15 minute walk from downtown.

The best of the medium-priced hotels is El Meson (tel 222154) with singles/doubles at US$31/42. This is the second best hotel downtown, and although it's not glamorous, many people prefer to stay here than at the top end, poorly managed Ducor. Downtown on lively Carey St, near Randall St, El Meson is well managed with a generator, a lively bar and one of the best restaurants in town. It's also usually full, so make a reservation.

Julia's (tel 222532) has singles for US$23 to US$34 and doubles for US$28 to US$40. It is comparable to El Meson and the Ambassador and has a popular tranquil bar and a good restaurant when there's electricity, but because it doesn't have a generator it isn't recommended. There are frequent blackouts in Monrovia, so your night may be candle-lit. It's a block from El Meson on lively Gurley St.

Avoid the Carlton Hotel (tel 221245,

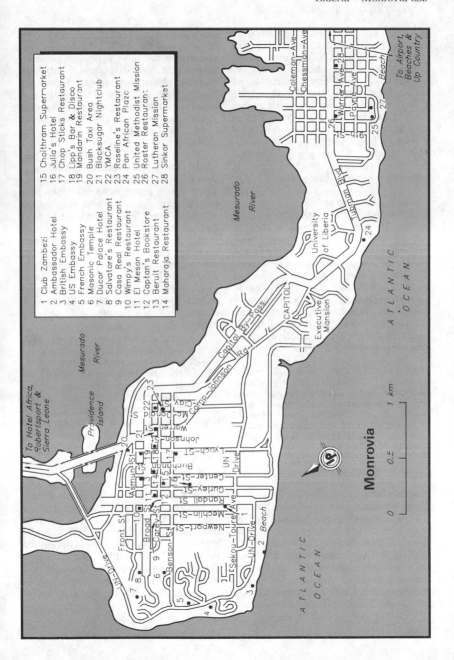

Monrovia

1 Club Zambezi
2 Ambassador Hotel
3 British Embassy
4 US Embassy
5 French Embassy
6 Masonic Temple
7 Ducor Palace Hotel
8 Salvatore's Restaurant
9 Casa Real Restaurant
10 Wimpy's Restaurant
11 El Meson Hotel
12 Captain's Bookstore
13 Beruit Restaurant
14 Maharaja Restaurant
15 Choithram Supermarket
16 Julia's Hotel
17 Chop Sticks Restaurant
18 Lipp's Bar & Disco
19 Mandarin Restaurant
20 Bush Taxi Area
21 Blacksugar Nightclub
22 YMCA
23 Roseline's Restaurant
24 Pan African Plaza
25 United Methodist Mission
26 Roster Restauran-
27 Lutheran Mission
28 Sinkor Supermarket

To Hotel Africa,
Robertsport &
Sierra Leone

Providence Island

Mesurado River

Mesurado River

University of Liberia

CAPITOL

Executive Mansion

To Airport,
Beaches &
Up Country

Tubman Blvd

Coleman Ave
Chessman Ave
Warner Ave
Payne Ave

Beach

ATLANTIC OCEAN

ATLANTIC OCEAN

Beach

Capitol By-Pass Rd

Camp-Johnson Rd

Front St
Broad St
Benson St
Carey St
Ashmun St

Randall St
Mechlin St
Newport St
Gurley Ave
Center St
Buchanan St
Lynch St
Warren St
McDonald St
Clay St
Johnson St

Sekou-Toure Ave
UN Drive

UN Drive

0   0.5   1 km

cards AE, MC) on Broad St. At US$28/38, it's way overpriced and it's amazing that anyone goes there other than those looking for young prostitutes.

Caesar's Beach Hotel (tel 721094), on an excellent beach about a 45-minute drive from Monrovia, has rustic rooms with fans for about US$25. It's a possibility for weekends or for those wanting a beach setting and tranquility. Unfortunately, it's not always open and not easy to reach by telephone. It sometimes has water shortages.

Places To Stay – top end

The top hotel is the ocean-front *Hotel Africa*. Its major drawback is the 15-minute taxi ride from downtown, and finding a cab can be a problem. The *Ducor Palace* is downtown and the next best. You'll rarely meet a guest there who has good things to say about it. Everyone seems to complain that the rooms are small and musty, the restaurants expensive and the area too dark and unsafe for walking at night. At the airport, you can stay at the three-star *Robertsfield Hotel*.

Hotel Africa (tel 224519, telex 4223) singles/doubles for US$45/60, large rooms, generator, pool, tennis, casino, nightclub, windsurfers and hobbycats, excellent restaurant, cards AE, MC. *Ducor Palace*, US$65/80, great view of Monrovia, pool, car rental, tennis, generator, a seven-minute walk from the heart of town, cards AE,V,MC,EC. *Robertsfield Hotel* (tel 224403), US$48/65, pool, generator, cards AE.

Places to Eat

Chop Houses There are 'chop houses' everywhere serving local fare for US$1.50 to US$2.50. Downtown, try the one across from Julia's Hotel– it's open until midnight. *The Rooster* offers fast-food-style fried and barbecued chicken and delicious cassava fries with hot sauce. A dinner costs US$3.50. It's in Sinkor at 9th St and Tubman Boulevard.

Liberian *Roseline's* (tel 222513) downtown at Carey and Warren St, is the best-known and one of the more expensive Liberian restaurants. Most dishes cost about US$6 each. It closes early (about 5 pm). In Sinkor near ACS, you can try *Angi's*, a small restaurant with good food. There's a Friday luncheon special – all you can eat from a large variety of African dishes for US$15.

Silver Spoons, at the Pan-African Plaza near the Presidential Palace and closed Sunday, is good only at lunchtime. They offer a few African selections plus non-African dishes. *Arlene's*, down on Warren St near Carey, offers some African dishes but mostly Western food. On Friday from 5 to 9 pm, they have a jazz band and serve South American food – all you can eat for US$10. *Chicken Nest*, on Mechlin near Carey has half chickens for US$4. It closes at 8.30 pm. *King Burger*, on Broad St which is open every day until 11 pm, is something like a Burger King but more expensive.

Italian *La Villa* (tel 261235) has good Italian selections, excellent steaks and numerous fish dishes. It's a 10-minute ride from downtown in Sinkor, on 14th St, and closed Sunday. *Salvatore's* (tel 222643) is a popular restaurant just down the hill from the Ducor, with an extensive menu, pleasant atmosphere, good service and open every day. Daily specials are about US$8 but à la carte dishes cost double that.

Chinese *Mandarin* (tel 222612) is a well-known restaurant in a restored old house downtown on Broad St. It is open every day and most dishes are US$7 to US$9 with tea. It's à la carte only and the service is slow. *Chop Sticks* (tel 222526), downtown on Carey and Lynch St and closed Monday, is also good and the prices are lower, plus there are special meals for about US$9.

French *El Meson*, at the popular downtown hotel, is one of the best restaurants in town but it's fairly expensive. You'll find an extensive menu, excellent seafood (when they have it), Spanish dishes and good sandwiches. It's open every day. *Julia's*, which is closed Sunday, has equally well-prepared food but fewer selections. It's known for the pepper steak and onion soup, and the wine selection is good. Unfortunately, the restaurant suffers greatly from the lack of a stand-by generator (this may change). *Casa Real*, downtown on Carey St near Mechlin, has well-prepared food, including seafood and some Portuguese specialities. The restaurant is dark and the service can be very slow. It's expensive.

Lebanese *Beruit* (tel 222891), downtown on Centre St above Broad St, is the best Lebanese restaurant in town, plus they offer many non-Lebanese dishes. Open every day, it has an uninteresting decor and moderately high prices. *Geegee*, on Gurley St, is open every day. It's a notch below the Beruit but prices are also slightly lower. Most dishes are US$7 to US$10.

Indian *Maharaja's*, on Centre St near Carey St, has excellent food and quite a few selections. Most dishes are US$5 to US$9. *Wimpy's*, on Broad St near Randall, is open every day and has lower prices but only seven Indian selections, plus some American and Liberian dishes. The service can be slow.

Something Special *Hotel Africa* may have Monrovia's best restaurant. Closed Monday, it's expensive and is relaxed and quiet. *Le Bistro*, at the top of the Ducor, is also excellent and expensive, with a great view and live music on weekends. The *Kenema Beach* restaurant, about a 20-minute drive from downtown, offers pleasant patio dining overlooking the beach and lagoon. The seafood is exceptionally good. Main dishes run US$8 to US$15.

Entertainment & Sports

Bars *El Meson*, popular with both locals and travellers, is the best known bar in town. *Julia's Hotel*, nearby on Gurley St, is also fairly popular. It has an aura of intrigue and is the perfect setting for making shady deals. *The Garden*, on Tubman Boulevard just beyond JFK Hospital, a 15-minute ride from downtown, is recommended. It's outdoors and inexpensive, and has music and sometimes dancing on weekends. It has a relaxed unpretentious African atmosphere, popular with both locals and foreigners.

Club Zambezi, on Randall St near one of Choitram's supermarkets, has very subdued lighting and is popular with some locals, less so with foreigners. *Lipp's Bar & Nightclub*, downtown on Lynch St, has a downstairs bar that is fairly lively and popular with locals and foreigners. *Katios* is Monrovia's plushest bar. There's a happy hour from 4 to 8 pm; the doors shut at 1 am. It is downstairs in the Pan-African Plaza building on Tubman Boulevard.

The Clubhouse on Tubman Boulevard beyond Sinkor consists of three thatched 'palaver huts' behind a rustic bamboo fence, flanked by a huge satellite TV dish. It has US cable television featuring all major US sporting events 'live'.

The bars across from King Burger have cheap beers (US$1.50 for a big bottle) and lively music but they're for the adventurous only. Don't be surprised if the locals are smoking joints; they're available for the price of a regular cigarette at many of the kiosks around town.

Nightclubs *Bacardi*, at the Hotel Africa, is popular with locals and foreigners and is the hottest nightclub in town, especially on weekends. The cover charge is US$10 and there's also a casino. *Black Sugar*, downtown on Warren St, has a good sound system and spacious dance floor, excellent for late night dancing. The US$10 cover charge is sometimes negotiable. The upstairs disco at *Lipps's Bar & Nightclub*, downtown on Lynch St, is fairly popular. There's a US$5 cover on weekends. There are 10 or so nightclubs on the appropriately named Gurley Street; prostitutes are everywhere. Roguings are not unknown, so take the maximum precautions.

Movie Theatre The *Relda Theater* is the best in town, which isn't saying much. They show mostly American films. It's on Tubman Boulevard in Sinkor, a 15-minute ride from downtown.

Sports Squash players can check out the squash club on Tubman Boulevard between 9th and 10th Sts. It's hidden behind the gas station. Annual membership is only about US$35. They might accept you on a short-term basis. Tennis players have two options – the Ducor or Hotel Africa. The Hotel Africa also rents hobiecats for US$15 for two hours. There's also a Hash House Harriers group that runs every Saturday around 3.30 pm or so. Ask the US Embassy marines.

Swimmers can try the pool at the Ducor, Africa or Ambassador hotels, or head for the beaches, which are popular only from November to April. You can swim downtown in front of the Ambassador Hotel, although few people do so because of the strong undertow.

You'll find eight softball teams in Monrovia; there are usually four games played every Saturday afternoon (two games on two different fields) during the dry season. One of the fields is Elwa Field near Elwa Hospital, about one km before the turn off to Cooper's Beach. Visitors are welcome. There's excellent fishing for barracuda and, further out, shark. There are no boats for charter, so you'll have to make friends with a local expatriate who has a boat.

There are two golf courses, a nine-hole course with sand greens at the VOA compound (tel 222585) in Brewerville, just west of Monrovia (a 30-minute drive), and one at the Firestone Plantation, an hour's drive from Monrovia near Roberts-field Airport. Both are open only to members and their guests, and there are no clubs for rent.

Things to Buy

Artisan Goods Liberia is a good place to buy masks, baskets, soapstone carvings, 'country cloth' and tie-dye materials. The tie-dye material is similar to that sold elsewhere in Africa but the tablecloths are a little unique and very popular. They have matching napkins and come in a variety of settings, for four to 12 people. The prices are very reasonable, about US$9 to US$14 depending on the size. The two best places are the shops downtown on Randall St between Broad and Carey, and outside the *Sinkor Supermarket* on Tubman Boulevard on 14th St. The ones that feel stiffer resist staining much better.

Another good buy are the African dresses and shirts. Three popular materials include: patterned Fanti cloth which is sold by the *lappa* (two metres); tie-dyes and wax prints; and country cloth, a thick, durable, hand-woven cotton material, sold in strips or ready-made outfits (warning: all are not colour fast). The best place to look for these materials are the sweat shops on Randall St between Carey and Broad Sts. For country cloth, check outside the Sinkor Shopping Centre and the *Liberian Cultural Centre* (LCC). The LCC is about 20 minutes from downtown on the road to the airport past Elwa Hospital – the sign says 'Kendeja'.

There are some very fine masks made of sapwood and used in the Sande and Poro rituals. The styles vary; one used in initiation ceremonies has an elongated beak, while another type has tubular eyes beneath a horn. Finding them is a problem and about the only way is to ask a local expatriate to lead you to his or her favourite door-to-door arts salesman ('Charlie'). For other types of African art, including brass jewellery and knick-knacks, African musical instruments and some wood carvings, try the LCC and the *FLY Shop* (Federation of Liberian Youth) or outside Sinkor Supermarket. The FLY Shop is on Camp Johnson Rd.

Basket lovers are in for a treat. Some are so large that you can't even get your arms around them and the shapes and painted designs can be unusual. The only problem is finding them. The best place by far is the institute for lepers in Ganta, also the crafts shop in Yekepa.

Music For records and cassettes of Liberian and African music, *SAM Music Shop* downtown at the corner of Carey and Centre, and *Soul Sound* at Broad and Gurley, are two among many. Some of the local stars are Morris Dorley and the group *Voice of Liberia*.

Getting There & Away
Air Air Liberia has such a terrible reputation that flying within the country is not recommended. Monrovia has air connections with most of the capital cities on the West African coast.

Bush Taxi Bush taxis leave from the centre of town next to the bridge. There are frequent bush taxis west to Buchanan and to the north, and several a day to Robertsport and the Sierra Leone border.

Getting Around
Airport Transport The airport departure tax is US$10. Robertsfield airport has no amenities other than a bar and does not even have a place to exchange money. Only 200 metres away, however, you'll find the airport hotel, which has a decent restaurant and bar. A taxi from the airport to Monrovia (60 km) is US$35. The only way to reduce the cost is to share a taxi. There is no bus service into Monrovia, however, Hotel Africa now runs a shuttle bus for many flights.

Taxi There's a zone system and fares are 40c for a shared taxi, 65c and 90c for longer trips. Monrovia is one of the few places in Africa where bargaining with cab drivers is not required. Drivers are remarkably honest and, unlike elsewhere in Africa, will invariably give you the shared taxi rate. This is not true of taxis waiting outside one of the major hotels. They're much more expensive because you rent the entire cab. Cabs are everywhere, even at night.

Car Rental Morgan Travel Agency (tel 223586) downtown at 70 Ashmun St, Box 1260; Brasilia Travel Agency (tel 222378) downtown on Broad St, Box 54; International Automobile Co (tel 222486); Mensah Travel Bureau (tel 222807); Yes Transport Co (tel 222970).

AROUND MONROVIA
There are several good beaches out of town to choose from if you're not up to adventure into the hinterland, or you can visit the world's largest rubber plantation.

Cooper's Beach
Cooper's Beach is about 10 miles from downtown towards the airport, about three km beyond the new stadium on your right – look for the sign. It can be reached by taxi. There is a good restaurant specialising in seafood, and there are bathroom facilities. The entrance fee is US$2; it's crowded on weekends.

Caesar's Beach
Better, perhaps, is Caesar's Beach further out on the same road, about a 45-minute drive from Monrovia going towards the airport. It's much quieter and, hence, preferred by those with wheels. The entrance fee is US$5.

Firestone Plantation
The Firestone plantation is an hour's drive from Monrovia near Robertsfield Airport. If you're lucky, you may get a tour.

The Coast

ROBERTSPORT

The beach town of Robertsport is a good place to spend a few days away from the bustle of Monrovia. Not that it's full of historical monuments or sights of interest, it's just that Robertsport doesn't have much competition. It's a sleepy town of about 3000 people with no seeming destiny other than to exist in tranquility surrounded by a tropical green hill with the surf pounding nearby. Most of the locals exist off the only thing keeping the town alive – fishing. If you like ocean fishing in a dugout canoe, for a few shekels the boatman will be glad to give you some equipment and have you tag along.

Before arriving at Robertsport, you'll pass by peaceful Lake Piso, the best spot for campers seeking a little tranquility. It's salt water and free of bilharzia, so you can swim there. During WW II, it was used as a seaplane base by the Allies. Robertsport itself is a good place to walk around and get to see and know the locals. You can walk from one end of town to the other in 20 minutes or so. Most important for those who don't like to rough it too much, there is, surprisingly, a fairly decent ocean-front hotel only 10 minutes walk from downtown.

Places to Stay

Wakorlor Hotel (tel 601060), with singles/doubles for US$15/20 (US$25/40 with air-con), is surprisingly large for such a small town. This relatively new hotel has about 50 rooms and water actually comes out of the taps. There's a breezy dining area overlooking the ocean, as well as a rundown tennis court. There's an air strip in town; expatriates from the nearby Mano River iron ore mine sometimes fly in for the weekend. Chances are, however, that there won't be other guests. *Josephine's Hotel*, with rooms for US$8 to US$15, is downtown one block from the water. It is not very clean and doesn't have a restaurant.

Places to Eat

Those who can't afford the hotel might try *Benisab's Coffeehouse*, a hole-in-the-wall drinking place downtown. You might be able to wrangle a meal from them if you are lucky.

Nightlife

For night entertainment, there's *The Zoe Bush*, a nightclub downtown which is open only on the weekends. Bring your dancing shoes.

Getting There & Away

Robertsport is only a two-hour drive, 100 km west of Monrovia, off the main trunk route to Sierra Leone. About half the distance is paved. There are several bush taxis a day connecting the two and the cost is only about US$5. They leave Monrovia downtown at the taxi area on your left just before crossing the bridge to the port.

BUCHANAN

Buchana is a two-hour drive east along the coast from Robertsport. It is Liberia's second major port and stopping point for the Lamco train from Yekepa. Except for the port itself and the many old houses in the older section of town, there's not too much of interest.

Places to Stay & Eat

The best hotel is *Louiza Hotel*, which is nothing special but it does have air-con. Another is *Sabra Hotel* on Atlantic St. There is a good Chinese restaurant.

HARPER

This remote port town of about 11,000 people is almost on the Ivory Coast border. There are some sites of historical interest, including the residence of the late President William Tubman and the Tubman Library & Museum. Nowadays, its primary reason for existence is to serve as an outlet for the rubber plantations, though it also has a small fishing industry.

If the town seems particularly pleasant,

Kids at Sotuba, Mali   (JJ)

part of the reason may be that the overland trip to get there is so arduous that anything resembling civilisation may seem like paradise. The trip is so exhausting, because of the bad roads, that it's not recommended unless you're on your way to or from the Ivory Coast via the slower coastal route, or you want to see some real tropical rain forests.

Places to Stay & Eat
The *Seaview Motel,* with singles/doubles for about US$30/40, is one of the three nicest hotels outside Monrovia. There's no air-con, but it's not really needed with the sea breeze. Nets hang everywhere and there are turtles in a pool, and you can eat outside as the waves lap nearby in the bay.

Getting There & Away
Getting there is difficult because there is no coastal road; you must go way upcountry and then back south. The route from Monrovia is via Ganta, Tapeta and Zwedru with an over-night stop usually in

Tapeta or Zwedru. Straight driving time from Monrovia is 15 to 17 hours during the dry season. During the rainy months, a 4WD is an absolute must, and even then you can expect to get stuck. The road passes through some of the thickest rainforests in all of Africa and this is part of what makes the journey interesting. It's another day and a half to Abidjan. Since there's an airstrip, you could also charter a plane or, with some risk, take Air Liberia.

The Interior

GBARNGA
Gbarnga is 204 km north-east of Monrovia. If you have time, stop by the Cuttington College museum; specialists from abroad have helped raise its quality significantly.

Places to Stay
Dafal Motel is pretty terrible and way overpriced at US$13 a room. It's just off

the main highway on the southern end of town, not far from the well-known casino which is a hang-out for students from nearby Cuttington College.

GANTA
One of the main attractions in this town is the craft shop of the leper institution where they make some of the most interesting baskets in West Africa.

Places to Stay
You have a choice between *Sister Rachael's Motel* and *Kinta Motel*; 'rustic' is one euphemism to describe them.

YEKEPA
Normally you wouldn't think that a mining town would be a place of interest to travellers. Yekepa, a town of over 20,000 people in the mountains of north-east Liberia, is one of the exceptions. It is best known for being the company town of Lamco. It was not until 1965 that some of the world's biggest and richest iron ore deposits were discovered there. The company has traditionally employed not only thousands of Liberians but hundreds of expatriates as well, though many have left as the ore deposits under exploitation are nearing exhaustion.

At about 350 metres above sea level, Yekepa has the best climate in Liberia. The climate plus the view of the lush surrounding mountains are what attract most people, especially those tired of the flatlands elsewhere in Liberia.

The more physically active may be attracted by the possibility of the best light hiking in West Africa. For those who want to build up a good sweat, there's Mt Nimba, 1752 metres high, just across the border in the Ivory Coast. For tourists, there's the possibility of getting a tour of the mines and picking up some interesting locally made baskets at a craft shop downtown. The final draw card is the hotel, probably the best outside Monrovia. Take your bathing suit because Lamco has a huge swimming pool, which you may be allowed to use. November to March is the best time to visit, when it's cooler and there's little rain.

Places to Stay & Eat
The *Mountain View Lodge*, with singles/doubles for US$29/39, is Lamco's rustic guest house, which has a nice view of the mountains. It's on the outskirts of town and the restaurant offers dishes such as boeuf bouguignon. You may be able to reserve by calling Lamco in Monravia. The *Travellers Inn* has doubles without electricity for US$6.

Getting There & Away
The most interesting way to get to Yekepa used to be by train from Buchanan. Those with bucks can charter a plane. Everyone else will take the six-hour, 320-km ride by car from Monrovia. The road is now in excellent condition, even the unpaved 50-km section north of Ganta. Bush taxis are fairly easy to catch in Monrovia downtown near the bridge, but you'll probably have to change at Ganta unless you hire the car to yourself (about US$100). Coming from the Ivory Coast, you can make it from Man in about five hours unless you're in a bush taxi, in which case the trip can take double that.

SARPO NATIONAL PARK
The Sarpo National Park in eastern Liberia has some of the best primal rain forest in all of West Africa. From January to March the park staff, including Peace Corps volunteers, run canoe trips on the Sinoe River to raise money for the park. This also presents an excellent chance to travel upcountry with a minimum of hassle, and to experience adventure to boot. The trips are three to four days, and the fee (US$80) covers all your needs. Reservations are necessary and can be made through the Peace Corps office in Monrovia on Tubman Boulevard. To get there, take one of the charter planes with others on the trip (about US$200 roundtrip), or go overland – a two-day trip to Sinoe County.

Mali

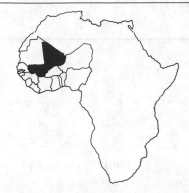

Timbuktu is that place you have always heard about but could never find on the map. But now you know, it's in Mali, where you can also see nomads on their camels languidly crossing the desert, fishermen in their long dugout canoes paddling slowly down the great Niger River and Africans carrying out their daily chores around their hobbit-like homes perched on rocky cliffs. These are only at the top of a long list of attractions that make Mali a gem of West Africa.

Mali is a Mecca for those wanting to see the real Africa and especially the Sahel. Alongside the Niger is Bamako, a vibrant, safe city large enough for numerous amenities but small enough to cover on foot. The market is one of the three or four best in West Africa and people everywhere are friendly.

To the far north of Bamako is Timbuktu, the northern most town on the southern fringe of the Sahara. Then there's Mopti and nearby Djenné, both on the banks of the Niger River. Mopti has the most active waterfront on the Niger, and Djenné is the best preserved city from the Middle Ages, when the Sahara trade routes dominated West African economic life. For adventure seekers, there's the possibility of taking a trip down the Niger in a boat or dugout canoe. Finally, there's the Dogon area, where Africans live on the side of cliffs, reminiscent of the famous cliff-dwelling Indians in the southwest of the US.

Unfortunately, there's a flip side to the story. Mali is one of the five poorest countries on earth. Part of this reality you can see, such as the considerable number of lepers and blind people in Bamako. There are other aspects not so readily visible – a life expectancy of 41 to 44 years, an average calorie intake that is about 30% below the required minimum, a literacy rate of about 10%, and a mortality rate of about 15% among children less than one year old. Poverty is nothing new to Malians. Indeed, they are an inspiration. Their fortitude despite the hardships, the friendliness of people everywhere, and the vibrancy of their city life and local markets are, ultimately, what leave the most lasting impression.

HISTORY

Timbuktu was and still is the mysterious terminus at the end of a camel route which brought Arabia to black Africa. Long ago it ceased being an influential centre of trade and learning in the medieval Islamic world. Its fame was enhanced by the rise of three of the greatest kingdoms in West Africa between the 9th and 16th centuries.

The wealth of these kingdoms was based on the trans-Saharan trade routes. Gold, ivory, kola nuts and slaves from the central area of West Africa were transported north, eventually making their way to Europe and the Middle East. Several of the principal trade routes ran through what is now Mali. In return, the Africans wanted salt which, as incredible as it may seem, traded pound for pound with gold. There is an important salt oasis in northern Mali and the Tuareg nomads transported it south on the backs of camels. Most of the nomads ended their journey at Timbuktu, strategically located on the southern edge of the Sahara Desert and at the northernmost loop of the Niger River. The Bozo fishermen took over from

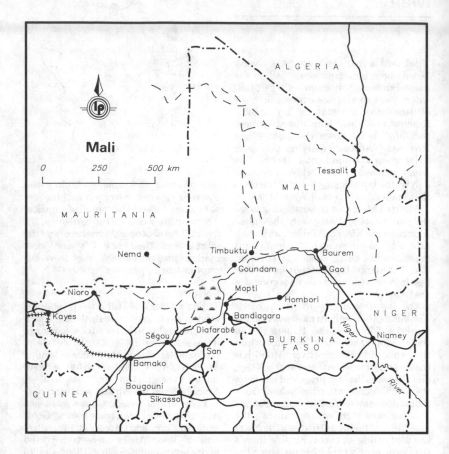

there, transporting the salt south on the Niger to Mopti.

The first kingdom was that of Ghana, which had no geographic connection whatsoever to the present day Republic of Ghana. The Empire of Ghana covered much of present day Mali and parts of Senegal and its capital was several hundred km north of present day Bamako. This empire was only marginally influenced by Islam during its 500-year life, until it was destroyed in the late 11th century by the better-armed Berber invaders from the north.

Empire of Mali

In the mid-13th century, the Mandinka Empire of Mali arose and stretched from mid-Senegal to the border of Niger. The empire's revenue sources originally were derived from the levying of taxes on those trading gold and ivory within its territory, but the kingdom expanded to include ownership of the actual gold and silver areas.

The trans-Saharan trade reached its peak during this period and served to finance not only new mosques designed by foreign Arabian architects but also the extensive growth of Timbuktu and Djenné into major centres of finance and culture. Timbuktu became an important commercial city with about 100,000 inhabitants by the 16th century (now about 15,000) and also a famous centre of learning. Its two Islamic universities once had over 2500 students.

When Emperor Kankan Moussa made his visit to Mecca via Egypt in 1324-26, he took with him an entourage of 60,000 people and 150 kg of gold. Because of his lavish gifts of the precious metal all over Egypt, he is said to have destroyed the value of the Egyptian currency for several years. As if this wasn't enough, whenever he stopped on Friday to pray, he had a mosque built – or so the story goes.

Songhai Empire
By the 15th century the Songhai Empire to the east in the area of Gao became powerful and well organised. It covered about the same area as the Empire of Mali, but its control was greater.

This was Mali's heyday as well as that of Timbuktu, Gao and Djenné, and it lasted well over a hundred years. A hallmark of this third empire was the creation, for the first time, of a professional army and a civil service with provincial governors. The government of the day even subsidised Muslim scholars, judges and doctors in places such as Timbuktu.

This golden period ended with the invasion, again, of Berber armies from Morocco in the late 16th century. At the same time the European maritime nations began circumventing the Saharan trade routes by sending ships down along the coast of West Africa. They not only broke the Muslim monopoly on trade but destroyed the base of the Sahel's wealth. Timbuktu was sent into oblivion.

Mali became a French colony in 1883 and was part of French Sudan until independence in 1960. Some of the remnants of the colonial period include the largest irrigation works (Office du Niger) and the longest railroad span (1200 km from Bamako to Dakar) in West Africa. France's chief interest was in developing a source of cheap exports to France, especially cotton and rice.

Independence
After independence and following a brief federation with Senegal, Mali embarked on an unsuccessful period of socialism, employing hundreds of Russian advisors while maintaining membership in the French Community. The Soviets went for politically popular projects, building Bamako's critical bridge over the Niger, the sports stadium and a hospital. Even more politically important was the Russian assistance to the Malian military.

Fired by a sense of nationalistic pride, Mali left the Franc zone in 1962 and established its own currency. State corporations took over many areas of the economy even down to the level of the supermarkets. Almost all of them began losing money except the cotton enterprise, which benefitted from French advisors and a fairly reliable world market. The ambitious planning schemes went awry, resulting in unpopular austerity measures. Eventually, in 1968, a successful coup was led by Moussa Traoré, who continues as president today.

In 1960 Mali was a net exporter of food and even embarked on a limited program of road improvement for the purpose of increasing its export potential. As a result of bad management, however, within a few years Mali became a net importer of food. The droughts in 1973-74 and 1983-84 only worsened the situation. Even in years of good rainfall, cereal production became insufficient to meet demand. Nearly everyone blamed the weather, saying a permanent climatic change had occurred. In fact, the droughts were only repeating a pattern that has continued over the centuries. With a population growth of about 2.5% the government had, and continues to have, its hands full just trying to keep conditions from deteriorating further.

The low prices offered by the government to farmers from the time of independence until the early 1980s certainly contributed to the decline per capita in food production. During this period, prices were easily one-quarter less than those on the open market. Farmers either stopped growing more than they needed, switched to cash crops, or smuggled their grain across the border to neighbouring countries where prices were more attractive.

One result is that since independence, the government has had a chronic financial deficit. Revenues barely cover the salaries of the bureaucracy and the government is usually four or five months behind in paying salaries. The remainder of the budget is always covered by the French.

Today

Politically, things are calm – at least by African standards. Still, there have been four coup attempts since 1970, and a well-publicised student strike in late 1979 that, according to Amnesty International, resulted in 13 young people being shot or tortured to death. A major political event occurred in late 1985 when Mali and Burkina Faso declared war over a long-standing border dispute. Burkina even dropped a small bomb on Sikasso. But it was over in five days – in part, perhaps, because neither side had the resources to continue.

Change is in the air. Two indications are the waning of Soviet influence in Mali and a steady movement towards the west, and the re-installation of a free enterprise system. The sheer size of the aid provided by the west compared to that from Russia may have been a factor. In 1984 Mali re-adopted the CFA franc, but not without first freezing salaries for three years. The country experienced significant inflation immediately following the change. A number of the state-owned enterprises are being dismantled. The SOMIEX supermarkets in all the major cities have been sold to private business people, with a noticeable improvement in service. The

government is gradually getting out of the business of buying and selling grain, for long a major recommendation of the western donor countries.

Corn and sorghum researchers in Mali say they are probably years away from any production breakthroughs. Still, by 1987, Mali had an estimated grain surplus of 150,000 tonnes – more than the grain deficit during the great 1983-84 drought. Adequate rainfall was the main reason, but policy change may have helped.

PEOPLE

Ethnically, Mali is a fascinating country, but for the traveller the multiplicity of ethnic groups complicates understanding the country. Three groups, however, stand out: the Bambara, Tuareg and Dogon.

The Bambara

The Bambara (BAM-bah-rah) are the most numerous, comprising about one-quarter of the population. Concentrated in the area around Bamako, they occupy most of the senior positions in the government, and are noted for their art. Indeed, there is no piece of African art more well known than the *chiwara*, a headpiece carved in the form of an antelope used in ritualistic dances. Air Afrique even uses the chiwara as its company logo.

The Tuaregs

The Tuaregs (TWA-reg) are known as the 'blue men of the desert' because of the swathes of indigo cloth wrapped around most of their face and head to keep out the sand. Concentrated in the northern area around Timbuktu, they are fiercely proud of their Caucasian descent and feel themselves to be superior to the Negro. So it is hardly surprising that they have historically had conflicts with the Bambara and others.

The Tuaregs were famous for both their fighting abilities and artwork which, not surprisingly, adorns mostly swords and other metal objects. They are considered by many to have mysterious characters, perhaps because of their typically cold eyes peering between the blue cloth.

As with the Songhai, the Tuaregs' lives have been totally altered by the recent droughts. The sheep, goat and camel herds have been decimated, and their camel caravans can no longer compete with small trucks, putting in serious jeopardy one of their major occupations, the transportation of salt and other produce from the north.

Forced to retreat south in search of water and vegetation for their animals, many have had to set aside their nomadic ways and become farmers and even urban residents. Others have not made the transition and live in camps just outside Timbuktu. During the droughts these camps swell in size, with no source of food other than that given out by relief organisations. It's a pathetic sight and yet one can only admire their resilience.

The Dogon

The Dogon (DOH-ghon), famous for both their farming and artistic abilities, are the incredibly industrious farmers living on the rocky escarpment east of Mopti. No serious African art collector visiting West Africa would miss a trip to 'Dogon Country'. While today's craftsmen may have lost some of the original inspiration, some of the older pieces fetch tens of thousands of dollars.

Other Groups

Three other groups are noteworthy: the Peuls, Bozos and Songhai. The Bozos (BOH-zoh) are mostly fishermen all along the river. The Peuls, scattered everywhere from Nigeria to Senegal and constantly on the move, are the professional herdsmen who, for a few sacks of rice, take care of the cattle owned by the farmers. Finally, the Songhai (SONG-guy) are primarily fishermen, farmers and herders, and are concentrated in the desert area around Gao.

Regardless of ethnic group, Malians tend to be very poor. Average per capita income is only $180, and may be falling in real terms.

GEOGRAPHY

Mali is the largest country in West Africa. It is twice the size of France but has only about one-seventh as many people.

The Sahara Desert covers the entire upper half of the country. Towards the south, near the Ivory Coast and Guinea borders, annual rainfall is entirely adequate, similar to that on the east coast of the US. It's the heavily populated and relatively flat 200 to 800 mm rainfall area in between, called the Sahel, where fluctuations in rainfall cause great havoc. It's also where the Niger River winds slowly through Mali, passing by Bamako, Ségou, Mopti, Timbuktu and Gao, on its way to Nigeria and the ocean.

Bamako, the capital, has about 550,000 inhabitants although, as with most African cities, it seems only half that size.

CLIMATE

The rainy season lasts four months, from June to September. The hot season is from March to May, when temperatures frequently exceed 40°C.

VISAS

Only the French do not need visas. Visas cannot be obtained at the border or from French embassies. They are valid for seven days only, however, you can get them renewed fairly easily in Bamako, Mopti or Gao. A four-week extension in Bamako, for example, is obtained in 24 hours and costs CFA 2600; forms are available from SMERT (the national tourist agency) across from the mosque. When you do this, ask SMERT for a white tourist card; it will avoid hassles with the police if you travel upcountry.

Overstaying your visa will cost you CFA 2600 a week. Exit visas are no longer required except for those staying a year or longer. Malian embassies in the US and Europe tend to charge considerably more than those in Africa, so those travelling on the cheap may want to wait until they get to Dakar, Abidjan or Algiers to get one.

The French Embassy in Bamako issues visas to the Ivory Coast, Burkina Faso, Togo and Chad. Tourist visas to Senegal, Guinea and Niger cannot be obtained in Bamako. In Senegal, however, they are issued at Dakar airport (not always at the border). Some people have reportedly travelled on the Bamako-Dakar train without visas and gotten through.

Diplomatic Missions Abroad
Abidjan, Accra, Algiers, Berlin, Bonn, Brussels, Conakry, Dakar, Ottawa, Paris, Washington. Consulate: Niamey.

MONEY
US$1 = 287 CFA
£1 = 537 CFA

The unit of currency is the CFA. Banking hours: Monday to Saturday 7.30 to 11.30 am (for cash transactions). Banks: BIAO, Banque de Développement de Mali.

LANGUAGE
French is the official language. Bambara, which is almost identical to Dioula (the market language in much of West Africa), is the most widely spoken African language, especially around Bamako. Songhai is spoken widely in the north around Gao and Timbuktu. Greetings in Bambara:

Good morning	e-nee-SOH-goh-mah
Good evening	e-nee-WON-lah
How are you?	e-koh-kay-nay-WAH
Thank you	e-nee-chay
Goodbye	khan-bee-ah-FOH

GENERAL INFORMATION
Health
A yellow fever vaccination is mandatory; also cholera if you come from an infected area. The Hôpital Gabriel Touré (tel 222712) in Bamako has an emergency room and is perhaps better for emergencies,

otherwise the Hôpital du Point G (tel 225002) on the plateau overlooking Bamako is better. Their standards are low. For doctors, inquire at one of the embassies. One of the best pharmacies in Bamako is at the Hôtel de l'Amitié. A cheaper one is Pharmacie Soudanaise in the heart of town near Air Mali.

Security
Bamako is one of the safest capital cities in Africa, though purse snatchings are occasionally reported.

Business Hours
Business: weekdays 8 am to 12 noon and 3 to 6 pm (approximately); Saturdays 8 am to 12 noon. Government: weekdays 7 am to 2 pm; Saturdays 7 am to 12 noon.

Public Holidays
1 January, 20 January, Easter Monday, 1 May, 25 May, End of Ramadan (17 May 1988, 6 May 1989), Tabaski (25 May 1988, 14 May 1989), 22 September (Independence Day), Mohammed's Birthday, 19 November, 25 December.

Photography
A permit is required and it's advisable to get one. The SMERT travel agency in the lobby of the Hôtel de l'Amitié in Bamako will issue them in 24 hours. Take CFA 2700 and a photo. If you'll be travelling upcountry, ask them for a tourist card too. For same day service but more hassle, go in person to the Sureté National downtown near the Air Mali offices. You'll need a CFA 200 fiscal stamp (*timbre fiscal*) from the Trésor and a photo plus money. If you arrive after 8 am, you're not likely to get same day service. If there's not enough time, you can get one in Mopti in 10 minutes at the Commissariat near the Campement, provided the official is there.

Time, Post, Phone & Telex
When it's noon in Mali, it's noon in London and 7 am in New York (8 am during daylight savings time). There are

international telephone facilities and telex machines at the Bamako post office and, more expensive, at the Hôtel de l'Amitié. The Poste Restante is reportedly not very reliable in Bamako.

GETTING THERE
Air
The only direct flights from outside black Africa are from Paris, Casablanca and Moscow. The cheapest way from London would be via Moscow on Aeroflot with a ticket purchased from a bucket shop.

From the USA, you could take Air Afrique from New York, transferring in Dakar or Abidjan, or go via Europe or Morocco.

Ethiopian Airlines offers direct flights from Addis Ababa. Air Mali, nicknamed Air Maybe, has one of the worst reputations of any airline in Africa.

Car
Your green card is not valid in Mali; you will have to buy insurance in Bamako (Gao if you're coming across the desert), such as at the Assurances Générales de France. A carnet de passage is also apparently required. Roads are paved Bamako-Mopti-Gao (16 hours straight driving time), Bamako-Abidjan via Sikasso (20 to 24 hours; not paved for 150 km between the border and Ferkéssédougou), and Bamako-Ouagadougou via Ségou and Bobo-Dioulasso (12 to 14 hours). Bamako-Conakry (12 hours to Kankan plus 20 hours to Conakry) is not paved between Bamako and Kankan (Guinea). You cannot be guaranteed of getting petrol in Mopti, Timbuktu and Gao, however, it is almost always available on the black market at a slightly higher price. So fill up in Bamako or Ségou and take jerry cans.

For Bamako-Dakar, travellers have two options. The most direct route is westward via Kayes. However, it is next to impossible to drive from Kayes to Tambacounda (Senegal) during the wet season, and difficult at other times. So many motorists put their cars on the train in Bamako and ride with them to Tambacounda (Senegal) or Dakar (50% more expensive).

The cost from Bamako to Tambacounda is about CFA 75,000 for vehicles of 1.5 tonnes and less, and another CFA 11,000 per passenger; it's more for heavier vehicles or those going to Dakar. One problem is that it usually takes one to three weeks, sometimes longer, to get a reservation. Coming from Senegal you can put the car on in Tambacounda and take it off in Kayes or Bamako; coming from Bamako, it is apparently more difficult or impossible to put your car on in Kayes. By road, the Bamako-Kayes section is terrible and the trip takes at least two days. The route is north via Nioro, not the road following the railway line.

A much better alternative is to drive north from Bamako to Néma (Mauritania) via Nara, even though the Nara-Néma stretch is sandy and difficult. From Néma it's paved all the way to Nouakchott and Dakar. It's difficult to get petrol in Néma but all along the Transmauritanienne is no problem. The road from Bamako to Néma isn't too bad except from July to August when it can get muddy.

There are two routes from Bamako to Néma. The first is north via Kolokani on a dirt road that has been improved and is in good condition all the way. The other is a longer route via Ségou and Niono that is asphalted two-thirds of the way, however, the remaining 168-km stretch between Niono and Nara is terrible; sometimes impassable from July to August, and apparently worse than the Nara-Néma section.

Bush Taxi
The best route by far from Bobo-Dioulasso (Burkina Faso) is via Ségou, not Sikasso; the latter takes a good two days. Coming from the Ivory Coast, it's far better to go via Ferkéssédougou and Sikasso than Odienne and Bougouni; the traffic on the latter is zilch. It's difficult to find a taxi direct to Bamako from

Abidjan. When you do, count on at least two days. Otherwise, it can take three days (one to Ferké, one to Sikasso, and one to Bamako).

Train

The Bamako-Dakar express takes about 30 hours. There are actually two trains. If possible, avoid the older Malian one. The Senegalese train is relatively new and possibly the best in West Africa; it has a dining car and berths (couchettes). Berths on both trains are for two people only.

Trains leave Bamako on Wednesdays and Fridays at 11.30 am. They leave Dakar the on same days at 10.30 am. The Senegalese train is the one that leaves Bamako on Friday and Dakar on Wednesday. The cost to Dakar of both trains is the same: CFA 27,600 for 1st class with air-con and berth, CFA 11,700 for 2nd class. Second class cannot be reserved, so arrive early to get a seat. There are no student discounts. Those on the cheap can save money by hitchhiking the Dakar-Tambacounda stretch. The very decrepit local train to Kayes is only CFA 2805. For information, call the Bamako train station (tel 225586).

GETTING AROUND
Air

Air Mali (tel 225741/2) has flights three times a week to Mopti, Timbuktu and Gao and once a week to Kayes and Nioro, but a good half seem to end up being cancelled. You can charter a plane from STA Mali (tel 329932, telex 454) or Mali Air Service (tel 224530, telex 418). Both are quite reliable.

Bush Taxi

The principal Gare Routière in Bamako is in Sogoniko, eight km from downtown on the road to the airport and Ségou. Go early in the day. Bamako-Mopti takes about 10 hours; Mopti-Gao eight to 10 hours on a new road; Bamako-Sikasso about seven hours. If you are headed towards Guinea, Kayes or Nioro, you must use the other

Gare Routière near the river and back of Les Trois Caimans. Going towards Guinea, you should count on one day to the border and one more to Kankan.

Boat

There's a river boat that plies the Niger River, connecting Koulikoro (60 km east of Bamako) and Gao, stopping at 16 villages and towns on the way, including Mopti and Timbuktu. The first part of December is the ideal time to do this because of the cooler weather. You'll see life along the Niger as the Malians know it. Particularly interesting is all the activity at the village ports along the way. This trip is not for those who dream of sipping piña coladas while lounging in deck chairs as the boat drifts slowly down the Niger. It's only for the adventurous, but US ambassadors have done it.

The boat operates only from August through December; the Mopti-Gao portion is usually open about a month longer. Koulikoro-Gao takes five days, six days for the return journey, but every now and then a boat gets stuck on the bottom and the trip takes much longer. Boats leave every Monday from Bamako. From Gao, the departure date is a little more erratic; it is supposed to leave every Monday at 8 pm and every other Wednesday at 8 pm.

You can take the boat in either direction, and you don't have to go the entire distance. Two days Mopti-Timbuktu or vice versa, for example, is for many people quite enough. Since Timbuktu is nine km from the river, the only way you can see it is to hop a taxi in Kabara and take a quick tour during the boat's stop of several hours. Those with time on their hands could, of course, stop over and pick up another a week later.

The two best boats are the new (1982) *Kankan Moussa* followed by the renovated *Général Soumaré*, inaugurated in 1965. The trip is not exactly luxurious, but 1st class deluxe is a double cabin with one or two beds, air-con, sink, refrigerator and a short-wave radio. The eight 1st-class cabins have two bunk beds, toilet and sink. Second class consists of four bunk beds and a sink, with outside toilets and showers. Third class consists of an eight or 12 berth cabin and allows you to sleep on the upper deck. This is not true of 4th class which is the absolute pits; there are people everywhere, screaming babies plus mounds of sacks and boxes. Each class has its own communal toilet and shower facilities.

There's a restaurant, bar, video TV, and a stereo blasting away. The water is filtered, but it's best to bring purification tablets or your own water. Approximate fares on the *Kankan Moussa*: Koulikoro-Gao CFA 150,000 (deluxe), CFA 68,000 (1st class), CFA 47,000 (2nd class), CFA 24,000 (3rd class). Prices include meals. The Mopti-Timbuktu portion (perhaps the most interesting section) is only about one-third this. Fares on the *Tombouctou* (1979) may be less; check this out. You can reserve by phone with the Navigation Company of Mali in Bamako (tel 223802).

Bamako

Mali is so poor that many people go there thinking that beggars must be everywhere and that the pace of life in Bamako must be pretty slow. Nothing could be further from the truth. The activity level in Bamako is amazing. It seems like everybody and his aunt has a motorbike. The main streets downtown are jammed with people banging on metal, music blasting away, engines running and people selling everything under the sun, Bamako can provide hours of entertainment even if you can't speak the language or don't like shopping. There are a few beggars, but not anything like what one might expect. Most are lepers or people blinded from the river blindness disease, oncho.

Information
Tourist Office The government tourist agency is SMERT (BP 222, tel 224355,

telex 516), downtown across from the mosque (hours: 7.30 am to 2.30 pm) and at the Hôtel de l'Amitié (open to 6 pm). They arrange four and five-day overland trips to the Dogon area, among other services. This is the place to go for visa extensions. Also, get a white tourist card; it will avoid hassles with the police if you travel upcountry.

Embassies Canada (tel 222236); France (tel 222951, telex 569); West Germany (BP 100, tel 223999, telex 529); USA (BP 34, tel 225834, telex 448). Consulates: Belgium (tel 222144); UK (tel 222064).

Other embassies include: Algeria, Ghana, Guinea (issues diplomatic visas only), Liberia, Mauritania, Morocco, Netherlands, Nigeria. Consulates: Netherlands.

Bookstores & Supermarkets The bookstore at the Amitié carries *Time*, *Newsweek* and *International Herald Tribune*, as well as the best selection of postcards and books on Mali. The one at the Grand is not as good. *Deves et Chaumet Papeterie*, one block from the Sabbague snackbar, is the best downtown but offers very little. Hours are 9 am to 3.15 pm.

As for supermarkets, *Malimag* and *Danaya*, both in the heart of town at the red light, are the best.

Travel Agencies The following three private agencies offer many of the same services as SMERT at a lesser price and with more flexible itineraries: Dogon Voyages (BP 2442, tel 225484, telex 566) on the same street as the Central Restaurant and, one block away, Manding Voyages (BP 2224, tel 224736, telex 992). Togu Nu-Mali Tour (BP 559) on Route de Koulikoro is apparently run by an affable Italian and organises tours to Timbuktu, Djenné and Dogon country.

Grand Marché
One of the major attractions of Bamako is the Grand Marché. You won't find pushy

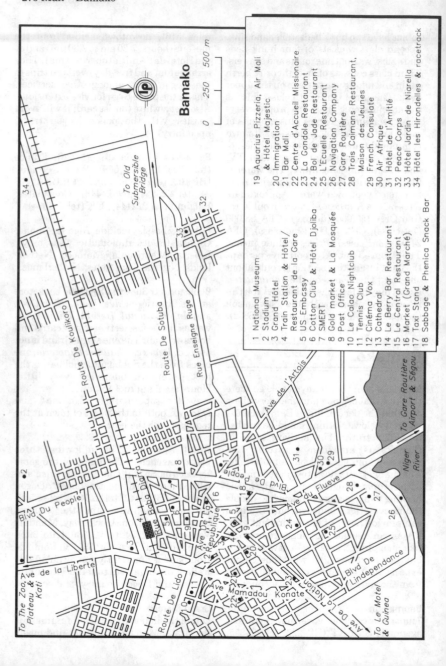

Bamako

0 250 500 m

1 National Museum
2 Stadium
3 Grand Hôtel
4 Train Station & Hôtel/
  Restaurant de la Gare
5 US Embassy
6 Cotton Club & Hôtel Djoliba
7 SMERT
8 Gold market & La Mosquée
9 Post Office
10 Le Calao Nightclub
11 Tennis Club
12 Cinéma Vox
13 Cathedral
14 Le Berry Bar Restaurant
15 Le Central Restaurant
16 Market (Grand Marché)
17 Taxi Stand
18 Sabbage & Phenica Snack Bar
19 Aquarius Pizzeria, Air Mali
  & Hôtel Majestic
20 Immigration
21 Bar Mali
22 Centre d'Accueil Missionaire
23 La Gondole Restaurant
24 Bol de Jade Restaurant
25 L'Ecuelle Restaurant
26 Navigation Company
27 Gare Routière
28 Trois Caimans Restaurant,
  Maison des Jeunes
29 French Consulate
30 Air Afrique
31 Hôtel de l'Amitié
32 Peace Corps
33 Hôtel Jardin de Niarella
34 Hôtel les Hirondelles & racetrack

merchants like those in Dakar and Abidjan. In Bamako they will take 'no' for an answer. Malians have a reputation for being very pleasant and you can take your time wandering around without people pulling at you.

Just finding out what most of the food items are could easily take all day. There's everything from beads, blankets, indigo cloth, gold and brass to incense, African spices and medicines. I have one friend who likes to wander around the market looking for scraps of metal, hoping he may find pieces of solid brass for making experimental waterpumps. Others get interested in things such as beads; the variety is amazing.

National Museum

Le Musée National is one of the better ethnographical museums in West Africa and certainly the one with the most interesting architecture – modern Sudanese inspired by some older mud architecture in Mali. There's a good selection of tapestries, masks, funeral objects and weapons. It's several blocks behind the Grand Hôtel on the road leading up the Plateau. Hours: 9 am to 7 pm. Closed Mondays.

Zoo

A good block from the museum is the zoo. Considerably more spacious than most zoos, it's a good picnic spot too. Open every day until sundown.

Plateau

The huge plateau overlooking Bamako affords a panoramic view of the city. It's on the same road as the museum and zoo. The Presidential Palace and other government buildings are located there as well as a hospital. The best place for viewing Bamako, however, is not at the top. Rather, go about half-way up the plateau until you see a sign 'Point de Vue Touristique' pointing to the left and follow it for about one km. The view is superb, especially at dusk.

Hippodrome

For a Sunday entertainment, go to the hippodrome (race track). You'll see Malians in their finest threads and, between races, wrestling matches and singing by a local star. There are three races; the first starts at 4 pm sharp. It is three km from downtown on the road to Koulikoro, behind Hôtel les Hirondelles.

Places to Stay – bottom end

There are three places where you can get decent accommodation for CFA 1500 a person. The Centre d'Accueil Missionaire has a big dormitory room with mattresses on the floor, hammocks, a clean bathroom, and washing facilities. Hours are 7 am to 1 pm and 4 to 10 pm. It's a two-storey, pink building downtown, back of Cinéma Vox and two blocks beyond Bar Mali.

The Centre d'Accueil des Soeurs Blanches, corner of 130th and 133rd Sts, has showers, mosquito nets and clean toilets. You can cook your own food if you have a stove. A better place to meet Africans is La Maison des Jeunes, downtown next to Les Trois Caimans and 200 metres from the bridge. The bathrooms are dirty but the dormitory rooms, with eight beds to a room, are relatively clean.

For ordinary hotels with rock bottom prices, you have four choices. The best of the lot is Hôtel Djoliba (tel 226006) at CFA 4465/6375 for singles/doubles. It's downtown 50 metres from the US Embassy and good for the price, with fans in the rooms. Not as good is Le Motel (tel 225622/24) at CFA 6000/7000 for singles/doubles with breakfast. It's inconveniently located about three km from downtown near the river, and the atmosphere is like a tomb. Hôtel Majestic (tel 225260) costs about CFA 3800 to CFA 7100 for singles and CFA 5000 to CFA 8200 for doubles and the cheaper rooms do not have air-con. This is a fairly popular hotel only because it's in the dead centre of town. You won't find mosquito nets, but you will find it very noisy. Three may no longer share a double. Bar Mali, downtown several blocks behind the Cinéma Vox, costs about CFA 5300/7800 CFA with breakfast. It's filthy, with prostitutes galore.

Camping If you're camping, the best spot is at or near *Le Lido* six km out of town.

Places to Stay – middle
The most popular of the medium price hotels is *Les Hirondelles* (tel 224435, telex 455) with singles/doubles at about CFA 11,000/15,400 with breakfast. This is a rundown, colonial era hotel with friendly management, quiet African ambience, a slightly dirty pool which is open sporadically, and a nightclub. It's on the road to Koulikoro, a good three km from the centre of town.

The best of the medium priced hotels however, is *Le Lido* (tel 222188) at about CFA 12,350/14,000 for singles/doubles with breakfast. It has a pleasant location in the hills outside Bamako, long pool, very good restaurant and pizzeria and it's patronised by foreigners. The problems with this hotel are that there are only about 10 rooms and they are almost always full, and the hotel is six km from the centre, with no taxis to take you into town. So it's recommended only if you have wheels.

Le Terminus (tel 223340/45) costs CFA 13,000/14,000 with breakfast. The rooms are slightly nicer than at the Hirondelles, plus there's a pleasant patio for drinks and a popular disco on weekends, but the ambience is dead. Since it's near the outskirts of town and you must walk a km just to hail a cab, it's recommended only for those with a car.

Hôtel de la Gare (tel 225968) is CFA 10,000/13,500 with breakfast and better than you'd expect from a train station hotel. It has air-con rooms, no windows but huge doors for light, and a very good, inexpensive restaurant. *Jardin de Niarella* (tel 223667) costs about CFA 10,500/12,500 including breakfast. This small hotel has an African ambience and very

decent air-con rooms, but it's three km from the centre of town, two blocks from the Peace Corps (Corps de la Paix) off the road to Sotouba.

Places to Stay – top end
Hôtel de l'Amitié is a four-star Sofitel and is a 10-minute walk from the market downtown. Alternatively the totally renovated colonial era *Grand Hôtel* has a quieter ambience than the Amitié with rooms that are almost as nice. It's a 15-minute walk from the market.

Hôtel de l'Amitié (tel 224321/95, telex 578) singles/doubles CFA 27,250/29,100, long pool, tennis, disco, movie theatre, pharmacy, SMERT, telex, car rental, cards AE, D.
Grand Hôtel (tel 222481, telex 578), rooms about CFA 22,500, pool, tennis, popular disco, Eurocar rental, cards AE, D, V.

Places to Eat
Cheap Eats *Restaurant de la Gare* at the train station is a good choice if you're looking for a decent meal for about CFA 1300. It has a number of selections, including some authentic African selections such as *fonio*. The better known *Le Central* is in the same category and in the heart of town, a half block from Le Berry. There are CFA 1200 daily specials plus a limited à la carte menu, good yoghurt, and quick service. It's open every day until midnight.

Bar Kassouf, only two blocks away and across from the Cathedral, is not as good but cheaper. A full meal runs CFA 500 to CFA 1000. *Sabbague* and, around the corner, *La Phoenica* are both several blocks from the market going towards the bridge. They are extremely popular with travellers and serve sandwiches including Lebanese shawarmas, pastry, beer and ice cream. They're open every day from 6 am to midnight.

African *La Savanne* offers only grilled chicken and fries, but they are very well prepared and inexpensive. Plus there are African bungalows and late night dancing on weekends. The problem is that it's a 25-minute ride from downtown, across the submersible bridge.

Chez Kadia is just as good and nearer to downtown. You can get stuffed pigeon, excellent Niger perch (capitaine), and the best fries in town. It's outdoors with an African ambience, but it's not for those with sensitive stomachs. It's a five-minute ride from downtown, one km across the bridge.

French *Le Dougouni* at the Amitié and *Le Bananier* at the Grand are two of the best French restaurants in town, but local expatriates tend to patronise other restaurants which are almost as good and more moderately priced. The one with the most pleasant setting is *Le Lido* (tel 225223) in the hills outside Bamako. The set five-course menu is about CFA 4300. Alternatively, the indoor pizzeria offers the best pizza in town and an à la carte menu. It's six km out of town; your taxi must wait for you.

La Gondole (tel 225223), downtown on Avenue de la Nation and closed Monday, is a longtime favourite with more moderate prices. It has great ratatouille and a good selection of steaks and pizza. *Aquarius Pizzeria* is equally good and has the best steaks in town, plus good fish, frog legs and fries at moderate prices. It's on the same street but three blocks down, in the heart of town next to Hôtel Majestic. You can eat outside or inside with air-con, and it's open every day.

The open-air *Les Trois Caimans* (tel 222380) is also good and best known for Mali's speciality, the Niger perch (*capitaine*) and the pepper steak. It's near downtown next to the bridge and is open only from October to May and is closed Tuesday. The adjoining nightclub gets going around 11 pm. *Le Berry* is a well-known bar in the dead centre of town and serves surprisingly good food. It's one block from Hôtel Majestic going towards the market and is open every day.

Vietnamese *Le Bol de Jade* gets good reviews from those who know, the Vietnamese. There's authentic Vietnamese cuisine, air-con, pleasant surroundings, good service and reasonable prices. It's downtown a half block from the main BDM bank and open every day. *New Asia* is equally good and has more seafood dishes. It's on Sotouba Road, a few km from downtown.

Lebanese *L'Écuelle* offers a few well-prepared Lebanese specialities along with numerous French dishes. This recommended restaurant is outdoors and has music and moderate prices. It's central, two blocks behind USAID.

Les Pyramides, one block away, is a notch down and many dishes must be ordered one day in advance, but the selection is larger, including a *mesa ordinaire* for about 4300 CFA. *Le Crésus* two blocks away should be avoided at all costs.

Entertainment & Sports

Bars *Sabbague* and *La Phoenica*, both with terraces for watching people, are also the most popular watering holes for travellers. *Le Berry* runs a strong second and is a good restaurant as well. It's in the dead centre of town, a half block from the Hôtel Majestic. Those seeking a little more tranquility go to the *Manantali* bar at the Grand. *Faguibine* at the Amitié is more expensive, with primarily hotel clientele, but it's popular after work and has live music.

At the opposite end of the scale is *Bar Kassouf*, downtown across from the cathedral. It's a cheap bar and good for meeting Africans; big beers are CFA 550. *Bar Coumba*, on Avenue de la Nation three blocks from Hôtel Majestic, is a well-known, disreputable Bamako landmark where everyone goes, especially the prostitutes, after 3 am when the nightclubs start slowing down. *Bar Mali*, about four blocks away and behind Cinéma Vox is even more disreputable.

280 Mali – Bamako

Nightclubs Nightclubs do not get going before 11 pm. Monday is not the night to go; they are either closed then or certainly dead. Drinks (included in the cover charge) are cheap by African standards, about CFA 1350/1650 weekdays/weekends unless otherwise stated. *Le Village* at the Grand Hôtel is the liveliest in town, with lots of dancing partners available. It's closed Mondays.

The *Cotton Club*, opposite the US Embassy, has recently become very popular and is well liked by many. It's open every day. *Black & White* near the centre of town has been around for years and is preferred by many Africans. It can easily get unpleasantly crowded and is considered by some expatriates to be a little dangerous. It's open every day. *Le Dogon*, a more expensive and spacious disco at the Amitié, is flash but frequently dead. It's closed Monday.

Le Calao across from the tennis club is fairly popular and has a mixture of African and disco music. It's open every day. *La Cabane Bambou* at the Hôtel Terminus on the outskirts of town is recommended only on weekends when there is usually special entertainment and prizes. *L'Africana* at the Hôtel les Hirondelles is usually lively even on weekdays and much more popular with the common man because of the lower prices.

Club les Loisirs is closed but look to see if it has reopened – it was the only place that regularly had live music.

Movie Theatres The best theatre by far, with air-con and daily showings at 9 pm, is at the Hôtel de l'Amitié. For karate flicks and Indian movies, there are four theatres downtown to choose from, including the Vox one block from the Cathedral.

Sports For tennis, the best players are at the tennis club in town about four long blocks from the Grand, but temporary membership is not available except from July to September when most of the

French are away on vacation. The best court is at the Hôtel de l'Amitié (CFA 1500 for each non-guest); you can hit with the hotel's pro for CFA 1500 to CFA 2000 extra. The courts at the Grand Hôtel are the same price, inferior and hence easier to reserve.

For swimmers, the best pool for doing laps is at the Lido (CFA 750), but it's out of town and it's impossible to get a return taxi. The pool at the Amitié is long and costs about CFA 1200 for non-guests; the one at the Grand is short and costs about CFA 700.

For softball fanatics, there are games every Sunday at 3.30 pm at the American Recreation Center except during the summer; inquire at the US Embassy for directions. If they need players, you can join in.

For windsurfing, there's a private club on the river near the Trois Caimans restaurant but the winds are frequently too light. Sunday is the most popular day.

Things to Buy

Artisan goods The *Grand Marché* in the centre of town is one of the best in West Africa. You can get all kinds of fabrics, tie-dye cloth, Mopti blankets, Fulani wedding blankets and rugs, brassware and beads. It's open daily until 6 pm.

The women's cooperative, *La Paysanne*, primarily sells fabrics. Prices are slightly higher and the selection is limited, but the clothes are more adapted to western tastes. It's off the road to the Lido restaurant, a five-minute taxi ride from downtown. The *Centre for the Blind* also has a limited selection of handmade items, such as tablecloths. It's downtown very close to the bridge. One of the most popular items with travellers are the handsome leather cassette boxes (*les caisses en cuir*). Unfortunately, they're a little bulky. You can usually find them in the dead centre of town near the traffic lights and Le Berry bar.

Gold & Silver The gold market next to the mosque, *l'Artisanat*, is one of the best places to buy gold and silver in West Africa. It's sold by the gram, about CFA 4500 a gram for gold and CFA 500 for silver. The quality of the silver is typical for West Africa, meaning it tarnishes easily. Bargaining is usually not possible. It's downtown next to the mosque and open until 6 or 7 pm.

There are also reputable gold shops downtown on the same street as the Gondole restaurant. You need not worry about getting cheated at any of these places, but if you do, just go to the police and they will help you get your money back.

Music For Malian music, there are no music shops, just street vendors. Most of the cassettes are of terrible quality. Local groups include Les Ambassadeurs du Mali, Super Rail Band, Super Biton National de Ségou, L'Ensemble Instrumental National du Mali. Some of the leading singers are Boncana Maiga, Alassane Soumano and Salif Keita.

Getting There & Away
Air Air Mali (tel 225741/2) at the Majestic Hôtel has flights to Mopti, Timbuktu, Gao, Kayes and Nioro.

Bush Taxi The principal Gare Routière for Ségou, Mopti, Gao and Sikasso is eight km from town in Sogoniko. Most leave early. For a bush taxi to Mopti, get there before 8 am; it costs CFA 5000 plus CFA 500 for luggage.

For bush taxis to Kayes, Nioro or Guinea, the Gare Routière is near the river behind Les Trois Caimans.

Train The train for Dakar (Senegal) leaves Bamako on Wednesday and Friday at 11.30 am. See the Getting There section at the start of this chapter for more details.

Getting Around
Air Transport At the Bamako airport, there's a departure tax of CFA 1500. You'll find a

restaurant and bank (not always open) but no car hire. A taxi into town (15 km) is CFA 2500 to CFA 3000; bargaining is required but rarely a hassle. A bus (CFA 500) meets every flight. Reconfirm your onward flight as soon as possible because the airlines do not have reservation terminals and must cable for confirmation. Check-in at the airport can be very crowded, so go early.

Taxi The fare is CFA 90 (double for long trips) for a shared taxi; CFA 500 for a taxi to yourself ('charter') or one stationed at a hotel; about CFA 1600 by the hour (more from the hotels); about CFA 11,000 plus gas by the day (bargaining definitely required). Finding cabs can be difficult.

For a shared taxi, walk to a major road and hail a cab going in the same direction. The problem is that they're frequently full. If you're downtown and don't mind paying the charter rate, go to a major hotel or, closer to the centre, one of the taxi stations (the Dabanaani circle near the Petit Marché, or in front of Cinéma VOX near the Cathedral).

Car Rental Eurocar (tel 222481, telex 578) at the Grand Hôtel; Falaye Keita (BP 1720, tel 224325/03, telex 433) at the Hôtel de l'Amitié; as well as the travel agencies in the information section.

AROUND BAMAKO
Those with wheels might consider an excursion to **Selingue Dam**; it's a two-hour drive. The lake behind the dam is popular with expatriates on Sundays. You can rent a two bedroom furnished villa for CFA 10,000. It has a pool and you can play tennis, volleyball or go fishing.

Or drive to **Sibi**; it's a one-hour drive on the road to Guinea. There are massive cliffs in the area, which are great for climbing, hiking and picnicking.

The Niger River Route

SÉGOU

One of the best one-day excursions from Bamako is a trip to Ségou, a town of 50,000 inhabitants noted for its still largely intact colonial buildings. Alongside the Niger River 235 km from Bamako on a good paved road, it is easily reached in three hours by private vehicle, up to an hour more by bush taxi. With numerous colonial buildings and abundant trees, this small town offers a glimpse of what a colonial town was like.

You can also get a better feeling than in Bamako of life along the Niger River. Take a short walk down to the river and observe the goings-on – boats being loaded and discharged, motors being repaired, people bathing, and dug-out canoes (pirogues) passing by. It's fascinating just watching and talking with the locals. The bar at the Auberge is an excellent place to get your questions answered; it's also the watering hole for most visitors.

Office du Niger

Ségou is also noted for having the headquarters of the Office du Niger, one of the largest rice-growing operations in West Africa. In the 1920s, the French constructed a huge irrigated area of thousands of hectares for growing rice and exporting it to France. For the system to operate successfully, the water must enter each farmer's plot at just the right moment. Coordinating the water flow in such a large system requires sophisticated management. The system also requires flat land and motivated farmers. If the land isn't perfectly level, some plants get too much water and others not enough.

In many areas, the plots are owned by school teachers, bureaucrats, soldiers – anybody but the sharecroppers who till the land. As a result, the system has been a failure from the beginning, with farmers getting yields one-quarter those in Asia. You can catch a glimpse of these fields by travelling north of Ségou towards Niono. For fields closer to town, inquire at the Operation Riz Ségou offices. The rice-growing season is from June to October.

Market

Market day is Monday, but it's active every day. Ségou is the centre for Bambara pottery and Ségou blankets, and these items are especially good buys here. Those interested in rugs should stop by the rug cooperative.

Places to Stay & Eat

Le Campement at the Office du Niger is about CFA 3000 a room. This is the best value for your money, but it's frequently full. The rooms have mosquito nets and fans, although the beds may be missing a few slats. You can eat well there or, more cheaply, at several places around the market.

Many travellers stay at *L'Auberge*, which costs about CFA 4500/5500 for singles/doubles. The rooms are dingy but some have air-con, plus the garden is nice and it's in the centre of town near the river. The restaurant is the best that Ségou has to offer, plus the bar is a meeting place and the management is a source of good humour, conversation and information.

Le GTM at CFA 5000/6500 for singles/doubles has air-con and the best rooms in town, which isn't saying much. At night, it's the hot spot in town – loud music, booze and women – which is why many travellers find it intolerable for lodging. In any event, it's a lively meeting place at night, especially Saturdays when frequently there's live music. It's a good walk from the town centre and the path is dark at night.

MOPTI

This area of Mali is one of the most fascinating in West Africa. With a beautiful mosque and the most vibrant port on the Niger River, coupled with side trips to the fascinating Dogon country and Djenné, the Mopti area offers enough to keep one fully occupied for quite a few days.

The approach itself to Mopti is a little unique. The first thing you'll notice leaving Sévaré on the mainland is the 12-km dyke connecting it and Mopti. Between the two, there are rice fields that are inundated half the year.

History
Until the 20th century, Mopti was eclipsed by Djenné. During the colonial period starting at the turn of the century, commerce increased significantly. Much of this passed on the Niger River. Mopti's proximity to the centre of this wide, shallow river (coupled with the 12-km dyke that the French constructed to connect it by road to the mainland) gave it a distinct advantage. Today, with approximately 40,000 inhabitants, Mopti quadruples Djenné's population.

Information
Banks are open 8.30 to 11.30 am and 2.15 to 3.15 pm, and closed Saturday and Sunday.

If you don't have a photo permit, you can get one in minutes at the Commissariat if the official is there; they require a photograph. You can also get your visa extended there, and you'll need photographs for that as well.

Mosque
Approaching Mopti you'll see the Sudanese-style, mud brick mosque, built in 1935, towering above the city. It compares favourably with the revered mosque in Djenné, which provided the inspiration for Mopti's mosque. If you're lucky, the guard may let you climb the stairs to the porch for a view of the city.

Waterfront & Market
Equally interesting is the waterfront. Packed with brightly painted pirogues and people selling their goods and repairing their boats and motors, the waterfront is the vital organ of Mali, one that keeps it going despite the poverty and disease everywhere.

Thursday is market day. Bozo fishermen converge on the city to sell their dry fish. If you see huge white slabs which resemble 18th century tombstones, it is salt from northern Mali brought down by the camel caravans. It's the same rock salt you'll see in most of the markets throughout West Africa.

Look for the famous Mali blankets and Fulani wedding blankets; you won't find better prices. The wool blankets can be rough to touch; the finer ones tend to be softer. The cotton ones are softer still, but are cheaper because they wear out more quickly. The long wedding blankets can

Man walking his fish - a CAPITANE
The fish salesman strolled the Niger with his impressive riverfish meekly in tow —
MOPTI, MALI

DOGON WOMAN WITH FIREWOOD COLLECTION GEAR...
Sancha, MALI

easily cost CFA 60,000 if they're 100% wool. (Many are mixed wool and cotton.)

Kakalodaga

Dusk is a good time to hire a pirogue. If you've got the time and money, take a trip over to the Bozo village of Kakalodaga. At dusk, the village buzzes with activity – women cooking, men repairing their nets and building boats. Pelicans, ibis and herons may contribute to the tranquility of the ride back. At the Bar Bozo, which has a beautiful view of the river scene at sunset, there's no lack of men offering to take passengers.

Places to Stay

Apart from Le Relais Sofitel Kanaga, all the hotels suffer from sporadic blackouts except at night, so even if there's a fan or air-con, you probably won't get to use it much.

Places to Stay – bottom end

Bar Mali costs about CFA 1700 for a room (CFA 1900 with fan). It has cold showers, fairly clean toilets, mosquito nets and a restaurant with edible food. But beware: the noise and prostitutes galore may drive you crazy.

Hôtel Oriental has rooms for about CFA 3300. This place is noisy and has dirty communal bathrooms, but hitchhikers love it because it's cheap, there's water, the food is decent, and you can get your clothes washed. Some people prefer to sleep on the terrace. It's near the mosque and Bar Mali.

Places to Stay – middle

Le Bateau costs about CFA 5500 for a 1st-class cabin for two people, CFA 6500 for a 2nd-class cabin which sleeps four. This boat without name has lots of charm and small but clean rooms, but there are no mosquito nets and the water is only on for several hours at night. The bar is open only at night, when you can have a big beer for about CFA 450 and watch the pirogues silently pass by. Not easy to locate, it's the large blue and white boat alongside the river near the restaurant Les Nuits de Chine.

A good place to meet people is *Le Campement*. It's about CFA 5300 to CFA 6350 for singles, and CFA 8800 to CFA 10,000 for doubles including breakfast and dinner (obligatory). You'll find cold showers, ceiling fans, candles, dirty bathrooms, mosquito nets and a decent bar. It's at the entrance to Mopti, on your right, and frequently full, so inquire early in the day.

Motel de Sévaré has singles for CFA 7000 to CFA 8000 and doubles for CFA 8000 to CFA 9250, with breakfast. It's in Sévaré a full 15 km from Mopti, this is the best hotel after Le Relais but a good notch down.

Places to Stay – top end

Le Relais Sofitel Kanaga at CFA 16,950/

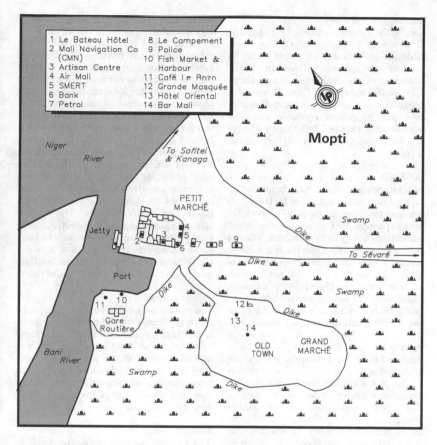

1 Le Bateau Hôtel
2 Mali Navigation Co (CMN)
3 Artisan Centre
4 Air Mali
5 SMERT
6 Bank
7 Petrol
8 Le Campement
9 Police
10 Fish Market & Harbour
11 Café Le Bozo
12 Grande Mosquée
13 Hôtel Oriental
14 Bar Mali

20,250 for singles/doubles, is an excellent three-star hotel with back-up generator but no pool. It's next to the river but, unfortunately, a good 20-minute walk to the centre of town. (If you feel lazy, you can rent a pirogue to take you there.)

Places to Eat

Sofitel Kanaga serves the best food in town but is pricey by Malian standards – about CFA 4500 for the set menu and CFA 1000 for a beer. You can save money by ordering less substantial meals from the á la carte menu. *Les Nuits de Chine*, downtown near the river, is no longer Vietnamese but the food, braised chicken and the like, is still good and inexpensive.

Le Bozo, downtown on the water's edge with the best possible view of the harbour, offers ordinary food which isn't particularly cheap and the service is notoriously slow. Even if you don't eat here, this is the most pleasant place for a drink and to meet people, even if it's not cheap. Full meals, such as fish and rice or chicken and fries, cost about CFA 1500. *Bar Mali*, *Hôtel Oriental* and *Le Campement* are all cheaper and offer acceptable fare.

Getting There & Away

Car Rental To rent vehicles for either the Dogon area (Sangha) or Djenné, both SMERT and Manding Voyages (near the Campement) have offices in Mali. Manding offers cheaper rates, eg about CFA 45,000 a day for a Land-Rover with chauffeur. It's best to reserve in Bamako to be sure of getting a vehicle. Petrol is occasionally rationed but there's always black market petrol at a slightly higher price.

DJENNÉ

A small town of about 8000 inhabitants, Djenné is sometimes missed by travellers pressed for time. It's a pity because for many people, this is one of the most interesting towns in West Africa. Djenné is located on an island on the Niger River Delta, a two-hour drive from Mopti, of which 29 km is on a dirt road which intersects with the Mopti-Ségou highway. Market day is Monday and the best day to be there, but by no means pass it by just because you can't arrive on a Monday.

History

Founded in the 9th century, Djenné is one of the oldest towns in West Africa and was in its prime during the 14th and 15th centuries when it profited, like Timbuktu, from the trans-Saharan trade. When the French explorer René Caillié visited there in the early 19th century, he reported that most of the inhabitants could read, no one went barefoot, everyone seemed to be usefully employed, and the inhabitants enjoyed a good standard of living and had plenty to eat.

Until the 14th century Djenné co-existed with Jenné-Jeno, a town three km up stream which dated back to about 250 BC. The latter is now only an archeological site. Iron implements and jewellery have been discovered there which suggest that it may have been one of the first places in Africa where iron was used. In the 8th century Jenné-Jeno was one of the two oldest fortified cities in West Africa with

walls three metres thick. Around 1400 it was abandoned; nobody knows why.

Today, modern Djenné is one of the most picturesque towns in West Africa. Little has changed for centuries. Almost all of the houses are of mud with thatched roofs, making for an aesthetically pleasing town which blends in with the environment. Many of the houses have more than one storey, with the top part being, historically, for the masters and the middle floor for the slaves, and the bottom floor for storage and selling. The porches of the houses are lined with wooden columns, while the wooden window shutters and doors are decorated with paint and metal objects. The narrow streets allow the sun to penetrate only rarely, making the town refreshingly cooler than most. You'll see artisans skilfully plying their crafts, particularly gold, silver and wooden *objets d'art*.

Things to See

Not to be missed in Djenné is a stroll to the river, especially nice at sunrise or sunset. If you hire a guide (many will offer their services), he will probably want to show you the place where young girls were buried alive in the hope of keeping the town prosperous by warding off destruction from the annual rise of the nearby river. Don't go; only the story is interesting.

Mosque

The elegant mosque in Djenné, built in 1905, is renowned. A previous mosque, famous even in Europe, was demolished in the 19th century because of political and religious strife. The present mosque is considered by many to be the best example of Sudanese mud architecture; photographs of it are shown in exhibits worldwide.

Just to keep the mosque from disintegrating during the rains is a major task and each year the mud structure must undergo considerable repair. Inside, there is a forest of a hundred or so massive columns, taking up almost half of the floor surface, while the outside is of a style common to all Sudanese mosques. You can get a superb view of the town from the mosque's upstairs terrace, but the guard may insist on a gift.

Places to Stay & Eat
If you're with SMERT, you can stay at their lodgings, which are clean with showers. The only alternative is *Le Campement* at about CFA 1500/2700 for singles/doubles. The owner is friendly, but only some of the rooms have mosquito nets, there is no running water (bucket showers only), the erratic electricity is on for a few hours in the evening, and the barely edible meals cost about CFA 1650. You'll do better eating at one of the rotisseries in the main square.

If you stay in town more than one night, register with the Commissariat de Police. They may make you pay for a tourist card from SMERT if you don't have one.

Getting There & Away
It isn't necessary to have a four-wheel-drive vehicle to get there except, sometimes, in July and August.

Bush Taxi If you go by bush taxi, the only time to get one in Mopti is early in the morning. From Mopti it should cost around CFA 1600 plus 250 for a pack. If you're coming from Ségou, you'll be much better off going to Mopti and getting a bush taxi there than trying to catch a ride at the 29 km entrance to Djenné. All the bush taxis will be completely full and they'll never pick you up.

Boat You can even take a pirogue from Djenné to Mopti; a one-day trip if you leave at 4 am from the Campement. The loading place is four km from town.

Car Rental The other alternative is renting a car with chauffeur in Mopti from either SMERT or Manding Voyage. SMERT's price per person for an all-day excursion varies according to the number of passengers: about CFA 39,000 for one person, CFA 17,500 for four people, and CFA 12,000 for up to eight people.

Manding Voyages' rates are lower. You can also rent a vehicle in Bamako from the same agencies. From February to June, vehicles pass over the submersible dyke crossing the Bani River which flows alongside the town. During the rest of the year, they must be put on a ferry and pulled across the Bani. Between July and September, the approach road can sometimes become impassable because of the rains.

DOGON COUNTRY
On everybody's list of the top 10 places to see in West Africa, this area is worth every bit of the extra effort it takes to get there. The Dogon live primarily on the escarpment which extends about 200 km from Bandiagara to Douentza. They number only about 250,000 and are animists, with a rather complex culture. What makes the Dogon special are their multi-storey houses and granaries built into the rock faces of the Bandiagara cliffs; their art, which is among the best-known in Africa; and their unique irrigated vegetable plots in the inhospitable rocky cliffs.

Around 1300, the Dogon began taking refuge from the more bellicose Muslims and built their villages in the Bandiagara cliffs, where they continue to resist Muslim influence. Extensive cereal agriculture was impossible in such an environment so they developed their unique agricultural system, which involves bringing topsoil from the flatland below to the water trapped in pools in the rocks.

The system works well and is very productive – their onions make their way all over the country. Foreign technicians trying to provide assistance have found little to improve upon except the water catchments, which can be made more water-tight with cement.

The photogenic villages resemble those of cliff-dwelling Indians in the southwest of the United States. While some villages

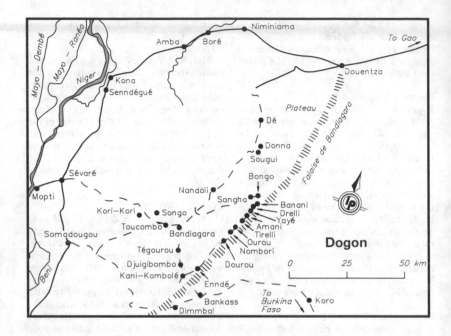

are built on the flat rocks below the escarpment, the more spectacular ones are built higher up on the steep slopes. The houses are of mud with flat roofs instead of the more common conical straw roofs. The smaller granaries, however, retain their traditional shape of a small African hut with a conical roof because they are assembled on the ground and then hoisted up. Some of the houses are multi-storeyed and quite old. The better ones have elaborately carved doors less than a metre high which art collectors are forever seeking. Some very good examples are still produced.

Dogon masks are very popular with many travellers. One of the most important masks is the snake mask because according to legend, the Dogon's first ancestor took the form of a snake when he died. If you're in Sangha, don't be surprised if you are led secretly to some outlying house where the owner purports to have some very old masks

and doors. They are rarely old but the quality of Dogon art remains fairly good compared to that being produced in other areas of Africa; just don't be surprised to find your piece coloured by shoe polish. As in most African communities, masks play an important role in Dogon religious ceremonies.

If you're lucky, you might even be able to see one of their celebrations (fêtes), such as l'Agguet around May in honour of the ancestors, l'Ondonfile three weeks before the first rains, or la Guinam Golo around January.

The Dogon are obsessed with raising children. Marriages are arranged by the parents, sometimes even before the birth of their children. A young man usually learns the name of his wife when she is circumcised around the age of 12. Sexual relations begin almost immediately, even before the girl's first menstruation. Until a man has produced a child, he is not

Top: Bororo men, Niger (EE)
Bottom: Unloading boats and marketing salt at the river market, Mopti, Mali (EE)

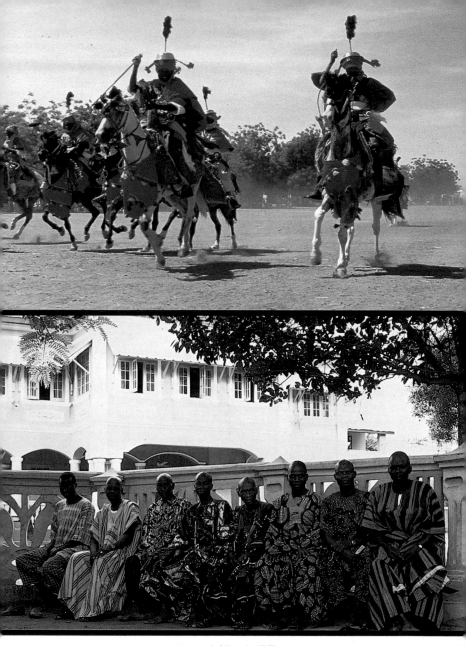

Top: The Emir of Katsina's bodyguard, Nigeria (EE)
Bottom: Yoruba men waiting outside Oni's palace, Ife, Nigeria (EE)

really considered to be a man. Considering the difficulty of growing things in the rocky cliff, it is not difficult to understand why procreation is also a common theme in Dogon statues and plays a strong role in Dogon mythology.

Getting There & Away

Most of the Dogon villages are difficult to reach. Because Sangha is one of the more accessible ones and has a striking *falaise* (cliff), most travellers end up there. It's 107 km, a three-hour drive, from Mopti via Bandiagara. Getting there requires a high clearance vehicle because of the sizeable boulders on the 44-km stretch between Bandiagara and Sangha. The route from Bandiagara to Dourou is just as bad. Try to avoid the months of February to May when it's hot and walking is uncomfortable. Those who plan to do several days of hiking should head to Bandiagara and then map out an itinerary that avoids Sangha because it has become too saturated with tourists.

Many travellers hook up with SMERT, Manding Voyages or Dogon Voyages in Mopti (or Bamako) for a one or two-day tour of Sangha. A one-day trip to Sangha with SMERT costs about CFA 70,000 for a vehicle and chauffeur. Manding does the same for about CFA 45,000; if you stay overnight in Sangha and come back by noon, the charge will be about CFA 70,000.

If you want to hitchhike, hang around the Sofitel in Mopti or the Campement in Djenné and try hitching up with other travellers; the chances are pretty good in the tourist season from December to January. You can also catch a truck from Mopti to Sangha on market day (once every five days, which is the length of the Dogon week) or, better, take a bush taxi to Bandiagara and try the same from there. It's not easy even there because trucks do not leave every day, although they always leave on market day in Sangha. Also, as a loner or couple you can tell SMERT that you wish to join another party going to Sangha. You can go with one group, and

arrange to return with another group a few days later. This is advisable because most groups don't stay overnight, and a few hours in Sangha isn't nearly enough time.

Bandiagara

Bandiagara, an hour's drive from Mopti on a good dirt road, is the first stop on almost every tour of Dogon country. Market day is Monday and Friday. You'll find other travellers here, and they may have some good suggestions for touring the area. Buy some cigarettes; they can come in useful as presents along the way. The water on the cliffs is fairly clean, but bring water tablets or a water container. Whatever you do, don't forget to stop by the police station on the outskirts of town leading towards Sangha; travellers failing to do so have been known to get into some pretty hot water with the police.

Places to Stay *Le Campement* costs about CFA 3000/4080 for singles/doubles with breakfast. The toilet and washing facilities are communal and it's on the outskirts of town leading towards Sangha.

Bar Kansaye has cleaner rooms for about CFA 1000. The owner is a friendly war veteran (*ancien combatant*) and will keep your excess baggage if you go trekking. You can also sleep on the roof of *Le Conseil* for about CFA 1400 and eat there as well. It's unmarked, on the river bank across the bridge from the Campement. *Faïda*, near the mosque, is another.

Sangha

The people have seen tourists before, so don't expect them to be too curious. They resisted the Muslims for 600 years and their resistance to tourists is just as strong. Nonetheless, the government is concerned that tourism may spoil the place, so you are not supposed to walk around without a guide, which you are required to hire at the entrance. SMERT officials have been known to demand stiff fines from people wandering around without guides. They aren't cheap, although you may be able to bargain down the price a little. If you're on your own get together with a group and share the cost.

Perhaps it's just as well because without a guide you would miss the significance of many things and might unintentionally do something to cause offence, such as taking off your shirt or touching one of the many sacred objects.

Everything plays a role in the Dogon cosmos. The niches outside the houses, for example, represent the family's lineage, and the eight pillars supporting the *toguna* represent the eight primordial spirits.

If you stay overnight, you'll get a better insight into Dogon life. Because the number of people visiting Sangha has the potential of destroying their culture, travellers need to be particularly sensitive to local customs and do as little as possible to intrude into their lives.

For those planning a walking trip of several days starting at Sangha, there are two routes. The most popular route leads south-west from Sangha along the falaise to Banani and Ireli followed by Yayé, Amani, Tireli, Ourou, Nombori and, finally, Dourou, a distance of about 30 km. At Dourou, you can get a vehicle back to Bandiagara 25 km to the west. Alternatively, from Banani you could walk in the opposite direction, north-east, along the falaise towards Soroli and Douentza, about 80 km away.

Places to Stay & Eat *Le Campement* costs CFA 3500/4500 for singles/doubles with breakfast. There's cold beer, a restaurant and *moustiquaires* (mosquito nets) for the beds. You may find it preferable to move your mattress outside onto the rocks where the wind will cool you off.

Le Bar de la Dogonne offers about the same level of accommodation with bucket showers, but it's cleaner with a more agreeable ambience and you can eat there. The family has a refrigerator and so can provide you with cold soft drinks and beer, and keep your food supplies chilled. It's near the Protestant church.

Getting There & Away Getting from Bandiagara to Sangha is an adventure in itself. Huge rocks make the going slow and bumpy; count on two hours, more in a truck. If you don't stay overnight, you'll have only three of four hours to walk around.

There are three routes, the seven km Petit Tour (Sangha to Gogoli) taking three hours, the 10 km Moyen Tour (to Gogoli and Banani), and the 15 km Grand Tour (to Gogoli, Banani and Ireli) taking six to eight hours. Be prepared for an arduous walk in the hot sun. Take water and a hat and, if possible, get up at dawn to go walking, rest, then walk again in the late afternoon so as to avoid the sun at its fiercest.

Other Dogon Villages

If you're going to be in the Dogon area for at least several days and you want to do some hiking, it's best to avoid Sangha altogether. One suggestion is to talk to the owner of the Bar Kansaye in Bandiagara. He has been known to arrange tours of several days to some of the lesser known villages, and you can get always some leads there. In any event, guides are not expensive (Sangha excepting) and they make trips more interesting. Otherwise, you risk missing insights into the local culture while at the same time running foul of the law. You could also rent a moped. Expect on paying about CFA 4000 for the moped and the same for a guide.

You could take the 40 km route south-east from Bandiagara through Tégourou, Djuigibombo, and Kani-Kombolé (there's a *case de passage*) to Bankass. Or you could take a taxi from Mopti to Bankass and start your trip there. The Monday market in Bankass is a good place to buy the indigo Dogon cloth. *Le Campement* in Bankass costs about CFA 1350 and has food and friendly people, or you can sleep on a mat at *Ben's Bar* for the same price. If you need help or advice, Ben is apparently more than willing to assist, including renting you a horse and cart. In Bankass, you can get a bush taxi to Koro (there's a campement) and onward to Burkina Faso, or return by bush taxi to Mopti (five hours). Or you could walk four hours back to Kani-Kombolé and then proceed north-east for 30 km to Dourou.

Another possibility is to catch a truck from Bandiagara to Dourou (30 km), and from there walk on the cliffs south-west to Kani-Kombolé or north-east 35 km to Sangha. Whatever you do, make sure you try some of the Dogon's millet beer (kojo). While still fermenting, it's usually poured into a large earthenware pot and then served in the shade to the men. It's an occasion to tell jokes and catch up on the news.

TIMBUKTU

In Timbuktu (Tombouctou), sand is everywhere. Even when you bite into the famous wholewheat bread of Timbuktu, you'll detect tiny particles. Sand is piling up on the outside of town, threatening to blanket everything. The only thing that seems to keep people here is tourism, trade and a small amount of farming on the nearby Niger River. Also, the salt trade continues to breathe life into the camel caravans which bring huge slabs of salt all the way from the Taudeni salt mines in northern Mali to be shipped down the river to Mopti. The fact that even today it's not easily reached seems only to make some people want to come here more than ever.

Timbuktu dates back to around 1100 AD when a group of Tuareg nomads settled here. The settlement was put in charge of an old woman while the men tended to the animals. Her name was Timbuktu, meaning 'mother with a large navel', possibly meaning she had a physical disorder. The settlement was named after her. The population is now 15,000, down from 100,000 centuries ago.

Many people find Timbuktu disappointing, others couldn't disagree more. If you are like most people with only a day to walk around and hop a camel for a short ride, you'll probably feel that a day is sufficient. In terms of interesting structures and commercial activity, Timbuktu cannot compete with Djenné and Mopti. But if you have the time, the Timbuktu area can be quite interesting, especially if you have a car.

If you like the desert, speak a little French, enjoy poking around, and especially if you can travel outside Timbuktu to Goundam and Lake Faguibine, or spend the night in a Tuareg camp, or see the wheat growing north of Dire, your journey is likely to be memorable.

Information

You should report to the police station as soon as you arrive in Timbuktu; you can get into problems if you don't.

SMERT is near Le Campement.

Things to See

The old section of Timbuktu is quite interesting. In the narrow streets of the old section you'll see two and three-storey houses with carved doorways similar to those in Djenné.

Mosques

Timbuktu has three of the oldest mosques in West Africa. They're not large, architecturally impressive, or in good repair – just historical.

Djingereyber (the Grande Mosquée) is the oldest of the mosques and dates from the 14th century. The Sankoré mosque was also a university and a major centre of Arabic learning with approximately 2500 students.

Markets

Entering the market, you'll think that with so little being sold, people must be starving. Any number of reporters visiting during the periodic droughts have been fooled into thinking the situation is bordering on catastrophic. In reality, commerce in Timbuktu is somewhat unique in that most staples are sold in bulk in merchants' homes.

There's also a small market, next to the large supermarket, where artisans work and sell their handicrafts.

René Caillié's House

You'll probably hear the name of the legendary René Caillié. When he was only 16 years old, he left France for Africa in the early 19th century when little was known about the Sahara. His initial attempts to reach the interior were unsuccessful, but in 1824 he returned to Africa and lived with the Moors. Disguised as an Arab, he learned all about the Arab culture. In 1828 he finally fulfilled his ambition and became the first European to reach Timbuktu, and live to tell the tale. His account of the trip and the cultures he encountered makes for fascinating reading. The house he stayed in is on the small list of 'must' places to see.

The house of another famous explorer, Gordon Laing, is nearby on the same street.

Taureg Camps

Touristy as it may be, a short camel ride from the Sofitel out to one of the Tuareg camps shouldn't be missed. The best time to go is in the late afternoon to see the desert sunset. SMERT will try to charge you CFA 5000 for this, but you can sometimes bargain the price down to CFA 3500 or so. You'll be entertained by a sword fight and energised by the strong, sweet Arab tea offered inside a Tuareg tent. It's prohibited to stay overnight in the Tuareg tents, but some people still manage to do it. If there's time, take the nine-km trip to Karaba on the Niger River and go for a pirogue ride.

Île de Paix

If you can get a ride, go by the Île de Paix, a privately run Belgian organisation which sponsors an irrigated rice scheme of several hundred hectares just outside town towards the river. You can take a walk around the perimeter to the pumping station. It's a successful project in terms of producing food, the only problem is that the technology (huge pumps) is a little too complex, making it impossible for the Belgians to leave without the system breaking down. So it cannot be duplicated elsewhere by Malians and is not useful as a development model. Still, the project is doing exactly what it's supposed to do – produce rice at a cost considerably less than shipping it in from Asia or the US. That's no mean accomplishment.

Places to Stay & Eat

Cheapest is the *Tombouctou* for about CFA 1000 a single. A five-minute walk from the Sofitel is *Le Campement* at about CFA 4500/6000 for singles/doubles including breakfast for rooms in the 22-room annex. The rooms are very basic and the building, though very attractive with a courtyard, is neglected. There are also some much better rooms with air-con in the main part of the hotel for about twice this amount. Meals run about CFA 2800. At the annex, it's more fun and cooler to drag your mattress to the roof and sleep under the stars.

Relais Sofitel Azalai (tel 921163, telex 994 Bamako) is CFA 16,900/20,250 for singles/doubles. This new 42-room hotel is very nice, with air-con and its own generator. There's no pool; the fixed menu (no à la carte) costs about CFA 4500. Reserve through Sofitel or at the Hôtel de l'Amitié in Bamako.

Unlike Gao, Timbuktu has virtually no bars outside the two hotels. *Kaleme Bar* behind the post office may be the only one.

Getting There & Away

Air This is a major problem. The only regularly scheduled flights from Bamako, Mopti and Gao are on Air Mali. Its service is very unreliable and many flights are cancelled. One plane crashed in 1985, killing everybody on board. It is still used by tourist groups, however, for lack of alternatives. STA Mali is a possibility, but it doesn't have regular flights. Mali

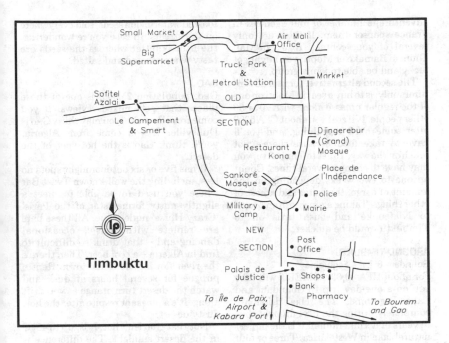

Timbuktu

Air Service charters planes for four to eight people.

Car It takes about three days overland from Bamako via Ségou, Niono, Niafounké and Goundam on the western side of the Niger River; Ségou to Timbuktu is 717 km. This route can become impassable at times between mid-July and the end of August.

You can also go overland from Mopti via Kona, Saraféré and Niafounké; this 434 km route can only be taken from mid-April to early June when the river is down. Now that the Mopti-Gao road is paved, the better route from Mopti may be north-east on the asphalted highway to Gossi and and then north to Gourma-Rharous, where there's a ferry. You could probably count on finding someone in Gossi who knows the route and would like to go along. Coming south from Gourma-Rharous, you will encounter two routes – one toward Mopti and other toward Gossi.

From Gao, you can try your luck with Air Mali, take the riverboat (late August to January), or go overland via Bourem. Trucks make the trip, but you may have to wait several days. The route is worse than anything on the Reggane (Algeria) to Gao route, and it can become impassible at times between mid-July and the end of August.

Boat The only other alternative is to go by boat. The riverboat takes about two days from Mopti (usually leaving on Thursdays) and four days from Koulikoro to Kabara (nine km south of Timbuktu). An alternative is to go on one of the large motorised boats (*pinasse*) plying the river. You could rent one to yourself, but for one or two people the price is prohibitive and it is only worthwhile for groups. Count on a minimum of four sun-baked days from Mopti to Timbuktu, five days in the opposite direction. This is quite an adventure; a number of tour agencies in France sponsor them. If there are only several of you, contact Togu Nu/Mali Tours in Bamako or Mopti; you might get lucky and be able to join a group.

The second alternative, for real adventurers only, is to buy a seat in Mopti on one of the regular pinasse along with 20 or 30 other people. It'll cost you about CFA 5000 after some hard bargaining, and you'll have to take food because there's not much on the way. To get to Timbuktu, you may have to change several times. Count on one to two weeks depending on the amount of cargo, the water and a host of other things. Taking a pinasse from Mopti to Niafounké and bush taxis on to Timbuktu would be quicker.

AROUND TIMBUKTU
Goundam & Lake Faguibine

For about CFA 80,000, SMERT will take you on a one-day trip to Goundam and Lake Faguibine. The lake dried up completely during the 1984 drought, but in years of normal rainfall it is the largest natural lake in West Africa. Three or four villages line the southern border. It's one of the three best places in the Sahel for seeing migratory birds. Goundam is nearby, about a three-hour drive from Timbuktu.

Diré is a 30-minute drive from Goundam and on the river. A few km north of Diré is the only place in West and Central Africa other than around Lake Chad where wheat is grown; the cool winter nights plus water nearby provide the essentials. Late November to March is the growing season. This is why you'll see the pita-like brown bread found everywhere in Timbuktu – always speckled with tiny sand particles that find their way into everything.

From December to February, you can watch farmers lift the water up several metres by swinging gourds heavy with water over their shoulders; it's definitely worth the trip alone. Then go into the Diré or Goundam market and eat some toasted watermelon seeds, sold everywhere on the streets. In case you're wondering, the fruit is bitter whereas the seeds are tasty when roasted and salted.

GAO

Gao, population 25,000, is one of those places that gets mixed reviews. If you come from Bamako, you may think Gao is Dullsville. If you come from Algeria, you'll think Gao is the hot spot of the desert.

It has five or six outdoor night spots no less, including the well-known Twist Bar where you used to be able to meet a slightly nutty former star of the Paris' 'Crazy Horse' nude revue. All these bars are replete with music, occasional dancing and – that drink so difficult to find in Algeria – a cool beer. Then there's the river flowing alongside town. Rent a pirogue for several hours at dusk and watch the desert turn orange as you drift along. It's a pleasant respite after the hot, dusty desert.

Not that Gao isn't hot. It is, up to 48°C in the desert sunlight. The difference is that you can cool off in the Hôtel Atlantide lounge, even if you don't stay there, and hear the stories of a wide spectrum of modern day adventurers. Some may not have anticipated the adventure they experienced, such as the couple from New York who read about the river cruise down the Niger River and pictured a small Caribbean cruise ship. What they found was loud African music blasting away, dirty toilets, and cargo spread everywhere with people on top.

Or maybe it'll be some French motorcyclists who have just come across the Sahara – over 1500 km – sometimes at reckless speeds with near fatal spills. Or maybe it'll be some Japanese helping the government search for uranium, or Peace Corps volunteers on vacation making the grand tour of Mali.

Besides the usual trip to the market, a pirogue ride, or a visit to the small museum next to the SNTN bus station, you can observe rural life in several of the outlying towns where rice is planted along the Niger.

The river starts rising around early July (from the heavy rains in Guinea, the source of the Niger). Rice is transplanted or scattered as the river rises, the plants growing just fast enough to keep their heads out of the waters. Dykes have been built to keep the river from flooding the plants too soon; maintaining them is no small job, particularly because they are eventually covered by the river each year. From November to January, this 'floating' rice is harvested from pirogues – not exactly what one learns in agricultural school.

As the river recedes, sorghum is planted on the wet banks and reaches maturity using only the residual moisture. Agriculture may not be your bag, but you're likely to find this interesting if you get the chance to talk to some Songhai farmers or others knowledgeable on the subject. Agriculture is, after all, a critical matter in this area of the world. Even when the rice and sorghum crops are decent, the area imports about half of its grain requirements. In a bad year, this can reach 90%. In droughts, the desperate are forced to eat even lily pads (*cram cram*).

Getting grain from the States to Gao and the outlying areas costs more than you may think. One million dollars of grain costs another US$2.5 million in transportation costs. You might wonder why people don't just get up and leave. Some do, but the Songhai who dominate this area are proud people who are not about to forget the once great Songhai empire and leave their homeland.

They and the Bambara do not get along and the fact that the Bambara have become the dominant ethnic group in Mali, with their centre Bamako as the capital of the country, only accentuates the animosity. Pity the Bambara civil servants who are stationed in Gao – many are social outcasts.

Information

Banks are open only from 8 to 11 am; the fee for cashing travellers' cheques is CFA 500. Don't forget to have your passport stamped; the police office closes for passport business at 12 noon. The police also issue visa extensions and photo permits; just make sure the photo permit is good for all of Mali.

Places to Stay

For those on the cheap, *Chez Yarga*, about three km from the centre of town on the Niamey road, has stood the test of time. It's a long-time favourite of trans-Saharan travellers and costs CFA 750 to CFA 1000 after negotiation. It consists of mud brick dormitory rooms without doors, with mats on the floor, plus showers. The food is cheap and good for the price, especially the capitaine.

Camping Dominque is closer into town, about 1½ km from the centre of town near the SNTN bus terminal, and costs about CFA 650. Your possessions are reportedly safe here, and meals are about CFA 900. It is illegal to camp within 10 km of Gao except at the camping grounds. *Camping Tizzi Mizzi*, on the edge of town on the road to the airport, charges CFA 500/person and has good facilities. Another place is the *Government Rest House*. It has mats on the floor, showers, toilets, and doors that lock; the price is about CFA 3300.

The only hotel is *Hôtel de l'Atlantide*. The price of the rooms varies considerably, from about CFA 3300/4400 to about CFA 10,000 including breakfast. The more expensive rooms have private baths and air-con, but they're dingy. You can usually get away with putting more than two people in a room. Despite the rundown appearance of the rooms and the erratic water supply and electricity, the hotel is a pleasant place for a drink and a good meeting place, and the restaurant can sometimes serve a fairly decent meal, from about CFA 1650 and up.

Another possibility is *Le Village de Cases*, which is a block behind the

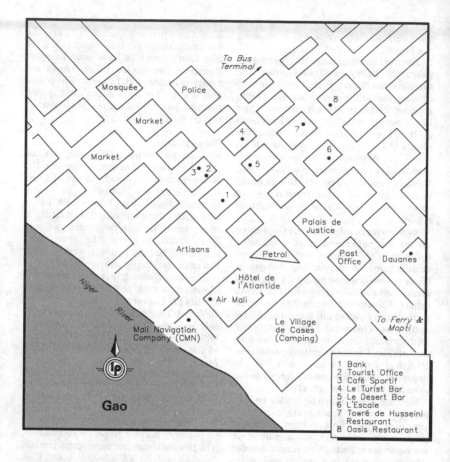

To Bus Terminal

Mosquée

Police

8

Market

4

7

Market

6

5

3 2

1

Palais de Justice

Artisans

Petrol

Post Office

Dauanes

Hôtel de l'Atlantide

Air Mali

Le Village de Cases (Camping)

To Ferry & Mopti

Niger River

Mali Navigation Company (CMN)

Gao

1 Bank
2 Tourist Office
3 Café Sportif
4 Le Turist Bar
5 Le Desert Bar
6 L'Escale
7 Towré de Husseini Restaurant
8 Oasis Restaurant

Atlantide and next to the river. You can camp here or use the bungalows equipped with cots, electricity and mosquito nets. The price of the bungalows is about one-third that of the hotel. You can also use the hotel's facilities and they will lock up your gear while you're out.

Places to Eat & Drink
In addition to the above, you can eat at several restaurants. *Snackbar L'Oasis* is about five blocks from the Atlantide in the direction of the SNTN; it has meals plus

it's a very animated meeting place. *Touré al Husseini* restaurant across the street from the Oasis also serves good cheap African food.

You can eat, meet Tuareg women and dance at *L'Escale*; it's fairly near the Oasis. *Le Desert* is another place for dancing. You can also eat and drink with good music at the well-known *Twist-Bar*, which is about three blocks from the Atlantide. *Sahel Vert* near the police station serves rice and steak and has a nice atmosphere.

If you just want to hear good music and have a drink in a garden setting, head for *Café Sportif*, three blocks from the Atlantide and next to the tourist office.

Getting There & Away

Air Air Mali is the only airline with a regular service, but it is not dependable. In principle, there is a plane to/from Niamey once a week. The only other alternative is to charter a plane.

Car It is now a cinch to get from Bamako to Gao; the road is asphalted all the way and takes about 16 hours straight driving time. You can catch an early morning bush taxi in Mopti without problem. If you're driving, you'll have to pass by the governor's office in Gao to get petrol coupons. If it's being rationed and you can't get enough, don't panic; you can always get black market petrol if you're willing to pay a premium. The road between Gao and Timbuktu (420 km) is worse than anything on the Gao-Algeria stretch. Trucks do it all the time, but if you're hitchhiking you may have to wait several days to get one.

Bus Between Niamey and Gao, you can take the very decent SNTN bus. Buses depart both cities on Monday and Friday between 10 am and 12 noon. The cost is about CFA 6500. The trip takes about 30 hours in the dry season, with a night at the border, but count on at least two days in July and August. Seats for the next bus go on sale as soon as a bus leaves. They go very quickly, so reserve as far in advance as possible, and take enough water for two days.

Boat The boat from Koulikoro only operates between August and December. From Mopti it usually continues to operate until late January or early February. In principal, the departure times are every Monday at 8 pm and every other Wednesday at 8 pm. Below Gao, there are some rapids, so it's not possible

to travel from Gao to Niamey by river boat or pinasse. It's also rare to find a pinasse headed to Timbuktu.

GOING TO NIGER

The buses for Niger leave form the SNTN station, about 1½ km from the centre of Gao next to the museum. Don't try hitchhiking to Niamey unless you're prepared to spend up to four days on the road. If you're hitchhiking to Algeria, there are trucks almost every day except during the July-September period when hitching becomes much more difficult. To find a truck, just ask the boys around the hotels to inquire.

If you're driving to Niamey, be prepared for some difficult sections south of Ansongo; it's sand and can be particularly difficult in the rainy season, occasionally impassable. The 443-km stretch between Gao and Niamey can be done in 12 to 15 hours, much longer in the July-August rainy season.

Fifty-five km south of Ansongo there's a very pleasant campement called *Chez Fata*. You'll find clean rooms for about CFA 3800, a bar, and very good food with lots of fish and rice but it's not cheap. There's also the possibility of taking a pirogue ride to see the hippos. People occasionally come here from Niamey to spend a long weekend. It's closed from July to August.

CATTLE CROSSING AT DIAFARABÉ

This is unquestionably the most captivating event in Mali and one of the most interesting in all of West Africa. Every year during December, in a rite that goes back more than 160 years, the sleepy village of Diafarabé is transformed into a centre of activity and celebration as hundreds of thousands of cattle (about a third of the total cattle population of Mali) are driven southward across the Niger River for greener pastures. It's a happy time for the herdsmen, who have been up in the Sahara for months on end. The crossing means reunion with their families and a time to celebrate. On the first day, a festival of music and dance is held.

A little known aspect is the democratic process preceding the crossing that determines when and in what order the herds will cross and where the herds will graze once they are on the other side. This is accomplished at a council of the local chiefs or elders. Cattle begin converging on the area well in advance of the crossing and must remain spread out to prevent complete destruction of the grazing grounds.

The major crossing is at Diafarabé because it's located at one of the narrowest places along the river. This is an event not to be missed. Diafarabé is about 200 km east of Ségou, on the western bank of the Niger River, about a six-hour drive from Bamako. A four-wheel-drive vehicle is not required.

The exact date is not set until November by the government's livestock agency (Ministère d'Élevage); the water level is an important determinant. The second weekend in December, give or take a week, is the approximate date. If you can't make the one at Diafarabé, inquire about the dates of the others; they continue through December.

HOMBORI

Hombori is on the new road between Mopti and Gao. What stands out about this place is, quite literally, a huge rock formation that rises straight up from the flat plains to over 1000 metres. At the village there is the 1155-metre-high Mt Hombori Tondo.

Twelve km to the south-west is a major rock formation called Le Main de Fatma, where the needle-like rocks look like fingers. It may be the single best place in West Africa for rock climbing and reportedly attracts climbers from Europe. There are some routes that purportedly have not been climbed. Non-experts who want to give it a try can get guides from the nearby villagers. They know the different routes, including the easier ones. You could easily get killed on some of the more difficult routes if you don't know what you're doing.

SAN

Hôtel Bazani and *Hôtel Bar Sangue* cost about CFA 1350. The *Campement* has doubles for about CFA 3300 and electricity for about four hours in the evening.

SIKASSO

Sikasso is 373 km from Bamako at the crossroad to Bobo Dioulasso (Burkina Faso) and Ferkéssédougou (Ivory Coast).

Places to Stay

The *Mamelon* is the best hotel. It has 25 rooms with air-con and a modest restaurant, and charges about CFA 7200 a room. *Le Lotto* at the truckstop (*Place Autogare*) offers very basic rooms for about CFA 1850 a single. The *Hôtel Solo-Khan*, at the Gare Routière about one km from the centre of town on the road to Ferkéssédougou, costs about the same.

KAYES

If you come from Senegal, Kayes is the first town of significance over the border.

Places to Stay

The *Hôtel du Rail* is the best hotel; rooms are about CFA 4000 to CFA 7000. It's a picturesque and pleasant old hotel directly behind the train station. For cheaper accommodation, try *Hôtel de la Pharmacie*, *Hôtel Amical* and *Hôtel l'Amitié*.

Mauritania

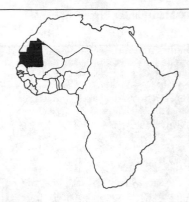

The Moors are the dominant ethnic group and the ones that give Mauritania its special character. It is the only country in West Africa controlled by people who are traditionally nomads, and the only country in sub-Saharan Africa where Islam is the official religion. In other countries, the nomads tend to be looked upon as a people out of step with the 20th century and a 'problem'. In Mauritania, they are in the majority and their settled descendants call the shots.

In Mauritania you can venture through towns half blanketed in sand, sip tea with nomads under their colourful tents in the middle of nowhere, cross plateaus that resemble the moon as much as the earth, and look at prehistoric rock drawings and ancient Saharan architecture. Even people who have lived in this 'God forsaken place' and would never do so again agree that it's a truly exotic and unforgettable place to visit.

Besides the desert, one of Mauritania's greatest attractions is the ocean. Mauritania is one of the best fishing and bird watching areas in the world. If you're into surf casting, Mauritania is No 1 in Africa and trout, bass, sea bream, bonita and ray abound. Air Afrique even has a special hotel just to cater for sports fishing charters. For birdwatchers, there's nothing quite like the 200-km-long Arguin Bank. It's the mating place for hundreds of thousands of sea birds, squashed side by side on islands of sand as far as the eye can see. If you're lucky or prepared to wait on the beach for several days, you might get to see a truly amazing event – Imragen fishermen using dolphins to round up the fish. The only drawback is that none of these places are very accessible. Mauritania is certainly not for everyone by a long shot and long drives in Land-Rovers or trucks are necessary to visit many of the sites.

HISTORY

It is hard to imagine that thousands of years ago Mauritania had large lakes, rivers and enough vegetation to support an abundance of elephants, rhinos and hippos. There is also evidence of early human habitation throughout Mauritania and you can find prehistoric rock drawings, arrowheads and the like scattered around the country. This came to an end when the Sahara started spreading about 10,000 years ago.

Around the 3rd century the camel was introduced to the Berbers from Morocco. For Mauritania this significant event also meant the arrival of the nomads. With the camel, the Berbers could cover long distances and they established trading routes all over the western Sahara. Salt was the primary commodity and in those times it traded on a par with gold. Later, gold and slaves were traded as well, giving rise in the 9th and 10th centuries to the first empire in all of West Africa, the empire of Ghana, the capital city of which is believed to have been in south-east Mauritania at Koumbi-Saleh. The Berbers in Mauritania were reduced to vassals.

Islamic Beginnings

Islam began spreading throughout the area about this time. One Muslim group, the Almoravids, gained control over the Berbers and established their capital in Marrakesh (Morocco), from where they ruled the whole of north-west Africa as

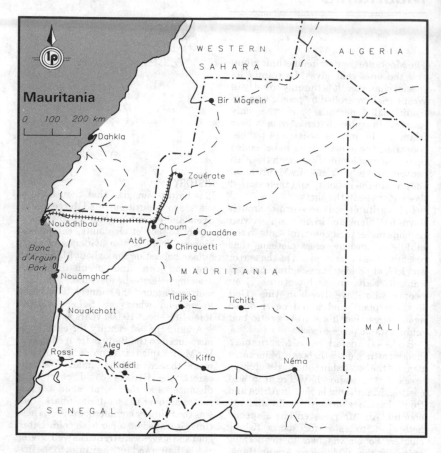

well as southern Spain. In 1076 they pushed south and, with the assistance of Mauritanian Berber leaders, destroyed the empire of Ghana. That victory led to the spread of Islam throughout the western Sahara – their most important legacy to Mauritania.

The Almoravids did not run a tight ship, however. What resulted was in effect two empires, one in Morocco and a southern one ruled by the Berbers of Mauritania. They, in turn, were subjugated by Arabs in 1674, after which virtually all the Berbers adopted Hassaniya, the language of their conquerors. This cross of Arab and Berber culture gave rise to the Moors. The stratified caste system of Moorish society, in which the losers were made slaves and the commoners made to pay tribute to the warriors, had its origins in this Arab conquest.

While Europe was busily draining the African continent of its people and its gold, starting in the late 15th century, Mauritania remained relatively unscathed.

Mauritania was less affected by European intervention than just about any country in Africa – no depopulation from slavery, no reorientation of the economy toward cash crops, no robbing of its minerals. Sand, it appears, wasn't a hot commodity. For the French, Mauritania was just a buffer zone, a place to station troops to protect French West Africa from tribal raiders and ambitious European powers.

Little developed until 1814 when the Treaty of Paris gave France the right to explore and control the Mauritanian coast. The French headquarters were installed in Senegal at St Louis on the Senegal river. Moors controlled the area along the river, and for security reasons the French wanted to take that control away. Playing one Moorish faction off against the other, they succeeded, and established the colonial territory of Mauritania in 1904.

It took the French another 30 years to subjugate the stubborn Moors in the northern areas. Yet, the French focused their attention elsewhere, and did not even discover the huge iron ore deposits there until just before independence.

Independence

With independence in 1960, the Moors, under President Mokhtar Ould Daddah, declared Mauritania an Islamic republic and set about building a new capital, Nouakchott. To take advantage of the country's sizeable iron ore deposits in Zouerate, they built a 675-km railway and a mining port. Production began in 1963.

The mines were operated by a foreign-owned consortium that paid its 3000 expatriate workers handsomely – their salaries accounted for two-thirds of the country's entire wages bill. When the Mauritanian miners went out on a two-month strike in the late '60s, the army intervened. It was a bloody mess, and eight miners were killed. Left-wing opposition to the government mounted and some miners formed a clandestine Marxist union in 1973. President Ould Daddah survived the challenge from left-wing opponents by nationalising the

company in 1974 and withdrawing from the Franc Zone, substituting the ouguiya in place of the CFA.

It was the Spanish Sahara issue that finally toppled the government. The government entered into an agreement in 1975 with Morocco and Spain to divide up the former colony. Mauritania was to take an empty slab of desert in the south and Morocco was to get the mineral-rich northern two-thirds, with Spain relinquishing all claims. Naturally the inhabitants of what became known as the Western Sahara were furious; the Polisario Front with the assistance of Algeria, Libya and Cuba launched a guerrilla war to oust both countries from the area.

Mauritania was very vulnerable; the railway linking the iron ore mines and the port ran practically on the border with the Western Sahara. The Polisario sabotaged it continually. In 1977 the country's iron ore exports were down by 18% due to the disruptions of the train service. A year later, exports were down 36% from the pre-war level. Twice the Polisario units travelled 1000 km from their base camps to lob mortars at Nouakchott.

The government increased its troops from 1800 men to 17,000, at great cost, but experience and morale were lacking. The Moors were more concerned with the danger of drought than that of an independent Western Sahara. To the black Africans of southern Mauritania, the war was meaningless. They were more concerned with the government's racial policies, inequitable political representation, and attempts to compel all school children to study in Arabic (potentially lessening their opportunities for university education in French-speaking countries).

A successful coup in 1978 brought in a new government that, with difficulty, extricated Mauritania from the conflict within a year by renouncing all territorial claims to the Western Sahara. Morocco reacted by simply claiming all the country, so the war continues without Mauritania (and continues to block the trans-Saharan route through Mauritania). Despite promises to get the economy back on the rails, the new government was unable to do so. The military wanted a change; so in 1984, there was a palace coup, called 'the re-structuring' by the new government, which brought in the present military ruler, Colonel Maaouya Sid'Ahmed Ould Taya.

Today

Thanks to its iron ore exports, Mauritania's per capita GDP is around US$450, placing it in the intermediate range of underdeveloped countries. But a single statistic can be misleading. The iron ore money is simply not filtering down to the majority of the population; their standard of living is very low. Infant mortality, for example, is 170 per 1000, about 80% higher than in the 30-odd countries which the World Bank classifies as the world's poorest (over half are in Africa).

The droughts of the early '70s and early '80s had a more devastating impact on Mauritania than on any other country in West and Central Africa. In 1965, the nomadic population was 65%; now it's less than 25%. The slums surrounding Nouakchott are evidence of the plight of the nomads.

Mauritania's high-grade ore deposits at Zouerate are due to run out in 1990. New mines are being developed, the first stage of which will cost about US$500 million, almost equal to Mauritania's entire GDP. However, they are inferior in ore content and will have to be enriched, requiring another US$90 million to construct an enrichment plant. One bright spot is the fishing industry, which now contributes about 15% to government revenues and could add considerably to export earnings. In any event, the 4% annual growth rate the country obtained between independence and the mid-1970s will be difficult to match.

PEOPLE

From photographs of Mauritania, you may get the impression that 90% of the 1.8 million people in Mauritania are Moors of Arab and Berber descent. Actually, the figure is closer to about 40%. The rest are black Africans, split into two groups. The *Harratin* or Black Moors, the descendants of blacks enslaved by the Moors, have assimilated the Moorish culture and speak their language, Hassaniya. Culturally, they have little affinity with the southerners, the Africans living in the south along the Senegal river. The southerners are primarily Fulani, Wolof, Toucouleur and Soninké – the same ethnic groups found across the border in Senegal. The Moors have political control, consequently, tensions between the southerners and the Moors are strong.

The Moors have one of the most stratified caste systems in West Africa. At the top are the upper classes, the light-skinned Bidan Moors descended from warriors and men of letters. Below them are commoners, mostly of Berber-Negroid stock. The lowest castes traditionally consisted of four groups: the Harratin Moors, artisans, bards, and slaves with no rights of any kind.

In 1980, there were an estimated 100,000 Harratin slaves in Mauritania. It wasn't until then that Mauritania declared slavery illegal – the last country in the world with slaves to do so! But it's one thing to declare slavery illegal; it's another for it to happen in fact. In Adrar, people are reportedly still being bought and sold. For one thing, freeing the slaves was conditional on the owners being compensated. Also, most 'slaves' have been attached all their lives to Bidan families. Once they walk out the door, they loose all their financial security. So it's not surprising that most continue living and working for their Bidan families while at the same time being part of, and cared for by, the greater family itself.

Traditionally, the Moors made their livelihood from raising camels, cattle, sheep and goats and from commerce, particularly transport with camel caravans.

For some, this came to an end during the severe droughts of the '70s and early '80s when most of their animals died and they had no choice but to come to Nouakchott and build shanty towns. But many had long ago given up their nomadic existence for life in the city as traders, indeed, Moorish merchants are a common sight all over West Africa. They're easy to spot. If you see a merchant with coffee-coloured skin and Arab facial features, wearing a long light blue African robe, he's probably a Moor.

If you talk with a Moor it won't be long before he offers you the traditional glass of Arab tea with mint. Traditionally, it's not one but three glasses that are served over a period of an hour or so. The glasses are small and even though it is very sweet and gets even sweeter the second and third time around, think of it as a liqueur with the punch of a strong cup of coffee, not something you drink because you're thirsty. It's an acquired taste, but if you're out in the enervating desert, chatting away and lying on cushions or mats under a tent for several hours, you'll find the taste has magically improved, and your energy restored.

The Moors are renowned as good craftsmen. In years past, the silver was of the highest quality, the kind that doesn't tarnish quickly. Those days are gone. Nothing is more sought after than the wooden chests with silver inlay for storing valuables, but there are also earth-tone rugs of camel and goat hair from Boutilimit, hand-woven carpets, hand-dyed leatherwork, cushions and saddles, silver daggers and jewellery. The quality was once excellent, now imitations are the norm.

GEOGRAPHY

Geography has not been kind to Mauritania. Although twice the size of West Germany, the northern two-thirds, including Nouakchott, is pure desert. Life there is extremely difficult – even during the best of times. Moreover, the desert is expanding southward, leading to a major exodus in recent years of nomads into the urban areas. Even in the lower third, which forms part of the Sahel, there are only a few areas in the extreme south that receive enough rainfall in good years to grow sorghum and millet. The country's total arable land consists of a 400-km strip 10 to 25 km wide, called the *chemana*, on the northern bank of the Senegal river which divides Mauritania and Senegal.

In the south it is fairly flat land with scrub, but as you move northward into the Sahara desert area, there are more sand dunes and the scrub begins to disappear. The rocky plateaux of this desert region offer the most spectacular sights in Mauritania. Most of the plateaux have been eroded, so that only isolated peaks remain. The highest and most well-known plateau area, over 500 metres, is the Adrar 450 km north-east of Nouakchott. This is where you'll find the 'must see' towns of Atâr, Chinguetti and Ouadâne. These plateaux are often rich in iron ore, especially at Zouerate about 200 km due north of Chinguetti. The other two major plateau areas are Tagant, 400 km due east of Nouakchott, and Assaba, to the south of the Tagant plateau.

Mauritania also has some 700 km of shoreline. The fishing town of Nouâdhibou in the extreme north is the second largest city. Between there and Nouakchott is the Arguin Bank National Park, a bird watchers' paradise where hundreds of thousands of birds migrate from Europe in the wintertime.

CLIMATE

It is very hot from April through October (highs of 40 to 45°C, June through August) throughout Mauritania except on the coast and Nouakchott where the trade winds blow and the average highs are about 5°C less. In December through March, the highs and lows in Nouakchott are typically 29°C and 13°C; a heavy sweater is definitely required.

VISAS

Only French, Italians and certain African

nationals do not need visas. All neighbouring countries and Las Palmas can provide you with a visa. In Dakar (Senegal), you can get them in 24 hours, but you may need a letter of recommendation from your embassy. You cannot get a Senegalese visa in Nouakchott, but if you fly to Dakar, Senegalese visas are issued free at the airport. Travelling overland, you will not get into Senegal without a visa. This is more of a problem for Americans because unlike most Europeans, they need visas to Senegal. The French embassy in Nouakchott issues visas to Burkina Faso, Togo and the Ivory Coast.

Diplomatic Missions Abroad
Abidjan, Algiers, Bamako, Banjul, Brussels, Dakar, Kinshasa, Lagos, Madrid, Paris, Rabat, Washington. Consulates: Geneva, Las Palmas (passports must be sent to Madrid for visas).

MONEY
US$1 = 74 UM
£1 = 117 UM

The unit of currency is the ouguiya (ou-GHEE-yah). The currency seems overvalued because the country is extremely expensive, but there is apparently no black market, at least not an open one. Mauritania takes its currency laws seriously. There is no restriction on the amount of foreign currency that you may bring in, but you must fill out a currency declaration form upon entering. You are strongly advised to declare all of your money including travellers' cheques. It is not unusual to be stopped four or five times by police between the Senegalese border and Nouakchott. If they find undeclared currency, you're in big trouble.

When you leave the country the police don't always count your money, but don't rely on it. If you have lost your currency declaration form expect a huge hassle. Also, don't take any ouguiya out of the country, not even coins; you risk confiscation of your luggage if they find any.

You can change money at Rosso, the Senegalese border station, but not between 12.30 and 3 pm. If you arrive in Nouakchott on a weekend (Thursday afternoon through Saturday evening), the bank at the airport in Nouakchott may be closed. If so, your only hope for changing money is at the Novotel.

Banking hours: Sunday to Thursday 7 am to 1 pm; closed Friday and Saturday. Banks: Banque Centrale de Mauritanie, Banque Arabe Africaine en Mauritanie, Banque Intenationale pour le Mauritanie, BIAO.

LANGUAGE
Both French and Arabic are the official languages. The everyday language of the Moors is a Berber-Arabic dialect called Hassaniya. The black Africans in the south have their own languages. Greetings in Hassaniya:

Good morning	sah-LAH-mah ah-LAY-koum
Good evening	mah-sah el-HAIR
How are you?	ish-TAH-ree
Thank you	SHOE-kran
Good-bye	mah-sah-LAM

GENERAL INFORMATION
Health
A yellow fever vaccination is mandatory for those arriving from an infected area or staying over two weeks, as is a cholera shot for those arriving within six days from an infected area. Nouakchott hospital has French doctors and a reasonably good intensive care unit for emergencies.

Security
Nouakchott remains one of the safest capitals in Africa despite a slight rise in crime brought on by migration from surrounding areas.

Business Hours
Business: Sunday to Thursday 8 am to 12 noon and 3 to 6 pm; closed Friday and Saturday. Government: Saturday to

Wednesday 8 am to 3 pm; Thursday 8 am to 1 pm.

Public Holidays

1 January, 26 February, 8 March (Mauritanian women only), 1 May, 25 May, End of Ramadan (17 May 88), 10 July, Tabaski (25 July 88), Mohammed's Birthday, 28 November (Independence).

Photography

A permit is apparently not required. Nevertheless, use great discretion and never photograph government buildings, the airport or military installations. About the only two places to buy film are the Novotel and Gralicoma bookstore at the Grand Marché in Nouakchott.

Time, Phone & Telex

When it's noon in Mauritania, it's noon in London and 7 am in New York (8 am during daylight savings time). The telephone system was recently connected to satellite, so you can now direct dial to almost anywhere. The cost is about US$5 a minute to the USA and US$3 to US$4 to Europe. There's a phone and telex machine at the post office.

GETTING THERE

Air

From Europe, the only direct flights are from Paris, three times a week. From the USA, you can take Air Afrique from New York and transfer in Dakar. Within Africa, there are flights five times a week to Dakar, thrice weekly to the Canary Islands, and weekly to Abidjan. Both Air Mauritanie and Air Senegal service the Dakar-Nouakchott route; the Air Mauritanie planes are newer and the service is more reliable. During the dusty, December-March *harmattan* season, Air Mauritanie usually flies, but many Air Senegal flights are cancelled, as are many of those on UTA and Air Afrique from Paris (they fly over Nouakchott).

Car

The 550-km drive to Dakar takes about eight hours; the road is paved all the way. There's a small ferry at Rosso which crosses about every 20 minutes; the wait for the three-minute crossing can be anywhere from five minutes to an hour, depending mostly on how many vehicles are waiting. The ferry operates from 7 am to 12.30 pm and 3 to 5 pm.

With the completion of the 1100-km asphalt road from Nouakchott to Néma in the far eastern region of the country, the drive to Bamako (Mali) is no longer a major problem. Averaging 100 km/hour on the asphalt stretch is not difficult. The entire 1768-km drive to Bamako via Néma can be done in three days, but that's really pushing it. Even from Dakar this is now the best route to Bamako (you can also put your car on the train). You can usually get petrol in all the major Mauritanian towns (Aleg, Kiffa, Ayoun el Atrous, Néma), but in Nara petrol is infrequent. If you're coming from Bamako, there's a bank in Néma where you can change money.

The 200-km stretch between Néma and Nara (Mali) is the worst section, but you can make it without four-wheel drive – it's speed that gets you through the soft sand spots, not traction. You may need sand ladders, however. This stretch is more of a problem during the rainy season in July and August than at any other time.

From Nara, the best route to Bamako is south via Kolokani, or you can east via Niono and Ségou. The Niono route is paved south of Niono, but getting stuck or lost in the northern 168-km stretch is a distinct possibility, especially in July and August. The Kolokani route is dirt road all the way (374 km) but it has been improved and is in good condition plus the overall distance is shorter by 180 km.

Bush Taxi

You can go by bush taxi from Dakar to Nouakchott, changing at the border town of Rosso. Ten to twelve hours is typical, depending on how long you have to wait at Rosso. The bush taxis on the Senegalese side are Peugeot 504s; those on the Mauritanian side are *bâches* (converted pickup trucks). You will find them at the Gare Routière.

Boat

Once in a while, you hear of someone hopping a ship from the Canary Islands or Marseilles to Nouâdhibou, but don't count on doing the same. Only an occasional ship passing south from Europe toward Dakar stops at this fishing town of 25,000 inhabitants. Travellers have reported having to wait for a month in Las Palmas before finding a boat headed for Africa. The best time is from October to January when private yachts are more numerous.

GETTING AROUND

Air

Air Mauritanie (Avenue Abd-el-Nasser, Nouakchott, tel 52212/52472) has twice daily flights to Nouâdhibou, thrice weekly flights to Atâr (3000 UM), and at least once a week flights to Néma, Zouerate, Tidjikja, Kaédi, Ayoun-el-Atrous, as well as light aircraft for chartering.

Car

From Nouakchott to Atâr (450 km), count on seven or eight hours driving time; over half the road is asphalted. The 120-km stretch from Atâr to Chinguetti and Ouadâne is very sandy and difficult. Unless you're an expert desert driver, you'll need a four-wheel-drive vehicle. The road is not as bad from Atâr to Choum (the northern limit of permitted travel). For the rest of Mauritania, whenever you're driving on an unasphalted road, you'll need a four-wheel-drive vehicle unless you're an experienced desert driver and you know what you're doing. In any case, sand ladders are a must.

Although truckers make the trip between Nouakchott and Nouâdhibou, you won't find many others doing it. The

first 155 km of the 525-km seaside road are on the beach itself. More than one experienced driver has gotten his vehicle stuck in soft beach sand and then seen it covered by the rising water. After the beach, you run into dunes. It can be done, but for safety reasons you must go with at least one other vehicle; a four-wheel-drive vehicle is a necessity, and getting lost is very easy without a guide. So forget it, or at least leave the driving to someone who has done it before.

Trucks

There are no bush taxis serving Nouâdhibou, but trucks reportedly make the trip. They leave from the market in the Cinquième district of Nouakchott; expect a 30-hour trip costing about 1500 UM including food. In addition to trucks, you may find bâches for Kaédi and Atâr, Mauritania's third and fourth largest cities.

Train

Those who like the hobo life can hop the iron-ore train that connects Nouâdhibou and Zouerate, stopping at Choum along the way. There are no longer passenger cars but it's apparently easy enough to hop a wagon; some travellers have even gotten a ride in the cab with the engineer.

Old Moor man (CB)

Nouakchott

Nouakchott, meaning 'the place of the winds', is one of the newest capitals in the world, created in 1960 at the beginning of independence. Prior to this, Mauritania was governed by the French from St Louis. When Senegal and Mauritania separated at independence, St Louis ended up on the Senegalese side, leaving Mauritania without a major city. So a new city had to be built. The site chosen was 200 km north of the Senegalese border and near the ocean, many days' walk from the Sahara. During the next 25 years the Sahara moved in, part of the desertification process that is occurring all along the 6000-km southern border of the Sahara. Now the city is in the Sahara surrounded by rolling sand dunes, with sand piling up against walls and fences like snow drifts.

The city was planned with wide streets, adequate water supply, and some space around public buildings and houses – quite unlike the typical African city. Some say that because the city is new and planned, the atmosphere is artificial and uninteresting. Maybe, but if you find the desert intriguing, you are less likely to agree. It's an easy place to meet people; browse around the souk and you'll be invited for tea.

Go to the beach for a jog and swim, then watch the fishermen arrive in the late afternoon with their catch. Watching the artisans at work can be fascinating too. The activity isn't vibrant, but because Nouakchott is so unlike other African capitals you may find it interesting.

Nouakchott's major problem is that it was designed for about 200,000 inhabitants but is now more than double that size because of the hordes of nomads attracted to the city during the recent droughts. Accordingly, the outskirts of Nouakchott are the antithesis of what the designers intended – a shanty town of tiny metal shacks and tents cluttered one against the other, far worse than anything in other African cities. Why far worse? Because in the rest of Africa, people migrating to the city usually end up living with relatives, even if it's only sleeping under the stars on a mat in an enclosed compound. But in the case of Nouakchott, there were almost as many nomads descending on the city as there were inhabitants. There was no way the city (or their relatives if they had any in Nouakchott) could absorb these numbers.

Some of these shanties are made out of shipping container crates converted into houses. An American businessman who made shipments to Mauritania using containers seized upon the following idea. If the containers are going to be used ultimately as houses, are there some simple modifications he could make in their design that would at least make them more habitable? What he found, however, was that once you start improving the containers, their value increases, thereby making them no longer affordable by the poorest of the poor for whom they were intended. Another nobly inspired development idea down the drain, and just one of hundreds conceived by well-intentioned foreigners that seem brilliant but are unworkable in the African milieu.

Information
Embassies Algeria, France (BP 231, tel 51740/5), Gabon, West Germany (BP 372, tel 52304), Guinea, Morocco, Nigeria, Spain, Tunisia, USA (BP 222, tel 52660/3), Zaire.

Bookstores & Supermarkets As for bookstores, the best has traditionally been *Gralicoma* next to the market; you can frequently pick up *Time, Newsweek*, postcards and French publications there. The new Novotel, however, may now have a better selection. For foreign grocery items, the two supermarkets on either side of the El Ammane are as good as any.

Travel Agencies Oasis Tours (BP 926, tel 51717, telex 531B), on the main drag

(Avenue Abd el Nasser) near the turn off for the hospital, is the best agency in town for tours to the Adrar area (Atâr, Chinguetti, Ouadâne) and the Parc du Banc d'Arguin. It's run by a young enthusiastic French couple and open every day except Friday. Lodgings and meals are usually arranged with local families. A Land-Rover with chauffeur runs about 7000 UM a day plus 17% tax plus 10 UM per km.

Others include Agence-Dayna Voyages et Tourisme (Avenue Abd el Nasser next to the BAAM bank), Inter Tour (BP 708, Avenue Abd el Nasser about 100 metres from Hotel El Ammane, tel 53217, telex 847), Soprage (next to Inter Tour), and Somavot (tel 52872).

Things to See
The three things that almost everybody tries to see are the **Central Market**, the shanty districts on the outskirts of town, and the two **Grande Mosquées**, one donated by Saudi Arabia, the other by Morocco.

National Museum
This museum has a display of pottery and other historical artefacts. It is at the Maison du Parti et de la Culture, built by the Chinese. It's open Tuesday to Saturday 10 am to 12 noon and 2.30 to 5.45 pm, and Sunday afternoons.

Port de Pêche
Much more interesting to some is the activity at the small wharf, Port de Pêche, every afternoon around 4 pm when the fishing boats return with the day's catch. If you're camping and cooking on the beach, this is the time and place to buy your fish.

Ksar
You can also take a stroll through the Ksar, an old Moorish settlement just outside town that was destroyed by a flood in 1950 and partially rebuilt. There's reportedly an outlet where rugs are sold, and a rug-making school for women.

Places to Stay – bottom end
There are no good cheap hotels in Nouakchott. For starters, try the *Mission Catholique*; they are reportedly friendly and sometimes allow people to stay there. The only other cheap alternative is the *Hôtel Adrar* (tel 52955), about 800 UM a night, or 1100 UM with air-con. It's a smelly dump with poor lighting; it's a brothel (figuratively and literally). You can ask for directions downtown in the area of the womens artisan cooperative; it's only three blocks away.

The next cheapest hotel is not cheap at all – the *Hôtel Oasis* (tel 52011/06) costs about 1800/2100 UM for singles/doubles. This hotel's bar has an atmosphere of intrigue and is a good place for meeting interesting characters. While the rooms are quite acceptable, they don't measure up to the price and the restaurant is mediocre at best. It's downtown on Avenue de Gaulle next to the Oasis Cinema.

The beach is six km from town, far enough away so that you shouldn't be pestered by intruders. Sleeping there is apparently not illegal. Indeed, the favourite weekend activity of the local expatriates is to go fishing and camping on the beaches for the weekends, but with their four-wheel-drive vehicles they head for more secluded places much further away.

Places to Stay – top end
There are two fairly decent hotels in the middle of town. The *Park Hôtel* (tel 51444), with singles/doubles for about 2000/2300 UM, is a small hotel with 17 very decent rooms, air-con, good lighting, balconies and a relatively good restaurant. The bar is dead, however, and the ambience is sterile. It's in the heart of the city on Avenue Abd el Nasser. *Hôtel El Ammane* (tel 52178) costs about 2000/2300 UM for singles/doubles. Even though the rooms are not quite as nice as the Park's, many people prefer this similarly sized hotel around the corner because the terrace bar is one of the most popular in

1	Stadium	11	Soprage Travel	19	US Embassy
2	French Embassy		Agency, Supermarket	20	Chez Riad Restaurant
3	Lebanese Club	12	Patisserie Hajjar	21	Post Office
4	Peace Corps	13	Parc Hôtel &	22	SNC Movie Theatre &
5	Hospital		Poussain Grocery		Museum
6	Oasis Tours	14	Hôtel Amane	23	Air Mauritanée
7	Zoubeida Restaurant	15	Hôtel Oasis	24	UTA
8	Artisanat Féminin	16	Phenicia Restaurant	25	Friday Mosque
9	Hôtel Adrar	17	Mosque	26	Artisan Centre
10	Gralicoma Bookstore	18	German Embassy		

Nouakchott

town, and the restaurant is one of the best in town.

Sabah Hôtel (tel 51552/64, telex 821) has singles/doubles for about 2600/3100 UM. The 40 air-con rooms are decent, there's a stand-by generator and the hotel is on the ocean. The restaurant is poor for the price, and credit cards are not accepted. Furthermore, the hotel is isolated six km from downtown, and taxis are sometimes impossible to get.

The best hotel by far is the brand new *Novotel*, with singles/doubles for 5500/6200 UM. It's behind the French embassy in the direction of the new Chinese-built stadium, about two km from the centre of town.

Places to Eat
Cheap Eats *Phenicia* is a plain restaurant with a TV blasting away. It is inexpensive, which explains its great popularity with the locals and Peace Corps volunteers. No alcohol is served. It's downtown across from *El Mouna* (also a theatre) across the street, which is slightly cheaper but has few choices on the menu. *Sinibad*, next to Gralicoma bookstore and across from the downtown market, matches El Mouna

price-wise and offers a few more selections, including chicken, steak and brochettes.

The new *Frisco Snack* downtown on the northern end of Avenue Kennedy is not cheap but serves low-budget fare including hamburgers, fries, ice cream, shawarma sandwiches and full meals. It's very popular and pleasant with tables on a terrace.

The locals tend to eat at places such as *Le Palmier* south of the market and all along Avenue Kennedy out beyond the downtown market – the desert cuisine of the Moors wins no culinary awards in Africa. You can also fill up at one of the two bread and pastry shops, *Au Petit Creux* which has tables and is next to the El Ammane, or *Patisserie Hajjar*, one block away with the best bread in town but it has no place to sit down.

Lebanese *Chez Riad* is clean and probably serves the best restaurant food in Nouakchott, which isn't saying much. It's frequented by Lebanese, which is some proof that this family-run restaurant serves very decent Lebanese fare. Prices are quite reasonable, about 500 UM for the fixed price menu, plus there's a wide à la carte selection but no alcohol. The main restaurant is in back; the front section serves a wide variety of sandwiches for only 80 UM. It's in the centre of town on Avenue Abd el Nasser, two blocks from the El Ammane, and open every day.

The *Lebanese Club* across from the French Embassy is equally good, but it's only open to non-members on Thursday nights. You can get a meal for about 600 UM followed by dancing starting around 11 pm. It's also a good place to meet the non-African community.

Continental *Hôtel El Ammane*, which serves alcohol, is recommended. You'll find excellent service, a nicely decorated interior, an international crowd and large portions. It's in the heart of town on Avenue Abd El Nasser and closed Friday. *Park Hotel* around the corner also serves

pretty good meals – and alcohol – at slightly lower prices. Friday lunch is their only break.

Sabah Hôtel, out on the beach and open every day, is not worth the effort getting there, and it's more expensive than the others. Fish is apparently the best thing on the menu. *Hôtel Oasis* is not recommended; it offers only a fixed no-choice menu for about 900 UM. Like I said, you don't come to Mauritania for the food. If you're a conservative eater, you'd better stick with the *Novotel*, which probably has the best meals in town, but at a price.

Moroccan *Zoubeida* serves tagine and other Moroccan specialities. The local expatriates give this place a bad review, especially the cleanliness. It has a Moroccan ambience with pillows to sit on, but don't expect anything plush. The price of a meal could easily run 1000 UM, a little high for the mediocre quality, plus they don't serve alcohol. For the money, the separate dining area in front is a much better deal. You can get cheap fare, such as couscous, for about 160 UM. It's on Avenue Abd El Nasser four or five blocks back of the now defunct Hôtel Marhaba; ask for the Moroccan restaurant.

Entertainment & Sports
Bars Moneyed travellers tend to prefer the terrace bar of the *El Ammane*. Those looking for intrigue head for the dumpier bar at the *Hôtel Oasis*, where you'll meet a few Africans as well.

Nightclubs Again, the pickings are slim. The international crowd shows up Thursday night at the *Lebanese Club*. The 600 UM entrance fee includes a drink; the similarly priced meal includes free entrance to the disco. *Hôtel El Ahmadi* and *Timiris* are less respectable and quite expensive. They are near the Sabah hotel, next to the ocean and close to each other. Thursday is the only night worth going.

Movie Theatres Both the Cinéma Oasis downtown and Cinéma El Mouna one block away occasionally have some pretty good films; show time is 9 or 9.15 pm. However, the best selection of films is at the government-operated SNC Theatre, one long block across the street from the post office. The screen is quite large but the sound system is poor. There's a different film every night at 9 pm; see the billboard next to the post office for showings.

Sports The sports scene is fairly limited – swimming at the Novotel or in the ocean (expect cold water December through February), jogging on the beach, running with the Hash House Harriers Tuesdays at 5 pm (inquire at the American embassy for details), and softball on Friday mornings at 9.30 am with the Americans.

Fishing is the major sport in Mauritania. Trout (*courbine*), speckled sea bass (*bar*), ray fish (*raie*), and shark (*requin*) are particularly plentiful, and in the late evenings and on weekends you'll see foreigners fishing along the beach. Indeed, this is the best surf casting area on the entire western African continent. It's no coincidence that Air Afrique has a resort for surf casting outside Nouâdhibou. The big drawback is that unless you're on one of Air Afrique's package tours, you won't find rental equipment anywhere. You could ask at the new Novotel, they may get something together, or try to borrow some.

Things to Buy

Artisan Goods The womens cooperative, *L'Artisanat Feminin* across from the central market, should not be missed. You can get tablecloths, clothes, purses, pillows, camel-hair rugs, colourfully painted leather cushions, huge decorated nomad tents, and fine straw mats at very reasonable prices. They're open every day except Friday, 8 to 11 am and 4 to 6 pm.

Le Grand Marché and *Le Souk*, one block off Avenue Abd El Nasser, offer a bit of everything, including leather sandals (*samaras*) and sacks, the popular but bulky Moroccan brass kettles for hand washing at meal time and, sometimes, tooled leather saddles.

For the best selection of the famous wooden boxes with silver inlay, daggers, copper and silver jewellery and other metal objects, head for the open-air *Centre Artisanal* on the outskirts of town on the road to Senegal or scrutinise the wares for sale in front of the Hôtel El Ammane. It is well worth a visit to see the silversmiths at work, but don't expect any great bargains. You can also bargain with the traders outside the El Ammane; their prices are as good as anybody's if you bargain well.

Rugs Mauritanian rugs are traditionally made of white, beige or chestnut-coloured wool with geometrical designs less complex and quite different from those in northern Africa. There's a rug factory, *Le Centre National du Tapis* on Rue Ghary, with a magnificent selection. They are very expensive and made to order, but you might find one or two for sale, or go just to see how they're made.

Getting There & Away

Air Air Mauritanie (tel 52212/52472), Avenue Abd-el-Nasser has flights to Nouâdibhou, Atâr, Néma, Zouerate, Tidjikja, Kaédi and Ayoun-el-Atrous.

Truck Trucks and bâches (converted pickup trucks) leave from the market in the Cinquième district. Mauritania is not noted for its fast and frequent public transport, but you should have no problems finding a truck or bâche to Nouâdhibou, Atâr or Kaédi. For Dakar, take a bâche to Rosso on the border and then a bush taxi from the Senegalese side.

Getting Around

Air Transport There is no longer an airport departure tax. The Nouakchott airport has a place to exchange money. A taxi into town (4 km) should cost about 250 UM, but bargaining is definitely required. There are no buses.

Taxi Fares are 125 UM for a short trip in town, and 10 to 20 UM for a 'seat' in a shared taxi. However, you cannot get the lower price except with taxis plying the two or three major routes in town. Taxis do not have metres, and they are somewhat scarce. You can recognise them by their green and yellow colour.

Car Rental Hertz (Avenue Abd el Nasser, tel 53615, telex 838), Eurocar (tel 51136, telex 853), Avis (tel 51713, telex 851), LVB Location Voitures (tel 53899/53321), Lovoto (tel 52814), Cotema (tel 52352), Lacombe (tel 52221). Expect to pay about 3700 UM (in town) or 7000 UM (out of town) per day plus 10% tax plus 10 UM a km.

The North

NOUÂDHIBOU

Fishing is the principal activity of Nouâdhibou, and it's big time, with huge refrigeration and processing plants. The waters here are loaded with fish, making it one of the best fishing areas in the world. The town's population is 25,000, and it's 525 km north of Nouakchott on a peninsula about 35 km long running north and south. The eastern side of the peninsula is Mauritania and the western side is Western Sahara. (Some travellers have found no guards at the border, making crossing surprisingly simple.)

The Cape Canarian *Tcherka* district is perhaps the most interesting section of town. The Cansado district, six km to the south, is a somewhat elegant residential area, and Port Mineralier, four km further south, is where the train ends and iron ore is loaded onto the ships. Those interested in catching a ship to Dakar or points north might want to try their luck here.

Places to Stay & Eat

Nouâdhibou offers no cheap places to sleep. You could try at the *Mission Catholique*; the priest there is reportedly friendly. Most people stay downtown at the 60-room *Hotel Sabah* (tel 2377), the town's best with air-con and pool. It costs about 2600/3100 UM for singles/doubles. The 21-room *Hôtel des Imraguens* (tel 2272), one km from the centre of town, may be a little cheaper. It has a restaurant and nightclub.

Getting There & Away

Most people get here by air because the road from Nouakchott is nothing but tracks in the sand. There are connections every morning and afternoon from Nouakchott; the roundtrip cost is about 8000 UM.

Fishing

The fishing is good yearlong. Trout and umbrine (*ombrine*) are the main catch from December to June; sea bass, ray and sea bream (*dorade*) are some of the main catch the rest of the year. If you don't have a lot of bucks to throw around, you can apparently find small fishermen in Nouâdhibou who'll take you out in their boats.

Sport fishing enthusiasts usually stay at Air Afrique's *Le Centre de Pêche* at the Baie de l'Étoile 14 km north of Nouâdhibou. It has seven bungalows. Air Afrique's nine-day package tour from Paris costs 8900 to 9550 FF (about US$1500) including airfare, meals, lodging and fishing gear. You can also get package deals leaving from Nouakchott (Air Afrique, BP 51, Nouakchott, tel 52084); the length of stay can vary from a few days to several weeks.

ARGUIN BANK NATIONAL PARK

The Banc d'Arguin is known around the world by bird watchers as an important crossroads for multitudes of aquatic birds migrating between Europe and northern Asia, and most of Africa. Over two million broad-billed sandpipers have been recorded in the winter. Other migrants include hundreds of thousands of black terns, tens of thousands of flamingoes, thousands of white pelicans and hundreds of spoonbills. Some species breed here as well, including terns, flamingoes, herons, cormorants, spoonbills and white herons.

During the mating season, the birds need lots of fish and seclusion from mankind. The Banc d'Arguin extends some 200 km north from Cape Timiris (155 km north of Nouakchott) and provides an ideal environment. The sea is crystal clear and shallow. Even 25 km from shore it's only several metres deep, so fish are easy to find, but not so the birds. Most of them are found on islands of sand and the only way you can get to see them is by small shallow boats.

Even in Nouakchott it's difficult to find anyone who has made the trip. Bird watchers know about it, however. They come down from Paris on organised trips with, among others, Explorator, 16 Place de la Madeleine, 75008 Paris, France (tel 01-42666624).

You reportedly can only take this trip with permission from the national parks service, and a guide. The opening dates and travel within the park are regulated. During the mating season, April to July and October to January, you may not get close to the birds because the slightest disturbance will apparently cause them to fly away and forsake their eggs. So the best viewing time may be August and September and the cooler months of February and March. Oasis Tours in Nouakchott would prefer you let them organise the trip, but they'll probably give you information even if you want to do it on your own.

Getting There & Away
Essential equipment includes a four-wheel-drive vehicle, two spare tires, sand ladders and a vehicle mounted compass among other things. You start at the Sabah Hôtel in Nouakchott and drive on the beach 155 km to Nouâmghâr, the fishing village at Cape Timiris; avoid the soft beach sand or it could put an early end to your trip.

Since you'll need a boat to get to the islands where the birds are, this may be the best place to rent one. From Nouâmghâr it's another 50 km on good sand track to a point where the track returns to the sea, with Tidra, the main island, across the way. Tidra is an island of sand 35 km long; it and some 13 other tiny islands are where most of the birds are.

NOUÂMGHÂR
If you pass through Nouâmghâr - stop. Nouâmghâr may not seem like anything special, but it is fascinating. This is the major fishing village of the Imragen, a people numbering only 300 or so and totally unlike those in the rest of Mauritania. What's unique is the way they catch the fish with the help of dolphins. When a migrating school of yellow mullet (mulets jaune) is spotted, a man hits the water with a long stick and the sound waves induce the dolphins, sometimes two km out in the sea, to drive the mullet toward shore and the nets. The Imragen can't fish every day - only when schools are spotted, which can be days apart - and it all happens very quickly. So your chances of seeing this fascinating event are very poor unless you're prepared to stick it out for a few days.

CAPE TAGARIT
A very interesting alternative to, or continuation of, a trip to see the birds is a trip to Cape Tagarit north of Tidra for fishing, snorkelling and camping. It does not involve getting government permission or a guide, but it does involve some very serious desert driving.

The view is magnificent and the water is crystal clear; you can see turtles and huge fish swimming around the rocks even from the cliff. A good catch of trout, sea bass and sea bream is almost guaranteed; just don't let the eerie wailing of jackals, or their presence near camp, bother you. All they'll do is stare at you with eyes that shine in the night like emeralds when a torch is pointed at them.

Getting There & Away
A journey to Tagarit is not to be undertaken lightly. You should talk to someone who has made the trip, and there aren't many who have, for detailed instructions.

Go north from Nouâmghâr for 70 km on good sand track towards Nouâdhibou until it divides; take the left track for 10 km, then go directly north by compass over sand dunes for 15 km until you regain the track. At km 106 from Cape Timiris, you reach two low rocky hills bisecting the track; at this point head directly west by compass over sand dunes for 25 km. Your trip ends at the edge of a cliff 100 feet above the ocean; this is Cape Tafarit. (The smaller Cape Tagarit five km to the north is a good camping spot.)

Adrar Region

If you have time to visit only one area outside of Nouakchott, head for the Adrar plateau area encompassing Atâr, Chinguetti and Ouadâne. This is where you'll see oases, nomads in their natural habitat, spectacular plateaux areas with deep canyons and ancient rock paintings, towns seemingly about to be buried under the encroaching desert, and the country's most historic sites.

ATÂR
With 10,000 inhabitants, Atâr is the major market centre for the nomads of northern Mauritania. It's a day's drive from Nouakchott and the starting point for a number of interesting side trips. The petrol supply is fairly reliable.

The town itself is divided into two sections, a new larger section with wide rectangular streets, and the more interesting

Ksar with narrow winding streets. Between the two is the market where you can find sandals, leather goods, silver jewellery and rugs among other things.

Places to Stay & Eat
There's both a cheap rest house and an old building that has been restored into a hotel and restaurant with air-con.

CHINGUETTI
More interesting is Chinguetti and the lunar-like Adrar plateau en route. You may be able to get a ride on one of the lorries that periodically makes the 120-km trip. There are various gorges leading into the plateau. One of these deep inhospitable gorges leads up to the Amorgar Pass and, at about the 70 km point, the summit of the Adrar Plateau, which is reminiscent of Colorado. The panoramic view on top is particularly beautiful at sunset. Just at the point where the plateau begins, you can see some rocks on your left just a few metres off the road. Amongst them are some prehistoric rock paintings (*peintures rupestres*) of giraffe, cows and people in a green and grassy landscape long since gone.

Chinguetti is one of the holy cities of Islam but now threatened on all sides by encroaching dunes some 10 to 20 metres high. Founded in the 13th century, it was the ancient capital of the Moors and once the seventh city of Islam, reputed for its poets and Muslim scholars. Each year this was where the pilgrims from all over Mauritania assembled to join the caravan to Mecca, sometimes taking several years. The town at one time boasted 11 mosques and witnessed huge caravans of 32,000 camels laden with salt.

Things to See
The only two notable things about the modern section are a solar demonstration pump no longer working and, dominating the town, an old **fort** converted into a hotel. It was recently renovated and air-

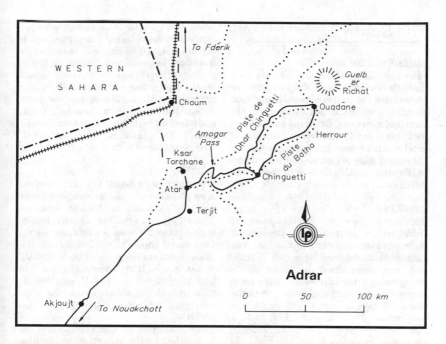

conditioning was installed for the actors in *Fort Saganne*, a French film shot here in the early '80s.

In the older Ksar, you'll see the often photographed 16th century **mosque** (non-Muslims are not allowed to enter) and a library housing some 1300 ancient manuscripts, certain of them dating from the 3rd century, which have passed for centuries through the hands of prestigious Muslim theologians.

Getting There & Away

There are two routes from Chinguetti to Ouadâne; the southerly route called the *piste du Batha* passes through sand dunes and requires a guide. The 120-km northerly *piste du Dhar Chinguetti* is better but requires a four-wheel-drive vehicle. There are few vehicles, so expect difficulty hitchhiking.

OUADÂNE

Ouadâne was once an important, prosperous camel caravan centre. It is now an imposing ruin hugging the hillside with an oasis setting below.

The best view is from the minimally furnished *Rest House*. Towards the west are date palms and the oasis; towards the east is a cliff covered with ruins, which include a mosque and the Ksar el Klali with its formidable stone walls. The only place that people are still holding out is the tiny 'modern' section on top of the cliff. Just how long they can continue weathering the storm of sand is anybody's guess.

ZOUERATE

This important iron ore centre has little to offer the visitor. If you make it this far north, the mining company there supports a hotel with restaurant.

The South

TAGANT REGION

Like the Adrar region, the Tagant area due east of Nouakchott offers impressive views from the plateau, prehistoric rock paintings, historical sites including old forts and fortresses, decaying towns such as Tidjikja and Tichitt with mountains of sand about to consume them, as well as the opportunity to look for neolithic items in the sand. Getting there is slightly more difficult.

TIDJIKJA

Tidjikja is one of those towns so infrequently visited that presenting yourself on arrival to the police is not just a courtesy but required. Founded in 1680 and now surrounded by sand dunes threatening its existence, the town supports a population of 6000, one of the country's more important palm groves, a rest house with little more than beds, a fort built by the French in 1905, a relatively busy market, and an old mosque reconstructed many times.

What's particularly interesting about the old section are the numerous traditional houses, some of which are vacant and easily visited. Notice the decorative niches with geometrical designs, the flat roofs serving as terraces with gargoyles to keep the water from stagnating, the double panelled doors in place of windows, and the elevated outdoor latrines made of stone – built 10 steps up because the rock is too hard to dig through!

Getting There & Away

If you're hitchhiking, be prepared for some long waits because the traffic is very light. If you're driving, the first leg, 425 km south-east on the Transmauritanienne highway to the village of Sangarafa (20 km beyond Magta-Lahjar), will take four or five hours. The remaining 190 km leg north-east to Tidjikja is well packed sand except for the sand dunes virtually blocking the entrance to Moudjéria. If you see huge cistern trucks stuck in the sand, you'll know you're there. For this reason finding petrol in Tidjikja can never be guaranteed. Just be prepared with sand ladders.

TICHITT

If you're really adventurous and want to see a ghost town in the making, head east from Tidjikja to the ancient town of Tichitt. The tracks are usually barely visible, so you'll need a guide and petrol for a round trip. The old houses and the mosque are said to be architecturally more beautiful than those in Tidjikja. It is like the arctic except that it's sand rather than snow that blankets everything.

KAÉDI

Some 437 km to the south-east of Nouakchott on the Senegal river, Kaédi is a large town famous for its interesting market. The FAO has a *Guest House* with six rooms, air-con and a pool – the only one in Mauritania outside Nouakchott.

KEUR MASSÈNE

Small game hunting is the attraction of this town on the northern bank of the Senegal river and practically on the ocean. Air Afrique (BP 51, Nouakchott, tel 52084) has a *Campement de Chasse* with eight bungalows. They offer package deals.

ROSSO

If you're trapped at this Senegal border post, you can stay at the *Hotel Traza*, which has nine air-con rooms.

Niger

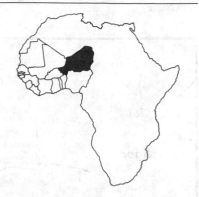

Camels walking down the main boulevards have long given Niamey its distinctive character. Sand, too, plays a role in giving the city its desert charm. For travellers flying from the coast, the change is dramatic – and a treat. You'll find almost as many trees in Niamey as in Dakar, Bamako and Ouagadougou, its sister Sahelian capitals, but the climate is noticeably drier.

Today, the camel seems to be going the way of the horse and buggy. Their numbers have dropped from 20,000 in Niamey at independence to 2000 today. You'll see other signs of change as well. During the 1970s, the city went through a building boom. As a result, you'll see some of the most interesting modern architecture in West Africa – modern Sudanese-style buildings – all financed, ultimately, by the country's uranium mines. The recent collapse in world uranium prices, however, has sent the country's economy into a tailspin. Begging is no longer confined to the handicapped.

Outside Niamey, you'll find one of the most fascinating countries in West Africa. North of Niamey, there's the famous Sunday cattle market in Ayorou, where the variety of people is as interesting as the number of animals. To the south is one of the better game parks in West Africa – Parc 'W'. In September, west of Agadez, you can observe one of the great spectacles in Africa – the Cure Salée, the week-long reunion of the Bororos when the unmarried men participate in a veritable beauty contest, make-up and all, wooing the opposite sex. Agadez is actually more interesting than Timbuktu, both teetering on the Sahara's southern edge. For travellers having just completed the Sahara desert crossing, it's a veritable paradise. And the Aïr mountains in the desert to the north-east of Agadez are incomparable. An excursion there would probably be your most lasting memory of this starkly beautiful country.

HISTORY

If you could step back into history 6000 years or so, you would find rivers running through grassy plateaux in areas of northern Niger (nee-JAIR in French) that are now pure desert. You would also meet migrating hunters and herdsmen, some of whom might be painting local animals – giraffe and rhino – on the cave walls. As the Sahara became drier, these people migrated southward. Even before the time of Christ, some of them had developed elaborate social organisations, with metal work and complex forms of trade.

Empires also arose, their wealth stemming invariably from control of the trans-Saharan trade in salt, gold and slaves. The first was the Kanem-Bornu empire in the east around Lake Chad starting around the 9th century; 500 years later the large Hausa population in Nigeria began spilling over into south-eastern Niger. In the 17th century, the western area along the Niger river witnessed the arrival of the Djerma, descendants of one of the greatest kingdoms in West Africa – the Songhai empire of the 15th and 16th centuries which stretched from Senegal to Niger.

Just 100 years ago, the slave trade, which no longer existed in most of West Africa, was still going strong in Niger and Chad. The sultans and chiefs were

Niger

ALGERIA

LIBYA

Ténéré Desert

Djado

In Guezzam

Asamakka

Aïr Mountains

Arlit

Bilma

Tegguidam Tessoumi

MALI

Agadez

NIGER

0   200   400 km

Tahoua

Tanout

Nguigmi

Lake Chad

Ayorou

Niamey

Maradi

Gouré

Birnin–NKonni

Zinder

Dossa

BURKINA FASO

Gaya

NIGERIA

Niger

River

BENIN

determined to keep it alive, as were the Sanusi traders on the northern side of the Sahara in Libya. With an army of up to 12,000 soldiers including a 2000-man cavalry, the sultan of Zinder had little trouble attacking his own Muslim villages whenever debts mounted. Slaves were cheap – about half the price of a camel – perhaps because the great majority of them died before reaching the Americas.

The slave trade was the only way the Sultan could support his 300 wives and 150 children. Gold, for instance, was no longer traded in great quantities. Agadez,

the great gold market, shrank from a population of 30,000 in 1450 to 3000 by the early 20th century. Salt was the prerogative of the Tuareg nomads; it was so rare in the Sahel that markets often traded it ounce for ounce for gold. It was salt that kept alive the huge Saharan camel caravans, sometimes extending 25 km or so. As late as 1906, a 20,000 camel caravan left Agadez to collect salt at Bilma, an oasis some 750 km to the east.

Islam came via the trans-Saharan trade, but the rural people stuck entirely to their traditional religions until the 19th century. Now 85% of the people are Muslim. Europe's first intruder was a Scot, the celebrated Mongo Park, who disappeared on the Niger river in 1806. Although the French didn't arrive until 1890, their conquest was rapid and savage with bloody massacres in 1898 and 1899. By 1901, Niger was a military territory and the slave trade was over. Tuaregs in the north kept resisting until the '20s when Niger became a colony. Thereafter, the French did very little for the area, except perhaps for the introduction of groundnuts in the '30s.

Independence

In 1958, Charles de Gaulle offered the 12 French colonies the choice between a plan for self-government in a French union, or immediate independence. Guinea shocked De Gaulle and made history by becoming the only colony to reject his plan. Unofficially, Niger may have voted the same way. As Basil Davidson says in *Modern Africa*, 'there seems little doubt that the true voting returns were falsified by administrative action'. The French-supported administration claimed that 370,000 people voted for the union, 100,000 against – and 750,000 didn't vote! It was clear, however, that nothing could stop Niger and the other 10 colonies from eventually gaining full independence. Infuriated at Djobo Bakari for campaigning for complete independence, the government banned his Sawaba party and sent Bakari into exile. This left Hamari Dori, leader of the Niger Progressive Party (PPN), in complete control and the only candidate for president when full independence arrived in 1960.

Dori maintained unusually close ties with the French and, despite several unsuccessful coups, survived until the great Sahelian drought of 1973-74. Niger was probably the worst hit country of all; over 60% of the livestock was lost. Stocks of food were discovered in the homes of several of Dori's ministers. Soon thereafter, Lt-Col Seyni Kountche (KOUNT-chay)

overthrew Dori in a bloody coup. Most people were jubilant. The new military government took a hard line on morality. In his early years, Kountche was known for sensationalism. If a ministry's books didn't add up, he would surround it with troops and demand an immediate accounting. He also kicked out the French troops, but still maintained good relations with France. Twice, in 1975 and 1976, members of his government attempted coups; neither succeeded.

Kountche was lucky in other ways. From 1974 to 1979, world prices for uranium quintupled. Production in Niger, which began in 1971, more than tripled and made Niger one of the five biggest uranium producers in the non-socialist world. Revenues rose to $200 million. No longer needing the traditional French budget subsidy, the government set out on a number of ambitious projects, building deluxe ministry headquarters all over Niamey, roads all the way from Niamey to the Chadian border, and the 'uranium highway' to Agadez and Arlit, the centre of operations of the majority French-owned Somair mining company. Not everyone was smiling. Prices rose dramatically, almost 25% in 1976 alone. The poorest of the poor were worse off than ever.

Today

Kountche's luck ran out in the early 1980s. Anti-nuclear protests around the world contributed to a collapse in world uranium prices. Government revenues from uranium took a nose dive – from $200 million in 1980 to $20 million in 1985. The construction boom was over. In 1983-84, another great drought hit. For the first time in recorded history, the Niger river stopped flowing. Then the expulsion of 'illegal aliens' from Nigeria sent foreign remittances tumbling and landed thousands of dispossessed returnees in Niger. Niamey now has the reputation for the most beggars of any city in the Sahel. The government has acquired such an enormous debt that it desperately wants to sell its unprofitable state enterprises. Predictably, buyers are not pounding down the door.

Kountche has weathered the storm, including an unsuccessful coup attempt in 1983. His reputation for honesty has helped. In the long-run, the country's hope for a better future may lie as much in the hands of organisations like Icrisat, an international, 'green revolution' organisation focusing on cereals and legumes in semi-arid areas. Luckily for Niger, they chose a site just south of Niamey for their major research station in Africa.

PEOPLE

With six million people, and only about five people per square km, Niger has one of the lowest population densities in West Africa. Nigeria, to the south, is three-quarters the size of Niger and has 17 times more people.

A little over half of the people are Hausa (HOW-sah). They live all along the border of Nigeria, their heartland where over 20 million additional Hausa live. Hausa is one of the most widely spoken and understood languages in West Africa largely because Hausa traders are so widely scattered throughout the region. On the beaches of Togo, for example, many of the traders you thought were Togolese may well be Hausa.

About a fifth of the people are Djerma (GHUR-mah), descendants of the great Songhai empire centred in Gao (Mali). About 400 years ago, they migrated south and settled along the Niger river. Today, they constitute over half the population of Niamey. Along the river, you'll see them cultivating rice and fishing. Ther are also many Djermas in the government because during colonial times, the French concentrated their educational efforts in Niamey, the Djerma-Songhai being the primary beneficiaries.

In the north, are the famous Tuareg (TWAH-reg) nomads, who constitute about 8% of the population. You can recognise these mysterious 'Blue Men of the Sahara' by their light-coloured skin,

sometimes grey or blue eyes, and faces covered with dark veils that reveal only their eyes. Proud and warlike in character, many still carry swords. Camels are the focus of their lives. They give them names, write songs about them, settle arguments with camel races, go courting on camels, measure a man's wealth by the size of his herds and judge his nobility by how well he rides.

Tuaregs are Muslim, yet their customs are distinct from the Arabs. While celebrating most Muslim holidays, they ignore the annual Ramadan fast. Women, too, play a totally different role. Tuaregs are one of the few matrilineal ethnic groups in West Africa. (They are also the only ones who traditionally eat with utensils – a large wooden spoon.) Tuareg women can own property, maintain it separately from their husband's during marriage, keep their social status even while marrying into a lower caste, and divorce their husbands. In Tuareg society, it's the men who must cover their faces, not the women! You are unlikely to see a Tuareg man unveil the lower half of his face in company. The veil, called a *taguelmoust*, is the symbol of a Tuareg's identity, and the way it is wrapped changes from tribe to tribe. Typically five metres long and made of indigo or black cotton, it helps keep out the desert winds and sand. Look at the Tuaregs' hands – they are usually blue from handling the material.

GEOGRAPHY

Over 6000 years ago, the area of Niger was fertile and well watered. Today, two-thirds of it is desert; the rest is in the Sahel.

Niger is West Africa's second largest country, over twice the size of France, and is land-locked, more than 650 km from the sea. The southern region receives just enough rainfall from July to September to grow crops, but the harvests are no longer sufficient to support the country's population. Much of the country's food

Top: Gorée Island, Senegal (EE)
Bottom: Senegalese boat carver (EE)

Top: Kara market, Togo (CL)
Bottom left: Mossi women at well, Burkina Faso (EE)
Bottom right: Baking bread, Timbuktu, Mali (EE)

supply comes from grains, mainly rice, grown along the Niger river, which meanders down the western side of the country for 500 km. Niamey, the capital, borders it. Sorghum is also grown near the country's only permanent lake, Lake Chad, on the north-east border.

Niger's most remarkable area is the Aïr (eye-EAR) Massif in the north-east, which you can see from the tallest buildings in Agadez. Rising over 2000 metres and built of dark volcanic formations culminating in the Bagzane peaks, the mountains afford some spectacular sights. Beyond the Massif is the Ténéré desert, with some of the most spectacular sand dunes in all of the Sahara.

CLIMATE
In the hottest part of the year, March to May, temperatures reach 45°C. From December to February, temperatures in the desert can drop to freezing, which is why this is the preferred period for crossing the Sahara and visiting Niger.

VISAS
Visas are required of everyone except nationals of Belgium, Denmark, Finland, France, West Germany, Italy, Luxembourg, Netherlands, Norway, Sweden and the UK. Visas are not issued at the airport or at the borders. If at all possible, get a visa before coming to Africa. The only countries in Africa where you can get them are Benin, Ivory Coast, Liberia (from the Ivory Coast embassy), Nigeria (Lagos and Kano) and Senegal – also Algeria, Tunisia (from the Ivory Coast embassy on Rue Ibn Charaf, Tunis), Egypt, Ethiopia and Sudan. French embassies do not have authority to issue visas to Niger. The embassy will ask to see your airline ticket proving that you have either a return or onward ticket (or a statement from your travel agency verifying such) or a statement from your bank that you have the equivalent of at least US$500, which they will hold until your return.

If you are travelling overland south from Algeria, border officials at Assamaka will demand that you produce not only one of the above but also hard cash – 3000 French francs (US$500) or the equivalent. This rule is strictly enforced and bribery rarely works. If you are coming south from Algeria, treat the border officials at Assamaka with tender loving care – the formalities there can take anywhere from several hours to a full day depending on whether or not they like your looks. Similarly, searches by custom officials vary greatly – from virtually none to very thorough. Sometimes, officials cause lots of problems, apparently hoping for bribes.

Reporting to the police in each town where you stay the night is apparently not required by law, but the police will tell you it is. So do it anyway unless you want to get in trouble. What is required is that you get your passport stamped by the police at various major towns en route, whether or not you stay the night. Travellers to/from Algeria, for example, must get them in Arlit, Agadez, Tahoua and Niamey. People not doing this have been sent from Niamey back as far as Arlit for the stamp.

Exit visas are no longer required. However, if you travel overland and have not had your passport stamped at the major cities en route, you may have problems at the border. If you're in Niamey, for example, and head off to Mali without going by the Sûreté, you risk being told at the border to go back and get the stamp (not an exit visa). With exit visas no longer required, however, travellers need not pass through Niamey. There's one exception. If you head east of Zinder towards Chad, you reportedly still need a special letter of authority from the Ministry of Interior in Niamey, obtainable in 24 hours – but verify this.

A white tourist card is also required, but only if you go to Niamey. This card is the government's official approval for you to travel about the country. The police will ask to see it and if you don't have one, you're asking for problems. They could even send you back to Niamey to get one. For CFA 100, they are issued automatically and on the spot, which makes you wonder what purpose they serve. Regardless, don't take a chance. Go to the Sûreté in downtown Niamey, two blocks from the Hôtel Rivoli and closed weekends. They'll ask for two photos.

In Niamey individual visas to all neighbouring countries take only 24 hours, including Mali and Nigeria. The French embassy issues visas to Togo, Burkina Faso, Chad and CAR.

Diplomatic Missions Abroad

Abidjan, Accra, Addis Ababa, Algiers, Bonn, Brussels, Cairo, Cotonou, Dakar, Kano, Khartoum, Lagos, New York, Ottawa, Paris, Washington, Yaoundé.

MONEY

US$1 = 287 CFA
£1 = 537 CFA

The unit of currency is the West African CFA. The best place to change money in Niamey is Citibank, (tel 733621) downtown at the Sonara II building, open weekdays 9 to 11 am and 4 to 5 pm. Normal banking hours: weekdays 8 am to 12 noon. Banks: Citibank, BIAO (Banque Internationale pour l'Afrique Occidentale).

LANGUAGE

French is the official language. Hausa is the most widely spoken African language, especially in the south. You'll hear more Djerma in Niamey, and Fulani and Tamachek in the north. Greetings in Hausa:

Good morning	ee-nah-KWA-nahlah-HEE-yah-low
Good evening	ee-nah-EE-neelah-HEE-yah-low
How are you?	BAR-kah
Thank you	nah-GOH-day

Greetings in Djerma:

Good morning	mah-teen-keh-NEE
Good evening	mah-teen-HEE-ree
How are you?	BAR-kah
Thank you	foh-foh
Goodbye	kah-LAH-ton-ton

GENERAL INFORMATION

Health

A vaccination for yellow fever is required but not for cholera unless you're travelling from a country where an outbreak has been reported. In emergencies, use Clinic de Gamkelly (tel 732033), which is better than the hospital (tel 722521) except for surgery. One of the better pharmacies in Niamey is Pharmacie Nouvelle downtown between Hôtel Rivoli and Air Afrique; they're open Sundays and close late.

Security

Despite the highest beggar population in West Africa, Niamey retains its triple A security rating.

Business Hours

Business: weekdays 8 am to 12.30 pm and 3 to 6.30 pm, Saturday 8 am to 12.30 pm. Government: weekdays 7.30 am to 12.30 pm and 3.30 to 6.30 pm, closed Saturday and Sunday.

Public Holidays

1 January, Easter Monday, 15 April, 1 May, End of Ramadan (17 May 88), Tabaski (25 July 88), 3 August, Mohammed's Birthday, 18 December, 25 December. The major government holiday is April 15, which in recent years has been toned down because of the recession.

Photography

A permit is required. They can be obtained on the spot at the Ministry of Interior (tel 722162) on Avenue Charles de Gaulle if you go there with a CFA 5000 fiscal stamp (*timbre fiscal*), obtainable at the Préfècture downtown across from the Sonara II building. In Agadez, you can get one at the Tourist Office, but it'll be valid for only that region. Even with a permit, you're not allowed to take photos of government buildings and personnel, airports, bridges or TV stations.

Time, Phone & Telex
When it's noon in Niger, it's 11 am in London and 6 am in New York (7 am during daylight savings time). International telephone service is by satellite and good. Calling from Niamey to Agadez is fairly easy. You'll find telex machines at the post office and the Gaweye Sofitel. Anybody can make international calls from the Gaweye, but the cost is expensive – CFA 2680 a minute to the USA, for example.

GETTING THERE
Air
From Europe, there are direct flights from Paris and Marseilles. From the USA, you'll have to transfer in Paris, Dakar or Abidjan. There are also flights from Nairobi and Addis Ababa. Within West Africa, there are direct flights to/from Dakar, Abidjan, Lomé, Ouagadougou and Cotonou.

Car
Driving time from the coastal cities of Lomé, Cotonou and Lagos is two days, each paved all the way. Driving time from Ouagadougou (Burkina Faso) is about 10 hours, all paved road now. The Niger-Benin border closes at 7.30 pm, the Burkina border at 6 pm. You'll have to buy Niger vehicle insurance at the border even if you have some – no exceptions. A carnet de passage, on the other hand, is not required for tourists.

Roads in Niger are excellent. Niamey-Agadez-Arlit, Niamey-Zinder-Chad border, and Niamey-Burkina border are all paved. Only the Zinder-Agadez route is still in bad condition. Niamey-Agadez and Niamey-Zinder (both over 900 km) take 12 to 14 hours straight driving time, Zinder-Ndjamena via Lake Chad takes about five days. En route to Agadez, you can stop in Tahoua; it's no longer closed to

travellers. You'll encounter about 10 police checkpoints along the way. The police are reportedly sometimes rude. Getting mad only makes matters worse. For vehicle repair, try Sonida (VW, Peugeot), Agence Centrale (Toyota) or Niger Afrique (Renault) in Niamey.

Bush Taxi
To/from Mali If you're headed for Gao and can't get a seat on the SNTN bus, try the Gare Routière next to the Camping Touristique in Niamey. Trucks leave from there on an irregular basis.

To/from Burkina Faso You may find that the bush taxi system has improved now that the Niamey-Ouagadougou road is paved the entire distance. The trip used to take a painfully slow 1½ days during the dry season, with a stop at the border and two or three changes of vehicles en route.

To/from Nigeria If you're headed from Zinder to Kano (Nigeria), you'll find vehicles probably every day but more on Thursday and Friday (Thursday is market day in Zinder).

Bus
The SNTN bus system in Niger is excellent by African standards.

To/from Mali Niamey-Gao costs about CFA 6500 plus CFA 35 per kilo of baggage. Buses leave in both directions on Monday, Wednesday and Friday at noon. The trip takes about 1½ days during the dry season, with an overnight stop at the border, but much longer during July-September.

To/from Benin Niamey-Gaya (Benin border) buses leave daily at 9 am and take four hours. In Gaya, you'll find bush taxis for the eight-km trip to the border, and an STB bus from there to Parakou, where you can hop the train to Cotonou.

To/from Nigeria Niamey-Maradi buses

(towards Kano, Nigeria) leave Niamey on Tuesday, Thursday and Saturday between 7 and 9 am and cost about CFA 7000.

GETTING AROUND
Air
Air Niger went back into operation in 1986, offering service to Agadez on Wednesday, perhaps expanding to Zinder, Maradi and Tahoua. For a charter plane, see Transniger Aviation (tel 732055).

Bush Taxi
Buses in Niger are fast and comfortable, so many travellers seem to prefer them to bush taxis – if they can get a seat. If not, you'll find bush taxis headed in all directions – Agadez, Zinder, and the borders of Nigeria, Benin and Burkina Faso. Trucks are another possibility but frequently no cheaper. You'll find trucks leaving virtually every day on most of the main routes, including Niamey-Agadez, Agadez-Arlit and Agadez-Zinder.

Bus
Travellers swear by the SNTN buses. Prices are low, so they're popular with everyone. Seats must be purchased in advance, and the buses fill up fast, starting from the moment the previous one leaves. They cover all the major routes except Agadez-Zinder, where trucks are your only choice. There's no longer a bus from Zinder to the Chad border.

Niamey

Few cities in Africa, even the world, can match Niamey's fantastic growth – from around 2000 people in the 1930s to 350,000 today. Still, it's fairly spread out and uncongested, requiring a little more walking than other Sahelian capitals. Niamey is on the eastern bank of the Niger river, spanned by Kennedy bridge. Dusk is the time to have a drink nearby and watch the camels crossing over it. You'll

find the street pattern confusing. The two major streets, running perpendicular to one another, are Rue de Kalley extending from Kennedy Bridge (where it is called Rue de Gaweye) to the market, and Boulevard de la Liberté, the wide street running in front of the Grand Marché and extending all the way to the airport. However, you'll find street names virtually useless – nobody knows them.

Information
Tourist Office The Office National du Tourisme (tel 723447) is downtown between the Rivoli and the Grand Hôtels.

Embassies Algeria (tel 723165) Avenue du Président Luebke, Belgium (tel 733314), Benin (tel 723919), Canada (BP 362, tel 733686/7), France (open 7.30 am to 12 noon, BP 240, tel 722722/3), West Germany (BP 629, tel 722534), Nigeria (tel 732410) Avenue du Président Luebke, USA (BP 201, tel 722661/2, telex 5444). Consulates: Netherlands (tel 732734), UK (tel 722032), Mali (tel 722883/735628) in an obscure office to the north of the Grand Marché.

Other embassies include: Senegal, Tunisia. Consulates: Italy, Liberia, Mauritania, Sweden, Switzerland, UK.

Bookstores & Supermarkets The two best bookstores are *Camico Papeterie* downtown across from Score and *Papeterie Burama* four blocks away between Avenue Coulibaly and Hôtel Maourey. The tabac behind the Rivoli sells *Time* and *Newsweek* as do the bookstores at the Gaweye and the Terminus.

The best supermarket is *Score* downtown one block from the Rivoli, across from the Petit Marché, the best place to buy fresh produce.

Travel Agencies The best is Temet Voyages (BP 12001, 723400, telex 5367), which arranges trips to Parc 'W', Ayorou on Sundays, and trips to the Aïr mountains starting from Agadez. Prices are sky-high.

A day trip to Ayorou costs about CFA 140,000 for a Peugeot 504 plus CFA 8000 a person (maximum five). A two-day trip to Parc 'W' costs about CFA 225,000 for two including room and board. A four-day trip from Agadez to the Aïr mountains costs about CFA 180,000 a person (minimum three people). The Office National du Tourisme (tel 732447) also conducts trips to the Aïr mountains, but they are arranged only in Agadez. Small-time entrepreneurs charge significantly less. The CLO officer at the US embassy may have names.

Grand Marché

This is one of the city's major attractions and is one of West Africa's best markets. It has been completely rebuilt since it burned down a few years ago.

Musée Nationale du Niger

This impressive 24-hectare museum (tel 734321) is one of the best in West Africa. You'll find life-size model dwellings (Tuareg, Hausa, Djerma, Fulani, Toubou) with mannequins dressed in typical dress and a series of pavilions based on traditional architectural styles, each with a different theme, eg handicrafts, costumes and weapons.

Zoo

The zoo is part of the museum and contains hippo, crocodile, lion, hyena, chimps, snakes and birds. Open from 9 am to 12 noon and 4 to 6 pm every day except Monday, the museum is in the middle of town, less than a five-minute walk from Score supermarket.

Franco Nigerian Cultural Centre

Virtually in the same complex, the FNCC (tel 734834) has a busy schedule of movies, lectures, exhibits, dance and theatre. Programs are available from the ticket windows, open Tuesday to Saturday 9 am to 12.30 pm and 4.30 to 7.30 pm.

La Grande Mosquée

Four or five km from the centre of town towards the Wadata market you'll find this impressive new mosque financed by Libya. Open to both male and female visitors, it has workers and guards who will be glad to give you a small tour.

Oumara Ganda Cultural Centre

Opposite the mosque, the OGCC sponsors a variety of African cultural activities including wrestling, dancing, films by local film makers, concerts and art exhibits. Activities are frequently advertised in Le Sahel and posted in store windows.

Le Stade de Lutte Traditionelle

On some Sundays, 4.30 to 7 pm, you can see African-style wrestling matches at Le Stade de Lutte Traditionelle, an arena with a covered viewing stand between the Grande Mosquée and the Marché Wadata, about four km from the heart of town. The crowds are very enthusiastic and the matches are definitely worth seeing. In one afternoon, you'll see about 30 matches, each usually lasting one to six minutes. The men employ lots of ritualistic hand movements, trying to get both knees of the opponent on the ground. Consult Le Sahel for events.

Le Hippodrome

The wrestling is far more interesting than this race track out near the airport where you can see horse races almost every Sunday, 3 to 5 pm.

Places to Stay - bottom end

Campers can stay at Camping Touristique, on the northern edge of town on the road to Tillabéri. The cost is CFA 1000 a person, plus CFA 500 per vehicle and CFA 300 for a motorcycle. It has a guard, fairly clean showers and wash basins. Finding a cab is easy. Le Camping Rio Bravo, 20 km to the north of town on the side of the river, is now rundown and not recommended.

The city's two cheapest hotels are the Hôtel Moustache (tel 734282) and Hôtel-

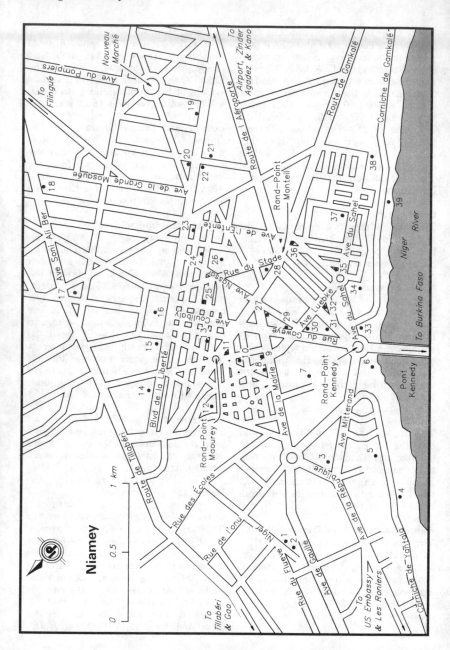

Niamey

1	British Consulate	22	Hôtel Ténéré
2	German Embassy	23	Hôtel Domino
3	French Consulate	24	Akalan
4	SNTN Bus Station	25	Marhaba Restaurant
5	La Flotille Restaurant	26	Stadium & Tennis Club
6	Hôtel Gaweye	27	Sûreté (Police)
7	Museum	28	Post Office
8	Petit Marché	29	Hôtel Rivoli
9	SCORE Supermarket	30	El Nsar Building, Chez Nouis
10	La Cascade Restaurant		Restaurant & Le Satellite Disco
11	Hôtel Maourey	31	Sonara I Building
12	Cathedral		& Le Damsi Restaurant
13	An Na Chouwa Restaurant	32	Nigerian Embassy & Tourist Office
14	Peace Corps	33	L'Oriental Restaurant
15	Mali Consulate	34	Grand Hôtel
16	Grand Marché	35	Au Feu du Bois Restaurant
17	Islam Restaurant	36	Le Viet Nam Restaurant
18	Hôtel Moustache	37	Hôtel Terminus
19	L'Ermitage	38	Hôtel Sahel
20	Le Flamboyant	39	Le Bateau Restaurant
21	American Recreation Centre		

Bar Dé. Moustache is about three km from downtown on Avenue Soni Ali Ber, not far from the new mosque, while Dé (ex-Domino) is a little closer to downtown, a block behind Hôtel Ténéré. At the Dé, you'll find a noisy bar and filthy ventilated dormitory rooms with four beds, about CFA 2500 a person, and doubles for about CFA 4000. The showers and toilets are fairly clean. Moustache charges virtually the same price per person for a shared room with two beds, fan and outside shower and toilet. For about CFA 5500, you can get a double with air-con, private shower and toilet at Moustache.

Places to Stay – middle

For years, the *Hôtel Rivoli* (tel 733849, telex 5205) has been the favourite of trans-Saharan travellers. It's in the dead centre of town and charges about CFA 7000/7800 for singles/doubles with air-con and fairly decent beds but no hot water. One of the best buys in town is the much nicer *Hôtel Terminus*, a 10-minute walk away. The cheaper rooms there cost no more than the Rivoli's but are frequently all taken. Ask

to see a room first; the air-con doesn't always work.

Places to Stay – top end

Niamey's finest is the well-managed *Gaweye Sofitel* downtown on the edge of the Niger river, a 10-minute walk to the centre of town. For half the price, however, the city offers a wide range of hotels that are quite pleasant and highly recommended. The best of the lot is *Les Rôniers*, with an excellent restaurant and 26 top quality bungalows. It's on the northern outskirts of town, 10 km from the centre and overlooking the river – a good choice if you want tranquility and don't care to see Niamey, but a poor choice if you don't have wheels. The hotel, however, will make arrangements for you to be taken into town in the mornings.

The old *Grand Hôtel* is the most popular because it has a pool and pleasant terrace overlooking the river and is only a 15-minute walk from the centre of town, with rooms in several price ranges. The newer *Hôtel Ténéré* has slightly better rooms for the same price. While it's several km from downtown, getting a taxi isn't a problem because it's on a main drag, Boulevard de la Liberté.

A better buy for the money is the *Terminus*, a tranquil hotel near downtown, two blocks from the Grand. The rooms are about as good as the Ténéré's and less expensive, plus the greenery is pleasant. If you're looking for a hotel with an African ambience, try the *Maourey*, in the heart of downtown at Carrefour Maourey, midway between the Petit Marché/Score and the Grand Marché, with 19 decent rooms but poor lighting.

Two hotels are not recommended. *Le Sahel* has rooms similar in quality to the Terminus and a fairly decent nightclub on weekends, but few clients, no pool and a mediocre restaurant. It's also a 20- to 30-minute walk from downtown, with few taxis in the area. Although a public, olympic-size pool is next door, there's no place to lie in the sun. The other is the *Sabka Lahiya*, which has a pleasant pool but is over-priced and in a terrible location – a good four km from downtown in a remote area with almost no taxis.

Gaweye Sofitel (tel 723400, telex 5367), CFA 25,000/27,000 for singles/doubles (CFA 3000 more for river-view rooms), pool, three tennis courts, TV/video in rooms, travel agency, Hertz, nightclub, cards AE and D.
Les Rôniers (tel 723138, telex 5428), CFA 9,900/10,900 for single/double bungalows, pool, tennis, cards AE and D.
Grand Hôtel (tel 732641, telex 5239), CFA 12,000 to CFA 15,000 for rooms, pool, cards AE and D.
Hôtel Ténéré (tel 732020, telex 5330), CFA 13,500/14,500 for singles/doubles, pool.
Hôtel Terminus (tel 732692/3, telex 5424), CFA 9900/10,500 for single/double bungalows (CFA 6500/7000 for rooms), pool, tennis.
Hôtel Sabka Lahiya (tel 740933, telex 5427), CFA 11,500/12,500 for singles/doubles, pool.
Hôtel Le Sahel (tel 732431/2, telex 5330), CFA 10,000/10,500 for singles/doubles, pool next door.
Hôtel Maourey (tel 732850), CFA 8500/9200 for singles/doubles with air-con.

Places to Eat

Cheap Eats The winner, hands down, for the most popular cheap restaurant in town is the open-air *Marhaba* (tel 732819) – a favourite of Peace Corps volunteers and world travellers. Most dishes (spaghetti, entrecôte, poisson grillé) are about CFA 800 to CFA 2000. Walking down Rue de Kalley towards the market, take a right two long blocks before reaching the Grand Marché. It's a block away and open every evening. The kitchen closes around 9.45 pm.

If you're famished, head for *L'Islam*, which is six blocks directly behind the Grand Marché (a continuation of Avenue Coulibaly). Meals with huge portions cost CFA 1300 to CFA 1700. The service is fast and the five or six selections, which change daily, are a mixture of African and western cuisines. They're open every day and don't serve beer. For a cheap restaurant in the heart of town, try the animated *An-Na Chouwa*, between Rue de Kalley and Hôtel Maourey and open every day late. You'll find excellent brochettes, steak and lots of beer, but nothing else. The ambience is 100% African – bare tables, loud music and stars.

The open-air *La Croissette* has cheap meals – CFA 1500 to CFA 2000 for steak au poivre, omelettes, Nile perch (*capitaine*) and other non-African dishes. For hamburgers, sandwiches, milkshakes and the least expensive French meals in town, there's *Damsi*, a block away in the Sonara I building overlooking Kennedy bridge.

African The best restaurant for African food is *Au Feu de Bois*, which is open every day and serves dishes from various African countries. The portions are large and prices reasonable, CFA 2000 to CFA 2700 for most courses. It is a stone's throw from the Grand Hôtel. Not far away, 100 metres from Lotus Bleu, there's a relatively obscure, rustic place called *Mai Biga* (tel 733424). Open every day except Monday, they offer about 20 authentic African dishes all in the CFA 1600 to CFA 2700 price range. Another is the very rustic *Le M'Backe*, nearby on a dirt road just beyond Hôtel Terminus and open every day until 11 pm. They serve Senegalese poulet yassa and six or seven other dishes, but no beer. For the price, about CFA 1300 a meal, this place is recommended. On the downtown side of the Terminus, you'll find another cheap outdoor restaurant with tablecloths – *La Tapoa*, with couscous for CFA 800, and other meals.

Russian The only place you'll find Russian cuisine in West Africa is at *La Flotille* (tel 723254), a marvellous restaurant run by quite a character – a merry red-cheeked Russian lady and her French husband. The service is sometimes slow but the quality is high with prices to match – four to six course meals for CFA 5500 to CFA 20,000. Closed Sunday, it's a 10-minute walk from the Gaweye on the Corniche road near the river.

Asian Two of Niamey's finest restaurants are Vietnamese, both moderately priced with most dishes in the CFA 2200 to CFA 3750 range. *Le Viet-Nam* (tel 732646), a 15-minute walk from the Rivoli and back of Hôtel Terminus, gets slightly higher marks from the local expatriates than *Lotus Bleu* (tel 722105) a block away. Both are open for dinner only and offer a choice of dining outside on a terrace or inside with air-con.

Several blocks away, across the street from the Grand Hôtel, is *Le Dragon d'Or* (tel 734423), a good Chinese restaurant with over 100 selections and open for lunch as well. Le Viet-Nam is closed on Monday, Lotus Bleu on Tuesday, and Le Dragon d'Or on Wednesday.

Lebanese One of Niamey's most popular restaurants, with moderate prices and highly recommended, is *L'Oriental* (tel 732015), which has an à la carte menu plus daily specials. Open for dinner only and closed Wednesday, it's now downtown midway between the Gaweye and the Grand.

French Niamey has seven top notch French restaurants that are expensive and, with one exception, open for dinner only. Choosing among them is not easy. The nod for the best food goes to *Chez Nous* (tel 733033), across from the Rivoli and closed Sunday. The highly recommended *Le Diamangou* (tel 735143), also called *Le Bateau*, is more unusual – a boat where you have drinks upstairs and eat downstairs. You'll find it below the Grand Hôtel on the dark Corniche road running along the river. *La Cascade* (tel 732832) is also highly recommended. The white and green decor is one of the most attractive and refreshing you'll find in West Africa, plus you have a choice between French and Italian specialities. Most main courses are CFA 3200 to CFA 4800. Open every day, it's in the heart of town on the street back of Score.

Four of the top French restaurants are at hotels. The food at the Gaweye's *La Croix du Sud* (closed Sunday), the Terminus' *Toukounia* (closed Monday) and the *Hôtel Les Rôniers* (open every day) is about as good as you'll find anywhere. The restaurant at the Rôniers is slightly less expensive and the only one open at lunchtime, every day. If you go on a Wednesday or Saturday night, you can eat fresh mussels and snails from France. However, if you don't have wheels, forget it.

Various Cuisines For Polynesian fare with French flare, attentive service and a riverside setting, try *Les Tropiques* next to the river, near Le Diamangou. Open for dinner only and closed Monday, it's fairly expensive.

For more reasonably priced meals, you could try *Marrakech* (tel 734250), a Moroccan restaurant downtown about a block from the Sûreté. However, the meals, about CFA 2500 to CFA 4000, are nothing to write home about. For the same price, you could eat better at the Gaweye's *La Potinière*, which serves the best pizza in town every evening.

Tunisian food is the speciality at the

Hôtel Sabka Lahiya, but the remote location beyond the Wadata Marché is a big drawback.

Entertainment & Sports

Bars One of the favourite pastimes in Niamey is watching the camels passing over Kennedy bridge at dusk. The patio at *Damsi* affords the best view. Most travellers, however, seem to prefer the view from the *Grand Hôtel*, where you can buy inexpensive brochettes and sip drinks around the pool overlooking the river. Others prefer the pool around the *Gaweye*. The best place of all may be *La Diamangou*, a riverboat restaurant below the Grand Hôtel where you can sit on the deck as the sun goes down.

The most popular watering hole for foreigners, excellent for meeting other travellers, is the bar at the *Hôtel Rivoli*. The central location is the attraction, not the relatively expensive drinks. You can get cheaper beers across the street at *La Croissette*, popular with both foreigners and Africans.

For a bar with African ambience, it's hard to beat *An-Na Chouwa*, between Rue de Gaweye and Hôtel Marourey and open late. Another is *L'Ermitage*, which has a huge outdoor beer garden open to 3 am and serves brochettes and other inexpensive food every night from 8 to 11 pm. It is on the wide Boulevard de la Liberté two blocks beyond Hôtel Ténéré, on the other side of the street. *Le Flamboyant*, across from the Ténéré, and *Le Rendez-Vous Restaurant*, near the stadium and opposite the Mercedes dealership, are similar.

To meet the American community, go to the *Marine House* (tel 722661) on Friday nights when they have their TGIF (Thank God It's Friday) open bar or Monday nights when they serve sloppy joes from 6 to 8 pm, followed by a movie. The movie costs CFA 500. You're supposed to be a guest of someone, but don't worry – everyone is usually welcomed. You'll find it about three km north from the centre of town next to the Tunisian embassy.

Nightclubs Niamey's most popular nightclub is unquestionably *Takoubakoyé* across from the Rivoli – the only one that is lively seven days a week. The cover is CFA 2000, which includes a drink, and you won't have problems finding a dancing partner. *Hi-Fi Club* is around the corner, *Le Satellite* a block away in the El Nasr building, and *Kakaki* two long blocks away at the Gaweye. They have similar covers/prices but are lively only on weekends and, except for Hi-Fi, close on Sunday. For a nightclub with predominantly African clientele, try *Fofo Club* at Hôtel Le Sahel. Closed Tuesday and fairly dead except on weekends, it has an interesting decor and similar prices.

If you're looking for an inexpensive nightclub with 100% African clientele, head for *Akolan*, a strobe-lit nightclub with cover/drinks for only CFA 500. The music is a mixture of African and western. You'll find it between the stadium and Boulevard de la Liberté as the crow flies. Open every night, it's a respectable place and livens up around midnight.

Movie Theatre The air-con *Studio* has fairly good films and is the best. It's downtown on the street behind Score, with shows nightly at 6.30, 8.30 and 10.30 pm. The FNCC (tel 734834), downtown across from the entrance to the zoo, has shows almost every night at 9 pm. Consult Le Sahel for what's showing at both places; movies change daily. Most Tuesday evenings around 8.30 pm, the American Recreation Centre has movies in English.

Sports The Gaweye has three tennis courts, free to hotel guests or CFA 1500 for others. The Hôtel Terminus also has courts, only for hotel guests. You can also play at the Rôniers, but it's 10 km from downtown. The top six hotels all have pools. If you're not staying at one, try the Grand's – their pool costs about CFA 600 while the Gaweye's costs about CFA 1000. The cheapest place to swim is the public olympic-size pool next to Hôtel Le Sahel;

the fee including dressing room is only CFA 250. If you have a drink at Les Rôniers, they'll let you use the pool free, perhaps the tennis courts as well. Indeed, for sports, lounging in the sun and a good meal, you can't beat it.

Others go to the American Recreation Centre next to the Ténéré and act like they're guests of members, using the pool and changing rooms and eating at their inexpensive snack bar (non-members pay a slight premium). On weekends, it's crowded; on weekdays, most of those sunning at the pool are Peace Corps volunteers. Sundays at 4.30 pm is volleyball time; Monday it's closed.

Things to Buy
Artisan Goods Downtown between the Rivoli and Score supermarket, you'll find a long row of artisan stalls with leather work, blankets, swords, calabash bowls, silver jewellery and unusual necklaces, some with the famous cross of Agadez. Nearby, across from the entrance to the zoo, you'll find *Le Centre des Métiers d'Art du Niger*. The Tuareg and Hausa leather work is perhaps better here than anywhere else, but prices are also higher. At the rebuilt *Grand Marché*, you'll find a wide selection of goods, enough to keep you busy for hours. What's truly spectacular are *les couvertures Djerma* – large bright strips of cotton partially sewn together which make great wall hangings and are unique to Niger. Most are not washable.

Music For records of African music, the two best shops are *Le Chant du Monde* (open to 9 pm) across from Hôtel Maourey and *Festival Musique* next to the Rivoli. Niger is not known for its singers. Some of the leading groups/singers are Les Ambassadeurs du Sahel, Orchestre Assode and Mamare Garba.

Getting There & Away
Bush Taxi There are bush taxis to all the major towns, but the bus is cheaper and good, if you can get a seat. Many bush taxis, trucks and private buses used to leave next to the Wadata market, but this may have changed with the recent reconstruction of the Grand Marché.

Bus In Niamey, the SNTN buses leave from the Gare Routière, a 15-minute walk north from the Gaweye hotel along the Corniche river road. Schedules occasionally change; call SNTN (tel 723020) to be sure.

Niamey-Agadez costs about CFA 12,500, leaving Niamey on Monday, Wednesday and Friday at 4 pm and Agadez on Tuesday, Thursday and Saturday at the same hour, arriving 8 am the following day.

The Niamey-Zinder express bus costs about CFA 10,000 and leaves Niamey on Monday and Friday at 7 am, arriving 14 hours later.

Getting Around
Air Transport At the airport, there's no departure tax. You'll find a restaurant, bank, Hertz and lots of vendors selling a wide variety of crafts at fairly good prices. A taxi into town (12 km) costs only CFA 1000. No buses serve the airport, but it is on a main road, making hitching possible.

Taxi Fares are CFA 100 for a shared taxi, CFA 500 for a taxi to yourself, about CFA 2000 by the hour, and about CFA 14,000 plus petrol by the day. Finding taxis is an art. Many may stop but none may be headed exactly where you're going. Take the cab and find another where he lets you off. Otherwise, you may wait an hour, cursing all the time. Around 9 to 10 pm, the taxis turn into pumpkins and are nowhere to be found, even at the Gaweye, unless you have arranged to be picked up.

Car Rental You'll find Niger Car/Hertz (tel 732331/6, telex 5327, cards AE, D) at the Gaweye Sofitel and the airport, Transcap Voyages (tel 732334/733635) downtown in Immeuble El-Hasr near the bridge. A chauffeur is obligatory if you'll be going out of town. Others include Afric Safari Car (tel 733582), Transniger (tel 733571), and Niger Afrique (tel 732228/9).

AROUND NIAMEY
Boubon
A 25-minute, 25-km drive north of Niamey on the paved road to Tillabéri will bring you to Boubon, a small village on the eastern side of the Niger river. It's off the road a bit and easy to miss; look for the small sign. What's special about this place is simply being so close to the river. During the rice harvest season, November to January, you may see farmers in their pirogues paddling around, cutting down the 'floating' rice with their machetes.

Places to Stay & Eat In the village you'll find someone with a dugout canoe (*pirogue*) to take you across to an island 200 metres away with a *Campement Touristique* (tel 732427), which is open all year round and includes a restaurant, pool (not working) and rustic cabins for about CFA 1800. Although they'll whip up a meal any day of the week, you're unlikely to find other guests except on Sunday when they anticipate a number of people from Niamey for lunch or, possibly, Wednesday, when there's a market. It's not necessary to order in advance unless you want something special.

Namaro
Driving 30 km further north of Boubon on the same road, you will come to a sign pointing to the *Complexe Touristique de Namaro* (tel 732123), a fairly popular weekend spot for expatriates wanting to escape Niamey. For those who haven't had an opportunity to explore African village life more closely, Namaro provides this opportunity. The hotel is across the river on a hill overlooking the village of Namaro. You'll find a man with a pirogue to take you across. Minimally furnished cabins with double beds, air-con and filthy toilets are about CFA 6000 to CFA 9000 (CFA 10,000 to CFA 14,000 for rooms

with four beds). The complex has a fairly decent bar-restaurant, pool, ping-pong and games room.

From June to September, it's less active and open only on weekends. During the rest of the year, it's open all week long; December to February is the most popular period. The hotel has a bus for those needing transportation. You should be able to get a taxi from Niamey to drop you off there for CFA 4000 plus 10 litres of petrol.

The North

AGADEZ
Unlike Timbuktu which seems to be dying, Agadez continues to thrive because of its location – the first city you come to after crossing the desert via the major trans-Saharan route. Its heyday, however, is long past. In the 16th century, with a population of 30,000 people, the city thrived off the gold trade between Gao (Mali) and Tripoli. Later, gold waned and salt became the principal item of trade, and the city's population dropped to 3000 people by 1900. Now, it's back up to 20,000 – uranium, the Trans Saharan highway and travellers all contributing.

Agadez is an interesting desert town, with sandy streets, excellent examples of Sudanese mud architecture, and Tuareg nomads (or Tamasheq as they prefer to be called).

Information
Whatever you do, don't forget to get your passport stamped by the police. If you neglect to do so and continue on to Niamey or Zinder, you may be forced to return to Agadez for the stamp.

Things to See
The city has only two historical landmarks – La Grande Mosquée of adobe construction and the three-storey Palais du Sultan.

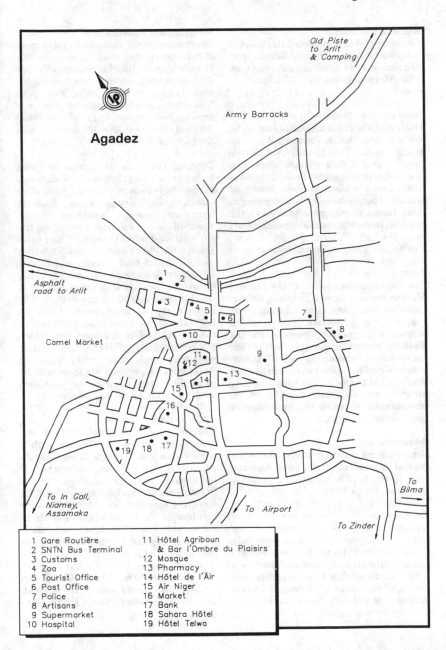

Agadez

Army Barracks

Old Piste
to Arlit
& Camping

Asphalt
road to Arlit

Camel Market

To In Gall,
Niamey,
Assamaka

To Airport

To Bilma

To Zinder

1 Gare Routière
2 SNTN Bus Terminal
3 Customs
4 Zoo
5 Tourist Office
6 Post Office
7 Police
8 Artisans
9 Supermarket
10 Hospital
11 Hôtel Agriboun
  & Bar l'Ombre du Plaisirs
12 Mosque
13 Pharmacy
14 Hôtel de l'Äir
15 Air Niger
16 Market
17 Bank
18 Sahara Hôtel
19 Hôtel Telwa

La Grande Mosquée

Dating from 1515 and rebuilt in 1844, the mosque's 27-metre, pyramid-like minaret with permanent scaffolding affords a view of the Aïr mountains. Only Muslims may enter.

Grand Marché

The Grand Marché nearby has a new metal roof and has lost its charm but not its animation. You'll find a variety of artisan goods, rugs and Tuareg leatherwork. The most popular souvenir by far is the famous Agadez cross in silver filigree – a stylised symbol of both sexes which, according to some Tuareg tribes, protects against 'the evil eye'. Inspect them closely; each desert town (In-Gall, Tahoua, Zinder, Bilma, etc) has a slightly different design.

Vieux Quartier

The hassling vendors of the Grand Marché are sometimes fatiguing. Many travellers prefer the more tranquil vieux quartier, the old section of town which surrounds the market, particularly the district facing the mosque. You'll find small shops, interesting old Sudanese houses with Hausa-inspired designs, and small crooked streets. The early morning around 7 am is the best time for taking photographs, catching the multitude of soft colours on the walls.

Animal Market

Another good morning adventure is the animal market on the paved highway beyond the SNTN station; the activity dies down by 10.30 am.

Cavalcade

The best time to be in Agadez is during one of the Muslim holidays, especially Tabaski when, following the feast, you can see one of the great spectacles of the desert – the 'cavalcade', a furious camel race through the narrow crowded streets between the Sultan's Palace and mosque.

Places to Stay – bottom end

The favourite for those on-the-cheap is *Hôtel Sahara* (tel 440197), opposite the Grande Marché. Double rooms cost about CFA 5000 with air-con; singles/doubles with fans cost about CFA 3000/3500. Meals are fairly expensive but the servings are copious. If it's full, try *Hôtel Agriboun*, between the Hôtel de l'Aïr and the post office.

Camping Trans Saharan travellers now have a choice of campsites. Most campers used to stay at Joyce's Garden, now called *Camping de l'Oasis*. Since changing names and owners, it has reportedly gone downhill. Seven km from town along the old Arlit road north of town, l'Oasis costs about CFA 1000 a person and CFA 1000 a vehicle. You'll find a restaurant (about CFA 2500 for a meal), washing facilities, erratic showers, and a small rock pool which has apparently become filthy. The better campsite may now be *Camping L'Escale*, about five km west of town on the new road to Arlit. Except for the lack of a pool, it has similar facilities, a better restaurant and lower prices, plus the Swiss-Nigerian owners are friendlier. As in all of Niger, camping on your own within five km of town is prohibited.

Places to Stay – top end

The best hotel is *Hôtel de l'Aïr* (tel 440147), in the centre of town with a perfect view of the Grande Mosquée and a popular place for drinks. Architecturally fascinating, the Aïr was formerly the Sultan's palace and charges about CFA 6000/7000 for singles/doubles with air-con and less for rooms with fans. There's no hot water but near the Sahara, who needs it. Groups headed for the Aïr mountains almost invariably stay at the Aïr, so it's a good place to look for a ride. If it's full, try the government-run *Hôtel Telwa* (tel 410164), two blocks west of the market, with air-con rooms for about CFA 5000 to CFA 7500.

Places to Eat

Agadez has a number of interesting watering holes and decent restaurants besides those at the hotels. One of the most popular restaurant-bars with young travellers is *Le Restaurant Senegalais* in the centre of town; it's also a good place to look for lifts. Another popular bar is *Bar L'Ombre du Plaisirs* next to Hôtel Agriboun. In the evenings, you may hear local musicians playing here and sample some of the local brew, maize beer.

For good, cheap, hearty meals, try *Restaurant Islamique*, 200 metres from the market on the same road as the BDRN bank. The ambience is pleasant, the owner affable, and the lamb stew highly recommended. You'll find *Tafadek* on the main road through town, near Hôtel de l'Aïr. Apparently well-known for serving Tuareg specialities, it has a peaceful setting and good food, including couscous. For cheaper meals, try one of the small restaurants near the market.

Getting There & Away

To get there, you can take the overnight bus from Niamey on Monday, Wednesday and Friday; it heads back the following days at 4 pm. The SNTN terminal is on the north side of Agadez on the new road to Arlit. On Wednesday, Air Niger offers a flight Niamey-Agadez and return.

If you have car problems, you risk having your vehicle butchered if you don't use a real garage. *Garage de l'Aïr* facing Hôtel Telwa, *Garage Franco* on the road to Zinder, and *Garage Yahaya Ango*, 300 metres from Hôtel Agriboun on the same path, have all been recommended.

AROUND AGADEZ

If you tire of Agadez altogether, head for In-Gall, 130 km to the west, a peaceful oasis of date trees, irrigated gardens and a market.

AÏR MOUNTAINS & TÉNÉRÉ DESERT

One of the principal attractions of Agadez is the desert area to the north-east. There are three principal zones: the Aïr mountains starting immediately to the north and north-east of Agadez, the Ténéré desert beyond and, further north-east, the Djado mountain range, about 1000 km from Agadez.

Aïr Massif

The Aïr Massif is one of the most spectacular sights in West Africa. Covering an area the size of Switzerland, these mountains are of dark volcanic rock capped with unusually shaped peaks, the highest being Mont Bagzane at 2022 metres, 145 km from Agadez. You'll see artefacts dating back to at least 1300 AD yielding lush greenery and an astonishing garden agriculture.

Some of the major destinations include the hot thermal springs at Tafadek, a waterfall five km from the oasis of Timia, the effervescent wells at Igouloulef, and a prehistoric site at the oasis of Iferouâne (160 km east of Arlit).

Ténéré Desert

The second principal destination is the Ténéré Desert – an area of sand dunes and monotonous flat areas of hard sand. There are two principal routes, both notoriously difficult – east towards Bilma or north/north-east over the Aïr Massif into the Ténéré desert.

If you choose the latter, head north to Iferouâne, then on to Temet and Adrar Bous – unquestionably, one of the most extraordinarily beautiful sand dune areas in the entire Sahara. Count on at least two days driving to reach them, ie, a minimum of five days for a trip to the Aïr mountains and the dunes and back. Allowing eight or nine days would permit you to see much more.

If instead, you head east towards Bilma, you'll come to Tazole after 100 km. To the south is one of the world's most important dinosaur cemeteries. The fossils are spread over a belt 150 km long; you might even see one at the top of a dune. Continually covered and uncovered

Air Mountains

To Algeria

Adrar Greboun
2310m

1800m

Tamgak Mtns

Iférouane

1700m

Tagmeurt
Mtns

1500m

Mt
Takolokouzet
1500m

Aguellal

Tin—Telloust

Akokano

Arlit

Gougaram

Assodé

Mt
Agalak
1700m

Timia

Kreb—Kreb

Bagzane
Mtns
1900m

To
Bilma

Puits de
Sekiret

Elmeki

Aouderas

Akrereb

Tafadek

Abardokh

Anou
Araren

Massif du
Taghouaji
900m

Tequida
in Tagaït

Tchirozerine

Tin Tibesgin

Tazolé

Assouas

Agadez

0   50   100 km

To Niamey

Marendet

To
Zinder

by the sand, they are silent witness to the fact that the whole Sahara desert was once green and fertile. You may see a number of species, maybe even fossilised crocodiles. After another 170 km, you'll pass the famous *arbre du Ténéré*, the only tree in Africa pointed out on the Michelin map – except there's no tree. This sole tree in the middle of the desert, over 400 km from the nearest tree – the last acacia of the once great Saharan forests – was hit in 1973 by a Libyan truck driver. Incredible. All you'll see is a metal replica; the remains are in the museum in Niamey.

Further east are the salt producing oases, Fachi and Bilma, where you'll see how salt is dug out of the earth and then dissolved in a pan, evaporating, and leaving salt crystals at the top and heavier impurities at the bottom. This process is repeated until the salt is pure, after which it's poured into moulds made from large palm trunks, giving the salt its loaf-like aspect (in contrast, for example, to the door-like slabs from Mali). Today, the camel caravans coming to pick it up are very rare.

Djado Plateau

If you continue on to the Djado Plateau (a 10- to 14-day roundtrip from Agadez), you'll see some of the prehistoric cave paintings of antelope, giraffe and rhino for which the area is noted.

Tours

A guide and government authorisation are required for all trips. For an organised tour, in Agadez contact Temet Voyages (BP 178, tel 440172, telex 8241), which also has offices in Niamey, Aligouran Voyages (BP 205), or the Office du Tourisme on the northern side of town across from the post office. In Arlit, contact Tamzak (tel 452278). The price per person runs about CFA 55,000 a day. Aligouran, for example, offers a seven-day excursion that includes most of the Aïr Massif and the dunes at Temet, and a 12-day excursion that includes much of the Aïr Massif and the Ténéré desert all the way to the Djado Massif. In Niamey, there are reliable and personable Tauregs who arrange equally good trips for much less. Ask the CLO (community liaison officer) at the US embassy.

LA CURE SALÉE

The Cure Salée (kure sal-AY) is an annual event of the herders in Niger. The Cure Salée of the Bororos, a unique sect of Fulani (Peul) herders, is famous Africa-wide – don't miss it if you're in Niger during September. Proud of their beauty, the men have long, elegant, feminine features. They are also playful and don't shy away from showing their friendship to one another, even sharing their women on occasion. Bororo women have the same features and, before marriage, enjoy unusual sexual freedom, sleeping with unmarried men whenever they choose.

During the year, the nomadic Peul Bororos are dispersed, tending to their animals. During the Cure Salée, you'll see men on camels – like cowboys – trying to keep their herds in order as well as racing their camels. The event serves above all as a social gathering – a time for wooing the opposite sex, marriage and seeing old friends.

To win the attention of the eligible women, the single men participate in a virtual beauty contest, the *Gerewol*. They form a long line and are dressed to the hilt with blackened lips to make the teeth seem whiter, lightened faces, white streaks down their foreheads and noses, star-like figures painted on their faces, braided hair, elaborate hats, anklets, all kinds of jewellery, beads and shiny objects. They dance for long hours. Then the women, dressed less elaborately, make their choices. This is at the end of the week, every day of which they dance, sometimes well into the night. Each sect is afraid the other will take away its women, so the rivalry can be fierce. Even the TV cameras don't show the event where men dance while others hit them with huge sticks, trying to make them fall over. All of this is magnificently recorded in *Nomads of Niger* by Carol Beckwith and Marion Van Offelen.

The Cure Salée takes place at the end of the rainy season; some of the cattle are then driven to Nigeria for sale. The location is usually between In-Gall and Tegguiddan Tessoum, 88 km to the north – about 200 km west of Agadez, a 10-hour drive from Niamey. Around Tegguiddan, the land and water are salty, the animals being driven there for the 'cure'. Each group of herders has its own Cure Salée. The Tuareg equivalent of the Gerewol is the *Illoudjan*. Top government officials attend only that of the Peul Bororos. Around August, the government sends out a team to select the site. It lasts a week, and the big event happens on the last two days.

ARLIT

Uranium was discovered here in 1965. Six years later, Somair, the uranium mining company, created Arlit, Niger's northern-most major town.

This dusty town has grown considerably.

You'll find a hospital, a colourful marketplace bustling with activity, a number of petrol stations and two banks, which offer terrible exchange rates and charge a high commission on travellers' cheques. Most important, don't fail to get your passport stamped by the police.

Places to Stay & Eat

Campers have a choice – a campsite three km north of town and another to the south, near where the paved road ends. Equally good, they cost about CFA 600 per person per night, CFA 1200 per vehicle and CFA 300 for a shower. The best restaurants are *Restaurant de l'Aïr* on the main drag, *Le Sahel* and *Tamesna*, with steak for CFA 700 or so. For about CFA 600, you can get a complete meal at *Ramada* in the centre of town near the post office. For a cheap beer, try the popular *Cheval Blanc*, which charges extra at night whenever they have music.

Getting There & Away

SNTN buses connect Arlit with Agadez (237 km) and Niamey (1188 km) via the all-paved Route de l'Uranium, which ends in Arlit. For a mechanic, look around Somair; they have a welding shop.

The South

AYOROU

The major attraction of Ayorou (ah-you-rou) is the famous animal market on Sundays, an interesting one-day excursion from Niamey and highly recommended during the dry season. You'll find the cattle, camel, sheep and goats in much larger numbers and the activity much more vibrant from November through April. It's not so much the animals as the people who make this an unforgettable trip. You'll see Africans of various ethnic groups – Tuareg, Peul, Bella, Moors – wearing their best garb, including elaborate head gear, swords and costumes. The market on Sundays in the large main square is packed with animals and people with dust everywhere. It doesn't get going until around noon. If you're there in the morning, go to the river to watch the cattle swimming across. Many travellers take a trip on the river. You can rent pirogues in Ayorou or, better, in Firgour, a small fishing village 11 km away with a hippo pool nearby. During the dry season, you may also see giraffes.

Places to Stay & Eat

On the river bank, you'll find a decent tourist hotel, the PLM *Hôtel Amenokal*, with a pool, bar, restaurant and air-con singles/doubles for about CFA 11,000/13,000. To reserve, call Transcap Voyages at the Gaweye. It's open only from November through April. (It was closed during the 1985-86 season; hopefully, it has reopened.) Otherwise, you'll have to ask the locals for a mat. For an inexpensive meal, try *Restaurant à la Pirogue* run by a Tuareg.

Getting There & Away

To get there, you may have to rent a car or take a dilapidated private bus. The trip takes three hours by car and six hours by bus. From July to September, the 88-km unpaved stretch north of Tillabéri becomes muddy, increasing the Niamey-Ayorou (208 km) driving time by an hour or more. If you're hitching a ride to Gao in Mali (235 km), the best time is Sunday after the market. On the way to Ayorou, stop at Tillabéri for a look at one of Niger's biggest rice growing areas. Sundays is market day there as well.

DOSSO

Only 138 km south-east of Niamey, Dosso is a Djerma town of no particular interest. For about CFA 6000 a double with air-con, you can stay at *Hôtel Djerma*, a fairly decent hotel. Or inquire whether the cheaper, rustic *L'Auberge du Carrefour* still exists.

SAY
During the first or second weekend in December, there's an interesting festival in Say, 50 km to the south of Niamey. Friday is market day.

PARC 'W'
One of the better game parks in West Africa, Parc 'W' has various carnivores, including lions, leopards, cheetahs, hyenas and jackals. Other animals you might see are elephants, crocs, hippos, buffalos, antelopes, duikers, baboons and wart hogs, as well as a wide assortment of birds, with migratory aquatic ones arriving between February and May. While the variety of game is large, their total numbers are small. So don't be surprised if you see few animals. Located on the western bank of the Niger river in an area of savannah woodland, the park is named after the double bend the Niger river takes at the park's northern border in Niger. It's open the last week of November to late May and a three-hour drive (145 km) south of Niamey on a conversation-stopping washboard road. November to February is the best viewing time.

Places to Stay & Eat
Camping in the park is prohibited, so most people stay at *Hôtel Relais de la Tapoa* at the park entrance. It is open the same period as the park and constructed to look like a Sahelian village. The cost for two people with half board and a bungalow with air-con is about CFA 26,000 (CFA 4500 less with fan). Without meals, a two-person bungalow costs about CFA 10,500 with air-con and CFA 5000 with fan. You'll also apparently find some cheaper bungalows. To reserve, call Transcap Voyages at the Gaweye; they can also arrange tours.

FELINGUÉ
If you're in Niamey and looking for a Sunday excursion, consider Felingué, 185 km north-east of Niamey by paved road. The market there on Sunday is surprisingly active for such a small town. Inhabited primarily by Fulani and Hausa, with examples of Hausa architecture, it's at the base of a hill which you can climb to get an excellent view of the town and the Dallol Bosso, the valley of a dried-up river. You'll find a rustic campement, *La Villa Verte*, and bush taxis heading to/from Niamey every day in the early morning.

TAHOUA
Niger's fourth largest city is an important market centre but not particularly interesting. Sunday is market day. About the only place to stay is the *Campement Administratif* (tel 610015), which has doubles with fans for CFA 3500 (CFA 5000 with air-con) and a friendly manager. Make sure the police stamp your passport.

BIRNIN-NKONNI
Only 93 km north of Sokoto (Nigeria), Birnin-NKonni is one of the three major border crossings with Nigeria. Market day is Wednesday. There's *Hôtel Kado* (tel 364) near the market and, cheaper, a rustic *Campement* on the outskirts of town on the road to Niamey, a good place to pick up cheap Nigerian petrol as well.

MARADI
With a population of about 55,000 inhabitants, Maradi is the peanut capital of Niger and the country's No 2 commercial city. It's not a particularly interesting city, but it does have a superb example of Hausa architecture, the **maison de chefs** with traditional geometric designs. You'll find it at the plaza, Place Dan Kasswa. Maradi also has two market days, Monday and Friday; both are quite animated.

Places to Stay & Eat
Hôtel Jangorzo (tel 410140, telex 8235) on the road to the airport is probably the best hotel in southern Niger. It has a pool and nightclub; expect to pay about CFA 7500/8800 for singles/doubles with air-con and CFA 600 for the pool if you're not staying there. For about half the price, you can

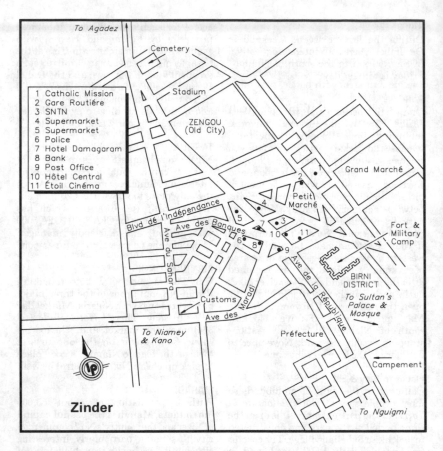

Zinder

1 Catholic Mission
2 Gare Routiére
3 SNTN
4 Supermarket
5 Supermarket
6 Police
7 Hotel Damagaram
8 Bank
9 Post Office
10 Hôtel Central
11 Étoil Cinéma

stay at the *Niger-Hôtel* (tel 420212) in the centre of town or the *Campement Administratif*, in a pleasant area on the outskirts of town. The city's most well-known restaurant is the Lebanese-run *Chez Naoum*; the grilled chicken is unbeatable.

ZINDER

When the French arrived in Niger at the end of the 19th century, the only significant city they found in the area was Zinder (zen-DAIR). So they made it the capital until 1926, when the administrative

offices were transferred to Niamey. The importance of this old Hausa trading town was due solely to its location on the trade route between Kano and Agadez. Now, most of the traffic passes over the Uranium highway via Tahoua, and the Zinder-Agadez route remains in terrible condition. So Zinder, the country's second largest city with 80,000 people, is pretty tranquil these days except on Thursday, the day of the market – one of Niger's largest. Look for leather goods; the best leather craftsmen (*artisans de cuir*) in Niger are here.

Things to See

The city has two old sections – the **Zengou district** to the north towards Agadez and the more interesting and picturesque **Birni district** to the south-east – separated by the modern area, with hotels, post office and wide streets.

A stroll through Birni is highly recommended. You'll find narrow streets, small gardens, friendly people, numerous old houses with typical Hausa geometrical designs, a **mosque** and, nearby, the **Sultan's Palace**, built around the mid-19th century. People from all around come to see the highly respected Sultan, seeking his advice on marriage, divorce, debts, inheritance matters, etc. To make an appointment, pass by city hall (*la mairie*).

Places to Stay

The noisy *Hôtel Central* (tel 512047) is where the British overland trucks stop for the night. This deteriorating old place is downtown and costs about CFA 5500 for a huge double with air-con that doesn't always work. The pleasant outdoor terrace is a popular rendezvous in the evenings for expatriates and Africans; occasionally, local musical groups play here. There's also the *Campement* on the road east towards Nguigmi.

You may find even cheaper places around the Auto Gare two blocks from the Central. Forget the *Peace Corps Hostel*; it's closed and the *Catholic Mission* no longer takes travellers.

Zinder's finest accommodation is at the new, tranquil *Hôtel Amadou Kourandaga* (tel 510642) on the outskirts of town on the road to Niamey. It has 48 singles/doubles for about CFA 7500/8800, air-con, no pool, a pleasant terrace bar and the best restaurant in town. Don't be surprised if there's running water only several hours a day. The next best is the similarly priced *Hôtel Le Damagaram* (tel (tel 512219, telex 8223), with air-con rooms, a shaded patio, modern nightclub with CFA 1200 drinks and decent restaurant. It's downtown near the Hôtel Central and is similarly rundown.

Places to Eat

Some of the best street food is in front of the Central. For a good inexpensive restaurant, try *Restaurant Dan Kasina* downtown by the Bar Rollo. They serve simple fare such as steak and frites. For the best African food in town, including brochettes and chicken in gumbo sauce, head for the *Scotch Bar*. It's on Rue du Marché, a good 10-minute walk from the market and next to *Le Moulin Rouge*, a popular Cameroonian nightclub. For a good African-style bar but no food, try *Oiseau Bleu* downtown past the market – a Peace Corps favourite.

Sports

If you're looking for a pool or tennis court, head for the *Club Privé*. It's near the old French fort, which you'll see on a hill in the distance when you're in Birni. Open to travellers, it has a pool for CFA 1000, a tennis court and bar.

Nigeria

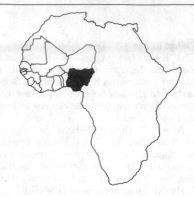

Nigeria is to Africa what China is to the world. One in five Africans is a Nigerian. Every 12 months, new births equal the combined populations of six West-Central African countries: Gabon, Mauritania, Cape Verde, Gambia, Equatorial Guinea and São Tomé. Nigeria is No 1 in Africa in oil production and its GNP is three times the rest of West Africa's. It has six vehicle assembly plants whereas the rest of West Africa has one (in Guinea-Bissau), and it brews over 30 different kinds of beer – more than the rest of West Africa combined. Nigeria is something else.

Lagos, however, has given Nigeria's reputation a black eye. It is West Africa's largest city and, by many criteria, Africa's worst city. It has the highest crime rate and is the most congested. It's hot and muggy and ugly as sin. Even Nigerians hate Lagos. What's good about it? The music is one thing and the low prices are another. Rated the most expensive city in the world for three years running in the early '80s, Lagos (and the rest of Nigeria) is fairly cheap now that the currency has been devalued.

The trick to enjoying Nigeria is avoiding Lagos. Not that it's the only city to avoid. You'll never see the sprawling, congested cities of Ibadan, Port Harcourt, Enugu or Onitsha on anybody's list of interesting places to visit. They're so spread out that you can never be sure where the centre is. If you spend most of your time in places such as Kano, Katsina, Zaria, Jos, Sokoto, Calabar, Ife and Maiduguri (most in the north), in villages, or in the mountains in the far east along the Cameroon border, the chances are you'll enjoy Nigeria. If you also attend one of the country's many festivals, especially the spectacular Durbar festivals in the north, your chances increase from good to guaranteed.

HISTORY

Northern and southern Nigeria are like two different countries. Their histories are equally disparate. Before the time of Christ, the Nok people around Jos were producing terracotta and casting iron. By the time Marco Polo set out for China, the first great kingdom in northern Nigeria, the Islamic Kanem-Borno empire around Lake Chad, was already in decline. It had acquired its wealth through the trans-Saharan trade, particularly the slave trade.

Around 1000 AD, Islamic Hausa states arose in the north at Kano and nearby areas. Like Kanem, they had powerful armies with imperial ambitions but no link with the outside world except through the trans-Saharan trade. The arrival of the Portuguese in the late 15th century on the southern coast affected them little. A major upheaval in the 18th century – the holy wars – occurred when Fulani religious zealots, sick of being discriminated against by the Hausa, formed cavalries and overthrew the Hausa kings, establishing Sokoto as their caliphate and revitalising Islamic values.

In the south, powerful pagan kingdoms arose in Ife, Benin and Oyo. The empire of Benin was particularly powerful. The king's palace occupied a sixth of the huge walled city and virtually all artists worked for the court, producing the finest bronze work in Africa. There are examples in virtually every museum in the country, but more so in Benin City. In the south-east, land of the Ibo, there were no great kingdoms. People depended on agriculture for a living; a strong military wasn't needed. In the late 15th century, the Portuguese began trading in ivory and peppers, later in slaves. Years later, the British gained the upper hand. You won't see old forts dotting the coast of Nigeria as in Ghana because the numerous estuaries provided a safe harbour, permitting the British to use the ships themselves for storing slaves.

Colonial Period

After the British outlawed slavery in 1807, they began looking for other ways to exploit Africa, financing explorers to discover inland waterways and other means of opening up trade. During the scramble for Africa in the late 19th century, Britain sent armies to gain political control over Nigeria, storming Kano in 1902. By then, tin was a well-organised industry in the north. The British were intent on finding the sources, artfully concealed by the Nigerians. They found them in the central plateau area around Jos and over 50 foreign companies came in and took over the Jos mines, employing nearly 40,000 tin-miners by 1928. Thus, the British destroyed the thousands of independent tin producers, converting them into wage earners with no other means of livelihood.

What they did to the farmers was worse. The British turned food crops to export crops until eventually there wasn't enough food to go around – for the first time ever. As a 1947 report to the British parliament stated, malnutrition had become widespread. The cocoa farmers were an exception and they clearly prospered. To their credit, the British were intent on keeping Nigeria a black colony, allowing no white settlers, even refusing to issue temporary work permits to foreigners who could not show that their presence was absolutely necessary.

Rather than taking direct political control, the British administered Nigeria – as it did throughout Africa – by indirect rule, delegating authority to village chiefs, thereby preserving local culture. In 1938 all of Nigeria was governed by only 380 British political officials. There were two problems. In the south-east, many Ibo communities had no chiefs. Undaunted, the British appointed them. The 'invented chiefs' and the people got on like cats and dogs. The second problem was that the British system of colonial rule did nothing to unify Nigeria or prepare it for independence. It isolated north from south, strengthening regional rivalry. Years later, Nigeria was to pay a huge price – the Biafran war.

Independence

The cry for independence rang loud during the '50s. The northerners began worrying that the south's educational advantages would enable the southerners to dominate. The British reacted by giving the northerners even more regional autonomy. When independence finally came in 1960, the British solution was to divide the country into three regions, each governed by a party representing the majority people in that region – the Hausa-Fulani in the north, the Yoruba in the south-west, and the Ibo in the south-east. It didn't work. Each region began governing itself as though it were a separate country, and tensions arose over who was to dominate the federal parliament in Lagos. The north had more people, so they dominated. But they didn't have a majority after the first elections in 1960; so the Hausa were forced into a coalition government with the Ibo, isolating the Yoruba.

The government was a disaster. Competition for civil service jobs became fierce, corruption was widespread, the gap between the haves and have-nots was wider than ever, and major strikes became an annual event. Elections in 1965 were so outrageously rigged that protesting groups went on a rampage. In early 1966,

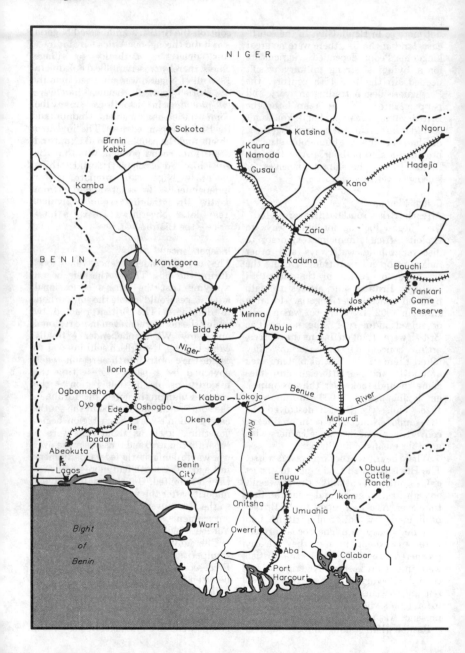

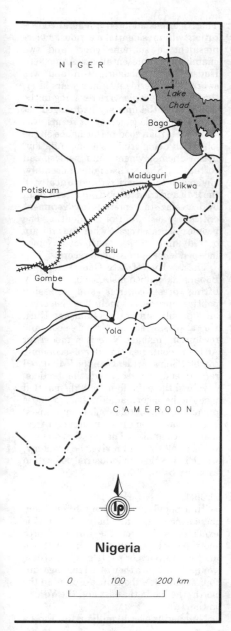

Nigeria

0   100   200 km

the military staged a bloody coup, assassinating the prime minister, the premiers in the north and west and most of the senior army officers! An Ibo general took over, declaring soon after that the public service was to become nationwide – an advantage for the better educated Ibo. Northerners staged anti-Ibo riots and killed hundreds. This was followed by a counter coup that reinstated northern control. A second wave of killings in the north followed; an estimated 10,000 to 30,000 Ibo were massacred.

In 1967, unable to take the abuse any longer, the Ibo declared an independent republic of Biafra. Civil war was on. Seeing an opportunity to secure drilling rights in oil-rich Biafra, France threw its support behind Biafra. So did the Ivory Coast, South Africa, Portugal and Rhodesia, all of which wished to see Africa's giant split up. Washington supported the federal government, but the press was pro-Biafra, showing scenes of mass starvation. The world responded with donations of food, much of which rotted in the harbours. Biafra printed its own money, issued its own stamps, and had its own TV station – on the back of a truck. After 2½ years and the death of a million people, Federal Nigeria won. Africa's worst post-independence tragedy was over.

Oil Boom
Within several years, the war was viewed like a prehistoric event – forgotten. Oil was the reason. Production jumped seven-fold between 1965 and 1973 and world prices skyrocketted. Overnight, well-placed people became millionaires. By 1975, Nigeria found itself with a US$5 billion surplus. The military government went on a spending spree. New construction projects began sprouting like plants following the first rains. Foreign contractors with their pockets stuffed with *dash* (bribe) money rushed to Lagos, and were shocked to find that driving from the airport to downtown took four hours – six

km an hour. Crime was rampant. People were advised not to abandon their vehicles for any reason as it would be a mere skeleton within hours.

The chaos became unbearable. When the president went away for a conference in 1975, he turned on the BBC news only to find that he had been overthrown in a coup. A group of military officers took over. A year later, military malcontents assassinated the head man, but the coup attempt failed. The spending spree continued. The five-year plan called for seven new universities, a new federal capital at Abuja, 13 new TV stations, 34 new prisons, 20,000 km of new paved roads and FESTAC, a black arts festival that won world acclaim but reportedly cost a staggering US$200 million.

In 1981 the world recession sent prices tumbling. Oil revenues fell from US$25 billion in 1980 to US$5 billion in 1986. Prices and salaries were frozen, new construction projects curtailed, and imports of non-essentials banned. Construction at Abuja slowed to a snail's pace. The boom had turned into a bust. Only brewing remained healthy.

Today

The average Nigerian is no better off today than at the end of the civil war in the late 1960s; real incomes are 25% less than in 1974. Population growth and almost total neglect of the agricultural sector are two reasons. In 1960, Nigeria was self-sufficient in food production and the world's largest producer of palm kernels and palm oil; food accounted for 70% of its exports. Now, it imports cooking oil and the food import bill is in the billions of dollars. Cocoa production is half what it was in 1970. Industry too is in the doldrums. In 1986, all six vehicle assembly plants stopped production for lack of parts. Debt servicing almost equalled total exports.

Politically, Nigeria is in constant flux. In 1979 it became the world's third largest democracy, behind India and the USA.

The Nigerians adopted a federal consti-tution with presidential elections, a vice-president, a supreme court and two chambers of representatives. A northern Hausa-Fulani, Shagari, won and was sworn in as president. Fours years later, the Nigerian people were rejoicing in the streets after the military had staged yet another coup. Democracy, it seems, was valued less than good performance on the job. With rising crime, soaring inflation, mass unemployment and widespread corruption, Shagari had failed miserably. His successor, Bahari, refused to deal with the IMF and tried to snuff out all criticism by decreeing stiff sentences to government critics. He lasted all of 20 months. The people celebrated again when the military ousted him in its sixth coup since independence – an African record.

The new head of state, General Ibrahim Babangida, gained instant popularity by lifting press controls and releasing political prisoners, including Nigeria's most popular singer, Fela Ransome-Kuti. He also started a virtual economic revolution, making Nigeria a model for African countries in deep economic trouble. Going further than the IMF dared recommend, he reopened the borders, devalued the naira four-fold, dismantled many of the major marketing boards, and is privatising unprofitable public enterprises. Nigeria has become the darling of the free-market economists. The question remains whether all this will revive the economy, which in 1987 had an industrial utilisation capacity below 30%.

PEOPLE

With a population of about 105 million, increasing 3.2% annually, Nigeria is expected to become the world's fourth most populous country on earth in another 30 years or so. It has 250 ethnic groups, most with their own language, but four stand out – the Hausa-Fulani in the north, the Ibo in the east and the Yoruba in the west.

Numbering over 10 million, the Yoruba

historically have been Africa's most prolific art-producers. In the museums, you may see one of the large helmet masks of the Epa cult, certainly the most spectacular of the Yoruba masks. During festivals, the wearer must jump onto an earth mound a metre tall – no small feat since masks can be up to 1½ metres tall and weigh 30 kg. Yoruba chiefs were treated royally. They wore beaded crowns; some had beaded umbrellas, cushions, a sceptre and slippers as well. Elaborately carved house posts and doors from their dwellings can be seen in the local museums.

The Hausa-Fulani are predominantly Muslim. Of all the celebrations in West Africa, the most elaborate are the Sallah celebrations in northern Nigeria at the two most important Islamic celebrations – the end of Ramadan and Tabaski, 69 days later. The principal event is the Durbar, a procession of ornately dressed men mounted on gaily bedecked horses covered from head to tail with decoration. The Hausa-Fulani horsemen wear breast-plates and coats of flexible armour, and on their scarlet turbans, copper helmets topped with plumes. An emir, draped in white and protected by a heavy brocade parasol embroidered in silver, rides in the middle of a cavalry of blue. He may be followed by traditional wrestlers flexing their huge biceps encircled by leather bracelets, and lute players with feathered head-dresses decorated with cowrie shells. The major Durbars are in the north – Kano, Zaria and, above all, Katsina. Don't miss them, but be prepared for every hotel in town to be booked.

Nigeria seems to have as many writers as the rest of black Africa combined. Chinua Achebe, Amos Tutuola, Cyprian Ekwensi and Wole Soyinka are perhaps the most famous. In 1986, Soyinka was awarded the Nobel Prize for Literature – only the fifth time that the prize has been awarded to a person from the third world. Having written over 20 plays, four volumes of poetry and two novels, he is the most versatile of Nigeria's writers. His plays, however, stand out. *A Dance of the Forests* written in 1963 for the independence celebration, *The Man Died*, *Opera Wonyosi* and *A Play of Giants* are some of the more well known.

Most of the writings of this new Nigerian hero, a Yoruba, are devastating denunciations of the corrupt government and commercial establishment which has arisen since independence, with a merciless lambasting of all who service and benefit from the set up. As he says in his introduction to *Opera Wonyosi*: 'Art should expose, reflect, indeed magnify the decadent, rotted underbelly of a society that has lost its direction, jettisoned all sense of values and is careering down a precipice as fast as the latest artificial boom can take it.' The masses find the writing style of this one-time playwright for the Royal Court Theatre in London too difficult to understand. However, his satirical comedies, such as *The Trials of Brother Jero*, are fairly popular. Others find his denunciations too bitter, a charge Soyinka replies to in *The Man Died*, written while he was in prison for 27 months during the Biafran war: 'The man dies in all who keep silent in the face of tyranny.'

GEOGRAPHY

Over three times the size of the UK, Nigeria is unexciting geographically. The only mountains are in the far east along the Cameroon border, affording some spectacular scenery but too far off the beaten path of most travellers and Nigerians. In the centre around Jos, you'll find a plateau area in the 1500 metre range and the most pleasant climate in the country. With short grass and open scenery, this central savannah area offers some fairly impressive sights. The north is largely savannah and has a drier climate, like that of the Sahel which it borders. Cutting north-west to south-east is the Niger river, Africa's third longest. A second river, the Benue, flows west from Cameroon, emptying into the Niger below Abuja.

The coastal oil-producing region is like a different country – lagoons, mangrove swamps, sandy beaches, innumerable streams and, as you move inland, thick forests. Before malaria tablets, the hot muggy coast, the Bight of Benin, was infamously hostile to foreigners – 'Beware, beware, the Bight of Benin, Where one comes out though forty go in.'

CLIMATE

Nigeria's weather pattern differs substantially between the north and the south. In the north, the climate is like that of the Sahel – hot and dry, with one long rainy season from late May through September. Between March and May, temperatures reach 45°C. Along the coast, temperatures average 5 to 10°C less, but the humidity can become unbearable. There, the rains fall heaviest between April and July, peaking in June; September and October is a second, minor rainy season.

VISAS

Everyone needs a visa. Getting them is no longer a major hassle and they are normally issued in four days. In Douala (Cameroon), they're reportedly issued in one day. Embassies in the USA and Europe issue visas valid for 90 days. If you wait until arriving in Africa to get one, you may find it's valid for only seven days, though easily renewable. You can obtain them in all four neighbouring countries. Most embassies request you present a roundtrip airline ticket or one with an onward destination. If you say you're on a business trip, they'll also demand a letter of introduction from a Nigerian – but not if you say you're a tourist.

Historically, British consulates have acted for Nigeria in those countries where Nigeria has no representation of its own, but this practice is becoming increasingly rare. Visas are supposed to be free for British citizens, but some embassies reportedly try to levy a fee anyway. As in most of Africa, you'll be denied a visa if your passport has a South African stamp;

moreover, Nigerian passport officials are particularly vigilant in looking for the stamp.

In Lagos, you can get visas to all neighbouring countries. You can also get visas to Cameroon in Calabar in 24 hours and visas to Niger in Kano.

Diplomatic Missions Abroad

Abidjan, Accra, Addis Ababa, Algiers, Athens, Bamako, Bangui, Berne, Bissau, Bonn, Brazzaville, Brussels, Cairo, Canberra, Conakry, Cotonou, Dar es Salaam, Dakar, Dublin, Freetown, The Hague, Hong Kong, Kinshasa, Libreville, Lisbon, Lomé, London, Madrid, Malabo, Monrovia, Nairobi, N'Djamena, New Delhi, Niamey, Nouakchott, Ottawa, Ouagadougou, Paris, Rabat, Rio de Janeiro, Rome, Stockholm, Tokyo, Vienna, Washington, Yaoundé. Consulates: Atlanta, New York, San Francisco.

MONEY

US$1 = N4.17
£1 = N7.80

The unit of currency is the naira (N) and the rates fluctuate daily. Starting in late 1986, Nigeria devalued the naira almost four-fold, virtually wiping out the black market. Prices of goods with foreign components shot up. A loaf of bread went from N1.5 to N2.5 and a VW Beetle (which didn't go out of production in Nigeria and Brazil until December 1986) from N6000 to N24,000. By 1987 overall prices had decreased by about two-thirds at the official exchange rate from a year earlier. Changing money on the black market used to be a widespread practice, especially around the Bristol hotel in Lagos, at the airport, and in neighbouring countries, especially in Lomé, Togo. Now, the black market rate is hardly any more favourable. It is illegal to import more than N50.

The airport is a good place to change money, as is the First Bank downtown near the Canadian High Commission.

Commissions on travellers' cheques are apparently much lower at the First Boston than at other banks. Not all banks accept the CFA; those that do tend to give a fairly poor exchange rate.

Banking hours: Monday and Friday 8 am to 3 pm; Tuesday to Thursday 8 am to 1 pm. Banks: Bank of America, Chase Merchant Bank, First Bank, National Bank of Nigeria, New Nigeria Bank, United Bank for Africa.

LANGUAGE

English is the official language. The three principal African languages are Hausa in the north, Ibo in the south-east and Yoruba in the south-west around Lagos. Greetings in Ibo:

Good Morning	ee-BOW-lah-chee
Good Evening	nah-NO-nah
How are you?	ee-MAY-nah ahn-GHAN
Thank you	ee-MAY-nah
Goodbye	kay-MAY-see-ah

Greetings in Hausa:

Good Morning	ee-nah-WAH-nah lah-HEE-yah-low
Good Evening	ee-nah-EE-nee lah-HEE-yah-low
How are you?	Barca
Thank you	nah-GOH-day
Goodbye	SAY-goh-day

GENERAL INFORMATION
Health

A yellow fever vaccination is required. For emergencies, the best hospitals in Lagos are Abimbola Awoliyi Memorial Hospital (tel 631520/630916) on Lagos Island and the clean, modern Medical Consultants Group. Dr C O Da Silva (tel 636997) is a general practitioner who accepts emergency cases without appointment. Dr B R Bahl (tel 683127) is another.

Security

Lagos is one of the two most dangerous cities in West and Central Africa (Kinshasa is the other); Ibadan is not far behind. Armed thieves are the major problem. Taxi drivers seem to be involved in most of the thefts involving foreigners, so be careful in picking a driver at the airport, particularly if you are arriving at night (to be avoided if at all possible). Drivers who are well known at the airport are safer; ask the luggage handlers or dispatchers. Conspicuously, write down the number of the taxi's licence plate. Also, avoid taxis where there is a second person riding along for some inexplicable reason. Carry your passport at all times – police stops are frequent – but keep it well hidden. Walking alone at night anywhere in Lagos is risky, particularly around hotels and other areas frequented by foreigners.

Despite the horror stories you may hear in Lagos, outside of Lagos and Ibadan, the security risk drops significantly. Leaving Lagos and Ibadan is like a breath of fresh air.

Business Hours
Business: weekdays 8.30 am to 5 pm. Government: weekdays 7.30 am to 3.30 pm, Saturday 7.30 am to 1 pm.

Public Holidays & Festivals
1 January, Good Friday, Easter Monday, 1 May, End of Ramadan (17 May 1988, 6 May 1989), Tabaski (26 July 1988, 14 July 1989) 1 October (National Day), Mohammed's Birthday, 25-26 December.

The Muslim holidays are also respected, the spectacular Sallah celebrations in the north coincide with the end of Ramadan and Tabaski.

Argungu Fishing & Cultural Festival In mid to late February this famous 3-day festival takes place on the banks of the Sokoto river in Argungu, 100 km south-west of Sokoto. It has acquired international status and attracts visitors from all over the world. Their customs and traditions are closely tied to Islamic religious practices. Several months before the festival, the Sokoto

River is damned. When the festival begins, hundreds of fisherman jump into the river with their nets and gourds and some come out with fish weighing over 50 kg. It's quite a sight.

Pategi Regatta If you'll be in Nigeria around August, don't miss Nigeria's most photographed festival – the Pategi Regatta. Pategi is on the Niger river, half way between Ibadan and Kaduna as the crow flies. You'll see swimming, traditional dancing, acrobatic displays and fishing. The highlight, however, is the paddling competition. There's a good hotel there – *River Niger Holiday Resort* with pool and tennis.

Oshun Festival Around July/August, this festival in Oshogbo, 86 km north-east of Ibadan, has music, dancing and sacrifices. It is well worth seeing.

Igue Festival In December, this week-long festival in Benin City includes traditional dancing.

Omumo Festival In late December/early January, there's the Omumo Festival, a week-long new year's celebration in the south-east around Owerri and Aba. You'll also find festivals in Nkpa and other villages.

Photography

No permit is required, but use great caution. You may find lots of people who are offended by photographs. Even when taking photos of crowd scenes, you should ask around to see if people would be offended. As usual, taking photos of bridges, airports, military personnel and installations, harbours, TV and radio stations is prohibited.

Time, Phone & Telex

When it's noon in Nigeria, it's 11 am in London and 6 am in New York (7 am during daylight savings time). Telephone services tend to be erratic. International

soft drink vendor
NIGERIA.

telephone, telegram and telex facilities are available at NET's principal office in Lagos (Necom House, 14 Marina) and at Net's offices throughout the country.

Hotel Tax

Hotel room bills are subject to a hefty 15% tax; prices quoted herein include it.

GETTING THERE
Air

From Europe, there are direct flights from London, Paris, Rome, Amsterdam, Geneva, Frankfurt, Madrid, Brussels, Vienna and Zurich. From the USA, Nigeria Airways has direct flights twice a week from New York; Pan Am no longer offers service. You can also fly direct from Bombay, Cairo and Nairobi.

The cheapest flights from London are on Aeroflot via Moscow with a ticket purchased from a bucket shop. The cost is about £400 roundtrip. Bucket shop tickets on Nigeria Airways will cost you about £50 more.

Within Africa, Nigeria Airways flies all along the coast and as far as Nairobi. The service varies between terrible and atrocious except when there aren't many passengers, which is very rare. At times, so many of the flights are full that you will not be able to reserve a seat for days. If you buy the ticket and later want a refund, keep dreaming. If you want to change your flight to another airline, Nigeria Airways may refuse to endorse the ticket. If the ticket was purchased with naira, other airlines will not accept it even though it's endorsed.

Car

The road system is excellent, second in Africa only to South Africa's. However, driving is dangerous, especially on the expressway between Lagos and Ibadan where it's like playing bumper cars at the carnival. Typical driving times are 2½ hours Lagos-Cotonou (longer during rush hour), one day Lagos-Enugu, two days Lagos-Kano, 2½ days Lagos-Douala via Ikom, three days Lagos-Agadez via Sokoto (Niger).

Bush Taxi

To/from Cameroon If you're headed to Cameroon, you should have no problem finding a taxi in Ikom for the 25-km trip to the border (Mfum-Ekok) or in Ekok for other points in Cameroon. If you get caught in Ikom, you'll find a dirt cheap hotel opposite the taxi park.

To/from Niger Travellers to Agadez (Niger) can go via Sokoto, Katsina-Maradi or, longer, Kano-Zinder. Vehicles leave every day from Kano but more so on Wednesday because Thursday is market day in Zinder.

To/from Benin There are direct bush taxis to Cotonou from Lagos Island at the end of Carter bridge.

Boat

You can travel to Cameroon via boat from Oron near Calabar. You have a choice of either a 15-metre fishing boat, for about N28 a person, which leaves around 8 am, arriving near Limbe 12 to 14 hours later, or a CFA 10,000 a person speedboat which leaves around 10 am and takes three hours. Either way, you must stay overnight in Oron because the erratic ferry connecting Calabar and Oron (departing daily around 8 or 9 am, 2.30 and 8 pm) doesn't arrive in Oron until both have departed. Rooms at the *King Kong Hotel* cost about N17; elsewhere, expect to pay about N45 for a double. You may find flying just as cheap. Calabar-Douala on Nigeria Airways is only about N50.

GETTING AROUND
Air

Within Nigeria, the service on Nigeria Airways is sometimes good. You may find that you cannot reserve – a possible advantage considering the mad-house nature of the Nigeria Airways office. Buy the ticket at the airport, but get there several hours in advance. Any number of expediters will offer to get your ticket. Many are reportedly crooked as mine was (he was beaten by the police for attempting to run off), so keep an eye on them. Flights are frequently not full, moreover, there are as many as three and four flights a day between many major cities. Flights for the interior do not originate at Murtala Mohammed airport but at an older airport roughly 10 km away. You can also fly to Kaduna, Kano and Jos on Kabo Air and to Port Harcourt, Benin City and Enugu on Okada Air, both private airlines. Flights are not expensive. Lagos-Kano, for example, is N105 one way.

Bush Taxi

The bush taxi system in Nigeria is unquestionably the fastest and most comfortable in Africa – and dangerous. There are two types of Peugeot 504 bush taxis – those that take only five passengers (more expensive) and those that take eight. Minibuses are cheaper. Because Nigeria has so many people, the typical waiting time on many routes is about 10 minutes! The major problem is that they travel at 140 km an hour. When an accident occurs, it's goodbye mama.

Bus
A safer, more comfortable and cheaper way to travel is by bus. You'll find lines connecting all the main cities. They are, however, slower with set schedules, and not much cheaper than the fast-loading bush taxis which leave at all hours.

Train
Nigeria has a decent rail system. Trains are the cheapest way to travel. They're also very slow. One line connects Lagos with Ibadan, Kaduna and Kano; the Port Harcourt-Maiduguri line passes through Enugu, Jos and Bauchi. The 200 km Kaduna-Kafanchan line connects the two.

The train leaves Lagos daily at 9 am and arrives in Kaduna at 10.20 am the next day and Kano five hours later. Late arrivals are common; 34 hours to Kano is typical. From Kano, it leaves daily at 9 am, arriving Kaduna at 2.45 pm and Lagos 4 pm the next day. The 32-hour Kano-Port Harcourt train departs Kano daily at 7.30 am and Port Harcourt at 11 am. You can also travel Lagos-Maiduguri, changing at Kaduna and at Kafanchan. The train takes 53 hours, leaving Lagos daily at 4.10 pm and Maiduguri at 10 pm. Schedules change periodically, so check.

The 1st class fare Lagos-Kano with sleeping berth, toilet and fan is about N45 plus bedding. Second class costs only about N12. Third class is crowded, uncomfortable and not recommended. The air-con train costs about N66 for 1st class with berth and bedding, leaving Lagos Wednesday, Friday and Sunday, and Kano Monday, Tuesday and Friday. The train without air-con is also good. Both have a dining car; fish soup seems to come with every meal.

Hitchhiking
Hitchhiking in Nigeria is relatively easy, especially in the north. However, unless you make it clear that you can't pay, chances are the driver will expect money – sometimes more than the normal fare.

Lagos

Most travellers detest Lagos. The city's reputation for crime is world-wide. It's size – four million inhabitants – doesn't help matters any. In 1970 it had 300,000 inhabitants. By 2025 it's predicted to be one of the world's five largest cities. The infamous transportation problems of the '70s, when the expressway system was being constructed and four hours was the typical driving time from the airport to downtown, are long gone. Wide expressways now connect the airport with downtown and encircle Lagos Island ('downtown') and nearby Ikoyi and Victoria Islands, where you'll find three of the four top hotels and posh residences. The main street downtown is Broad St. Saka Tinubu Square, on Broad, is the heart of the city.

One of the city's attractions is the music. Sunny Ade has his own nightclub. This hardly makes up for its other faults – hassles with the taxi drivers and police, a dearth of good restaurants, high prices and suspicious people. If you hear of people liking Lagos, chances are they stayed with Nigerians. This seems to be the requirement for enjoying Lagos.

Information
Banks Bank of America (136 Broad St), Chase Merchant Bank (23 Awolowo Rd), First Bank (Unity House, 37 Marina), National Bank of Nigeria (82-6 Broad St), New Nigeria Bank (4 Sanni Adewale St), United Bank for Africa (a French bank at 97/105 Broad St).

Embassies The addresses of some of the embassies are:

Top: Drying crabs at Lomé beach, Togo (CL)
Left: Lomé beach, Togo (JTJ)
Right: Lomé market, Togo (JTJ)

Dogon mask dancers, Mali (EE)

Algeria (tel 683155) 26 Maitama Sule St, SW Ikoyi

Australia 14 Adeola Hopewell St, Box 2427

Benin (tel 614411) 4 Abudu Smith St, Victoria Island

Burkina Faso (tel 681001) 15 Norman Williams St, Ikoyi

Cameroon 5 Femi Pearse St, Victoria Island

Canada (tel 612382) 4 Idowu Taylor St, PMB 54506

France (tel 680026) 1 Queens's Dr, Ikoyi, Box 567

Ghana (tel 630015) 23 King George V Rd

West Germany (tel 611551) 15 Eleke Crescent, Victoria Island, Box 728

Ivory Coast (tel 610963) 5 Abubu Smith St, Victoria Island

Japan (tel 613797) 24-5 Apese St, Victoria Island, PMB 2111

Kenya (tel 682768) 52 Queens Drive, Ikoyi

Niger (tel 613510) 15 Asdeola Odeku St, Victoria Island

Senegal (tel 614226) 14 Kofo Abayomi Rd, Victoria Island

Switzerland (tel 625277) 7 Anifowashe St, Victoria Island, Box 536

Togo (tel 617449) 96 Awolowo Rd, SW Ikoyi

UK (tel 611551/920) 11 Eleke Crescent, Victoria Island, PMB 12136

USA (tel 610050/78) 2 Eleke Crescent, Victoria Island, Box 554

Other embassies include: All countries of Western Europe, Argentina, Brazil, CAR, Egypt, Equatorial Guinea, Ethiopia, Gabon, Gambia, Guinea, India, Liberia, Mauritania, Morocco, Sierra Leone, Tanzania, Togo, Zaire, Zambia and Zimbabwe.

Bookstores & Supermarkets *Falomo Shopping Centre* has a little bit of everything including *Bestseller* bookstore (the best in town and especially good for their selection of West African writers and art books), *Quintesseme* (records, art, books), three pharmacies, a bakery and a small supermarket with bottled water.

You'll also find books and magazines at the Eko Holiday Inn, the Federal Palace Suites Hotel, and *CSS Bookshop* downtown at Broad and Odunlami St. For supermarkets, try the Swiss-owned *UTC*

downtown on Broad St or the Greek-owned *Leventis* nearby at 42 Marina.

Travel Agencies Transcap Travel Bureau (tel 665063) CFAO Building, 1 Oladip Davies St, is the agent for Thomas Cook. Others include Five Stars Travel Agency (tel 603160) Falomo Shopping Centre, and Mandilas Travel (tel 662130) 96 Broad St, an agent for Hertz. You'll find lots of others at Tafawa Balewa Square.

National Museum

This is a good museum by African standards and definitely worth seeing. The Benin bronzes are the star attraction. Also interesting are the numerous wooden doorways, masks (some covering the entire body) and house posts. Open every day except Sunday 9 am to 6 pm, it's downtown on Lagos Island near Tafawa Balewa Square.

Portuguese Houses

Some of the city's most interesting buildings are the old Portuguese houses of the late 19th and early 20th centuries. Most notable is the dilapidated Ilojo Bar at 2 Bamgbose St, which runs into Tinubu Square. It was built by a successful slave family which returned home to Nigeria from Brazil. The style is gothic, with attractive arched doorways and windows and iron balustrades. Other fine examples of Brazilian architecture are Ebun House (1914) on Odunfa St and Maja House at Glover Square.

Iga Idunganran

This is the official residence of the king (*Oba*) of Lagos, built during the 18th century. The old part of the Oba's Palace is built of mud, with bronze pillars and the original parlour. For inspection, call the secretary (tel 656397).

Other Sights

The **Tafawa Balewa Square** is a huge arena adorned by gargantuan horses. You'll find most of Lagos' airline offices and travel

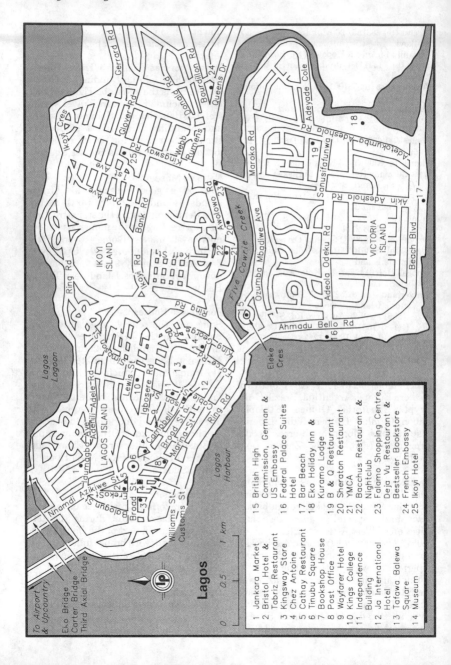

Lagos

To Airport & Upcountry
Eko Bridge
Carter Bridge
Third Axial Bridge

0   0.5   1 km

1 Jankara Market
2 Bristol Hotel &
   Tabriz Restaurant
3 Kingsway Store
4 Chez Antoine
5 Cathay Restaurant
6 Tinubu Square
7 Bookshop House
8 Post Office
9 Wayfarer Hotel
10 Kings College
11 Independence
   Building
12 Ja International
   Hotel
13 Tafawa Balewa
   Square
14 Museum
15 British High
   Commission, German &
   US Embassy
16 Federal Palace Suites
   Hotel
17 Bar Beach
18 Eko Holiday Inn &
   Kuramo Lodge
19 B & Q Restaurant
20 Sheraton Restaurant
21 YMCA
22 Bacchus Restaurant &
   Nightclub
23 Falamo Shopping Centre,
   Deja Vu Restaurant &
   Bestseller Bookstore
24 French Embassy
25 Ikoyi Hotel

agencies on one side of the square and shops and restaurants on the other.

A block away is the 26-storey **Independence House**, constructed in 1963 to commemorate Nigeria's independence.

Remembrance Arcade across the street contains memorials to Nigeria's WW I, WW II and civil war victims. The guard changes on the hour, and there's a parade on Saturday from 9.30 to 11 am.

Places to Stay – bottom end

The cheapest place downtown is the *YMCA* (tel 680516) at 77 Awolowo Rd in Ikoyi. You'll find four beds to a room and a supermarket nearby. The Y offers an excellent opportunity to meet young Africans. The cost is about N7 a person. You can also pitch a tent in the garden.

The *YWCA* downtown on Maloney St, a block from Tafawa Balewa Square, charges over double the rate at the YMCA, but the price includes breakfast and it's not so dirty. Also on Lagos Island are the *Ritz Hotel* on Abibu St, south of Broad, with singles/doubles for about N33/45 and *Hotel Wayfarers* (tel 630113) at 52 Campbell St, with a lively bar and singles/doubles for about N33/46.

If Wayfarers is full, try *Ja International* at 60 Campbell St, with singles/doubles for about N38/50 including breakfast. The *Zeina Hotel* several blocks north-east of Saka Tinubu Square has similar prices, but is usually booked.

Places to Stay – middle

Of the centrally located hotels, it's hard to beat the single rooms at the *Federal Palace Hotel* (see top end hotels) on Victoria Island, with slightly shabby singles/doubles for about N58/115 in its older section. You'll get better value for the money by staying in the suburbs. One among many is *Crossroads Guest House* (tel 863320) at 6 Ikorodu Rd in Yaba, across from Sunny Ade's nightclub, between downtown and the airport. Rooms with TV cost about N38 to N50, and buses to downtown pass right by the hotel.

Airport Area The closest hotel to the international airport is the new, no-frills *Stop-Over Motel* two km away, with rooms for about N58 a night. They'll sometimes let you pay in naira if you say you've cashed all your foreign currency. The run-down *Maryland Hotel* (tel 964465) near the Sheraton has 39 singles/doubles for about N55/66 including pool, nightclub and TV/videos. For cheaper hotels, go to the area of the Airport hotel and the Hilton; you'll see quite a few. Rooms for N38 to N45 are probably about as cheap as you'll find.

Places to Stay – top end

All the top hotels require a deposit, paid when registering, equal to almost double the price of the room. The best hotel is the *Sheraton*, the only hotel in town where your reservation is guaranteed. But it's out near the airport, nearly 20 km from downtown. So most people prefer the *Eko Holiday Inn/Kuramo Lodge* which is near downtown on Victoria Island. Do not plan a night arrival because they will not hold your reservation that long unless it's pre-paid. They'd like you to believe it's a real Holiday Inn. It isn't, but the quality is similar. Rooms at the Kuramo Lodge are highly recommended because they are decent and a real bargain compared to those at the Eko, which is part of the same complex.

The suites at the poorly managed *Federal Palace Suites*, also on Victoria Island, are huge, nicer and less expensive, but the hotel's dead ambience and refusal to guarantee reservations except when pre-paid are why travellers prefer the Holiday Inn. If these two hotels are full, your best bet is the *Ikoyi* on Ikoyi Island, near Lagos Island, followed by the *Mainland* just across the river from Lagos Island. Only pre-paid reservations are guaranteed. The only advantage of the *Bristol Hotel* is that it's smack in the heart of downtown on Martins St. Remember – prices herein include tax.

Sheraton Hotel (tel 900930, telex 27202), N220/233 for singles/doubles, pool, cards AE and D.

Eko Holiday Inn (tel 615000/614554, telex 22650), N190/230 for singles/doubles with breakfast, N91/104 with breakfast for singles/doubles in the *Kuramo Lodge* section, pool, bookstore, casino, nightclub, cards AE only.

Federal Palace (tel 610030/31, telex 21432), N230 with breakfast for suites in the newer 'suites' section and N58/115 for singles/doubles in the hotel section, long pool, TV/videos, bookshop, cards AE.

Ikoyi Hotel (tel 603200/8, telex 22632), N75/92 for singles/doubles with breakfast, pool, casino, mini-refrigerators, TV/video, no cards.

Mainland Hotel (tel 800300/9, telex 21595), N65/80 for singles/doubles with breakfast, mini-refrigerators, travel agency, bookstore, casino, nightclub, cards AE.

Bristol Hotel (tel 661201/07/12, telex 21144), about N67/80 for singles/doubles, downtown location, cards AE.

Airport Area A taxi to hotels in the airport area shouldn't cost more than N10. The best hotel by far is the *Sheraton*, 15 minutes from the airport. In addition, there's the unpretentious *Hilton* (tel 900604, telex 26329, no cards). One look at the place and you'll know it isn't part of the Conrad Hilton chain. About 10 and 20 minutes from the national and international airports respectively, it has 56 singles/doubles for about N96/124, a pool and a nightclub. The older *Airport Hotel* (tel 901001/5, telex 26203, no cards) not far away has 275 rooms for about N68, olympic-size pool, a tennis court in fair condition, bookshop, car rental, nightclub, TV/videos.

Places to Eat

Cheap Eats Don't miss the *Museum Kitchen Restaurant* at the National Museum, which serves palm wine and a different regional speciality each weekday at lunch for N6. If you're staying at the Holiday Inn, you could try *B & Q*, which serves a decent meal for about N13 and is several blocks from the hotel, beyond the nearest intersection. If you're looking for hamburgers (N6 to N7) and simple meals

(N9 to N16), try *Deja Vu*, an attractive restaurant at Falomo Shopping Centre on Ikoyi island.

UTC Department Store on Broad St, the cafeteria at *Leventis* supermarket at 42 Marina Rd, and *Kingsway Rendezvous Restaurant*, in the heart of town next to the old First Baptist Church, are popular with middle-class Nigerians looking for inexpensive meals. They are highly recommended.

French/Lebanese A number of restaurants serve both Lebanese and French or continental cuisine. You can dress casually at all of them. One of the best is *Quo Vadis* (tel 635152), downtown at Western House, 8 Broad St, with a good view of the harbour from the 17th floor. Closed Sunday, they serve especially good seafood, although the menu is mainly Lebanese.

Three other French-Lebanese restaurants downtown, all with pleasant ambiences, closed Sunday and moderately priced, are *Chez Antoine* (tel 664881) at 61 Broad St, *Tabriz* behind the Bristol hotel at 19/21 Breadfruit St, and *Tam Tam* at 16 Market St.

Continental dishes are served at the *Phoenicia* (tel 663156), 35 Martins St near the Bristol Hotel. The main attraction, however, is the African band which plays most evenings. Dress is casual. Open every day and late (until 3 am), they levy a cover of about N6 (double on Saturday).

One of the city's more popular restaurants is *Bacchus Dining Restaurant* (tel 681653) at 57 Awolowo Rd on Ikoyi Island, closed Sunday. Dancing is as much an attraction as the food.

Chinese Four of the top Chinese restaurants are at hotels. The best of the lot may be *Club Panache* (tel 800300 x 4681) at the Mainland hotel – excellent food, good service, smartly decorated, expensive, and open for dinner only except Sunday. Reservations are recommended.

The Chinese restaurant on the 14th

floor of the *Eko Holiday Inn* is similarly priced, with a good view. *Café de Chine* at the Federal Palace hotel also has a good reputation and pleasant service, better perhaps than *China Restaurant* at the Ikoyi hotel. Downtown at 88 Broad St you'll find *Cathy* (tel 664926), another expensive restaurant which serves good food and is closed Sunday. The other good ones are far from downtown.

Indian *Club Bagatelle* (tel 662410) downtown at 208 Broad St is elegant, expensive, with a good reputation and a 4th floor view of the harbour. Smartly decorated with mirrors, glass and chrome and a dancing floor, the restaurant serves continental cuisine and a number of spicy Indian and middle-eastern specialities. For less expensive Indian cuisine, try *Sherlaton* at 108 Awolowo Rd on Ikoyi island.

Entertainment & Sports

Nightclubs Lagos' most famous nightclub, where juju music reigns, is Sunny Ade's *Ariya Nightclub* at 12 Ikorodu Rd in Yaba, a 15-minute ride from downtown in the direction of the airport. Sunny sings most Saturday nights, sometimes Friday. The cover is N10. Don't go before 11 pm unless you're coming to eat. Open-air, it's open every evening until dawn. Several hundred metres away on the same road is *Faze 2*, a popular fancy disco with a cover of N10 and closed Sunday. Women are admitted free until midnight. Further out is *Stadium Hotel*, a large nightclub with Nigerian music.

Downtown, the most sophisticated nightclubs, all attached to expensive restaurants, are *The Bacchus* (tel 681653) on Ikoyi Island at 57 Awolowo Rd, *Club Bagatelle* (tel 662410) downtown at 208 Broad St, *The Summit* at the Eko Holiday Inn with live music (suit and tie required), and *Club Panache* (tel 800300) at the Mainland hotel.

Much more interesting are the seedier nightclubs. Foremost among these is the lively *Ritz Hotel*, which has a band in the evenings until 8 pm and cheap drinks. You'll find it in the heart of downtown, a block south of Broad St on Abibu St. About five blocks away, several blocks north-east of Saka Tinubu Square, is *Zeina Hotel*, with live music, a small cover and women.

Theatre Opened in 1976 for FESTAC, the National Theatre (tel 830200) is the huge round building you'll see coming in from the airport. Call the theatre or consult the local newspapers for events – dancing, film and drama.

Sports You'll find pools at the top four hotels. The one at the Federal Palace is the longest but also the dirtiest. Of the major hotels, only the Federal Palace has a tennis court, and it's not in usable condition. Golfers could try the nine-hole Ikeja Golf Club out towards the airport. Joggers can join the all-male Hash House Harriers, who meet at a different location every Monday at 6 pm. Call the British High Commission; someone there should know the location.

Beaches The most popular beach is Bar Beach on Victoria Island, not far from the Eko Holiday Inn. Because it's crowded on weekends, most expatriates prefer Tarkwa Bay (no undertow) and, nearby, Lighthouse Beach (strong undertow), both across the harbour. Launches are available on weekends and holidays. You'll find them on Victoria Island along Eleke Crescent, across from the Russian embassy. A typical roundtrip journey costs N6 per person. Agree on a price beforehand but don't pay until you've been picked up at the agreed time.

Things to Buy

Artisan Goods The national museum has a non-profit *Crafts Centre*, with batiks, calabashes, wood carvings and textiles at fixed prices. Most interesting of all, you can see batiks being made and woodcarvers at work. *Jankara Market* just north of Saka Tinubu Square is the largest market in Lagos, but nothing special by West African standards. You'll find dyed and woven fabrics, African prints by the yard, beads, Nigerian-made jewellery and pottery plus a fetishers' market where they sell Ju-Ju beads and various medicines. Speaking a few words of Yoruba helps.

Not to be missed is *Bar Beach*, particularly on weekends. On the south end of the beach towards the Eko Holiday Inn, you'll find traders selling batiks, baskets, calabashes, old coins and antiquities. They are also outside the *Federal Palace Hotel*, the *Ikoyi Hotel* and *Falomo Shopping Centre*, on Awolowo Rd, Ikoyi Island. The wooden carvings are generally of low quality. For higher quality art, go to *Quintesseme* at Falomo Shopping Centre.

Music *Quintesseme* is also the best music shop. For cheaper cassettes of lower quality, try the market. Nigeria has some of Africa's most well-known singers. Foremost are Fela Anikulapo Kuti and Sunny Ade, followed by Sonny Okosun, the group *Ghetto Blaster* and Ebenezer Obey. Sunny Ade is the king of juju music, a new style of music unique to Nigeria and extremely popular. Sonny Okosun plays a funk/highlife/Afro-pop synthesis called Afro Soul, while Ebenezer Obey plays a form of highlife, now somewhat passé.

Of the four, Fela stands out – probably Africa's most famous musician. Three of the musicians with *Ghetto Blaster* are former members of his group. Immensely popular in Nigeria, he's also the most politically vocal, frequently criticising government policy in his lyrics. Various Nigerian governments have taken revenge. Travelling to Los Angeles in 1964, he met Malcolm X, who stirred black consciousness in Fela. On the musical front, James Brown influenced him greatly. Returning to Nigeria, he took Brown's jazz and mixed it with the many cultural intricacies

of Nigerian music, to create Afro-Beat. During the '70s, Fela formed the Kalakuta Republic, a commune for playing music. The government burned it down in 1977, resulting in his mother's death two days later. Exiled in Ghana from 1978 to 1980, he returned to Nigeria and continued playing music with lyrics critical of the regime. In 1985 he was put in jail on currency smuggling charges, then released a year later when the judge – under the present regime – changed his tune and admitted it was a frame-up.

Getting There & Away
Air International flights leave from Murtala Mohammed airport and internal flights leave from the older airport 10 km away.

Bush Taxi In Lagos, Onipanu Bus Stop on Ikorodu Rd, between downtown and the airport, is the departure point to Ibadan and many other cities. Lagos island, at the end of Carter bridge, is the departure point for taxis to Cotonou and Lomé. Fares are low. Lagos to Ibadan is about N5 to N6, Lagos to Benin City about N17.

Train The train to Kano leaves Lagos daily at 9 am and arrives in Kaduna at 10.20 am the next day and Kano five hours later. Late arrivals are common; 34 hours to Kano is typical. The 1st class fare Lagos-Kano is about N45, 2nd class costs only about N12. Third class is crowded, uncomfortable and not recommended. The air-con train costs about N66 for 1st class with berth and bedding, leaving Lagos Wednesday, Friday and Sunday. The train without air-con is also good. Both have a dining car; fish soup seems to come with every meal.

For Maiduguri you have change at Kaduna and at Kafanchan. The train takes 53 hours, leaving Lagos daily at 4.10 pm. Schedules change periodically, so check.

Getting Around
Air Transport At Murtala Mohammed

international airport, you'll find Hertz, a restaurant, bank and shops. The departure tax is N5 for interior flights and N20 (N100 if you buy your ticket in Nigeria) for flights with foreign destinations; the cost of a taxi from the international airport is N25 to N30 to downtown (22 km) and N7 to N12 to the local airport. There are no buses to downtown. To cut the cost in half, take a taxi to the expressway into town and hail a shared taxi from there.

Taxis A shared cab costs only about N0.60 for a short trip on one of the major islands in Lagos, but you'll never be quoted this price. Expect to pay about N3 to N6 from Victoria or Ikoyi Islands to downtown (Lagos Island). Taxis are plentiful and go out of their way to pick up foreigners because they expect you to pay the cab-to-yourself price. Expect to pay about N17 for a taxi by the hour in Lagos, though it is only N7 to N9 in other cities.

Car Rental Hertz (Mandilas Travel, tel 660536/630266/834483, telex 21383) 96 Broad St; National Eurocar (Cross Keys Travel, tel 662572/662892, telex 21089) Investment House, 21 Broad St; Avis/Nigerian Rent-a-Car (tel 846336, telex 21324) Apapa Rd, Inganmu; Safedrive (tel 844615) 19 Adam St, Yaba; Intra (tel 634884) 11 Martin St.

The South

IBADAN
The largest city in West Africa in 1960, now roughly half the size of Lagos, Ibadan (ee-BAH-dan) is an ugly sprawling city. There's little of interest other than the university and the International Institute of Tropical Agriculture (IITA), a research centre six km beyond the university on the northern edge of town.

Information
The university bookstore is one of the best

in West Africa. The heart of downtown is Cocoa House, slowly being rebuilt after a fire. You'll find the huge sprawling Dugbe market nearby and the British High Commission in the Finance Corp Building on Lebanon St.

Places to Stay – bottom end
For the money, it's hard to do better than *Sijuwade Motel* (tel 317855), which has singles/doubles for about N28/41 including breakfast. Only 250 metres from the bus stop (Molete Park), opposite UBA, it has rooms with air-con, TV, carpeting, comfortable beds and chairs, telephones and a decent restaurant. *Cityman Inn* is nearby at Molete Park and cheaper, with rooms for about N22/28, but the quality is much inferior.

The *CUSO* hostel may be cheaper still. For the key, call or drop by their office (tel 414032), 836 Adelabu Rd in the direction of 'Ring Challenge'. The hostel is nearby.

Places to Stay – middle
Foreigners looking for a moderately priced hotel prefer the 52-room *Lafia Hotel* (tel 316750, telex 31175) on the southern outskirts of town in Apata Ganga, which has decent but small singles/doubles with TVs for about N38/56, or the somewhat more centrally located *K S Motel* (tel 712238) which charges N43/56 including breakfast, and has one of the best nightclubs in town. The only advantage of the *J K International* (tel 415569) is that it's only 200 metres from the university on Awolowo Rd. Decent singles/doubles with TVs cost about N38/50, with a 20% reduction on Friday and Saturday.

On Kudeti Avenue is *Onireke Rest House* (tel 414607). Preferred by Nigerians, it has a lively indoor/outdoor bar, a tranquil ambience and greenery. Bungalows cost about N42/55.

Places to Stay – top end
The old *Premier Hotel* (tel 400340/1), with 87 singles/doubles for about N63/76, is the city's most expensive hotel but

rundown and a bad buy. Its advantages are the hill location with commanding views, the large pool and the Chinese restaurant, *Dragon d'Or*.

Places to Eat

Besides the hotel restaurants, the city's best restaurant is probably *Fortune* (tel 410077) on Kudeti Avenue near Onireke Rest House, three km or so from the Premier and not conveniently located. Run by friendly Chinese and open every day, it has an attractive dining room.

AROUND IBADAN

Rather than staying in congested Ibadan, consider heading on to Ife, Ilesha or Oshogbo, all centres of traditional Yoruba culture and roughly 100 km to the east.

Ife

In Ife, the legendary home of the founder of the Yoruba, Oranmiyan, you'll find a small museum, a university with an ethnological museum and the Oni's palace.

Places to Stay There is the medium-priced *Jolly Friends Hotel* and the cheaper *Mayflower Hotel*.

Ilesha

Ilesha is between Ife and Oshogbo. The principal attraction is St Joseph's Workshop, which sells wooden carvings. You can camp there as well.

Oshogbo

This town is famous for its dyed cloth, the shrine to the river goddess Oshuno (a grove enclosed by a wall designed by a local artist), and the Oshun festival in July or August.

Places to Stay The best hotel is *Oshun Presidential Hotel* (tel 2299, telex 34240), with singles/doubles for about N43/53, car hire, movie theatre and nightclub. On Ede Rd, you'll find two much cheaper hotels – *R A Alli Guest House* (tel 2332) and *Trans Nigeria Motels* (tel 2353).

BENIN CITY

Until the British sacked it, Benin City was one of the great cities of West Africa, dating back to the 10th century. Human sacrifice was a part of Bini culture. When a British contingent arrived in 1897, a ceremony was, coincidentally, in progress. Upon entering the walled city, the conquering troops encountered a shocking, seemingly savage sight – countless decapitated corpses. However, what they carted back to Europe – 2000 bronze statues from the Oba's palace – was hardly produced by 'savages'. The western world was amazed by the high quality of the art and museums pounced on it. Thus, the bronzes of Benin became one of the first styles of African art to win major world-wide recognition.

Now, Benin City is a sprawling, undistinguished place. There are, however, several interesting sites.

National Museum

It's in the dead centre of town, encircled by Ring Rd and open every day from 9 am to 6 pm. The star attraction is the bronze work for which the Bini were famous – virtually all produced for the king's court. Photographs of major pieces make up a good part of the collection. Upstairs, you'll see masks, stools, doorways, terracotta, pottery and carvings in ivory.

Oba's Palace

The mud-walled Oba's palace a block away doesn't look very intriguing from the outside, but inside it's quite spectacular. You need the secretary's permission, but he's a busy man. Moreover, you're supposed to request permission a week or so in advance, so few travellers see it.

Places to Stay & Eat

Among the cheaper hotels, an advantage of the *Edo Guest House* (tel 242722) on the main drag at 128 Akpakpava St, and *City Garden Hotel* (tel 242871) at 61 Sapele Rd, is their relatively central location. *Lixbor Hotel* (tel 243078), however, is

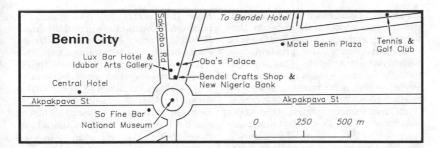

better. It has clean bathrooms, carpeting, restaurant and bar, TVs with double rooms and air-con for about N30/37 (singles/doubles). It is conveniently located 100 metres from Ring Rd on Sakpoba Rd, in a part of the Idubor Arts Gallery building. In the back, you can watch them carving away.

The *Central Hotel* (tel 200780) on the main drag is not as good and costs more, about N33/45. However, it's one of the two best places to hear live music, especially on weekends. The other is *So Fine*, a bar-nightclub opposite the museum.

The new *Bins Hotel* (tel 242197), has a decent dining room and singles/doubles with TVs for about N38/51. You'll find it on the edge of town on Ekenwa Rd, a major street with a fair number of taxis.

The two best hotels are the old *Bendel Hotel* (tel 200120) about one km from downtown, and the newer *Motel Benin Plaza* (tel 201430) nearby. The Bendel is set in extensive grounds and has a lot more character – old-style furnishings, carpets, and bathrooms where everything works. You'll feel as though the British left yesterday. At about N35/45 for singles/doubles, it's a steal. The Benin Plaza has a small pool, two bars, one of the best restaurants in town, and modern rooms with TVs that cost about N52/63. Forget about the *University Palace Hotel*, which is as expensive as the Benin Plaza and a poor buy.

Things to Buy

If you want to purchase art, try the *Idubor* *Arts Gallery* (open 8 am to 5 pm) at 2 Sakpoba Rd, 100 metres off Ring Rd, or *Bendel Crafts Shop* in the New Nigeria Bank building one block away.

ONITSHA

Onitsha is in the heart of eastern Nigeria, the most densely populated area in Africa after the Nile valley. Before the Biafran war, traders from as far away as Cameroon converged on the market, the largest in West Africa at the time. During the war, fighting destroyed major parts of the city, including the market.

Today, this rebuilt city has regained its vitality but it has little to offer unless you're interested in African writing. Onitsha is famous for its authors – the Onitsha market writers. They write about many things, but love and romance are most popular, also unsuccessful forced marriages. This is a conversation from a very popular play called *Husbands and Wives Who Hate Themselves*:

MARK: I hate not marry you further you are a useless, hopeless, stupid, disobedient and nonsense wife.

VICTORIA: Bad man, bokom man, silly man, wicked man, bush man, I am packing quick quick and must move today. You could remember that I refused to marry you but my illiterate father forced me. You deceived and corrupted him with a bottle of White Horse.

It all began in the 1950s when Onitsha was growing and people wanted books that were cheap and easy to read, books about their own country and problems. So ordinary Onitsha people – taxi drivers, traders, farmers – began writing and buying second-hand printing presses to produce cheap books. They knew how to catch their readers' interest. One writer advertises: 'This book entertains more than two bottles of beer.' If you browse through the market, you may find a few of these books – highly entertaining and, for foreigners, educational.

Places to Stay – bottom end

For cheap (N33/45) but quite decent accommodation, there's the *Travellers Palace Hotel* (tel 211013) in the centre of town near a taxi park, and *People's Club Guest House* 250 metres from Columbus International. People's is a particularly good buy – the rooms have TV and a refrigerator plus there is a good restaurant and an active bar – but it's not so conveniently located as Travellers. For rock bottom prices, about N17 a room, try *A P 2 Hotel* behind the market.

Places to Stay – middle

Two good middle range hotels are the *Belingo Hotel* (tel 210877) one km from downtown and *Hotel de Columbus International* (tel 210503), not far from the centre of town but near nothing in particular.

At the Belingo, you'll find rooms with TVs for about N46, one of the best restaurants in town with Chinese food, a run down lobby, and the Belingo Entertainment Centre across the street, with two tennis courts and a pool. The Columbus has decent singles/doubles with TVs and refrigerators (doubles only) for N38/50, an adequate restaurant and *Garden Nite Club*, reportedly the town's best.

Places to Stay – top end

The two best hotels are the *Nkisi Palace Hotel* (tel 211711), on Nkisi Rd on the northern outskirts of town, and the *Niger Heritage Regency Hotel* (tel 211769), on the eastern outskirts towards Enugu.

The Nkisi has singles/doubles with TV, refrigerator, carpeting and comfortable lounge chairs for about N50/62, plus a decent bar and restaurant. The new Niger Heritage has a pool, a pleasant ambience and a lobby with a fountain and a four-storey atrium. However, even though the rooms are well maintained and have TVs and carpets, they don't quite measure up to the Nkisi's. The old government-run *Paramount Hotel*, several hundred metres from the Nkisi, is run down and way over-priced at N55 a room.

OWERRI

After passing through so many huge, noisy, congested cities, you'll find Owerri's tranquility delightful.

Places to Stay

The *Ivory Hotel* (tel 230902) at km four on Okigwe Rd is a decent, moderately priced hotel. The city's best, about 45 minutes from the Port Harcourt airport, is the new four-star *Imo Concorde Hotel*, with pool, tennis, nightclub, casino, telex, bookstore and 228 rooms for about N77, followed by the *Pinewood Hotel* (tel 230135), with pool and car hire.

ENUGU

The centre of Nigeria's coal mining area, Enugu in Anambra State is another one of Nigeria's sprawling cities in Iboland with little of interest to most travellers. With trees along the streets providing shade and rolling green hills in the suburbs, it is prettier than many. Visiting the Ekulu mines several km out of town is apparently permitted. You could also drop by the Enugu Sports Club. It's fantastic – nine tennis courts, a superb indoor badminton court (possibly the only one in Africa), a squash court, a clean pool and an active bar and restaurant. A three-month membership costs only N50.

Places to Stay - bottom end

For cheaper hotels centrally located, try *Palacia Hotel*, which charges about N28 for a small room with air-con and has an active bar and decent restaurant. *Cool Spot*, at 19 Annang St, with air-con rooms for about N30, is not as good.

Places to Stay - middle

Of the medium-priced hotels, the two best are *Astoria Guest House* (tel 330180), in a quiet residential area near the Gemini, with singles/doubles for about N45/52, and the similarly priced *Metropole Guest House* (tel 338178) next door. Finding taxis could be a major headache. Downtown on the main drag to Port Harcourt (Agbani Rd), there's *Royal Palace Hotel* (tel 334082), with singles/doubles for about N51/63. *Joe Continental Hotel* (tel 254578) is nearby on the same road and a better buy at N33/45.

Places to Stay - top end

The city's three best hotels are the *Zodiac Hotel* (tel 256297, telex 51242), *Gemini Inn* (tel 331595, telex 51281), and the state-run *Hotel Presidential* (tel 337451), all in the same area of town.

The oldest and by far the largest is the slightly rundown Presidential, with rooms for about N65, four well-lit tennis courts (N2 an hour), long clean pool, casino, bookshop, nightclub, pharmacy and a cold ambience. The Zodiac's singles/doubles with TV and refrigerator, which cost about N58/76, are better. The grounds are also well maintained, plus the bar is more active and the hotel better managed.

The Gemini is equally as good as the Zodiac but more expensive, with singles/doubles for about N70/95, but it's not on a main road like the Zodiac and Presidential, making transportation a problem if you're without wheels.

OBUDU CATTLE RANCH

In the far east of Nigeria on the Cameroon border, 110 km from Ogoja on asphalt road, you'll find this well known but unlikely resort. Driving east from Ogoja, you'll pass through dense forests with trees so high that their branches form a canopy, shading out the sun entirely - Nigeria's Amazon. Driving up to the plateau, you'll see rolls of mountain ranges. Don't be surprised if it's a little chilly on top. At 1890 metres with no mosquitoes, you'll think you're in Scotland.

Built during the 1950s by Scots, the ranch is rundown. At one time, it was full of cattle, with meat from the ranch gracing tables in many cities and towns in the eastern part of the country. Now there's a task force to bring the ranch back to its former state.

Places to Stay

The *Obudu Ranch Hotel* is one of the main attractions. There are 23 chalets, tennis courts and horses for riding. The rooms are not cheap, but you can always pitch a tent. Sometimes you have to - at Easter and Christmas, they are usually fully booked. For reservations, call their booking office in Bauchi (tel 077-42174).

PORT HARCOURT

Built as a port for exporting coal from Enugu, Port Harcourt in Rivers State now has another *raison d'etre* - oil. All around town you can see oil flares at night. Wealth has made it one of Nigeria's most expensive cities but not one of its most interesting. New Market, two km from the heart of town, and the port are the only sights.

Information

If you need a travel agency, try Tamsaki at the Presidential Hotel or Benjosy Travel Agency (tel 221420) at 20 Asa Rd at the corner of Aba Rd (the main drag leading into town) near the bridge. Golfers can try the 18-hole Port Harcourt Club, open every day with sand greens, a sports shop and club rentals for N10.

Places to Stay - bottom end

Of the medium-priced hotels, *Delta Hotels Training School* (tel 338333/1) is by far the best – excellent service, well-maintained spacious rooms with air-con for about N38/52 that come with TVs and telephones, spacious grounds, downtown location, pleasant ambience, and a decent bar and restaurant. If it's full, you'll have to pay more for similar quality. *Zuru Hotel* (tel 332047), several km from the Presidential, has top quality rooms with TVs and plush carpeting for about N45/65 and a decent restaurant. The atmosphere is dead, in contrast to the livelier *Hotel Chez Therese* (tel 330820) nearby on Aba Rd, with 50 identically priced rooms that are a notch below.

Other hotels in the same price range as the Delta are near the bottom of the barrel. *Anon Lodge Hotel*, a km from the Presidential at 157 Aba Rd, has TVs and refrigerators in its singles/doubles. They are about N38/45 and better than similarly priced rooms at *Alhaja Titilope Hotel* and *Biddy's Hotel*, both several hundred metres from the top-end Presidential. The only advantage of the over-priced *Cedar Palace Hotel*, with shabby singles/doubles for about N45/52, is its downtown location near the port, with a popular bar where sailors change money on the black market.

Places to Stay – top end

Hotel Presidential (tel 335649/335100, telex 61308, cards AE) on Aba Rd, a 10-minute drive from downtown, is the best hotel. It has 330 rooms for about N80 (N150 deposit), a music shop, bookstore, movie theatre, casino, car rental, a tennis court and a long pool that's slightly dirty. Others prefer the somewhat smaller *Hotel Olympia* (tel 333706, no cards) near downtown – TVs and refrigerators in all rooms, the cleanest pool in town, and the golf club next door. Don't stay at the huge *Port Harcourt International Airport Hotel* – a 30-minute drive into town!

Places to Eat

Finding a restaurant downtown is no easy task. *Luna's Restaurant* at 157 Victoria St serves inexpensive Nigerian fare.

Another place serving Nigerian dishes, roughly N5 to N6, is the small air-con *Annsby Restaurant* at 17 Ogbunabali St several km from downtown toward the Presidential.

In all of Nigeria, you'll be hard pressed to find a restaurant serving better Nigerian food than *Labake Hotel*, several hundred yards from the Presidential, off Aba Rd. The town's most elegant restaurant is nearby – *Insular Sea Food Restaurant* 200 metres behind the Presidential, just off Aba Rd. Seafood, including lobster, is the speciality but meat dishes are also served, most in the N17 to N33 range.

Texas oilmen will feel right at home at the popular *Shaka's Place*, a km from the Presidential at 171 Aba Rd. It has checked tablecloths, country & western music, luncheon specials for about N13, hamburgers, steak, fish & chips, plus several Nigerian dishes. Next door is *Omar Khayam Restaurant*, which serves decent Nigerian food.

Nightlife

Next to Shaka's Place is one of the city's two most popular nightclubs, *Aquarius*, which has a cover of N10 on weekends and is slightly fancier and more reputable than *Uncle Sam*, the hottest nightclub in town, with whores galore.

Getting Around

The airport is a good half-hour drive from downtown. You'll find rental cars, taxis and a bus (N6 per person) awaiting every flight. In town, taxis by the hour are N9.

ABA

Only 65 km north of Port Harcourt, Aba is noted for its flourishing market.

Places to Stay

The city has a number of inexpensive hotels; three are on Pound Rd – *Voyage Guest House*, *Grace Guest Inn* and *City Guest Home*. The top hotels are *Imo Hotel* (220111), with singles/doubles for about

N45/72, *Enitona Hotel* (tel 220200), with singles doubles for about N57/72, and *Crystal Park Hotel* (tel 221930).

CALABAR

In the far south-east, only 25 km from Cameroon with twice as much rainfall as Lagos, Calabar has a beautiful setting, high on a hill, commanding a fine view of the water. People are friendly and walking around town is a pleasure.

Places to Stay

For a moderately priced hotel, try the *Government Guest House*. For rock bottom prices, try *Ropsop Guest House* on Palm St near the Cameroon consulate, with rooms for roughly N22. The 154-room *Metropolitan Hotel* (tel 222527) has the best accommodation.

The Centre

JOS

Travellers come to Jos for two principal reasons – the cooler climate and the Jos Museum. At 1200 metres above sea level, the Jos plateau is noticeably cooler than most other areas of the country. The rolling hills also make it more scenic.

Jos Museum

Four km from downtown, the museum includes a zoo, railroad museum, art museum and museum of traditional architecture. Pottery lovers have hit the jackpot. The collection is superb. Most unusual, however, is the museum of traditional architecture. Spread out over some 20 hectares are full-scale reproductions of buildings from each of Nigeria's major regions. You can see a reconstruction of the Kano wall, the old Zaria mosque with a Muslim museum inside, the Ilorin mosque, and examples of the major styles of village architecture region by region, such as the circular *katanga* buildings of the Nupe people,

with beautifully carved posts supporting a thatched roof. Open every day 10 am to 6 pm, it's highly recommended.

Jos Wildlife Game Reserve

Another major attraction is this reserve, which is half zoo and half park. It's about 10 km south of town off the road to Bukuru and open from 10 am to 6 pm. You'll see the usual – elephant, lion, hippo, baboon, monkey, ostrich – and the unusual – a manatee (sea cow). In the huge reserve section, animals walk around freely and pelicans think nothing of wandering into the bar, looking for a drink perhaps. Drive around – you're in a game reserve.

Tin Mines

The tin mines around Jos made the area extremely important to the British; building a railroad to Jos was one of their first major projects. Bukuru, just south of Jos, is the site of some major mines. To see them, you'll need permission from the Ministry of Trade & Industry.

A final major attraction is **Yankari Game Reserve**, a three-hour drive to the east.

Places to Stay - bottom end

Jos has a number of hotels with rock bottom prices. The best buy is the *Moonshine Hotel* (tel 55645), which has decent singles/doubles for about N12/17. They also have a new *Annex* (tel 54361) next door, an excellent buy at about N28/33 for an air-con room with TV, refrigerator, hot water and carpets. It's also a good place to eat. It is about two km from the heart of town towards the museum.

If the Moonshine is full, try *Jubilee Jenta Hotel* closer to town or the noisy *Terminus Hotel* in the heart of town across from the market. The price is virtually the same, about N12/18. Another possibility is one of the church missions, two of which are behind Challenge Bookshop.

Places to Stay - top end

The city's number one hotel is *Hill Station* (tel 55399, telex 81130, cards AE). About four big blocks from the museum, it has singles/doubles with TV for about N55/62 (about N67 for a double with air-con), tennis, a pool and two restaurants, one Chinese. A notch down is the new *Summit Hotel* (tel 54476), about three km from downtown towards the museum. The rooms have TV, air-con and refrigerators.

Nigerians seem to prefer the new *Tati Hotel* (tel 52554), two km from the town centre. It has similar quality rooms for N33 (N70 deposit) and a popular nightclub Friday and Saturday nights.

If you have wheels, you might try the older *Naraguta Country Club* on the outskirts of town just before the university. They have a good restaurant, ventilated rooms for about N31 and bungalows with air-con, TV and refrigerators for about N44. For a more central location, about a km from downtown, try the *Paas Hotel* (tel 53581), which seems fairly popular but is slightly over-priced at about N38/53 with air-con, or the less lively *Daula International* (tel 53340) – about N38/45 for singles/doubles with air-con, refrigerators and TV.

Places to Eat
For the price, it's hard to beat the wood-panelled restaurant at the *Moonshine Hotel Annex*. They serve a three-course special for N7 and à la carte selections for N3 to N7, including some Nigerian specialities. For a good Nigerian meal at rock bottom prices, head for *Pat's*, a well-known tiny restaurant about a km from the central market. It closes about 8 pm.

Jos has few top quality restaurants. Your best bet is the *Cedar Tree Restaurant* (tel 54890), roughly eight km from downtown on the road south to Bukuru. Don't confuse it with the Cedar Restaurant on the same road. A typical meal should run about N17 to N22. The *Sharazad*, on the same road closer to town, used to be the best but has gone down hill. Avoid the *Palace Restaurant* at the Hill Station; one reviewer called the Chinese food there 'awful'. Another

possibility is the *Naraguta Country Club* on the opposite edge of town near the university.

Nightlife
If you're looking for a place to drink and dance, try *Tati Hotel*, the most popular place in town but open on weekends only, with a cover of N5. Downtown, not far from the Moonshine is another popular nightclub, *Joe K*. A third, well-liked by foreigners, is *Sharazad*.

ABUJA
During the oil boom days, the government decided to construct a new capital. Like Brasilia, it's in the centre of the country. Construction is going slowly. The first ministry isn't scheduled to move from Lagos until late 1987. It won't be an interesting place to visit for years.

Places to Stay
For less expensive hotels, try *Sunny Guest Inn* and, cheaper, *Mayfair Guest Inn*.

The new *Hilton*, *Sheraton* and *Hyatt Regency* hotels should be open by 1988; until then, the best hotel will remain the 216-room *Agura Hotel*.

KADUNA
Laid out by the British, Kaduna is less crowded than other Nigerian cities, but you'll find little of interest.

Information
Several countries maintain consulates here, including the UK (United Bank of Africa Building, Hospital Rd, tel 212178/243080), West Germany (Ahmadu Bello Way 22, tel 23696) and the USA (No 2, Maska Rd, tel 213074). For a travel agent, try *Habis Travels* between the Durbar and Hamdala hotels. Golfers can try the local course.

National Museum
The museum (open daily 9 am to 6 pm) on the main drag (Ahmadu Bello Way) across from the Emir's palace has a little bit of

1 Railway Station
2 Post Office
3 Jacaranda Restaurant
4 Durbar Hotel
5 Maharaja Rest
6 Outdoor Grilled Meats
7 Habis Travels Ltd
8 Hamdala Hotel
9 Kaduna Club
10 Golf Course
11 Arewa Chinese Restaurant
12 Market
13 Safari Hotel
14 Fatma Guest House
15 Durncan Hotel
16 Gloria Maria Hotel
17 Flamingo Hotel
18 Stadium
19 Tati Hotel
20 Kimbo Hotel
21 Fina White House Hotels

Kaduna

everything – masks, pottery, musical instruments, brass work, door posts, wooden carvings and leather displays.

Places to Stay - bottom end

Travellers on the cheap should check out the *YMCA* and the *SIM Mission* for rooms. Otherwise, the cheapest place may be the *Safari Club* (tel 211838) near downtown at 10 Argungu St, about four blocks off the main drag. It has air-con singles/doubles for N17/22, filthy toilets, poor lighting and a popular bar, with tolerable noise levels even on weekends.

The *Fatma Guest House* (tel 213097), one block behind the Safari Club on Katsina Rd, is not recommended – N28 for rooms that are no better. If the Safari is full, try the *Durncan Hotel*, also nearby on Katsina Rd, air-con singles/doubles with TVs cost N28/33.

Places to Stay - middle

Nigerians obviously prefer the three new *Fina White House* hotels (tel 210125/ 211852/216418) – all frequently full. Virtually identical, they are near each other, one km from downtown on or near

Constitution Rd. The N45 rooms – better than the more expensive Hamdala – have TVs and mini-refrigerators.

Others prefer the new, similarly priced *Country Club*, three km or so from downtown, because it has a pool and a pleasant relaxing atmosphere. On the main drag, you'll find *Gloria Moria Hotel* (tel 214501), which is similar to the Fina hotels and has rooms with TVs for N40. If these are full, try the *Flamingo Hotel* (tel 213514) on Constitution Rd near the Fina White House hotels, with slightly frayed singles/doubles for N33/38, or *Kimbo Hotel* a block away, with air-con rooms for N31.

Places to Stay – top end

The *Durbar Hotel* (tel 201100, telex 71134) is one of the best hotels outside Lagos. It has 302 rooms for N60 (N120 deposit) including tennis courts, TV and mini-refrigerators in all rooms, an excellent bookstore, pharmacy, bank, and a long, clean pool – the 'in' place to be on weekends.

Until the Durbar was constructed in 1977, top honours went to the nearby eight-storey *Hamdala Hotel* (tel 211005, telex 71163). It's now a good notch down, with singles/doubles for N42/56 including TV/video, a pool, a good Chinese restaurant on top, and few clients. Some people prefer it, however, because the service is better than at the Durbar.

Places to Eat

For cheap eats, try the excellent grilled meats sold across from the Durbar. People from all over Kaduna come by in their cars to pick it up. In the centre of town on the main drag, you'll find a small inexpensive restaurant, *Nanet*. *Bleka Democratic Restaurant* is convenient to the hotels on Constitution Rd; they serve Nigerian specials for N4 to N5.

Jacaranda Restaurant (tel 210419) in a house on Waff Rd, 300 metres from the Durbar and poorly marked, is definitely one of Nigeria's finest restaurants. Open every day for lunch and dinner, they serve Continental cuisine with a variety of selections including seafood. You'll find the owner friendly and the decor fresh and bright. A second restaurant with the same name but different management is outside town and is also excellent. The delightful *Maharaja Restaurant* (tel 212662), in the NIDB building across from the Durbar, serves good Indian food for lunch and dinner in a pleasant setting.

The city's most popular restaurant – packed on Saturday night – is *Arewa Chinese Restaurant* (tel 212380) in the centre of town on the main drag, Ahmadu Bello Way. Open every day with over 140 choices in the N12 to N22 range, it is highly recommended. For good Chinese food that is less expensive, with over 100 choices, try the restaurant at the Hamdala hotel, open every day. On Saturdays between 5 and 10 pm, the all-you-can-eat, pool-side buffet for N18 at the Durbar is quite popular.

Nightlife

For late night dancing and drinking, the rich go to *After 6* at the Durbar, *La Cabana* on Junction Rd, and *Costain Club* at Jaofami Estate. The poor go to *Club 69* near the centre of town; you can eat there as well.

ZARIA

An old city, once one of the seven Hausa emirates, Zaria retains its traditional character. It's definitely worth visiting if you'll be in Kaduna or Kano. Partly surrounded by a 14-km mud wall, the old section of Zaria has an Emir's palace and some fine examples of houses with patterned mud walls. There's also the restored Friday mosque with magnificent interior vaulting, a military museum and the Zaria Club, with tennis and golf.

Places to Stay

The three best hotels are *Hotel Kuta* (tel 33268) with TV and refrigerator in all 35 rooms, *Kongo Conference Hotel* (tel

32873), and *Zaria Hotel*. For a medium-priced hotel, try the old *Catering Rest House* (tel 32451).

YANKARI GAME RESERVE

Open for game viewing from 1 November to June 30, Yankari is a three-hour drive east of Jos (225 km) and covers an area of 2244 square km. Bush buck and horned waterbuck are the most common animals, followed by approximately 500 elephants, 200 buffalos, 35 hippos, 50 lions, also baboon, monkey, wart hog, waterbuck and crocs.

Another great attraction of Yankari is its eight-metre-wide, two-metre-deep lake formed by the Wikki warm springs. The crystal clean mineral water is free of bilharzia and has a constant temperature of 31°C. The best time for animal viewing is late February and March, before the rains, when the animals congregate at the Gaji river.

Driving vehicles is permitted in the park, but most people take advantage of the park's tours at 7.30 am and 3.30 pm in specially converted trucks. If you're in Kaduna, talk to the travel agent at the Durbar hotel. They apparently organise bus trips.

Places to Stay

Wikki Warm Springs Hotel in the park is often full. It has 85 renovated circular bungalows starting from about N17 for a single room, some with air-con, an unreliable generator and an adequate restaurant. If the hotel is full, you could stay at *Awalah Hotel*, the best hotel in Bauchi, two hours away.

The North

KANO

Dating back more than a thousand years, Kano is the oldest major city in West Africa. For centuries it was one of the most active commercial centres in West Africa.

Today, it is Nigeria's third largest city – number one on most travellers' list of places to see in Nigeria.

Information

You'll find Habis Travels (tel 3271) on Post Office Rd near Air Afrique, the British Liaison Officer (open Monday to Friday 8 am to noon) at 64 Murtala Mohammed Way, Chase Manhattan Bank on the same street, the Niger consulate just south of the racecourse on Alu Avenue, and money changers behind Sheila Cinema.

Things to See

The centre of the city is Sabon Gari Market. From there, it's 1½ km south-west via Ado Bayero Rd and Kofa Mata Rd to Kofa Mata Gate, the main gate leading into the old city, and another 1½ km on to Kurmi Market (KOUR-mee), the city's major attraction. You might expect the main gate of this 17 km partially standing wall to be impressive. It isn't. However, just beyond it you'll see the dye pits, reputedly the oldest in Africa, where men dip cloth into pots in the ground filled with indigo dye.

Kurmi Market

With thousands of stalls in a 16-hectare area, Kurmi is probably the largest market in Africa. It's a centre for African crafts, gold, bronze, silver and all types of fabrics, from the ancient religious Hausa gowns and a huge selection of hand-painted African cloth, to the latest imported suits. Guides will certainly approach you. You may find them quite helpful. They'll expect a tip.

Central Mosque

After passing through the gate, instead of heading towards the market, you could continue straight for over a km to the central mosque, which you may no longer enter. The Friday prayer around 12.30 pm attracts 50,000 or so – a sight to see.

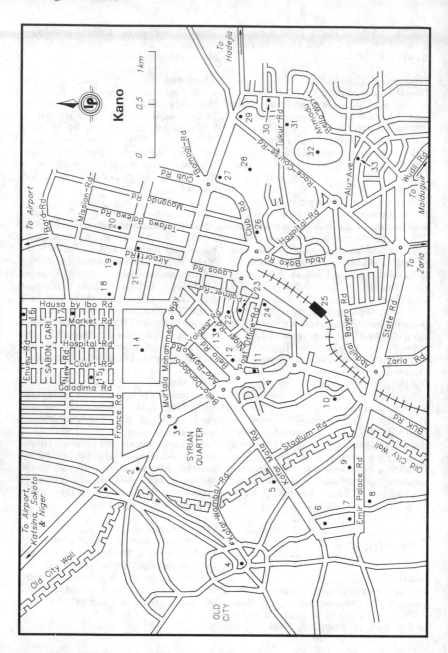

1	Akija Hotel	18	JYC Hotel
2	Truck Park	19	Stadium
3	Kano Guest Inn	20	SIM Guest House
4	Kurmi Market	21	Concorde Restaurant
5	Dye Pits	22	Barclays Bank
6	Central Mosque	23	Nigeria Airways
7	Emir's Palace	24	Post Office
8	Gidan Makama Museum	25	Train Station
9	British Council	26	Central Hotel & Camp Site
10	Kandara Palace Hotel	27	Kano Guest Inn
11	Danish Bakery	28	Golf Course
12	JJ Nightclub	29	Daula Hotel
13	Moulin Rouge	30	Castle Restaurant & Nightclub
14	Salon Gari Market	31	Palace Restaurant
15	Criss Cross Hotel	32	Racetrack
16	International Hotel	33	Niger Consulate
17	Remco Hotel		

Emir's Palace & Museum

Next door to the mosque is the huge mud-walled Emir's palace, where visitors are not allowed without invitation. On the opposite end of the Emir's palace is Gidan Makama Museum, built in the 15th century for the 20th Emir of Kano and open every day 9 am to 5 pm – well worth a visit. You'll find on display photographs of Kano architecture, an interesting photographic history of Kano, including the taking of Kano in 1902 by the British, and various crafts – leather, baskets and fabrics.

Gida Dan Hausa

Another outstanding example of Kano's architecture, blending Hausa and Arab styles, is the Gida Dan Hausa, the remarkable early 20th century home of the first British administrator.

Zoo

On the southern end of town off the road to Zaria and west of Gyadi-Gyadi village, there's an attractive zoo, open every day 7.30 am to 6.30 pm. The largest city zoo in Nigeria and the only zoo in West Africa housing kangaroos and wallabies, it has over 50 variety of animals including rhino.

Places to Stay – bottom end

Travellers on the cheap are in luck. Near downtown behind the Central Hotel on State Rd is the *Kano Tourist Camp* (tel 2341). It has 64 beds, including dormitory rooms with eight beds and mosquito nets. Expect to pay about N10 per bed, N18 for a double private room, N4 for pitching a tent and N3 per vehicle. They also have a tennis court, an inexpensive restaurant, and a common room with air-con and TV! If it's full, try the similarly priced *SIM Mission* guest house, several large blocks north-east of the central market and beyond the stadium, off Mission Rd near the SIM Eye Hospital.

Among the cheap hotels, one of the best is the *Criss Cross Hotel* (tel 1399/3385) two blocks north of the central market at the corner of Church and Ibadan Rd in Sabon Gari. It has singles for about N17/22 (fan/air-con) and doubles with air-con for about N66. Seven blocks further north on Enugu Rd is the *International Hotel* (tel 3284), another decent hotel with singles for about N20 (N27 with air-con) including breakfast.

For a dirt cheap hotel, try *Challenge Guest Inn* three blocks north of the market on Yoruba Rd. It has singles/doubles with fan for about N12/15. Another cheap one is *Universal Hotel* a block south on Church Rd, with ventilated rooms for about N33. With both hotels, the noise comes free.

Places to Stay – middle

The three best moderately priced hotels are the well-maintained *Remco Hotel* (tel 8600) five blocks from the central market at 61 New Rd in Sabon-Gari, with modern singles for about N38 and doubles for N45 to N50, followed by the *Tower Hotel* (tel 7107) seven short blocks further north at 64 Aba Rd (N33 rooms with TV and refrigerators), and the *Akija Hotel* (tel 3514). At about N32/38 for singles/doubles with TV and refrigerator, the Akija is frequently full. It's two km west of downtown on a main highway, Murtala Mohammed Way.

The similarly priced *Kandara Palace Hotel* (tel 3612) is poorly maintained, inconveniently located and not recommended. If these are full, try the *Kano Guest Inn* (tel 2717/2282) near the central market on Ibrahim Taiwo Rd. At about N26/40 for singles/doubles with air-con, TV and a decent Nigerian restaurant, it's a good buy and quite popular.

Places to Stay – top end

The top hotel, one km from downtown, is *Central Hotel* (tel 3051/3062, telex 77151, cards AE), with 195 singles/doubles for about N56/67, pool, tennis, bookshop, hair salon, Chinese restaurant, Nigeria Airways office, shops, bank, and a popular terrace for drinks. The *Daula Hotel* (tel 5311, telex 77241, cards AE) has mostly Nigerian clients and is almost as good, with rooms for about N65 and a pool. It is two km from downtown beyond the Kano Club.

Places to Eat

For cheap meals downtown, you'll find numerous places north of the market in Sabon Gari. The restaurant at the Remco Hotel is one of the best. For sandwiches, pastries, ice cream and Nigerian meals, try the air-con *Danish Bakery &*

Restaurant south of the market on Ibrahim Raiwo Rd, near the intersection of Post Office Rd – Kano's answer to MacDonald's.

You'll be hard pressed to find a better restaurant than the *Palace Restaurant* (tel 2309) on Race Course Rd next to the racetrack, a km south-east of the Central hotel. Open every day for lunch and dinner, it serves Chinese dishes in the N11 to N22 range and has an extensive menu, attentive service and attractive ambience. *China House* at the Central hotel is also quite good, especially the full-course special for about N16.

For decent Lebanese cuisine, head for *Castle Restaurant* (tel 7337) on Ahmadu Bello Way, three km south-west of the central market, beyond the racecourse. Open every day, they charge about N7 to N17 for main courses and have a nightclub upstairs. On the same street, look for a small sign with a top hat saying *Toppers Restaurant*, which is off the street and serves American meals for about N6 and up. Around the corner from Toppers you'll find *Shangri-La*, which serves reasonably priced Indian food.

Entertainment & Sports

Kano Club One of the best buys in town is a meal at the *Kano Club* (tel 4040/2831). If you request temporary membership and can prove to them that you are not residing in Kano, they'll give you use of all facilities for up to a month, including two squash courts, four tennis courts, a badminton court, pool, popular bar and restaurant with inexpensive meals. Don't expect them to offer this if you look like you just crossed the desert. They'll charge you either nothing, as they did me, or about N7/11 for singles/couples. You'll find it 500 metres from the Central Hotel on Bompai Rd. It's one of the two most popular watering holes for expatriates and Nigerians; the other is the terrace at the Central Hotel.

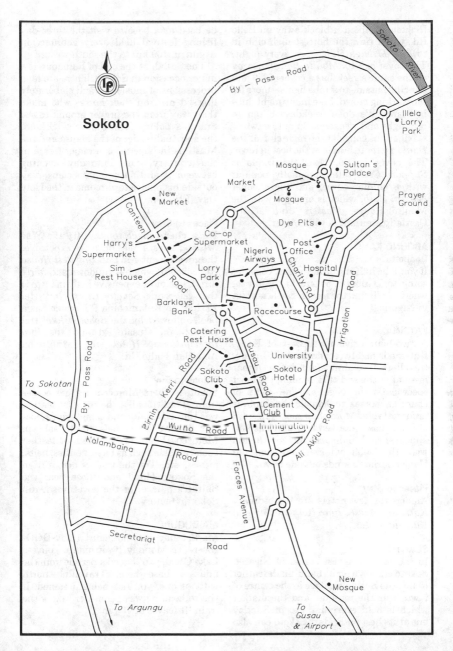

Sokoto

Sokoto River

By – Pass Road

Illela
Lorry Park

Sultan's
Palace

Mosque

Market

Mosque

Prayer
Ground

New Market

Canteen

Dye Pits

Co-op
Supermarket

Post
Office

Harry's
Supermarket

Nigeria
Airways

Charity Rd

Hospital

Sim
Rest House

Road

Lorry
Park

Barklays
Bank

Racecourse

Irrigation Road

Catering
Rest House

Kerri Road

Gusau Road

University

To Sokotan

Sokoto
Club

Sokoto
Hotel

Birnin

Cement
Club

By – Pass Road

Wurno Road

Immigration

Ali Akzu Road

Kalambaina

Road

Forces Avenue

Secretariat   Road

To Argungu

To
Gusau
& Airport

New
Mosque

Nightclubs About a block away on Bello Rd, you'll find the hottest nightclub in town – *JJ Nightclub*, open every night. The cover is N10. *Moulin Rouge*, nearby on the same street, has a cover of N3 and dancing outside to strobe lights – more for the working crowd. Like many nightclubs in Kano, it's open weekdays 8 pm to midnight and weekends 8 pm to dawn.

Nigerians consider the nightclub at the *Daula Hotel* to be one of the best in town. The cover is N6. Near the Daula is *Support Club*, almost equally popular with a similar cover, and the cheaper *Federal Club*, which is on a par with the Moulin Rouge. *Masters Club* at the Castle Restaurant is yet another.

AROUND KANO
Danbatta
If you'll be in Kano on a Sunday, consider going to Danbatta 50 km to the north, where you'll find the largest cattle market in Nigeria.

KATSINA
A two-hour drive north-west of Kano, Katsina is highly recommended by many travellers. Its claim to fame is the Durbar festival at the end of Ramadan, the most spectacular in Nigeria. The sight of charging horses to honour the Emir is unforgettable. More than most Nigerian cities, it has preserved its traditions and appearance. Landmarks include the old wall, the Gobir Minaret and some old Hausa burial mounds outside town.

Places to Stay
Among the few hotels are the ordinary *Katsina Guest Inn* (tel 30313) and *Katsina Motel*.

SOKOTO
In the far north-west corner of Nigeria, Sokoto is known for its hand-made leather items, the Sultan's palace in the centre of town near the mosque, and the market which is held every day except Sunday but at its best on Friday. Sokoto can also be used as a base to visit the three-day fishing festival held every February in Argungu, 100 km to the south-west.

The Sallah at the end of Ramadan is a major occasion in Sokoto. There are long processions of musicians and elaborately dressed men on their horses who make their way from the prayer ground to the Sultan's palace. The Sultan of Sokoto, the spiritual leader of the Hausa and the Muslims in Nigeria, is a major figure in the country. On Thursday evening between 9 and 11 pm musicians play outside his palace to welcome in the Holy Day (Friday).

Places to Stay
For a cheap place to stay, try the *SIM Mission* guest house or, more expensive, the government-run *Catering Rest House* (tel 232505), which is rundown and fairly dirty. The most expensive hotel in town is the 120-room *Sokoto Guest Inn* (tel 233205) on Kalambaina Rd, which has a pool, followed by the *Sokoto Hotel* (tel 232412) on Gusau Rd and the *Ibro International Hotel* (tel 232510) on Abdullah Fodio Rd.

Things to Buy
Sokoto is where 'Moroccan leather' comes from. Traditionally, the red goat leather was tanned locally and then taken across the Sahara on camels to be sold in Morocco. There are all sorts of leather goods for sale such as bags, pouffes, belts, purses, etc. Try the traders across from the Sokoto Hotel and those near the Sultan's palace, or the government-run Sokotan factory.

MAIDUGURI
Market day in Maiduguri (may-DOO-gou-ree) is Monday. If you plan on going to Lake Chad, you'll need a permit from the military base here. Travelling north without one, you risk being detained. If you're heading west, consider taking the train. It leaves at 10 pm.

Places to Stay

The government's *Guest House* and the *West End Hotel* are decent, inexpensive hotels, about N22 to N28. The top hotel is *Lake Chad Hotel* (tel 232746), with a pool and singles/doubles for about N46/62, followed by *Deribe Hotel* (tel 232662), all 98 rooms with TV, air-con and refrigerators.

Senegal

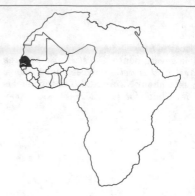

Senegal gets far more travellers – over 250,000 a year – than any other country in West-Central Africa. One reason for this must be Dakar, the favourite West African city of most travellers. While Abidjan may be amazing, Dakar is more liveable. It has a cooler climate, half the population, good beaches nearby, and a lower cost of living. It also has a more African ambience and a greater sense of history, particularly with Gorée Island, the first European settlement in West Africa.

Dakar is by no means the only reason for Senegal's popularity. The southern Casamance region is another. Years ago the government, in a stroke of brilliance, gave money to villages to build interesting African-style quarters that would be cheap but suitable for travellers. They have foam mattresses, running water, clean bathrooms, mosquito nets, and they serve meals. As a result, you can travel all over the Casamance region, live in villages and experience rural Africa. Others head for the beach and live in luxury; it's no accident that Senegal has two of the three Club Meds in black Africa. You can also visit one of West Africa's major game parks and St-Louis, the picturesque former capital of Senegal.

On the negative side, Dakar has some of the most persistent traders in Africa. If you can learn how to deal with them without losing your cool, your stay will be a lot more enjoyable.

HISTORY
The history of all of French West Africa is closely tied to that of Senegal because it was here that the French directed the major part of their colonial policy. In the 20th century, much of that history has centred around one man – Leopold Senghor – who stands out as the country's most influential statesman of all time.

Senegal was one of the earliest inhabited regions of West Africa – dating from at least 13,000 BC. More recently, it was part of the first two great empires of West Africa, the Ghana Empire of the 9th to 11th centuries and the empire of Mali (13th to 14th centuries). Between these two empires, Islamic invaders from Morocco made great inroads into the area of Senegal, bringing their religion with them. At the same time, the Sahara was experiencing long droughts, forcing large migrations of Wolof, Serer, Fulani and Toucouleur people south into Senegal.

European Arrival
The year 1444 marks medieval Europe's first direct contact with West Africa. The Portuguese landed at Cap Vert that year and soon set up shop on nearby Gorée Island, just off present-day Dakar. For the next 150 years, Portuguese ships plied the coast in search of slaves. The Dutch and the English then entered the scene. St-Louis and Gorée Island changed hands several times until they were finally secured by the French in the late 1600s.

Wherever Europeans settled, slaves were always the main export. While slaving was not new – the Arab caravans had been operating the interior for centuries – with the arrival of the Europeans it became a coastal operation. Had it not been for the powerful ruling kingdoms in the interior like the Djolof, who periodically conducted raids on each other to procure these slaves, the

Europeans could not have conducted their operations so easily. The brutality of the slave trade is evident in the dark dungeons at Gorée Island where the slaves were held.

The banning of the slave trade in 1815 by the Council of Vienna forced the French to look for new sources of wealth. Their efforts to develop commercial crops were a failure until Louis Faidherbe was appointed governor in 1845. Stationed in the capital, St-Louis, he set out to conquer the lower Senegal valley, believing this would eventually open up trade to West Africa's interior. Within only 10 years, he had completed his mission. To the French treasury officials, he was a darling. By encouraging farmers to cultivate a cash crop, groundnuts (peanuts), he had made the colonial administration self-financing.

French Imperialism
Culturally, the French were the most imperialistic of all the colonialists. Their doctrine of assimilation was, in effect: 'Act like us and we'll forget your colour.' As a result those Africans who integrated into French culture were treated quite fraternally. Starting in 1848, France started allowing Senegal to send a delegate to the French parliament. Over 110 years later, Britain had still not done the same in its colonies. Initially, the delegates were all white or mulatto.

By 1887, France had given all the Africans living in the four largest coastal towns (Dakar, Gorée, St-Louis, Rufisque) limited French citizenship. In 1914, they elected their first black delegate, Blaise Diagne. The same year saw the birth of the first political party in West Africa. It soon became fashionable, however, for politically conscious Senegalese to join the political parties of France. Since the leftists in France were gaining increasing power from 1936 onward, many French West Africans joined the French socialist and communist parties.

Meanwhile, the French moved slowly in implementing their policy of assimilating Africans into French culture. Apart from the four large coastal towns with their 80,000 black *citoyens* with full political rights, only about 2000 of the 14 million French West Africans had received French citizenship. Compared to the British, the French did little to educate Africans. The only blacks who received secondary education were those whom they needed in the colonial administration. Nearly all of the French secondary education for West Africa was given in three institutions in one city – Dakar, which the French had made the administrative capital of French West Africa, a huge territory extending to Niger.

Between WW I and WW II, a number of Senegalese intellectuals went to France to study. One was Léopold Senghor, a Serer from a wealthy family. Georges Pompidou was a classmate. Following graduation, he became the first African to qualify as a secondary-school teacher in France. During this period, he began writing poems. After WW II, he and Alioune Diop founded *Présence Africaine*, a magazine promoting the values of African culture.

Politically, Senghor began a popular movement in Senegal that got him elected to the French Assembly. With independence in the wind, he defended the idea of a strong federal union as the only way to achieve real independence. France, he felt, would balkanize her former colonies to keep them weak and dependent. His rival was Houphouet-Boigny of the Ivory Coast who wanted French West Africa split into various small countries. Houphouet-Boigny feared that within a federal union the richer colonies (ie the Ivory Coast) would have to subsidise the weaker ones.

Independence
In the late '50s, Senghor gained support from Soudan (now Mali), Upper Volta (now Burkina Faso) and Dahomey (now Benin) to form a single union, the Mali Federation. But the last two countries withdrew almost immediately on pressure

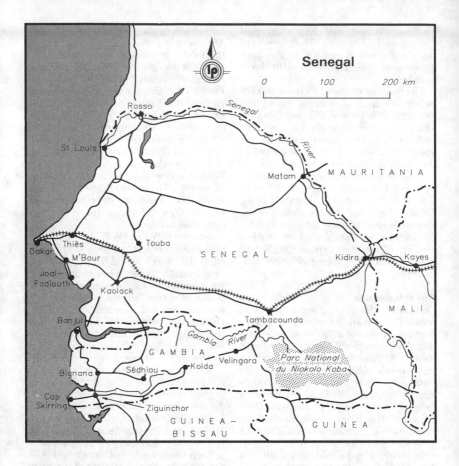

from France and the Ivory Coast. Only two months after independence in 1960, the Senegal-Mali union broke up. Houphouet-Boigny had won the day and French West Africa was composed of nine totally separate republics.

A minister in the French cabinet, Senghor made no bones about his love for the French. He married a French woman, took his vacations on a farm in Normandy, became one of the leading authorities on French grammar, and is still an eminent published poet.

By African standards, Senegal has been very stable and is the least politically repressive of the former French colonies. However, Senghor did not always have a smooth run. In 1962, the Prime Minister allegedly attempted a coup. Six years later, in the wake of the student riots in France in May 1968 and with mounting economic difficulties at home, students rioted at the University of Dakar. Senghor sent in troops to occupy the school. The national trade union threw its support behind the students, and called for a general strike. The situation was potentially revolutionary. Even with a strong show of force supported by the 1000-odd French troops stationed in Senegal, Senghor had to make concessions to the union and the students. Ultimately, however, he was able to undermine the union's effectiveness when a new single confederation was formed. In 1976, he felt secure enough to introduce constitutional changes allowing three legally sanctioned political parties; two years later, a fourth was added.

Economically, the country had been over-dependent on groundnuts for more than a century. When the droughts struck in the 1970s, Senegal was severely affected. Still, Senghor remained popular. In 1980, after 20 years as president, he did what no other African head of state had ever done before – he voluntarily stepped down. The imposing, 195-cm tall prime minister, Abdou Diouf, took over and remains president today.

Today

Senegal is the only country in West Africa that might be called a democracy. Eight parties contested the 1983 elections, which Diouf won with over 83% of the vote. His major opponent, Abdoulaye Wade, received most of the rest. Wade remains a major critic, arguing that Diouf has sold out to the IMF.

Economically, Senegal is getting nowhere – ditto for the Senegambia confederation. Real per capita income – about US$500 – remains exactly where it was at independence in 1960, when Senegal and the Ivory Coast were on a par. Now, income per capita in the Ivory Coast doubles that of Senegal, and Senegal is still a one-crop economy – groundnuts. Less than half are sold to the government as legally required; the rest are sold on the parallel market or, in some years, smuggled into The Gambia. Production of corn, millet and sorghum is stagnant or declining. Even when producer prices rise, farmers don't seem to respond. The Senegalese now import more than 35% of what they eat.

Meanwhile, although foreign reserves are at a new low, Senegal continues to receive more foreign aid per capita than just about any country in Africa. Seemingly every six months or so, the Paris Club reschedules the debt. By continuing to pour millions into the economy, western governments may simply be permitting the government to forestall taking tough measures, such as reducing government payrolls.

PEOPLE

Of the country's 6.5 million people, about 35% are Wolof. Almost all of the remainder are Serer, Diola, Fulani (or Peul), Toucouleur, or Mandinka. You'll find the Wolof everywhere, but more in the area north of Dakar and Thiès, the Serer in the region just east and south-east of Dakar, the Diola in the Casamance, the Toucouleur in the north and east along the Senegal river, and the Fulani and Mandinka more in the central and eastern regions.

Ethnically, what distinguishes Senegal from much of West Africa is the high degree of homogeneity among the major groups. One reason is that most of them speak or understand a single native language – Wolof. Another is that about 80% are Muslim, and also that during the colonial era, the French espoused assimilationist policies, minimising ethnic culture.

You don't have to go to Senegal to meet the Wolof. On Fifth Avenue in the heart of New York, you'll see them hawking everything from cut-rate umbrellas, neckties and scarfs to phoney Rolex watches. In New York, shoppers seek them out; in Dakar, their never-say-no trading technique drives tourists crazy. Most Wolof in Senegal, however, are groundnut farmers and bureaucrats.

As with many African tribes, their society is highly stratified and status is determined by birth. At the top are the traditional noble and warrior families, followed by the farmers, traders and persons of caste – blacksmiths, leather-workers, woodworkers, weavers and *griots*

(GREE-oh). Griots are the lowest of the castes but highly respected as it is they who pass on the oral history and are usually the only ones who can recite family or village history. As musicians or song writers, they used to entertain the royal families. Today, if you're fortunate enough to hear someone playing the harp-like *kora* he'll almost certainly be from a griot family.

At the bottom of the social hierarchy were the slaves, taken in wars or bought from traders. Slavery is long gone, but many descendants of former slaves still work as tenant farmers for their former masters. Modernism is eroding this hierarchy. Today, the government official who manifests contempt of the uneducated peasants (even the chief) may actually be a member of a caste or slave family who went away to the city and became educated.

The Muslim religion as practised in Senegal is rather unique, blending magic with a reliance on the clergy and the veneration of saints. Virtually all adherents are members of one of five brotherhoods, the two principal ones being the Mourides, centred in Touba and Diourbel, and the Tidjanes. At the head of each is a Grand Caliph, the chief *marabout* (mah-rah-bou), or holy man. The Grand Marabout at Touba is held in as much awe by his followers as the Pope is by Catholics. He has secular as well as religious influence and no one high or low would make a major decision without consulting him. This is at odds with orthodox Islam, which says that Allah is directly accessible to each believer without intermediaries. Senegalese Muslims hold that a disciple, or *talibé*, is also linked to Allah through his marabout. The Grand Marabout has only to say the word and his zealots will do it. If you're in Senegal during a Muslim holiday or the Great Magal, head for Touba. Go to the palace of the Grand Caliph for his benediction. Otherwise, you may be treated in the streets with disdain. You'll see the faithful offering him gifts, while he spits into their hands as a sign of blessing.

GEOGRAPHY

Senegal is the western-most country on the African continent. It is a country of monotonous flat plains in the middle of the arid, sandy Sahel. The only mountains are in the far south-east along the Guinea border – the northern tip of the Fouta Djalon plateau – and further east along the Malian border. The country's major game park, the Parc National du Niokolo-Koba, is here as well. In the forested south-west, the popular Casamance area, is one of the country's most beautiful stretches of beaches – Cap Skirring. You'll also find Ziguinchor, the attractive regional capital along the Casamance river. To get there overland, you'll have to pass through The Gambia, which looks like a bent nail in the side of Senegal.

In the north the Senegal River, originating in the Fouta Djallon, forms the dividing line with Mauritania. St-Louis is the old colonial city at the river's mouth. The wide flood plains are one of the country's most productive areas, and are cultivated with peanuts and millet as the waters retreat. Dakar, the capital, is on a rocky plateau overlooking the ocean, roughly half-way between St-Louis and Ziguinchor.

CLIMATE

Dakar is one of the cooler, breezier spots in West Africa. If you go to rocky Cap Vert peninsula 15 km north-west of Dakar, a popular beach area, you'll find it even breezier. Average temperatures lie between 18°C and 31°C, and the rainy season only lasts three months, from July through September. In the Casamance, the rainfall is two to three times heavier and longer, from late May to early October. November to March is the best time to visit, but don't be surprised if the skies are cloudy from the dusty harmattan winds that blow down from the desert.

VISAS

Nationals of Belgium, Denmark, France, West Germany, Italy, Luxembourg and the Netherlands do not need visas. If you arrive by plane, visas are issued at Dakar airport and are valid for three months. You're supposed to have an onward airline ticket, but this is rarely enforced. Visas are not issued at the borders. You can get Senegalese visas in all neighbouring countries except Mali; the French embassy there does not issue them. Some travellers without visas have made it into Senegal overland from Mali via the Bamako-Dakar train and from Mauritania via the Rosso border. If you do this, you risk big hassles with the police.

In Dakar you can get visas to all neighbouring countries. The Spanish embassy issues visas to the Canary Islands and the British embassy to Kenya and Sierra Leone.

Diplomatic Missions Abroad
Abidjan, Addis Ababa, Algiers, Banjul, Berne, Bissau, Bonn, Brasilia, Brussels, Cairo, Conakry, Geneva, Lagos, Libreville, London, New York, Niamey, Nouakchott, Ottawa, Paris, Rabat, Rome, Stockholm, Tokyo, Tunis, Washington, Yaoundé.

MONEY
US$1 = 287 CFA
£1 = 537 CFA

The unit of currency is the West African CFA. Currency declaration forms are not used. Despite regulations prohibiting the export of more than CFA 25,000, exporting CFA is almost never a problem unless you're found with large quantities. In Ziguinchor and near the Gambian border, you'll find a black market in Ghanaian dalasi. The bank at Dakar airport is open 24 hours every day; the No 8 SOTRAC bus passes there. Banking hours: Monday to Friday 8 to 11.30 am and 2.30 to 4.30 pm. Banks: Citibank, BIAO (Banque Internationale pour l'Afrique Occidentale), BICIS (Banque Internationale pour le Commerce et l'Industrie Senegalaise), BCS (Banque Commerciale du Senegal), USB (Union Senegalaise de Banque).

LANGUAGE
French is the official language and Wolof the principal African language. Expressions in Wolof:

Good morning	ya-MAN-gah fah-NIN
Good evening	ya-MAN-gah YEN-lou
How are you?	nang-gah-DEF
Thank you	jair-ruh-JEF
Goodbye	mahn-gah-DEM

GENERAL INFORMATION
Health
A yellow fever vaccination is required, but not cholera. For emergencies, try Hôpital Principal (tel 217780/214919) or Clinique Hubert (tel 216848), both in Dakar. Two general practitioners who speak English are Dr Hassan Bahsoun (tel 213614) and Dr Majdi Kaouk (tel 225612). For a night pharmacy (*pharmacie de garde*) in Dakar, consult *Le Soleil*.

Security
Petty thieves are a major problem everywhere in Dakar, especially at night when the dark streets make Dakar a pickpocket's paradise. In the beach areas, even muggings have been reported. Beware of people trying to give you a gift. Petty thefts are common at all the major beaches.

Business Hours
Business: weekdays 8 am to 12 noon and 2.30 to 6 pm, Saturday 8 am to 12 noon. Government: same except closed Saturday.

Public Holidays
1 January, 1 February, 4 April (National Day), Easter Monday, 1 May, End of Ramadan (17 May 1988, 11 May 1989), Ascension Thursday, Whit Monday, Tabaski (25 July 1988, 14 July 1989), 15 August, 1 November, Mohammed's Birthday, 25 December. The major public holidays are National Day, the end of Ramadan and Tabaski. The Grand Magal is 40 days following Ramadan.

Photography

Taking photographs in Senegal is not a problem. The government here is the least uptight in this respect in West Africa. You can even take photographs of the presidential mansion. Nevertheless, avoid photographing military installations.

Time, Phone & Telex

When it's noon in Senegal, it's noon in London and 7 am in New York. International telephone connections to/from Dakar are good. *Telesenegal* at 6 Rue Wagane-Diouf is open 7 am to midnight and you can dial direct. Hôtel Teranga in Dakar has public telex facilities. Telegrams can be sent from any post office.

GETTING THERE
Air

From Europe, there are direct flights from Brussels, Frankfurt, Geneva, London, Madrid, Paris, Rabat and Rome. From New York, you'll have to fly on Air Afrique; Pan Am has discontinued service. There are also flights to/from Rio de Janeiro. In Africa, there are direct connections to/from Rabat, Las Palmas and Addis Ababa as well as flights to most capital cities in West Africa and the coastal cities of Central Africa.

Car

A carnet de passage is no longer required. For free, the customs office will give you a 30-day, renewable *passavant de douane*. They'll accept your international insurance as well. The road system in Senegal is excellent. Typical driving times from Dakar are six hours to Ziguinchor via the Transgambian Highway (longer via Banjul), five hours to Tambacounda, five or six hours to Banjul (Gambia), three hours to St-Louis and seven or eight hours to Nouakchott (Mauritania). If you're heading to/from Conakry (Guinea), a three-day trip in the dry season, anticipate terrible roads in Guinea, especially June to October.

Most travellers heading to/from Mali

put their vehicles on the train or go via Mauritania because the road between Tambacounda and Nioro (Mali) is in terrible condition and almost impossible to pass during the rainy season. If you want to take the express train from Dakar, you'll have to reserve a week to a month in advance; expect to pay about CFA 120,000 for the vehicle alone. Most people drive to Tambacounda and put their vehicle on the much slower non-express, a trip that can take up to three days with a long stop in Kayes. Get your carnet de passage stamped there. The cost is roughly a third less – about CFA 75,000 for a vehicle weighing 1.5 tonnes or less (more for heavier ones) and CFA 11,000 for passengers. Thievery is a big problem, so everyone sleeps in their cars.

Bush Taxi

To/from Gambia Dakar-Ziguinchor via the Transgambian Highway (cutting The Gambia mid-way) in a bush taxi (CFA 4500) takes seven to 10 hours, depending on the wait for the ferry, and longer for buses (about CFA 3000). To Banjul (Gambia), you can apparently save money by taking the *GPTC* (Gambia Passenger Transport Corp) bus to Barra, the ferry point for Banjul. One leaves Dakar every day or every other day in the morning, reportedly from LeClerc bus terminal.

To/from Mauritania Dakar-Nouakchott (Mauritania) takes roughly 10 hours and, altogether, costs about CFA 7000, with a change of taxis at Rosso (the border/river crossing). The ferry operates from 7 am to 12.30 pm and 3 to 5 pm.

Train

To/from Mali The Dakar-Bamako express takes about 30 hours, sometimes up to 36 hours. There are actually two trains. If possible, avoid the older Malian one. The Senegalese train is relatively new and one of the best in West Africa; it has a dining car and berths (*couchettes*). Berths on both trains are for two people only. Take toilet paper. Trains leave Dakar on Wednesday (Senegalese train) and Friday (Malian train) at 10.30 am. They leave Bamako the same days. The cost to Bamako of both trains is the same: CFA 27,600 for 1st class with air-con and berth, CFA 18,400 for 1st class and CFA 11,700 for 2nd class. Second class cannot be reserved, so arrive early to get a seat. There are no student discounts. When they take your passport at the Malian border, don't expect to see it again until Kayes.

Those travelling on the cheap can save money by hitchhiking the Dakar-Tambacounda stretch, the only problem is that the train is 150% full when it arrives there around 10 pm. Another way to save is getting off in Kayes (Mali) and taking the decrepit, daily local on to Bamako for only about CFA 3000.

Boat

For a freighter headed for Europe or along the coast of West Africa, ask at Socopao (tel 222416) or Croisières Paquet (tel 212621/214040) in Dakar. Expect to pay about double the airfare.

GETTING AROUND

Air *Air Senegal* (tel 210970) at the Place de l'Indépendance in Dakar has twice weekly flights to Simenti (the game park area) and daily flights to Ziguinchor in the southern Casamance area, five of which continue to Cap Skirring, the beach area. Air Senegal makes reservations on all its flights only when someone walks into their office; they will not accept reservations by phone or computer. If you're with a tour group, no problem – reservations are usually made through a local agent. If not, even though your Dakar-Ziguinchor ticket may read 'OK', your name will not be on the list. If your travel agent knows an agent in Dakar who will make the reservation personally, you're in luck. Regardless, go immediately to the Air Senegal office upon arriving in Dakar. To charter a plane, contact *Air Afric Service* (tel 200388).

Bush Taxi

Taxis de brousse in Senegal are of two types – Peugeot 504s and the inferior buses and minibuses, which are slower and typically about a third cheaper.

The Peugeots are as fast as private vehicles – once they're are on the way. Tourists should not shy away from taking them. They seat only three people across, not four as in some poorer countries, and you can always buy an extra seat. If the driver honours you with the front seat, remember it's more dangerous.

Train

If you're headed for St-Louis, for lots of laughs, take the seven-hour train – twice as long as the bush taxis but cheaper, about CFA 1300 for 2nd class. It leaves daily from Dakar at 1.40 pm and from St-Louis at 7 am. In Dakar, *la gare* is only a 10-minute walk from the Place de l'Indépendance.

Boat

The *Casamance Express* plows the ocean between Dakar and Ziguinchor, leaving Ziguinchor on Thursday mornings at 10 am and Dakar on Fridays at 6 pm – every two out of three weeks. The trip takes 16 hours. Deck costs about CFA 3500 and pullman (seats with head rests and air-con) about CFA 5000. A 1st-class cabin with air-con, access to the restaurant and berths with two, four, or six beds costs about CFA 16,500, 13,000 and 11,000 per person, respectively. Contact Sun Travel (tel 218073) in Dakar and L'Inscription Maritime (tel 917161) near the train station in Ziguinchor.

Africatour's elegant cruise boat, *African Queen*, sails from Dakar to the Casamance area and back, taking about eight days. Transcap Senegal (tel 213928) has the details. Or charter the 23-metre *Gitana III* and go wherever you want; see La Brocante (tel 225322) at 22 Rue Jules Ferry in downtown Dakar.

Dakar

With tree-lined streets and a relatively small downtown section, Dakar is uncrowded and easy to walk around despite its population of almost one million inhabitants. The centre is the Place de l'Indépendance, around which you'll find Hôtel Teranga, Bruno's African art shop, Citibank, Hôtel de l'Indépendance, Librairie Clairafrique, Air Senegal, Air Afrique and Cinéma Le Paris. Streets radiate from the plaza, two of the principal ones being Avenue Roume in the direction of the Presidential Palace and Avenue Pompidou (formerly Avenue Ponty and still called by that name), lined with shops, cafés and bars. Near either end of Pompidou, you'll find one of the city's two major markets – Marché Sandaga and, towards the port, Marché Kermel (a block off Pompidou).

About 18 km to the north-west of Dakar is the Pointe des Almadies, a favourite weekend retreat for Africans and expatriates. You'll find the major beaches, the Meridien, N'Gor Island, seafood restaurants and the airport. All along the Corniche Rd, which runs along the Atlantic Ocean from Dakar towards Almadies and the airport, you'll see joggers. The city's nicest residential section is also along this road.

Despite Dakar's charm, some people hate it. There are two reasons for this – thieves and pestering traders who won't take no for an answer. The traders can ruin your walk around town. No technique works perfectly. Some people refuse to speak or look them in the eye. A better technique may be to look very closely at their goods, then make it quite clear you don't like anything.

Information

Embassies Canada (BP 3373, tel 210290), Cape Verde (downtown at 1 Rue de Denan, tel 211873), France (BP 4035, tel 210181), Gambia (11 Rue de Thiong, tel 214476), West Germany (BP 2100, tel 224884), Guinea (Route de Ouakam, tel 218606), Guinea-Bissau (in the suburbs at 6 Rue Tolbiac, tel 215922), Japan (BP 3140, 210141), Mali (46 Boulevard de la République, tel 220473), Mauritania (37 Boulevard du General de Gaulle, tel 214343), Netherlands (BP 3262, tel 220483), Switzerland (BP 1772, 225848), USA (BP 49, tel 214296/213681), UK (BP 6025, tel 217392, telex 517).

Other embassies include: Algeria, Argentina, Belgium, Brazil, Cameroon, Egypt, Ethiopia, Gabon, Italy, Ivory Coast, Niger, Nigeria, Portugal, Spain, Tunisia, Zaire.

Bookstores & Supermarkets Dakar has some good bookstores, but few books are in English. Three of the best are *Librairie Clairafrique* on the plaza next to the old Chamber of Commerce building, *Librairie Universitaire* on Avenue Pompidou two blocks off the plaza, and *Librairie aux Quatres Vents* (tel 210176) two blocks further down at 91 Rue Blanchot, 30 metres from Avenue Pompidou.

For a modern supermarket downtown, there's *Score* on Avenue Sarraut near the Novotel, and *Ranch Filfili* at 18 Boulevard de la République, several blocks from the Presidential Palace.

Travel Agencies You'll find three agencies on or just off the Place de l'Indépendance: Senegal Sun Travel (2 Place de l'Indépendance, tel 218073, telex 3371), Senegal Tours (5 Place de l'Indépendance, BP 3126, tel 214040, telex 687), Socopao Voyages (51 Avenue Albert-Sarraut, BP 233, tel 222576/222416, telex 521). Others are nearby: Transcap (24 Boulevard Pinet-Laprade, BP 58, tel 216063/213928, telex 484), Inter Tourisme (3 Allees Delmas, tel 224529, telex 683), Transtours Senegal (Rue Victor Hugo, Maginot Building, BP 8117, tel 212676). Inter Tourisme, for example, has three-day, all-inclusive tours of the Casamance for

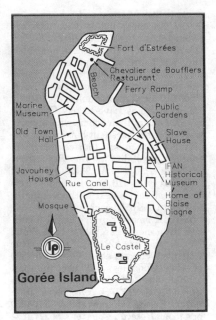

Fort d'Estrées

Chevalier de Boufflers
Restaurant

Beach

Ferry Ramp

Marine
Museum

Public
Gardens

Old Town
Hall

Slave
House

Javouhey
House

Rue Canel

IFAN
Historical
Museum
Home of
Blaise
Diagne

Mosque

Le Castel

(IP)

Gorée Island

about CFA 65,000, Joal and Fadiouth for CFA 10,000, Lac Rose for CFA 5,000.

Things to See

Many people start out with a visit to the two major markets, **Marché Sandaga** and **Marché Kermel** (see Things to Buy). Two of the most beautiful colonial buildings in West Africa are in Dakar – the **Presidential Palace**, built in 1906 and six short blocks from the Place de l'Indépendance along Avenue Roume, and the **train station**. You can take photographs of both. Another must is a stroll along the **Corniche Rd** in the direction of the university, which you can do following a visit to **Le Village Artisanal**.

Near the museum, the **Cathedral** is open to the public daily. The striking **Grande Mosquée**, built in 1964, no longer allows visitors, but go there anyway to walk through **La Medina**, the most African section of town – picturesque.

Musée d'Art Négro-Africain (IFAN African Art Museum)

This museum (tel 214015) is one of the best African art museums in West Africa. It is a testimony to ex-President Senghor's interest in promoting African art and culture. You can even take photographs. Open Tuesday to Sunday, 8 am to 12 noon and 2 to 6 pm, it's attached to the University of Dakar and is a centre for black studies. One floor displays the Senegalese collection. The second floor displays art from other areas, including a good collection of African masks and statues, Ashanti weights and royal bronzes from Benin. It is a good km from the Place de l'Indépendance at Place Tascher, on the same street as the US embassy.

Gorée Island

Dakar's major attraction is Gorée Island, about three km from Dakar in the Atlantic and probably the most famous of all the West African slave centres. Only 28 hectares, it is wonderfully peaceful, with 1000 inhabitants, no asphalt roads, no cars, no bicycles. You'll find numerous 18th century homes with wrought-iron balconies (including one lived in by a retired US ambassador), the old town hall, the former home of Blaise Daigne, Le Fort d'Estrées (now a jail) near the ferry ramp, and Le Castel, a plateau at the far end of the island where you can get a good view of the island and Dakar. Next to the ferry ramp is the beach, popular on the weekends when you'll see people sunning, boys jumping off the sea wall into the greenish-clear water, and pleasure boats from Dakar.

A visit to Gorée, however, is no light-hearted affair. The **Maison des Esclaves** (Slave House), built by the Dutch in 1776, is where slaves were stored for three months or so awaiting shipment to the Americas. If you take the 3 pm tour, you'll meet the delightful and amusing curator, Jo N'Diaye, who has made this his life's work. He'll explain how slaves were stuffed into pens six by 10 metres, inspected and priced as though they were animals, how the obstinate ones were chained to the walls and sea water piped into their rooms to keep them partially submerged, how the slaves fought for food, the weaker ones dying on the island and being fed to the fish, and how the slaves were branded with the shipping company's insignia and packed like sardines into the holds of ships. There are two other museums – the IFAN Historical Museum across the street from the Slave house and the Musée Maritime. All are open 8.30 am to 12 noon and 2.30 to 6 pm except on Monday.

On the island you can eat good seafood at the wonderful restaurant near the ferry ramp – *Chevalier de Boufflers* (tel 225364). Closed Tuesday evening and all day Wednesday, they have a terrace overlooking the harbour. For cheap beers, try *Chez Michou* behind the historical museum, or the bar facing the ferry ramp. It is also possible to find cheap accommodation on Gorée, see Places to Stay.

Les Almadies

One of Dakar's major attractions is the beach area, Les Almadies, a 20-minute drive from Dakar. On Sunday afternoons, half of Dakar seems to be there, at the beach next to the Meridien or on N'Gor Island, several hundred metres away. At Almadies, you'll find several excellent restaurants and, nearby, some rocky beaches and the Club Med. Several km away, next to the Meridien hotel, there's a popular sandy beach, packed on weekends, and some more restaurants nearby. Other, less crowded beaches are between the Meridien and the Lighthouse. From the Meridien, you'll see N'Gor, a small island which you can reach in five minutes by pirogue (CFA 200) from the beach. There, many of the bathers are Senegalese; you can rent huts with kitchens for about CFA 5000 to CFA 7500 a night, depending on your bargaining skills.

Places to Stay – bottom end

Of the dirt cheap hotels downtown, my favourite is *Hôtel Le St-Louis* (tel 225423), a large old Portuguese house at 68 Rue Félix-Faure with a pleasant central patio, about five blocks from the plaza. The rooms without air-con (about CFA 5500/6000 for singles/doubles) are usually full, so you may have to pay CFA 1500 more for one of their rooms with air-con. Meals here are excellent but not cheap – CFA 2500 for a set four-course meal. Another possibility is the *Restaurant l'Auberge Rouge* (tel 217256), several blocks away at 116 Rue Blanchot, with seven clean rooms next to the restaurant for about CFA 6500 each.

You can, however, find cheaper rooms, with little more than a hard bed. *Hôtel Provençal* (tel 221069), at 17 Rue Malenfant, charges about CFA 4000/4500 for singles/doubles and has the best location, just off the plaza. *Hôtel du Marché* (tel 215771), one block from Marché Kermel, charges about CFA 4500 for a room. *Hôtel du Coq* (tel 225522) at 34 Rue Raffenel, and *Mon Logis* (tel 220371) at 57 Rue Blanchot, three blocks off Avenue Pompidou, are about as cheap as you'll find downtown – about CFA 4000 a room.

Around Dakar For really cheap accommodation, try Gorée Island. With a little searching, you can reportedly find people who rent rooms for CFA 400 or so – what you pay for tax alone at any hotel.

Another possibility is *Campement Touristique de Malika Peul*, 25 km north-east of Dakar and on the ocean. The cost per person is only about CFA 1700; they serve inexpensive meals as well. To get to Malika (seven km north-east of Thiaroye), take Sotrac bus No 21 on Avenue Lamine-Gueye in Dakar. Renting a hut on N'Gor Island might also be interesting, but it'll cost more even if you bargain well.

Places to Stay – middle

Two of the best medium priced hotels are the *Croix du Sud* (tel 212947, telex 576) and the *Nina* (tel 212230, telex 3105) both in the heart of town only one block from the Place de l'Indépendance. The Croix du Sud is a well-managed, old-style hotel with a French ambience, one of the best restaurants in town and, on request, small refrigerators in your room. The small Nina, at 43 Rue du Dr Thèze, has a mixed African/expatriate clientele and an active bar. Singles/doubles cost CFA 15,500/18,500 at the Croix du Sud and CFA 13,500/17,300 at the Nina. Both accept credit cards (AE, Visa, D). The brand new (Al Baraka (tel 225532), on Rue A K Bourgi, charges CFA 12,400/14,800 for singles/doubles but is not as centrally located.

Two more moderately priced hotels are *Hôtel de la Paix* (tel 222978), with decent singles/doubles for CFA 10,500/13,000 (CFA 1000 more for many rooms), and the similarly priced *Hôtel du Plateau* (tel 221526, telex 3252, cards AE, CB). Five blocks from the plaza at 38 Rue Assane Ndoye in a lively but dark area, the Paix has a first-rate restaurant. Others prefer the Plateau, near the US embassy at 68 Rue Jules Ferry, because it's in a safer area and still within walking distance of downtown. If you want to be in the dead centre of town, try the popular *Hôtel Central* (tel 217217) at 16 Avenue Pompidou (formerly Ponty), one block from the plaza. Their entirely renovated singles/doubles cost about CFA 9000/11,000.

The award for the best hotel in town for the price goes to *Hôtel Atlantic* (tel 216380), a block away at 52 Rue Dr Thèze and ever-popular with world travellers and Africans alike. The mattresses sag, but it's a well-managed hotel with spotless rooms, air-con that works and hot water. It costs about CFA 6500/7500 for singles/doubles. If it's full, try *Hôtel Farid* (tel 216719), several blocks away at 52 Rue Vincens. Their rooms without air-con cost about the same (more expensive with air-con), plus the restaurant serves some of the best Lebanese fare in town.

Places to Stay - top end
Beach-lovers stay at the *Méridien* complex near the airport, a good 20-minute drive from downtown and considered by many people to be the city's best hotel. It's really three hotels in one, the best being the *N'Gor*, followed by the *Diarama*, both with magnificent views. The simple, thatched-roof bungalows at the *Village Huts* are an excellent buy because you get to use all the facilities of the Méridien for 33 to 50% less. Nearby, Club Med's action-packed, architecturally striking *Les Almadies* accepts travellers for one or two nights whenever one of its 300 rooms is available.

Of the four top hotels downtown, Sofitel's 264-room *Teranga* is the favourite of the tour groups. It's also the most centrally located, at one end of the Place de l'Indépendance. From the pool, you'll have a magnificent view of the sea. The *Novotel* is about five blocks off the plaza, modern and not particularly interesting. A much better buy for the money is the more reasonably priced *Lagon II*, just down the hill from the Novotel and right next to the sea. It's like being on an ocean liner. It has one of the best bars and restaurants in town, top bartenders and free windsurfers.

Many people prefer Frantel's *Le Savana*, which has a beautiful setting on a cliff overlooking the ocean, an olympic-size pool and many other amenities, without the hustle and bustle of the Teranga and closer to town than the Méridien. If you don't mind being three km from the heart of town, it's a good choice. A bad choice would be the tall *Hôtel Indépendance*, a poorly managed, over-priced hotel right on the plaza. The pool on top is its only plus.

Méridien (tel 231005, telex 682), CFA 30,600/33,200 for singles/doubles at the N'Gor (CFA 3100 to CFA 3700 more for a sea-view room), CFA 26,240/30,600 at the Diarama (CFA 2700 to CFA 3500 more for a sea-view room), CFA 17,000 a room at the Village Huts (tel 200540), pools, tennis, windsurfers, sailboats, horseback

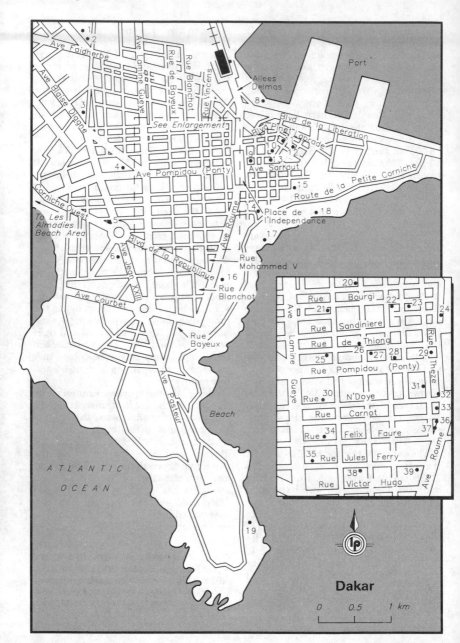

Dakar

0   0.5   1 km

1	Grande Mosquée	20	Hôtel Mon Logis
2	Peace Corps	21	La Pizzeria
3	Mauritanian Silversmiths	22	Hôtel Farid & Restaurant
4	Marché Sandago	23	Chez Vous
5	Ifan Museum	24	Hôtel Provençal
6	US Embassy	25	New James Restaurant
7	Train Station	26	Keur N'Deye Restaurant
8	Gorée Island Ferry	27	Al Kayam Restaurant
9	Hôtel Croix du Sud & La Region	28	Librairie Universitaire
	du Fleuve Restaurant	29	Hôtel Indépendance
10	Marché Kermel & du Marché	30	Hôtel de la Paix
11	Le Dagorne/Le Vietnam Restaurant	31	Hôtel Atlantic
12	Safari 2000 Restaurant	32	Bruno's Art Shop
13	Le Sarraut Restaurant	33	Hôtel Nina
14	Hôtel Teranga	34	Hôtel Le St-Louis
15	Novotel	35	Black & White Nightclub
16	Presidential Palace	36	La Trastevère Restaurant
17	Lagon I Restaurant	37	Le Bilboquet Restaurant
18	Hôtel Lagon II	38	L'Auberge Rouge Restaurant
19	Hôtel Le Savana	39	Keur Samba Nightclub

riding, life-size chess game, miniature golf, shops, nightclub, casino nearby, Eurocar, cards AE, D, Visa.

Les Almadies (tel 200951, telex 234), about CFA 30,000 a person, pool, tennis, windsurfers, etc, cards AE.

Teranga Sofitel (tel 231044, telex 469), CFA 28,500/30,000 for singles/doubles (CFA 3000 more for a sea-view room), long pool, tennis, sauna, Hertz, shops, nightclub, cards AE, D, Visa.

Le Savana (tel 226023, telex 3331), CFA 32,000/34,000 for singles/doubles, pool, tennis, nightclub, windsurfers, sauna, gym, cards AE, D, Visa.

Novotel Dakar (tel 218849, telex 3363), CFA 27,500/29,000 for singles/doubles, pool, tennis, cards AE, D, Visa.

Lagon II (tel 211780, telex 214), CFA 20,000/22,000, windsurfers, Eurocar, cards AE, D, Visa, CB.

Hôtel Indépendance (tel 231019, telex 454), about CFA 22,400/26,800 for singles/doubles, pool, cards AE, D, Visa.

Places to Eat

Cheap Eats In addition to the cheap African restaurants and the Lebanese *Al Khayam*, you can get a splendid, home-style Portuguese meal at *Chez Nenette* on Rue Vincens, a block behind Hôtel Atlantic as the crow flies. A three-course meal costs CFA 1600 - highly recommended. For meals half this price, try *Gargotte Diarama* at 56 Rue Félix-Faure for steak, chips, salad, kidneys, potatoes, etc. For rock bottom prices, CFA 300 to CFA 500 a meal, try one of the many small restaurants along Rue Sandiniery or Avenue Jean Jaurés. In the Meridien area, you'll find an African restaurant near La Madrague restaurant which serves meals for about CFA 1500. At Almadies beach is a nem stand with cheap nems and Vietnamese soups.

African Senegal is known for having some of the best cuisine in West Africa, and Dakar is an excellent place to sample West African cuisine. In the Food section in the Facts for the Visitor chapter, you'll find the recipes for *poulet yassa*, chicken with onions and lemon juice, and *mafé* (mah-fay), a meat stew in peanut sauce. Other specialties include *tiebou dienne* (chey-bou-jen), the 'national dish of Senegal' consisting of rice, fish and a variety of vegetables, and *bassi-salété*, a Senegalese couscous made with millet. If you don't like hot dishes, try the poulet yassa.

Downtown, there are four good choices. *La Region du Fleuve* is a favourite of many – a different African specialty every day for only CFA 1400 to CFA 1600, plus à la carte selections. It's one block off the plaza at 15 Rue Dantec, behind Hôtel Croix du Sud. It is closed Wednesday. The inexpensive, highly recommended *Keur N'Deye* (tel 214973) is at 68 Rue Vincens, two blocks off Avenue Pompidou. Open every day, they serve meals for about CFA 1300. *Restaurants des Plates Africaines* at 95 Rue de Bayeux is similar. The city's best African restaurant, *Keur Samba* (tel 216045) at 13 Rue Jules Ferry near Le Bilboquet, is fairly expensive and also has a jazz club. In the Meridien beach area, try *M'Baye Barrick* (closed Monday) at Almadies beach, which has a rustic outdoor setting and strolling kora players.

French What's amazing about some of Dakar's French restaurants is the low cost. For the price, the following three restaurants offer some of the best value in all of West Africa, none are more than a 10-minute walk from the plaza: *Le Dagorne* (tel 222080) at 11 Rue Dagorne behind the Marché Kermel, *L'Auberge Rouge* (tel 217256) at 116 Rue Blanchot (between the plaza and the US embassy as the crow flies), and *Le Bilboquet* at 20 Avenue Roume, between the plaza and the Presidential Palace. At all three, you can get a three-course meal for CFA 3000. The immensely popular Dagorne (closed Monday) has a bustling, energetic atmosphere, the Auberge Rouge (closed Wednesday) a garden setting and the Bilboquet (closed Sunday) a charming sidewalk setting. The *Hôtel de la Paix* (closed Sunday) also gets good reviews and has a large menu, including a CFA 3000 special. If you're in the Meridien area, head for popular *Ramatou* nearby, run by the brother of the owners of Le Dagorne.

Dakar's best French restaurants, however, are expensive. *Safari 2000* (tel 21 2719), at 4 Rue Parent a block from Marché Kermel and closed Monday, gets top marks from many local expatriates. The three runner-ups are all in the same area, roughly between the plaza and the US embassy: *Le Bambou* at 19 Rue Victor Hugo and open every day, the sparkling new *La Colisée* at the corner of Avenue Lamine-Gueye and Rue Félix-Faure and closed Monday, and the new *La Cambrouse* on Boulevard de la République, several blocks from the Presidential Palace. Among the hotels, *Lagon II* is also good.

Seafood Most of the restaurants known for serving good seafood are at Les Almadies and near the Meridien. Downtown, three good choices are *Safari 2000*, where seafood is the speciality, *Lagon I*, a five-minute walk down from the Teranga, and *Hôtel La Croix du Sud*, a block off the plaza, which specialises in seafood. Of these, Lagon I is probably the most popular because of its location next to the water, and the slightly lower prices. *Le Chevalier de Boufflers* (tel 225364) on Gorée Island is another good choice. It is closed Tuesday evening and all day Wednesday. The last ferry returns around 11 pm.

At Almadies beach, if you want lobster, head for the ever-popular, moderately priced *La Pointe des Almadies* (tel 200140), closed Thursday. For a greater seafood selection, try the similarly priced *L'Armatan* (tel 200555) next door, open until midnight every day except Monday. For the best seafood and a range of choices, you'll have to pay a little more – either at *La Madrague* (tel 200223) next to the Meridien and open every day, with superb service and a roaring fire in the winter, or *Le Virage* (tel 200657) between the Meridien and the airport. Closed Monday, they are known for their excellent bouillabaisse and the splendid ocean view.

Vietnamese Dakar has four fine Vietnamese restaurants, all reasonably priced and similar in quality. *La Pointe des Almadies* (tel 200140), closed Thursday, is the most popular restaurant in the Almadies area and highly recommended. In addition to Vietnamese food, they serve good seafood, steaks, chops and excellent banana splits. On Saturday and Sunday, you have to reserve.

The other three are downtown. *Le Samson*, between the plaza and the cathedral at 61 Rue Assane Ndyoe and closed Thursday, has a very simple setting and is quite popular. *Le Hanoi* (tel 213269) nearby at 85 Rue Carnot, has a more pleasant ambience but a limited menu. For real home-style Saigon cooking, try the tiny *Le Vietnam* on the other side of the plaza at 9 Rue Dagorne near Marché Kermel. It's open every day.

Lebanese The favourite of Peace Corps volunteers and travellers is *Al Khayam* (closed Sunday), on Avenue Pompidou opposite Le Bruxelles ice cream parlour. For CFA 1200 to CFA 2000, you can get a filling meal; the wine is cheap as well. The best Lebanese fare, however, is served at *Hôtel Farid* nearby – two blocks off Avenue Pompidou at 52 Rue Vincens and closed Wednesday.

Italian One of Dakar's best restaurants for the price, with the best pizza in town and other Italian fare, is the popular *La Pizzeria* (tel 210926). It is open to 5 am! Not easy to find, it's several blocks off Avenue Pompidou at 47 Rue A K Bourgi and closed Monday. *La Trastevere* (tel 214920), 26 Rue Mohammed V, is closed Tuesday, moderately expensive and nothing special.

Pastry Shops Dakar has some excellent pastry shops/ice cream parlours, most of them open to midnight and very popular: *Le Bruxelles* on Avenue Pompidou, four blocks off the plaza; *La Palmeraie N'Diogonal* nearby at 20 Avenue Pompidou; *Gentina* on Avenue Sarraut, a block off the plaza; *Candy* on Avenue Roume across from the Bilboquet, and *Lutétia* across from the Cathedral.

Entertainment & Sports

Bars If you want to feel like you're on the QE II, try *Hôtel Lagon II*, where the bartenders are real professionals. There's nothing professional about the *Hôtel Indépendance*, but the top floor pool and bar affords a spectacular view of the city at sunset. Two of the better sidewalk cafés are *Le Bilboquet* on Avenue Roume and *Le Sarraut* on Avenue Sarraut, both two blocks off the plaza. For a sleazy bar with whores galore, try *Le Ponty Bar* on Avenue Pompidou.

Nightclubs To mingle with the African jet set, head for *Keur Samba* at 13 Rue Jules Ferry, near the Bilboquet. It's a fancy jazz club with great live music on weekends, mainly rich African clientele and expensive drinks. A half a block away on the same street is the poor man's alternative, an 'in' spot to some – *New Experience* – with mixed African and expatriate clientele, low prices and similar music. For more traditional African music, sometimes live, try *Les Toundes* (Caves) at 12 Rue Victor Hugo.

For a reputable nightclub with dancing, expect to pay a cover charge of CFA 3000 to CFA 4000; this always includes a drink. No one goes before 11 pm. Clients at the Keur Samba who want to dance go to the owner's other nightspot, the posh *Play Club* at 46 Rue Jules Ferry. Nearby at 32 Rue Victor Hugo is the equally fancy *King's Club*. Other possibilities include *Harry's Club* nearby on Boulevard de la République, *Le Mandingo* at the Teranga, *Aldo's* back of the Hôtel Indépendance and, a block away, the slightly cheaper *La Plantation*.

Dakar is famous for its sleazy nightclubs, foremost of which is *Chez Vous* on Rue Wagon Diouf, three blocks off Avenue Ponty, replete with a madame or two, a pool outside and rooms upstairs. The low price of the drinks, about CFA 1200, is a come-on. For African women, cheap drinks, a strobe-lit dance floor and Michael Jackson music, you've got innumerable choices – *Chez Claudette*, *Imperator* and *Verseau*, all likewise on Rue Wagon Diouf, plus *Tropicana* and *Cauri* nearby at 58 Rue A K Bourgi (near Rue Raffenel), and *Black & White* on the other side of Pompidou on Rue Bayeux, two blocks down from Hôtel de la Paix.

About the only choices in the Meridien area are the hotel's nightclub plus the nearby *Casino du Cap Vert* (tel 200974), which has a floor show in addition to gambling and is open every night. For CFA 10,000, you can go to the nearby *Club Med* from 5 pm to the wee hours of the morning. The price includes dinner, a show and the discotheque, and no reservation is required.

Theatres There are many cultural events at the Théâtre National Daniel Sorano (tel 213104) on Boulevard de la République, near the US embassy. However, they are seldom well-publicised, so it's best to check the box office. Of special interest are the Ensemble Instrumental, the Ballet National and the Théâtre National. Also watch out for the *Semaines Culturelles* when there are presentations by other African countries. The Centre Culturel Blaise Senghor on Boulevard Dial Diop is frequently the site of exhibits and cultural presentations, usually of African origin.

Dakar has some good movie theatres but they're all in French – Le Paris next to the Teranga and Le Vog and Le Plaza, both on Avenue Pompidou. Movies are at 6.30 and 9.15 pm. Consult *Le Soleil* for what's showing. The British Senegalese Institute at 18 Rue Juin has movies twice weekly in English.

Sports If you're looking for a beach not far from downtown, head for Plage Belle Aire beyond the train station. It has windsurfers and catamarans for rent, and a bar and entry costs CFA 300. Le Plage des Enfants is a more secluded beach of the Petit Corniche, beyond Hôtel Lagon II. In the Almadies area, the major beaches are between the Meridien and the Lighthouse.

Those looking for a more secluded beach prefer those between the Meridien and the airport.

All the major hotels except the Lagon II have pools. Non-guests cannot swim at the Teranga on a daily basis. The Savana has a superb, olympic-size pool and charges CFA 1500 for non-guests (CFA 2000 on weekends); the pool on top of the Indépendance is not as nice but may be cheaper. To rent a windsurfer, go to the Meridien, Lagon II, Teranga or Savana. The Cercle de la Voile (tel 221152) is a private sailing club and doesn't rent boats. You could also splurge and go to the Club Med. For about CFA 8000, you can spend the day there, 10 am to 5 pm. The price includes lunch and use of most of their facilities; no reservation is required.

Most of the major hotels also have tennis courts which non-guests can usually pay to use. The best players are at the Cercle de l'Union, a private club that's a five-minute walk down from the Teranga. You'll also find squash courts there. If you see the African squash pro and tell him you want to take a half-hour lesson, he'll probably manage to find a racket and get a court during off hours – for CFA 1000, it's in his interest.

Golfers can try the nine-hole Golf Club (tel 224069) in Cambérène, a CFA 3500 taxi ride from downtown Dakar and open year round. You may think the sand greens and terrible fairways are a joke but the locals don't. Non-members can play for about CFA 4000 weekdays and CFA 6000 weekends. Clubs cost CFA 3000.

If you're a jogger, join the Hash House Harriers on Saturday at 5.30 pm sharp for their weekly run through millet fields, African villages, crowded markets – you name it. The meeting place changes weekly and is published in the American Embassy's weekly rag, *La Palabra*. Bring CFA 1000 for the beer drinking festivities afterwards. Because Dakar is cool by African standards, you'll see more joggers here than anywhere else in West Africa. The favourite route is along the Corniche

Rd leading towards the university and Les Almadies.

Fishing & Scuba Diving Dakar is one of the best places in the world for landing sailfish (*espadon*). It's also an excellent place for blue marlin. Fishermen in large numbers fly in from France and the USA to try their luck. The season begins around the first of June for marlin and the end of June for sailfish, and usually lasts well into September. Other fish caught in the area include shark, barracuda, tuna, wahoo and tarpon.

The *Centre de Pêche Sportive* (BP 3132, tel 212858), at the Gorée Island pier, charter nine-metre boats for up to four people including all equipment for about CFA 150,000 during the high season, 1 June to October 31, and for about a third less during the rest of the year. From June to August, there are competitive events almost every Sunday. On weekends during the high season you have to reserve well in advance. If you're alone, they may be able to hook you up with somebody.

The coast off the Pointe des Almadies is one of the two best places along the West African coast for scuba diving (*plongee sous-marine*); the other is Sierra Leone. Around N'Gor Island, there are protected places where the water is fairly clear with lots of interesting fish. The waters are clearer from February to April. *Sports et Pêche* (tel 225464), at 13 Avenue Albert-Sarraut, and *La Civette* (tel 221320), at 6 Boulevard Pinet-Laprade, rent or sell equipment and can give you more details, as can the Centre de Pêche Sportive.

Things to Buy
Artisan Goods For high quality African art, you won't find a shop with better quality – or higher prices – in all of West Africa than *Bruno's* (tel 121519) at 2 Place de l'Indépendance. There's also a tiny gallery at 32 Rue Ndoye.

For cheaper souvenirs, take a five-minute taxi ride to *Le Village Artisanal de Soumbédioune* on the Corniche Rd.

A good time to go is in the late afternoon when the area next to the Artisanal comes alive with pirogues returning from their day's fishing. There is also a lively food market. You'll find a tremendous display of African crafts including wooden carvings, metal work, tablecloths, gold and silver jewellery, ivory, blankets, leather goods, dresses.

If you don't speak French, don't worry. Chances are the vendor will whip out a pocket calculator. The game begins by the seller typing in an outrageously high number, then your typing in an outrageously low one. Play continues by his lowering and your raising until a price is finally agreed upon. Giving a defiant take-it or leave-it expression each time, even sticking it in his face, are acceptable strategies.

For locally woven fabrics of high quality, head for *Caritas Tissage Traditional*, a traditional weavers' workshop on the Route de Ouakam, about four blocks beyond Hypersahm supermarket. You'll find tablecloths, bedspreads and cotton purses in material with intricate patterns. Prices are fixed. If you do this, stop at Hypersahm for a look at the artisan goods (gold, silver, etc) sold outside.

For gold and silver, the best place is *La Cour des Mours*, an alley at 69 Avenue Diagne with numerous Mauritanian silversmiths. It's priced by weight. Even if you're not interested in jewellery, a trip to this fascinating old district near Marché Sandaga is highly recommended. Rue Raffenel, nearby, also has a number of shops with rock bottom prices; you'll find them several blocks away from Avenue Pompidou.

For ordinary jewellery shops near the plaza with good prices, try *Galeries* at the Hôtel Indépendance, *Taj Mahal* several blocks down at 18 Avenue Pompidou, or *Bijouterie* at 7 Rue Félix-Faure, near the Teranga.

Markets You won't find as many artisan goods at the city's two major markets, but the atmosphere is more chaotic and fun. They are on either side of the plaza, the *Marché Kermel* four blocks towards the port and the *Marché Sandaga* six blocks up Avenue Pompidou. Marché Kermel closes early, around 1 am and has slightly higher prices and fewer artisan goods than the larger Marché Sandaga, which slows down from 12.30 to 3.00 pm and is the best place in town for fabrics. Note the baggy cotton pants being worn by some of the men. What they consider to be traditional dress is 'in' for foreigners, particularly women. You may see some ready-made for sale, but local expatriates, men and women, prefer to pick their own fabrics and have them tailor-made, usually within 24 hours.

Music Senegal is well known for its musicians, several of whom have made world tours. For records, try *Musiclub* at 60 Avenue Pompidou or *Le Radio Africaine* at 15 Avenue Jean Jaurès. The most popular are all men: Youssou N'Dour, Touré Kunda, Thionne Seck, Lamine Konté and the group Xalam (African jazz).

Getting There & Away
Air *Air Senegal* (tel 210970) flies twice weekly to Simenti and daily to Ziguinchor. Some of the Ziguinchor flights continue on to Cap Skirring.

Bush Taxi In Dakar, bush taxis leave from the Gare Routière (or Gare Pompierre) on Avenue Malick Sy. To get there, take bus No 5 at the Sandaga market facing Ciné Malik, or buses No 6 or No 18.

Bus The government GPTC buses are slower and less comfortable than the bush taxis, but considerably cheaper. Buses to Barra, the ferry point for The Gambia, leave from the Le Clerc terminal at 9.30 am.

Train The trains to Bamako in Mali leave Dakar at 10.30 am on Wednesday and Friday. Get there early to get a seat if you

travel 2nd class. See the Getting There section earlier in this chapter for more details.

The train to St Louis leaves at 1.40 pm daily. The bush taxis are much quicker.

Getting Around
Airport Transport At Dakar's Yoff airport, there's no departure tax. There's a bank open 24 hours with a good exchange rate, a poorly maintained hotel, restaurant, shops, Hertz, Avis and Eurocar. The Meridien hotel complex is only several km away.

Taxis have meters, but they are not used for trips to/from the airport. The official rates for taxis to downtown Dakar are posted in the luggage reception area – CFA 2500 during the day and CFA 3300 at night. However, bargaining is required. The drivers will swear to Allah that the posted rate is old. It isn't. You'll be doing well if you can negotiate them down to within CFA 500 of the posted rate. Locals do not tip; many tourists do. You could also walk to the main highway several hundred metres from the airport and wait for one of the cheap (CFA 100) SOTRAC buses headed for downtown.

Bus & Car Rapide You'll find cheap SOTRAC buses going all over town and the suburbs, including the Almadies area (No 7) and the airport (No 8). Destinations are marked on front. Most of them pass by the Place de l'Indépendance. Or, at the Gare Routière, take one of the similarly priced *car rapides* – dilapidated blue and yellow minibuses with 20 people stuffed like sardines and a maximum downhill speed of 60 km. To rent a bicycle, see Locavel (tel 218427) downtown at 109 Rue Carnot.

Taxis Taxis have meters and are cheap and plentiful. Rates double between midnight (drivers will say earlier) and 5 am. By the hour, they cost about CFA 1750 if you stay within the downtown/Almadies area. CFA 11,000 plus petrol is reasonable for an all-day rental, but they're not accustomed to this type of arrangement. Figuring out the petrol consumption is usually the only problem.

Ferry The ferry to Gorée Island takes 20 minutes, leaving Monday to Saturday at 6.30, 7 and 10 am, and 12.30, 2.30, 4, 5.30, 6.30, 8, 8.30 and 10.30 pm, with a slightly different schedule Sunday. Check the schedule in *Le Soleil* to be sure. The ferry ramp in Dakar is a 10-minute walk from the Place de l'Indépendance in the direction of the train station.

Car Rental Agencies in Dakar include Avis (71 Rue Blanchot, tel 213232/223726, telex 414), Hertz (Hôtel Teranga and 64 Rue Félix-Faure, tel 222016/215623, telex 655), Eurocar (Hôtel Lagon II and the Meridien, tel 221780, telex 214), Soatour (12 Allees Delmas, tel 210943), Senegalauto (19 Rue Blanchot, tel 224270), Car-Afric (25 Avenue Pompidou, tel 218867), Tourauto (29 Rue Assane Ndoye, tel 215719). One of the cheaper ones is Clinic Auto (58 Rue Vincens, tel 222425).

You'll also find Avis in Ziguinchor (Hôtel Albert and Rue de Gaulle, tel 911038), the airport in Cap Skirring (same tel) and at the Total petrol station (tel 571084) in Nianing on the Petite Côte.

AROUND DAKAR
Benedictine Monastery

If you've got wheels, take a Sunday morning drive to this monastery at Keur Moussa, about an hour's drive from Dakar off the road to Rufisque. The 10 am mass is a major attraction because of the music, which combines African musical instruments and Gregorian chants. After mass, the monks sell beautifully made koras (African-style harps), records and cassettes of their music, goat cheese and jams. For a tour, contact Senegal Tours.

Lac Rose

Another possibility is Lac Rose (or Lac Retba) – Senegal's answer to the Dead Sea. Surrounded by dunes, it's 10 times saltier than the ocean but suitable for

swimming – on your back, to keep the salt from burning your eyes. Everyone finds it unusual, but few find it interesting, which doesn't mean you won't. To get there (only 25 km) take the road towards Rufisque; you'll see the sign a few km beyond Thiaroye.

Places to Stay & Eat *Campement Niaga-Peul* charges CFA 5000 a person for one its huts and double that with full pension. The chances of it being full are nil. A single meal costs CFA 3000. On the way, just outside of Dakar, you'll pass by *Charlie's*, a good place for a French meal or chili con carne. What's unusual about Charlie's is its menagerie of exotic birds, monkeys, peacocks and snakes.

Thiès

If you go east to Thiès, an hour's drive from Dakar, don't miss seeing the world famous tapestries of Thiès made at the Manufactures Senegalaises des Arts Decoratifs (tel 511103). Established in 1966 under the guidance of French artists, the factory is but one of a series of artistic endeavours inspired by president Seneghor during the '60s, such as: l'École des Arts Plastiques, le Conservatoire de Musique et de Danse, l'École d'Architecture et d'Urbanisme, le Théâtre Daniel Sorano, le Musée Dynamique, etc.

The tapestries are based on paintings by Senegalese artists. Portraying the daily lives of fishermen, farmers and mothers with children, they are a sort of visual distillation of African life. Hundreds of paintings are submitted for consideration; only a few are chosen. The number of different coloured wools used is typically around 20, but can be as many as 100. Prices can range in the thousands of US dollars (about CFA 350,000 per square metre), but they're worth seeing even if you have no intention of buying. You can see them on weekends at the factory's exhibition room, which has an entrance fee of about CFA 750; they usually allow people to see them being made as well. Or

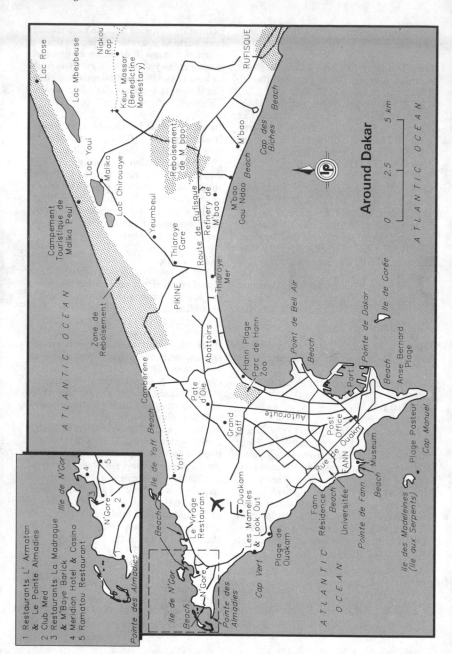

Around Dakar

0   2.5   5 km

1 Restaurants L' Armatan
   & Le Pointe Almadies
2 Club Med
3 Restaurants La Madrague
   & M'Baye Barick
4 Meridian Hotel & Casino
5 Ramatou Restaurant

ATLANTIC OCEAN

Pointe des Almadies

Ile de N'Gor

N'Gore

Ile de N'Gor

Beach

Ile de Yoff Beach

Cambérène

Zone de Reboisement

Campement Touristique de Malika Peul

Lac Rose

Lac Mbeubeuse

Niakou Rap

Keur Massar (Benedictine Monestary)

Lac Youi

Malika

Lac Chirouaye

Yeumbeul

Reboisement de M'bao

M'bao

RUFISQUE

Cap des Biches

Beach

M'bao
Gou Ndao Beach

Refinery de M'bao

Route de Rufisque

Thiaroye Gare

Thiaroye Mer

PIKINE

Pate d'Oie

Grand Yoff

Yoff

Abattoirs

Hann Plage
Parc de Hann Zoo

Point de Bell Air

Beach

Autoroute

Post Office

Rue de Ouakm

FANN

Pointe de Dakar

Port

Ile de Gorée

Anse Bernard Plage

Beach

Cap Manuel

Plage Pasteur

Museum

Fann Résidence

Universitée

Beach

Pointe de Fann

Fann Beach

Ile des Madeleines
(Ile aux Serpents)

Cap Vert

Plage de Ouakam

Ouakam

Les Mamelles & Look Out

Le Virage Restaurant

ATLANTIC OCEAN

ATLANTIC OCEAN

see them at their Dakar office (tel 211636), 38 Boulevard de la République. For a good place to eat in Thiès, ask for directions to the Vietnamese restaurant.

La Petite Côte

The 150-km stretch of coast starting south of Dakar is called the Petite Côte. The principal attractions are the beautiful beaches around M'Bour and the twin villages of Joal-Fadiouth.

SALI, M'BOUR & NIANING
Going south from Dakar, you'll pass Sali Portudal (75 km), M'Bour (82 km) and then Nianing (93 km). This is one of Senegal's most famous beach areas (the other is Cap Skirring). There is a series of ocean-front hotels packed with European tourists in the winter time, all 100% full around Christmas and Easter. People flock here for several reasons – clean white beaches, sports, guaranteed sunshine every day during the winter – experiencing a new culture is not one of them. The time to come here is May through October when you'll have the place to yourself and accommodation is cheaper.

Places to Stay & Eat
The seven major hotels all offer virtually the same activities – fishing, water skiing, sailing, windsurfing, tennis, swimming, pétanque and horse riding. The newer hotels are in Sali.

Sali Prices at the 92-room *Sali Novotel* (tel 571167, Dakar tel 210386, telex 7761) are typical – CFA 30,800/45,600 for singles/doubles with half board and CFA 33,300/50,600 with full board. The *Palm Beach* (tel 571137, telex 7755) has 246 rooms, a good Sunday lunch buffet and special weekend and off-season rates. The 226-room *Savana Koumba* (tel 571112) is another.

M'Bour In M'Bour, the largest town in the area with 35,000 inhabitants, there's the 70-room *Centre Touristique de la Petite Côte* (tel 571004), which is apparently much cheaper than the others, especially during the low season. It costs around CFA 7000 for a double with air-con.

Those on a low budget can take a 1½ hour bush taxi ride from Dakar and stay at *Relais 82*, a decaying, unmarked hotel at the northern entrance to M'Bour and run by a Frenchman. You can eat fairly cheaply in an agreeable setting at *Izabelita*.

Nianing In Nianing, you'll find several more – the 300-room *Club Aldiana* (tel 571084, telex 7756), which caters to Germans, and the 100-room *Domaine de Nianing* (tel 571085, Dakar tel 222573, telex 7786), a French-run camp. CFA 7500 will buy you entrance to the Aldiana and a buffet lunch with wine. AVIS is there as well.

JOAL-FADIOUTH
Fadiouth is touristy, picturesque and unusual. It is an island village of oyster and clam shells accumulated over the centuries. Shells are everywhere, embedded in the walls of houses and in the streets. Even the topsoil is shells. Joal is on the mainland and is the birthplace of ex-President Senghor – not an interesting town. The two are connected by a wooden bridge. Boys, however, will beg you to let them take you across in a canoe (*pirogue*). They can also take you to a small adjacent island where you'll see some curious basket-like granaries on stilts. If you're turned off by places overrun with tourists, Fadiouth may not be your cup of tea.

Places to Stay & Eat
The top hotel, with 10 comfortable air-con bungalows, is *Hôtel le Finnio* (tel 57 6112) on the southern outskirts of Joal overlooking the ocean. The restaurant serves some very good African dishes in addition to standard continental fare. *Relais 114*, in

the centre of Joal near the gare routière, is cheaper but still expensive. The *Mission Catholique*, 100 metres before the bridge over to Fadiouth, supposedly allows travellers to sleep in their garden hut.

The Sine-Saloum

Below the Petite Côte and inland along the Gambian border, the Sine-Saloum is one of the most beautiful regions of Senegal with sand islands, lagoons, mangrove swamps, sand dunes and open forest. There are numerous remote villages along the way, perfect for fishing and hunting. At the eastern end of the Saloum river, 190 km south-east of Dakar, Kaolack is the capital of the area, also the groundnut capital of Senegal. It's the base of many trips to the Sine-Saloum.

The major towns and villages besides Kaolack are Foundiougne, Toubacouta, Ndangane and Djiffer. Saloum Delta National Park, near Djiffer and the ocean, is at least as interesting for the scenery as for the wildlife. You'll see lots of birds but no large mammals except, possibly, for an occasional sea cow (manatee) in the lagoons. A pirogue trip down the river to some of the island villages would likely be the most memorable part of your trip around Senegal. Whether you allow one of the hotels along the river to make the arrangements or, cheaper, you do it yourself, the price could be stiff.

KAOLACK
Except for the magnificent market and a beautiful mosque, the prize of the Tidjana brotherhood, Kaolack (population 170,000), mid-way between Dakar and The Gambia, offers little of interest to travellers. Don't miss seeing the picturesque old market on the outskirts of town though. It has Sudanese mud architecture with Oriental arcades, a grand entrance, a large central patio and is quite active.

Places to Stay & Eat
For really cheap accommodation, try *Hôtel Napoléon* three blocks east of the market and over-priced at about CFA 3500 for a dirty double without air-con. Another possibility is the *Mission Catholique*, which has six-bed dormitories.

The best hotel is *Le Dior* (tel 411513), with a pool, restaurant and 30 air-con rooms, each with a terrace. Two others are *Le Paris* (tel 411019) with 17 air-con rooms and the 10-room *Centre Touristique de Kahone* (tel 411116).

FOUNDIOUGNE
This village is a good place to find pirogues for taking trips down the Saloum River.

Places to Stay & Eat
Your only choice is between *Les Piroguiers* (tel 451129) tourist hotel and a bare minimum room at *Chez Anne-Marie* bar-restaurant. On a beautiful spot along the river, the Piroguiers has 21 air-con rooms, a pool, a good restaurant and a nightclub, and it offers windsurfing, sailing, hunting and fishing.

TOUBACOUTA
Toubacouta is also a good place to explore the Saloum River region.

Places to Stay
You have a choice between two tourist hotels – *Les Paletuviers* (Dakar tel 218773) or *Keur Saloum* (Dakar tel 213882, Kaolack tel 411019). Both have air-con bungalows and a pool, and offer hunting, fishing and pirogues for hire.

NDANGANE
This is the spot for taking a pirogue over to Djiffer and Saloum park. To get here, you'll have to go via Thiadiaye (east of M'Bour) rather than Joal-Fadiouth.

Places to Stay
Le Pelican, built in the early 1980s and quite attractive, has a pool and a superb location over-looking the ocean.

DJIFFER

The attraction here is the Saloum Park.

Places to Stay

To stay at the *Campement de Djiffer*, you absolutely must reserve in advance; they usually accept only group reservations and are closed from July to October. Contact Transcap Voyages (tel 216083) in Dakar or the owners at Hôtel de Thiès (tel 511226).

The Casamance

The Casamance, south of The Gambia, attracts more travellers than any other area of the country. One reason is the environment. The Casamance river is a labyrinth of creeks and small islands not unlike parts of the Amazon basin in South America – an area of palm trees, forests, mangrove swamps and lush estuary vegetation, perfect for touring in a pirogue. During the dry season it's a temporary home to millions of migratory birds. Another attraction is Ziguinchor, a small city on the southern bank of the Casamance river, with wide avenues bordered by flowering trees. A third reason is the unique system of cheap campements all over the area, allowing tourists to live in villages and view rural life as Africans know it. A fourth reason is Cap Skirring, the finest beach area in the country.

ZIGUINCHOR

At first glance, Ziguinchor may not seem like anything special. But most people who stay here a while grow to love it despite the influx of tourists during the winter months. For one thing, the city is not big, about 100,000 inhabitants. You can easily cover downtown on foot, and the shade trees everywhere cut off the sun. There's also an element of vitality here. The money from tourism helps.

Things to See

The **Marché St Maur** is quite colourful and well worth a visit. You'll find it between the Gare Routière and the **Centre Artisanal**, on the road to Hôtel Néma-Kadior. At the Artisanal, open every day from 7.30 am, you'll find wooden carvings, dresses, metal objects, silver, fabrics – nothing unusual. Another place for crafts is *Deco Shop*, in the dead centre of town near Hôpital Silence. They also sell maps of the city and the Casamance for about CFA 600. On Sunday afternoons around 4 pm, ask some of the kids to take you to l'arène, where they have wrestling matches almost every week. Each section of town has its favourites at these festive occasions – highly recommended, with few tourists.

Places to Stay – bottom end

For cheap accommodation, try *Hôtel N'Dari Kassoum*, with spacious ventilated singles/doubles for about CFA 3300/4600 (CFA 2000 more with air-con) and clean private bathrooms. Meals cost about CFA 1500 and are served in the central garden under paillotes. The friendly owner of *Chez Astou Goudiaby*, between the market and the Artisanal, is recommended for the price – small rooms with tiny lights and no fans for about CFA 2500. He also serves decent meals, about CFA 500 steak and potatoes. *Hôtel Mama Djanke Waly Sames* nearby at the Gare Routière has similar prices but isn't as clean or friendly.

The most popular place for backpackers is the eight-room *Hôtel du Tourisme* (tel 911227), a well-run family operation – the 'hippy' hotel. They have decent singles/doubles with air-con for about CFA 5000/6000 plus tax (CFA 1000 less with fan). It's right in the centre of town and the city's best meeting place, a good choice for a drink and a very popular eating place. Low-budget tourist groups eat here too. Meals are not cheap, however, at about CFA 3000 for the three-course special.

If the Tourisme is full, often the case,

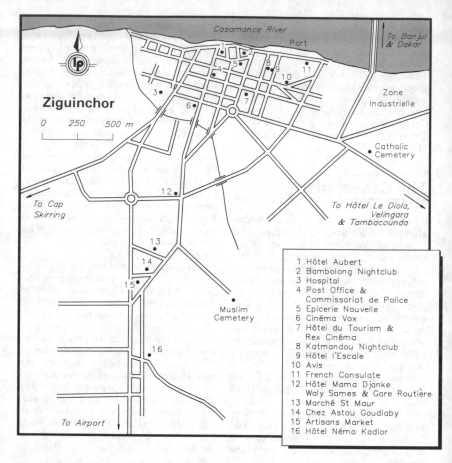

Ziguinchor

0   250   500 m

To Cap
Skirring

To Hôtel Le Diola,
Velingara
& Tambacounda

To Airport

Casamance River   Port   To Banjul
& Dakar

Zone
Industrielle

Catholic
Cemetery

Muslim
Cemetery

1 Hôtel Aubert
2 Bambolong Nightclub
3 Hospital
4 Post Office &
   Commissariat de Police
5 Epicerie Nouvelle
6 Cinéma Vox
7 Hôtel du Tourism &
   Rex Cinéma
8 Katmandou Nightclub
9 Hôtel l'Escale
10 Avis
11 French Consulate
12 Hôtel Mama Djanke
   Waly Sames & Gare Routière
13 Marché St Maur
14 Chez Astou Goudiaby
15 Artisans Market
16 Hôtel Néma Kadior

try *Hôtel l'Escale* (tel 911204) nearby, where the rooms with air-con are equally good and similarly priced and the restaurant slightly cheaper. Their singles/doubles with fans cost only CFA 2500/3500, and you can get beers for about CFA 350 at the bar, which is fairly popular with Africans.

Places to Stay – top end
The city's top two hotels are *Hôtel Diola* (tel 911262, telex 7320) and the almost identical *Hôtel Néma-Kadior* (tel 911052, Dakar tel 217313, telex 7320, cards Visa, CB). Geared to the tourist trade, both are peaceful and have attractive single/double bungalows for about CFA 13,500/17,000 and pools (CFA 1000 for non-guests). The restaurant menu is about CFA 5000. Only the Néma-Kadior offers tennis. It's also more conveniently located, two km from the heart of town and on the same street as the market and artisan centre. The Diola, on the other hand, is a good three km from town on a less-travelled road.

The best hotel in the heart of town is *Hôtel Aubert* (tel 911879, telex 732), which has a small pool, AVIS, singles for about CFA 9500 to CFA 10,500 and doubles for about CFA 10,000 to CFA 11,500.

Entertainment
For entertainment, you'll find several movie theatres, including the Cinéma Rex next door to Hôtel Tourisme and, better, Le Vox. Show time is 9.15 pm. One of the two most popular discos is *Katmandou Night-Club*, downtown one block behind Hôtel l'Escale and open every night, with a cover of about CFA 1200 (doesn't include a drink). The other is *Bambolong* nearby, two blocks east of Hôtel Aubert. The city's largest supermarket, *Épicerie Nouvelle*, faces the nightclub.

Getting There & Away
Most travellers from Dakar come by bush taxi (about seven hours) or on the daily Air Senegal flight.

Bush Taxi Bush taxis leave from the Gare Routière, between downtown and the Centre Artisanal. Most travellers heading for Bissau take the long route via Tanat because the roads are better and the traffic higher. Taxis to Banjul (Gambia) take about three hours and cost CFA 2500. If you wait until the afternoon, you may not find one. The drive to Cap Skirring takes only an hour.

Hitchhiking Hitching to Cap Skirring is fairly easy, but take only a ride that gets you to your destination. If they drop you off in Oussouye, for example, you may not find another ride for hours.

Boat The most interesting way, however, is by boat. The *Casamance Express* leaves from Dakar on Friday at 6 pm (and for Dakar on Thursdays at 10 am), two out of every three weeks, arriving 16 hours later. Prices range from about CFA 3500 for deck class to CFA 11,000 to CFA 16,500

a person for a cabin. Contact L'Inscription Maritime (tel 917161) near the Ziguinchor train station or Société Maritime Casamançaise (tel 911056).

Getting Around
A taxi from the airport to downtown (three km) costs only about CFA 300.

You can rent a car from AVIS (tel 911038), a block from the port, but renting a taxi by the day is cheaper – about CFA 10,000 a day plus petrol if you bargain well.

For a bicycle, try AVIS or Hôtel Diola. For a mobylette, try *Chez Diatta* facing *La Cité Ossu*.

RURAL CASAMANCE
The Casamance is famous for its integrated tourist campements, built by villagers with government loans and run as cooperatives. Profits are reinvested in the village for the construction of schools, maternity clinics and health centres – an exemplary way to improve village life without introducing many of the noxious effects generally associated with western tourism in developing countries. Well over 20,000 tourists stay in them each year.

The first campement was constructed in 1973. There are now eight: three west of Ziguinchor in the Basse Casamance (Enampor, Oussouye and Elinkine) and five on the northern side of the Casamance river in the Haute Casamance (Koubalan, Affiniam, Thionk-Essyl, Baila and Abéné). The last one is the hardest to get to and the only one on the ocean – 18 km from Diouloulou. At all these places, the price of a bed, usually with mosquito net, is about CFA 1200. Lunch or dinner runs about CFA 1000. During the peak winter tourist season, you'll probably need a reservation. Contact Adama Goudiaby at the Centre Artisanal (tel 911084) in Ziguinchor.

Architecturally, the two most interesting campements are in Enampor and Oussouye.

Enampor

The tourist campement in Enampor, 23 km directly west of Ziguinchor, is a huge, round mud house, called the *Case a Impluvium*. During wartime, they'd shut the doors and get their water from the huge opening in the middle, which trapped the rain. The main reason for the opening, however, is to let in a wonderful diffuse light.

Getting There & Away Unless you have a vehicle, you'll have to rent a taxi because bush taxis don't travel here and taking a mobylette over the 10-km section of rough dirt road is difficult.

Oussouye

In Oussouye, roughly halfway between Ziguinchor and Cap Skirring on a paved road, there is a superb two-storey campement made of mud. It's one km north of town on the road leading northwest towards Elinkine and the island of Carabane.

Elinkine & Carabane Island

In Elinkine, there is a campement of two large houses bordering the river. Chances are you might see one of the tour groups from Ziguinchor that come here on all-day excursions.

One of the attractions of Carabane is the ruins of an old settlement, including a Breton church. Another is *Hôtel de Carabane* (Ziguinchor tel 911304), a tranquil hotel next to the water and a pleasant place to stay for several days. It's also a bargain at about CFA 3000/3500 for clean singles/doubles and CFA 2300 for a full meal. You'll also find a cheaper campement with neither toilet nor shower but facing a beautiful beach.

Getting There & Away Every day around 2.30 pm, you can get a bus at the Gare Routière in Ziguinchor headed for Elinkine; it returns the next day at 7 am.

A motorised pirogue from Elinkine to Carabane takes half an hour and costs

CFA 5000 for one to five persons, and CFA 1000 for each additional person.

M'Lomp

An alternative is to head north from Oussouye for 10 km north to M'Lomp, where you'll see something unique in this part of the world – several two-storey houses made of mud (banco). The walls are quite thick in order to carry part of the weight of a banco floor and a heavy thatched roof. The owner will give you a tour.

Pointe St George

Pointe St George is further north along the Casamance river. There, you'll find a delightful tourist hotel, *Hôtel Pointe St George*. It has 30 modern bungalows for about CFA 16,000 a person with full pension (about CFA 2000 more if you're alone), pool, tennis, windsurfers, catamarans, ping pong, boule, archery and water skiing (CFA 3500 for 15 minutes). What's particularly nice about this hotel is that it's next to a village, Ponta Da Reya; the two exist in complete harmony. In Ziguinchor, you can make reservations at Hôtel du Tourisme.

Getting There & Away Getting there is tricky. Unless you have a four-wheel drive vehicle, you'll have to ask them to meet you west of M'Lomp with their rugged van. Or take a motorised pirogue from Ziguinchor, 40 km away.

Tours

If you're thinking about taking a guided tour of the Casamance, consider also the possibility of hiring a taxi by the day. For a guided tour, contact Senegal Tours (tel 911052) at the Hôtel Néma-Kadior. A one-day excursion costs about CFA 14,500 to Cap Skirring and CFA 15,500 to Carabane Island – about what you'd pay for a taxi. The Casamance is also a popular area for small game hunting. Orchape (6 Rue d'Armaille, 75017 Paris, tel 01-43803067) organises eight-day trips from November to May. A package tour

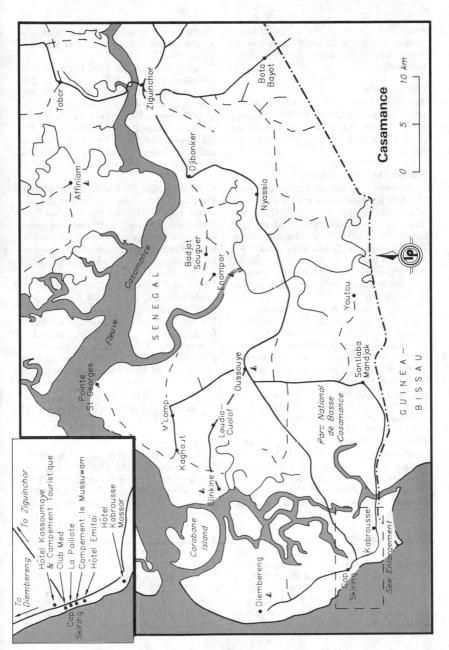

Casamance

from Paris costs about 13,500 French francs, including lodging at a deluxe campement in Kolda or at *Relais Fleuri* in Badioure.

CAP SKIRRING

The coast here is superb, which is why you'll find a Club Med. The finest beaches in Senegal are around here, and this is the place to lie back and enjoy the sun and water.

Places to Stay – bottom end

In the main hotel area south of Club Med, the cheapest beach hotel is *Campement le Mussuwam*, a steal at CFA 3000 a room. You can camp there as well. Meals cost about CFA 2000. The 27-room *Hôtel Emitaï*, next door, costs only about CFA 9200 with half board. Like all the hotels, it's right on the water, with a great breeze. You can also rent a bicycle there as well as at the Paillote.

In the village just to the north of the Club Med, you'll find cheap places to eat and two hotels, *Hôtel Kassoumaye* about 300 metres off the ocean and, better, *Campement Touristique* 100 metres away. At both places, you can get very basic singles/doubles for about CFA 2000/ 2500 and meals for CFA 1000. Sleeping on the beach is reportedly not dangerous, although you'll have to watch the kids.

To escape the tourists, head for Diembering, 10 km to the north and easily reached by bicycle. You'll find two inexpensive places to sleep – *Campement Chez Albert*, a large traditional-style house on the ocean, and the newer and cleaner *Campement Khalil* at the entrance to town.

Places to Stay – top end

Club Med (tel 911043) has 206 bungalows, serving those on package tours and closed to travellers. The adventurous try getting in through the beach. *Kabrousse Mossor* (telex 7320, cards Visa, CB), four km to the south, has 120 single/double bungalows for about CFA 16,000/21,500 and a superb

garden environment. The facilities include a pool, tennis court, mini-golf and free windsurfers.

Just south of Club Med is *La Paillote* (Ziguinchor tel 911379, telex 7321). For the money, it's a better buy – 30 single/ double bungalows for about CFA 12,500/ 15,000 (about CFA 11,000 per person more with full pension). Reservations for the Kabrousse Mossor or La Paillote can be made in Ziguinchor at Cabrousse Autos (tel 911192) on Avenue Dr Carvalho.

PARC NATIONAL DE BASSE CASAMANCE

For an excursion from Cap Skirring, you could take a trip to the nearby Parc National de Basse Casamance, as interesting for its vegetation (tropical forests, wooded savanna and mangrove swamp) as for the animals (lots of birds during the dry season, a few monkeys and an occasional hippo and antelope). More interesting might be a pirogue trip up to Elinkine and back, a round-trip distance of about 30 km. You can find pirogues near the bridge, a few km east from the ocean on the road to Ziguinchor. If you take a motorised pirogue, the price per person will be stiff unless you get 10 or so persons together.

The Northern Region

TOUBA

Touba is sacred city of the Mouride Islamic Brotherhood and the site of one of the major events in Senegal – the Magal. This is an annual pilgrimage when 250,000 or so zealots of the brotherhood descend on Touba for several days to celebrate the return from exile of their founder, Amadou Bamba. (Feeling threatened by the potential power of this great marabout, the French kept him in exile outside Senegal for 16 years until 1903.) The centre of attention is, of course, the mosque, probably Senegal's most beautiful, which holds his tomb. You can visit inside except during prayer hour.

For those interested in Islamic culture, a visit here can be very interesting. If you're lucky enough to be in Senegal at the time of the Magal, by all means go. During the three days preceding the holy night (39 days following the end of Ramadan and 30 days prior to Tabaski, ie around 24 June in 1988), it is almost impossible to find an empty seat in a vehicle headed for Touba from towns within a 100-km radius. Don't expect to find a hotel room or a taxi back to Dakar, 164 km to the west. And, whenever you go to Touba, be very careful of what you wear and how you act – no alcohol, no cigarettes and, for women, no pants.

ST-LOUIS

For a glimpse of what towns looked like in the colonial period, head for St-Louis, the first French settlement in Africa, dating from 1659. The city has scores of old houses with gracious wrought-iron and wooden balconies and verandas. It is the New Orleans of West Africa.

The heart of town is not the mainland, where you'll find the train station and taxi gare. Rather, it's the sausage-like island on the other side of the main bridge, Pont Faidherbe.

Things to See

Immediately after crossing the bridge, you'll see the old Hôtel de la Poste, the most interesting hotel in town. Go inside; the bar looks like the headquarters for the Order of the Moose – heads of buffalo and gazelle, bamboo walls and sturdy wooden furniture. Have a drink there or at the sidewalk café outside; seemingly everyone in St-Louis passes by sometime during the day.

The old governor's palace, a fort during the 18th century, and the cathedral dating from 1828, are both nearby. North and south of Place Faidherbe, which has a statue of the famous colonial administrator, are many 19th century houses.

After cutting across this narrow island of St-Louis, you'll come to another bridge, Pont Servatius. On the other side, and

parallel to the island, is a long thin peninsula, La Langue de Barbarie, beyond which is the Atlantic Ocean. After the bridge, if you take a right (north), you'll come immediately to N'Dar Toute market. If you take a left (south), you'll eventually come to the quartier des pêcheurs, the picturesque section of town with grass huts where most of the fishermen live. Every morning, they launch some 200 pirogues into the sea and return in the late afternoon – quite a spectacle. Further south, is a rather unique cemetery, with each tomb marked by a stake with the net of the dead fisherman draped over it. If you continue further south across the dunes, you'll come to a bird sanctuary, the Parc Marin de la Langue de Barbarie.

Places to Stay

The cheapest hotels, about CFA 4500 a room, are Hôtel Maïmaïdo, two blocks from the Residence and, worse, Hôtel Battling Siki.

The most interesting hotel is the old Hôtel de la Poste (tel 611118/48) at the Place de l'Indépendance. It has 27 rooms with and without air-con (roughly CFA 6000 without air-con), a good restaurant and a fabulous bar. Four blocks behind it on Avenue Brière de l'Isle, you'll find a hotel with slightly better rooms, Hôtel Résidence (tel 611260), with air-con doubles for roughly CFA 7800 and cheaper singles.

The most modern hotel is the 50-room Mame Coumba Bang (tel 611850), with a pool, tennis court and nightclub. At the entrance to town, about six km from the centre, it's a bad choice for anyone without a vehicle.

PARC NATIONAL DES OISEAUX DU DJOUDJ

An outstanding bird sanctuary 70 km north-east of St-louis, on the delta of the Senegal river, Djoudj is well worth a visit. From November to April, some three million birds migrating south from

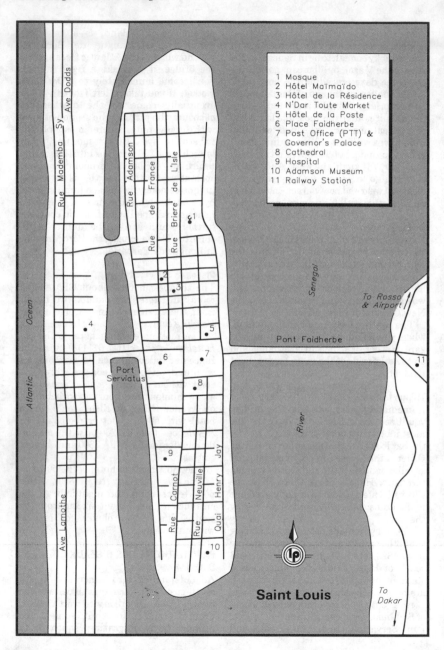

1 Mosque
2 Hôtel Maïmaïdo
3 Hôtel de la Résidence
4 N'Dar Toute Market
5 Hôtel de la Poste
6 Place Faidherbe
7 Post Office (PTT) &
  Governor's Palace
8 Cathedral
9 Hospital
10 Adamson Museum
11 Railway Station

Saint Louis

Europe pass through, mainly ducks and waders, but also pink flamingoes, white pelicans, geese, herons, spoonbills and tree-ducks. From St-Louis, take the paved road towards Rosso for about 45 km until Ross-Bethio, then due north on dirt road for about 25 km.

January, when the water's salinity is rising due to evaporation, is the best time of the year for seeing flamingoes. From May to October, you'll see little birdlife. You can take a vehicle through the park, but because much of the park is covered by a lake and swamp, using a pirogue is perhaps a better way to see them.

Places to Stay
Air Afrique runs a hotel with attractive bungalows, *Campement du Djoudj*. As the campement is often full, reservations in Dakar are essential.

MAKA-DIAMA
Hunters may be more interested in Maka-Diama, an 80,000 hectare hunting reserve 30 km north-east of St-Louis. Contact Air Afrique, which operates the *Campement de Chasse*, for details. The season is approximately December to April, when the principal trophies are wart hog, gazelle and numerous small animals. About 60 km north as the crow flies, on the northern banks of the Senegal river in Mauritania, Air Afrique runs another hunting campement, *Keur Massene*. So taking in both reserves on the same trip is quite feasible.

The Eastern Region

TAMBACOUNDA
A flat savannah area full of baobab trees, Tambacounda is a crossroads. Some people head east to Mali, others south to the Niokolo-Koba game park, others west to Dakar or The Gambia.

Places to Stay
For accommodation under CFA 1000, try *Voluntaires du Progrès*. They have a hostel near the expensive Hôtel Asta Kebé. If they're full, your only alternatives are the run-down *Maison de Jeunes* or the *Mission Catholique*, which has clean rooms but is reportedly unfriendly.

In the mid-range try the 10-room *Hôtel de la Gare* (Ocean-Niger) or, about five blocks away, *Bar Marina* (or Chez Dessert), where the friendly old French owner has been known to let travellers sleep in the bar after closing time. His wife can apparently whip up a good meal as well.

The best hotel is the *Hôtel Asta Kebé* (tel 811028, telex 851), two km out of town on a slight hill overlooking a village of huts. It has a pool and tennis courts.

NIOKOLO-KOBA NATIONAL PARK
Senegal's major park (over 800,000 hectares) is an eight-hour drive (600 km) on paved road from Dakar, 144 km south-east of Tambacounda near the Guinea border. Niokolo-Koba is on the Gambia river where it meets two tributaries, giving it a lush, varied vegetation. Elephant, lion, leopard and the giant derby eland are among the 84 species of mammal in the park, but don't bet on seeing them. You're more likely to see hippo, crocodile, green monkey, wart hog, buffalo, gazelle and other species of antelope. Open from December to June, the park has over 600 km of roads. The roads are dry at this time of year, so a four-wheel drive vehicle is not essential.

The park entrance fee is CFA 2000 a person and CFA 5000 per vehicle, both good for three days. You have a choice of routes through the park, the best area is around Badi. Ask at the park entrance for one of their maps and a guide.

The area east of the park is the major hunting zone in the country. Small and medium-size game such as antelope, kob and wart hog are the principal trophies. The season is 15 December to 30 April, although in some areas it extends from 15

November to 30 June. There are people at the Hôtel Asta Kebé who organise trips. Or contact Air Afrique; they can make the necessary arrangements, including getting the hunting licence, gun licence and insurance.

Places to Stay & Eat

All three major villages in the park have lodgings. In Badi, near the entrance to the park, you'll find the cheapest lodgings, the *Campement de Badi*, which has some bare minimum bungalows. Bring food and water. There are also free camping spots with huts, but you'll need the park ranger's permission, which is more or less automatic. Since the best time for viewing the animals is at the crack of dawn and at sunset, camping affords the best chance of seeing them.

The closest camp site to the park entrance is the *Camp du Lion*, in a superb spot nine km from Simenti.

The best accommodation is *Hôtel de Simenti*, ideally located on the river's edge in Simenti, near the park's northern entrance. Animals come here to drink early in the morning and again in the late afternoon. The hotel has 50 superb

looking, thatched-roof huts with air-con, a restaurant and a pool. Prices are very reasonable – about CFA 9500 for a room with air-con (CFA 1000 less without). For a 4½ hour morning or afternoon safari, they charge about CFA 6000. For reservations, call the Meridien in Dakar, which manages the hotel.

Hôtel du Niokolo-Koba (Dakar tel 231005) has a pool, restaurant and 30 attractive bungalows, with and without air-con. Travel agents in Dakar can make reservations.

Getting There & Away

If you're without a vehicle, getting to the park won't be easy. Trucks are few, so you'll probably have to hitch to Dar es Salaam at the park entrance, where you may be able to radio for a ride.

Senegal Sun Travel in Dakar offers three-day, all-inclusive excursions for approximately CFA 95,000 a person, minimum six people. You could also take bush taxis or one of *Air Senegal's* twice-weekly flights to Simenti. For further information, contact the Direction des Parcs (tel 230793/214221) in Dakar.

Sierra Leone

For tourists seeking warm weather and beautiful beaches, Sierra Leone is a West African Mecca. The country's three large beach hotels are packed every winter with Brits and northern Europeans attracted by low-priced tours that allow them to enjoy a little of the exotic – Africa – along with the beach. The most popular beach is next to these hotels, but more romantic beaches are further down the peninsula where you'll find crystal-clear water perfect for skin diving and fishing. Hire a dugout canoe and visit the exotic small islands nearby. Both the country's major travel agencies offer a number of potential side trips to these and other places, including hunting trips, visits to an old slave-trading post, and an inland excursion to the diamond-mining area.

Those wanting to avoid the tourist sites will have no problem. Few tourists stay in downtown Freetown or travel upcountry, where accommodation is frequently nonexistent or at best rustic. Or you could stay on some of the more remote beaches on the southern end of Freetown peninsula so long as you keep an eye out for thieves.

Other than the beaches and skin diving sites, Sierra Leone doesn't have spectacular attractions, but it does have tropical scenery, a dry climate for at least half the year, and friendly people. As you cross the harbour separating the airport and Freetown, you'll see lush green tropical mountains which form a backdrop to the capital – quite a contrast to the city, with its shabby old buildings, crowded narrow streets, and daily blackouts which put a damper on the city's nightlife. The country's economy is in a mess, but if your hotel has a generator, you shouldn't be too adversely effected – unless the brewery shuts down again.

HISTORY
Sierra Leone is the British equivalent to American sponsored Liberia. Around 200 years ago, British philanthropists sent freed slaves here to start a better life. With one of the unhealthiest economies in West Africa today, the country and its people have yet to fully realise that dream.

Sierra Leone's contact with the west began when the first Portuguese navigators landed in 1462 and called the area Sierra Leone or 'Lion Mountain'. Almost 120 years later, Sir Francis Drake stopped here during his voyage around the world, but the British did not gain ascendancy until the 1700s.

In 1772 Britain declared slavery illegal and over 15,000 ex-slaves began drifting into London, where they suffered from acute poverty and unemployment. Fifteen years later, a group of philanthropists – men inspired by John Wesley's religious revival to improve the condition of the downtrodden – purchased 52 square km of land around Freetown from a local chief for the purpose of founding a 'Province of Freedom' in Africa for these unfortunates. The same year, 1787, they sent the first group of 411 freed men and women, including 100 whites.

Within three years, all but 48 settlers had died of disease or from hostilities with the natives, or deserted. The British press soon nicknamed Sierra Leone 'the white man's grave'. Undaunted, the British philanthropists sent a second band of

Sierra Leone

0   50   100 km

settlers in 1792, this time 1200 freed slaves who had fled from the USA to Nova Scotia during the American Revolution. Later, they sent 550 ex-slaves from Jamaica who had escaped into the mountains there. The settlers were hardly moralists. According to Richard West in *Back to Africa*, most of the whites were probably 'debtors, adventurers, men who had failed in other colonies or disgruntled officers from the army or navy'. To the chagrin of the philanthropists, some settlers, both white and black, joined in the slave trade,

which wasn't outlawed in the British Empire until 1807. The following year, Britain declared Sierra Leone a colony.

Colonial Period

During the next 60 years, British war ships plowed the West African coast, trying to intercept slave ships destined for America. Freetown became the depot for thousands of 'recaptives' as well as thousands of indigenous migrants from the hinterland. Congo Town, a section of Freetown, began in 1816 when recaptive

Congolese were deposited there. By 1850, over 100 ethnic groups were represented in the colony. Yet they lived in harmony, each group in a different section of town.

Like the previous settlers, the recaptives became successful traders and inter-married, so that all non-indigenous blacks became known collectively as Krios. Cut off from their homes and traditions, they assumed the English style of living and began regarding themselves as superior to the indigenous people. Many were Christian and adopted British culture and became well educated by attending Fourah Bay College outside Freetown, the first English-speaking university in Africa. So the British administrators and missionaries naturally favoured the Krios and even appointed them to senior posts in the civil service.

Towards the end of the 19th century, the tide started turning against the Krios, who were outnumbered 50 to one by the indigenous people. Britain declared the hinterland a protectorate and imposed a hut tax, which led to a war between the two groups that killed many Krios. Lebanese merchants began migrating to the area, and by WW I, had displaced the Krios as the leading traders with the interior tribes. In Freetown, British entrepreneurs began favouring the more tractable indigenous people, thereby squeezing Krio merchants out of business.

In 1924 the British administrators established a legislative council with elected representatives, to the advantage of the more numerous indigenous people. The Krios, who continued to monopolise positions within the civil service, reacted by clinging to the British. While other colonies clamoured for independence, they proclaimed loyalty to the Crown. One group even petitioned against the granting of independence. They were far from enamoured with Wallace Johnson, a liberal Krio journalist who led the independence movement in the 1930s and whose name now adorns one of Freetown's major streets.

Then the country had a diamond rush. Before the 1950s, a subsidiary of an international corporation had a monopoly on diamond mining. When the public learned that machinery wasn't required to mine the alluvial deposits of diamonds in the river beds, people rushed from all over the country to the diamond-filled streams which abounded between Sefadu and Kenema. Eventually, the government allowed them to prospect under government licence, thereby distributing the wealth considerably. At independence, Sierra Leone had about the seventh highest per capita income in West Africa. The economy has gone downhill ever since.

Independence

When independence came in 1961, it seemed that western democracy would work. There were two parties of roughly equal strength but, not unusual for Africa, they became divided on ethnic lines. The Sierra Leone People's Party (SLPP) was the party of the southerners, the Mende, and represented the tribal structure of the old colony. The All People's Congress (APC), formed by a trade unionist, Siaka Stevens, became identified with the Temne of the north and voiced the dissatisfaction of the small, modernising elite. The Krio community threw their support behind the SLPP, whose leader, Milton Margai, became the first prime minister. A Mende from the south, he was profoundly traditional and tried to delay the end of colonial rule. He even used his membership in one of the traditional secret societies to further his political ends.

Following Margai's death in 1964, his brother Albert took over and set about replacing the Krios in the bureaucracy with Mende. The Krios took revenge in the 1967 elections by supporting the APC, which won a one-seat majority. A few hours after the APC was declared victorious, a Mende military leader led a coup, placing Stevens under house arrest. This was followed two days later by another coup, whose military leaders vowed to end corruption now blatantly widespread under the Margai brothers. Stevens went into exile in Guinea and with a group of Sierra Leoneans began training in guerrilla warfare for an invasion. This became unnecessary when a group of private soldiers mutinied and staged a third coup 13 months later – an African record for coups in such a short period of time. Stevens returned and formed a new government.

Siaka Stevens' first decade in office was turbulent. He declared a state of emergency, detained people left and right, banned breakaway parties from the APC and tried a number of SLPP members for treason. Fearing for his life after two assassination attempts in one day in 1971, Stevens took the unusual step of asking Sekou Touré of Guinea, with whom he made a military pact, for Guinean troops to act as his bodyguards. He held on to them for two years. Following a trial in 1974 of 65 accused traitors, eight were publicly hanged.

Meanwhile, the economy continued to deteriorate. The iron ore mine closed, revenues from diamonds dropped, the cost of living steadily increased, students rioted, and Stevens again declared a state of emergency. The 1978 election campaign resembled a mini civil war between the major ethnic groups and the death toll topped 100. Stevens won and Sierra Leone had become a one-party state.

Sierra Leone experienced relative political calm but the economy continued to stagnate. Craving international publicity, Stevens nevertheless went ahead with plans to host the 1980 Organisation of African Unity conference, involving huge expenditures for two deluxe hotels, 60 luxury villas for the visiting heads of state and three new ferries, among other things. The country sank deeper in debt by approximately US\$150 million.

This was followed a year later by the 'Vouchergate Scandal' which revealed that about US\$1 million had been paid out by government departments on fictitious invoices. Despite the changeover to a one-party system, the 1982 elections were the most violent ever. Elections in a fifth of the constituencies had to be re-held. Stevens decided it was time to give the Mendes equal representation in the cabinet with the Temnes. But economic conditions continued to deteriorate – queues for food and fuel became an everyday part of survival in Freetown, inflation soared and the city was almost totally blacked out every night. Students rioted, rampaging through Freetown and looting shops, stoning security forces and setting up road blocks.

Today

With virtually no support left, the 'old man' finally stepped down in 1985 at the age of 80. No longer trusting his vice president to protect him in his retirement, Stevens hand-picked as his successor 'the choice of God', Major-General Joseph Momoh, the head of the army. The economic situation Momoh inherited, however, was far from divine. By 1987 the inflation rate was the highest in Africa (well over 100% annually), people were hoarding food, budget deficits were astronomical, and smugglers – allegedly with close government connections – were continuing to rob Sierra Leone of about a third of its diamond revenue. Foreign exchange reserves had completely dried up and the government has only been able to forestall a virtual economic collapse with occasional loans from the country's most powerful Lebanese businessman.

Momoh clearly has his work cut out for him. The toughest part may be breaking the close links between big business and government, which are widely criticised.

PEOPLE

Sierra Leone has 18 ethnic groups. The two largest are the Temnes and Mendes, who are about equal in number and comprise 60% of the country's four million people. The Temnes (ex-President Stevens is Temne) are the main tribe in the north and are predominantly Muslim. The Mendes and kindred tribes inhabit most of the southern and eastern provinces, and are predominately animist.

With both groups, African traditions remain strong. Village chiefs, for instance, still wield considerable power and they, not the civil judges, have primary jurisdiction over most domestic disputes. Secret societies, such as the Poro society for men and the Bundu society for women, are still going strong. The Bundu masks are highly prized but difficult to find. These societies train children over many months, sometimes years, in a number of matters including tribal law and crafts, thus helping to keep traditional culture alive. If you see some pubescent children with their faces painted white, you'll know that they're in the process of being initiated.

The creoles number less than 2% of the people – roughly 60,000. Residing mostly in the Freetown area, they have held on to western traditions and Christianity and make up many of the country's intellectuals and professional people. You'll also see a lot of Lebanese and Indian merchants, who began migrating here in the 1880s and now number about 10,000. The much smaller European community is involved mainly in business and government service.

GEOGRAPHY
Some countries in West Africa have a fairly monotonous terrain – not Sierra Leone. One of the most scenic areas is the hilly, 40-km-long Freetown peninsula. It's the only place along the West African coast where mountains rise near the sea, and one of the few areas where the beaches are generally safe for swimming.

Sierra Leone, about the same size as Austria, has three regions, starting with the coastal belt, which consists of mangrove swamps and beaches and is flat except for the peninsula. There are also small islands just off the coast such as Shebro, Taso, Plantain, Banana, Turtle and York. As you move inland, the countryside becomes heavily forested and extensively cultivated.

Still further inland, to the north and north-east, is a forested area of plateaux and mountains, the highest peak being Mt Bintumani (1948 metres) north of Sefadu. This is the country's most scenic area. You'll find two picturesque waterfalls – Binkongo falls five km from Sefadu and the Bumbuna falls about 50 km north-east of Magburaka. This is also the diamond area. The National Diamond Mining Co operates 15 km west of Sefadu in Yengema, but you'll need a government permit to visit them. In 1972, they found the world's third largest diamond of 969.8 carats. South of Sefadu towards Kenema, you may see prospectors looking for diamonds along the small streams. These alluvial deposits are rapidly diminishing.

In the north-west, along the Great Scarcies (or Kolente) river which forms the boundary with Guinea, is Outama-Kilimi National Park, the country's largest game reserve. There is a much smaller park near Magburaka.

CLIMATE
Sierra Leone is one of the wettest countries in West Africa – averaging over 3150 mm (125 inches) of rainfall a year in most of the country. The rainy season stretches from May through October, the wettest months being July through September. While the humidity is particularly high in the coastal regions, the sea breeze affords considerable relief. The country's annual average temperature is a fairly moderate 27°C (80°F). Temperatures drop in December and January, but the skies are frequently hazy from the harmattan winds that carry sand from the Sahara.

VISAS
Visas, or entry permits for nationals of Commonwealth countries and some European countries, are required of everyone. Entry permits are free, visas are not. South Africans are denied entry.

Visas are normally valid for 30 days and extensions of up to six months are available from the immigration office at 14 Siaka Stevens St, Freetown. If you're in a country without a Sierra Leonean embassy, try the British Embassy as they frequently have authority to issue them. Visas are not issued at the border, however, border officials have been known to grant entry to travellers on condition that they go immediately to immigration for a visa.

In Freetown, you can get a Liberian visa in 24 hours from their embassy; bring three photos. For a Malian visa, you'll have to go to Conakry (Guinea) or Abidjan (Ivory Coast). The British embassy in Freetown does not handle visas to other countries as is frequently the case elsewhere; the consulate section closes at 1 pm.

Diplomatic Missions Abroad
Addis Ababa, Banjul, Bonn, Brussels, Conakry, Lagos, London, Lusaka, Monrovia, Paris, Rome, Washington.

MONEY
US$1 = Le 22
£1 = Le 41

The unit of currency is the leone. Importing more than the equivalent of about US$5 in leones is illegal. In 1986, the government adopted a floating exchange rate, thereby eliminating the black market. At the same time they began printing money like mad. In 1987, with inflation progressing at an annual rate over 100%, prices and the exchange rate were both literally increasing weekly. The local joke is that stores may start weighing money instead of counting it. So prices, which in real terms are fairly stable, are quoted in dollars herein. At the top hotels, you have to pay in hard currency.

Banking hours: weekdays 8 am to 1.30 pm (2 pm on Friday); closed Saturday and Sunday. Banks: Barclays (tel 22501) Siaka Stevens/Charlotte Sts, Box 12, Sierra Leone Commercial Bank, Standard Bank.

LANGUAGE
English is the official language, however, Krio is more widely spoken. The major ingredient of Krio is English, but it's enriched by various West African languages. Expressions in Krio:

Good morning	MOH-nee-noh
How are you?	how-dee body
Thank you	TANK-kee
Goodbye	we go see you
Food	chop

GENERAL INFORMATION
Health
A vaccination against yellow fever is required, as is cholera if you come from an infected area. For emergencies, there is the Connaught Hospital (tel 22001) and West End Clinic (tel 23918), both in Freetown.

Security
Security is a problem because the hordes of tourists at the beach hotels during the winter months attract thieves and muggers. The beaches directly in front of the beach hotels are fairly safe, but several hundred metres away they become dangerous. If you jog on the beach, don't tempt them by wearing a watch and carrying a wallet. Downtown Freetown has no street lights, so walking around town at night can be quite dangerous.

Business Hours
Business: Monday to Saturday 8 am to 12 noon and 2 to 5 pm. Government: weekdays 8 am to 12 noon and 12.30 to 3.45 pm, plus alternate Saturdays 8 am to 12 noon.

Public Holidays
1 January, Easter Friday, Easter Monday, 19 April (Republic Day), End of Ramadan, Tabaski, Mohammed's Birthday, 25-26 December.

Photography
The government is not uptight about travellers taking photographs. No photo

permit is required. However, you should not photograph major government buildings, military sites, airports, harbours and religious ceremonies.

Time, Phone & Telex

When it's noon in Sierra Leone, it's noon in London and 7 am in New York (8 am during daylight savings time). From Freetown it is easy to call Europe, the USA and other non-African countries, but the only place to make a call is at Sierra Leone External Telecommunications (SLET) on Wallace Johnson St, not at the post office or the hotels. SLET (tel 22801) has telex facilities as well; it's open daily 8 am to 7 pm. There is also a public telex booth at Mercury House (7 Water St).

GETTING THERE
Air

From Europe and North Africa, there are direct flights to Freetown from Amsterdam, London, Paris and Casablanca. From London, the cheapest flights are on Sierra Leone Airlines with tickets purchased from a bucket shop. Some bucket shops do not deal with Sierra Leone Airlines because of occasional flight cancellations. From the USA, you can take Air Afrique from New York, transferring in Dakar or Abidjan, or go via Europe.

Car

The 335-km trip from Conakry (Guinea) to Freetown takes six hours in the dry season, a little longer in the rainy season; about two-thirds of the road is paved. The border is closed from 6 pm to 6 am.

From Liberia, there are two routes, both of which converge at Joru a few km east of Kenema. The borders at both these routes also close at 6 pm. Most people travelling to/from Monrovia take the coastal route via Zimmi and the Mano River bridge south-east of Fairo. During the dry season, it's a 10-hour drive from Monrovia to Freetown, but in the wet this route can be impassable along the 45-km stretch between Zimmi and the border.

The northern route via Gbarnga, Voinjama and Pendembu is dirt road but is possibly better than the coastal route during the rainy season. Normally, there's petrol in Gbarnga, Voinjama, Pendembu and Kenema, but because Liberia and Sierra Leone are in such dire economic straits, you may encounter difficulty finding some. Occasionally the northern border has been closed due to smuggling, so check to make sure it's open.

Most of the major towns inland are connected to Freetown by asphalt roads, but they are winding and dangerous. The best stretch is Bo-Kenema.

Bush Taxi

Bush taxis and minibuses are called *poda poda*, the buses being much cheaper. The trip from Conakry to Freetown takes a full day and requires a change at the border. Most people heading to Monrovia go via the coastal road, changing at Kenema. During the dry season count on two days (three days during the rainy season). You may be able to find a taxi direct from Kenema to Monrovia; expect to pay US$20 or so.

GETTING AROUND
Air

Sierra Leone Airlines offers service to Kenema, Bonthe and Monrovia (Liberia). Even those travelling on the cheap sometimes recommend flying when travelling upcountry because the planes are fairly cheap and fly low enough to give a good view of the countryside. They leave from Hastings airport near Freetown, not Lungi international airport.

Bus

Most people prefer to take the government buses instead of the poda poda. They connect Freetown with all the major towns and are fast, fairly cheap and have fixed rates. They are safer than the poda poda, whose drivers stuff people inside like sardines. The only problem is getting a ticket because they are so popular; so go to the bus station several hours in advance. It's downtown in the old railway station at Rawdon and Wallace Johnson. (The train no longer operates.)

Freetown

Freetown (population 400,000) is the type of city where you avoid elevators because chances are they haven't been inspected since independence. It's a shanty town with a capital S. If a bucket of paint has been sold in the last 20 years, you wouldn't know it. Eighty-year-old buildings with shutters falling off and rusting roofs, congested streets, dirt and disorder are all part of the scene. Most major streets are barely two cars wide and all it takes for a traffic jam is one stalled car or rudely parked vehicle. At rush hour, you might as well go have a drink and wait it out. If you're an average tourist, that means heading to the Paramount Hotel because there's not another decent place downtown to have a drink. There's usually not enough oil in the country to keep the generators going, so most evenings downtown Freetown is pitch black except for the small flickering kerosene lights up and down the streets where people sell cigarettes, gum, candy and food. If it's the rainy season, there may not even be that.

Places that are run-down, decadent and chaotic can also be intriguing. Some travellers like Freetown and the acid test is to have a drink at the run-down City Hotel. If you get good vibes from this derelict haven, you'll probably like Freetown. It's where Graham Greene wrote his highly acclaimed novel, *The Heart of the Matter*, while in the British Colonial Service during WW II.

Some people say they like Freetown because it's very African. On a continent where over half the countries are worse off now than at independence, Freetown is certainly closer to the African norm than Dakar or Abidjan.

Beneath the city's shabby exterior, you may find some surprises. Inside the Law Courts building, for instance, you'll see lawyers – almost all educated in England – with white wigs and formal gowns arguing cases before various courts and conferring outside with their clients. So give Freetown a try. There's more to the city than initially meets the eye.

Information
Embassies France (tel 22477, Box 510) 13 Lamina Sankoh St; West Germany (tel 22511, Box 728) 10 Howe St; Ghana (tel 23461); Guinea (tel 22331) 4 Liverpool St; Italy (tel 30995) Congo Cross; Ivory Coast (tel 23983); Liberia (tel 40322) 30 Brookfields Rd; Nigeria (tel 22444); UK (tel 23961/5) Standard Bank, Lightfoot Boston St; USA (tel 26481) Walpole/ Siaka Stevens St.

Other embassies include: Egypt, Niger. Consulates: Belgium, Denmark, Netherlands, Norway, Sweden, Switzerland.

Travel Agencies *Yazbeck Tours* (tel 22063/ 24423, telex 3412), Siaka Stevens and Charlotte Sts, and the Mammy Yoko hotel, is the Thomas Cook representative and highly recommended, especially for tours of the interior. They offer all-day fishing and hunting trips, half and full-day river boat cruises, a Freetown shopping tour, an African village tour and an all-day trip to Paradise Island where snorkelling and fishing are possible, among others.

Another good agency is Africa Tours at the Cape Sierra which offers similar excursions. Additional agencies include Ace Tours (tel 24244) Ludgate House, Rawdon St, Freetown Travel Agency (tel 23109) Walpole St, and Aureol Travel Agencies (tel 25571) Rawdon St.

Cotton Tree & Law Courts
The first order of the day should be a walk up and down Freetown's major street – Siaka Stevens. The heart of town and the

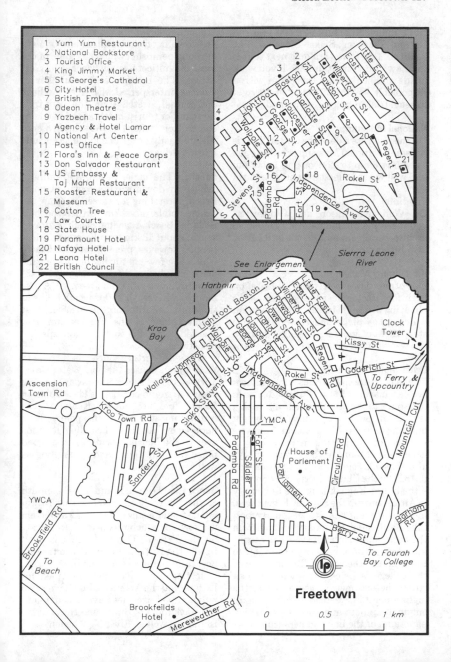

1 Yum Yum Restaurant
2 National Bookstore
3 Tourist Office
4 King Jimmy Market
5 St George's Cathedral
6 City Hotel
7 British Embassy
8 Odeon Theatre
9 Yazbech Travel
  Agency & Hotel Lamar
10 National Art Center
11 Post Office
12 Flora's Inn & Peace Corps
13 Don Salvador Restaurant
14 US Embassy &
   Taj Mahal Restaurant
15 Rooster Restaurant &
   Museum
16 Cotton Tree
17 Law Courts
18 State House
19 Paramount Hotel
20 Nafaya Hotel
21 Leona Hotel
22 British Council

See Enlargement

Sierrra Leone River

Harbour

Krao Bay

Clock Tower

Kissy St

Goderich St

To Ferry & Upcountry

Rokel St

Ascension Town Rd

Kroo Town Rd

Lightfoot Boston St
Wallace Johnson
Wilberforce St
Little East St
Regent Rd

Independence Ave

Wallace Johnson

Siaka Stevens St

Pademba Rd

Fort Soldier St

YMCA

House of Parlement

Parliament Rd

Circular Rd

Mountain Cut

YWCA

Sanders St

Brooksfield Rd

To Beach

Barham Rd

To Fourah Bay College

Berry St

Brookfeilds Hotel

Mereweather Rd

Freetown

0   0.5   1 km

city's major landmark is a 500 year-old Cotton Tree on Siaka Stevens. The beautiful two-storey building next to it is the Law Courts built in 1905. If you walk inside and strike up a friendship with a responsible looking official, you may get to see a trial in process – wigs and all.

National Museum
On the opposite side of the Cotton Tree is the small National Museum, which is open weekdays 8 am to 12 noon and 1 to 4 pm and well worth at least a 30-minute tour.

City Hotel
On Wallace Johnson and Gloucester, you'll see the dilapidated City Hotel, an architectural gem built in the late 1920s; step inside for a drink.

King Jimmy Market
One street down from the City Hotel on Lightfoot Boston near the hospital, is the old King Jimmy Market, a food market which takes place under a bridge on a steep flight of stone steps leading down to the waterfront.

Other Sights
The wooden-frame Old Houses in Freetown are fascinating. Most of the older ones date back to the late 19th century, with a few even older. The new Parliament building is on the hill inland from the Paramount hotel; tours are possible.

On top of Mount Aureol (Freetown lays at its base) is Fourah Bay College, founded in 1827 by the Church Missionary Society – the oldest English-language university in Africa south of the Sahara. To get there, most people take a taxi to the top. By foot, take Parliament Rd passing inland from the Paramount Hotel. It eventually turns into Berry St, from where you turn off to Barham and the college. To the south of the college is Leicester, where you can climb the 595 metre Leicester Peak, the highest point in Freetown. The hike takes only half an hour and affords a sweeping panorama of the bay and peninsula.

Around Freetown
Freetown is on the northern end of a 40-km-long peninsula which has some of the most magnificent sandy beaches in West Africa. The beaches and a number of villages, interspersed with tree-clad bays and coves, stretch from the country's three major tourist hotels at the northern end to Kent village at the southern end. All are easily accessible along the scenic marine drive.

Beaches The major beach, a 15-minute drive from downtown Freetown, is Lumley Beach, stretching for three km from the beach hotels. Five km further south is Goderich Beach. Hamilton Beach is further south, about 18 km from Freetown. Most people, however, prefer River No 2 Beach, which is a few km further on the marine drive but before York – roughly a 45-minute drive south from Freetown. At the mouth of River No 2, this beach is one of the most beautiful on the coast of West Africa. None of the beaches are well marked; ask the natives for specific directions.

A few km further south you'll come to York, which houses the Fori Water Cave. York is a good diving site because of the clear water and coral, as is Black Johnson Beach, five km out of Kent. At the southernmost point of the peninsula is Kent, where you can take a dugout canoe over to the Banana Islands, another good place for skin diving and snorkelling as well as fishing.

Bunce Island Bunce Island is at the mouth of the Sierra Leone river, about 15 km inland from Freetown. The major attraction is a fortress which was held alternatively by the French, Dutch, Portuguese and finally the British. It started as a trading post and later became notorious as a collection point for slaves destined for Europe and the Americas. Freetown's two major travel agencies have half-day and full-days tours of Bunce and the Banana islands as well as River No 2 beach.

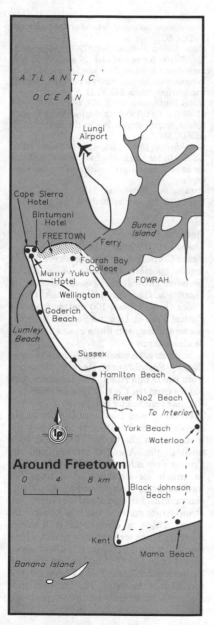

Around Freetown

0   4   8 km

Places to Stay – bottom end

Make sure you have a good torch or candles because you'll spend most nights in the dark. For the money, the best place is the six-room *YMCA* (Box 243, tel 23608) at 32 Fort St, which is a five-minute walk directly behind the Paramount hotel. The cost of singles/doubles is roughly US$3/5 including breakfast. Opened in 1981, it's by far the best YMCA in West Africa, with a library, TV room and a fully equipped kitchen. Unless you reserve in advance by letter, you're unlikely to get a room. They also operate *Lakka Beach Camping Centre*, a camping spot on the beach about 18 km from Freetown, a km or two from the leprosy centre. The cost is only about US$1 a night. The *YWCA* is about three km away on Brookfields Rd, a major road leading to the beach area.

City Hotel on Gloucester St provides singles/doubles for US$1/1.50 but you get what you pay for. Two other possibilities for about 50c are the *Canadian Volunteers Hostel* (CUSO) on Siaka Stevens and the *Christian Youth Centre* on Garrison St, which reportedly allows people to sleep on the floor. Sleeping on the beach is illegal. If the cops don't get you, the muggers probably will.

As for hotels catering to Africans, the following four are in the same downtown area near Siaka Stevens St, starting four blocks down from the Cotton Tree. The first is *Lamar Hotel* (tel 25903) at 21 Howe St, 40 metres inland from Siaka Stevens. It's the cheapest of the four, and it has rooms with private baths for about US$3. The best of the lot is the brand new *Nafaya Hotel* a block further down on Rawdon St, one block inland from Siaka Stevens. Another block down on Regent Rd, three blocks inland from Siaka Stevens, you'll find *Leona Hotel* (tel 23380/1), a decent hotel with a restaurant and air-con when the electricity is on. The price is approximately US$5/8 for singles/doubles. Another block down, at 23 East St, half a block off Siaka Stevens, is the unmarked *Ritz Hotel* (tel 22704), which charges about US$5 including breakfast for a double with a hallway bathroom.

Others include the *Lido Hotel* (tel 22947) on Garrison St and *Dabo Hotel* (tel 22747) on Fourah Bay Rd.

Places to Stay – top end

Most people stay at one of the three beach hotels, all with stand-by generators and within a 10 or 15-minute walk of each other. The best may now be the newly renovated 200-room *Mammy Yoko*, which up until now has not been one of the better Sofitels. A better buy for the money is Frantel's recently renovated *Cape Sierra*, which is well managed and is the closest hotel to the beach. Unlike the others, it has some bungalows which are a real bargain, one-quarter less than the rooms, but available only during the high season.

The 150-room *Hotel Bintumani*, built for the OAU conference in 1980 on top of Aberdeen Hill, has an excellent view. It is the best buy for the money and is the only one with all rooms facing the ocean, however, its mediocre restaurant and location, a 10 or 15-minute walk to the beach, are definite drawbacks.

In the heart of town is the old *Paramount Hotel* with decent rooms for about half the price of the beach hotels. It has no pool, tennis court or generator, but it's in an area where the electricity usually stays on at night. For the same price, you can stay in larger rooms and swim at the *Brookfields Hotel*, which is also in an area where the electricity usually stays on at night. Its major disadvantage is that it's several km from the centre of town and you need a taxi to go anywhere.

The decent, well-maintained *Lungi Airport Hotel* (tel 025-345), with singles/doubles for US$42/50, is only 300 metres from the airport. Many business people and tourists who have early morning flights stay there.

Mammy Yoko Sofitel (tel 37448, telex 3416), US$100/120 for singles/doubles (about 25% more for an ocean-view room), newly renovated, purified water system, two pools, tennis, windsurfers, car rental, tourist office, cards AE, V, D, CB.

Cape Sierra Frantel (tel 37266, telex 3367), US$70/100 for one of the 75 singles/doubles including breakfast (25% less for one of the 80 bungalows), mini-refrigerators, pool, tennis, windsurfers, cards AE, V, D.

Hotel Bintumani (tel 37019, telex 3316), US$ 31/46 (Le 1000/1500) for singles/doubles, pool, tennis, hourly shuttle bus to the beach, cards AE, D, MC.

Brookfields Hotel (tel 41860, telex 3424), US$30-45 for singles/doubles (about 40% less for an older room), pool, no generator, no credit cards.

Paramount Hotel (tel 24531, telex 3257), US$32/38 for singles/doubles, no generator, cards AE, D.

Places to Eat

Cheap Eats It's hard to beat *Flora's Inn*, a Peace Corps hangout which serves a daily lunch special consisting of a choice between two Sierra Leonean dishes for about 50c. This tiny place is next to the Peace Corps offices, 100 metres from the Cotton Tree on Lamina Sankoh near the petrol station, and Flora closes the doors at about 5 pm.

You can get a meal for the same price at *Big Boy Restaurant* on Back St, 20 metres from the Leona Hotel. The *Laminco*, two blocks from the Cotton Tree on Pademba Rd, has lunches for 50c to 75c.

For beer and fried chicken, head for *Rooster* on Siaka Stevens St, about 100 metres from the Cotton Tree and open until 10 pm. Also 100 metres from the Cotton Tree is *Khadra* on Walpole St; it's as much for drinking as eating. For hamburgers, sandwiches, Lebanese shawarmas, full meals and ice cream – all at moderate prices – your best bet is *Yum Yum*, which is clean and is a social meeting place for the younger set. Open every day until 5.30 pm, it's about seven blocks from the Cotton Tree on Rawdon St, several blocks off Siaka Stevens in the direction of the water. The *International Bakery* is apparently on the same street.

Downtown Restaurants *Don Salvador* probably has the best reputation of the restaurants downtown. It has Spanish and Italian dishes, including a good pizza selection, quick service, moderate prices and a pleasant ambience. Closed Sunday, it's a block and a half from the Cotton Tree, on Pultney St behind the US embassy.

Almost next door to the US embassy you'll see the sign for *Taj Mahal* (tel 23750), which is upstairs and open every day except Sunday. The Indian food is good and prices are moderate, but the atmosphere is disappointing. The *Paramount Hotel* is another possibility. The luncheon special is reasonably priced, and the service is quick.

If you want to experiment with African food, try *Provilac* (tel 31704), which serves an all-Sierra Leone buffet every Wednesday at lunch for about US$2. It's several km from downtown on Congo Cross Rd leading towards the beach. Some typical Sierra Leonean dishes are potato-leaves sauce, okra sauce, palm oil stew, groundnut stew and pepper soup.

The *Bacardi* on the hill overlooking Freetown serves Lebanese food and is the best in town according to some. It's also the city's top nightclub.

Beach Hotel Area The restaurant with the best location is *The Lighthouse* – right next to the water. The cuisine is Armenian and Lebanese and quite good, plus prices are moderate. It is down the hill from the Bintumani – go to the hotel's gate and take the path to your left just before entering.

Between the Mammy Yoko and the Cape Sierra are three restaurants right next to each other, overlooking a bay. All three are very good and moderately priced. *El Ancla*, closed Tuesday, serves Spanish cuisine, lobsters when in season, and other seafood. The bar is a good place to have a drink even if you're not hungry. *Chez Alex's*, closed Monday, also has great lobster and other seafood, plus meat dishes. You can eat at the lively bar, talk to Alex and buy one of his T-shirts, or eat under the palm trees on the sand. *Cape Club* serves similar food and is closed Tuesday.

By reputation Freetown's best restaurant is *The Atlantic*. It's about three km from the beach hotels towards Freetown just before you turn away from the coast. The shrimp, lobster and barracuda are recommended. Open every evening plus Sunday lunch, it has tables that are very near the beach and it has music later in the evening, sometimes even an orchestra on Saturday. You won't find a taxi afterwards unless you arrange to be picked up. You can also eat Chinese food at the *Jade Garden* in the casino between the Mammy Yoko and the Cape Sierra, but the food is mediocre.

Entertainment & Sports

Bars The only decent place for a drink downtown is the *Paramount Hotel*. At the beach hotels, the bars at *Chez Alex's* and *El Ancla* are quite popular, with a relaxed atmosphere.

For cheap bars, *City Hotel*, run by a fascinating old Swiss guy, is high on atmosphere – where drunken derelicts mingle with the adventurous. *Khadra* on Walpole St, 100 metres from the Cotton Tree, is typical of the Freetown bars. At *Flora's Inn* a block away, you're likely to meet Peace Corps volunteers.

Nightclubs The best in town is *Bacardi*, which has its own generator and is on the hill overlooking Freetown. There's a casino and restaurant there as well, and a cover charge on weekends. The *Atlantic Restaurant*, the *Mammy Yoko*, the *Rokel Club* at the Cape Sierra, and the *Brookfields Hotel* all frequently have live music on weekends but it's more for listening than dancing. For gambling, there's also the *Casino Leone* between the Mammy Yoko and the Cape Sierra.

All other nightclubs are for the common people and offer dancing. They are open only when there's electricity in that section of town. *Count Down* on Pademba Rd is one of the better ones. If you're looking for a disreputable place, try the *City Hotel Disco*. Dancing partners are easy to find, but going alone may be risky. Others include *La Tropicana* on Walpole St, *Planza* on Kissy Rd, *Blow Up* on Howe St, *Storm* and *Kiss*.

Movie Theatres The theatres show only Kung Fu type films. Your choices include the *Odeon Theatre* at Siaka Stevens/ Howe St, with shows at 9 pm; the *Roxy Theatre* on Walpole St next to the US embassy, with shows at 6 and 9 pm; and the *Strand Theatre* on Waterloo St.

Sports All three beach hotels have tennis courts. If you're staying at one of them, be sure to ask for a card to prove you're a guest. It will allow you to play golf for free at the Freetown Golf Club, which has clubs for rent for about US$1.70. The club also has two good squash courts, which are usually occupied from 5.20 to 6.40 pm only but you be able a free court sometime outside those hours. There are no rackets for rent, but if you play with the African pro he'll find you a racket. The Aqua Club also has squash clubs, but you have to be invited to play.

The three beach hotels plus the Brookfields have pools, but none of them are suitable for doing laps. However, the ocean is calm and swimming is both possible and safe and conditions are also good for novice windsurfers. Several places in front of the beach hotels rent windsurfers for about US$10 an hour but they close around 5 pm.

If you're interested in fishing or hunting, see Yazbeck or Africa Tours travel agencies. The principal fish are large mackerel, jack, shark, barracuda and red mullet. You have the choice of fishing from rented power boats or from dugout canoes launched in the surf and paddled by local fishermen.

Things to Buy
Artisan Goods The best buy is the tie-dye cloth. You'll find some for sale along Wilberforce St near Wallace Johnson. For ready made clothes of African materials, try *Afro-Cheedonian Boutique* nearby on Rawdon St, across from the Yum Yum restaurant. Baskets and leather goods in Sierra Leone are of fairly good quality. You'll find them and other handicrafts at the *African Art Handicraft Centre* (3 Oxley St, Fourah Bay) a few km from downtown, as well as at the beach hotels. The main shopping areas for goods of all kinds are along Kissy, Wilberforce, Siaka Stevens, Wallace Johnson and Garrison Sts.

Music For cassettes of Sierra Leonean music, the two most well-known places are *Tapes International* at 27 Regent St and *Pat Paul* on Kroo Town Rd, three blocks from the intersection with Siaka Stevens. Both places are open late. Some of the leading groups and singers are Bosca, God Fathers and Afro National.

Getting There & Away
Bush Taxi You can catch poda poda in Freetown for Conakry around 8 am at the Regent Rd Parking Ground, near Free St; the trip takes four or six hours. You'll find poda poda in Freetown at the Dan St Parking Ground (for Kenema), on Fyabon St, and on Kissy St at the Shell station.

Bus The buses are downtown in the old railway station at Rawdon and Wallace Johnson. (The train no longer operates.)

Getting Around
Airport Transport At old Lungi airport, the departure tax is now in foreign currency (US$10). You'll find a bar and a place to change money 24 hours a day.

Getting from the airport to Freetown (24 km) is a problem because the journey involves a 40-minute ferry ride and a road journey at either end. Most people take the airport bus which drops you off at the

Paramount hotel in the centre of town. Old but reliable, it costs several US dollars in leones. If you prefer to take a taxi, take one only to the ferry and then catch another on the opposite side, otherwise the trip will be quite expensive. Apart from the occasional ferry breakdown, the problem is timing. You may arrive just as the ferry is leaving, so the trip may take anywhere from 1½ to 3½ hours. When you leave Freetown, call the Paramount (tel 24531) for the bus departure time, which is usually three hours before every flight. Reservations are not required.

Travellers staying at one of the beach hotels can take advantage of the ferry service offered by the Sierra Beach Hotel, which has a ferry waiting for most international flights. The cost is US$15. Or you can even take a helicopter. The cost is US$300 if you charter it to/from the Mammy Yoko, and US$40 if you take one of their regular flights and pay only for a seat.

Taxi Taxis do not have meters. In theory, fares are fixed and posted; in practice, they must be negotiated. A shared taxi costs only about Le 1 for a short trip in town; a poda poda costs 25c. Invariably, however, drivers will give you the 'charter' fare, which is about five times higher. A taxi from downtown to the beach hotels (15 km) takes a good 15 minutes – longer at rush hour. The fare is posted in the hotel lobbies but most drivers will accept less if you bargain. For a taxi by the hour, drivers will accept about half the official price to the beach area if you stick to the downtown area.

Taxis are plentiful during the day unless there's a petrol shortage; at night, they're difficult to find except at the beach hotels and the Paramount Hotel, where there's 24-hour service.

Bus The buses are even cheaper than the shared taxis. No 3 takes you to the beach area, but expect a long wait.

Car Rental Apex (tel 024-385/475) 20 Freetown Rd, Lumley; Freetown Travel Agencies (tel 25850) Walpole St, Freetown; Gamsieco Ltd (tel 24205) Bathurst St, Freetown.

The Interior

Accommodation outside Freetown is primitive. Various government agencies and organisations operate guest houses throughout the country and they frequently allow travellers to use them, but sometimes only if you make reservations. For information and reservations contact the Ministry of Interior (tel 23447) on State Avenue, before leaving Freetown.

KENEMA
Kenema is 263 km east of Freetown on the main road. Three hotels, in descending order and price, are *Capital Hotel*, *Eastern Motel* for about US$1.50 and, for about half that amount, *Travellers' Lodge* at the Mobil station.

BO
Bo is the major town between Freetown and Kenema. There's little of interest but if you stop over the *Demby Hotel* and *Sugar Ball Hotel* are the two choices.

MAGBURAKA
Magburaka is the major town between Monrovia and Sefadu. The tiny Mamunta Game Reserve is nearby. The *Hotel Adams* may still be in business.

MAKENI
The market here is vibrant and well known for its tie-dye cloth. There's no hotel in town but the Peace Corps reportedly allows travellers to stay at its rest house; expect to pay about 50c.

GAME RESERVES
Sierra Leone is not noted for its game reserves. Few people see them because

they are not easily accessible, no hotels are nearby, and the wildlife doesn't begin to compare with that in many game parks in East Africa. However, if you've never been to a game park in Africa, you may find the two in Sierra Leone interesting. You'll see the countryside to boot.

Mamunta Game Reserve

This new game reserve is the easiest to get to, about 250 km from Freetown near Magburaka in central Sierra Leone. Covering an area of only 31 square km of swampland, it supports a wide variety of wild animals and birds including baboon, monkey, leopard, buffalo, antelope and two threatened species of dwarf-crocodile.

Outama-Kilimi National Park

This park is over 30 times larger than Mamunta and has a greater variety of wildlife, but it's also more remote – in the north-west in the Bombali district on the Guinea border. The drive on the all-weather road from Freetown, via Kambia or Kamakwie, takes about eight hours. The park is in an area of grasslands, woods, flood plains and rain forests, and is divided into two separate units, with the Great Scarcies river (or the Kolente) forming the western boundary. You'll find a mixture of animals and birds – chimpanzee, monkey, bush baby (a nocturnal animal resembling a monkey), baboon, leopard, hippo, buffalo, wart hog, crocodile as well as numerous birds including kingfisher, hornbill, heron, goose, hawk, eagle, touraco weaver and sunbird. Those with camping gear can stay at sites in the park.

Togo

If there were a popularity contest among countries in West Africa, Togo would probably win. It's only a pencil-thin strip of land, about the size of Belgium, but interesting enough to get rave reviews from travellers. Lomé, the thriving capital city, and the nearby beaches are the main reasons. The ocean is only a block from the heart of town, and you can reach several good beaches without even taking a taxi.

The market is one of the five best in Black Africa and equally famous throughout Africa are the women traders themselves – nicknamed 'Nana Benz' because they all seem to own Mercedes Benz. Elsewhere in town, you can buy everything from good pieces of African art and the best sandals in West Africa, to smuggled goods and black market currency. Taxis are everywhere, more than half of them owned by the Nana Benz, but the centre of Lomé is small enough to explore on foot. Plus the selection of restaurants and nightclubs is outstanding, so relax and have a good time – which is what most people do.

There's more to Togo than Lomé and the beaches. For starters, the people are friendly, and beer Benin, by reputation one of the best beers in Africa, makes it even easier to strike up a friendship. Togo is the only country in West Africa that allows Americans and Canadians to enter without visas, and the same honour is bestowed on most Europeans as well.

Upcountry, you'll pass through some beautiful hills on your way to the game parks where you can stalk a few animals, and you can see the famous fortress-like houses of the Tamberma, who used to go naked and occasionally still do. For a totally different environment, travel down the coast to Aného and observe life in a fishing village where the men on the beach slowly haul in their long fishing nets accompanied by the rhythm of guttural singing. Or cross Lake Togo in a canoe and visit Togoville, a centre of the fetish cult in Togo. In short, there's a lot more to do in Togo than just soaking up the sun on the beach.

HISTORY

Togo was the only German colony in West Africa before it came under French and British rule. The entire British section of Togo eventually became part of Ghana and the resulting boundaries, which resemble a finger poking into the side of West Africa, are totally artificial. Since this partition, Togo and Ghana have bickered constantly like a separated couple, despite their cultural affinities and the constant cries for reunification since independence.

Little is known of Togo prior to the late 15th century when the Portuguese first arrived. Various tribes migrated into Togo from the surrounding regions – the Ewe (EH-vay) from Nigeria and Benin, and the Mina (MEE-nah) and Guin from Ghana – and settled along the coast. When the slave trade began in earnest in the 16th century, the Mina prospered and became ruthless agents for the European slave-traders, travelling north to buy slaves from the Kabyé and other northern tribes. The Europeans built forts at Elmina in neighbouring Ghana and at Ouidah in Benin, but not in Togo, which had no natural harbours. Some of the slaves that were sent off to Brazil were

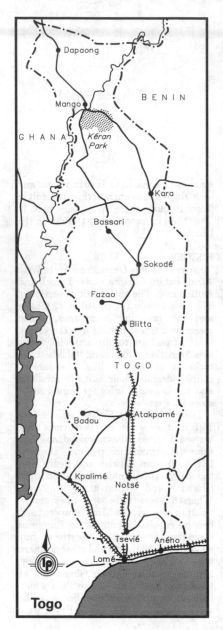

eventually freed and returned to settle along the coast from Accra (Ghana) to Lagos (Nigeria). They, in turn, became heavily involved in the slave trade. The father of Sylvanus Olympio, Togo's first president, was one of these 'Brazilians'.

Colonial Period

When the slave trade started dying out in the mid-19th century, the Europeans turned their attention to trade in commodities – palm and coconut oil, cocoa, coffee and cotton. The rivalry between Britain and France was fierce, while Germany, which initially showed no interest in colonial expansion, surprised the main colonial powers by sending a ship to the coast of 'Togoland' in 1884. In Togoville they signed a treaty with a local king, Mlapa, that agreed to 'protect' the natives in return for German sovereignty.

German Togoland, like neighbouring Gold Coast (Ghana), went through an economic miracle before WW I. Through the introduction and scientific cultivation of cocoa, coffee and cotton, the colony's agricultural resources boomed and soon paid for all of Germany's colonial expenses. Local tax revenues equalling 5% of GNP, which were large for the time, were enough to pay for everything, including a harbour and breakwaters at Lomé, a telegraph system, excellent roads, a brewery, a powerful radio transmitter to Germany, three railroads and the highest level of educational development in Africa – nine out of 10 school age children were in school in 1914.

The Togolese, however, had to suffer the forced labour, direct taxes and 'pacification' campaigns of the Germans which killed thousands of people. Large numbers of Togolese migrated to the Gold Coast and in 1914, with the outbreak of WW I, the country welcomed the British forces with open arms. Encircled by British and French colonies, Togoland was defenceless and so the Germans blew up their expensive radio station and surrendered – the Allies' first victory in WW I.

After the war, Togoland was no longer a colony *per se*. According to the League of Nations mandate, France was to administer the eastern two-thirds of Togoland and Britain the other third. This virtually ended development in Togoland until the 1950s.

During the colonial period, the Mina, by virtue of their position on the coast and long association with Europeans, came to dominate Togo's economic and political life to the exclusion of northern groups, whom they treated as savages and systematically excluded from any significant participation in the government and economy.

Independence

The dissection of Togoland divided the Ewes. After WW II, political groups on both sides agitated for reunification, which the French violently opposed. Sylvanus Olympio, a Mina from the south, led the cause on the Francophone side. In 1956, hopes of reunification were dashed when British Togoland, in a plebiscite which was irregular and unilateral, voted to be incorporated into Ghana, then on the brink of independence.

When independence on the French side came in 1960, the French backed a northern-based party, but Olympio's party won and he became the first president. The outside world was impressed with what they saw of Olympio's regime. The Mina were able and competent and knew how to manipulate western opinion. The government, however, was repressive, violent and discriminatory, driving thousands into exile and infuriating the Northerners.

In 1963, Togo became the first country on the continent to experience a military coup following independence. (They proved just how easy it is to stage a coup and the continent has averaged over two a year since then, plus many more unsuccessful ones.) It was provoked by Olympio's refusal to hire some 600 Togolese, mainly Cabrais from the north, who had served in the French army and returned to Togo after the Franco-Algerian war. Because they were *petits nordiques* as Olympio called them, he refused to employ any of them in his small, 250-man army. Out of work, they were furious with Olympio for having denied northerners the means for advancing in the army or in the civil service. All it took was a few shots by a band of these men to kill Olympio at the gates of the US embassy as he sought refuge. Thousands of exiles returned and one of them, Nicolas Grunitzky, Olympio's brother-in-law, was put in charge. He lasted four years until he was deposed in a bloodless coup headed by Colonel (now General) Etienne Eyadéma, a northerner.

Eyadéma set out to unify the country, insisting on one trade union confederation and one political party. Every time he makes a public appearance, he is accompanied by a cheering, dancing crowd of hundreds of women all in identical traditional dress. Chances are you'll see one of those cheering choruses if you stay very long. There is also a huge bronze statue of *Le Guide* at the Place de l'Indépendance in Lomé, and you can even buy wristwatches with a picture of Eyadéma that fades and reappears every 15 seconds, plus a comic book where he appears as a Superman character – all in the name of national unity.

The comic book recounts the most historic event of the 1970s, when Eyadéma's private plane crashed in Sara-Kara on 24 January 1974. Most of those on board, including Eyadéma, survived, but four didn't. Only two weeks before, he had announced the government's decision to increase Togo's share in the lucrative foreign-owned phosphate mines to 51%. Convinced that 'imperialists' had attempted to assassinate him for this action, nine days later on 2 February, he announced the complete nationalisation of the company. About the same time, following the example of Zaire's Mobutu, he ordered all Togolese with French first names to replace them with African ones;

Etienne Eyadéma became Gnassingbé Eyadéma.

Today

Under Eyadéma's guidance, Togo's economy grew dramatically from 1967 to 1980 and Togo experienced the highest real growth rate in West Africa. Phosphates were the reason and they account for about half of export earnings, making Togo one of the world's largest producers. To attract tourists, the government constructed many new hotels, including two five-star hotels, increasing the number of rooms from 200 to over 3000 today. A new steel plant, a cement works, an oil refinery and sugar operations were other new initiatives. Some of the projects were not so production-oriented, such as the lavish presidential palace, the political party (RPT) headquarters, the RPT's training school, and the huge Hôtel du Deux Février.

It was all a bit too ambitious, and when the recession of the early 1980s hit and phosphates prices tumbled, the economy was devastated. The cost of servicing the debt reached a staggering 50% of the budget. The IMF stepped in to help and forced the government to sell at least 10 unproductive government enterprises, lease the state-owned oil refinery to multinationals and reduce the bureaucracy. But even in 1986, the picture was still gloomy. On the brighter side, revenues from tourism grew, and Togo's Green Revolution program, started in 1977, was doing extremely well. The country is now virtually self-sufficient in food production in non-drought years.

Politically, relations with the west are excellent. Togo and the US became much closer in the late 1970s when the Americans tipped Eyadéma off about a rumoured coup attempt. American travellers are the beneficiaries – they no longer need visas. Relations with Ghana continue to be bad, as a result of the division of the Ewe and other ethnic groups at the end of WW I. Every two years or so there's another coup

attempt against Eyadéma. Each time Togo closes the border for months, claiming it was staged in Ghana. The Ghanaians do the same when they have coup attempts. In 1984, bombs exploded in Lomé on the eve of Pope John Pauls' visit. In 1986, dissidents within Togo – not outside mercenaries – staged a coup that came very close to being successful. Eyadéma himself fired many of the shots that killed 13 of the attackers. Some of these are backed by the sons of Olympio and other Mina supporters exiled in Paris, possibly by Libya as well. But Eyadéma is a survivor, and after 20 years in power, he has become one of Africa's elder statesmen.

PEOPLE

With about 40 ethnic groups and a population of three million people, Togo has one of the more heterogeneous populations in Africa. The two largest groups are the Ewe and the Kabyé. The Kabyé, who count President Eyadéma among their numbers, are concentrated in the north around Kara and central Togo and are known as hard working people skilled in terrace farming. Travelling north of Atakpamé, you'll know when you reach the Kabyé area by the design of the houses. The predominantly rectangular huts give way to the round Kabyé houses that have conical roofs and are joined together by a low wall. The compound is known as a *soukala* (SOU-kah-lah) and is designed for an extended family, where a father and his sons and their wives all live. The granaries are often more interesting than the houses. They are also circular but slightly elevated and about half the size of the regular houses.

The Ewe-speaking people are concentrated in the south, particularly on the cocoa and coffee plantations in the southwest. They include people who call themselves Ewe, such as Anlo, Adja, Peda, Plah, Mina, Guin, etc. However, some of these groups, such as the Mina and the Guin, are not ethnic Ewe. The Guin are Ga people from Accra while the

Mina are Fanti people from the Ghanaian coast. In Togo, the Mina tend to be somewhat better educated than other groups; many are bureaucrats and merchants.

One of the more interesting things about the Ewe-speaking people is their strong attachment to animist beliefs even though many are Christians. They believe Mahou, the Supreme Being, created some 600 deities, many representing natural phenomena such as thunder and disease. The Ewe can communicate with these deities by joining a cult and worshipping them, but only these spirits can communicate with God. A person's soul can be reincarnated and you can influence this by casting a spell. When someone dies, relatives go through a series of funeral rites during the following year to help free the soul of the deceased. Each newborn child is the reincarnation of some deceased person in the area, and a week after birth they determine by divination who that ancestor is.

The Ewe consider the birth of twins a great blessing and hope to increase the chances of this happening by offering kola nuts and water to figurines embodying the spirit of twins. You may see some of these figurines in the market. Not all Togolese consider twins to be a blessing, however. The Bassari regard them as a misfortune, and used to kill one of the twins, or even both of them if this happened a second time to the same mother.

GEOGRAPHY

Togo is long and narrow and measures roughly 540 km by 110 km. A good road dotted with coconut palms and fishing villages runs along the 55-km coast from Lomé at the Ghana border to Benin, passing near Lake Togo on the way. Northeast of the lake is where all the phosphate is quarried. In Lomé and along the flatlands of the coast, there are lagoons which extend intermittently across the country just behind the sandy coast.

Inland, there are rolling hills covered with forests. The hills around Kpalimé are excellent for growing coffee, while those around Atakpamé afford some pleasant vistas. Central Togo is also the area of a major national park, the Forêt de Fazao. Further north above Lama-Kara, the hills drop down to savannah plains where you'll find the traditional houses of the Tamberma and another small park, the Réserve de la Kéran. Sokodé, about half way between Lomé and the northern border, is the largest city in the interior, with about 40,000 inhabitants, followed by Lama-Kara, Kpalimé and Atakpamé.

CLIMATE

Rains fall from May through October. In the south including Lomé, there's a dry spell from approximately mid-July to mid-September. In the drier northern areas, there's no such interlude. The best time to visit is the dry season, but don't stay away just because you may encounter rain. The coast, including Lomé and up to 10 km inland, is a fairly dry area. Mid-February to mid-April is the hottest period.

VISAS

Nationals of the following countries do not need visas: Belgium, Canada, Denmark, France, Germany, Italy, Luxembourg, Netherlands, Norway, Sweden and the USA. Getting a visa is simple because French embassies generally have authority to issue them where there is no Togolese embassy. Visas extensions are available from the Sûreté National in Lomé and usually take a good three days.

An exit permit (*permit d'embarquement*) is required if you stay in Togo more than 10 days. You must apply at the Sûreté at least 48 hours prior to departure.

One month tourist visas to Ghana take one to three days at the Ghanaian embassy in Lomé (open 8 am to 2 pm) and cost CFA 9000. Visas to Benin can be obtained at the southern border (Ouidah). The border is open 24 hours, but visas are obtainable only from 8 am to 12.30 pm and 3 pm to

6.30 pm on weekdays, and Saturday 8 am to 12.30 pm. This is the only Benin border station that issues visas. The Nigerian embassy takes three full days to issue visas to Nigeria. The French embassy issues visas to Burkina Faso, CAR, Chad, Ivory Coast, Mauritania and Senegal. Visas to Niger cannot be obtained in Togo; the nearest Niger embassies are in neighbouring Benin and Ghana.

Diplomatic Missions Abroad
Accra, Bonn, Brussels, Kinshasa, Lagos, Libreville, London, Ottawa, Paris, Washington. Consulates: Geneva.

MONEY
US$1 = 287 CFA
£1 = 537 CFA

The unit of currency is the West African CFA. Lomé has a thriving black market in Ghanaian cedis. If you're near the market and hear someone hiss at you, it will almost certainly be one of the dealers. The rate is good but count your notes carefully as some dealers try to cheat you.

Banking hours: weekdays 7.30 to 11 am and 2.30 to 4 pm. Banks: BIAO, UTB (Union Togolaise de Banque), BTCI (Banque Togolaise pour le Commerce et l'Industrie).

LANGUAGE
French is the official language. About half the people speak or understand Ewe. The second most widely spoken African language is Kabre. Greetings in Ewe:

Good morning	mou-DOH-boh-no, nee-fon
Good evening	mee-LIE-nee-ah
How are you?	nee-FOH-ah
Thank you	mou-DOH, ack-pay-noh
Goodbye	mee-AH-gah-DOH-goh

GENERAL INFORMATION
Health
A yellow fever vaccination is required, as is a cholera shot if you come from an

infected area. Hôpital Tokoin (tel 212501) in Lomé is a typical African hospital and should be avoided like the plague, which you might pick up there.

Security
Lomé is a fairly safe city. Pickpockets frequently operate around the Grand Marché, the cathedral and the downtown area around the Hôtel du Golfe. Walking along the beach after dark is not safe.

Business Hours
Business: weekdays 8.30 am to 12 noon and 3.30 to 6.00 pm; Saturday 8.30 am to 12.30 pm. Government: weekdays 7 am to 12 noon and 2.30 to 5.30 pm.

Public Holidays
1 January, 13 January (Liberation Day), 24 January, Easter Monday, 24 April, 27 April (Independence Day), 1 May, End of Ramadan (17 May 88, 6 May 1989), Ascension Day, Whit Monday, 21 June, Tabaski (25 July 88, 14 July 1989), 15 August, 1 November, 25 December.

Photography
A photo permit is not required, but be sure not to photograph government buildings and personnel, the airport, the harbour or major industries.

Time, Phone & Telex
When it's noon in Togo, it's noon in London and 7 am in New York (8 am during daylight savings time). The international telephone service is good. The post office and major hotels have telex facilities.

GETTING THERE
Air
From Europe, there are direct flights from Paris, Geneva, Amsterdam and Frankfurt. From the USA, you'll have to take Air Afrique or Nigeria Airways from New York (transferring in Dakar, Abidjan or Lagos), or go via Europe. At Christmas and in July, Friends of Togo (Box 666,

Durham NC 27702) sponsors two-week excursions on Air Afrique from New York for US$760.

Car

Roads in Togo are excellent and paved from Lomé to the northern border and all along the coast. Both Accra (Ghana) and Cotonou (Benin) are only three to four hours by car from Lomé on asphalt road. The more interesting route to Accra is not via the coast but north-west to the mountainous area of Kpalimé. From there, you travel west to Ghana and south-west along Volta Lake, the largest man-made lake in Africa, passing by Akosombo Dam at the southern end. The road is 60% longer but tarred all the way.

Ouagadougou (Burkina Faso) to Lomé is 967 km, an easy two-day drive on asphalt road. Niamey to Lomé takes two full days, whether you go via Benin (1217 km) or northern Togo (1192 km). The road is now paved all the way on both routes. All the borders close at 6 pm except at Ouidah on the coastal road connecting Lomé and Cotonou, which is open 24 hours.

Bush Taxi

Bush taxis from Lomé to Cotonou and Accra take only three to four hours. You'll find those for Cotonou near the Grand Marché in Lomé, and those for Accra just across the border in Ghana.

Ouagadougou-Lomé takes about two days in taxi or minibus. A direct taxi or minibus from Lomé to Ouaga or vice versa, costs about CFA 13,000, but only about half that much if you go only as far as Dapaong and catch another there. You'll find decent accommodation in Dapaong.

GETTING AROUND
Air

Within Togo, don't count on flying; almost everybody goes overland. Air Togo (Rue du Commerce, tel 213310), however, charters small planes.

Bush Taxi

The bush taxi system in Togo is excellent. In Lomé, you'll find new minibuses at the Gare Routière; they leave at all hours of the day to towns throughout Togo. Those for Aného leave from near the market.

Train

For total submersion into African life for a few hours, try the train from Lomé to Kpalimé. The local expatriates occasionally have a whale of a time taking loads of beer on board and having a six-hour drinkathon. There are two trains a day, leaving Lomé at 6.30 am and 3.15 pm; the journey takes at least six hours even though the schedule says much less. You could also take the train to Blitta via Atakpamé, but it's dangerous – a wreck in the mid-1980s resulted in many fatalities. The Blitta line train leaves Lomé at 5.45 am, arriving 1 pm or so, and returns to Lomé that evening around 9 pm.

There's no air-con in 1st class, but it's quite comfortable; 2nd class is fairly crowded and costs less than half the price, about CFA 575 from Lomé to Kpalimé.

Lomé

Lomé is the pearl of West Africa. Seemingly half of the Peace Corps volunteers living within 2000 km of Lomé spend at least part of their vacations here. Travellers motoring their way across West Africa almost invariably spend a few days camping on the beach outside Lomé. It's not just on-the-cheap travellers who are attracted to Lomé. French and German tourists flock here in the winter time. The city has two five-star hotels and one of them, 35-storeys high, is the tallest building in black Africa outside of South Africa.

For a city of half a million inhabitants, Lomé has more than its fair share of attractions. On the top of the list are the beaches and the good ones are only a 10-minute walk from the heart of town. In no

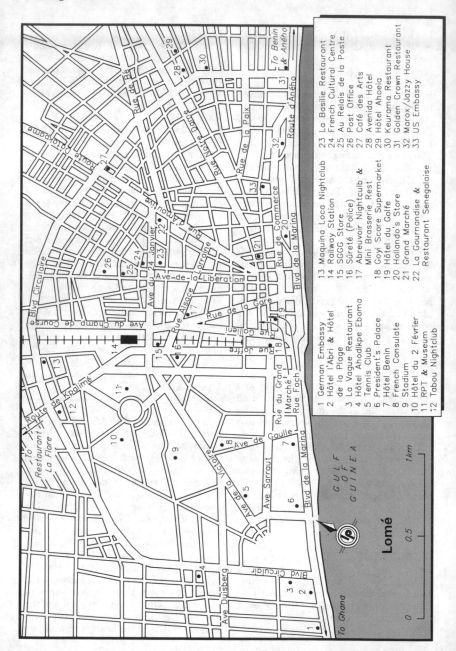

Lomé

GULF
OF
GUINEA

To Ghana
To Benin & Aného

1 German Embassy
2 Hôtel l'Abri & Hôtel de la Plage
3 La Vague Restaurant
4 Hôtel Ahodlkpe Eboma
5 Tennis Club
6 President's Palace
7 Hôtel Benin
8 French Consulate
9 Stadium
10 Hôtel du 2 Février
11 RPT & Museum
12 Tabou Nightclub
13 Maquina Loca Nightclub
14 Railway Station
15 SGGG Store
16 Sûreté (Police)
17 Abreuvoir Nightclub & Mini Brasserie Rest
18 Goyi Score Supermarket
19 Hôtel du Golfe
20 Hollando's Store
21 Grand Marché
22 La Gourmandise & Restaurant Senegalaise
23 La Basilie Restaurant
24 French Cultural Centre
25 Au Relais de la Poste
26 Post Office
27 Café des Arts
28 Avenida Hôtel
29 Hôtel Ahoeia
30 Keurama Restaurant
31 Golden Crown Restaurant
32 Marox/Jazzy House
33 US Embassy

other major West African city is the beach so convenient. For as little as US$10, you can get a room at a beach hotel, or pay US$2 and sleep on the beach at a camping spot out of town. Or splurge US$80 on a double at a five-star beach hotel, which is good value compared to prices in the USA and Europe.

The range of restaurants is outstanding – from some of the best home-style African cooking on the continent (US$2 a meal) to fancy French and seafood restaurants that hold their own against those in Abidjan and Dakar. As for the market, the selection of African materials is fantastic.

At night, you have a wide choice of nightclubs – from the ultra fancy to the lively African. And with a major highway along the beach and a semi-circular one (Boulevard Circulaire) passing around the urban centre, it's hard to get lost.

Information

Embassies Belgium (tel 210323); Egypt; France (BP 337, tel 212571/3); Gabon (BP 4872, tel 215363); West Germany (BP 1175, tel 212338/70); Ghana (BP 92, tel 213494); Nigeria (BP 1189, tel 213925); Tunisia; USA (BP 852, tel 212991/2); Zaire (BP 1102, tel 215155).

Bookstores & Supermarkets The two best bookstores are *Librairie Bon Pasteur* across from the cathedral on Rue du Commerce and *La Bouquinerie* nearby, across from Hôtel du Golfe. Try the bookstores at the Sarakawa and the Deux Février for colourful books on Togo.

Goyi Score is the major supermarket, and *SGGG* the major department store (also a supermarket).

Travel Agencies There's no lack of tour agencies offering excursions to the interior. Those in the heart of town are: Pronto Voyages (Rue du Commerce across from Hôtel du Golfe, BP 250, tel 210914); Togo Palm Tours (1 Rue du Commerce, BP 3316, tel 215784, telex 5278); Afrique

Excursions (Rue Gallieni facing SGGG, BP 4113, tel 210268); Gazelle Tours (13 Rue de la Gare near SGGG, BP 538, tel 210767, telex 5002); and Togo Voyages (13 Rue du Grand Marché, BP 1078, tel 211277). Togo Touristc (1 Avenue de la Libération and at Hôtels Bénin and 2 Février, BP 7543, tel 210932, telex 5050) caters to Germans. STMP Voyages (2 Rue du Commerce near the cinema, tel 215793) is recommended for airline tickets. Typical prices for a three-day group tour of the north is CFA 80,000 per person.

Place de l'Indépendance

Shopping and just living in Lomé are more interesting than seeing the few sights. Still, the Place de l'Indépendance is a good place to start exploring. There stands the gilded bronze statue of President Eyadéma, carved by North Koreans. Across the way is the **Hôtel de Deux Février**. No visit would be complete without a trip to the 35th floor for a drink – best at dusk when the sun is going down, along with the price of drinks (happy hour). On the Place, you'll also see the **RPT Building**, the headquarters of Togo's unique political party.

National Museum

The entrance to the museum is behind the RPT Building. It houses historical artefacts, pottery, costumes, musical instruments, wood carvings, traditional medical remedies, including powders for pregnant women, and 'thunder stones' and cowrie shells, both formerly used as legal tender. The hours are weekdays 8 to 12 noon and 3 to 6 pm, Saturday 3 to 6 pm.

Bé

The adventurous will head to the African sections of town. Bé is about three km from the heart of town behind the Hôtel de la Paix. It is Lomé's oldest and most animated section (*quartier*). This is where you'll find the famous fetish market and a remarkable supply of traditional medicines used by sorcerers, including skulls of monkeys and birds, porcupine skin, wart hog teeth and all sizes of bones. The market there, quite unlike the one downtown, resembles that in a rural village. If a draft beer sounds tempting, look around for STC bar – you won't find any cheaper in town.

Amoutive

This is another interesting section of town, starting around the intersection of Boulevard Circulaire and the Route d'Atakpamé. This is a very animated area and one of the best places for late night street food.

Places to Stay – bottom end

In town, of the hotels along the beach, the cheapest is the long-standing and ever-popular *Hôtel de la Plage* (tel 213264), an excellent buy at about CFA 3300 to CFA 3800 a double without fan (CFA 6000 with air-con). You'll sleep to the pounding of ocean waves. Don't keep valuables in the room – the hotel has a reputation for thieves. It's a good km west from downtown, at the intersection of Boulevard Circulaire and the beach road, two km from the Ghanaian border. If it's full, try *Hôtel Lily* between the Plage and the Ghanaian border, next to the L'Auberge Provençale. A room with fan goes for about CFA 3800 to CFA 4400.

For something a little nicer on the beach, *Hôtel l'Abri* (tel 213584/58) next door to the Plage is highly recommended. Singles without air-con or hot water are about CFA 5500 to CFA 6500 and doubles CFA 6500 to CFA 8800. The rooms are bright, clean and, if you get an ocean-side room, breezy. There's a terrace and indoor bar-restaurant. Next door is *Hôtel le Maxime* (tel 214126), with air-con singles/doubles for about CFA 5800/6500. It has a new and improved French management. It also has a pleasant patio and a fine restaurant, although the portions are small.

At the opposite end of town beyond the Sarakawa and several hundred metres from the beach, is the *Foyer des Marins*

(tel 214126), which is unbeatable at about CFA 4500/5500 for a single/double with air-con (CFA 6000/7000 for the better rooms). Plus there's a video room, outdoor cinema, outdoor bar and pool, with an international telephone service that is popular because the rates are relatively low. The ambience can change dramatically. If you go when the Foyer's religious director is there, it's like a morgue but when he's on vacation, it's fun city – the bar is packed and women abound. The major problem with the Foyer is the location – a minimum CFA 350 taxi ride from downtown.

For a cheap hotel in the dead centre of town, there's *La Paloma* on Rue du Marché back of the UTB bank. A grubby double, sometimes with no running water, will cost you about CFA 3300. Or, you can get a similar quality room for about CFA 2200 at *Hôtel Atlantique* behind the customs building.

The three-storey *Hôtel Ahodikpé Eboma* (tel 214780) costs a little less and is recommended. It is less centrally located on Boulevard Circulaire, several blocks down from the Hôtel de la Plage and recommended. But the rooms have fans and super comfortable double beds for about CFA 3800 (CFA 5500 with air-con). The locks on the doors, however, are terrible and offer little deterrence to thieves.

Camping Campers are in luck. Nine km to the east beyond the port is *Robinson Plage*, *Le Ramatou* (tel 210875) and *Alice Place*. The first two are next to each other and are about equal in quality with friendly managements. Forget Alice's; it has filthy toilets, no showers and no ocean view. Robinson Plage is on the beach, while La Ramatou is 100 metres away. At Ramatou, you can pitch a tent for CFA 500 or rent a hut (*paillotte*) for about CFA 2200 – one sleeps at least four people, and some beds have mosquito nets. A paillotte at Robinson Plage costs around CFA 3600 for two people. Both places have clean bathrooms and showers.

Keep an eye on your luggage because thievery is not uncommon. Travellers have even been robbed at gun point during the day in this beach area. The restaurants are not cheap, around CFA 3800 for the special menu, but they serve some of the best seafood in town. On weekends, you'll find expatriates here with their children because there are areas with no undertow.

Places to Stay – middle

Of the mid-range hotels, the two best are *Hôtel du Golfe* (tel 215141, telex 5290, cards AE, D, V, CB) in the dead centre of town and *Hôtel le Bénin* (tel 212485, telex 5264, cards AE, D) on the ocean, a 10 to 15-minute walk from downtown. Good singles/doubles are about CFA 12,000 to CFA 16,000/CFA 14,000 to CFA 18,000 plus tax (CFA 300) at the Golfe, and CFA 12,000 to CFA 13,500/CFA 14,000 to CFA 15,500 plus tax at the Bénin. Both places have pools but the Bénin's is much longer. The Bénin, a big renovated hotel of the independence era, is 200 metres from the ocean and preferred by beach lovers. The well-managed Golfe is livelier and a favourite of many because of the central location, choice of two restaurants, and popular terrace bar with bands almost every evening after work.

For hotels with African management and ambience and decent air-con rooms, you have three choices. *Hôtel Agni* (tel 214734, telex 5047), several km from downtown across the lagoon in Tokoin, charges about CFA 9500/11,000 plus tax for small but decent singles/doubles with, typically African, low lighting. The roof-top restaurant is very popular with Africans.

Less expensive and closer to town is the new *Avenida Hôtel*, one block from Boulevard Circulaire on the eastern end, with singles/doubles for about CFA 8600/10,000. Four blocks away on a back street is the 20-room *Hôtel Ahoefa*, with singles/doubles for about CFA 8000/9500. You'll find bathrooms with hot water, a bar and restaurant, plus polite service – the hotel's hallmark.

Places to Stay – top end

Bizarre as it may seem, the most deluxe hotel south of the Sahara – the glittery *Hôtel du Deux Février* – has a low occupancy rate even though the price is quite reasonable. In a land of sunshine and beaches, who wants to stay in a skyscraper a km or two from the ocean? It's the government which is losing millions a year, not Sofitel which manages it. The name commemorates the day the Togolese government nationalised the phosphate company, nine days after Eyadéma's famous crash. Most peoples' favourite, with an olympic-size pool and a real winner in every way, is the five-star PLM *Hôtel Sarakawa*, on the ocean three km from downtown.

Near the Sarakawa and a better buy for the money is the ever-popular, four-star Frantel *Hôtel de la Paix*, which has a private beach across the street. It's an architectural landmark in Lomé and has small, very modern rooms and, better, bungalows with kitchenettes, living rooms and TVs for about the same price. Those interested primarily in the beach may prefer the more informal atmosphere at the *Hôtel Tropicana*, 18 km east of Lomé. The horse riding on the beach there is something you won't soon forget. You could also stay overnight at the *Hôtel du Lac* on Lake Togo. Both it and the Tropicana are closed after Easter until 1 July.

Hôtel de Deux Février (tel 210003, telex 5347), CFA 26,000/28,000 for singles/doubles, long pool, tennis courts, casino, shops galore, movie theatre, disco, cards AE, D, CB, V.
PLM Hôtel Sarakawa (tel 216590, telex 5354), CFA 24,000/27,000 for singles/doubles (CFA 28,500/31,500 with ocean view), windsurfers, casino, horseback riding, tennis, hairdresser, shops, cards AE, D, V, CB.
Hôtel de la Paix (tel 215297, telex 5252), singles/doubles for CFA 20,000/23,000 (CFA 3000 more for an ocean-view room), pool, tennis, casino, disco, mini-golf and a private beach across the street, cards AE, D, V, CB.
Hôtel Tropicana (tel 213406, telex 5269), single/double bungalows for about CFA 15,000/

19,000 with breakfast, tennis, two pools, disco, mini-golf, a terrific beach for horseback riding, cards AE, D, V, CB.

Hôtel Restaurant du Lac, singles/doubles starting around CFA 11,000/13,000, pool, windsurfers, reservations through the Tropicana.

Places to Eat

Cheap Eats For inexpensive non-African food, two of Lomé's most popular places are the *Mini-Brasserie*, downtown near SGGG and open every day 6 am to 1 am, and *Chez Marox*, open to 10 pm and near the ocean, between downtown and the eastern end of Boulevard Circulaire. Marox is an open-air German delicatessen/ beer parlour with real knotty-pine decor, while Mini Brasserie is possibly Lomé's most popular restaurant, a meeting place with a convivial atmosphere and good food.

For rock bottom prices downtown, about CFA 550 a meal, there's *Restaurant de l'Amitié*, back of the UTB bank, popular with French hitchhikers and open every day until 11.30 pm, plus *Snack Vendome* and *Boulangerie Bopato* across from the BIAO bank, *Snack Domino* in the centre of town on Rue de la Gare and, further out on Boulevard Circulaire between the train tracks and Rue de Kpalimé, *Le Chawarama*, a Lebanese fast food joint. Then treat yourself one morning before 10 am to the unforgettable all-you-can-eat breakfast at the Sarakawa for CFA 1800, or the most yummy ice cream in town at *La Gourmandise* at the far eastern end of Rue 24 Janvier.

Togolese In most of Africa, it takes a lot of searching to find authentic African food other than in someone's home or on the street. Lomé is the exception and has a number of restaurants serving superb African cuisine with lots of good ingredients. *Keurama*, on the eastern end of Boulevard Circulaire and closed Monday, is recommended for those who want to experiment but are uncertain. The restaurant is clean, and it's a favourite of both Africans and Europeans. The cuisine is Senegalese and Togolese. Try the *poulet yassa* (chicken with onions and lemon juice), *tiebou dienne* (fish, vegetables and rice) or *agouti*, an animal which resembles rat and looks positively disgusting but is, in fact, tender and tasty.

Togolese food and CFA 100 draft beer is served at *Pili Pili*, on Rue de l'OCAM in the Ablogame area. It is closed Tuesday. The menu is varied, plus you'll hear some of the best sounds in town. There's even a show on weekends except Sunday, the day of rest. *Tanti Hanou* is where you go to eat African style – with your hands if you like (they'll offer you a spoon). You might not think it's known outside Lomé, but it's famous way beyond Togo. You can choose one or more of six spicy sauces to put on your corn pate. You'd really have to pig out to spend more than CFA 500. It closes at 7.30 pm, so go for lunch or early dinner. It is a block off Boulevard Circulaire on Rue Champs de Course. In the heart of town, you can't do better than *Goldfinger*, on a short side street leading from the Hôtel du Golfe towards the ocean. Ghanaian and Senegalese dishes are the specialities. Gourmets order in advance – the only way to get certain specialities of the house. It is closed Sunday.

Seafood *L'Auberge Provençale* (tel 211682), on the coastal road near the Ghanaian border, has become a culinary institution – their seafood is the best in town. Highly recommended are the mussels (*moules*), fish soup, groper (*merou*) and snails (*escargots*). The cuisine is southern French, and you can dine inside or outside except Tuesdays, the day-off. Less expensive but nine km east of town are *Le Ramatou* (tel 210875) and *Robinson Beach*, both open every day and specialising in seafood, with daily menus for about CFA 3800. At Ramatou, you can also get paella and Togolese dishes. Expect a long wait at both.

French Of the more moderately priced

French restaurants, *Au Relais de la Poste* (tel 214678), the favourite of French *coopérants* and those 'who know' is highly recommended. Go there. The atmosphere is friendly, sometimes boisterous, plus wandering minstrels play during the meal. It's downtown next to the post office and open every day. If the idea of a small quiet French bistro with 19th century decor sounds appealing, try *Le Lautrec* (tel 215021), downtown near Air Afrique and closed Sunday. Another moderately priced restaurant with a nice setting, attentive service, and a few Lebanese specialities as well, is *Las Vegas*, downtown on Rue 24 Janvier. It is closed Monday.

It's difficult to choose between the top five, all expensive. *Le Berry* (tel 215133), on the east end of Boulevard Circulaire and closed Sunday, is Lomé's most exclusive restaurant, with a formal ambience, excellent quality food, and outstanding service. The lamb, vegetables and escargots are recommended. Also one of the best is the attractively decorated *Alt München* (tel 216321), closed Tuesday and just beyond the Sarakawa. The seafood is also good here, and the service is excellent. *Le Cahors*, downtown on Rue 24 Janvier opposite the police station and closed Monday, offers French provincial cooking with individually prepared dishes. Inevitably, you'll be offered a *digestif* on the house. On the same street opposite the French Cultural Centre is *Le Basilic* (tel 215021), closed Monday. It has exquisite Mediterranean cuisine, but small portions. Finally, for good food and atmosphere, you cannot do better than *Le Panoramique*, the top-floor restaurant of the Deux Février.

Chinese If popularity means anything, then the moderately priced *Shangai* on Boulevard Circulaire near the Commissariat, must be one of the best restaurants in town for the money. *Golden Crown*, at the eastern intersection of the ocean highway and Boulevard Circulaire, is in the same price and quality range. If you are American, tell them so – they'll give you a 10% discount.

Lebanese The two best, both moderately priced and closed Monday, are *Le Phénicien* (tel 212816), downtown on Rue d'Amotive, and *La Vague* (tel 213264), at the western end of Boulevard Circulaire near the ocean. La Vague has good food and a pleasant Middle Eastern atmosphere, while Le Phénicien, with the special touches of Romeo, its owner, is simply fabulous.

Italian *Oceano* (tel 210119), across from Hôtel Sarakawa and down two short streets, serves the best pizza in town. The breezy roof-top setting is only icing on the cake. If you're on the opposite end of town, try *La Pizzeria* on Avenue Duisberg, another roof-top restaurant and connected to Le Petit Cabanon bar. If you want something more than pizza, your best bet is *Ristorante da Silvia* near the eastern end of Boulevard Circulaire opposite the Nigerian embassy. Built in the style of a colonial Italian villa, this restaurant serves fine Italian cuisine as well as pizza at moderate prices.

Entertainment & Sports

Bars The most popular place with expatriates and travellers is the terrace of the *Hôtel du Golfe*. One of the big attractions is the live band that usually shows up in the early evening. The best deal in town, if not all of West Africa, is atop the *Hôtel Deux Février*. The plush top floor bar has a Happy Hour from 5.30 to 8 pm when beers sell for only CFA 400. The plush environment, spectacular view and munchies are all free. *Le Bistroquet*, at the eastern end of Rue 24 Janvier, is a sophisticated pub-like bar with music on the weekend.

At the other end of the scale is the rustic *Café des Arts*, maybe the liveliest bar of its kind on the West African coast. It's a Peace Corps favourite with cheap draft beers (*pressions*), good music, and Davis, the friendly manager. This gem is on Boulevard Circulaire, near the intersection with the Route d'Atakpamé.

The immortal, investigative journalist John Braniff, a Peace Corps volunteer from Chicago, who apparently found work too tiring and the CFA 100 pressions at the Café des Arts too expensive for his meagre salary, undertook a painstaking cultural survey in 1985 of the local establishments serving pressions under CFA 75 (less than US 25c) and came up with 20. In the heart of town, he came up with four, thereby plotting for you a perfect afternoon of bar-hopping: *Panjar Bar* (or Jungle Bar) on the marché side of Goyi Score with brochettes and yam fries, *Bar Mawuena* on the south-east corner of the Grand Marché, *Petit Barroque* one block west and two blocks north of the American Cultural Centre and, half a block away, the winner for the marché area – at CFA 55 a pression – *La Mesure*.

If that's too expensive, there's always *Sweet Mother* in Tokoin, four streets north of the lagoon on the Route de Kpalimé, then three or four streets west. This not-so-hidden treasure has pressions for CFA 50 – with two bars no less, jukebox, pinball and a football table. After publishing his 'Cultural Guide To Togo: Pressions under 75 CFA', and admitting his limits, Braniff begged readers 'to take the baton' in the quest for additional qualifiers. Happy hunting.

Nightclubs Lomé's hottest *boîte de nuit* is *Abreuvoir*, downtown next to Mini-Brasserie and open every night. The clientele is European and African, with dancing partners galore, beers for CFA 1500, and a snack bar on the roof. Nearby, and lively on weekends, is *Z*, a big, plush joint with adult films and drinks for CFA 2000.

There are four more nightclubs near Boulevard Circulaire, not far from the Deux Février. The long-standing *Maquina Loca*, opposite the Mairie, is a popular disco with drinks for CFA 2000 and occasional live bands. Nearby is *Le Tabou*, an expensive, overly fancy disco that has good music and is open every night. Also nearby is *Le Tango*, the largest and best ventilated disco in town. The crowd is mostly European and the music varied, with beers for about CFA 2000 and open every night. Prices are half those of the other clubs, and the mix of tunes is good. *The Chess* at the Deux Février is lively only on weekends.

One of the 'in' spots, with a fair share of teenagers, is *Safari Club*. It has a flashy, noisy, crowded floor and western sounds. It's on the Kpalimé road at the lagoon, about a km beyond the Boulevard Circulaire. The newest, flashiest, most expensive nightclub in town is *Oro*. It requires reservations on weekends and has European blondes behind the bars – a bit too much. It is two blocks north of Rue de l'OCAM at the pharmacy cut-off.

For *boîtes* with an African ambience, try *Cascade*, on Boulevard Circulaire between Pharmacie de l'Avenir and Rue de Kpalimé, a nightclub that caters to the Togolese lycée and university crowd and half the price of those catering to the European crowd. Somewhat cheaper and more for the common man is the *African Queen*. It's outdoors, always crowded, open every night and a great place for dancing. The price is right – CFA 175 for a large beer and, on weekends only, a CFA 200 admission charge. Don't miss it. Take the Rue d'Atakpamé a km beyond the Boulevard Circulaire and a block past the lagoon; it is on your left.

Movie Theatres The best cinema is at the Deux Février, with shows at 6.30 and 9 pm. The *24 Janvier* and *Club* are twin theatres downtown behind Goyiscore with the same show times, and are also comfortable with air-con.

Sports The surf in Lomé is dangerous because of a strong undertow, so be very cautious. As for the beaches, the locals use them as a toilet. Most people not at the

Lomé Market (JTJ)

If sailing sounds interesting, you can reserve a boat with crew at Le Bistroquet; the price is reasonable if there are four of you. Captains wanting to earn a few extra shekels also put notices up at the hotels, particularly Hôtel de la Paix; CFA 6500 per person for a day sail on a 14-metre sailboat is typical.

Things to Buy
Artisan Material The 2nd and 3rd floors of the *Grand Marché*, in the centre of town, are the domain of the Nana Benz and loaded with colourful cotton material, most of it wax cloth from Holland and, less expensive, from Africa. If you saw women at the airport with huge sacks and wondered what was inside, it was probably wax cloth they were bringing from Europe.

It's sold by the *pagna* (PAHN-yah), almost two metres, the complete package being three pagnas. Don't be surprised if they sometimes refuse to sell less than the entire three pagnas – it's not always easy to sell the remainder because most African women want three pagnas, the amount needed for a complete outfit. Don't expect to bargain much either. If you can get the price down 10%, you're probably doing well. Nonetheless, prices here are lower than anywhere else in West Africa. With handmade African material, such as the kente cloth from Ghana, it's a different ball game – you can bargain all day. The market is open every day except Sunday, and closes at 4 pm sharp.

For well-tailored, female fashions with the latest African styles and materials, head for *Brigitte Nahodje* at the Hôtel de la Paix and downtown in Immeuble Taba back of Goyi Score. She also offers a broad selection of accessories such as handbags, hats, belts and jewellery.

Artisan Goods For wooden carvings and brass work, take a walk on the short *Rue des Artisans* downtown alongside the Hôtel du Golfe; you'll find lots of Senegalese and Malian traders. For much

Sarakawa or Paix head for the beach in front of Hôtel le Bénin. You can get drinks there, plus the beach is not polluted. Others prefer the private beach in front of the Hôtel de la Paix, which is easy to crash if you look respectable. Or take a cab and head for the more secluded and protected Robinson's Beach area nine km to the east of town.

As for pools, the Sarakawa's is olympic size and, quite simply, the best in West Africa. Those at the Hôtel Benin and the Paix charge only about CFA 600 for non guests, while at the Deux Février it's free if you take the CFA 2000 cold buffet lunch or the superb CFA 2000 Sunday morning brunch.

The four top hotels all have tennis courts. Those not staying at the hotels can play for CFA 2000 at the Deux Février and CFA 1000 at the Sarakawa and Paix (both a little windy). You can rent windsurfers at Lake Togo (30 km) and, during the cooler part of the day, ride horses at the Sarakawa and Tropicana. If you can cope with playing on flat dry land with sand greens, fork over CFA 1500 to the Golf Club du Togo, just north of Lomé on the Atakpamé road, and try their nine holes.

higher quality art, try *Art d'Afrique* on the street behind the Hôtel du Golfe and, several blocks away, *L'Afrique Historique*, a tiny shop facing the BIAO bank. Downtown across from the Goyi Score parking lot is *Scupture Africaine*, which has a good collection of jewellery and high quality brass and wooden pieces.

Then head for the *Village Artisanal* on Avenue de la Nouvelle Marché, between Rue 24 Janvier and Boulevard Circulaire. You'll see Togolese artisans weaving cloth, carving statues, making baskets and lampshades of rattan, sewing leather sandals, and constructing cane chairs and tables – all for sale at reasonable, fixed prices. You can also pick up jewellery, ivory, table cloths, napkins and ceramic pottery. Throughout West Africa, Lomé is famous for its leather sandals. You can tell when a traveller has been to Lomé – they're usually wearing them. They were originally all made at the Village Artisanal. Now, you can also buy them around the market for about CFA 1900.

Another place for Togolese handicrafts, mostly cloth items with tie-dye designs, is *Prohandicap*, an outlet for a sheltered workshop in Niamtougou. It is one block up from the ocean on the eastern end of the Boulevard Circulaire.

Various For photo supplies, the best places are *Bdekpé* downtown behind the cathedral, *Colorama* just past the main post office, and *Photo Degbava* on Rue 24 Janvier opposite Walters bookstore. Try the Sarakawa or the Deux Février for records of African music. Leading Togolese musicians include the group As du Golfe, Ouye Tassane, Dama Damaozan, and the female vocalist, Akofa Akoussah, who has a beautiful voice.

Getting There & Away
Bush Taxi Taxis to Cotonou leave from near the Grand Marché and cost CFA 1500. For Accra, catch a taxi to the Ghana border and then another from the border. There are taxis to Ouagadougou for CFA

13,000 but it is cheaper to do it in stages via Dapango. New minibuses leave regularly from the Gare Routière for towns throughout Togo.

Train There is a train to Kpalimé for around CFA 575 in crowded 2nd class; twice as much in 1st class. It departs at 6.30 am sharp and takes a leisurely six hours or more. There are also trains to Aného (CFA 250), and one to Blitta that departs at 5.45 am and arrives around 1 pm.

Getting Around
Airport Transport At the airport, there's no departure tax. You'll find a bar, restaurant, bank, Hertz, Avis, Eurocar and Budget, but no bus service. A taxi into Lomé (9 km) will cost you CFA 2000, but only half that from town to the airport.

Taxi Fares are CFA 175 for a taxi (CFA 200 after 6 pm), more to the outlying areas, and CFA 500 for a *course* (short trip in a taxi to yourself). At the hotels, you'll pay more. Rates double at midnight. A taxi by the hour will cost you CFA 1500 to CFA 2500, depending on your bargaining skills. By the day, you can get a taxi for about CFA 12,000 plus petrol if you bargain well. Taxis are without meters and abundant, even at night.

Car Rental Hertz (tel 215052, telex 5208), Avis (tel 211030, telex 5214), Eurocar-National (Africom, Rue Agnes Gaba, tel 211324, telex 5275) and Budget (tel 210931, telex 5244) all have booths at the airport. Others include Loc-Auto (tel 214250) and Tele Taxi (tel 213931). Avis is on Boulevard Circulaire, Hertz is opposite the Hôtel du Golfe, and Budget is behind Texaco. For one day, the cost of a Toyota Starlet with air-con will run you roughly CFA 22,000 plus petrol if you travel 150 km.

AROUND LOMÉ
Lake Togo
This bilharzia-free lake is 30 km east of Lomé, just off the road to Benin. It is a

popular weekend retreat for sailing, windsurfing and water skiing enthusiasts. You can lunch or stay overnight at the hotel there, as well as rent a pirogue for a ride across the lake to Togoville, where you'll find a museum containing artefacts from the German colonial period, an interesting cathedral and a tie-dye cooperative. It was from this region that voodoo practitioners were taken as slaves to Haiti, now a major centre for voodoo.

If you have wheels, a good day trip would be to take in Lake Togo and the nearby original capital of Togo, Aného. You can combine this with a trip north to Vogan where there's an interesting Friday market.

Aného

A 45-minute drive east of Lomé brings you to Aného, the colonial capital of Togo until 1920. It's interesting to walk around and look at the old buildings that are still standing. Particularly interesting are the daily activities of the fishermen, including their deft navigation of the boats and the hauling in of the nets in the late afternoon.

Guin Festival

If you're in Togo during the second week in September, don't miss the Guin festival in Glidji, four km north of Aného. It lasts four days, ending on the second Sunday in September. Thursday is the opening day, attended with great pomp and ceremony, and this is when they determine the colour of the sacred stone that will be used in the various celebrations. If it's white, the year will be good; if black, the opposite. On Friday the people pay tribute to the elders, while the last two days are for celebrating, with much dancing and drinking.

Places to Stay & Eat Most people don't stay overnight, but there is reasonable accommodation in Aného. The five-room *Hôtel de l'Oasis* (tel 70) has rooms for about CFA 4400 (about CFA 6600 with air-con) and serves very decent meals, including

cassoulet and couscous. Other hotels in the same price range include the *Royal Holiday Hotel* (tel 310127), which has a restaurant and nightclub, and the cheaper *Hôtel Nous les Jeunes* at the eastern entrance to town. For a cheap restaurant, try *As des Picques*, which also rents rooms for CFA 2800 a double. For a good restaurant, try the French-run *Oceano*.

The South

KPALIMÉ

A 1½ hour drive (120 km) north-west of Lomé brings you to Kpalimé (PAH-lee-may), a mountainous cocoa and coffee region – considered by many to be the prettiest area in Togo. At 250 metres altitude, Kpalimé is noted for its mild climate, the market, the artisans' cooperative, and nearby Mt Agou (986 metres), Togo's highest peak.

Markets

Saturday is market day and the best day to visit. The kente cloth is a good buy here. There are also cloth shops on either side of Bar Domino, and cloth weaving across from Hôtel 30 Août. More famous than the market is the Centre Artisanal (tel 410077), a 20-minute walk north-west from the market off the road to Kpandu and the Campement. You'll find a vast array of wooden carvings, including chiefs' chairs and tables carved out of solid blocks of wood, as well as pottery, macrame and batiks – good for souvenirs but not serious art collections. It is open Monday to Saturday, 7 to 12 noon and 2.30 to 5.30 pm, Sunday and holidays, 8.30 to 1 pm.

Places to Stay – bottom end

With singles/doubles for about CFA 800/1100, *Hôtel Solo* is the cheapest and isn't bad for the price. The restaurant *Mini-Brasserie* is good value and has a few clean doubles for CFA 1500 with fan. The

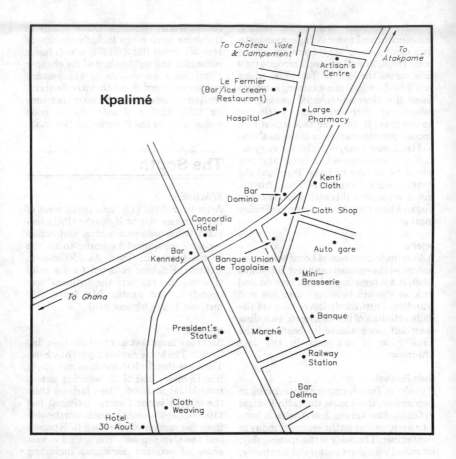

Kpalimé

To Château Viale & Campement

To Atakpamé

Artisan's Centre

Le Fermier (Bar/Ice cream Restaurant)

Hospital

Large Pharmacy

Kenti Cloth

Bar Domino

Cloth Shop

Concordia Hotel

Bar Kennedy

Banque Union de Togolaise

Auto gare

Mini-Brasserie

To Ghana

Banque

President's Statue

Marché

Railway Station

Bar Delima

Cloth Weaving

Hôtel 30 Août

popular *Bar Delima*, downtown near the railway station, has austere rooms for about CFA 1800 (CFA 300 more for a fan), water in a bucket and a primitive toilet. There's a movie theatre in the courtyard, so don't be surprised if it's noisy at night.

In the centre of town near the market, you can stay at the five-storey *Hôtel Concordia* (tel 410072), which has 18 fairly clean singles/doubles with fans for about CFA 2500/3600 (CFA 500 more for a private bath), an erratic water supply, plus a

shaded terrace for cheap drinks and music. The restaurant isn't bad for the price. The big drawback is the noise at night.

Around Kpalimé Many travellers prefer the 15-room *Campement de Kloto* because of its location on top of a mountain, 12 km north-west of Kpalimé on the road to Kpandu. Up there, it is quiet, shady and cool, with a constant breeze. On weekends it's busy but on weekdays you may be the only guest. Expect to pay about CFA 3800/5000 for singles/doubles with clean sheets, good ventilation, electric lights, and decent bathrooms with cold showers, soap and toilet paper. You'll also find a ping pong table and a restaurant serving a copious three-course meal, though it's not cheap at CFA 3000. To get there, charter a taxi from Kpalimé for CFA 1500 or, cheaper, take a taxi to the *douane* and from there another to the campement. For the return journey, pay a kid to find you a taxi.

Places to Stay - top end
The three-storey *Grand Hôtel du 30 Août* (tel 410095/6, cards AE, D, V), one km south of town, has 41 air-con singles/doubles for about CFA 6500/8000 (CFA 9000 for a huge room for three). Even though it doesn't have a pool or tennis court, it's still fairly luxurious and popular with tour groups. The nicest hotel in the area, *Hôtel Auberge Bethania*, has a pool and tennis courts, but it's 30 km south of Kpalimé on the road to Lomé.

Places to Eat
For cheap eats, you can choose between *Lion* (a Togolese restaurant owned by a Frenchman), *Hôtel Concordia*, *Bar Delima* and *Bar Domino*, which serves good chop from 8 pm on and is located at the point where the roads to Atakpamé and the Campement diverge. A good watering hole is *Bar Kennedy* across from Concordia Hôtel, with pictures of John Kennedy and Stevie Wonder hanging side by side.

Tourists usually eat at the *Hôtel du 30 Août*, which now has a big thatched-roof eating area and dance floor. The *Mini-Brasserie*, however, is better for the price and has draft beer for CFA 115 and good meals with large portions for CFA 1700 to CFA 2100. It's downtown across from the market and managed by Jean Sodatonou, an affable rotund guy who ran Lomé's Mini-Brasserie for many years. *Le Fermier*, between the market and the artisan centre, is noted for having the best ice cream in town.

Getting There & Away
If you don't have wheels, it's very simple to catch a taxi in Lomé near the Grand Marché; the trip takes two hours and the taxis are not stuffed to the limit. For laughs, take the antiquated seven-hour train, leaving Lomé at 6.30 am and Kpalimé at 2.30 pm daily.

AROUND KPALIMÉ
A good diversion is to take a car or taxi up 986-metre-high **Mt Agou**, a good 20 km south-west of Kpalimé. About 10 km north of town you'll find **Kpimé Falls** (Cascades de Kpimé); they range from spectacular during the rainy season to totally uninteresting during the rest of the year.

On the way to the Campement you may see **Chateau Viale** from a distance, an astonishing medieval-style fortress of stone built by a visionary Frenchman in 1944 as a retreat for his wife. She spent three days there, then split for France. On a clear day, there were views of Lake Volta (Ghana), but since the government purchased it, the chateau has been off limits to the public.

ATAKPAMÉ
A 2½ hour drive north of Lomé brings you to Atakpamé (ah-TAC-pah-may). At 500 metres altitude in the heart of a mountainous area, it was the favourite residence of the German administrators. It's also the centre of Togo's cotton-growing belt and has a textile mill. You may see tourist posters in Lomé of dancers on stilts, sometimes five metres high – they come from here.

If you're driving north from Lomé, stop off on the way in Davié (dah-vee-AY) for a look at the unusual cemetery, which has gravestones depicting the occupation of the deceased, eg a chauffeur's grave will have a steering wheel.

Places to Stay - bottom end
For cheap accommodation, you'll have to walk a little. On the southern outskirts of town on the road to Sokodé is the *Hôtel*

Obandge, with a restaurant, hallway bathroom, and small rooms with a bed and fan for CFA 2200. The hotel's name is not well-known; just ask for the Station Total next door. Further away in Hiheatro, two km out of Atakpamé on the road to Kpalimé, there's *Hôtel Alaifa*, with bar and restaurant and rooms for about the same price.

Bar le Retour, in front of the Shell station, has been recommended as one of the cheapest in town. Doubles cost CFA 1500, CFA 300 extra for a fan, and it serves cheap food.

Places to Stay – top end
The 27-room *Roc Hôtel* (tel 400237), one km from the heart of Atakpamé on a hill with a panoramic view of the city and surrounding hills, is the best hotel. Air-con singles/doubles cost about CFA 6200/7800 plus tax. Next in line is *Hôtel du Kapoke* (tel 400213), with air-con singles/doubles for about CFA 4400/5000 (CFA 6000 for double beds) plus tax. Downtown on the main drag, with a terrace bar-restaurant overlooking a football court, the hotel has a lively ambience. Not far away on the main drag, half a km from the bus station, is the French-run *Relais des Plateaux*, which has singles/doubles with fans for about CFA 3300/4400 (CFA 4400/5000 with air-con). The rooms have showers and are about as nice as the Kapoke's, plus there's a central bar.

Getting There & Away
The daily train takes twice as long as the time it does to drive. The train leaves Lomé at 5.45 am and Atakpamé at about 4 pm.

AROUND ATAKPAMÉ
Ayomé Falls These cascades, about 17 km from town on the asphalt road to Kpalimé, are picturesque in the rainy season.

Badou
Badou, in the heart of the cocoa area, is an hour's drive west of Atakpamé. The 35-metre waterfalls, les Cascades d'Akrowa,

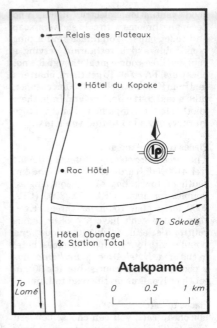

are the major attraction. The 40-minute climb up the hill from town is not easy, but once there you can swim in the shallow pond beneath the waterfalls. The water is reputedly therapeutic.

Places to Stay You can stay at the *Hôtel Abuta*, with 15 air-con rooms for about CFA 3800 to CFA 7700.

FAZAO NATIONAL PARK
Fifty km south of Sokodé is Ayengré, the turn-off to Fazao National Park, 23 km to the west on a dirt road – a four-hour drive from Lomé. You'll find a very comfortable tourist hotel at the park, which is open November to June. The forest scenery is interesting, but the park has not been well managed. So the chances of seeing wildlife other than birds and monkeys are not good. If you're very lucky, you might see buffalo, hippo, kob, wart hog, bongo, possibly even elephant and lion. Early

morning and late afternoon are the best viewing times.

Places to Stay & Eat

Perched on a hill and shaped like an African village with a swimming pool in the centre, where monkeys sometimes play, *Hôtel du Fazao* has 25 air-con rooms, each with a sitting room, and an interesting restaurant with gourds used as lighting fixtures. In the evening, the locals frequently perform dances of hunting scenes. Expect to pay about CFA 11,500/14,500 for singles/doubles. You can make reservations at the Sarakawa Hôtel in Lomé.

SOKODÉ

There's little of interest to see and do in Sokodé (SOAK-oh-day), Togo's second largest city with about 40,000 inhabitants, but it's a pleasant town and the streets are lined with flamboyants and mango trees. The market is particularly active on Mondays.

Places to Stay – bottom end

Of the cheap places in town, the best for the money is *Le Campement* (tel 90), up the hill from the *douane* (customs house) on the southern end of town. It has 14 rooms (three with air-con) and a restaurant. *Hôtel Tchaoudjo*, however, is more conveniently located. It's next to the market and bush taxi station, with grubby rooms, sagging mattresses and filthy outside bathrooms for CFA 1800 – the mosquitoes are free.

The rooms are simple but better at *Hôtel Almandou*, a km from the town centre, with ventilated rooms for about CFA 1100 to CFA 2200 (CFA 3300 with air-con). The hotel has a restaurant. The CFA 3000 rooms are clean and bigger at *Hôtel La Cigale*, between downtown and the southern end of town. The big problem is that this is one of the most popular dancing places in town and very noisy.

Places to Stay – top end

The best hotel is *Hôtel Central* (tel 500003/23) at the southern entrance to town, with a restaurant, straw hut bar and 15 very decent air-con rooms and 7 bungalows for about CFA 7800 (CFA 6700 with fan) plus tax.

Also on the main drag, but at the northern end of town, is the Swiss-run *La Bonne Auberge* (tel 500235), which has decent but plain rooms with air-con and a hallway bathroom for about CFA 4700 (CFA 3000 with fan). Not far away on the same road is *Hôtel A V Kedia* (tel 500103), which has a more African ambience. The small rooms are quite clean with double beds and spotless bathrooms; the cost for a room is about CFA 2750 with fan and CFA 5500 with air-con (CFA 6000 with inside bathroom). There's also a restaurant.

Places to Eat

The terrace restaurant at *La Bonne Auberge* has a pleasant ambience and is the best in town. There are many choices on the French menu, with most main dishes costing CFA 1300 to CFA 2500. You may meet some of the local Peace Corps volunteers at *Bar Sans Souci*, which is well known for its brochettes.

BASSAR

Bassar is 57 km on asphalt road to the west of Sokodé. It is the site of the annual yam (*igname*) festival at the beginning of September, involving lots of dancing, including fire dances, and traditional clothing.

The North

LAMA-KARA

Because President Eyadéma comes from a village not far to the north, he has pumped a lot of money into Lama-Kara often called simply Kara), including a second brewery and a modern radio station. As a result, it has grown quickly to about 30,000 people. It is spread out, and all in all, it's a fairly pleasant town. The three-star Hôtel Kara is a major reason why travellers to the north stop here for the night. Even if you don't stay there, you can use the pool, which isn't expensive. Much more interesting than Kara is the area to the north, where most tourist buses are headed.

Places to Stay – bottom end

The cheapest of all, with clean bunk beds, are *La Bourse de Travail* (labour centre) on the south side of town on the main road, and *Affaires Sociales* on the north-east side leading towards Kétao. Both are a good long walk from the centre of town.

For about CFA 2400/2700 for singles/doubles with mosquito nets and clean bathrooms, you can stay at *Hôtel Sapaw*, which is about half a km from the main highway on the road passing by the Hôtel Kara. It has a pleasant atmosphere and is popular with Africans, but the music goes until midnight.

Hôtel Mon Village, *Hôtel Bakassi* and *Hôtel Campement* are other cheap ones.

Places to Stay – top end

Hôtel Kara (tel 606020/1) has a pool, tennis court, nightclub and 75 singles/doubles for about CFA 15,000/19,000, including 21 bungalows. The next best place is the Swiss-run *Hôtel Mini-Swiss*, which has rooms for about CFA 6000 with air-con and TV and one of the town's best restaurants.

Places to Eat

The popular *Wax Restaurant* offers hamburgers and wiener schnitzel among other dishes. It is 100 metres from the Hotel Sapaw.

For drinks and food, in addition to the Wax, the Peace Corps volunteers seem to like the *Mini-Rizerie*, across from the post office. The food is decent, but the cook sometimes has to go out and buy the ingredients while you wait. Near the market, are some good cheap bars.

SARA-KAWA

Sara-Kawa, 23 km to the north-west of Lama-Kara, is not worth visiting, but if you pass through check out the huge monument commemorating the site where Eyadéma's plane crashed in 1974. The statue has Eyadéma pointing to the ground and saying, 'They almost killed me here'.

KPAGOUDA

Kpagouda is 25 km north-east of Kara; take the major road leading east from Kara towards Benin for 15 km or so to Kétao, which has a good market on Wednesday, then north on a dirt track to Kpagouda. The attractions there are the scenic mountains and the stunningly located tourist hotel.

Places to Stay & Eat

The 10-room *Tourist Hôtel* has a bar-restaurant and a tennis court and charges CFA 6000/6500 for air-con singles/doubles.

NIAMTOUGOU

Niamtougou is 34 km to the north of Lama-Kara on the main highway and is frequently used as a base camp for side trips because of the tourist hotel. The Sunday market there is one of the most vibrant in Togo – don't miss it.

Places to Stay & Eat

The *Tourist Hôtel* is similar to the one in Kpagouda and has singles/doubles for CFA 6000/6500.

VALLEY OF THE TAMBERMA

Between Niamtougou and Kanté, 28 km further to the north, a dirt track leads east for about 25 km to the Valley of the Tamberma, whose fortress-like houses are the major attraction.

Their compounds consist of a series of towers connected by a thick wall with only one doorway to the outside. Inside, is a huge elevated terrace of clay-covered logs where they cook and dry the millet and corn. The Tamberma do all the work by hand, using only clay, straw and wood, the walls being a mixture of clay and straw, creating a cooler environment than, say, cement dwellings. They use the towers, capped by picturesque conical roofs, for storing grain and other rooms for sleeping, bathing and cooking in the rainy season. Downstairs, they keep the animals. Unfortunately, many Tamberma aren't very hospitable, perhaps irritated by tourists staring at them, but if you are lucky, you might get to see inside one of their compounds. If you see any animal skulls, they are probably fetishes.

Some people hike the 27 km from Kanté to the Tamberma villages. Not only is walking more interesting, but the people are much more likely to give you a warm welcome. From Kanté, walk east for 20 km to Warengo, then another 7 km to Nadoba, the most important village. Bring your own food.

KÉRAN NATIONAL PARK

The other major attraction during the dry season is Kéran National Park. As you're driving north from Kanté towards Dapaong, look for a sign pointing to the park's entrance. They will insist you take a guide. You are forbidden to stop the vehicle, speed or take photographs on the international highway cutting through the park.

The park rangers are known for giving stiff fines frequently and arbitrarily, with no excuses accepted. Taking less than 92 minutes may be used as evidence that you were speeding; taking more than 92 minutes will be taken as proof that you stopped along the way. So synchronise your watch with the ranger at the park entrance. Going north to south, at the 62-minute mark, you should be in Naboulgou, the site of another tourist hotel. You can forget about this mad trip schedule if you're staying overnight there.

Don't expect to see lots of animals. If you're lucky, there are elephant, giraffe, buffalo, antelope, wart hog, hippo, monkey and various birds including stork, crane and marabou. Sorry – no lions. The best viewing time is the crack of dawn and the late afternoon.

Places to Stay

Kanté At the southern end of the park, Kanté has a *Campement* with rooms for about CFA 2200 (CFA 500 more with fan). It's on the main drag.

Mango At the northern edge of the park, Mango is a small town without electricity. In addition to hippos in the nearby Oti River, you'll find a *Campement* at the entrance to town and *Hôtel Cercle de l'Amitié* and a restaurant, *Au Bon Coin des Savanes*, near the market.

Naboulgou The *Tourist Hôtel* has round bungalows designed like African *soukalas*. Comfortable air-con singles/doubles cost CFA 6000/6500.

DAPAONG

In the far north only 30 km from Burkina Faso, Dapaong sits on a hillside and is noted for its mild climate and the market. Saturday is the big day. In the corner of the market you'll find *chakpa*, the only indigenous beer with a good head. It's made from millet.

Places to Stay & Eat

Near the market is *Hôtel Cercle de l'Amitié*, with clean singles/doubles for about CFA 2750/3300. *Hôtel l'Union*, opposite the douane, has a decent medium-priced restaurant and charges about the same as the Amitié for its clean rooms.

The renovated *Campement* is Dapaong's best hotel. It has rooms for about CFA 4500 and a thatched-roof bar open 24 hours, with draft beer and even sandwiches available in the middle of the night. On the south side of town on the old road to Kara, it's a short walk to downtown and far superior to the morgue-like *Hôtel le Vergier*, the town's second best hotel.

Getting There & Away

If you're headed north to Ouagadougou, start early because the numerous police stops make it an all-day journey. There are direct connections to Ouaga and trucks also go to Koupéla in Burkina Faso for CFA 2500. From Koupéla there are connections to Ouagadougou or Niamey in Niger.

The night I spent in Dapaong was totally unexpected. I was coming from Ouagadougou to Lomé, having paid CFA 13,000, the normal price for a non-stop ride. It only took us about five minutes into the journey to realise that our driver had none of the required papers, causing big hassles with the police all along the way. When we finally reached the Togo border, he met a Togolese taxi driver waiting for passengers, whereupon an agreement was reached that the Togolese driver would take us the rest of the way. When we arrived 30 minutes later in Dapaong, the new driver stopped the car, told us that was as far as he had agreed to go, and offered us each CFA 2900 for the rest of the journey – the price of a slow cattle car to Lomé. The passengers were furious, ranted and raved with the police until 2 am, but the police took the side of the local boy and blamed it all on the Burkinabé. You'll have more experiences like this travelling 2nd class. A sense of humour and a beer help.

Index

MAPS

Temperature

To convert °C to °F multipy by 1.8 and add 32

To convert °F to °C subtract 32 and multipy by ·55

Length, Distance & Area

	multipy by
inches to centimetres	2.54
centimetres to inches	0.39
feet to metres	0.30
metres to feet	3.28
yards to metres	0.91
metres to yards	1.09
miles to kilometres	1.61
kilometres to miles	0.62
acres to hectares	0.40
hectares to acres	2.47

Weight

	multipy by
ounces to grams	28.35
grams to ounces	0.035
pounds to kilograms	0.45
kilograms to pounds	2.21
British tons to kilograms	1016
US tons to kilograms	907

A British ton is 2240 lbs, a US ton is 2000 lbs

Volume

	multipy by
Imperial gallons to litres	4.55
litres to imperial gallons	0.22
US gallons to litres	3.79
litres to US gallons	0.26

5 imperial gallons equals 6 US gallons
a litre is slightly more than a US quart, slightly less
than a British one

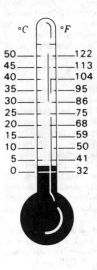

°C		°F
50		122
45		113
40		104
35		95
30		86
25		75
20		68
15		59
10		50
5		41
0		32

454

Lonely Planet

Lonely Planet published its first book in 1973. Tony and Maureen Wheeler had made a lengthy overland trip from England to Australia and, in response to numerous 'how do you do it?' questions, Tony wrote and they published *Across Asia on the Cheap*. It became an instant local best-seller and inspired thoughts of a second travel guide. A year and a half in South-East Asia resulted in their second book, *South-East Asia on a Shoestring*, which they put together in a backstreet Chinese hotel in Singapore in 1975. The 'yellow book', as it quickly became known, soon became *the* guide to the region and has gone through five editions, always with its familiar yellow cover.

Soon other writers started to come to them with ideas for similar books – books that went off the beaten track and took an adventurous approach to travel, books that 'assumed you knew how to get your luggage off the carousel,' as one reviewer described them. Lonely Planet grew from a kitchen table operation to a spare room and then to its own office. It also started to develop an international reputation as the Lonely Planet logo began to appear in more and more countries. In 1982 *India – a travel survival kit* won the Thomas Cook award for the best guidebook of the year.

These days there are over 60 Lonely Planet titles. Nearly 30 people work at our office in Melbourne, Australia and another half dozen at our US office in Oakland, California.

At first Lonely Planet specialised exclusively in the Asia region but these days we are also developing major ranges of guidebooks to the Pacific region, to South America and to Africa. The list of walking guides is growing and Lonely Planet is producing a unique series of phrasebooks to 'unusual' languages. The emphasis continues to be on travel for travellers and Tony and Maureen still manage to fit in a number of trips each year and play a very active part in the writing and updating of Lonely Planet's guides.

Keeping guidebooks up to date is a constant battle which requires an ear to the ground and lots of walking, but technology also plays its part. All Lonely Planet guidebooks are now stored and updated on computer, and some authors even take lap-top computers into the field. Lonely Planet is also using computers to draw maps and eventually many of the maps will be stored on disk.

The people at Lonely Planet strongly feel that travellers can make a positive contribution to the countries they visit both by better appreciation of cultures and by the money they spend. In addition the company tries to make a direct contribution to the countries and regions it covers. Since 1986 a percentage of the income from each book has gone to aid groups and associations. This has included donations to famine relief in Africa, to aid projects in India, to agricultural projects in Nicaragua and other Central American countries and to Greenpeace's efforts to halt French nuclear testing in the Pacific. In 1988 over $40,000 was donated by Lonely Planet to these projects.

Lonely Planet Distributors

Australia & Papua New Guinea Lonely Planet Publications, PO Box 617, Hawthorn, Victoria 3122.
Canada Raincoast Books, 112 East 3rd Avenue, Vancouver, British Columbia V5T 1C8.
Denmark, Finland & Norway Scanvik Books aps, Store Kongensgade 59 A, DK-1264 Copenhagen K.
Hong Kong The Book Society, GPO Box 7804.
India & Nepal UBS Distributors, 5 Ansari Rd, New Delhi – 110002
Israel Geographical Tours Ltd, 8 Tverya St, Tel Aviv 63144.
Japan Intercontinental Marketing Corp, IPO Box 5056, Tokyo 100-31.
Netherlands Nilsson & Lamm bv, Postbus 195, Pampuslaan 212, 1380 AD Weesp.
New Zealand Transworld Publishers, PO Box 83-094, Edmonton PO, Auckland.
Singapore & Malaysia MPH Distributors, 601 Sims Drive, #03-21, Singapore 1438.
Spain Altair, Balmes 69, 08007 Barcelona.
Sweden Esselte Kartcentrum AB, Vasagatan 16, S-111 20 Stockholm.
Thailand Chalermnit, 108 Sukhumvit 53, Bangkok 10110.
UK Roger Lascelles, 47 York Rd, Brentford, Middlesex, TW8 0QP
USA Lonely Planet Publications, PO Box 2001A, Berkeley, CA 94702.
West Germany Buchvertrieb Gerda Schettler, Postfach 64, D3415 Hattorf a H.
All Other Countries refer to Australia address.

Guides to Africa

Africa on a shoestring
From Marrakesh to Kampala, Mozambique to Mauritania,
Johannesburg to Cairo – this guidebook gives you all the
facts on travelling in Africa. It provides comprehensive
information on more than 50 African countries – how to
get to them, how to get around, where to stay, where to
eat, what to see and what to avoid.

East Africa – a travel survival kit
Whether you want to climb Kilimanjaro, visit wildlife
reserves, or sail an Arab dhow, East Africa offers a
fascinating pastiche of cultures and landscapes. This
guide has detailed information on Kenya, Uganda,
Rwanda, Burundi, eastern Zaire, Tanzania and the
Comoros Islands.

Swahili phrasebook
Swahili is widely spoken throughout East Africa – from
the coast of Kenya and Tanzania through to Zaire.

Egypt & the Sudan – a travel survival kit
The sights of Egypt and the Sudan have impressed
visitors for more than 50 centuries. This guide takes you
beyond the spectacular pyramids to discover the villages
of the Nile, diving in the Red Sea and many other other
attractions.

Jordan & Syria – a travel survival kit
Roman cities, ancient Petra, Crusader castles – these sights, amongst many others, combine with Arab hospitality to make this undiscovered region a fascinating and enjoyable destination.

Yemen – a travel survival kit
One of the oldest inhabited regions in the world, the Yemen is a beautiful mountainous region with a unique architecture. This book covers both North and South Yemen in detail.

Central Africa – a travel survival kit
Central Africa offers the visitor incomparable wildlife and scenery, and the exxence of African culture. Traditional village life continues, little affected by the outside world, and the mighty jungles retain their mystery. This guide tells where to go to meet gorillas, how to contact a village sorcerer, and much more. Countries covered are: Cameroon, Central African Republic, Chad, The Congo, Equatorial Guinea, Gabon, São Tomé Principe, and Zaïre.

Forthcoming in 1989

North Africa – a travel survival kit

Lonely Planet Guidebooks

Lonely Planet guidebooks cover virtually every accessible part of Asia as well as Australia, the Pacific, Central and South America, Africa, the Middle East and parts of North America. There are four main series: 'travel survival kits', covering a single country for a range of budgets; 'shoestring' guides with compact information for low-budget travel in a major region; trekking guides; and 'phrasebooks'.

Australia & the Pacific
Australia
Bushwalking in Australia
Papua New Guinea
Bushwalking in Papua New Guinea
Papua New Guinea phrasebook
New Zealand
Tramping in New Zealand
Rarotonga & the Cook Islands
Solomon Islands
Tahiti & French Polynesia
Fiji
Micronesia

South-East Asia
South-East Asia on a shoestring
Malaysia, Singapore & Brunei
Indonesia
Bali & Lombok
Indonesia phrasebook
Burma
Burmese phrasebook
Thailand
Thai phrasebook
Philippines
Pilipino phrasebook

North-East Asia
North-East Asia on a shoestring
China
China phrasebook
Tibet
Tibet phrasebook
Japan
Korea
Korean phrasebook
Hong Kong, Macau & Canton
Taiwan

West Asia
West Asia on a shoestring
Trekking in Turkey
Turkey

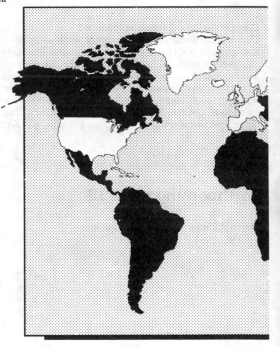

Mail Order

Lonely Planet guidebooks are distributed worldwide and are sold by good bookshops everywhere. They are also available by mail order from Lonely Planet, so if you have difficulty finding a title please write to us. US and Canadian residents should write to Embarcadero West, 112 Linden St, Oakland CA 94607, USA and residents of other countries to PO Box 617, Hawthorn, Victoria 3122, Australia.

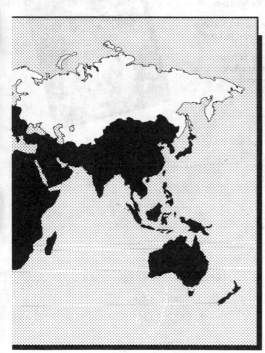

Eastern Europe
Eastern Europe

Indian Subcontinent
India
Hindi/Urdu phrasebook
Kashmir, Ladakh & Zanskar
Trekking in the Indian Himalaya
Pakistan
Kathmandu & the Kingdom of Nepal
Trekking in the Nepal Himalaya
Nepal phrasebook
Sri Lanka
Sri Lanka phrasebook
Bangladesh

Africa
Africa on a shoestring
East Africa
Swahili phrasebook
West Africa
Central Africa

Middle East
Egypt & the Sudan
Jordan & Syria
Yemen

North America
Canada
Alaska

Mexico
Mexico
Baja California

South America
South America on a shoestring
Ecuador & the Galapagos Islands
Colombia
Chile & Easter Island
Bolivia
Peru

Lonely Planet Update

We collect an enormous amount of information here at Lonely Planet. Apart from our research there's a steady stream of travellers' letters full of the latest news. For over 5 years much of this information went into a quarterly newsletter (and helped to update the guidebooks). The new paperback *Update* includes this up-to-date news and aims to supplement the information available in our guidebooks. There will be four editions a year (Feb, May, Aug and Nov) available either by subscription or through bookshops. Subscribe now and you'll save nearly 25% off the retail price.

Each edition has extracts from the most interesting letters we have received, covering such diverse topics as:
- how to take a boat trip on the Yalu River
- living in a typical Thai village
- getting a Nepalese trekking permit

Subscription Details
All subscriptions cover four editions and include postage. Prices quoted are valid until 1988.
USA & Canada – One year's subscription is US$12; a single copy is US$3.95. Please send your order to Lonely Planet's California office.
Other Countries – One year's subscription is Australian $15; a single copy is A$4.95. Please pay in Australian $, or the US$ or £ Sterling equivalent. Please send your order form to Lonely Planet's Australian office.

Order Form

Please send me

☐ One year's subscription – starting next edition.   ☐ One copy of the next edition.

Name (please print) ....

Address (please print) ....

....

....

Tick One

☐ Payment enclosed (payable to Lonely Planet Publications)

Charge my   ☐ Visa   ☐ Bankcard   ☐ MasterCard   for the amount of $ ....

Card No .... Expiry Date ....

Cardholder's Name (print) ....

Signature .... Date..

US & Canadian residents
Lonely Planet, Embarcadero West, 112 Linden St,
Oakland, CA 94607, USA
Other countries
Lonely Planet, PO Box 88, South Yarra, Victoria 3141, Australia